THE
Pillsbury
COOKBOOK

BANTAM BOOKS

NEW YORK • TORONTO • LONDON • SYDNEY • AUCKLAND

*This edition contains the complete text
of the original hardcover edition.*
NOT ONE WORD HAS BEEN OMITTED.

THE PILLSBURY COOKBOOK

*A Bantam Book / published by arrangement
with The Pillsbury Company*

PUBLISHING HISTORY
*Doubleday edition published September 1989
Bantam premium edition published 1995
Bantam edition / April 1996*

*Poppin' Fresh® figure, Bake-Off® and Classic® Cookbooks
are registered trademarks of The Pillsbury Company.*

ISBN 0-553-57534-1

Published simultaneously in the United States and Canada

*Bantam Books are published by Bantam Books, a division of
Bantam Doubleday Dell Publishing Group, Inc. Its trademark,
consisting of the words "Bantam Books" and the portrayal of a
rooster, is Registered in U.S. Patent and Trademark Office and
in other countries. Marca Registrada. Bantam Books, 1540
Broadway, New York, New York 10036.*

PRINTED IN THE UNITED STATES OF AMERICA

OPM   0 9 8 7 6 5 4 3 2 1

Contents

An Invitation To Good Cooking

The world of cooking, good food and marvelous recipes is an ever-changing one. As publisher of Classic® Cookbooks, the leading cookbook magazine, we are keenly aware of the latest preferences in food and cooking, from a growing interest in more healthful eating, to microwave cooking, simple-to-prepare meals and reliable recipe information. We are

and from Pillsbury's extensive food research, we know how cooking

and that is the universal attraction to Pillsbury's Bake-Off® recipes. Gathered from forty years of competition, our selected requested favorites from famous desserts to whole some meals clearly reflect our changing styles, and we feel meal planning is so important to the success and satisfaction of cooking that we've devoted an entire chapter to menu and entertaining ideas that demonstrate the ease and simplicity of many creative new ways with food.

To ensure the highest-quality results, every recipe was tested in Pillsbury's Test Kitchens by experienced home economists. Each recipe was evaluated for flavor, simple and appearance, that one cook's results may be another's

An Invitation To Good Cooking

The world of cooking, good food and marvelous recipes is an ever-changing one. As publisher of *Classic® Cookbooks*, the leading cookbook magazine, we are keenly aware of the latest preferences in food and cooking, from a growing interest in more healthful eating, to microwave cooking, simple-to-prepare meals and reliable recipe information. We are proud of the intense loyalty and involvement of our readers. Whether our contact is through the thousands of letters and phone calls Pillsbury receives each year or through Pillsbury's extensive food research, we know how cooking styles and preferences have evolved and changed since we last produced an all-purpose cookbook.

Indeed, cooking styles have changed! In direct response to our readers' interests, we set out to make THE PILLSBURY COOKBOOK the most helpful, up-to-date source of recipes and food information available today. Its contents were chosen to *mirror* the many changes in how you, the nation's cooks, prepare food—from quick meals for a busy family to the increasing use of exotic flavors and foods from around the world. Despite changing preferences one constant remains, and that is the universal attraction to Pillsbury's Bake-Off® recipes. Gathered from forty years of competition, our selected requested favorites from famous desserts to wholesome meals clearly reflect our changing styles. And we feel meal planning is so important to the success and satisfaction of cooking that we've devoted an entire chapter to menu and entertaining ideas that demonstrate the ease and simplicity of many creative new ways with food.

To ensure the highest-quality results, every recipe was tested in Pillsbury's Test Kitchens by experienced home economists. Each recipe was evaluated for flavor, texture and appearance. But one cook's genius may be another's shake of the head! So we ran daily taste panels to help us create new recipes that everybody will enjoy—recipes that meet your demanding criteria for convenience, flavor and nutrition. Once developed, each recipe was analyzed for key nutrient information: calories, cholesterol, fat, fiber, sodium, calcium and iron. We've placed this pertinent information right with the recipe for greatest use and convenience.

With THE PILLSBURY COOKBOOK and its full array of enticing recipes and helpful information, it is a pleasure to extend our invitation to good cooking from Pillsbury.

Menus & Entertaining

Menus & Entertaining

An Invitation to Good Eating

Never has creative, healthful eating been more popular than today. Never has abundant fresh produce been more available year-round. And never has cooking been more adventuresome as we enjoy new foods, new tastes and new products. Whether influenced by the many ethnic groups living throughout the country, our own extensive travels or the media, we are increasingly trying wider varieties of foods and new cooking techniques.

Along with these new interests has come a change in lifestyles. Concern for fitness, health and the role food plays in them makes lighter foods with less salt, sugar, fat and calories the choice for more and more meals. Our families have changed too. Many of them are smaller and a majority of women work outside the home, leaving less time for food preparation. Convenience foods and new appliances like the microwave oven and food processor have changed how we cook and the amount of time we spend on it.

The recipes gathered in this cookbook reflect these varied new interests; they retain the best of traditional favorite foods while including fresh ideas for meals from breakfast to party buffets. Use these recipes and the suggested menus that follow to spark your own imagination and creativity as you plan meals for your family and for special occasions. We hope you enjoy our invitation to good eating.

Weekend Family Breakfast

Serves 4 to 6

Orange or Tomato Juice

Vegetable Scrambled Eggs—page 396
or
Filled Omelet—page 390

Bacon Strips or Sausage

Cinnamon Doughnut Drops—page 132

Favorite Beverage

On weekend mornings when everyone is home and the pace is more relaxed, it's fun to turn breakfast or brunch into a family affair. This hearty, home-style menu is as fun to fix as it is enticing to eat. Fresh doughnuts are a special treat, easily prepared using a mini deep-fat fryer, and the handy microwave oven cooks bacon and sausage to perfection in minutes. Tasks are easily shared, including table setting and juice pouring, according to age and skill levels. It's an ideal opportunity to enjoy time and food together. Remember this menu, too, when you have sleepover guests who love to cook.

Breakfast on the Go

Serves 4 to 6

Egg Salad Breakfast Muffins—page 398
or
Whole Wheat Pancakes with Syrup—page 135

Homemade Granola with Yogurt—page 78

Fresh Fruit

Favorite Beverage

Getting up in the morning *can* be a pleasure when nutritious, appealing make-ahead foods await. These first-meal-of-the-day options offer speedy assembly and require only jiffy heating or toasting. The protein-packed **Egg Salad Breakfast Muffins** can be eaten en route if necessary, and for cholesterol watchers the wholesome pancakes can be ready and waiting in the refrigerator or freezer for microwave or conventional oven heating. Seasonal fresh fruits, yogurt and **Homemade Granola** make healthful staples for beat-the-clock breakfasts and anytime snacking.

Company Brunch

Serves 8

Orange Juice Spritzer—page 84

Vegetable Strata Supreme—page 403
or
Shrimp Asparagus Pasta Toss—page 502

Easy Fruit-Filled Braid—page 170
or
Bright Day Banana Muffins—page 116

Orange-Lemon Sorbet—page 347
or
Fruit with Caramel Cream—page 310

Beverage

This menu offers many tasty reasons why brunch time entertaining is all the rage with guests and hosts alike. Last-minute steps are minimal with **Vegetable Strata Supreme** that can be partially prepared the night before, a refreshing **Orange Lemon Sorbet** which is completely make-ahead, and baked goods that can be reheated before serving or served warm from the oven. Bite-sized muffins always add a festive touch, and any favorite muffin recipes can be used. Grease small tins on bottoms only, fill cups two thirds full and adjust baking time so the little gems don't overbake. Both entrees are perfect for light suppers or lunches as well as brunches.

Mexican Brunch

Serves 4

Banana Slush—page 88
or
Apple Grape Punch—page 85

Vegetable Nachos—page 79

Sundance Eggs—page 404

Avocado and Orange Salad—page 669

Spice Refrigerator Cookies—page 266

Mexican Coffee—page 105

It's fun to do and, with a little forethought, menus can be developed around a theme. This Mexican-oriented meal is well suited to a variety of happy occasions. A fiesta feeling comes naturally with the lively flavors and bright colors. Whether served on patio, porch or in the dining room, this is cuisine to enjoy to the fullest.

Patio Luncheon

Serves 4 to 6

Chilled Raspberry Soup—page 769

Smoked Turkey Jarlsberg Salad Supreme—page 705
or
Fresh Tomato and Basil with Vermicelli—page 435

Flaky Butter Brioche—page 163
or
Popovers—page 130

Chocolate Praline Layer Cake—page 186
or
Apple Nut Lattice Tart—page 357

Best Minted Iced Tea—page 101

When sunny days and warm breezes spell the need for light dining, you will find this menu a perfect midday repast. It's refreshingly cool, flavors and colors are delicate and it won't slow you down for the rest of the day. Chilled soups are elegant starters and this raspberry-flavored rendition is just right as a prelude to the sensational main course options. Each of the dessert ideas is captivating and make-ahead.

Brown Bag Lunch

Serves 1 or 4

Garden-Style Tuna Salad—page 714
or
Chunky Tomato Soup—page 756

Crusty Roll
or
Bow Knot Roll—page 161

Maxi Chippers—page 245
or
Chewy Granola Bars—page 282

Milk

Enliven everyday lunches with an appealing variety of tota-
bles. Carry a marvelous nutrition-packed salad such as this
or treat yourself to a soup or casserole. You will want to purchase a wide-mouthed thermal container to keep foods
fresh, the right temperature and safe from spoilage. Instead
of the usual sliced sandwich breads, different rolls, crackers,
flat breads or bread substitutes can add interest. The cookies
or bars are not only tasty and wholesome, they are great
travelers for lunches and take-along snacks.

Beat-the-Heat Barbecue

Serves 6

Sunny Citrus Cooler—page 82

Artichoke Appetizer with Easy Cream Dip—pages 41, 42

Barbecued Turkey Breast—page 647

Grilled Vegetables—page 827

Layered Lettuce Salad—page 673

Dilly Casserole Bread—page 155
or
French Bread

Fresh Strawberry-Rhubarb Pie—page 364

With the dip, salad, bread and fruit pie prepared in advance, there is no need to heat up the kitchen with mealtime indoor cooking except for microwaving the turkey breast before grilling. While guests are sipping and nibbling, the host can keep an eye on the turkey as it cooks to a golden brown. Have vegetables grill-ready to cook while the turkey is being sliced for serving. The turkey breast will serve 10, so there may be leftovers for great post-party sandwiches or salad making.

Quick and Easy Microwave Fare

Serves 4

Salmon-Filled Flounder—page 466

Lemon Buttered New Potatoes—page 815

Sweet 'n Sour Spinach Salad—page 671

Dinner Rolls

Favorite Beverage

For the **Salmon-Filled Flounder** dinner, the salad is prepared first. Microwave the potatoes while preparing the fish. Stand time will keep the covered container of potatoes warm while the fish microwaves. Make-ahead or purchased rolls can be heated just before serving.

30-Minute Turkey Dinner

Serves 4

Turkey Slice Saute—page 648

Tossed Salad—page 668

Baked Apples—page 312
or
Baked Pears—page 320

Favorite Beverage

For the **Turkey Slice Saute,** simply follow the microwave directions. Toss the salad and prepare the apples. While enjoying your dinner, microwave the **Baked Apples or Pears**.

Easy Everyday Dinner

Serves 4

Beef Oriental with Rice—page 547
or
Light Lemon Chicken—page 624

Fresh Tomato Slices

Tapioca Pudding—page 349
or
Frozen Yogurt

Favorite Beverage

Skillet cooking means dinner can be table-ready in less than an hour with delicious, nutritious results. The first step for the **Beef Oriental with Rice** preparation is marinating the meat. This gives you time to catch your breath after a busy day and complete other food preparation steps. The **Light Lemon Chicken** is also quick to fix, and both entrees are congenial with rice or noodles. Enjoy the pudding without chilling or pick up yogurt on the way home to end the meal with a complementary cooling finale.

Deluxe Dinner

Serves 4

Seafood Cocktail—page 61

Chicken Cordon Bleu—page 621

Cashew-Rice Pilaf—page 450

Fruit and Nut Tossed Salad—page 667

Oats 'n Wheat Dinner Rolls—page 162

Fruit with Caramel Cream—page 310

Dinner Beverages

Definitely aristocratic when it comes to cuisine. Dining deluxe, shall we say. We won't pretend that this menu isn't a bit more extravagant and a little more time-consuming. But then, there are certainly those occasions when we take pleasure in making an extra effort, when the guests are as special as the reasons to celebrate. You can depend on this meal to be memorable . . . an impressive marker for such milestones as a birthday, anniversary or promotion. Sneak in some time-savers, if you choose. Perhaps your butcher will bone and flatten the chicken breasts. By the way, the secret for keeping the cheese from melting out of the chicken is to use large breasts and take care to seal, coat thoroughly and chill as directed. If cost is a concern, substitute a moderately priced appetizer or a soup for the **Seafood Cocktail**. The dessert is an ideal complement for the rich entree—light and colorful.

Formal Dinner for Four

Serves 4

Escargots—page 60
or
Creamy Brie Spread—page 52

Cracker Bread
or
Melba Toast

Fruit and Nut Tossed Salad—page 667

Apricot Glazed Cornish Hens—page 661

Wild Rice-Sausage Stuffing—page 644

English Mushroom and Cream Bake—page 806

Julienned Vegetable Bundles—page 71

Crown Dinner Rolls—page 161

Herb Butter—page 141

Pear Tart Elegante—page 359
or
After Dinner Irish Cream—page 106

Dinner Wine

Coffee or Tea

This menu can provide a dash of elegance for a special occasion. Begin with a French accent and follow up with **Apricot Glazed Cornish Hens** where beautiful presentation belies the simplicity of preparation. The fresh vegetables and fruits featured in the accompaniments complement the hens with added color, textures and nutrients. Serve the **Crown Rolls** with herb-sparked butter if you choose, and ring down the culinary curtain with one of the two ravishingly rich dessert options.

Teen Celebration

Serves 6

Old-Fashioned Lemonade—page 84

Dilled Garden Dip—page 43

Back Pack Snack—page 75

Sloppy Joes—page 560 & Creamy Coleslaw—page 677
or
Pizza Deluxe—page 417

Confetti Balloon Cake—page 215
or
Black-Bottom Cups—page 207

Ice Cream

When it's time for a gathering to celebrate, you can turn to these favorite menu choices. There are lots of make-ahead options here so the cook doesn't miss any of the fun. The theme is informal—great for colorful, casual paper or pottery dishes and accessories. Let the **Confetti Balloon Cake** double as a centerpiece and dessert or treat guests to the irresistible **Black-Bottom Cups,** adding ice cream if you wish. Just spoon up a variety of colors and flavors and freeze on cookie sheets for speedy serving with no last-minute scooping to be done.

Hints for Successful Entertaining

When cooking for more people than usual at party and celebration times, planning, preparation and serving can be more demanding. Our menu suggestions and information can help dispel concerns and allow you to enjoy your own parties to the fullest.

Successful parties are a combination of many factors—relaxed hosts, congenial guests, pleasing ambiance and good food. It is important for you to select a style of entertaining that is comfortable and realistic for you.

Planning is the first step for a smoothly running, festive event for even the most casual of gatherings requires forethought and preparation on someone's part. As you recall delightful parties, the hosts welcomed you in a relaxed manner and the food, no matter how simple, was presented attractively and tasted terrific. The ambiance was enjoyable for guests and host.

Elements of Party Planning

• When making your guest list, consider the number you can accommodate, your budget and congeniality of the group. Whether you call or send written invitations, do it well ahead of time and include all the pertinent information—date, time, place plus directions, attire, theme or type of gathering, and special instructions like what to bring and whether the party is a surprise.

• For decor or theme, imagination is much more important than money in creating an inviting atmosphere. Theme entertaining can provide an opportunity for you to be especially creative, using your originality for bold and attractive decorations, dress and entertainment as well as menus.

• Plan a menu in keeping with the occasion, your budget, time available for food preparation, culinary skills required, cooking and baking space, refrigerator and freezer space for make-aheads, and the manner of serving. Choose foods and garnishes that complement one another and offer variety in colors, flavors, textures, temperatures and suitability to serving style.

• Make several lists to help keep track of tasks to do and when to do them. Include your menu with cookbook page numbers, shopping lists for nonperishable and perishable items, foods to prepare in advance, serving dishes, tableware and decorations, extras and a cooking time chart. Thinking each aspect through and putting it on paper can save time, money and energy.

• The type of party you are planning will determine the type of serving. Sit-down service adapts well to a smaller number and is the most comfortable for guests. Buffet service offers flexibility in terms of space and equipment for larger groups. Buffet serving can be formal or casual; the occasion will set the tone.

• In planning a buffet setup, the primary concern in determining menu and serving sequence is the convenience and comfort of your guests. Foods must be easy to serve and easy to eat. The number of guests and the space available will determine the number of serving lines and placement of serving table or tables. Often beverages and/or desserts can be served away from the main buffet table.

• Plan the arrangement of items on a buffet table in a sequence that makes serving oneself as easy as possible. Begin with the plates, then the main course followed by other foods from hot to cold. If guests will need two hands to serve themselves a salad, for instance, allow space for their plate to be set down. Flatware, napkins and beverages come last.

• At sit-down dinners, the host can fill plates in the kitchen or at the table. Or family-style, food can be passed around the table, but for safety's sake don't attempt to pass hot serving dishes.

• For the comfort of your guests, don't overlook pleasant ambiance with adequate outside lighting, space for coats or gifts, guest towels in the bathroom and ashtrays and coasters—touches as practical as they are thoughtful.

Buffet Setting

Serving food buffet style is the perfect solution for serving more people than could be comfortably seated around your dining room table. Guest convenience is foremost in determining buffet menu and serving sequence. Foods must be easy to serve and easy to eat. The number to serve and space available will determine the number of serving lines and table placement. Often beverages and/or desserts can be served away from the main buffet tables.

A logical sequence for serving oneself determines arrangement of items on a buffet table. Begin with plates, then the main course followed by other foods from hot to cold. If guests need two hands to serve themselves a food such as a salad, allow space for their plate. Flatware, napkins and beverages come last.

Amounts of Food to Purchase for Home Entertainment

Food Items	Serving Size	25 Servings	50 Servings	100 Servings
Meats, Cheeses and Buns				
Ham, turkey, cold cuts (1/2 oz. slices)	2 to 3 oz.	3 to 5 lb.	7 to 9 lb.	14 to 18 lb.
Cheese slices (1/2 oz. slices)	1 to 1 1/2 oz.	1 1/2 to 2 1/2 lb.	3 to 5 lb.	6 to 10 lb.
Buns	1 1/2 buns	3 dozen	6 dozen	12 dozen
Prepared Foods				
Chicken or Potato Salad	1/2 cup	1 gallon	2 gallons	4 gallons
Condiments				
Mayonnaise	1 to 2 teaspoons	1/2 to 1 cup	1 to 2 cups	2 to 4 cups
Mustard	1 teaspoon	1/2 cup	1 cup	2 cups
Olives (small or medium)	2 to 3	6 oz.	1 lb.	2 lb.
Pickles (medium spear)	1	1 quart	2 quarts	4 quarts
Desserts				
Cake	2x2-inch piece	1/4 sheet cake (24 pcs.)	1/2 sheet cake (48 pcs.)	1 sheet cake (96 pcs.)
Ice Cream	1/2 cup	1 gallon	2 gallons	4 gallons
Ice Cream Toppings	2 tablespoons	3 cups	6 cups	12 cups
Mixed Nuts	1 1/2 tablespoons	1/2 to 3/4 lb.	1 to 1 1/2 lb.	2 to 3 lb.
Mints				
small pillow	1 to 2	1/4 to 1/2 lb.	1/2 to 1 lb.	1 to 2 lb.
Wafer	1	3/4 lb.	1 1/2 lb.	3 lb.
Beverages				
Coffee	3/4 cup (6 oz.)	1/2 lb.	1 lb.	2 lb.
Coffee Cream	1 teaspoon	1/2 pint	1 pint	1 quart
Punch	1/2 cup (4 oz.)	1 gallon	2 gallons	4 gallons
Sugar Cubes	1 cube	6 oz.	3/4 lb.	1 1/2 lb.

Traditional Holiday Buffet

Serves 8

Wassail Bowl—page 90

Glazed Baked Ham—pages 583, 584
or
Microwave Glazed Ham—page 583

Mashed Sweet Potatoes—page 847

Sunny Sprouts—page 794

Jeweled Cranberry Shimmer—page 695

Quick Pickles—page 728
or
Summer Harvest Relish—page 726

Holiday Cranberry Bread—page 121

Cloverleaf Rolls—page 161

Cherries 'n Cream Dessert Squares—page 341
or
Steamed Plum Pudding—page 322

No one needs more to do during the busy holiday season and yet, what a wonderful time to entertain family and friends. And so we have fashioned a festive but simply prepared buffet menu with a magnificent **Glazed Ham** as the focal point. Several make-aheads help keep party day free for last-minute assembling and before-serving cooking. If oven space is limited or time at a premium, you can microwave the ham with excellent results. The traditional flavors in this menu will appeal to all ages, and the dishes are perfect for buffet presentation—colorful and easily served. The **Wassail Bowl** offers cups of good cheer to all your guests and begins the party with a hearty Old English welcome. If an appetizer is desired, try a savory Cheddar cheese spread and rye crackers.

Open House Buffet

Whether you elect to serve hors d'oeuvres only or heartier fare, you will appreciate these two open house options because almost every recipe is either totally or partially make-ahead. If the hours of your party are midafternoon or later into the evening, the lighter food array is preferred. However, if guests are expected around the usual dinner hours, the more complete menu will be appreciated by hungry partygoers. Adjust recipe yield to suit your needs.

Appetizer Buffet

Apple Grape Punch—page 85
or
Tart 'n Tangy Citrus Punch—page 89

Cheese Shrimp Puffs—page 70

Tortellini Kabobs—page 73

Barbecued Riblets—page 64

Curry Dip with Fresh Vegetable Dippers—page 44

Nippy Zippy Cheese Logs with Snack Rye Bread—page 53

Chocolate-Dipped Strawberries—page 860

Lemon Kiss Cookies—page 259

Coffee or Tea

For the Appetizer Buffet, **Barbecued Riblets** can be kept warm in a slow cooker or chafing dish until serving and the **Cheese Shrimp Puffs** can be microwaved just before serving. Chilled items can be arranged on serving plates 1 to 2 hours ahead, but must be refrigerated until serving time. This delectable spread offers a tantalizing array of hot and cold, loads of color plus texture and flavor contrasts—just the right presentation any time of year.

Small Meal Open House

Banana Slush—page 88

Cocktail Nuts—page 75

Hot Cheesy Clam Dip—page 43

Barbecued Beef Sandwiches—page 551

Cauliflower and Broccoli Make-Ahead—page 674

Watermelon Fruit Basket—page 689

Cookies 'n Cream Cake—page 179

The Small Meal Open House is a do-ahead dandy with all-American favorites. Although the **Watermelon Fruit Basket** is definitely warm weather fare, the other recipes are as agreeable in midwinter as they are in midsummer. Just substitute a hot or chilled fruit compote or a winter fruit salad when melons are unavailable. This is a menu tailor-made for casual, informal entertaining—after a game, for a patio or deck, a christening or a neighborhood roundup. With no last-minute fuss, dishes are simply set out when it's time to eat. It's a serve-yourself meal that will have them coming back for seconds (and the recipes)!

Meal Planning for Good Health

Eating for good health on a day-to-day basis doesn't just happen. Translating nutritional needs into adequate and delicious meals begins with thoughtful planning and consideration for each individual's dietary requirements, food preferences and schedules. Such planning begins with basic food groups and also involves your imagination and cooking skills to create meals that you and your family enjoy making and eating.

The following reference chart can guide you in meal planning. Because there is no one perfect food to supply all the body-building maintenance nutrients, a healthful diet requires a broad variety of foods from each group, except Other Foods, in appropriate amounts. Everyone requires the same nutrients; however, the number of calories differs with age, size, sex, activity level and state of health. Adjust the size and number of servings to individual needs, for even a well-balanced diet can provide too many calories when eaten in excess.

Remember that snack foods count as part of a daily diet—for better or worse. Snacks and mini meals chosen from fresh fruits, yogurt, cheese and fresh vegetables, for instance, provide wholesome eating and help eliminate "empty calories." Having these foods readily available in the refrigerator or pantry makes it easier for everyone to eat healthfully.

Guide to Daily Food Needs

Food Group	Minimum Daily Requirement	Serving Size	Principal Nutrients
Milk and Milk Products	2 to 4 servings (children, teens and women have the greatest need)	1 cup (8 oz.) milk 1½ oz. cheese 1 cup yogurt 2 cups cottage cheese	calcium, riboflavin, protein, for strong bones, teeth, healthy skin, good vision
Meat, Fish, Poultry, Dried Peas and Beans, Nuts and Seeds	2 servings (balance vegetable protein for complete amino acids when served without animal protein)	2 to 3 oz. cooked meat, fish or poultry (without fat or bone) 1 cup legumes ½ cup nuts or seeds	iron, protein for muscle, bone and blood cells and healthy skin and nerves
Fruit and Vegetables	4 servings (1 Vitamin C source daily)	½ cup juice 1 cup cooked vegetable or fruit 1 cup raw vegetable 1 medium apple, banana or orange	vitamin A vitamin C for night vision and to resist infections
Enriched and Whole Grain Cereals and Bread	4 servings	1 slice bread ½ cup cooked cereal, rice or pasta 1 cup ready-to-eat cereal	carbohydrates, thiamin, iron, niacin for energy and healthy nervous system
Combination Foods Like Chili, Lasagna, or Beef Stew	These count as servings or partial servings from food groups from which they are made	1 cup soup or stew 1 cup pasta dishes ¼ 14-inch pizza 1 sandwich	
Other Foods Like Sweets, Fats and Oils, Chips and Related Snack Items, Alcoholic Beverages, Condiments	There are no recommended servings for these foods	Select these foods if additional calories are needed after the recommended amounts from the above food groups	

Planning Menus

Let menus in this chapter and the recipes throughout this cookbook embellish your own creative ideas for wholesome, tasty meals your family and guests will enjoy. Using these few simple guidelines, menu planning will be easier, quicker and more rewarding for you.

• Begin with an inventory of foods on hand and consider how you might use them in the week's menus.

• Decide on your main dish for each meal and then on appropriate side dishes. For economy and efficiency, try to use foods you already have on hand.

• Variety is the key to an appealing meal or week's menu. Vary flavors, colors, textures and temperature of foods to create interesting contrasts. Use of special relishes and garnishes can also provide added interest.

• Expand your usual menu repertoire with new recipe ideas from cookbooks, magazines or friends.

• Introduce ethnic foods for a change of pace and let the family have the fun of an occasional theme dinner.

• Vary menus to suit the season. For instance, in warm weather serve nutritious cold soups, hearty main-dish sandwiches requiring brief oven time and foods that can be microwaved rather than cooked in the oven.

• Be realistic about the amount of time you have for meal preparation. Plan quick-to-fix foods for busy days and more elaborate dishes when time is available. Plan meals that can be kept hot in a slow cooker or low oven or quickly reheated in the microwave for days when family members eat at different times.

Timesaving Ideas for Shopping

Menu planning and grocery shopping are definitely not a "chicken or an egg" situation. It is faster, easier and more economical to shop with a shopping list in hand following your weekly meal plan. Among other advantages, you return home with ALL necessary ingredients rather than only the ones you could recall at the store. When planning your shopping, be on the lookout for advertised specials and seasonal options, both of which can provide good value and fresh appeal.

When you shop, keep your storage limitations in mind. Purchase only the size and number of goods you can store safely and use within the time allotted for optimum quality.

In the real world, menu planning is not always precise. Having basic pantry goods on hand is helpful for last-minute or impromptu meals. Our suggestions for the family pantry:

• **Packaged goods:** flour, sugar, salt, baking powder, baking soda, yeast, cornstarch, baking chocolate, pasta, rice, dry soup mixes, cereals, dry bread crumbs, pancake and other mixes, crackers, nuts and bouillon.

• **Refrigerated items:** Milk, eggs, butter or margarine, cheeses, bacon, luncheon meats, lemon juice, fruits and vegetables.

• **Freezer items:** Meats, fish and poultry in family-sized packages, vegetables, fruits and fruit juice concentrates, bread, dessert items and ice cream products.

• **Canned goods:** meats, fish, poultry, vegetables, soups, fruits, juices, pie fillings, cocoa, coffee, tomato sauce and paste.

• **In bottles and jars:** mustard, catsup, mayonnaise, sauces, salad dressings, peanut butter, preserves, corn syrup, vinegar, oil, maple syrup, honey, wines and liqueurs.

Herbs, spices and extracts: thyme, oregano, basil, dill, paprika, chili powder, poultry seasoning, garlic and onion powders or salts, instant minced onion, dry mustard, cinnamon, cloves, ginger, nutmeg, poppy and sesame seeds, vanilla and almond extracts.

Nutrition for Good Health

To assist in planning healthful, wholesome meals, specific nutritional information is provided with each recipe. This unique NUTRI-CODED system, a computerized method designed by Pillsbury research scientists, utilizes information compiled by the U.S. Department of Agriculture in the revised Agriculture Handbook No. 8, and represents Pillsbury's strong, continuing commitment to nutrition education for the consumer. Every effort has been made to ensure accuracy of information; however, The Pillsbury Company does not guarantee its suitability for specific medically imposed diets.

The NUTRI-CODES for each recipe provide information on a per serving basis about:

calories, protein, carbohydrates, fat, cholesterol, dietary fiber, sodium, potassium, calcium and iron.

Protein, carbohydrates and fats are expressed in grams; sodium and potassium in milligrams. The amounts of calcium and iron are expressed as percentages needed by the body on a daily basis (U.S. Recommended Daily Allowance).

Guidelines Used in Calculating the Nutrition Information:

• When the ingredient listing gives one or more options, the first ingredient is analyzed.

• When an ingredient range is given, the larger amount is analyzed.

• When an ingredient is listed as "if desired," it is analyzed.

• When a serving suggestion is listed in the ingredients, it is analyzed.

• When each bread recipe is analyzed, a serving of yeast-leavened bread is a 1-ounce slice; a quick-bread serving is ¹⁄₁₆ of the loaf. Recipes that vary are indicated.

• Many ingredients are given generically. The following generic ingredients were analyzed:

Generic Ingredient	Used for Analysis
cottage cheese	creamed small curd
cream	whipping
eggs	large
fish fillets	cod
flour	all-purpose
ground beef	regular, 70% lean
ice cream	vanilla, 10% fat
milk	lowfat, 2% fat
nuts	walnuts
oil	corn oil
orange juice	reconstituted from frozen concentrate
oysters	Eastern
parsley	fresh
rice	enriched white
tomato paste	with salt
vinegar	white, distilled
yogurt	lowfat

• Occasionally foods, particularly rice, vegetables and pasta, are cooked in salted water. Extra sodium as a result of absorption was not calculated.

• The **VARIATIONS** given at the end of many recipes are not included in the nutrition information.

• In some instances, variations in the recipe itself make it impossible to calculate nutrition.

• **Symbol Reference**

<2 Less than 2% of the nutrient
<1 Less than one gram (or milligram) of the nutrient

Using NUTRI-CODE Information

NUTRIENTS PER ⅛ OF RECIPE	
Calories............................120	Dietary Fiber...........2 g
Protein..............................4 g	Sodium ....260 mg
Carbohydrate..................8 g	Potassium............460 mg
Fat......................................8 g	Calcium......4% U.S. RDA
Cholesterol.................20 mg	Iron.........6% U.S. RDA

Sample Nutrition Information from Broccoli-Mushroom Saute

Serving Size

A typical serving for each recipe as determined by our home economists. If you eat more or less, adjust the nutrition information accordingly.

Calories

The amount of calories a person needs is determined by age, size and activity level. The recommended daily allowances generally given are: 1800 to 2400 for women and 2400 to 2800 for men.

Protein

Protein provides the principal building blocks for all muscles and organs and is essential to life. Complete protein, containing all 20 of the essential amino acids in the right proportion, is found in meats, poultry, fish, eggs, milk and cheese. Dried beans and peas and certain nuts and seeds also are rich in protein, although their quality is somewhat lower. By combining them appropriately with grains, their quality can be made as good as that of meat proteins.

The amount of protein needed daily is determined by age and size; the general U.S. RDA for adults is 65 grams.

Carbohydrates

A principal source of energy, digestible carbohydrates consist primarily of starches and sugars. The starches are found in cereals (wheat, rice, corn, oats), breads, pasta, potatoes, beets, yams and turnips. The chief sugar sources are honey, syrup, table sugar and fruit.

The amount of carbohydrates and fat needed in the daily diet is dependent upon the daily caloric requirement. The amounts should be adequate so the body does not have to burn protein for energy. The American Heart Association and other nutrition authorities advise that 50% to 55% of calories should come from carbohydrates.

Fats

Fats are the most concentrated source of energy for the body. They supply essential fatty acids, which is important as the body cannot manufacture them. They are carriers of the fat-soluble vitamins A, D, E and K. Fats contain slightly more than twice as many calories per gram or per ounce as do pure proteins and carbohydrates.

Food fat is available in two forms. One form, saturated fat (usually solid at room temperature), generally comes from animal sources such as meat and milk. Some vegetable fats, such as coconut oil and cocoa butter, are also saturated. The other form is unsaturated fat. There are two kinds of unsaturated fat: monounsaturated and polyunsaturated. Both are usually liquid at room temperature and come mainly from vegetable sources. Exceptions are fish and fish oil which contain varying amounts of mono- and polyunsaturated fats. Common sources of monounsaturated fats are peanut oil, olive oil, nuts including peanuts and olives. Sources of polyunsaturated fats are sunflower oil and seeds, soybeans and soybean oil, corn oil and safflower oil.

Nutritionists believe that obtaining no more than 30% of

your calories from fat would result in less incidence of obesity, heart disease and other chronic diseases.

Cholesterol

Cholesterol, a fatlike substance synthesized by the body, is found in every living body cell. It has important body functions; however, a high blood cholesterol level is a major risk factor in coronary heart disease. Saturated fats in food tend to raise blood cholesterol levels. Saturated fat is found in meat, especially in heavily marbelized beef cuts; fat attached to poultry skin; processed meats such as sausages and hot dogs; egg yolks; milk products like ice cream, whole milk, hard and cream cheeses; cream and sour cream; cocoa butter (found in chocolates); coconut oil, palm oil, and palm kernel oil (found in many commercially prepared baked goods).

The American Heart Association advises that no more than 30% of calories should come from fat and of this 30%, no more than 10% should be saturated fats, with cholesterol intake limited to about 300 mg. per day.

Dietary Fiber

Fiber is a complex carbohydrate and is generally defined as the part of plant material that cannot be digested and absorbed into the bloodstream. Fiber can be water-soluble or insoluble. Water-soluble fibers help to slow food absorption and promote a "full" feeling and may help to lower blood cholesterol levels. Water-insoluble fibers pass quickly through the digestive tract, which aids regularity. Food sources of fiber are whole grains, cereals, legumes and beans, nuts, fruits and vegetables.

Nutritionists recommend a dietary fiber intake of 20 to 35 g. per day from a variety of food sources.

Sodium and Potassium

A proper balance of sodium and potassium within the body is necessary for normal functioning of the nervous system. Sodium is needed to maintain normal body fluid volume. Potassium is found principally within cells and is essential to their function.

The most common sources of sodium are table salt (1 teaspoon = 2132 mg. of sodium), milk, cheese, leavenings, soy sauce and monosodium glutamate (MSG). Nutrition authorities recommend that the "safe and adequate" range of sodium intake per day is 1100 to 3300 mg. Most Americans consume 4000 to 8000 mg. daily.

Important sources of potassium are meat, fish, poultry, cereals, vegetables and fruits, especially bananas. One average banana has 440 mg. of potassium. The minimum daily requirement for potassium has not yet been determined; however, the "safe and adequate" range of potassium intake per day is in the range of 1875 to 5625 mg.

Calcium

Calcium is one of the most commonly deficient minerals in the diet. The main sources of calcium are milk and milk products (yogurt, cheese, ice cream), canned fish with edible bones (sardines, salmon), tofu, beans and leafy vegetables.

The RDA for adults is 800 mg. per day. Women typically consume 500 to 700 mg. per day. Recent research studies have indicated that women over the age of fifty benefit from 1500 mg. per day.

Iron

Iron is important because it transports oxygen in the body. Children during growth periods and women in childbearing years have additional iron needs.

The RDA for adults is 18 mg. per day for women and 10 mg. for men. Half of women consume less than two thirds of the RDA for iron.

Vitamins and Minerals

These are other vitamins and microminerals, not listed with this NUTRI-CODE information, that are required to stay healthy. Eating a wide variety of foods from the basic food groups each day should supply your body with sufficient quantities of these nutrients.

Any questions regarding nutrition information in this book should be addressed to:

THE PILLSBURY COMPANY
Pillsbury Center—Suite 2866
Minneapolis, MN 55402

Appetizers, Snacks & Beverages

Appetizers, Snacks & Beverages

Appetizers

Appetizers are tempting food creations that have become a symbol of hospitality around the world. They are as varied as the chefs who prepare them and are a tasty way of welcoming guests and setting the stage for conviviality.

Selection

Choosing appetizers depends on several factors: other foods to be served, number of servings needed, style of service, serving equipment, oven and refrigerator space, special dietary guidelines and personal preference. The primary consideration in selecting appetizers is to achieve a balance of flavors with other items on the menu.

Appetizers offer contrast in flavors, textures, temperatures, colors, piece size and overall appearance. When served before a meal, appetizers should be light enough to just stimulate, not satisfy, the appetite. A single special appetizer can be chosen for a formal first course. It is often heartier and more elaborate than are appetizers when more than one is served. Some soups and fruit salads are also appropriate as first-course appetizers. When two or more appetizers are served before a meal, select one or two nibbler-type appetizers along with a dip or spread.

When appetizers are the main food event, plan to serve a variety of nibblers, spreads and dips. Select items that are easy for guests to serve themselves. As a general rule, for a party of 6 to 8 people, select 4 to 6 different kinds of appetizers to serve. This amount will vary depending on the number and type of appetizers available, when they will be served and the appetite of your guests.

Preparation

To avoid spending time in the kitchen away from your guests, plan only one or two items that must be prepared at the last minute. Many appetizers cook and reheat well in the microwave oven, making preparation and serving easier. Some assembly procedures should be done near serving time to maintain appealing textures. Hot appetizers should be served promptly after cooking or heating or kept at ideal temperature with electric trays, chafing dishes, slow cookers or fondue pots. If an electric outlet is needed, plan to set up the appetizers where one is available.

Make-ahead options are plentiful. In fact, some dips and marinated mixtures improve on standing and may be made one or two days ahead. Many appetizers adapt well to freezing; however, appetizers with ingredients like hard-cooked eggs, mayonnaise, gelatin and fresh vegetables do not. Frozen appetizers should be used within three months and not be refrozen after thawing. To preserve appearance, place appetizers on a tray in a single layer; freeze until firm. Move to a suitable container that can be tightly sealed. If stacking is necessary, place waxed paper between layers. Separate layers and thaw frozen appetizers in refrigerator to avoid danger of spoilage.

Presentation

Let imagination and practicality be your guide for appetizer preparation. Presentation makes good food great food, but it should also help make the food easy to eat. Select complementary serving dishes of various heights, shapes and sizes. Be creative with baskets, napkins, flowers and other novelties. Be aware of balance and design when arranging the food, but avoid overly artful arrangements. Garnishing (see Index) can also enhance presentation. Garnishes should relate to the appetizer flavors and be arranged so they do not interfere with serving. Choose recipes that will remain attractive until the last person is served, or have filled trays ready to replace those that begin to look depleted.

Serving tongs, knives, spoons and forks should be plentiful. Small napkins should be passed with the appetizers and be readily available in the entertaining area. When several appetizers are served, small plates, napkins and forks should be available. For an appetizer buffet featuring many selections, luncheon-sized plates and napkins are appropriate, along with utensils. Food should be placed so guests can easily circulate and help themselves quickly.

Artichoke Appetizer

2 large artichokes
8 cups water
1 tablespoon lemon juice
2 garlic cloves, halved
   Any Easy Cream Dip (page 42)

Using sharp knife, cut off stem even with base. Cut off top
⅓ of artichoke; pull off small coarse lower leaves. Using
scissors, cut off thorny tips of remaining leaves. Rinse well.

In 5-quart Dutch oven or large saucepan, bring water, lemon
juice and garlic to a boil. Place artichokes stem end down in
boiling water. Return to a boil. Reduce heat; cover and simmer 35 to 45 minutes or until base can be easily pierced with
fork. Drain; cool slightly.

Pull out small center leaves; slightly spread remaining
leaves. Using a spoon, remove light green fuzzy center,
scraping out a little at a time, being careful not to remove
heart. Cool; cover and refrigerate for 1 hour or overnight.

To serve, place in serving bowl; gently spread leaves of artichoke. Remove a few leaves for garnish, if desired. Fill
center with cream dip. Use leaves as dippers. When outer
leaves are gone, cut heart into small pieces and serve with
toothpicks. **6 to 8 servings.**

MICROWAVE DIRECTIONS: Trim artichoke as directed
above. Brush with 2 tablespoons lemon juice. Place in 1-
quart round casserole with ¼ cup water. Cover with plastic
wrap. Microwave on HIGH for 4 to 5 minutes, rotating ½
turn after 2½ minutes, or until base can be easily pierced
with a fork. Continue as directed.

NUTRIENTS: Variables in this recipe make it impossible to calculate
nutrition information.

Easy Cream Dips

In small bowl, combine 1 cup dairy sour cream or an 8-oz. pkg. cream cheese, softened, with 1 to 2 tablespoons milk. Stir in desired flavor additions. Cover; refrigerate several hours or overnight to blend flavors.

VARIATIONS:

ONION DIP: Add 3 tablespoons dry onion soup mix. **1 cup.**

HAM DIP: Add 4½-oz. can deviled ham, 2 tablespoons pickle relish and ¼ teaspoon Worcestershire sauce. **1¾ cups.**

ITALIAN DIP: Add 1.5-oz. pkg. spaghetti sauce seasoning mix. **1 cup.**

CLAM DIP: Add 6½-oz. can minced clams, drained, 1 teaspoon finely chopped onion, ¼ teaspoon salt, 1 tablespoon lemon juice, 1 teaspoon Worcestershire sauce and 3 drops hot pepper sauce.

NUTRIENTS PER 1 TABLESPOON ONION DIP

Calories	35	Dietary Fiber	<1 g
Protein	1 g	Sodium	110 mg
Carbohydrate	1 g	Potassium	30 mg
Fat	3 g	Calcium	2% U.S. RDA
Cholesterol	6 mg	Iron	<2% U.S. RDA

Hot Cheesy Clam Dip

½ cup chopped green pepper
¼ cup chopped onion
3 tablespoons margarine or butter
¼ teaspoon cayenne pepper
¼ cup catsup
1 tablespoon Worcestershire sauce
2 (6-oz.) cans minced clams, well drained
4 oz. American cheese, cubed or sliced

In medium saucepan, saute green pepper and onion in margarine until tender. Stir in cayenne pepper, catsup, Worcestershire sauce and clams; cook over medium heat until hot and bubbly. Add cheese, stirring constantly until melted. Reduce heat; cover. Simmer 10 to 15 minutes or until mixture has slightly thickened. Serve warm with crackers, tortilla chips or fresh vegetable dippers. **1½ cups.**

MICROWAVE DIRECTIONS: In medium microwave-safe bowl, combine green pepper, onion and margarine. Cover with microwave-safe plastic wrap. Microwave on HIGH for 1½ to 3 minutes or until tender; stir. Add cayenne pepper, catsup, Worcestershire sauce and clams. Microwave on HIGH for 1 to 2 minutes or until hot. Add cheese; stir until well blended. If cheese is not melted, microwave on HIGH for additional 1 to 2 minutes. Stir before serving.

NUTRIENTS PER 1 TABLESPOON

Calories 40	Dietary Fiber........................<1 g
Protein ....2 g	Sodium ....130 mg
Carbohydrate..........................1 g	Potassium ....40 mg
Fat ....3 g	Calcium ....2% U.S. RDA
Cholesterol ....8 mg	Iron.......................2% U.S. RDA

Dilled Garden Dip

1½ cups creamed cottage cheese
1 tablespoon lemon juice

    2 tablespoons shredded carrot
    1 tablespoon sliced green onions
    1 tablespoon chopped fresh parsley
 1½ teaspoons chopped fresh dill or
       ½ teaspoon dill weed
    1 teaspoon sugar
       Dash pepper

In blender container, combine cottage cheese and lemon juice. Cover; blend 3 to 5 minutes at medium speed or until smooth. Stir in carrot, onions, parsley, dill, sugar and pepper. Cover; refrigerate several hours or overnight to blend flavors. Serve with crackers or fresh vegetable dippers. **1½ cups.**

NUTRIENTS PER 1 TABLESPOON

Calories	14	Dietary Fiber	<1 g
Protein	2 g	Sodium	55 mg
Carbohydrate	1 g	Potassium	20 mg
Fat	0 g	Calcium	<2% U.S. RDA
Cholesterol	2 mg	Iron	<2% U.S. RDA

Curry Dip

       1 cup dairy sour cream
       1 cup mayonnaise
       1 tablespoon catsup
       2 teaspoons chopped green onions
 ½ to 1 teaspoon curry powder
      ¼ teaspoon garlic salt
      ¼ teaspoon Worcestershire sauce

In small bowl, combine all ingredients. Cover; refrigerate several hours or overnight to blend flavors. Serve with vegetable dippers. **2 cups.**

NUTRIENTS PER 1 TABLESPOON

Calories 70	Dietary Fiber........................<1 g
Protein ....0 g	Sodium..............................65 mg
Carbohydrate..........................1 g	Potassium ....15 mg
Fat ....7 g	Calcium.............<2% U.S. RDA
Cholesterol..........................6 mg	Iron ....<2% U.S. RDA

Taco Dip

8-oz.	pkg. cream cheese, softened
8-oz.	carton dairy sour cream
6-oz.	pkg. frozen avocado dip, thawed
1	teaspoon lemon juice
4	drops hot pepper sauce
4-oz.	can chopped ripe olives
4-oz.	can chopped green chiles, drained
4	green onions, chopped
2	cups torn lettuce
1	tomato, peeled, chopped
4 oz.	(1 cup) shredded Cheddar cheese

In small bowl, blend cream cheese, sour cream, avocado dip, lemon juice and hot pepper sauce. Spread mixture on large serving plate. Top with remaining ingredients. Serve with tortilla chips. **10 to 12 servings.**

TIP: Dip can be made several hours ahead; store in refrigerator. Just before serving, top with olives, chiles, onions, lettuce, tomato and cheese.

NUTRIENTS PER ½ of RECIPE

Calories 190	Dietary Fiber..........................1 g
Protein ....5 g	Sodium............................280 mg
Carbohydrate..........................5 g	Potassium ....120 mg
Fat ....16 g	Calcium.............10% U.S. RDA
Cholesterol........................40 mg	Iron ....2% U.S. RDA

Salsa

28-oz.	can tomato wedges or whole tomatoes, drained, chopped*
½	cup thinly sliced green onions
4-oz.	can green chiles, seeded, chopped**
1	teaspoon grated lemon peel, if desired
½	teaspoon salt
½	teaspoon oregano leaves
⅛	teaspoon pepper
2 to 3	tablespoons lemon juice
2	tablespoons oil

In large bowl, combine all ingredients; mix well. Cover; refrigerate several hours to blend flavors. Serve with tortilla chips. **2½ cups.**

TIPS: *Two cups (2 to 3 medium) chopped, peeled tomatoes can be substituted for canned tomatoes.

**One to 2 fresh jalapeño peppers, seeded and finely chopped, can be substituted for green chiles.

NUTRIENTS PER 1 TABLESPOON

Calories	12	Dietary Fiber	<1 g
Protein	0 g	Sodium	50 mg
Carbohydrate	1 g	Potassium	45 mg
Fat	1 g	Calcium	<2% U.S. RDA
Cholesterol	0 mg	Iron	<2% U.S. RDA

Classic Guacamole

2	large ripe avocados, peeled, mashed
¼	cup finely chopped onion
2	tablespoons lemon juice
2 to 5	drops hot pepper sauce, if desired
¼ to ½	teaspoon garlic powder
¼	teaspoon salt
	Dash pepper

> 1 medium tomato, chopped
> 2 tablespoons finely chopped green chiles or
>   1 small chile pepper, chopped

In blender container or food processor bowl with metal blade, combine all ingredients except tomato and green chiles. Blend until smooth. Stir in tomato and green chiles. Cover; refrigerate at least 30 minutes to blend flavors. Serve with tortilla or corn chips. **3 cups.**

TIP: To use avocado shells for serving, cut unpeeled avocado in half lengthwise. Remove pit and scoop fruit out of shell with spoon. Continue as directed above. Fill shells with dip and refrigerate until serving time.

VARIATIONS:

CREAMY GUACAMOLE: Add ¼ cup mayonnaise or dairy sour cream.

BACON GUACAMOLE: Stir in 2 slices bacon, crisply cooked, crumbled, with the tomato and green chiles.

NUTRIENTS PER 1 TABLESPOON

Calories	14	Dietary Fiber	<1 g
Protein	0 g	Sodium	10 mg
Carbohydrate	1 g	Potassium	60 mg
Fat	1 g	Calcium	<2% U.S. RDA
Cholesterol	0 mg	Iron	<2% U.S. RDA

Shrimp Cocktail Dip

> 4½-oz. can small shrimp, rinsed, drained and coarsely
>   chopped
> 1 cup dairy sour cream
> ¼ cup chili sauce
> 2 teaspoons lemon juice
> ½ to 1 teaspoon prepared horseradish
> ¼ teaspoon seasoned salt
>   Dash hot pepper sauce

In small bowl, combine all ingredients. Cover; refrigerate several hours or overnight to blend flavors. Serve with crackers or baguette slices. **1¾ cups.**

NUTRIENTS PER 1 TABLESPOON

Calories	25	Dietary Fiber	<1 g
Protein	1 g	Sodium	55 mg
Carbohydrate	1 g	Potassium	30 mg
Fat	2 g	Calcium	<2% U.S. RDA
Cholesterol	10 mg	Iron	<2% U.S. RDA

Hot Broccoli Dip

¼   cup margarine or butter
½   cup chopped onion
2   (4-oz.) cans mushroom pieces and stems, drained
2   (10¾-oz.) cans condensed cream of mushroom soup
8   oz. pasteurized process cheese food, cut into cubes
2   (5-oz.) jars sharp pasteurized process cheese spread
2   (9-oz.) pkg. frozen cut broccoli, thawed, drained, cut into bite-size pieces
⅓   cup slivered almonds
½   teaspoon garlic powder
1   teaspoon Worcestershire sauce
3 to 4   drops hot pepper sauce

In large skillet, melt margarine. Add onion and mushrooms; saute until onion is tender, about 3 minutes. Add soup and cheeses; cook until mixture is smooth and bubbly, stirring constantly. Add broccoli, almonds, garlic powder, Worcestershire sauce and hot pepper sauce. Simmer 10 minutes, stirring occasionally. Serve warm with tortilla chips, assorted crackers, bread chunks or fresh vegetable dippers. **7 cups.**

NUTRIENTS PER 1 TABLESPOON

Calories 25	Dietary Fiber.........................<1 g
Protein......................................1 g	Sodium..............................105 mg
Carbohydrate...........................1 g	Potassium...........................30 mg
Fat ....2 g	Calcium.................2% U.S. RDA
Cholesterol...........................2 mg	Iron ....<2% U.S. RDA

Late Summer Fruit Kabobs

  3 pears or apples, cored, cut into wedges
     Lemon juice
  3 plums, pitted, cut into wedges
 24 seedless green grapes
 24 seedless red grapes or watermelon cubes

Dip pear or apple wedges in lemon juice to prevent discoloration. On wooden skewers, place fruit to contrast in shape and color. Refrigerate until serving. Serve with Frosty Fruit Dip or Raspberry Cream Dip. **12 kabobs.**

NUTRIENTS PER 1 KABOB

Calories 35	Dietary Fiber.........................1 g
Protein......................................0 g	Sodium..................................0 mg
Carbohydrate...........................9 g	Potassium...........................90 mg
Fat ....0 g	Calcium...............<2% U.S. RDA
Cholesterol...........................0 mg	Iron ....<2% U.S. RDA

Raspberry Cream Dip

  6 oz. cream cheese, softened
  1 tablespoon brown sugar
 ½ teaspoon ginger
  1 tablespoon red wine vinegar
  1 cup raspberries, crushed

In small bowl, combine cream cheese, brown sugar, ginger and vinegar; blend until smooth. Stir in raspberries; refrigerate. Serve as dip or dressing for fresh fruit. **1¼ cups.**

NUTRIENTS PER 1 TABLESPOON

Calories 40	Dietary Fiber.........................<1 g
Protein ....1 g	Sodium ....25 mg
Carbohydrate...........................2 g	Potassium ....25 mg
Fat ....3 g	Calcium..............<2% U.S. RDA
Cholesterol...........................8 mg	Iron ....<2% U.S. RDA

Frosty Fruit Dip

In small bowl, combine 8-oz. pkg. cream cheese, softened, and 8-oz. carton fruit-flavored yogurt; blend well. Serve with fresh fruit dippers or fruit kabobs. Store tightly covered in refrigerator. **2 cups.**

NUTRIENTS PER 1 TABLESPOON

Calories 40	Dietary Fiber.........................<1 g
Protein ....1 g	Sodium ....25 mg
Carbohydrate...........................2 g	Potassium ....20 mg
Fat ....3 g	Calcium..............<2% U.S. RDA
Cholesterol...........................8 mg	Iron ....<2% U.S. RDA

Molded Cucumber Spread

> 1 envelope unflavored gelatin
> ¼ cup boiling water
> ¼ cup cold water
> ½ teaspoon salt
> 1½ cups mayonnaise
> 1 large cucumber, peeled, seeded, cut up (2 cups)
> 2 stalks celery, cut up (1 cup)
> 1 medium onion, quartered
> 1 small green pepper, quartered, seeded

Lightly oil 5-cup mold or 1½-quart mixing bowl. In medium bowl, dissolve gelatin in boiling water; stir in cold water and salt. Add mayonnaise; mix well. In blender container or food processor bowl with metal blade, coarsely chop vegetables; add to mayonnaise mixture. Mix well. Pour mixture into prepared mold. Refrigerate until firm. Unmold onto serving plate. Garnish as desired. Serve with assorted crackers or snack rye bread. **4½ cups.**

NUTRIENTS PER 1 TABLESPOON

Calories	35	Dietary Fiber	<1 g
Protein	0 g	Sodium	40 mg
Carbohydrate	0 g	Potassium	15 mg
Fat	4 g	Calcium	<2% U.S. RDA
Cholesterol	2 mg	Iron	<2% U.S. RDA

Hot Crab Meat Spread

8-oz. pkg. cream cheese, softened
6-oz. can crab meat, drained and flaked
 ½ cup dairy sour cream
 2 tablespoons finely chopped green onions
 1 tablespoon milk
 1 teaspoon lemon juice
 ¼ teaspoon garlic salt
 ⅛ teaspoon pepper
 ⅓ cup toasted sliced almonds

Heat oven to 375°F. In medium bowl, combine all ingredients except almonds; mix well. Spread in ungreased 9-inch pie pan or shallow 1-quart casserole; sprinkle with almonds. Bake at 375°F. for 15 to 20 minutes or until thoroughly heated. Serve with crackers. **2 cups.**

NUTRIENTS PER 1 TABLESPOON

Calories	50	Dietary Fiber	<1 g
Protein	2 g	Sodium	70 mg
Carbohydrate	1 g	Potassium	25 mg
Fat	4 g	Calcium	<2% U.S. RDA
Cholesterol	15 mg	Iron	<2% U.S. RDA

Gruyere Apple Spread

3-oz. pkg. cream cheese, softened
2 oz. (½ cup) shredded Gruyere cheese
  2 teaspoons milk
  1 teaspoon prepared mustard
  ¼ cup shredded peeled apple
  1 tablespoon finely chopped pecans
  1 teaspoon chopped chives

In small bowl, beat cream cheese; stir in shredded cheese,
milk and mustard until well blended. Stir in remaining ingredients. Cover; refrigerate 1 hour. Serve on assorted
crackers. **1 cup.**

NUTRIENTS PER 1 TABLESPOON

Calories	35	Dietary Fiber	<1 g
Protein	1 g	Sodium	40 mg
Carbohydrate	1 g	Potassium	15 mg
Fat	3 g	Calcium	<2% U.S. RDA
Cholesterol	10 mg	Iron	<2% U.S. RDA

Creamy Brie Spread

4 oz. Brie cheese, softened
3-oz. pkg. cream cheese, softened
  ½ teaspoon seasoned salt
  2 tablespoons sliced almonds

Line 10-oz. custard cup or bowl with plastic wrap. In
medium bowl, blend Brie (including crust), cream cheese
and seasoned salt until smooth. Spoon into prepared cup;
press firmly to pack. Refrigerate several hours or overnight
to blend flavors. Unmold onto serving plate; remove plastic
wrap. Press almonds on top and sides of cheese. Serve with
cracker bread, melba toast or assorted crackers. **1¼ cups.**

NUTRIENTS PER 1 TABLESPOON

Calories 30	Dietary Fiber.........................<1 g
Protein..1 g	Sodium...............................40 mg
Carbohydrate...........................0 g	Potassium...........................15 mg.
Fat ....3 g	Calcium...............<2% U.S. RDA
Cholesterol.........................10 mg	Iron ....<2% U.S. RDA

Herbed Salmon Ball

8-oz.	pkg. cream cheese, softened
½	cup small curd creamed cottage cheese
¼	cup finely chopped onion
1	teaspoon fines herbes, crushed
½	teaspoon thyme leaves
1	garlic clove, minced
15½-oz.	can salmon, drained, flaked
¾	cup chopped fresh parsley
½	cup chopped nuts

In large bowl, combine cream cheese, cottage cheese, onion,
fines herbes, thyme and garlic; blend well. Stir in salmon.
Cover; refrigerate at least 3 hours or overnight. Shape into
ball. In small bowl, combine parsley and nuts. Roll salmon
ball in parsley mixture to coat evenly. Serve with assorted
crackers or thinly sliced snack rye bread. **3 cups.**

NUTRIENTS PER 1 TABLESPOON

Calories 40	Dietary Fiber.........................<1 g
Protein..3 g	Sodium...............................50 mg
Carbohydrate...........................0 g	Potassium...........................50 mg
Fat ....3 g	Calcium.................2% U.S. RDA
Cholesterol...........................8 mg	Iron ....<2% U.S. RDA

Nippy Zippy Cheese Log

8-oz.	pkg. cream cheese, softened
2 to 4-oz.	pkg. blue cheese, crumbled
4 oz.	(1 cup) shredded Cheddar cheese

¼ cup finely chopped onion
1 tablespoon Worcestershire sauce
1 tablespoon lemon juice
¾ cup chopped pecans
½ cup finely chopped fresh parsley

In large bowl, combine all ingredients except pecans and parsley. Beat 2 minutes at medium speed until well blended. Stir in ¼ cup of the pecans (reserve ½ cup for coating). Cover; refrigerate mixture 1 hour or until firm.

Spread chopped parsley and reserved pecans evenly on sheet of plastic wrap or waxed paper. Form chilled cheese mixture into log shape; roll in parsley and pecans. Wrap; refrigerate several hours. Serve with crackers, chips or thinly sliced snack rye bread. **3 cups.**

NUTRIENTS PER 1 TABLESPOON

Calories	50	Dietary Fiber	<1 g
Protein	2 g	Sodium	35 mg
Carbohydrate	1 g	Potassium	25 mg
Fat	4 g	Calcium	2% U.S. RDA
Cholesterol	8 mg	Iron	<2% U.S. RDA

Chicken Liver Pâté

1 lb. chicken livers
1½ cups water
⅓ cup margarine or butter, melted
1 medium apple, peeled, chopped
1 medium onion, chopped
1 garlic clove, minced
Dash thyme leaves
Dash marjoram
⅓ cup sherry
¼ teaspoon salt
Dash pepper

In medium saucepan, simmer chicken livers in water 2 to 3 minutes. Drain and reserve ¾ cup liquid. In medium skillet, cook livers in margarine until brown. Add apple, onion, garlic, thyme, marjoram, sherry and reserved liquid. Simmer uncovered for 15 to 20 minutes or until liquid is absorbed, stirring occasionally. Grind finely in food chopper or puree in blender or food processor. Add salt and pepper. Refrigerate to chill. Serve with melba toast or crackers. **2 cups.**

NUTRIENTS PER 1 TABLESPOON

Calories 40	Dietary Fiber.........................<1 g
Protein.......................................3 g	Sodium...............................50 mg
Carbohydrate...........................2 g	Potassium...........................45 mg
Fat ....2 g	Calcium...............<2% U.S. RDA
Cholesterol........................60 mg	Iron........................6% U.S. RDA

Party Sandwiches

For party sandwiches, the visual appeal is worth the effort. For best results, start with a 1-lb. loaf of unsliced sandwich bread. If possible, have bread machine-sliced lengthwise into ½-inch slices. Many bakeries will cut bread as you request. If bakery does not provide this service, freeze bread for 30 minutes; trim crust and slice lengthwise into ½-inch slices. Use toothpicks for a cutting guide to mark widths. (Freeze bakery-sliced bread 30 minutes for easier crust removal.) To make ribbon sandwiches you'll need both white and whole wheat bread.

To prevent sogginess, spread bread with softened margarine or butter, topping with spreads. Any desired combination of spreads may be used. Mix and match garnish to accent the color and flavor of the spread.

Many sandwiches can be prepared a day ahead. Wrap in plastic wrap, then in a damp towel. Refrigerate until ready to serve. Freezing is not recommended.

Garnishes:

Capers	Mushrooms, sliced
Cherry tomatoes, halved	Nuts
	Olives, sliced
Cucumbers, sliced	Parsley
Dillweed	Pickles, sliced
Egg, hard-cooked and sliced	Pimiento strips
	Shrimp

Ribbon Sandwiches

Use 2 lengthwise slices whole wheat bread and 2 lengthwise slices white bread. Spread 2 slices whole wheat bread and 1 slice white bread with softened margarine or butter. Top buttered slices with ½ to 1 cup spread. Stack slices with spread, alternating whole wheat slices with white. Top with remaining bread slice. If necessary, trim edges. Wrap in plastic wrap; refrigerate 2 to 3 hours. To serve, cut loaf crosswise into ½-inch slices; cut each slice in half.

Open-Faced Sandwiches

Use lengthwise slices of bread. If desired, use cookie cutters or, using knife, cut into square or diamond shapes. Top with various spreads. Garnish as desired.

Pinwheel Sandwiches

Use 1 lengthwise slice of bread; flatten slightly with rolling pin. Spread with softened margarine or butter. Top with ½ to 1 cup desired spread. Beginning at short end, roll up tightly in jelly roll fashion. If desired, frost with softened cream cheese and roll in chopped nuts. Refrigerate 2 to 3 hours before slicing. To serve, cut crosswise into ½-inch slices.

Frosted Sandwich Loaf

Use 5 lengthwise slices of bread. Spread 4 slices with soft-ened margarine or butter. Top with ½ to 1 cup spread. Stack slices with spread; top with remaining slice. In small bowl, beat two 8-oz. pkg. softened cream cheese with ½ cup half-and-half until soft enough to spread. Frost loaf. Refrigerate 2 to 3 hours. Garnish as desired. To serve, cut crosswise into ½-inch slices.

Seafood Spread

6½-oz. can crab meat, tuna or shrimp,
        drained and flaked
    2 tablespoons chopped dill pickle
    2 tablespoons mayonnaise or salad
        dressing
    ½ teaspoon lemon juice

In small bowl, combine all ingredients; mix well. Refrigerate.
1 cup.

NUTRIENTS PER 1 TABLESPOON

Calories 20	Dietary Fiber..........................0 g
Protein.......................................1 g	Sodium.............................105 mg
Carbohydrate...........................0 g	Potassium...........................10 mg
Fat ....2 g	Calcium...............<2% U.S. RDA
Cholesterol ....8 mg	Iron ....<2% U.S. RDA

Chicken Salad Spread

    ¾ cup finely chopped cooked chicken
    ⅓ cup finely chopped celery
    2 tablespoons chopped pimiento
    2 tablespoons mayonnaise or salad dressing
        Salt and pepper

In small bowl, combine all ingredients; mix well. Refrigerate. **1 cup.**

NUTRIENTS PER 1 TABLESPOON

Calories	25	Dietary Fiber	<1 g
Protein	2 g	Sodium	20 mg
Carbohydrate	0 g	Potassium	40 mg
Fat	2 g	Calcium	<2% U.S. RDA
Cholesterol	6 mg	Iron	<2% U.S. RDA

Chicken Cashew Filling

2½ cups finely chopped, cooked chicken
½ cup chopped cashews
½ cup finely chopped celery
2 tablespoons finely chopped onion
½ cup mayonnaise or salad dressing
Salt and pepper

In small bowl, combine chicken, cashews, celery, onion and mayonnaise; mix well. Salt and pepper to taste. Store in refrigerator. **3 cups.**

NUTRIENTS PER 1 TABLESPOON

Calories	150	Dietary Fiber	<1 g
Protein	9 g	Sodium	150 mg
Carbohydrate	3 g	Potassium	125 mg
Fat	11 g	Calcium	<2% U.S. RDA
Cholesterol	25 mg	Iron	4% U.S. RDA

Pineapple Cheese Spread

In small bowl, combine 5-oz. jar pasteurized process cheese spread and ¼ cup well-drained, crushed pineapple; mix well. Refrigerate. **¾ cup.**

NUTRIENTS PER 1 TABLESPOON

Calories	45	Dietary Fiber	<1 g
Protein	3 g	Sodium	170 mg
Carbohydrate	1 g	Potassium	25 mg
Fat	4 g	Calcium	6% U.S. RDA
Cholesterol	10 mg	Iron	<2% U.S. RDA

Egg Salad Spread

4 eggs, hard-cooked, chopped
1 teaspoon chopped pimiento
½ teaspoon chopped chives
⅛ teaspoon salt
3 tablespoons mayonnaise or salad dressing
    Dash pepper

In small bowl, combine all ingredients; mix well. Refrigerate. **1 cup.**

NUTRIENTS PER 1 TABLESPOON

Calories	40	Dietary Fiber	<1 g
Protein	2 g	Sodium	50 mg
Carbohydrate	0 g	Potassium	20 mg
Fat	3 g	Calcium	<2% U.S. RDA
Cholesterol	70 mg	Iron	<2% U.S. RDA

Ham Salad Spread

8 oz. (1 cup) ground, cooked ham
1 to 2 tablespoons pickle relish
1 tablespoon minced onion
2 tablespoons mayonnaise or salad dressing

In small bowl, combine all ingredients; mix well. Refrigerate. **1 cup.**

NUTRIENTS PER 1 TABLESPOON

Calories 35	Dietary Fiber........................<1 g
Protein.....................................3 g	Sodium.............................190 mg
Carbohydrate...........................1 g	Potassium............................45 mg
Fat ....2 g	Calcium..............<2% U.S. RDA
Cholesterol..........................8 mg	Iron ....<2% U.S. RDA

Escargots

½ cup margarine or butter, softened
 1 tablespoon finely chopped fresh
    parsley
½ to 1 teaspoon garlic powder or instant
    minced garlic
    Dash nutmeg
4½-oz. can snails (about 24)
   24 snail shells

Heat oven to 400°F. In small bowl, combine margarine, parsley, garlic and nutmeg. Place 1 snail in each shell; top with about 1 teaspoon margarine mixture. Place shells on cookie sheet or jelly roll pan. Bake at 400°F. for 10 to 12 minutes or until snails are firm. Serve immediately with remaining margarine mixture for dipping. **4 to 6 servings.**

NUTRIENTS PER ⅙ OF RECIPE

Calories 150	Dietary Fiber........................<1 g
Protein.....................................3 g	Sodium.............................190 mg
Carbohydrate...........................1 g	Potassium............................90 mg
Fat ....15 g	Calcium..............<2% U.S. RDA
Cholesterol..........................8 mg	Iron........................4% U.S. RDA

Oysters or Clams on the Shell

Purchase live in the shell oysters or clams. Allow 6 to 8 oysters per serving. Clean and shuck; set aside deeper half of each shell. Refrigerate oysters or clams to chill. Serve each on deeper half of shell, arranging shells on bed of crushed ice. Serve with cocktail sauce, lemon wedges and crackers.

NUTRIENTS PER 6 OYSTERS

Calories	80	Dietary Fiber	0 g
Protein	8 g	Sodium	125 mg
Carbohydrate	4 g	Potassium	260 mg
Fat	3 g	Calcium	4% U.S. RDA
Cholesterol	60 mg	Iron	40% U.S. RDA

NUTRIENTS PER 6 CLAMS

Calories	90	Dietary Fiber	0 g
Protein	15 g	Sodium	65 mg
Carbohydrate	3 g	Potassium	380 mg
Fat	1 g	Calcium	6% U.S. RDA
Cholesterol	40 mg	Iron	90% U.S. RDA

Seafood Cocktail

SAUCE

    1 cup catsup
    1 tablespoon lemon juice
2 to 3 teaspoons prepared horseradish
  ¼ teaspoon Worcestershire sauce
      Few drops hot pepper sauce

COCKTAIL

    1 small avocado, peeled, cubed
    1 teaspoon lemon juice
    3 cups cooked shrimp, chilled*
      Lettuce or curly endive
      Lemon wedges

In small bowl, combine all sauce ingredients. Cover; refrigerate to blend flavors. In medium bowl, sprinkle avocado with lemon juice; combine gently with shrimp. Serve in lettuce cups with sauce and lemon wedges. **6 to 8 servings.**

TIP: *If desired, use a combination of cooked fresh or frozen crab meat, lobster and shrimp—½ to 1 cup of each.

Or, use 2 (6½-oz.) cans crab meat, drained and flaked, and a 4½-oz. can tiny shrimp, drained.

NUTRIENTS PER ⅛ OF RECIPE

Calories	140	Dietary Fiber	2 g
Protein	13 g	Sodium	428 mg
Carbohydrate	11 g	Potassium	360 mg
Fat	5 g	Calcium	6% U.S. RDA
Cholesterol	60 mg	Iron	10% U.S. RDA

Sausage Snack Wraps

Heat oven to 375°F. Separate 2 (8-oz.) cans refrigerated crescent dinner rolls into 16 triangles. Cut each triangle into thirds lengthwise. Place 1 fully-cooked, small smoked sausage link on shortest side of each triangle. Roll up, starting at shortest side of triangle and rolling to opposite point. Place on ungreased cookie sheet. Bake at 375°F. for 12 to 15 minutes or until golden brown. Serve warm with catsup and mustard, if desired. **48 appetizers.**

TIP: To make ahead, assemble as directed. Cover; refrigerate up to 2 hours before serving. Bake as directed above.

NUTRIENTS PER 1 APPETIZER

Calories	60	Dietary Fiber	N/A
Protein	2 g	Sodium	170 mg
Carbohydrate	4 g	Potassium	40 mg
Fat	4 g	Calcium	<2% U.S. RDA
Cholesterol	6 mg	Iron	<2% U.S. RDA

Marinated Antipasto Tray

½ cup oil
⅓ cup tarragon vinegar
1 tablespoon sugar
2 tablespoons water
3 garlic cloves, minced

    6 drops hot pepper sauce
    1 envelope Italian salad dressing mix
    2 medium onions, thinly sliced
    2 (4.5-oz.) jars whole mushrooms, drained
    1 pint (2 cups) cherry tomatoes
    1 cup pitted ripe olives
      Leaf lettuce
   12 oz. salami slices
      Assorted cheeses, if desired

In small bowl or jar, combine oil, vinegar, sugar, water, garlic, hot pepper sauce and salad dressing mix; mix well. In large bowl, place onions, mushrooms, tomatoes and olives. Pour dressing over vegetables; toss gently. Cover; refrigerate at least 4 hours or overnight.

To serve, arrange drained marinated vegetables on lettuce-lined serving tray. Cut salami slices in half; roll into cones. Insert salami cones and assorted cheeses around base of vegetables. **12 servings.**

NUTRIENTS PER ¹⁄₁₂ OF RECIPE

Calories	310	Dietary Fiber	1 g
Protein	12 g	Sodium	710 mg
Carbohydrate	6 g	Potassium	190 mg
Fat	26 g	Calcium	25% U.S. RDA
Cholesterol	50 mg	Iron	6% U.S. RDA

Carrot-Pineapple Frappe

       3 cups thinly sliced carrots
       2 cups water
       1 tablespoon lemon juice
      ¾ teaspoon ginger
8¼-oz. can crushed pineapple in heavy syrup, undrained
      ½ cup vanilla yogurt
        Lettuce leaves, if desired
        Fresh pineapple wedges, if desired

In large saucepan, combine carrots, water, lemon juice and ginger. Bring to a boil. Reduce heat; cover and simmer 20 to 25 minutes or until vegetables are tender. Pour mixture into food processor bowl with metal blade or blender container; add pineapple. Process until smooth, about 2 to 3 minutes. Add yogurt; process until well blended. Pour mixture into ungreased 9-inch square pan. Cover; freeze until firm but not hard, at least 3 hours.* Spoon or scoop into individual lettuce-lined shallow bowls or sherbet dishes. Garnish each serving with pineapple wedge. **8 servings.**

TIP: *If mixture is frozen overnight, thaw at room temperature 1 hour or until mixture can be scooped.

NUTRIENTS PER ⅛ OF RECIPE

Calories 70	Dietary Fiber ....2 g
Protein ....1 g	Sodium ....25 mg
Carbohydrate ....15 g	Potassium ....240 mg
Fat ....0 g	Calcium ....4% U.S. RDA
Cholesterol ....0 mg	Iron ....2% U.S. RDA

Barbecued Riblets

7 to 8 lb. pork spareribs, cut into appetizer-size pieces*

SAUCE
  ½ cup firmly packed brown sugar
  2 teaspoons salt
  2 teaspoons celery seed
  ½ teaspoon instant minced garlic
  2 cups catsup
  2 cups chili sauce
  1 cup finely chopped onions
  ¼ cup lemon juice
  ¼ cup Worcestershire sauce
  2 teaspoons prepared mustard

In 8-quart saucepot, cover spareribs with salted water. Bring to a boil. Reduce heat to low; simmer 20 minutes. Drain; place in glass baking dishes or large non-metal containers. In large saucepan, combine all sauce ingredients; mix well. Bring to a boil. Reduce heat; simmer 15 minutes, stirring occasionally. Pour sauce over ribs, stirring to coat. Cover; refrigerate several hours or overnight to blend flavors, stirring occasionally.

Heat oven to 350°F. Remove ribs from sauce; place on 2 foil-lined 15x10-inch jelly roll pans. Bake at 350°F. for 45 minutes, spooning sauce over ribs several times during baking. Serve immediately. **About 6 to 7 dozen riblets.**

TIP: *Have butcher cut spareribs lengthwise and crosswise into small individual serving pieces.

NUTRIENTS PER 1 RIBLET

Calories	100	Dietary Fiber	<1 g
Protein	6 g	Sodium	270 mg
Carbohydrate	6 g	Potassium	130 mg
Fat	6 g	Calcium	<2% U.S. RDA
Cholesterol	20 mg	Iron	2% U.S. RDA

Garden Harvest Squares

　2　(8-oz.) cans refrigerated crescent
　　　dinner rolls
8-oz.　pkg. cream cheese, softened
　½　cup dairy sour cream
　1　teaspoon dill weed
　⅛　teaspoon garlic powder
　20　small broccoli florets
　20　cucumber or zucchini slices
　10　cherry tomatoes
　　　Fresh parsley, if desired

Heat oven to 375°F. Separate dough into 4 long rectangles. Place rectangles crosswise in ungreased 15x10-inch jelly roll pan; press over bottom and 1 inch up sides to form crust. Firmly press perforations to seal. Bake at 375°F. for 13 to 17 minutes or until golden brown. Cool completely.

In small bowl, combine cream cheese, sour cream, dill weed and garlic powder; blend until smooth. Spread evenly over cooled crust. Cover; refrigerate 1 to 2 hours. At serving time, cut into squares. Garnish with broccoli, cucumber, cherry tomato and parsley. **60 appetizers.**

NUTRIENTS PER 1 APPETIZER

Calories 45	Dietary Fiber.........................<1 g
Protein......................................1 g	Sodium...............................75 mg
Carbohydrate..........................3 g	Potassium...........................40 mg
Fat ....3 g	Calcium.................<2% U.S. RDA
Cholesterol...........................6 mg	Iron ....<2% U.S. RDA

Sweet-Sour Chicken Wings

    12 chicken wings, tips removed
    ⅔ cup cornstarch
     1 teaspoon garlic salt
     1 egg, well beaten
    ¼ cup oil
    ¾ cup sugar
    ¼ cup catsup
    ¼ cup vinegar

Cut each chicken wing in half. In large saucepan, place chicken wings; add water to cover. Cover; simmer 15 minutes. Drain; reserve ½ cup broth. In plastic bag, combine cornstarch and garlic salt. Dip chicken wings in egg; shake in bag to coat. In large skillet, brown coated chicken wings in oil; drain. In small bowl, combine sugar, reserved ½ cup chicken broth, catsup and vinegar. Heat oven to 375°F. Place chicken wings in ungreased 13x9-inch pan; pour sauce over chicken. Bake at 375°F. for 15 minutes or until thoroughly heated, basting once. **24 chicken wings.**

NUTRIENTS PER 1 CHICKEN WING

Calories 90	Dietary Fiber.........................<1 g
Protein.................................3 g	Sodium.............................110 mg
Carbohydrate....................10 g	Potassium...........................15 mg
Fat ....4 g	Calcium...............<2% U.S. RDA
Cholesterol......................25 mg	Iron ....<2% U.S. RDA

Quick Cuke Canapes

2 medium cucumbers, chilled
3-oz. pkg. cream cheese, softened
2 tablespoons finely chopped fresh parsley
2 tablespoons finely chopped chives
1 tablespoon dairy sour cream or mayonnaise
1 teaspoon prepared horseradish
½ teaspoon lemon juice
½ cup finely chopped cooked shrimp

Draw lines of fork lengthwise through cucumber peel to
score; cut into ¼-inch thick slices. Dry on paper towels. In
small bowl, combine cream cheese, parsley, chives, sour
cream, horseradish and lemon juice; beat until smooth. Stir
in shrimp. Spread or pipe with pastry tube each cucumber
slice with 1 teaspoon cream cheese mixture. Garnish as desired. Serve immediately or refrigerate up to 2 hours. **About
36 appetizers.**

NUTRIENTS PER 1 APPETIZER

Calories 12	Dietary Fiber.........................<1 g
Protein...1 g	Sodium...............................10 mg
Carbohydrate............................1 g	Potassium...........................30 mg
Fat ....1 g	Calcium...............<2% U.S. RDA
Cholesterol..............................4 mg	Iron ....<2% U.S. RDA

Open-Faced Mini-Reubens

¼ cup prepared Thousand Island dressing
24 slices snack rye bread

½ lb. thinly sliced corned beef
1½ cups chopped sauerkraut, well drained
4 oz. sliced Swiss cheese

Heat oven to 400°F. Spread about ½ teaspoon dressing on each slice of bread; top each with slice of corned beef and about 1 tablespoon sauerkraut. Cut cheese to fit bread; place over sauerkraut. Place on ungreased cookie sheet. Bake at 400°F. for 10 minutes or until cheese is melted. **24 appetizers.**

TIP: Can be made up to 2 hours ahead. Prepare and place on cookie sheet; cover with foil. Refrigerate. Remove foil and bake as directed above.

NUTRIENTS PER 1 APPETIZER

Calories	80	Dietary Fiber	1 g
Protein	4 g	Sodium	380 mg
Carbohydrate	5 g	Potassium	50 mg
Fat	5 g	Calcium	4% U.S. RDA
Cholesterol	15 mg	Iron	2% U.S. RDA

Toasty Swiss 'n Onion Snacks

1-lb. loaf thinly sliced snack rye bread
8 oz. (2 cups) shredded Swiss cheese
1 cup mayonnaise
⅓ cup finely chopped green onions

Toast bread slices on 1 side under broiler. In medium bowl, combine cheese, mayonnaise and onions until well blended; spread on untoasted side of bread. Broil 2 to 4 minutes or until bubbly and light golden brown. Serve immediately. **40 snacks.**

TIP: Spread can be prepared ahead. Broil snacks as needed.

NUTRIENTS PER 1 SNACK

Calories 90	Dietary Fiber...........................1 g
Protein.......................................3 g	Sodium...............................135 mg
Carbohydrate............................6 g	Potassium.............................25 mg
Fat...6 g	Calcium.................6% U.S. RDA
Cholesterol...............................8 mg	Iron ....<2% U.S. RDA

Spicy Beef Turnovers

15-oz. pkg. refrigerated pie crusts

FILLING
> ½ lb. ground beef
> ¼ cup chopped onion
> 1 garlic clove, minced
> 2 teaspoons curry powder
> 1 teaspoon finely chopped fresh gingerroot or
> ½ teaspoon ground ginger
> ½ teaspoon sugar
> ¼ teaspoon salt
> ⅛ teaspoon cayenne pepper
> Chutney, if desired

Allow both crust pouches to sit at room temperature for 15 to 20 minutes. In medium skillet, brown ground beef, onion and garlic; drain. Stir in remaining filling ingredients; cool.

Unfold each pie crust; peel off top plastic sheets. Press out fold lines. Invert and remove remaining plastic sheets. Cut about four 4 to 5-inch circles from each pie crust. Cut each circle in half. Place 1 tablespoon filling on half of each semi-circle; brush edges with water. Fold over; seal edges with fork. Place on ungreased cookie sheet. Bake at 375°F. for 18 to 23 minutes or until light golden brown. Cool on wire rack. Serve with chutney. **16 turnovers.**

NUTRIENTS PER 1 TURNOVER

Calories 170	Dietary Fiber.......................1 g
Protein...................................3 g	Sodium.............................220 mg
Carbohydrate.......................17 g	Potassium...........................70 mg
Fat ....10 g	Calcium...............<2% U.S. RDA
Cholesterol............................8 mg	Iron.....................2% U.S. RDA

Cheese Shrimp Puffs

32 crackers
¼ cup margarine or butter
8 oz. (2 cups) shredded Cheddar cheese
1 egg, separated
4½-oz. can small shrimp, drained

MICROWAVE DIRECTIONS: Arrange crackers on 2 napkin-lined plates. In medium microwave-safe bowl, microwave margarine on HIGH for 10 seconds to soften. Add cheese; blend well. Stir in egg yolk and shrimp. In small bowl, beat egg white until stiff peaks form. Fold into cheese-shrimp mixture. Top each cracker with spoonful of mixture. Microwave 1 plate at a time uncovered on HIGH for about 1 minute or until hot. **32 snacks.**

NUTRIENTS PER 1 SNACK

Calories 70	Dietary Fiber........................<1 g
Protein...................................3 g	Sodium...............................90 mg
Carbohydrate.........................3 g	Potassium...........................20 mg
Fat ....5 g	Calcium.................6% U.S. RDA
Cholesterol.........................20 mg	Iron ....<2% U.S. RDA

Snappy Glazed Meatballs

1½ lb. ground beef
¼ cup dry bread crumbs
¼ cup chopped onion
1 teaspoon salt
1 egg, slightly beaten

1 cup chili sauce
10-oz. jar (1 cup) grape jelly

In medium bowl, combine ground beef, bread crumbs, onion, salt and egg; mix well. Shape into 1-inch balls. In large skillet, brown meatballs, turning occasionally; drain. Add remaining ingredients; simmer 15 minutes, stirring occasionally to coat meatballs with glaze. Serve warm. **36 meatballs.**

TIP: To make ahead, prepare and brown meatballs. Cool slightly; wrap and freeze. Thaw slightly before combining with sauce ingredients; simmer until heated through.

VARIATION:

SNAPPY GLAZED FRANKS: Use 1 lb. wieners, cut up, or cocktail franks for meatballs.

NUTRIENTS PER 1 MEATBALL

Calories 70	Dietary Fiber.........................<1 g
Protein.....................................4 g	Sodium.............................170 mg
Carbohydrate............................8 g	Potassium.........................100 mg
Fat ....3 g	Calcium..............<2% U.S. RDA
Cholesterol.........................20 mg	Iron.......................2% U.S. RDA

Julienne Vegetable and Cheese Bundles

MARINADE

1 garlic clove, crushed
¼ cup water
¼ cup vinegar
2 tablespoons oil
¼ teaspoon seasoned salt
¼ teaspoon dill weed

2 medium carrots, cut into twelve
   2½-inch thin strips
1 small zucchini, cut into twelve 2½-inch thin strips

1   small red bell pepper, cut into twelve 2½-inch thin strips

12   (2½-inch) thin strips Monterey jack cheese
Green onion tops, cut into 12 thin strips

Place all marinade ingredients in shallow glass baking dish; blend well. Add vegetable strips; toss to coat. Cover; refrigerate several hours or overnight. To prepare bundles, remove vegetable strips from marinade; place on paper towels to drain. For each bundle, use one strip each of carrot, zucchini, red pepper and cheese. Tie each bundle with onion strip.* **12 bundles.**

TIP: *Thin, limp green onion tops tie best.

NUTRIENTS PER 1 BUNDLE

Calories	40	Dietary Fiber	1 g
Protein	2 g	Sodium	50 mg
Carbohydrate	2 g	Potassium	105 mg
Fat	3 g	Calcium	6% U.S. RDA
Cholesterol	6 mg	Iron	<2% U.S. RDA

Sauterne Stuffed Mushrooms

1   lb. medium to large fresh mushrooms (about 15 to 20)

½   cup margarine or butter, melted

¼   cup finely chopped green onions

¼   cup sauterne wine

1   cup herb seasoned croutons, crushed

Heat oven to 350°F. Brush or wipe mushrooms with damp cloth. Remove stems from mushrooms; finely chop. Set aside. Dip mushroom caps in melted margarine; place crown side up in shallow baking pan.

In small skillet, saute chopped mushrooms and onions in remaining margarine. Remove from heat; add wine and croutons. Toss lightly. Spoon mixture into mushroom caps. Bake at 350°F. for 10 to 15 minutes or until hot.

NUTRIENTS PER 1 MUSHROOM

Calories	60	Dietary Fiber	1 g
Protein	1 g	Sodium	85 mg
Carbohydrate	2 g	Potassium	100 mg
Fat	5 g	Calcium	<2% U.S. RDA
Cholesterol	0 mg	Iron	<2% U.S. RDA

Tortellini Kabobs

   8 oz. fresh or frozen cheese tortellini
  ½ lb. thinly sliced salami
5-oz. jar pimiento-stuffed green olives
  ½ cup prepared Italian dressing

Cook tortellini to desired doneness as directed on package. Drain; rinse with cold water.

Cut each piece of salami in half. In large bowl, combine all ingredients. Cover; refrigerate 4 to 6 hours or overnight to blend flavors. To serve, thread tortellini on 3 to 4-inch bamboo skewers alternating with folded salami slices and olives. **3 dozen kabobs.**

NUTRIENTS PER 1 KABOB

Calories	50	Dietary Fiber	<1 g
Protein	2 g	Sodium	210 mg
Carbohydrate	2 g	Potassium	25 mg
Fat	4 g	Calcium	2% U.S. RDA
Cholesterol	10 mg	Iron	2% U.S. RDA

Bacon-Wrapped Appetizers

Heat oven to 375°F. Cut 8 slices bacon into thirds; wrap around any of the following fillings; secure with toothpicks. Arrange on broiler pan or on rack in shallow baking pan.

Bake at 375°F. for 20 to 25 minutes or until bacon is crisp. Serve hot. **24 appetizers.**

VARIATIONS:

WATER CHESTNUTS: Combine 8-oz. can (about 24) whole or halved water chestnuts, drained, ¼ cup soy sauce and 1 tablespoon sugar. Marinate about 30 minutes. Drain and continue as directed.

SMOKED OYSTERS: Use two 3¾-oz. cans (about 24) smoked oysters, drained.

OLIVES: Use 24 stuffed green olives.

CHICKEN LIVERS: Cut 8 oz. chicken livers into 24 pieces. Combine ½ cup prepared French dressing and ¼ teaspoon garlic salt. Marinate livers in dressing about 15 minutes. Drain and continue as directed.

PINEAPPLE: Use 24 fresh, canned or frozen pineapple chunks, drained. Marinate pineapple in prepared French dressing. Drain and continue as directed.

SCALLOPS: Use 8 oz. (about 24) fresh or frozen scallops, thawed. (Cut large ones in half.)

NUTRIENTS PER 1 BACON-WRAPPED WATER CHESTNUT

Calories	20	Dietary Fiber	<1 g
Protein	1 g	Sodium	210 mg
Carbohydrate	2 g	Potassium	30 mg
Fat	1 g	Calcium	<2% U.S. RDA
Cholesterol	2 mg	Iron	<2% U.S. RDA

Snacks

Almost anything we eat in small quantities can be considered a snack, from mini-meals to tidbits to tide us over between meals. Sweet or savory, snacks figure prominently in many daily diets, particularly if they are consumed regularly and serve as a substitute for breakfast, lunch or dinner. Therefore, it is important that the caloric and nutritional content of snacks be recognized to avoid the pitfall of eating foods that add calories without adequate nutrition.

Back Pack Snack

3 cups granola cereal
½ cup peanuts
½ cup candy-coated chocolate pieces
  or semi-sweet chocolate chips
½ cup raisins
½ cup chopped dried apricots
½ cup chopped dates

In large bowl, combine all ingredients. Store in tightly covered container. **5½ cups.**

NUTRIENTS PER ½ CUP

Calories	280	Dietary Fiber	3 g
Protein	6 g	Sodium	5 mg
Carbohydrate	37 g	Potassium	410 mg
Fat	14 g	Calcium	2% U.S. RDA
Cholesterol	0 mg	Iron	10% U.S. RDA

Cocktail Nuts

2 tablespoons margarine or butter
¼ teaspoon seasoned salt
¼ teaspoon garlic powder
  Dash hot pepper sauce
1 lb. (3 to 4 cups) mixed nuts
3 tablespoons Worcestershire sauce

Heat oven to 300°F. In 15x10-inch jelly roll pan or 13x9-inch pan, melt margarine with salt, garlic powder and hot pepper sauce; mix well. Add nuts, tossing to coat. Bake at 300°F. for 15 minutes, stirring occasionally. Sprinkle with Worcestershire sauce and continue baking 15 minutes or until crisp. **3 to 4 cups.**

NUTRIENTS PER ¼ CUP

Calories 200	Dietary Fiber............................3 g
Protein...5 g	Sodium....................................75 mg
Carbohydrate.............................7 g	Potassium..............................170 mg
Fat ....17 g	Calcium...................2% U.S. RDA
Cholesterol ....0 mg	Iron.......................4% U.S. RDA

Caramel Corn

  6 cups popped popcorn
 ½ cup slivered almonds, toasted if desired
 ¾ cup firmly packed brown sugar
  2 tablespoons water
  2 tablespoons light corn syrup
 ½ cup margarine or butter
 ¼ teaspoon baking soda
 ⅛ teaspoon salt

Arrange popcorn in 13x9-inch pan; sprinkle almonds over popcorn. In large saucepan, combine brown sugar, water and corn syrup. Cook, stirring occasionally, until candy thermometer reaches soft crack stage (280°F.). Stir in margarine and cook to 280°F. again. Remove from heat; stir in baking soda and salt. Slowly pour over popcorn and almonds; toss until coated. Spread on foil or waxed paper to cool. Store in loosely covered container. **6 cups.**

VARIATIONS:

POPCORN BALLS: Follow recipe for caramel corn. After tossing mixture to coat, use buttered hands to quickly and firmly press mixture into balls. Wrap each ball in plastic wrap.

OVEN BAKED CARAMEL CORN: Heat oven to 250°F. Arrange popcorn in 15x10-inch jelly roll pan; sprinkle almonds over popcorn. In large saucepan, combine brown sugar, water, corn syrup and margarine; bring to a boil over medium heat. Boil 2 minutes, stirring constantly. Remove from heat. Stir in baking soda and salt; mix well. Pour over popcorn and almonds; toss until coated. Bake at 250°F. for 35 minutes; stir after baking 15 minutes. Stir again after baking 30 minutes. Remove from oven; spread on foil or waxed paper to cool.

MICROWAVE CARAMEL CORN: Combine popcorn and almonds in large microwave-safe bowl. In 4-cup microwave-safe measuring cup, combine brown sugar, corn syrup, margarine and salt. Omit water. Microwave on HIGH for 2 minutes; stir. Microwave on HIGH for 2 to 3 minutes or until mixture comes to a rolling boil. Stir in baking soda; pour over popcorn and almonds. Mix well; microwave on HIGH for 2 minutes. Spread on foil or waxed paper to cool.

NUTRIENTS PER 1 CUP

Calories	350	Dietary Fiber	1 g
Protein	3 g	Sodium	280 mg
Carbohydrate	38 g	Potassium	190 mg
Fat	21 g	Calcium	6% U.S. RDA
Cholesterol	0 mg	Iron	10% U.S. RDA

Herb-Seasoned Popcorn

    6 cups popped popcorn
    2 tablespoons margarine or butter, melted
   ½ teaspoon basil leaves
   ¼ teaspoon oregano leaves
       Dash to ⅛ teaspoon cayenne pepper
    1 tablespoon grated Parmesan cheese

Place popcorn in large bowl. Combine margarine, basil, oregano and cayenne; pour evenly over popcorn. Sprinkle with Parmesan cheese; toss gently. **6 cups.**

NUTRIENTS PER 1 CUP

Calories 60	Dietary Fiber ....5 g
Protein ....1 g	Sodium ....65 mg
Carbohydrate ....5 g	Potassium ....25 mg
Fat ....4 g	Calcium ....<2% U.S. RDA
Cholesterol ....0 mg	Iron ....<2% U.S. RDA

Homemade Granola

4 cups quick-cooking rolled oats
1 cup sunflower nuts
1 cup coconut
½ cup slivered almonds
½ cup unsalted raw pumpkin seeds
½ cup wheat germ
¼ cup oil
¼ cup honey
⅓ cup water
1 cup finely chopped dried apricots
1 cup finely chopped prunes
1 cup raisins

Heat oven to 250°F. Lightly grease two 13x9-inch pans. In
large bowl, combine oats, sunflower nuts, coconut, almonds,
pumpkin seeds and wheat germ. In small bowl, combine oil
and honey. Add oil-honey mixture to dry ingredients, stirring until well mixed. Sprinkle water over mixture, a tablespoon at a time, while tossing and stirring. Divide mixture
into prepared pans. Bake at 250°F. for 1 hour, stirring every
15 minutes until mixture starts to turn light brown. Stir in
apricots, prunes and raisins. Return to oven for an additional
15 minutes or until desired dryness; fruit should be slightly
soft, not dried out. Cool. Store in tightly covered container.
10 cups.

NUTRIENTS PER ½ CUP

Calories	260	Dietary Fiber	6 g
Protein	7 g	Sodium	5 mg
Carbohydrate	33 g	Potassium	365 mg
Fat	12 g	Calcium	2% U.S. RDA
Cholesterol	0 mg	Iron	15% U.S. RDA

Vegetable Nachos

2	medium tomatoes, finely chopped, well drained
1	green pepper, finely chopped
2	green onions, finely chopped
4¼-oz.	can chopped ripe olives, drained
36 to 48	round tostada or tortilla chips
4 oz.	(1 cup) shredded Cheddar cheese

In medium bowl, combine all vegetables. Place tostada chips in single layer on ungreased cookie sheet. Sprinkle each chip with 1 teaspoon cheese; top with 1 tablespoon vegetable mixture. Broil about 6 inches from heat for 2 to 3 minutes or until cheese is melted. Serve immediately. **3 to 4 dozen snacks.**

TIP: Vegetable mixture may be prepared ahead and refrigerated for several hours before serving. Drain well before assembling.

NUTRIENTS PER 1 SNACK

Calories	30	Dietary Fiber	<1 g
Protein	1 g	Sodium	55 mg
Carbohydrate	2 g	Potassium	20 mg
Fat	2 g	Calcium	2% U.S. RDA
Cholesterol	2 mg	Iron	<2% U.S. RDA

Beverages

Drinks may be warm and soothing or cool and refreshing. They can be as hearty as a milk-based, fruit-filled combination or as light as a wine spritzer. They are selected to complement accompanying foods and should be appropriate for the weather, occasion, time of day and preferences of host and guests. Since most beverages can be prepared quickly and conveniently, there is little need for make-ahead steps other than to have necessary ingredients on hand.

Selection and Preparation

• **Punches:** Fruit bases for punch may be combined ahead and refrigerated. However, ingredients like alcohol and carbonated beverages should be added just before serving, mixing only to blend so "bubbles" remain. Chill all ingredients before mixing to keep ice from melting.

Punch Planning Guide

No. of People	Before Dinner	Party
4	1–1½ qt.	2–2½ qt.
6	1½–2 qt.	3–4 qt.
8	2–3 qt.	1–1½ gal.
12	1–1½ gal.	1½–2 gal.
20	1½–2 gal.	2½–3 gal.
50	3–4½ gal.	6–7½ gal.

An ice ring or mold is preferable to cubes for a punch bowl. Garnish ice block by freezing colorful fruits and/or mint leaves into the ring or mold. Make sure ice mold fits into punch bowl. For beverages served in glasses, cups or mugs, select garnishes that complement beverage flavors and will not interfere with sipping. In hot weather, chilled glasses add an elegant, refreshing touch.

To keep hot punches hot, serve in large chafing dish or slow cooker. If using a punch bowl, make sure it is heat-resistant. Warm bowl with hot water before adding hot punch.

The amount of punch to prepare will depend on the number of guests, kind of party, outdoor and indoor temperatures and whether other beverages are available. If the punch is to be served before dinner, plan 2 to 3 (½-cup) servings per person. If the punch is to be served for the duration of the event, plan 4 to 5 (½-cup) servings per person.

• **Coffee:** Coffee is available in the form of beans, ground, instant and freeze-dried, any of which can be caffeinated or decaffeinated. Freshly ground beans enhance flavor and aroma. If you do not grind your own beans, be sure to select the grind most appropriate for your coffee maker.

• **Tea:** Tea varieties offer a seemingly endless array of aromas, flavors and grades. However, teas can be grouped into three basic classifications: black, green and oolong. The differences lie in the quality of the plant leaves, degree of fermentation, flavor, color and aroma. *Black* teas have a rich aroma and amber color. Varieties include Ceylon, Darjeeling, Earl Grey, English breakfast and Lapsang souchong tea. *Green* tea is slightly bitter in taste and brews to a pale green color. *Oolong* tea is a cross between black and green tea. Popular varieties include jasmine and Formosa oolong. Herbal teas are blends of herbs, spices and aromatic ingredients. They are caffeine-free unless otherwise stated.

Wine

Wines, like foods, are vastly different in taste and character. When it comes to choosing a wine, there are no strict rules, just guidelines to help with the selection. Personal taste is the most important guideline.

Which Wine to Drink

Wines can be divided into categories based on when they are generally served.

- **Appetizer:** Dry Sherry, Vermouth and flavored wines.
- **Red Dinner:** Burgundy, Zinfandel, Pinot Noir, Cabernet Sauvignon, Gamay, Chianti and Barbera.
- **White Dinner:** Chablis, Rhine, Chenin Blanc, Sauternes (dry), Chardonnay, White Riesling, French Colombard and Sauvignon Blanc.
- **Rosé:** Vin Rosé Sec, Gamay Rosé, Light Rosé and Rosé.
- **Sparkling:** Champagne, Cold Duck, Sparkling Burgundy and Sparkling Rosé.
- **Dessert:** Port, Tokay, Sherry (cream or sweet), Sauternes (sweet), and Muscatel.

Sunny Citrus Wine Cooler

750 ml bottle (3¼ cups) light white wine, chilled
3 cups orange juice, chilled
1 cup unsweetened pineapple juice, chilled
2 (12-oz.) cans (3 cups) lemon-lime flavored carbonated beverage, chilled

In large non-metal pitcher, combine all ingredients except lemon-lime beverage; mix well. Just before serving, slowly add lemon-lime beverage; stir gently to blend. Serve over ice cubes or crushed ice. **10 (1-cup) servings.**

NUTRIENTS PER 1 CUP

Calories 140	Dietary Fiber.........................0 g
Protein ....1 g	Sodium ....0 mg
Carbohydrate........................23 g	Potassium ....180 mg
Fat ....0 g	Calcium..............<2% U.S. RDA
Cholesterol ....0 mg	Iron ....<2% U.S. RDA

Peach Pizazz

In 5-cup blender container, combine 2 (10-oz) pkg. frozen peach slices, partially thawed, 6-oz. can frozen lemonade concentrate, partially thawed, and ⅔ cup rum. Cover; blend at medium-low speed 30 seconds. Add 12 ice cubes, one at a time, blending at low speed until slushy. Pour into non-metal pitcher. If desired, garnish with peach or lemon slices. **10 (½-cup) servings.**

NUTRIENTS PER ½ CUP

Calories	130	Dietary Fiber	1 g
Protein	0 g	Sodium	0 mg
Carbohydrate	24 g	Potassium	85 mg
Fat	0 g	Calcium	<2% U.S. RDA
Cholesterol	0 mg	Iron	<2% U.S. RDA

Wine Spritzer

At serving time, in large pitcher or punch bowl combine 750 ml bottle (3¼ cups) dry white wine, chilled, with 28-oz. bottle (3½ cups) lemon-lime flavored carbonated beverage or sparkling water, chilled. Stir gently to mix. Add ice, if desired. Garnish with fresh raspberries or strawberries. **12 (½-cup) servings.**

NUTRIENTS PER ½ CUP

Calories	100	Dietary Fiber	<1 g
Protein	0 g	Sodium	0 mg
Carbohydrate	12 g	Potassium	0 mg
Fat	0 g	Calcium	<2% U.S. RDA
Cholesterol	0 mg	Iron	<2% U.S. RDA

Orange Juice Spritzer

6-oz. can frozen orange juice concentrate, thawed
1 cup cold water
1 tablespoon lemon juice
12-oz. can (1½ cups) lemon-lime flavored carbonated
beverage
Orange slices

In large pitcher, combine orange juice concentrate, water
and lemon juice. Just before serving, slowly add carbonated
beverage; stir gently to blend. Serve over ice in glasses.
Garnish with orange slices. **8 (½-cup) servings.**

NUTRIENTS PER ½ CUP

Calories	70	Dietary Fiber	0 g
Protein	1 g	Sodium	0 mg
Carbohydrate	16 g	Potassium	180 mg
Fat	0 g	Calcium	<2% U.S. RDA
Cholesterol	0 mg	Iron	<2% U.S. RDA

Old-Fashioned Lemonade

4 lemons
½ to ¾ cup sugar
1 quart (4 cups) cold water
Ice cubes

Cut lemons into very thin slices; remove seeds. Place in
large non-metal bowl; sprinkle with sugar. Let stand about
10 minutes. Press fruit with back of spoon to extract juice.
Add cold water, stirring and pressing fruit until well-
flavored. Remove fruit slices. Serve over ice. If desired, garnish with lemon slices. **4 (1-cup) servings.**

VARIATIONS:

LIMEADE: Use 2 limes and 2 lemons. Prepare as directed
above, increasing sugar to 1 cup.

ORANGEADE: Use 2 oranges and 3 lemons. Prepare as directed above, using ½ cup sugar.

NUTRIENTS PER 1 CUP

Calories 160	Dietary Fiber.........................<1 g
Protein.......................................0 g	Sodium ....0 mg
Carbohydrate.........................41 g	Potassium...........................65 mg
Fat ....0 g	Calcium...............<2% U.S. RDA
Cholesterol............................0 mg	Iron ....<2% U.S. RDA

Apple Grape Punch

ICE RING

- 2 cups apple juice
- 2 cups water
  - Apple slices or wedges, unpeeled
  - Lemon juice
  - Grapes

PUNCH

- 1½ quarts (6 cups) apple juice, chilled
- 1 quart (4 cups) grape juice, chilled
- 6-oz. can frozen lemonade concentrate, thawed
- 32-oz. bottle (4 cups) lemon-lime flavored carbonated beverage, chilled

To prepare ice ring, combine 2 cups apple juice and water. Toss apple slices in lemon juice to prevent browning. Arrange grapes and apple slices in an attractive design in 5-cup ring mold. Pour apple juice-water mixture into mold to partially cover fruit (about ¾ cup); freeze. When frozen, add remaining mixture; freeze completely.

In punch bowl, combine apple juice, grape juice and lemonade concentrate; refrigerate. Just before serving, add carbonated beverage, stirring gently. Unmold ice ring and float fruit side up in punch bowl. **28 (½-cup) servings.**

NUTRIENTS PER ½ CUP

Calories 80	Dietary Fiber.........................1 g
Protein..............................0 g	Sodium................................0 mg
Carbohydrate.......................21 g	Potassium.........................95 mg
Fat ....0 g	Calcium...............<2% U.S. RDA
Cholesterol.........................0 mg	Iron ....<2% U.S. RDA

Mai-Tai Punch

2 quarts (8 cups) pineapple juice
3 cups light rum
1 cup orange juice
½ cup sugar
½ cup prepared limeade
⅓ cup lemon juice

In 4-quart non-metal container, combine all ingredients; refrigerate. Serve over ice. **12 (1-cup) servings.**

TIP: If desired, serve in a punch bowl; float orange and lime slices for a garnish. If served in tall glasses, garnish with a fresh pineapple spear.

NUTRIENTS PER 1 CUP

Calories 280	Dietary Fiber.........................<1 g
Protein.....................................1 g	Sodium..................................5 mg
Carbohydrate.........................35 g	Potassium..........................300 mg
Fat ....0 g	Calcium................2% U.S. RDA
Cholesterol............................0 mg	Iron......................2% U.S. RDA

Strawberry Party Punch

3-oz. pkg. strawberry flavor gelatin
1 cup boiling water
2 (6-oz.) cans frozen pink lemonade concentrate, thawed
6-oz. can frozen orange juice concentrate, thawed
6 cups cold water

28-oz. bottle (3½ cups) ginger ale, chilled
    1 pint (2 cups) fresh strawberries with stems, frozen*

Dissolve gelatin in boiling water; cool. In large punch bowl, combine gelatin mixture, lemonade concentrate, orange juice concentrate and cold water; refrigerate. Just before serving, gently stir in ginger ale and frozen strawberries. **28 (½-cup) servings.**

TIP: *To freeze strawberries, wash and gently pat dry (leave stems on to add color, if desired). Arrange in single layer on cookie sheet; freeze until firm.

NUTRIENTS PER ½ CUP

Calories	70	Dietary Fiber	<1 g
Protein	1 g	Sodium	10 mg
Carbohydrate	17 g	Potassium	85 mg
Fat	0 g	Calcium	<2% U.S. RDA
Cholesterol	0 mg	Iron	<2% U.S. RDA

Mock Margarita Punch

12-oz. can frozen lemonade concentrate, thawed
12-oz. can frozen limeade concentrate, thawed
    1 cup powdered sugar
    4 egg whites
    6 cups crushed ice
    1 quart (4 cups) club soda, chilled
       Lime slices
       Coarse salt

In 4-quart non-metal container, combine lemonade and limeade concentrates, powdered sugar, egg whites and crushed ice; mix well. Cover; freeze, stirring occasionally. Remove container from freezer 30 minutes before serving. Spoon 2 cups slush mixture into blender; add 1 cup of the club soda. Cover; blend until frothy. To serve, rub rim of glass with lime slice and dip in coarse salt; fill glass. Garnish with lime slices. **24 (½-cup) servings.**

NUTRIENTS PER ½ CUP

Calories 90	Dietary Fiber.......................<1 g
Protein................................1 g	Sodium..............................10 mg
Carbohydrate.......................22 g	Potassium...........................30 mg
Fat ....0 g	Calcium..............<2% U.S. RDA
Cholesterol...........................0 mg	Iron ....<2% U.S. RDA

Banana Slush

2	cups sugar
3	cups water
3	ripe bananas, mashed
3	cups pineapple juice
1½	cups orange juice
2	tablespoons lemon juice
32-oz.	bottle (4 cups) lemon-lime flavored carbonated beverage, chilled

In large saucepan, combine sugar and water. Bring to a boil; boil 5 minutes. Cool.

In large non-metal container, combine mashed bananas, juices and sugar mixture; mix well and freeze. Two hours before serving, remove frozen mixture from freezer; let stand at room temperature. Just before serving, stir carbonated beverage into slushy fruit mixture. Serve immediately. **20 (½-cup) servings.**

NUTRIENTS PER ½ CUP

Calories 150	Dietary Fiber.........................1 g
Protein................................0 g	Sodium..................................0 mg
Carbohydrate.......................37 g	Potassium.........................160 mg
Fat ....0 g	Calcium..............<2% U.S. RDA
Cholesterol...........................0 mg	Iron ....<2% U.S. RDA

Tart 'n Tangy Citrus Punch

    6-oz. can frozen lemonade concentrate, thawed
    6-oz. can frozen grapefruit juice concentrate, thawed
    6-oz. can frozen pineapple juice concentrate, thawed
       2   cups water
   28-oz. bottle (3½ cups) club soda, chilled
   28-oz. bottle (3½ cups) ginger ale, chilled
           Ice ring or ice mold, if desired
           Fresh fruit slices, if desired

In large non-metal pitcher or punch bowl, combine concentrates and water; refrigerate. Just before serving, add club soda and ginger ale; stir to blend. Garnish punch bowl with ice ring and fresh fruit slices. **25 (½-cup) servings.**

NUTRIENTS PER ½ CUP

Calories 60	Dietary Fiber.........................<1 g
Protein.....................................0 g	Sodium.................................0 mg
Carbohydrate.........................14 g	Potassium...........................95 mg
Fat ....0 g	Calcium..............<2% U.S. RDA
Cholesterol...........................0 mg	Iron ....<2% U.S. RDA

Frosty Fruit Cooler

       1   quart (4 cups) apricot nectar, chilled
       2   cups pineapple juice, chilled
       2   cups orange juice, chilled
   32-oz. bottle (4 cups) lemon-lime flavored carbonated
           beverage, chilled
       1   pint pineapple sherbet
       1   pint orange sherbet

In 4-quart non-metal container or punch bowl, combine apricot nectar, pineapple juice and orange juice; refrigerate. Just before serving, pour in carbonated beverage. Float scoops of sherbet on top. Serve immediately. **25 (½-cup) servings.**

NUTRIENTS PER ½ CUP

Calories 110	Dietary Fiber........................<1 g
Protein ....1 g	Sodium ....15 mg
Carbohydrate.........................26 g	Potassium ....150 mg
Fat ....1 g	Calcium ....2% U.S. RDA
Cholesterol ....2 mg	Iron ....<2% U.S. RDA

Sangria

    1 cup sugar
    1 cup fresh lemon juice
    1 cup orange juice
    ½ cup orange-flavored liqueur
    2 (750 ml) bottles red Burgundy wine
    1 lemon, sliced
    1 orange, sliced

In 4-quart non-metal container, combine sugar, lemon juice,
orange juice, liqueur and wine. Refrigerate several hours.
Just before serving, pour into pitcher; add lemon and orange
slices. Serve over ice. **12 (¾-cup) servings.**

TIP: For bubbly sangria, add 2 (10-oz.) bottles club soda,
chilled, just before serving.

NUTRIENTS PER ¾ CUP

Calories 210	Dietary Fiber........................<1 g
Protein ....0 g	Sodium ....5 mg
Carbohydrate.........................34 g	Potassium ....180 mg
Fat ....0 g	Calcium ....<2% U.S. RDA
Cholesterol ....0 mg	Iron ....2% U.S. RDA

Wassail Bowl

       Whole cloves
    1 large orange
    2 quarts (8 cups) apple juice
    3 tablespoons lemon juice
    4 cinnamon sticks

Heat oven to 350°F. Insert whole cloves about ½ inch apart into orange. Place in ungreased shallow baking pan. Bake at 350°F. for 30 minutes. Pierce orange in several places with tines of fork.

In large saucepan, combine apple juice, lemon juice, cinnamon sticks and baked orange. Cover; simmer over low heat 30 minutes. Remove cinnamon sticks and orange. Pour apple juice mixture into heat-proof punch bowl. If desired, float clove-studded, baked orange in punch bowl. Serve hot. **16 (½-cup) servings.**

NUTRIENTS PER ½ CUP

Calories	60	Dietary Fiber	<1 g
Protein	0 g	Sodium	0 mg
Carbohydrate	15 g	Potassium	130 mg
Fat	0 g	Calcium	<2% U.S. RDA
Cholesterol	0 mg	Iron	<2% U.S. RDA

Raspberry-Cranberry Champagne Punch

64-oz. bottle (8 cups) raspberry-cranberry drink, chilled
   2 (750 ml) bottles champagne, chilled
   1 quart (4 cups) club soda, chilled

In large punch bowl, combine all ingredients; stir gently to blend. **38 (½-cup) servings.**

NUTRIENTS PER ½ CUP

Calories	80	Dietary Fiber	<1 g
Protein	0 g	Sodium	0 mg
Carbohydrate	14 g	Potassium	20 mg
Fat	0 g	Calcium	<2% U.S. RDA
Cholesterol	0 mg	Iron	<2% U.S. RDA

Burgundy Berry Sipper

       3 cinnamon sticks
       6 whole cloves
       6 whole allspice
       2 cups cranberry juice cocktail
     ½ cup sugar
     ½ cup water
    750 ml bottle (3¼ cups) red burgundy
         wine

Tie spices in a cheesecloth bag. In large saucepan, combine cranberry juice cocktail, sugar, water and spice bag. Bring to a boil; reduce heat and simmer 15 minutes. Remove spice bag; add wine. Serve hot in mugs or cups. Garnish as desired. **12 (½-cup) servings.**

NUTRIENTS PER ½ CUP

Calories	110	Dietary Fiber	<1 g
Protein	0 g	Sodium	5 mg
Carbohydrate	18 g	Potassium	60 mg
Fat	0 g	Calcium	<2% U.S. RDA
Cholesterol	0 mg	Iron	2% U.S. RDA

Holiday Eggnog

       6 eggs, slightly beaten
     ¼ cup sugar
     ¼ teaspoon salt
       4 cups milk
       1 teaspoon vanilla
       1 cup whipping cream, if desired
    ¾ to 1 cup light rum or ½ to 1 teaspoon
         rum extract
         Nutmeg

In large non-aluminum saucepan, combine eggs, sugar and salt; stir in milk. Cook over low heat, stirring constantly, until mixture thickens and coats spoon. Remove from heat; stir in vanilla and whipping cream. Cool; refrigerate immediately. At serving time, pour into punch bowl. Stir in rum; sprinkle with nutmeg. **12 to 16 (½-cup) servings.**

NUTRIENTS PER ½ CUP

Calories	150	Dietary Fiber	0 g
Protein	5 g	Sodium	95 mg
Carbohydrate	7 g	Potassium	130 mg
Fat	9 g	Calcium	8% U.S. RDA
Cholesterol	130 mg	Iron	2% U.S. RDA

Fluffy Eggnog

    6 eggs, separated
   ¼ cup sugar
   ¼ teaspoon salt
    4 cups milk
    1 teaspoon vanilla
   ¾ teaspoon cream of tartar
¾ to 1 cup light rum or ½ to 1 teaspoon
        rum extract
        Nutmeg

In large non-aluminum saucepan, combine egg yolks, 2 tablespoons of the sugar and salt; stir in milk. Cook over low heat, stirring constantly, until mixture thickens and coats spoon. Remove from heat; stir in vanilla. Cool; refrigerate immediately. At serving time, in medium bowl, beat egg whites with cream of tartar until frothy. Gradually add remaining 2 tablespoons sugar, beating until soft peaks form. Fold chilled eggnog and rum into beaten egg whites. Pour into punch bowl; sprinkle with nutmeg. **24 (½-cup) servings.**

NUTRIENTS PER ½ CUP

Calories	60	Dietary Fiber	0 g
Protein	3 g	Sodium	60 mg
Carbohydrate	4 g	Potassium	80 mg
Fat	2 g	Calcium	6% U.S. RDA
Cholesterol	70 mg	Iron	<2% U.S. RDA

Party Hot Chocolate

3 oz. (3 squares) unsweetened chocolate
½ cup water
½ cup sugar
Dash salt
½ cup whipping cream, whipped
5 cups milk
Nutmeg, if desired

In large saucepan, combine chocolate and water over low heat, stirring constantly. Blend in sugar and salt; simmer 4 minutes, stirring occasionally. Cool; fold in whipped cream. Refrigerate until serving time. Heat milk to scalding. Place 1 heaping tablespoon chocolate mixture in each cup; fill with hot milk. Sprinkle with nutmeg. **7 (1-cup) servings.**

TIP: Chocolate mixture will keep up to 1 week in the refrigerator.

VARIATION:

MOCHA HOT CHOCOLATE: Omit nutmeg; add ½ teaspoon instant coffee granules or crystals to each cup.

NUTRIENTS PER 1 CUP

Calories	280	Dietary Fiber	<1 g
Protein	7 g	Sodium	115 mg
Carbohydrate	29 g	Potassium	360 mg
Fat	15 g	Calcium	25% U.S. RDA
Cholesterol	35 mg	Iron	4% U.S. RDA

Hot Cocoa

⅓ cup sugar
3 tablespoons unsweetened cocoa
Dash salt
½ cup hot water
3 cups milk

In medium saucepan, combine first 4 ingredients; simmer 2 minutes. Add milk; heat. Before serving, beat until frothy. If desired, top with marshmallows or whipped cream. **4 (1-cup) servings.**

TIP: To make in mugs, combine 2 tablespoons sugar, 1 tablespoon cocoa, dash salt and 2 tablespoons hot water in each mug. Heat milk. Pour into mugs; mix well.

NUTRIENTS PER 1 CUP

Calories	170	Dietary Fiber	<1 g
Protein	7 g	Sodium	150 mg
Carbohydrate	27 g	Potassium	310 mg
Fat	4 g	Calcium	25% U.S. RDA
Cholesterol	15 mg	Iron	2% U.S. RDA

Yogurt Shake

In blender container or mixer, blend until frothy 8-oz. carton (1 cup) vanilla yogurt, ¼ cup milk and one of the following.

VARIATIONS:

VANILLA: Add 1 teaspoon vanilla.

BANANA: Add 1 small banana, sliced.

FRUIT: Add ½ cup cut-up fruit or berries; 1 tablespoon sugar can be added.

TIP: For added nutrition, add 1 to 2 teaspoons wheat germ for each shake.

NUTRIENTS PER 1 VANILLA YOGURT SHAKE

Calories	260	Dietary Fiber	0 g
Protein	12 g	Sodium	160 mg
Carbohydrate	46 g	Potassium	540 mg
Fat	4 g	Calcium	40% U.S. RDA
Cholesterol	15 mg	Iron	<2% U.S. RDA

Peanut Butter Banana Shake

In blender container, combine 1 cup milk, 1 cup vanilla ice cream, 1 medium banana cut into 1-inch pieces and ½ cup creamy peanut butter. Cover; blend at medium-low speed until smooth and thick, about 30 to 45 seconds. Pour into glasses. **3 (¾-cup) servings.**

NUTRIENTS PER ¾ CUP

Calories	440	Dietary Fiber	4 g
Protein	16 g	Sodium	330 mg
Carbohydrate	30 g	Potassium	615 mg
Fat	29 g	Calcium	20% U.S. RDA
Cholesterol	25 mg	Iron	6% U.S. RDA

Orange Soda

In large pitcher, combine 4 (12-oz.) cans (3 cups) orange-flavored carbonated beverage and 3 cups orange juice; stir to blend. Divide mixture equally into 4 tall glasses. Add 2 scoops orange sherbet to each glass. Garnish with orange slice and cherry. Serve with straws. **8 (1¾-cup) servings.**

NUTRIENTS PER 1¾ CUPS

Calories	270	Dietary Fiber	<1 g
Protein	2 g	Sodium	45 mg
Carbohydrate	61 g	Potassium	280 mg
Fat	2 g	Calcium	6% U.S. RDA
Cholesterol	0 mg	Iron	<2% U.S. RDA

Rise 'n Shine Shake

    1 cup strawberries
    1 medium banana, cut into pieces
    1 cup milk
    ½ cup plain or flavored yogurt
1 to 2 tablespoons honey
       Nutmeg

Reserve 3 strawberries. In blender container, combine remaining strawberries, banana, milk, yogurt and honey. Cover; blend at medium-low speed until thick and smooth. Pour into chilled glasses; sprinkle with nutmeg. Garnish each with whole strawberry. **3 (¾-cup) servings.**

NUTRIENTS PER ¾ CUP

Calories	160	Dietary Fiber	2 g
Protein	6 g	Sodium	70 mg
Carbohydrate	31 g	Potassium	470 mg
Fat	2 g	Calcium	20% U.S. RDA
Cholesterol	8 mg	Iron	2% U.S. RDA

Milk Shake

In blender container or mixer, blend until smooth ¼ cup milk, 1 cup vanilla ice cream and one of the following.

VARIATIONS:

BANANA: Decrease ice cream to ½ cup. Add 1 small banana, sliced.

CHOCOLATE: Add ¼ cup chocolate-flavored syrup or ice cream topping. Chocolate ice cream can be substituted for vanilla.

COFFEE: Dissolve 1 teaspoon instant coffee granules or crystals in milk.

FRUIT: Decrease ice cream to ½ cup. Add ½ cup cut-up fruit or berries.

MOCHA: Dissolve 1 teaspoon instant coffee granules or crystals in milk; add ¼ cup chocolate-flavored syrup or ice cream topping.

PEANUT BUTTER: Add ¼ cup peanut butter.

VANILLA: Add 1 teaspoon vanilla.

NUTRIENTS PER 1 VANILLA MILK SHAKE

Calories	310	Dietary Fiber	0 g
Protein	7 g	Sodium	150 mg
Carbohydrate	35 g	Potassium	350 mg
Fat	16 g	Calcium	25% U.S. RDA
Cholesterol	60 mg	Iron	<2% U.S. RDA

Tea

Keys to Successful Tea

• Begin with cold, freshly drawn water and fresh tea. For each serving, use 1 teaspoon or tea bag with ¾ cup water.

• Heat water just to boiling. Warm teapot with a rinse of boiling water; immediately pour fresh-boiled water over tea leaves or bag.

• Steep tea not less than 3 minutes or more than 5 minutes. Depend on the clock and taste rather than color, since tea varieties vary in color as well as other characteristics.

• When steeping is completed, strain out leaves or remove tea ball or bag to avoid bitterness.

Basic Tea Recipe

Fill a pottery or heat resistant serving pot with boiling water; let stand to warm pot. Meanwhile, heat 5 to 6 oz. cold water just to boiling. (Do not use a copper, brass or iron pot.) Pour out water in serving pot. Add 1 teaspoon tea leaves or 1 tea bag; cover with hot water. Steep 3 to 5 minutes. Strain tea leaves or remove tea bag. Serve immediately. Do not reheat tea or reuse tea leaves or tea bag. **1 serving.**

Hot Fruited Tea

　　5　cups boiling water
　　4　tea bags or 4 teaspoons tea leaves
　10　whole cloves
　¼　teaspoon cinnamon
¼ to ½　cup sugar
　2 to 4　tablespoons lemon juice
　⅓　cup orange juice
　　　Orange slices or wedges

In large teapot, pour boiling water over tea, cloves and cinnamon. Cover; let stand 5 minutes. Strain tea; stir in sugar, lemon juice and orange juice. Heat to simmering. Serve hot with orange slice. **11 (½-cup) servings.**

NUTRIENTS PER ½ CUP

Calories	40	Dietary Fiber	<1 g
Protein	0 g	Sodium	0 mg
Carbohydrate	11 g	Potassium	20 mg
Fat	0 g	Calcium	<2% U.S. RDA
Cholesterol	0 mg	Iron	<2% U.S. RDA

Russian Tea

3 cups sugar
2 cups orange-flavored instant breakfast drink
1 cup instant tea
1 teaspoon cloves
1 teaspoon cinnamon

In medium bowl, combine all ingredients; mix well. Place 2 rounded tablespoons of mix in each cup. Fill with 1 cup boiling water; stir well. Store dry mix in tightly covered container. **32 servings.**

NUTRIENTS PER 2 TABLESPOONS MIX

Calories	130	Dietary Fiber	0 g
Protein	1 g	Sodium	0 mg
Carbohydrate	33 g	Potassium	330 mg
Fat	0 g	Calcium	<2% U.S. RDA
Cholesterol	0 mg	Iron	<2% U.S. RDA

Iced Tea

Brew strong tea, steeping 5 minutes. Strain and pour over ice cubes. Add additional water until of desired strength. Serve with sugar, lemon slices or mint leaves.

TIP: When tea is steeped or cooled too long, it may become cloudy when added to ice. Add a small amount of boiling water to make it clear.

VARIATION:

SUN TEA: Place cold water in 1-quart glass jar. Add tea. Cover; let stand in full sun 2 to 3 hours or until desired strength.

Best Minted Iced Tea

      4 cups boiling water
    ½ cup instant tea
      1 cup sugar
 2 to 4 tablespoons slightly crushed mint leaves
      2 quarts (8 cups) cold water
 6-oz. can frozen lemonade concentrate, thawed

In 4-quart non-metal container, combine water, tea, sugar
and mint leaves; let stand 15 minutes. Stir in cold water and
lemonade concentrate; serve over ice. **12 (1-cup) servings.**

NUTRIENTS PER 1 CUP

Calories	110	Dietary Fiber	<1 g
Protein	0 g	Sodium	0 mg
Carbohydrate	28 g	Potassium	135 mg
Fat	0 g	Calcium	<2% U.S. RDA
Cholesterol	0 mg	Iron	<2% U.S. RDA

Spicy Citrus Cooler

      2 tea bags or 2 teaspoons tea leaves
    ½ teaspoon whole cloves
      1 cinnamon stick
      2 cups boiling water
      1 quart (4 cups) grapefruit juice
 6-oz. can frozen orange juice concentrate

Place tea, cloves and cinnamon in teapot. Pour boiling water
over tea mixture. Cover; let stand about 10 minutes.

In 2-quart non-metal container, combine grapefruit juice and
orange juice concentrate. Remove tea bags and strain spices
from tea; pour into juice mixture. Refrigerate. Serve over
ice, stirring to combine. Garnish as desired. **6 (1-cup) servings.**

NUTRIENTS PER 1 CUP

Calories 130	Dietary Fiber...........................1 g
Protein.......................................2 g	Sodium...................................5 mg
Carbohydrate............................30 g	Potassium.......................500 mg
Fat ....0 g	Calcium.................2% U.S. RDA
Cholesterol............................0 mg	Iron........................4% U.S. RDA

Cranberry Tea Punch

>   4   tea bags
>   2   cups boiling water
>   6   cups water
>   1   cup sugar
>   1   quart (4 cups) cranberry juice cocktail, chilled
>   2   cups apple juice, chilled
> 6-oz.   can frozen orange juice concentrate, thawed
>   Orange slices, if desired
>   Ice ring, if desired

Prepare tea by combining tea bags with 2 cups boiling water. Cover; let stand 10 minutes. Remove tea bags. Cool to room temperature; refrigerate.

Meanwhile, in medium saucepan bring 6 cups water and sugar to a boil, stirring constantly until sugar is dissolved. Cool to room temperature; refrigerate.

Just before serving, combine chilled tea, sugar mixture, cranberry juice cocktail, apple juice and orange juice concentrate in large punch bowl. Garnish with orange slices and ice ring. **30 (½-cup) servings.**

NUTRIENTS PER ½ CUP

Calories 70	Dietary Fiber.........................<1 g
Protein.......................................0 g	Sodium...................................0 mg
Carbohydrate............................18 g	Potassium.........................70 mg
Fat ....0 g	Calcium...............<2% U.S. RDA
Cholesterol............................0 mg	Iron ....<2% U.S. RDA

Coffee

Keys to Successful Coffee

• Start with a clean coffeepot. Wash pot with hot soapy water and rinse well after each use.

• Always start with freshly drawn cold water. For each serving, use 1 to 3 level tablespoons of ground coffee for every ¾ cup water, depending on the strength of the desired brew.

• Serve coffee as soon as possible after brewing. If necessary to hold, remove grounds and keep over very low heat. Avoid boiling coffee, as it will become bitter-tasting and lose its aroma.

• Store ground coffee and coffee beans, tightly covered, in refrigerator or freezer. Unopened cans of vacuum-packed coffee and jars of instant or freeze-dried coffee will keep one year at room temperature if stored in a cool, dry place. Once opened, coffee will maintain its freshness 2 to 3 weeks in a cool place, 8 weeks in the refrigerator and 6 months in the freezer.

Basic Coffee Recipe

Servings (¾-cup each)	Ground Coffee	Water
6	¼ to ½ cup	4½ cups
12	¾ to 1¼ cups (about ¼ lb.)	9 cups
25	2 to 2½ cups (about ½ lb.)	5 quarts
50	4 to 4½ cups (about 1 lb.)	10 quarts

Note: Plan for 1½ to 2 (¾-cup) servings per person. Serve with cream or milk and sugar.

To Brew Coffee

• **Percolator:** Use regular-grind coffee. Pour water into percolator. Assemble stem and basket. Add ground coffee; cover with lid. The water is forced up through the basket of coffee. For electric percolator, plug in coffeepot. For non-electric pot, bring water to a boil; reduce heat. The coffee should perk slowly for about 6 to 8 minutes.

• **Drip:** Use drip-grind coffee. Place ground coffee in filter section. Pour boiling water into filter and allow to drip through grounds and filter. When water has dripped through, the coffee is ready to serve.

• **Vacuum:** Use fine-grind coffee. Place cold water in lower bowl of pot; place filter and ground coffee in top bowl. Heat water until it rises to top bowl. Remove pot from heat. The coffee will filter back into the bottom pot as it cools slightly.

• **Steeped or Boiled Coffee:** Use regular-grind coffee. Place cold water in an enamel pot. Add ground coffee to water. If desired to improve clarity and flavor, mix one uncooked egg with coffee grounds before adding to water. Heat just to boiling; let steep 2 minutes. Add a small amount of cold water to cause grounds to settle to bottom.

International Brews

ARABIAN COFFEE: Place 1 crushed cardamom seed in each serving cup. Fill cup with hot strong coffee. Stir with cinnamon stick.

BRAZILIAN COFFEE: Place 2 tablespoons instant cocoa mix in each serving cup. Fill cup with hot strong coffee. Stir with cinnamon stick. Top with whipped cream or topping.

FRENCH COFFEE: To prepare cafe au lait, two pots are needed—one for hot strong coffee and one for an equal amount of hot milk or cream. Pour from both pots at the same time into each serving cup.

ITALIAN COFFEE: Fill each serving cup with hot strong coffee. Serve with a twist of lemon.

MEXICAN COFFEE: Place 2 teaspoons chocolate-flavored syrup and ⅛ teaspoon cinnamon in each serving cup. Fill cup with hot strong coffee; stir well. Top with whipped cream or topping; sprinkle with cinnamon and nutmeg.

SWEDISH COFFEE: Combine ¼ cup firmly packed brown sugar, ¼ teaspoon cinnamon, ¼ teaspoon ground cloves and ¼ teaspoon nutmeg; mix well. Place 1 teaspoon spice mixture in each serving cup. Add strip of orange peel. Fill cup with hot strong coffee; stir. Top with whipped cream.

TURKISH COFFEE: Place 1 tablespoon honey or sugar and 1 crushed cardamom seed in each serving cup. Fill cup with hot strong coffee; stir. Top with whipped cream or topping.

VIENNESE COFFEE: Fill each serving cup with hot strong coffee. Stir in 1 teaspoon sugar. Top with whipped cream or topping; sprinkle with nutmeg.

NUTRIENTS: Variables in these recipes make it impossible to calculate nutrition information.

Iced Coffee

Brew extra-strong coffee. Pour over ice cubes. Add additional cold water until of desired strength. Serve with sugar, if desired.

TIP: Iced coffee can also be prepared using ½ cup brewed coffee plus ½ cup cold milk poured over ice cubes.

Coffee Cordial

1½ cups sugar
1   cup firmly packed brown sugar
2   cups water
⅓   cup instant coffee granules or crystals
2   cups brandy
2   cups vodka
1   vanilla bean

In medium saucepan, combine sugar, brown sugar and water. Bring to a boil; simmer uncovered 10 minutes, stirring occasionally. Stir in coffee until dissolved. Cool. Poor into 2-quart glass jar with lid. Add brandy, vodka and vanilla bean; blend well. Cover tightly with lid. Allow to stand at room temperature for 2 weeks, stirring occasionally. Pour into decorative bottles; cap tightly. **7 cups.**

SERVING SUGGESTIONS:

AFTER DINNER COFFEE COOLER: Pour 3 tablespoons Coffee Cordial over crushed ice in 6-oz. drink glass. Fill glass with milk; stir well. **1 serving.**

HOT MOCHA MAGIC: Pour 2 tablespoons Coffee Cordial into cup of steaming hot chocolate; stir. Garnish with whipped cream, if desired. **1 serving.**

NUTRIENTS: Variables in this recipe make it impossible to calculate nutrition information.

After Dinner Irish Cream

2   cups whipping cream
1¾   cups brandy
14-oz. can sweetened condensed milk (not evaporated)
3   eggs

    2 tablespoons chocolate-flavored syrup
1½ teaspoons vanilla

In 6-cup blender container, blend all ingredients at low speed until frothy. Serve immediately or cover and refrigerate up to 4 weeks. Blend again before serving. **18 (⅓-cup) servings.**

NUTRIENTS PER ⅓ CUP

Calories	230	Dietary Fiber	<1 g
Protein	3 g	Sodium	45 mg
Carbohydrate	14 g	Potassium	110 mg
Fat	13 g	Calcium	8% U.S. RDA
Cholesterol	90 mg	Iron	<2% U.S. RDA

Chocolate Crinkle Cups

Melt semi-sweet or sweet cooking chocolate. Brush melted chocolate on inside of miniature paper candy cups until about ⅛ inch thick. Wipe off any chocolate that may have dripped over sides of cups. Refrigerate cups about 10 minutes. Apply second coat of chocolate over first layer. Refrigerate until chocolate is set. Carefully peel paper from cups. Store in refrigerator or freezer until ready to use. Fill with nuts, candy or liqueur.

Cran-Raspberry Liqueur

    2 cups frozen whole raspberries, thawed
    2 cups fresh whole cranberries, coarsely chopped
    2 cups sugar
    1 tablespoon lemon juice
    2 cups vodka

In 2-quart glass jar with lid, combine all ingredients; stir until sugar is dissolved. Cover tightly with lid. Allow to stand at room temperature 2 weeks, inverting jar every day. Strain through cheesecloth. Pour into decorative bottles; cap tightly. **3½ cups.**

SERVING SUGGESTIONS:

CRAN-RASPBERRY CHEER: In punch bowl or decanter, add 1 cup Cran-Raspberrry Liqueur to 750 ml bottle (3¼ cups) sparkling Burgundy wine, chilled; blend well. Serve immediately in chilled glasses. **16 (½-cup) servings.**

HOT CRAN-RASPBERRY COCKTAIL: Pour 2 tablespoons Cran-Raspberry Liqueur into cup of hot apple cider; stir. Serve with cinnamon stick and apple wedge, if desired. **1 serving.**

NUTRIENTS: Variables in this recipe make it impossible to calculate nutrition information.

Breads

Breads

There are home-baked bread variations today to suit and satisfy every taste, timetable, skill level and purpose. Contemporary techniques and ingredients, modern appliances and innovative recipes mean that the fragrance of homemade breads baking and the resulting unsurpassed flavor can be enjoyed by every cook.

Bread baking in this country includes a rich tradition of international influence. Such specialties as scones, crepes and French and challah bread are as much at home on our tables as some of America's regional favorites like sourdough, casserole and spoon breads, biscuits and corn bread.

Breads are divided into two main categories, *quick* and *yeast*. *Quick breads* are leavened by the addition of baking soda or baking powder and, as their name implies, are quickly made because no kneading or rising is required. Favorite quick breads include fruit and nut loaves, muffins, biscuits, corn bread, some doughnuts, pancakes, waffles, many coffee cakes and popovers.

Yeast breads rely on properties of the sensitive yeast plant for rising and include kneaded breads, batter breads, rolls, many sweet holiday breads, French and Italian loaves, bagels, croissants, brioches, English muffins, pita or pocket bread, some doughnuts and yeast coffee cakes.

Bread Baking Hints

• Dry ingredients do have a shelf life, especially leavening ingredients. Check expiration date on packages and store in tightly sealed containers away from heat and moisture. For best results, use flour within 12 to 13 months of purchasing. Whole grain flours are more susceptible to spoilage. If they are to be kept longer than 6 months, whole grain flours should be stored in the refrigerator or freezer and warmed to room temperature before using.

• Measure ingredients carefully and combine according to recipe instructions.

• Use size of pan or dish specified in recipe and prepare pan according to instructions. Use solid shortening, not butter or margarine, for greasing pans. Baking pans that are dull or dark will produce products with well-browned crusts. Bread products will not get as brown when baked in shiny pans.

• Follow oven temperature and timing stated in recipe. Since doneness tests vary, follow recipe instructions for each particular type of bread.

• Cool baked breads on wire racks before slicing. Using a sharp bread knife with a thin blade, slice with a back-and-forth sawing motion rather than pressing straight down.

• Wrap cooled breads in plastic wrap or foil; store in cool, dry place. Refrigeration retards molding but doesn't keep bread from becoming stale. Baked quick and yeast breads freeze well up to 3 months. To freeze, seal in freezer bags or wrap, date and place in freezer. To thaw, loosen wrap and let bread stand at room temperature. To reheat, heat oven to 350°F. and wrap bread in foil. Heat rolls, muffins and biscuits for 10 to 15 minutes, loaves and coffee cakes 15 to 20 minutes. If bread has a crispy crust, open foil last 5 minutes of reheating. The microwave oven is useful for quickly thawing and reheating breads. See your microwave oven manual for instructions.

Quick Breads

Keys to Successful Quick Breads

• **Loaves:** Accurate measuring is important to avoid a heavy loaf that seems dry on the outside and underdone on the inside. Adding more or less fruit than specified can cause this and other problems.

• Use a shiny baking pan that is the size called for in the recipe so bake time will be accurate.

• Successfully baked quick bread loaves are well shaped, with a thin, golden-brown crust. Texture is even, interior is fairly moist and ingredients such as fruit bits and nuts are evenly distributed. The lengthwise crack across the top is a common characteristic.

• Quick bread loaves should be completely cooled before slicing to avoid crumbling. Often quick breads will improve in flavor and be easier to slice if cooled, tightly wrapped and allowed to stand for at least one day.

• **Muffins:** Combine ingredients just until all dry particles are moistened; batter will be slightly lumpy. Overmixing causes a tough texture, unattractive tunnels and peaked rather than rounded tops.

• Bake in shiny pans that have been greased on bottom only of each cup. If there is not enough batter to fill every cup, fill empty cups with water before baking. Muffins should be removed from tins immediately after baking to prevent soggy texture.

• **Pancakes:** Heat griddle to 375° to 400°F.; grease evenly to avoid sticking. Avoid overgreasing, as grease will be absorbed into the pancakes.

• Turn pancakes only once during cooking. They are ready to turn when tops are puffed and full of bubbles that are just beginning to burst and edges are dry.

• Batter that becomes too thick on standing can be thinned with a little more liquid.

• **Waffles:** Heat waffle iron *before* adding batter. Grease lightly. To avoid sticking, iron may need additional greasing between waffles.

• Pour batter into center of waffle iron. Use amount specified by manufacturer's directions.

• Do not open when waffle is baking. Generally, when iron stops steaming, waffle is ready to eat.

How to Prepare Muffins

For tender, moist muffins, combine dry ingredients and additions such as blueberries by stirring together in a large bowl. Push this flour mixture up sides of bowl to make a well. Combine liquid ingredients and pour all at once into this well.

Stir only to moisten dry ingredients, counting 12 to 15 strokes. Batter will remain lumpy.

Muffin cups can be lightly greased or lined with paper baking cups. Fill each cup ⅔ full with batter for pebbly-topped, rounded muffins.

Muffins

2 cups all purpose flour
½ cup sugar
3 teaspoons baking powder
½ teaspoon salt
¾ cup milk
⅓ cup oil
1 egg, beaten

Heat oven to 400°F. Grease bottoms only of 12 muffin cups or line with paper baking cups. In medium bowl, combine flour, sugar, baking powder and salt; mix well. In small bowl, combine milk, oil and egg; blend well. Add to dry ingredients all at once; stir just until dry ingredients are moistened. Fill prepared muffin cups ⅔ full. Bake at 400°F. for 18 to 22 minutes or until light golden brown. Cool 1 minute before removing from pan. Serve warm. **12 muffins.**

MICROWAVE DIRECTIONS: Prepare muffin batter as directed above. Using a 6-cup microwave-safe muffin pan, line each cup with 2 paper baking cups to absorb moisture during baking. Fill muffin cups ⅔ full. Microwave on HIGH for 1 minute. Rotate ½ turn. Microwave on HIGH for 1 to 1½ minutes or until toothpick inserted in center comes out clean. Remove muffins from pan and discard outer paper baking cups immediately. Repeat with remaining batter.

VARIATIONS:

APPLE MUFFINS: Reduce sugar to ¼ cup and add 1 teaspoon cinnamon to flour; stir 1 cup finely chopped apple into dry ingredients. Substitute apple juice for milk. Bake at 400°F. for 18 to 22 minutes.

BLUEBERRY MUFFINS: Stir 1 cup fresh or frozen blueberries and 1 teaspoon grated lemon or orange peel into dry ingredients.

CHOCOLATE CHIP MUFFINS: Add ¾ cup miniature chocolate chips with flour. Sprinkle tops of muffins before baking with a combination of 3 tablespoons sugar and 2 tablespoons brown sugar.

JAM MUFFINS: Place ½ teaspoon favorite jam on each muffin before baking; press into batter. If desired, sprinkle with finely chopped nuts.

LEMON MUFFINS: Add 1 tablespoon grated lemon peel with flour.

ORANGE MUFFINS: Add 1 tablespoon grated orange peel with flour and substitute orange juice for milk.

STREUSEL-TOPPED MUFFINS: In small bowl, blend ¼ cup firmly packed brown sugar, 1 tablespoon softened margarine or butter, ½ teaspoon cinnamon and ¼ cup chopped nuts or flaked coconut with fork until crumbly. Sprinkle over muffins before baking.

SUGAR-COATED MUFFINS: Brush tops of hot muffins with 2 tablespoons melted margarine or butter; dip in mixture of ¼ cup sugar and ½ teaspoon cinnamon.

WHOLE WHEAT MUFFINS: Use 1 cup all purpose flour and 1 cup whole wheat flour.

NUTRIENTS PER 1 MUFFIN

Calories	180	Dietary Fiber	1 g
Protein	3 g	Sodium	180 mg
Carbohydrate	25 g	Potassium	50 mg
Fat	7 g	Calcium	6% U.S. RDA
Cholesterol	25 mg	Iron	6% U.S. RDA

Bran Muffins

    2 cups shreds of whole bran cereal
   2½ cups buttermilk
    ½ cup oil
    2 eggs
   2½ cups all purpose flour
   1½ cups sugar
   1¼ teaspoons baking soda
    1 teaspoon baking powder
    ½ teaspoon salt
    ¾ cup raisins (optional)

In large bowl, combine cereal and buttermilk; let stand 5 minutes or until cereal is softened. Add oil and eggs; blend well. Stir in remaining ingredients; mix well. Batter can be baked immediately or stored in tightly covered container in refrigerator for up to 2 weeks.

When ready to bake, heat oven to 400°F. Grease desired number of muffin cups or line with paper baking cups. Stir batter; fill prepared muffin cups ¾ full. Bake at 400°F. for 18 to 20 minutes or until toothpick inserted in center comes out clean. **24 to 30 muffins.**

NUTRIENTS PER 1 MUFFIN

Calories	150	Dietary Fiber	2 g
Protein	3 g	Sodium	160 mg
Carbohydrate	25 g	Potassium	120 mg
Fat	4 g	Calcium	4% U.S. RDA
Cholesterol	20 mg	Iron	6% U.S. RDA

Bright Day Banana Muffins

MUFFINS

- 1 cup all purpose flour
- ¾ cup whole wheat flour
- ½ cup sugar
- 2 teaspoons baking powder
- ½ teaspoon salt
- ¼ teaspoon nutmeg
- ½ cup (1 medium) mashed ripe banana
- ½ cup milk
- ⅓ cup oil
- 1 egg, slightly beaten

TOPPING

- ¼ cup sugar
- ½ teaspoon cinnamon
- 2 tablespoons margarine or butter, melted

Heat oven to 400°F. Grease bottoms only of 12 muffin cups or line with paper baking cups. In large bowl, combine all dry ingredients for muffins; stir in remaining muffin ingredients just until dry particles are moistened. Fill prepared muffin cups ⅔ full.

Bake at 400°F. for 18 to 22 minutes or until golden brown. Immediately remove from pan. In small bowl, combine ¼ cup sugar and cinnamon. Brush tops of hot muffins with melted margarine; dip in sugar-cinnamon mixture. Serve warm. **12 muffins.**

NUTRIENTS PER 1 MUFFIN

Calories 210	Dietary Fiber ....2 g
Protein ....3 g	Sodium.............................170 mg
Carbohydrate........................29 g	Potassium ....100 mg
Fat ....9 g	Calcium.................4% U.S. RDA
Cholesterol ....25 mg	Iron......................4% U.S. RDA

Banana Bread

¾ cup sugar
½ cup margarine or butter, softened
2 eggs
1 cup (2 medium) mashed ripe bananas
⅓ cup milk
1 teaspoon vanilla
2 cups all purpose flour
½ cup chopped nuts, if desired
1 teaspoon baking soda
½ teaspoon salt

Heat oven to 350°F. Grease bottom only of 9x5 or 8x4-inch loaf pan. In large bowl, cream sugar and margarine until light and fluffy. Beat in eggs; blend in bananas, milk and vanilla. In small bowl, combine flour, nuts, baking soda and salt; mix well. Add to creamed mixture; stir just until dry ingredients are moistened. Pour into prepared pan. Bake at 350°F. for 50 to 60 minutes or until toothpick inserted in center comes out clean. Cool in pan 5 minutes; remove. Cool completely on wire rack. Wrap and store in refrigerator. **1 (16-slice) loaf.**

HIGH ALTITUDE: Increase flour to 2 cups plus 1 tablespoon. Bake at 375°F. for 45 to 55 minutes.

VARIATION:

APPLESAUCE BREAD: Substitute 1 cup applesauce for mashed bananas and add ¾ teaspoon cinnamon with flour.

NUTRIENTS PER 1 SLICE

Calories	190	Dietary Fiber	1 g
Protein	3 g	Sodium	210 mg
Carbohydrate	26 g	Potassium	110 mg
Fat	9 g	Calcium	<2% U.S. RDA
Cholesterol	35 mg	Iron	4% U.S. RDA

Zucchini Orange Bread

BREAD

- 4 eggs
- 1½ cups sugar
- ¾ cup oil
- ⅔ cup orange juice
- 2 cups shredded unpeeled zucchini
- 3¼ cups all purpose flour
- 1½ teaspoons baking powder
- 1½ teaspoons baking soda
- 1 teaspoon salt
- 2 teaspoons grated orange peel
- 2½ teaspoons cinnamon
- ½ teaspoon cloves
- ½ cup chopped nuts, if desired

GLAZE

- 1 cup powdered sugar
- 2 to 3 tablespoons orange juice

Heat oven to 350°F. Grease and flour bottoms only of two 8x4 or 9x5-inch loaf pans. In large bowl, beat eggs until thick and lemon colored; gradually beat in sugar. Stir in oil, ⅔ cup orange juice and zucchini. Stir in remaining bread ingredients; mix well. Pour batter into prepared pans. Bake at 350°F. for 45 to 55 minutes or until toothpick inserted in center comes out clean. Cool 10 minutes. Remove from pans; cool slightly. In small bowl, blend glaze ingredients; spread over warm loaves. Cool completely on wire rack. Wrap tightly and store in refrigerator. **2 (16-slice) loaves.**

HIGH ALTITUDE: Increase flour to 3¼ cups plus 3 tablespoons. Bake at 350°F. for 45 to 50 minutes.

NUTRIENTS PER 1 SLICE

Calories	170	Dietary Fiber	1 g
Protein	2 g	Sodium	140 mg
Carbohydrate	24 g	Potassium	55 mg
Fat	7 g	Calcium	2% U.S. RDA
Cholesterol	35 mg	Iron	4% U.S. RDA

Nut Bread

¾ cup sugar
½ cup margarine or butter, softened
2 eggs
1 cup buttermilk
2 cups all purpose flour
1 cup chopped nuts
½ teaspoon baking powder
½ teaspoon baking soda
½ teaspoon salt

Heat oven to 350°F. Grease bottom only of 9x5 or 8x4-inch loaf pan. In large bowl, cream sugar and margarine until light and fluffy. Beat in eggs; blend in buttermilk. In small bowl, combine flour, nuts, baking powder, baking soda and salt; mix well. Add to creamed mixture; stir just until dry ingredients are moistened. Pour into prepared pan. Bake at 350°F. for 55 to 65 minutes or until toothpick inserted in center comes out clean. Cool in pan 15 minutes; remove. Cool completely on wire rack. Wrap and store in refrigerator. **1 (16-slice) loaf.**

HIGH ALTITUDE: Increase flour to 2 cups plus 1 tablespoon. Bake at 375°F. for 50 to 60 minutes.

NUTRIENTS PER 1 SLICE

Calories	210	Dietary Fiber	1 g
Protein	4 g	Sodium	200 mg
Carbohydrate	23 g	Potassium	85 mg
Fat	11 g	Calcium	4% U.S. RDA
Cholesterol	35 mg	Iron	6% U.S. RDA

Peach Kuchen

½	cup margarine or butter, softened
¼	cup sugar
1	teaspoon vanilla
1	egg
1	cup all purpose flour
½	teaspoon baking powder
¼	teaspoon salt
29-oz.	can sliced peaches, well drained
3	tablespoons sugar
1	teaspoon cinnamon

Heat oven to 350°F. Grease 9-inch springform pan. In large bowl, beat margarine and sugar until light and fluffy. Add vanilla and egg; beat well. Add flour, baking powder and salt to margarine mixture; blend well. Spread dough over bottom and 1 inch up sides of pan. Arrange peach slices in spoke fashion over dough. Sprinkle with sugar and cinnamon. Bake at 350°F. for 30 to 35 minutes or until edges are golden brown. Cool 10 minutes; remove sides of pan. **8 servings.**

NUTRIENTS PER ⅛ OF RECIPE

Calories	260	Dietary Fiber	2 g
Protein	3 g	Sodium	230 mg
Carbohydrate	35 g	Potassium	160 mg
Fat	12 g	Calcium	6% U.S. RDA
Cholesterol	35 mg	Iron	6% U.S. RDA

Holiday Cranberry Bread

        1   cup sugar
        1   tablespoon grated orange peel
     ¾   cup water
     ⅓   cup orange juice
        2   tablespoons oil
        1   egg
        2   cups all purpose flour
    1½   teaspoons baking powder
        1   teaspoon salt
     ½   teaspoon baking soda
        1   cup halved fresh or frozen whole
            cranberries
        1   cup chopped nuts

Heat oven to 350°F. Grease 9x5-inch loaf pan. In large bowl, blend sugar, orange peel, water, orange juice, oil and egg; mix well. Add flour, baking powder, salt and baking soda, stirring just until moistened. Stir in cranberries and nuts. Pour into prepared pan. Bake at 350°F. for 50 to 60 minutes or until toothpick inserted in center comes out clean. Cool 10 minutes; remove from pan. Cool completely. Wrap tightly and store in refrigerator. **1 (16-slice) loaf.**

NUTRIENTS PER 1 SLICE

Calories	160	Dietary Fiber	1 g
Protein	3 g	Sodium	200 mg
Carbohydrate	21 g	Potassium	70 mg
Fat	7 g	Calcium	2% U.S. RDA
Cholesterol	15 mg	Iron	6% U.S. RDA

Baking Powder Biscuits

        2   cups all purpose flour
        3   teaspoons baking powder
     ½   teaspoon salt
     ½   cup shortening
    ¾ to 1 cup milk

Heat oven to 450°F. In large bowl, combine flour, baking powder and salt. Using fork or pastry blender, cut shortening into flour until consistency of coarse meal. Add milk; stir with fork until mixture leaves sides of bowl and forms a soft, moist dough. On floured surface, toss lightly until no longer sticky. Roll out ½-inch thick; cut with 2-inch floured cutter. Place on ungreased cookie sheet. Bake at 450°F. for 8 to 12 minutes or until light golden brown. Serve hot. **12 to 14 biscuits.**

FOOD PROCESSOR DIRECTIONS: In food processor bowl with metal blade, combine flour, baking powder and salt. Cover; process with 5 on/off turns to mix. Add shortening to flour mixture. Process until mixture resembles coarse crumbs. Add ½ to ⅔ cup milk; process with on/off turns *just* until ball starts to form. On lightly floured surface, roll or press dough to ½-inch thickness; cut with floured cutter. Continue as directed above.

VARIATIONS:

BUTTERMILK BISCUITS: Add ¼ teaspoon baking soda to flour. Substitute buttermilk for milk.

CHEESE BISCUITS: Add 4 oz. (1 cup) shredded Cheddar cheese to flour-shortening mixture. Bake on *greased* cookie sheet.

DROP BISCUITS: Increase milk to 1¼ cups. Drop dough by spoonfuls onto *greased* cookie sheets. Bake as directed above.

SOFT-SIDED BISCUITS: Place biscuits in 9-inch round or square pan or on cookie sheet with sides touching. Bake at 450°F. for 12 to 14 minutes.

SOUTHERN-STYLE BISCUITS: Reduce shortening to ¼ cup.

THIN-CRISPY BISCUITS: Roll dough ¼-inch thick. Cut biscuits with 3-inch cutter.

NUTRIENTS PER 1 BISCUIT

Calories	140	Dietary Fiber	1 g
Protein	2 g	Sodium	135 mg
Carbohydrate	14 g	Potassium	45 mg
Fat	8 g	Calcium	2% U.S. RDA
Cholesterol	0 mg	Iron	2% U.S. RDA

Quick Orange Coffee Cake

BASE

 2 cups all purpose flour
 ½ cup sugar
 3 teaspoons baking powder
 ½ teaspoon salt
 6 tablespoons margarine or butter
 1 cup milk
 ½ teaspoon vanilla
 1 egg, slightly beaten

FILLING

11-oz. can mandarin orange segments, well drained

TOPPING

 ¼ cup sugar
 2 tablespoons flour
 2 tablespoons margarine or butter, softened
 ¼ cup chopped nuts
 1 teaspoon grated orange peel

Heat oven to 350°F. Grease and flour 9-inch square pan. In medium bowl, combine 2 cups flour, ½ cup sugar, baking powder and salt; blend well. Using pastry blender or fork, cut in 6 tablespoons margarine until mixture is crumbly. Add milk, vanilla and egg; mix well. Spread batter in prepared pan. Arrange orange segments over batter. In small bowl, combine all topping ingredients until crumbly; sprinkle over orange segments. Bake at 350°F. for 35 to 45 minutes or until toothpick inserted in center comes out clean. Cool slightly; cut into squares. Serve warm. **9 servings.**

VARIATIONS:

BLUEBERRY COFFEE CAKE: One cup frozen blueberries, thawed and drained, can be substituted for mandarin orange segments. For topping, increase sugar to ⅓ cup and flour to ¼ cup. Omit nuts and orange peel, add ¼ teaspoon nutmeg. Follow above directions.

PINEAPPLE-COCONUT COFFEE CAKE: One-half cup coconut and 8-oz. can crushed pineapple, well drained, can be substituted for mandarin orange segments. For topping, ¼ cup firmly packed brown sugar can be substituted for sugar. Omit nuts and orange peel. Follow above directions.

NUTRIENTS PER ⅑ OF RECIPE

Calories	320	Dietary Fiber	2 g
Protein	5 g	Sodium	375 mg
Carbohydrate	44 g	Potassium	130 mg
Fat	14 g	Calcium	6% U.S. RDA
Cholesterol	35 mg	Iron	6% U.S. RDA

Sour Cream Coffee Cake

COFFEE CAKE
- ¾ cup sugar
- ½ cup margarine or butter, softened
- 1 teaspoon vanilla
- 3 eggs
- 2 cups all purpose flour
- 1 teaspoon baking powder
- 1 teaspoon baking soda
- ⅛ teaspoon salt
- 1 cup dairy sour cream

FILLING AND TOPPING
- 1¼ cups firmly packed brown sugar
- 1 cup chopped walnuts
- 2 teaspoons cinnamon
- 3 tablespoons margarine or butter, melted

Heat oven to 350°F. Grease and lightly flour 10-inch tube pan. In large bowl, cream sugar and margarine; add vanilla and eggs. Mix well. Combine flour, baking powder, baking soda, salt. Add flour mixture and sour cream alternately to sugar mixture, beginning and ending with flour mixture. In small bowl, combine filling and topping ingredients; mix well. Spread half of batter in prepared pan; sprinkle with half of brown sugar mixture. Repeat with remaining batter and brown sugar mixture.

Bake at 350°F. for 35 to 40 minutes or until toothpick inserted in center comes out clean. Cool upright in pan 15 minutes. Invert onto large plate or cookie sheet; then invert again onto serving plate, streusel side up. **16 servings.**

NUTRIENTS PER ¹⁄₁₆ OF RECIPE

Calories	330	Dietary Fiber	1 g
Protein	4 g	Sodium	225 mg
Carbohydrate	40 g	Potassium	145 mg
Fat	17 g	Calcium	4% U.S. RDA
Cholesterol	60 mg	Iron	8% U.S. RDA

Fluffy Dumplings

- 1½ cups all purpose flour
- 2 teaspoons baking powder
- ½ teaspoon salt
- ⅔ cup milk
- 2 tablespoons oil
- 1 egg, slightly beaten

In medium bowl, combine flour, baking powder and salt; blend well. Add milk, oil and egg; stir just until dry ingredients are moistened. Drop dumpling dough by rounded tablespoons onto boiling stew mixture. Reduce heat; cover tightly and cook 13 to 16 minutes or until dumplings are fluffy and no longer doughy on bottom. **12 dumplings.**

VARIATIONS:

PARSLEY-SAGE DUMPLINGS: Add 1 tablespoon chopped fresh parsley and ½ teaspoon sage leaves, finely crushed, to flour.

CHIVE-BASIL DUMPLINGS: Add 1 tablespoon chopped fresh chives and ½ teaspoon basil leaves, crushed, to flour.

NUTRIENTS PER 1 DUMPLING

Calories 90	Dietary Fiber ....1 g
Protein.......................................3 g	Sodium..............................155 mg
Carbohydrate.........................13 g	Potassium............................40 mg
Fat ....3 g	Calcium.................2% U.S. RDA
Cholesterol...........................25 mg	Iron........................2% U.S. RDA

Spoon Bread

1	cup cornmeal
1	cup milk
8½-oz.	can cream style corn
½	cup margarine or butter
2	eggs
4 oz.	(1 cup) shredded colby cheese
¼	cup chopped stuffed green olives
¼	teaspoon dill weed

Heat oven to 375°F. Grease 1-quart casserole. In medium saucepan over medium heat, combine cornmeal, milk and corn. Bring to a boil, stirring constantly. Remove from heat and stir in margarine. Add eggs, one at a time, beating by hand after each addition. Stir in cheese, olives and dill weed.

Pour batter into prepared casserole. Bake at 375°F. for 30 to 35 minutes or until golden brown. Serve immediately topped with additional margarine or butter, if desired. Refrigerate leftovers. **4 servings.**

NUTRIENTS PER ¼ OF RECIPE

Calories	550	Dietary Fiber ... 6 g
Protein	16 g	Sodium ... 850 mg
Carbohydrate	39 g	Potassium ... 320 mg
Fat	38 g	Calcium ... 30% U.S. RDA
Cholesterol	170 mg	Iron ... 10% U.S. RDA

Corn Bread

1 cup all purpose flour
1 cup cornmeal
2 tablespoons sugar
4 teaspoons baking powder
1 teaspoon salt
1 cup milk
¼ cup oil or melted shortening
1 egg, slightly beaten

Heat oven to 425°F. Grease 8 or 9-inch square pan. In medium bowl, combine flour, cornmeal, sugar, baking powder and salt. Stir in remaining ingredients beating by hand *just* until smooth. Pour batter into prepared pan. Bake at 425°F. for 18 to 22 minutes or until toothpick inserted in center comes out clean. **9 servings.**

HIGH ALTITUDE: Decrease baking powder to 1½ teaspoons.

VARIATIONS:

BACON CORN BREAD: Fry 4 to 5 slices bacon until crisp; drain on paper towel. Substitute bacon drippings for oil. Sprinkle batter with crumbled bacon before baking.

CORN BREAD RING: Bake in greased 1½-quart (6-cup) ring mold for 15 to 20 minutes. Immediately remove from mold and fill center with creamed meat or seafood mixture.

CORN MUFFINS: Spoon batter into greased muffin cups and bake 15 to 20 minutes. Immediately remove from pan. **12 muffins.**

CORN STICKS: Bake in well-greased, hot (place in oven to heat) corn stick pans, filling ⅔ full. Bake 12 to 15 minutes. Immediately remove from pan. **18 corn sticks.**

MEXICAN CORN BREAD: Prepare batter using 2 eggs, slightly beaten. Stir in ½ cup shredded Cheddar cheese, ¼ cup chopped green chiles and ¼ cup finely chopped onion. Bake 20 to 25 minutes.

NUTRIENTS PER ⅙ OF RECIPE

Calories 190	Dietary Fiber ....2 g
Protein......................................4 g	Sodium...............................390 mg
Carbohydrate.........................25 g	Potassium.........................100 mg
Fat ....8 g	Calcium..............10% U.S. RDA
Cholesterol.........................35 mg	Iron.......................4% U.S. RDA

Easy Crepes

1 cup complete or buttermilk complete pancake mix
1 cup water
2 eggs

Heat crepe pan or 7 or 8-inch skillet over medium-high heat (375°F.). A few drops of water sprinkled on the pan sizzle and bounce when heat is just right. Grease pan lightly with oil. In small bowl, combine all ingredients. Beat with rotary beater until batter is smooth. Pour scant ¼ cup batter into hot skillet, immediately tilting pan until batter covers bottom. Cook until edges start to dry and center is set. If desired, turn to brown on other side. Fill with desired fillings. **9 to 12 crepes.**

NUTRIENTS PER 1 PLAIN CREPE

Calories	50	Dietary Fiber	<1 g
Protein	2 g	Sodium	160 mg
Carbohydrate	8 g	Potassium	20 mg
Fat	1 g	Calcium	2% U.S. RDA
Cholesterol	NA	Iron	4% U.S. RDA

Crepes

    4 eggs
 1⅓ cups milk
    2 tablespoons oil, margarine or butter, melted
    1 cup all purpose flour
  ½ teaspoon salt, if desired

In medium bowl, beat eggs slightly. Add remaining ingredients and beat until smooth. Batter may be covered and refrigerated up to 2 hours or cooked immediately. Heat crepe pan or 7 or 8-inch skillet over medium-high heat (375°F.). A few drops of water sprinkled on the pan sizzle and bounce when heat is just right. Grease pan lightly with oil. Pour scant ¼ cup batter into pan, tilting pan to spread evenly. When crepe is light brown and set, turn to brown other side. Fill with desired filling. **About 20 crepes.**

TIP: To prepare crepes ahead, prepare, wrap well in foil and store in refrigerator up to 3 days or in freezer up to 3 months. To thaw, place package of crepes in 300°F. oven for 10 to 15 minutes.

VARIATION:

DESSERT CREPES: Add 2 tablespoons sugar.

NUTRIENTS PER 1 PLAIN CREPE

Calories	50	Dietary Fiber	<1 g
Protein	2 g	Sodium	70 mg
Carbohydrate	5 g	Potassium	25 mg
Fat	3 g	Calcium	<2% U.S. RDA
Cholesterol	60 mg	Iron	2% U.S. RDA

Popovers

3   eggs, room temperature
1¼ cups milk, room temperature
1¼ cups all purpose flour
¼   teaspoon salt

Heat oven to 450°F. Generously grease 10 popover pans or ten 6-oz. custard cups.* Be sure eggs and milk are at room temperature. In small bowl, beat eggs with rotary beater until lemon-colored and foamy. Add milk, blend well. Add flour and salt; beat with rotary beater just until batter is smooth and foamy on top. Pour batter into prepared cups, about ⅔ full. Bake at 450°F. for 15 minutes. (DO NOT OPEN OVEN.) Reduce heat to 350°F.; bake 25 to 35 minutes or until high, hollow and deep golden brown. Remove from oven; insert sharp knife into each popover to allow steam to escape. Remove from pan. **10 popovers.**

TIP: *Standard muffin pans can be used. Fill alternating greased cups with batter to prevent sides of popovers from touching.

HIGH ALTITUDE: Increase flour to 1¼ cups plus 2 tablespoons. Bake at 450°F. for 15 minutes and at 350°F. for 20 to 30 minutes.

NUTRIENTS PER 1 POPOVER

Calories	100	Dietary Fiber	<1 g
Protein	4 g	Sodium	90 mg
Carbohydrate	13 g	Potassium	80 mg
Fat	2 g	Calcium	4% U.S. RDA
Cholesterol	80 mg	Iron	4% U.S. RDA

Currant Scones

2   cups all purpose flour
¼   cup sugar
3   teaspoons baking powder

  ¼ teaspoon salt
  ¼ cup margarine or butter
  ⅔ cup dried currants
5.33-oz. can evaporated milk
    1 egg
       Sugar

Heat oven to 400°F. In medium bowl, combine flour, sugar, baking powder and salt; blend well. Using pastry blender or fork, cut in margarine until mixture is crumbly. Stir in currants. Combine evaporated milk and egg; add all at once, stirring just until moistened. On well floured surface, knead dough gently 5 or 6 times. Press into an 8-inch circle, about 1 inch thick; place on ungreased cookie sheet. Cut into 8 wedges; do not separate. Sprinkle with sugar. Bake at 400°F. for 15 to 20 minutes or until golden brown. Serve warm. **8 servings.**

NUTRIENTS PER ⅛ OF RECIPE

Calories	230	Dietary Fiber	2 g
Protein	6 g	Sodium	290 mg
Carbohydrate	34 g	Potassium	130 mg
Fat	8 g	Calcium	8% U.S. RDA
Cholesterol	35 mg	Iron	6% U.S. RDA

Cake Doughnuts

  4 cups all purpose flour
  1 cup sugar
  3 teaspoons baking powder
  1 teaspoon baking soda
  1 teaspoon salt
  ½ teaspoon nutmeg
  1 cup buttermilk
  ¼ cup margarine or butter, melted, or ¼ cup oil
  1 teaspoon vanilla
  2 eggs, slightly beaten
     Oil for deep frying

In large bowl, combine flour, sugar, baking powder, baking soda, salt and nutmeg. Stir in remaining ingredients except oil for frying *just* until dry ingredients are moistened. If desired, refrigerate dough for easier handling.

Fill large saucepan or electric skillet ⅔ full with oil. Heat to 375°F. On well floured surface, knead dough 1 to 2 minutes or until dough is no longer sticky. Roll half the dough at a time to ½-inch thickness; cut with floured doughnut cutter. With pancake turner, slip doughnuts and holes into hot oil. Fry doughnuts and holes 1 to 1½ minutes on each side or until deep golden brown. Drain on paper towel. If desired, roll doughnuts and holes in powdered or granulated sugar, cinnamon-sugar mixture or drizzle with glaze. **About 30 doughnuts.**

VARIATIONS:

CHOCOLATE DOUGHNUTS: Omit nutmeg and increase sugar to 1¼ cups. Add 1 oz. (1 square) melted unsweetened chocolate or 1 envelope premelted chocolate baking flavor with eggs.

ORANGE DOUGHNUTS: Omit nutmeg and add 2 tablespoons grated orange peel. Decrease buttermilk to ½ cup; add ½ cup orange juice.

NUTRIENTS PER 1 DOUGHNUT

Calories	130	Dietary Fiber	1 g
Protein	2 g	Sodium	170 mg
Carbohydrate	20 g	Potassium	35 mg
Fat	5 g	Calcium	2% U.S. RDA
Cholesterol	20 mg	Iron	4% U.S. RDA

Cinnamon Doughnut Drops

Oil for deep frying
1½ cups all purpose flour
⅓ cup sugar
2 teaspoons baking powder

  ½ teaspoon salt
  ¼ teaspoon cinnamon
  ¼ teaspoon nutmeg
  ½ cup milk
  2 tablespoons oil
  ½ teaspoon vanilla
  1 egg, slightly beaten
  ½ cup sugar
  1 teaspoon cinnamon

In large saucepan, heat 2 to 3 inches oil to 375°F. In large bowl, combine flour, ⅓ cup sugar, baking powder, salt, ¼ teaspoon cinnamon and nutmeg. Stir in milk, oil, vanilla and egg with a fork *just* until dry ingredients are moistened. Drop by teaspoonfuls into hot oil (375°F.), 5 to 6 at a time. Fry doughnut drops 1 to 1½ minutes on each side until deep golden brown. Drain on paper towel. Mix ½ cup sugar and 1 teaspoon cinnamon; roll warm doughnut balls in sugar-cinnamon mixture. **24 to 30 doughnut balls.**

HIGH ALTITUDE: Decrease baking powder to 1½ teaspoons; increase milk to ½ cup plus 2 tablespoons. Reduce oil temperature to 360°F.

VARIATIONS:

PUMPKIN DOUGHNUT DROPS: Decrease milk to ¼ cup and add ½ cup canned pumpkin and ¼ teaspoon ginger.

WHOLE WHEAT DOUGHNUT DROPS: Use ¾ cup whole wheat and ¾ cup all purpose flour.

NUTRIENTS PER 1 DOUGHNUT BALL

Calories	80	Dietary Fiber	<1 g
Protein	1 g	Sodium	50 mg
Carbohydrate	9 g	Potassium	15 mg
Fat	5 g	Calcium	<2% U.S. RDA
Cholesterol	8 mg	Iron	<2% U.S. RDA

Puffy Oven Pancakes

  2 eggs
  ½ cup all purpose flour
  ½ cup milk
  2 tablespoons margarine or butter
  4 cups sliced fruit*
  ½ cup firmly packed brown sugar
8-oz. carton dairy sour cream

Heat oven to 425°F. In medium bowl, beat eggs slightly. Add flour and milk to eggs, beating with rotary beater until combined. Melt 1 tablespoon margarine in each of two 9-inch glass pie plates in oven; spread to cover bottom. Pour batter into prepared pie plates. Bake at 425°F. for 10 to 15 minutes or until golden brown. (Pancakes will form a well in the center and edges will puff up.) Spoon fruit or combination of fruits into center of pancakes. Sprinkle with brown sugar and top with sour cream. Serve immediately. **4 servings.**

TIP: *Any of the following fruits can be used: strawberries, bananas, pineapple, raspberries, peaches and blueberries.

NUTRIENTS PER ¼ OF RECIPE

Calories	490	Dietary Fiber .... 3 g
Protein	9 g	Sodium .... 155 mg
Carbohydrate	65 g	Potassium .... 590 mg
Fat	22 g	Calcium .... 15% U.S. RDA
Cholesterol	160 mg	Iron .... 15% U.S. RDA

Pancakes

  2 eggs
  2 cups buttermilk*
  ¼ cup oil
1¾ cups all purpose flour
  2 tablespoons sugar

2 teaspoons baking powder
1 teaspoon baking soda
½ teaspoon salt

Heat griddle to medium-high heat (400°F.). In large bowl, beat eggs; stir in buttermilk and oil. Add remaining ingredients; stir *just* until large lumps disappear. For thicker pancakes, thicken with additional flour; for thinner pancakes, thin with additional milk. Lightly grease heated griddle. A few drops of water sprinkled on griddle sizzle and bounce when heat is just right. Pour batter, about ¼ cup at a time, onto hot griddle. Bake until bubbles form and edges start to dry; turn and bake other side. **16 (4-inch) pancakes.**

TIP: *To prepare pancakes using milk, decrease milk to 1¾ cups, increase baking powder to 4 teaspoons and omit baking soda.

VARIATIONS:

APPLE PANCAKES: Add ½ cup peeled shredded apple and ½ teaspoon cinnamon to batter.

BLUEBERRY PANCAKES: Add 1 cup drained fresh or frozen blueberries (thawed and drained) to batter.

CHEESE PANCAKES: Add ½ cup shredded cheese to batter.

NUT PANCAKES: Add ½ cup chopped nuts to batter.

WHOLE WHEAT PANCAKES: Use 1 cup all purpose flour and ¾ cup whole wheat flour.

NUTRIENTS PER 1 PANCAKE

Calories 110	Dietary Fiber.........................<1 g
Protein.......................................3 g	Sodium...............................215 mg
Carbohydrate..........................14 g	Potassium............................70 mg
Fat ....5 g	Calcium.................6% U.S. RDA
Cholesterol..........................35 mg	Iron.......................4% U.S. RDA

Waffles

2 eggs, separated
2 cups buttermilk*
2 cups all purpose flour
2 teaspoons baking powder
1 teaspoon baking soda
½ teaspoon salt
½ cup margarine or butter, melted, or oil

Heat waffle iron. Place egg yolks in large bowl; whites in small bowl. To yolks add buttermilk; beat well. Add flour, baking powder, baking soda and salt; beat until smooth. Stir in melted margarine. Beat egg whites until soft peaks form; fold into batter. Bake in hot waffle iron until steaming stops and waffle is golden brown. **4 waffles.**

TIP: *To prepare waffles using milk, decrease milk to 1¾ cups, increase baking powder to 4 teaspoons and omit baking soda.

VARIATIONS:

APPLE WAFFLES: Add 1 peeled shredded apple and ½ teaspoon cinnamon.

BANANA WAFFLES: Brush waffle iron with oil before heating it. Place banana slices on batter before closing lid of waffle iron.

BLUEBERRY WAFFLES: Add 1 cup fresh or frozen drained blueberries to batter.

NUT WAFFLES: Add ⅓ to ½ cup chopped nuts with flour.

WHOLE WHEAT WAFFLES: Use 1½ cups all purpose flour and ½ cup whole wheat flour.

NUTRIENTS PER 1 WAFFLE

Calories	520	Dietary Fiber	3 g
Protein	14 g	Sodium	1120 mg
Carbohydrate	54 g	Potassium	290 mg
Fat	27 g	Calcium	25% U.S. RDA
Cholesterol	140 mg	Iron	20% U.S. RDA

French Toast

> 2 eggs, slightly beaten
> 1 tablespoon sugar
> ½ teaspoon salt
> ¼ teaspoon cinnamon, if desired
> ½ cup milk
> 2 tablespoons margarine or butter
> 4 to 6 slices bread or 6 to 8 slices French bread, cut diagonally about 1-inch thick

Heat griddle to medium heat (340°F.). In shallow bowl or pie pan, combine all ingredients except margarine and bread; mix well. Melt margarine on griddle. Dip bread in egg mixture, turning to coat both sides. Cook on griddle over medium heat, about 4 minutes on each side or until golden brown. If desired, sprinkle with powdered sugar. **4 to 6 slices toast.**

TIP: To make ahead, dip bread in egg mixture and place in 13x9-inch glass baking dish. Pour any remaining egg mixture over bread. Cover; refrigerate 8 to 12 hours. Use a pancake turner to remove bread slices to hot griddle; continue as directed.

VARIATION:

OVEN FRENCH TOAST: Melt margarine in jelly roll or broiler pan. Place egg-coated slices in margarine and broil 3 to 4 inches from heat about 3 minutes or until golden brown. Turn and broil other side.

NUTRIENTS PER ¼ OF RECIPE

Calories 150	Dietary Fiber..........................<1 g
Protein..5 g	Sodium....................................390 mg
Carbohydrate..........................17 g	Potassium................................85 mg
Fat ....7 g	Calcium..................6% U.S. RDA
Cholesterol..........................90 mg	Iron.........................6% U.S. RDA

Pancake and Waffle Syrups

BROWN SUGAR SYRUP: In medium saucepan, combine 1 cup firmly packed brown sugar and 1 cup water; bring to boil stirring constantly. Boil 5 minutes and remove from heat. Stir in 1 tablespoon butter or margarine and ½ teaspoon maple flavoring. **1 cup.**

CURRANT BUTTER SYRUP: In small saucepan, combine 2 tablespoons butter and 10-oz. jar currant jelly. Cook over low heat until melted, stirring constantly. **1 cup.**

EASY BLUEBERRY TOPPING: In small saucepan, combine 21-oz. can blueberry prepared fruit filling and ¼ cup butter. Cook over low heat until butter is melted. **2 cups.**

HONEY 'N MAPLE SYRUP: In small saucepan, combine 1 cup maple-flavored syrup with 2 tablespoons honey. Cook until thoroughly heated. **1 cup.**

ORANGE SYRUP: In small saucepan, combine ½ cup sugar, ¼ cup frozen concentrated orange juice and ¼ cup butter. Cook over low heat, stirring constantly, until sugar is dissolved. **¾ cup.**

SPICED MAPLE SYRUP: In medium saucepan, melt ½ cup butter or margarine. Stir in 1 cup maple-flavored syrup, ½ teaspoon cinnamon, ⅛ teaspoon nutmeg and ⅛ teaspoon allspice; bring to boil. Cook over low heat, stirring occasionally, for 5 minutes. Stir well before serving; serve immediately. **1½ cups.**

STRAWBERRY TOPPING: In small saucepan, heat 10-oz. jar strawberry preserves or jam. **1 cup.**

WHIPPED MAPLE SYRUP: In medium bowl, cream together 1½ cups powdered sugar, ½ cup softened butter, ½ cup maple-flavored syrup and 1 egg yolk. **1¾ cups.**

TIP: Store these toppings in the refrigerator.

Cinnamon Cider Syrup

- ½ cup sugar
- 1 tablespoon cornstarch
- ⅛ teaspoon cinnamon
- 1 cup apple cider or juice
- 1 tablespoon lemon juice
- 2 tablespoons margarine or butter

In medium saucepan, combine sugar, cornstarch and cinnamon; stir in apple cider and lemon juice. Cook, stirring constantly, until mixture thickens and boils, about 1 minute. Remove from heat; stir in margarine. **1¼ cups syrup.**

NUTRIENTS PER 1 TABLESPOON

Calories	35	Dietary Fiber	<1 g
Protein	0 g	Sodium	15 mg
Carbohydrate	7 g	Potassium	15 mg
Fat	1 g	Calcium	<2% U.S. RDA
Cholesterol	0 mg	Iron	<2% U.S. RDA

Easy Apple Syrup

- ¼ cup sugar
- 4 teaspoons cornstarch
- ¼ teaspoon allspice
- 6-oz. can frozen apple juice concentrate, thawed
- 1 cup cold water

In medium saucepan, combine sugar, cornstarch and all-spice. Add apple juice concentrate and water; cook over medium heat until slightly thickened, about 10 minutes. **1½ cups.**

MICROWAVE DIRECTIONS: In medium-size microwave-safe bowl or 4-cup glass measuring cup, combine sugar, cornstarch and allspice. Add apple juice concentrate and water; microwave on HIGH for 4 to 5½ minutes or until mixture boils and thickens, stirring twice during cooking.

NUTRIENTS PER 1 TABLESPOON

Calories 20	Dietary Fiber.........................<1 g
Protein.....................................0 g	Sodium....................................0 mg
Carbohydrate...........................5 g	Potassium...........................30 mg
Fat ....0 g	Calcium..............<2% U.S. RDA
Cholesterol............................0 mg	Iron ....<2% U.S. RDA

Molded Flavored Butter

Smoothly line 6-oz. (¾-cup) custard cup or gelatin mold with plastic wrap. In small bowl, combine ½ cup softened unsalted butter and desired flavoring. Beat 2 to 3 minutes at medium speed until light and creamy. Press butter mixture into prepared mold; smooth top. Fold plastic wrap over butter. Refrigerate 8 hours or overnight to blend flavors.* Unmold onto serving plate; remove plastic wrap. If desired, cover entire outside surface with desired coating; lightly press into butter. Serve at room temperature. **⅔ cup.**

TIP: *Butter mixture can be refrigerated up to 5 days or frozen up to 1 month. If refrigerated, continue as directed above. If frozen, unmold onto serving plate; remove plastic wrap. Let stand 1 hour before coating. Continue as directed above.

VARIATIONS:

GARLIC BUTTER: Add ⅛ to ¼ teaspoon garlic powder or 1 to 2 garlic cloves, pressed. Coat with about 1 tablespoon toasted sesame seed.

HERB BUTTER: Add ⅛ to ¼ teaspoon thyme leaves, finely crushed. Coat with about 2 tablespoons finely chopped fresh parsley.

ONION BUTTER: Add ½ teaspoon grated fresh onion. Coat with about 2 tablespoons chopped fresh chives.

PARMESAN BUTTER: Add ¼ cup grated Parmesan cheese. Coat with about 1 tablespoon poppy seed.

PEPPER BUTTER: Coat with about 1½ teaspoons coarsely ground pepper.

WINE BUTTER: Add 2 tablespoons burgundy wine, ¼ teaspoon sugar and dash garlic salt.

NUTRIENTS PER 1 TABLESPOON

Calories 90	Dietary Fiber..........................0 g
Protein....................................0 g	Sodium.................................0 mg
Carbohydrate..........................0 g	Potassium.............................5 mg
Fat ....10 g	Calcium...............<2% U.S. RDA
Cholesterol.........................25 mg	Iron ....<2% U.S. RDA

Whipped Cream Cheese

In small bowl, cream 8-oz. pkg. cream cheese until soft. Gradually beat in 3 to 4 tablespoons milk until light and fluffy. **1½ cups.**

VARIATIONS:

HONEY CREAM CHEESE: Omit milk and gradually add ¼ cup honey; beat until light.

MAPLE CREAM CHEESE: Substitute maple-flavored syrup for milk.

MARMALADE CREAM CHEESE: Omit milk and gradually add ¼ cup marmalade; beat until light.

NUTRIENTS PER 1 TABLESPOON

Calories 35	Dietary Fiber...........................0 g
Protein...................................1 g	Sodium............................30 mg
Carbohydrate..........................0 g	Potassium..........................15 mg
Fat ....3 g	Calcium..............<2% U.S. RDA
Cholesterol.........................10 mg	Iron ....<2% U.S. RDA

Whipped Butter

In small bowl, cream ½ cup butter or margarine until soft. Slowly beat in 2 tablespoons milk or cream. Beat at highest speed until light and fluffy. Refrigerate leftovers. **1 cup.**

VARIATIONS:

HONEY BUTTER: Omit milk; gradually add ¼ cup honey. Beat well.

MAPLE BUTTER: Substitute maple-flavored syrup for milk.

ORANGE BUTTER: Substitute orange juice for milk and add 1 tablespoon grated orange peel.

PEANUT-HONEY BUTTER: Decrease butter to ¼ cup and add ¼ cup peanut butter. Omit milk; beat in ¼ cup honey.

NUTRIENTS PER 1 TABLESPOON

Calories 50	Dietary Fiber...........................0 g
Protein...................................0 g	Sodium............................70 mg
Carbohydrate..........................0 g	Potassium............................5 mg
Fat ....6 g	Calcium..............<2% U.S. RDA
Cholesterol.........................15 mg	Iron ....<2% U.S. RDA

Crunchy Garlic Toast

½ cup margarine or butter, softened
⅛ to ¼ teaspoon garlic powder*
16 to 20 (½-inch) slices French bread or 8 to 10
hamburger buns, split

Heat oven to 250°F. In small bowl, blend margarine and garlic powder. Spread margarine generously on both sides of French bread; spread on cut side only of buns. Place on ungreased cookie sheet. Bake at 250°F. for 1 to 2 hours or until dry, crisp and lightly browned; turn French bread slices over halfway through baking. **16 to 20 pieces toast.**

TIP: *One to 2 garlic cloves, pressed, can be substituted for garlic powder. Combine with margarine; let stand 2 to 4 hours to blend flavors.

NUTRIENTS PER 1 PIECE OF TOAST

Calories	80	Dietary Fiber	<1 g
Protein	1 g	Sodium	145 mg
Carbohydrate	8 g	Potassium	15 mg
Fat	5 g	Calcium	<2% U.S. RDA
Cholesterol	0 mg	Iron	<2% U.S. RDA

Buttered Croutons

10 slices bread
½ cup butter or margarine, melted

Heat oven to 300°F. Trim crusts from bread; cut slices into ½-inch cubes. Spread cubes in 15x10-inch jelly roll pan. Drizzle butter over cubes; toss to coat. Bake at 300°F. for 30 to 35 minutes or until dry, crisp and golden brown, stirring occasionally. Store covered in refrigerator. **4 cups.**

NUTRIENTS PER ¼ CUP

Calories	90	Dietary Fiber	<1 g
Protein	1 g	Sodium	140 mg
Carbohydrate	7 g	Potassium	20 mg
Fat	6 g	Calcium	<2% U.S. RDA
Cholesterol	15 mg	Iron	<2% U.S. RDA

Buttered Bread Crumbs

In small saucepan, melt 2 to 3 tablespoons butter or margarine. Add ½ cup dry bread crumbs and ⅛ teaspoon salt; mix well. **½ cup.**

NUTRIENTS PER 1 TABLESPOON

Calories	30	Dietary Fiber	<1 g
Protein	0 g	Sodium	65 mg
Carbohydrate	1 g	Potassium	5 mg
Fat	3 g	Calcium	<2% U.S. RDA
Cholesterol	10 mg	Iron	<2% U.S. RDA

Yeast Breads

Keys to Successful Yeast Breads

• **Dissolving the Yeast:** In most of the recipes in this book we have used the method of mixing the yeast with some of the dry ingredients before combining it with the warm liquids. This method is easier and more foolproof, but does require warmer liquid temperatures. Yeast is very sensitive to temperature. Its growth is what causes bread to rise. Liquids that are too hot will kill it, and liquids that are too cool will stunt its growth. Whether the yeast is dissolved first in liquids or combined with dry ingredients, follow the liquid temperatures stated in a recipe. We suggest purchasing a thermometer to take away the guesswork.

• **Kneading the Dough:** Proper kneading technique distributes ingredients evenly throughout the dough and develops the protein in the flour for the structural framework. To knead, sprinkle work surface lightly with flour. Turn dough out onto floured area. With floured hands, form dough into a ball; sprinkle lightly with flour. Fold edges of dough toward center. Push dough down and away with heels of both hands. Give dough a quarter turn. Repeat folding, pushing and turning until dough is smooth and elastic and small blisters appear on the surface. It is important to knead as long as recipe directions specify. During kneading, continue to add flour in small amounts until dough is no longer sticky and can be easily handled. The bread will be crumbly, dry and heavy if not sufficiently kneaded. A range of flour is given to accommodate various flour conditions. Flour can gain or lose moisture depending on weather conditions and how it is stored.

• **Letting the Dough Rise:** Place dough in a lightly greased bowl large enough for it to double in size. Turn dough to coat with grease. This helps prevent surface of dough from drying out. Cover bowl with plastic wrap and cloth towel to further prevent drying out. Yeast dough needs a warm place (80° to 85°F.) to rise. To provide a warm place, turn on oven at 400°F. for 1 minute, turn off oven and place the bowl of dough on the center rack. Let rise with oven door closed. Or place dough on a wire rack over a pan of very hot water in a draft-free place. Rising times will vary with the recipe. When the dough is doubled in size, a dent will remain in the dough when you poke it lightly with 2 fingers. If the dent fills up rapidly, let the dough rise a little longer.

• **Punching Down the Dough:** Punch down center of dough with fist. Pull edges of dough to the center and turn out of bowl onto lightly floured surface. This step removes large air bubbles so that the bread will be fine-textured.

• **Letting the Dough Rest:** With some recipes, after the dough is punched down, it is covered with an inverted bowl and allowed to rest 10 to 15 minutes. This allows the dough to relax and makes it easier to shape.

• **Shaping the Dough:** Each recipe will give specific directions for shaping the dough. To shape into a loaf, roll out dough on lightly floured surface to a 14x7-inch rectangle. Starting with the 7-inch side, roll up tightly, jelly roll fashion, pressing out any air. Pinch edges and ends firmly to seal. Place loaf seam side down in well-greased loaf pan. To shape dough into a round loaf, knead dough several times to form a smooth, even ball. Bring edges together and seal well. Place loaf seam side down on greased cookie sheet; lightly flatten to form a rounded shape.

• **After Shaping:** Place dough in pan prepared according to recipe directions. Let dough rise until doubled in size. Dough has risen enough if an indentation remains when dough is pushed lightly with a finger. Bake bread in a preheated oven. The top of each pan should be at about the middle of the oven. Arrange pans so that they do not touch each other or the sides of the oven. Bake to the minimum time suggested in the recipe, then check for doneness. Bread loaves are done when they sound hollow when lightly tapped. Crust color is not always an indicator of doneness. If excessive browning occurs before loaves sound hollow, cover with foil before they get too dark. Remove from pan immediately; cool on wire rack.

Delicious White Bread

5 to 6 cups all purpose flour
3 tablespoons sugar
2 teaspoons salt
2 pkg. active dry yeast
¼ cup oil or shortening
   Melted margarine or butter, if desired

Grease two 8x4 or 9x5-inch loaf pans. In large bowl, combine 2 cups flour, sugar, salt and yeast; blend well. In small saucepan, heat water and oil until very warm (120 to 130°F.).

Add warm liquid to flour mixture. Blend at low speed until moistened; beat 3 minutes at medium speed. By hand, stir in an additional 2½ to 3 cups flour until dough pulls cleanly away from sides of bowl.

On floured surface, knead in ½ to 1 cup flour until dough is smooth and elastic, about 5 minutes. Place dough in greased bowl; cover loosely with plastic wrap and cloth towel. Let rise in warm place (80° to 85°F.) until light and doubled in size, about 45 to 60 minutes.

Punch down dough several times to remove all air bubbles. Divide dough in half; shape into balls. Shape into 2 loaves by rolling dough into two 14x7-inch rectangles. Starting with shorter side, roll up each tightly; pinch edges and ends firmly to seal. Place seam side down in prepared pans. Cover; let rise in warm place until dough fills pans and tops of loaves are about 1 inch above pan edges, about 30 to 35 minutes.

Heat oven to 375°F. Bake 40 to 45 minutes or until loaves sound hollow when lightly tapped. Remove from pans immediately; cool on wire racks. Brush with melted margarine. **2 (18-slice) loaves.**

VARIATIONS:

RAISIN BREAD: Add ½ teaspoon cinnamon with the salt and stir in 1 cup raisins after beating step.

CINNAMON SWIRL BREAD: Brush each 14x7-inch rectangle of dough with melted margarine or butter; sprinkle each with mixture of ¼ cup sugar and 1 teaspoon cinnamon. Starting with 7-inch side, roll up. Seal edges and place seam side down in greased loaf pans. Let rise and bake as directed above.

BREADSTICKS: After first rise time, punch down dough. Divide dough in half. Cut each half into 32 pieces; shape each into 8-inch long breadstick. Place on greased cookie sheets. Brush with beaten egg white; sprinkle with sesame seed. Cover; let rise in warm place about 30 minutes or until doubled in size. Bake at 400°F. for about 14 minutes.

PIZZA CRUST: After first rise time, punch down dough. Divide dough into 4 parts; press each part to cover bottom and sides of greased 12-inch pizza pan. Cover; let rise in warm place about 15 minutes. Top with desired sauce and toppings. Bake at 400°F. for about 25 minutes.

HAMBURGER BUNS: After first rise time, punch down dough. Divide dough in half; shape each half into eight 2-inch balls. If desired, flatten slightly. Place on greased cookie sheets. Let rise in warm place about 30 minutes. Bake at 400°F. for about 15 minutes.

NUTRIENTS PER 1 SLICE

Calories	100	Dietary Fiber	1 g
Protein	2 g	Sodium	125 mg
Carbohydrate	17 g	Potassium	30 mg
Fat	2 g	Calcium	<2% U.S. RDA
Cholesterol	0 mg	Iron	4% U.S. RDA

Rye Bread

        2 pkg. active dry yeast
        1 cup warm water
        1 cup warm milk
       ½ cup molasses
       ¼ cup shortening, melted
        2 teaspoons salt
3 to 3½ cups all purpose flour
        3 cups medium rye flour
        1 tablespoon water
        1 egg yolk

Grease 2 cookie sheets. In small bowl, dissolve yeast in warm water (105 to 115°F.). In large bowl, combine warm milk (105 to 115°F.), molasses, shortening and salt; blend well. Add dissolved yeast. Add 2 cups all purpose flour;

blend at low speed until moistened. Beat 3 minutes at medium speed. Stir in 3 cups rye flour and an additional ¾ to 1 cup all purpose flour until dough pulls cleanly away from sides of bowl.

On floured surface, knead in ¼ to ½ cup all purpose flour until dough is smooth and elastic, about 5 minutes. Place dough in greased bowl; cover loosely with plastic wrap and cloth towel. Let rise in warm place (80 to 85°F.) until light and doubled in size, about 45 to 60 minutes.

Punch down dough several times to remove all air bubbles. Divide dough in half; shape into balls. Shape dough into two 12-inch oblong loaves; round ends. Place on prepared cookie sheets. With sharp knife, make four ¼-inch deep diagonal slashes on top of each loaf. Cover; let rise in warm place until doubled in size, about 20 to 30 minutes.

Heat oven to 350°F. Combine water and egg yolk; brush on loaves. Bake at 350°F. for 35 to 45 minutes or until loaves sound hollow when lightly tapped. Remove from pans immediately; cool on wire racks. **2 (22-slice) loaves.**

HIGH ALTITUDE: Decrease first rise time 15 to 30 minutes. Decrease second rise time 10 minutes.

NUTRIENTS PER 1 SLICE

Calories	90	Dietary Fiber	2 g
Protein	2 g	Sodium	100 mg
Carbohydrate	15 g	Potassium	75 mg
Fat	2 g	Calcium	2% U.S. RDA
Cholesterol	6 mg	Iron	4% U.S. RDA

Whole Wheat Bread

> 2 pkg. active dry yeast
> ¼ cup warm water
> ½ cup firmly packed brown sugar or honey
> 3 teaspoons salt
> 2½ cups hot water

¼ cup margarine or butter
4½ cups whole wheat flour
2¾ to 3¾ cups all purpose flour

Generously grease two 8x4 or 9x5-inch loaf pans. In small bowl, dissolve yeast in warm water (105 to 115°F.). In large bowl, combine brown sugar, salt, hot water and margarine; cool slightly. To cooled mixture, add 3 cups whole wheat flour. Blend at low speed until moistened; beat 3 minutes at medium speed. Add remaining whole wheat flour and dissolved yeast; mix well. Stir in 2¼ to 2¾ cups all purpose flour until dough pulls cleanly away from sides of bowl.

On floured surface, knead in ½ to 1 cup all purpose flour until dough is smooth and elastic, about 10 to 15 minutes. Place dough in greased bowl; cover loosely with plastic wrap and cloth towel. Let rise in warm place (80 to 85°F.) until light and doubled in size, about 45 to 60 minutes.

Punch down dough several times to remove all air bubbles. Divide dough in half; shape into balls. Allow to rest on counter covered with inverted bowl for 10 minutes. Shape into 2 loaves by rolling dough into two 14x7-inch rectangles. Starting with shorter side, roll up each; pinch edges and ends firmly to seal. Place seam side down in prepared pans. Cover; let rise in warm place until light and doubled in size, 30 to 45 minutes.

Heat oven to 375°F. Bake 30 minutes. Reduce oven to 350°F. and continue baking an additional 10 to 15 minutes or until loaves sound hollow when lightly tapped. Remove from pans immediately; cool on wire racks. **2 (16-slice) loaves.**

NUTRIENTS PER 1 SLICE

Calories	140	Dietary Fiber	3 g
Protein	4 g	Sodium	220 mg
Carbohydrate	27 g	Potassium	100 mg
Fat	2 g	Calcium	<2% U.S. RDA
Cholesterol	0 mg	Iron	6% U.S. RDA

Speedy Whole Wheat Bread

2½ to 3   cups all purpose flour
     3   tablespoons toasted sesame seed
     2   teaspoons salt
     3   pkg. active dry yeast
   2¼   cups water
    ¼   cup honey
     3   tablespoons margarine or butter
     3   cups whole wheat flour
     1   egg white, beaten
        Toasted sesame seed, if desired

Grease large cookie sheet or 15x10-inch jelly roll pan. In large bowl, combine 2 cups all purpose flour, 3 tablespoons sesame seed, salt and yeast; blend well. In small saucepan, heat water, honey and margarine until very warm (120 to 130°F.). Add warm liquid to flour mixture. Blend at low speed until moistened; beat 3 minutes at medium speed. By hand, stir in whole wheat flour and an additional ¼ to ½ cup all purpose flour until dough pulls cleanly away from sides of bowl.

On floured surface, knead in ¼ to ½ cup all purpose flour until dough is smooth and elastic, about 5 to 8 minutes. Place dough in greased bowl; cover loosely with plastic wrap and cloth towel. Place bowl in pan of warm water (about 95°F.); let rise 15 minutes.

Punch down dough several times to remove all air bubbles. Divide dough in half; shape into round balls. Place diagonally, 3 inches apart, on prepared cookie sheet. With sharp knife, make three ⅛-inch deep slashes on top of each loaf. Carefully brush loaves with egg white; sprinkle with sesame seed. Cover; let rise in warm place until light and doubled in size, about 15 minutes.

Heat oven to 375°F. Bake 25 to 35 minutes or until loaves sound hollow when lightly tapped. Remove from cookie sheet immediately; cool on wire racks. **2 (16-slice) loaves.**

NUTRIENTS PER 1 SLICE

Calories	110	Dietary Fiber	1 g
Protein	3 g	Sodium	150 mg
Carbohydrate	19 g	Potassium	75 mg
Fat	2 g	Calcium	<2% U.S. RDA
Cholesterol	0 mg	Iron	6% U.S. RDA

Challah Bread

4½ to 5½ cups all purpose flour
    2 tablespoons sugar
    1 teaspoon salt
    2 pkg. active dry yeast
    1 cup water
   ⅓ cup margarine or butter
    4 eggs
    1 egg white
    1 tablespoon water
      Poppy seed

Grease large cookie sheet. In large bowl, combine 2 cups flour, sugar, salt and yeast; blend well. In small saucepan, heat 1 cup water and margarine until very warm (120 to 130°F.). Add warm liquid and 4 eggs to flour mixture. Blend at low speed until moistened; beat 3 minutes at medium speed. By hand, stir in an additional 2 to 2½ cups flour until dough pulls cleanly away from sides of bowl.

On floured surface, knead in ½ to 1 cup flour until dough is smooth and elastic, about 5 minutes. Place dough in greased bowl; cover loosely with plastic wrap and cloth towel. Let rise in warm place (about 80 to 85°F.) until light and doubled in size, about 35 to 45 minutes.

Punch down dough several times to remove all air bubbles.

Divide dough in half; roll into two 14x6-inch rectangles. Cut each rectangle lengthwise into three 14x2-inch strips. Braid strips together; tuck ends under to seal. Place crosswise on prepared cookie sheet. Cover; let rise in warm place until doubled in size, about 15 to 25 minutes.

Heat oven to 400°F. Bake 10 minutes. Brush with mixture of egg white and 1 tablespoon water; sprinkle with poppy seed. Return to oven; bake an additional 5 to 10 minutes or until loaves sound hollow when lightly tapped. Remove from cookie sheet immediately; cool on wire racks. **2 (15-slice) loaves.**

HIGH ALTITUDE: Decrease each rise time 10 to 15 minutes.

NUTRIENTS PER 1 SLICE

Calories	120	Dietary Fiber	1 g
Protein	4 g	Sodium	105 mg
Carbohydrate	20 g	Potassium	45 mg
Fat	3 g	Calcium	<2% U.S. RDA
Cholesterol	35 mg	Iron	4% U.S. RDA

French Bread Braids

4¾ to 5¾	cups all purpose flour
1	tablespoon salt
1	tablespoon sugar
2	pkg. active dry yeast
2	cups water
2	tablespoons shortening
1	tablespoon water
1	egg white

Grease large cookie sheet. In large bowl, combine 3 cups flour, salt, sugar and yeast. In small saucepan, heat 2 cups water and shortening until very warm (120 to 130°F.). Add warm liquid to flour mixture. Blend at low speed until moistened; beat 3 minutes at medium speed. Stir in 1½ to 2¼ cups flour to form a stiff dough.

On floured surface, knead in ¼ to ½ cup flour until dough is smooth and elastic, about 8 minutes. Place dough in greased bowl; cover loosely with plastic wrap and cloth towel. Let rise in warm place (about 80 to 85°F.) until light and doubled in size, about 1 hour.

Punch down dough several times to remove all air bubbles. Divide dough in half; divide each half into 3 parts. Roll each part into a 14-inch rope. Braid 3 ropes together; seal ends. Place on prepared cookie sheet. Repeat with other half of dough. In small bowl, combine 1 tablespoon water and egg white; beat slightly. Carefully brush over loaves. Cover loosely with greased plastic wrap; let rise in warm place until light and doubled in size, about 20 to 30 minutes.

Heat oven to 375°F. Brush loaves again with egg white mixture. Bake at 375°F. for 25 to 30 minutes or until golden brown. Remove from cookie sheet immediately. Cool on wire racks. **2 (18-slice) loaves.**

NUTRIENTS PER 1 SLICE

Calories	80	Dietary Fiber	1 g
Protein	2 g	Sodium	180 mg
Carbohydrate	16 g	Potassium	30 mg
Fat	1 g	Calcium	<2% U.S. RDA
Cholesterol	0 mg	Iron	2% U.S. RDA

Italian Cheese Bread Ring

2	tablespoons sesame seed
4½ to 5¼	cups all purpose flour
¼	cup sugar
1½	teaspoons salt
2	pkg. active dry yeast
1	cup water
1	cup milk
½	cup margarine or butter
2	eggs

FILLING

    4 oz. (1 cup) shredded mozzarella cheese
    ½ teaspoon Italian seasoning
    ¼ teaspoon garlic powder
    ¼ cup margarine or butter, softened

Generously grease 12-cup fluted tube or 10-inch tube pan; sprinkle with sesame seed. In large bowl, combine 2½ cups flour, sugar, salt and yeast; blend well. In small saucepan, heat water, milk and ½ cup margarine until very warm (120 to 130°F.). Add warm liquid and eggs to flour mixture. Blend at low speed until moistened; beat 3 minutes at medium speed. By hand, stir in 2 to 2¾ cups flour to form stiff batter. In small bowl, combine all filling ingredients; mix well. Spoon half of batter into prepared pan; spoon filling evenly over batter to within ½ inch of sides of pan. Spoon remaining batter over filling. Cover; let rise in warm place (80 to 85°F.) until light and doubled in size, about 30 minutes.

Heat oven to 350°F. Bake 30 to 40 minutes or until golden brown and bread sounds hollow when lightly tapped. Remove from pan immediately; serve warm or cool. **1 (24-slice) ring.**

NUTRIENTS PER 1 SLICE

Calories	200	Dietary Fiber	2 g
Protein	5 g	Sodium	225 mg
Carbohydrate	24 g	Potassium	65 mg
Fat	9 g	Calcium	6% U.S. RDA
Cholesterol	25 mg	Iron	6% U.S. RDA

Dilly Casserole Bread

  2 to 2⅔ cups all purpose flour
      2 tablespoons sugar
  2 to 3 teaspoons instant minced onion
      2 teaspoons dill seed

    1   teaspoon salt
    ¼   teaspoon baking soda
    1   pkg. active dry yeast
8-oz.   carton (1 cup) creamed cottage cheese
    ¼   cup water
    1   tablespoon margarine or butter
    1   egg
        Margarine or butter, melted
        Coarse salt, if desired

Generously grease 1½ or 2-quart casserole. In large bowl, combine 1 cup flour, sugar, onion, dill seed, salt, baking soda and yeast; blend well. In small saucepan, heat cottage cheese, water and 1 tablespoon margarine until very warm (120 to 130°F.). Add warm liquid and egg to flour mixture. Blend at low speed until moistened; beat 3 minutes at medium speed. By hand, stir in remaining flour to form a stiff batter. Cover; let rise in warm place (80 to 85°F.) until light and doubled in size, 45 to 60 minutes.

Stir down dough. Place in prepared casserole. Cover; let rise in warm place until light and doubled in size, 30 to 45 minutes. Heat oven to 350°F. Bake 30 to 40 minutes or until deep golden brown and loaf sounds hollow when lightly tapped. Remove from casserole immediately; place on wire rack. Brush warm loaf with melted margarine and sprinkle with coarse salt. Cool completely. **1 (20-slice) loaf.**

FOOD PROCESSOR DIRECTIONS: In food processor bowl with metal blade, combine *1½ cups* of the flour, sugar, onion, dill seed, salt, baking soda, yeast and 1 tablespoon margarine. Cover; process 5 seconds. Add cottage cheese. Cover; process about 10 seconds or until blended. With machine running, pour *⅓ cup hot tap water* through feed tube; continue processing until blended, about 20 seconds. Add egg; process about 10 seconds. Add *½ cup* flour; process 10 to 20 seconds longer or until dough forms a stiff batter. With rubber scraper, carefully pull dough from blade and bowl; place in lightly greased bowl. Continue as directed above.

HIGH ALTITUDE: Bake at 375°F. for 35 to 40 minutes.

NUTRIENTS PER 1 SLICE

Calories	90	Dietary Fiber	1 g
Protein	4 g	Sodium	180 mg
Carbohydrate	15 g	Potassium	40 mg
Fat	2 g	Calcium	<2% U.S. RDA
Cholesterol	15 mg	Iron	4% U.S. RDA

Sourdough Bread

STARTER

> 1   pkg. active dry yeast
> 2   cups warm water
> 3½ cups all purpose flour
> 1   tablespoon sugar or honey

BREAD

> 1   cup starter
> 5½ to 6   cups all purpose flour
> ¼   cup sugar
> 1   tablespoon salt
> 1⅔   cups warm water
> ⅓   cup oil

In large non-metal bowl, dissolve yeast in 2 cups warm water (105 to 115°F.); let stand 5 minutes. Add 3½ cups flour and 1 tablespoon sugar; blend well. Cover loosely with plastic wrap and cloth towel. Let stand in warm place (80 to 85°F.) for 5 days, stirring at least once each day. When the starter is ready for use, it is bubbly and may have a yellow liquid layer on top. Stir well before using.*

Place 1 cup starter in large bowl.** Add 2 cups flour, ¼ cup sugar, salt, 1⅔ cups warm water (105 to 115°F.) and oil; blend well. Stir in 2½ to 2¾ cups flour until dough pulls cleanly away from sides of bowl. On floured surface, knead in remaining 1 to 1¼ cups flour until dough is smooth and elastic, about 5 minutes. Place dough in greased bowl; cover loosely with plastic wrap and cloth towel. Let rise in warm place 8 to 10 hours or overnight.

Grease 3 cookie sheets or 9-inch round cake pans.*** Punch down dough several times to remove air bubbles. Divide dough into 3 parts. Work dough with hands to remove all air bubbles. Shape into round loaves. Place on prepared cookie sheets. Cover; let rise in warm place until doubled, 2 to 3 hours. Heat oven to 400°F. With sharp knife, make three ¼-inch deep slits on top of each loaf. Bake 20 to 25 minutes or until loaves sound hollow when lightly tapped. Remove from cookie sheets immediately. **3 (16-slice) loaves.**

TIPS: *If starter will not be used immediately, cover and refrigerate until ready to use. Return to room temperature before using.

**If desired, starter can be replenished for future use. After removing 1 cup starter, add to remaining starter 1 cup flour, ⅔ cup warm water (105 to 115°F.) and 1 teaspoon sugar or honey; blend well. Cover loosely with plastic wrap and cloth towel. Let stand in warm place (80 to 85°F.) 10 to 12 hours or overnight. The starter will become bubbly and rise. Stir, cover and store in refrigerator. Repeat this process each time the starter is used. If starter is used once a week it will remain active. If not used, stir in 1 teaspoon sugar or honey weekly.

***Three 8x4-inch loaf pans can be used. Bake at 400°F. for 25 to 30 minutes.

NUTRIENTS PER 1 SLICE

Calories	100	Dietary Fiber	1 g
Protein	3 g	Sodium	135 mg
Carbohydrate	18 g	Potassium	25 mg
Fat	2 g	Calcium	<2% U.S. RDA
Cholesterol	0 mg	Iron	4% U.S. RDA

English Muffin Batter Bread

Cornmeal
4 to 4½ cups all purpose flour
¼ cup sugar
2 teaspoons salt
2 pkg. active dry yeast
1¼ cups water
½ cup oil
2 eggs

Grease and sprinkle with cornmeal two 8x4-inch loaf pans. In large bowl, combine 1½ cups flour, sugar, salt and yeast. In small saucepan, heat water and oil until very warm (120 to 130°F.). Add warm liquid and egg to flour mixture. Blend at low speed until moistened; beat 2 minutes at medium speed. By hand, stir in 2½ to 3 cups flour to form a stiff batter. Cover loosely with plastic wrap and cloth towel. Let rise in warm place (80 to 85°F.) until light and doubled in size, about 45 to 60 minutes.

Stir batter vigorously 30 seconds; spoon into prepared pans. Cover; let rise in warm place until doubled in size, about 30 to 45 minutes. Heat oven to 375°F. Bake 20 to 30 minutes or until loaves sound hollow when lightly tapped. Remove from pans immediately; cool on wire racks. **2 (12-slice) loaves.**

NUTRIENTS PER 1 SLICE

Calories	150	Dietary Fiber	1 g
Protein	4 g	Sodium	185 mg
Carbohydrate	22 g	Potassium	40 mg
Fat	5 g	Calcium	<2% U.S. RDA
Cholesterol	25 mg	Iron	6% U.S. RDA

Dinner Roll Dough

5¾ to 6¾ cups all purpose flour
    ¼ cup sugar
    2 teaspoons salt
    2 pkg. active dry yeast
    1 cup water
    1 cup milk
    ½ cup margarine or butter
    1 egg
      Melted margarine or butter, if desired

In large bowl, combine 2 cups flour, sugar, salt and yeast; blend well. In small saucepan, heat water, milk and ½ cup margarine until very warm (120 to 130°F.). Add warm liquid and egg to flour mixture. Blend at low speed until moistened; beat 3 minutes at medium speed. By hand, stir in an additional 2½ to 3 cups flour until dough pulls away from sides of bowl.

On floured surface, knead in 1¼ to 1¾ cups flour until dough is smooth and elastic, about 8 to 10 minutes. Place dough in greased bowl; cover loosely with plastic wrap and cloth towel. Let rise in warm place (80 to 85°F.) until light and doubled in size, about 45 to 60 minutes.

Punch down dough several times to remove all air bubbles. DIVIDE DOUGH IN HALF; SHAPE EACH HALF ACCORDING TO VARIATION DESIRED. Cover; let rise in warm place until light and doubled in size, about 20 to 30 minutes. Bake at 400°F. as stated in shaping directions. Remove from pans immediately; cool on wire racks. Brush with melted margarine.

TIP: To make dough a day ahead, after first rise time, cover and refrigerate dough overnight. Shape dough as directed in recipe; let rise a second time until light and doubled in size, about 25 to 35 minutes.

VARIATIONS:

PAN ROLLS: Lightly grease 13x9-inch pan. Divide dough into 16 equal pieces. Shape each into a ball, pulling edges under to make a smooth top. Place balls smooth side up in prepared pan. Bake 16 to 20 minutes or until golden brown. **16 rolls.**

CLOVERLEAF ROLLS: Lightly grease 12 muffin cups. Divide dough into 12 equal pieces; divide each into thirds. Shape each into a ball, pulling edges under to make a smooth top. Place 3 balls smooth side up in each prepared muffin cup. Bake 14 to 18 minutes or until golden brown. **12 rolls.**

CROWN ROLLS: Lightly grease 12 muffin cups. Divide dough into 12 equal pieces. Shape each into a ball, pulling edges under to make a smooth top. Place 1 ball smooth side up in each prepared muffin cup. Using kitchen shears dipped in flour, cut balls of dough into quarters almost to bottom. Bake 14 to 18 minutes or until golden brown. **12 rolls.**

SWIRL ROLLS: Lightly grease cookie sheets. Divide dough into 16 equal pieces. On lightly floured surface, roll each piece into an 8-inch rope. Beginning at center, make a loose swirl with each rope; tuck end under. Place 2 to 3 inches apart on prepared cookie sheets. Bake 12 to 15 minutes or until golden brown. **16 rolls.**

BOW KNOT ROLLS: Lightly grease cookie sheets. Divide dough into 16 equal pieces. On lightly floured surface, roll each piece into a 9-inch rope. Tie each into a loose knot. Place 2 to 3 inches apart on prepared cookie sheets. Bake 12 to 15 minutes or until golden brown. **16 rolls.**

CRESCENT ROLLS: Lightly grease cookie sheets. Divide dough in half; shape into a ball. On lightly floured surface, roll each ball to a 12-inch circle. Spread each with 1 tablespoon softened margarine or butter. Cut each circle into 12 wedges. Beginning at wide end of wedge, roll toward point. Place point side down 2 to 3 inches apart on prepared cookie sheets. Curve ends to form a crescent shape. Bake 12 to 15 minutes or until golden brown. **24 rolls.**

NUTRIENTS PER ¹⁄₁₆ OF RECIPE

Calories	280	Dietary Fiber	3 g
Protein	7 g	Sodium	360 mg
Carbohydrate	46 g	Potassium	100 mg
Fat	8 g	Calcium	2% U.S. RDA
Cholesterol	20 mg	Iron	15% U.S. RDA

Oats 'n Wheat Dinner Rolls

1¾ to 2¾ cups all purpose flour
    ⅓ cup rolled oats
    ¼ cup sugar
    1 teaspoon salt
    1 pkg. active dry yeast
    1 cup milk
    3 tablespoons margarine or butter
    1 egg
    ¾ cup whole wheat flour

TOPPING
    1 egg
    1 tablespoon water
    1 tablespoon rolled oats

Grease 9-inch square pan. In large bowl, combine 1 cup all purpose flour, ⅓ cup rolled oats, sugar, salt and yeast; blend well. In small saucepan, heat milk and margarine until very warm (120 to 130°F.). Add warm liquid and egg to flour mixture. Blend at low speed until moistened; beat 2 minutes at medium speed. By hand, stir in whole wheat flour and an additional ½ to 1¼ cups all purpose flour until dough pulls cleanly away from sides of bowl.

On floured surface, knead in ¼ to ½ cup all purpose flour until dough is smooth and elastic, about 5 minutes. Place dough in greased bowl; cover loosely with plastic wrap and cloth towel. Let rise in warm place (80 to 85°F.) until light and doubled in size, about 1 hour.

Punch down dough several times to remove all air bubbles. Divide dough into 16 equal pieces; shape into balls. Place in prepared pan. Cover; let rise in warm place until light and doubled in size, about 35 to 45 minutes.

Heat oven to 375°F. In small bowl, combine egg white and water; beat slightly. Carefully brush over rolls; sprinkle with 1 tablespoon rolled oats. Bake at 375°F. for 20 to 30 minutes or until golden brown. Remove from pan immediately; serve warm. **16 rolls.**

NUTRIENTS PER 1 ROLL

Calories	150	Dietary Fiber	2 g
Protein	5 g	Sodium	170 mg
Carbohydrate	26 g	Potassium	90 mg
Fat	3 g	Calcium	2% U.S. RDA
Cholesterol	35 mg	Iron	8% U.S. RDA

Flaky Butter Brioche

4¼ to 4¾ cups all purpose flour
⅓ cup sugar
1 teaspoon salt
2 pkg. active dry yeast
1¼ cups milk
½ cup butter or margarine
3 eggs

Generously grease 24 brioche or muffin cups. In large bowl, combine 2 cups flour, sugar, salt and yeast; blend well. In small saucepan, heat milk and butter until very warm (120 to 130°F.). Add warm liquid and 2 of the eggs to flour mixture. Blend at low speed until moistened; beat 3 minutes at medium speed. By hand, stir in an additional 2 to 2¼ cups flour until dough pulls cleanly away from sides of bowl.

On floured surface, knead in ¼ to ½ cup flour until dough is smooth, about 2 to 3 minutes. Divide dough into 24 equal parts. Remove about ⅓ of dough from each part; shape all parts into smooth balls. Place larger balls in prepared pans. With finger, make a deep indentation in center of each ball. Place smaller balls in indentations, pressing down slightly. Cover, let rise in warm place until light and doubled in size, about 45 minutes.

Heat oven to 350°F. Beat remaining egg; carefully brush over rolls. Bake at 350°F. for 15 to 20 minutes or until golden brown. Remove from pans immediately. **24 rolls.**

NUTRIENTS PER 1 ROLL

Calories 150	Dietary Fiber...........................1 g
Protein......................................4 g	Sodium.............................150 mg
Carbohydrate.........................23 g	Potassium............................65 mg
Fat..5 g	Calcium.................2% U.S. RDA
Cholesterol.........................45 mg	Iron.........................6% U.S. RDA

Hawaiian Sweet Bread

6½ to 7   cups all purpose flour
    ¾   cup mashed potato flakes
    ⅔   cup sugar
    1   teaspoon salt
    ½   teaspoon ginger
    2   teaspoons vanilla
    2   pkg. active dry yeast
    1   cup milk
    ½   cup water
    ½   cup margarine or butter
    1   cup pineapple juice,
        room temperature
    3   eggs

Grease three 8 or 9-inch round cake pans. In large bowl, combine 3 cups flour, mashed potato flakes, sugar, salt, ginger, vanilla and yeast. In medium saucepan, heat milk, water and margarine until very warm (120 to 130°F.). Add warm liquid, pineapple juice and eggs to flour mixture. Blend at low speed until moistened; beat 4 minutes at medium speed. By hand, stir in 3 cups flour to form a stiff dough. On floured surface, knead in ½ to 1 cup flour until smooth and elastic, 5 to 8 minutes. Place dough in greased bowl; cover loosely with plastic wrap and cloth towel. Let rise in warm place (80 to 85°F.) until light and doubled in size, 1 to 1½ hours.

Punch down dough. Divide dough into 3 parts; form into round balls. Place in prepared pans; flatten slightly. Cover; let rise in warm place until light and doubled in size, about 1 hour. Heat oven to 375°F. Bake 25 to 35 minutes or until loaves sound hollow when lightly tapped. Remove from pans immediately. Cool on wire racks. **3 (16-slice) loaves.**

NUTRIENTS PER 1 SLICE

Calories	110	Dietary Fiber	1 g
Protein	3 g	Sodium	75 mg
Carbohydrate	18 g	Potassium	55 mg
Fat	3 g	Calcium	<2% U.S. RDA
Cholesterol	20 mg	Iron	4% U.S. RDA

Holiday Bread

5½ to 6½ cups all purpose flour
    ½ cup sugar
    1 teaspoon salt
    1 teaspoon cardamom, if desired
    2 pkg. active dry yeast
    1 cup milk
    ½ cup water
    ⅔ cup margarine or butter
    3 eggs
    ¾ cup mixed candied fruits
    ½ cup candied red cherries, cut in half
    ½ cup golden raisins

GLAZE
   1½ cups powdered sugar
   2 to 3 tablespoons milk
   ¼ teaspoon almond extract

Grease 2 large cookie sheets. In large bowl, combine 2 cups flour, sugar, salt, cardamom and yeast; mix well. In small saucepan, heat 1 cup milk, water and margarine until very warm (120 to 130°F.). Add warm liquid and eggs to flour mixture. Blend at low speed until moistened; beat 3 minutes at medium speed. Stir in remaining flour and fruits to form a soft dough. On floured surface, knead until smooth and elastic, about 8 minutes. Place dough in greased bowl; turn dough to grease all sides. Cover loosely with plastic wrap and cloth towel. Let rise in warm place (80 to 85°F.) until light and doubled in size, about 55 to 60 minutes.

Punch down dough several times to remove all air bubbles. Turn dough onto lightly floured surface. Divide dough into thirds. Shape each into a 12x7-inch oval. Fold in half length-wise. Place on prepared cookie sheets. Cover; let rise in warm place until light and doubled in size, about 45 minutes.

Heat oven to 350°F. Bake 30 to 35 minutes or until golden brown. Immediately remove from cookie sheets; cool on wire racks. In small bowl, combine all glaze ingredients until smooth. Drizzle over cooled loaves. **3 (24-slice) loaves.**

NUTRIENTS PER 1 SLICE

Calories	90	Dietary Fiber	1 g
Protein	2 g	Sodium	55 mg
Carbohydrate	16 g	Potassium	40 mg
Fat	2 g	Calcium	<2% U.S. RDA
Cholesterol	10 mg	Iron	2% U.S. RDA

Apricot Danish Squares

2 pkg. active dry yeast
¼ cup warm water
3 tablespoons sugar
¾ teaspoon salt
¼ cup orange juice
¼ cup margarine or butter, softened
½ teaspoon grated orange peel
2 eggs
2 to 2½ cups all purpose flour

TOPPING

½ cup sliced almonds
3 tablespoons margarine or butter
2 tablespoons brown sugar
½ teaspoon cinnamon
¼ teaspoon grated orange peel
¾ cup apricot preserves

GLAZE

¾ cup powdered sugar
1 to 2 tablespoons orange juice

Grease 15x10-inch jelly roll pan. In large bowl, dissolve yeast in warm water (105 to 115°F.). Blend in sugar, salt, ¼ cup orange juice, ¼ cup margarine, ½ teaspoon orange peel and eggs. Add 1 cup flour to yeast mixture. Blend at low speed until moistened; beat 3 minutes at medium speed. By hand, stir in remaining flour to form a soft, sticky batter. Cover loosely with plastic wrap and cloth towel. Let rise in warm place (80 to 85°F.) until light and doubled in size, about 30 to 45 minutes.

In small saucepan, saute almonds in 3 tablespoons margarine until almonds are light golden brown. Remove from heat; blend in remaining topping ingredients. Stir down dough; spread in prepared pan. Spoon topping over batter; spread gently. Let rise in warm place until light and doubled in size, about 30 minutes.

Heat oven to 350°F. Bake 25 to 35 minutes or until golden brown. In small bowl, blend all glaze ingredients until smooth; drizzle over warm coffee cake. **18 servings.**

NUTRIENTS PER ⅟₁₈ OF RECIPE

Calories	200	Dietary Fiber	1 g
Protein	3 g	Sodium	150 mg
Carbohydrate	32 g	Potassium	90 mg
Fat	7 g	Calcium	<2% U.S. RDA
Cholesterol	30 mg	Iron	6% U.S. RDA

Basic Sweet Dough

6 to 7 cups all purpose flour
  ½ cup sugar
  2 teaspoons salt
  2 pkg. active dry yeast
  1 cup water
  1 cup milk
  ½ cup margarine or butter
  1 egg

In large bowl, combine 2 cups flour, sugar, salt and yeast; blend well. In small saucepan, heat water, milk and margarine until very warm (120 to 130°F.). Add warm liquid and egg to flour mixture. Blend at low speed until moistened; beat 3 minutes at medium speed. By hand, stir in an additional 3 cups flour until dough pulls cleanly away from sides of bowl.

On floured surface, knead in 1 to 2 cups flour until dough is smooth and elastic, about 8 to 10 minutes. Place dough in greased bowl; cover loosely with plastic wrap and cloth towel. Let rise in warm place (80 to 85°F.) until light and doubled in size, about 45 to 60 minutes.

Punch down dough to remove all air bubbles. DIVIDE DOUGH IN HALF; SHAPE EACH HALF ACCORDING TO VARIATION DESIRED.

TIP: To make dough a day ahead, after first rise time, cover and refrigerate dough overnight. Shape dough and let rise as directed in recipe.

VARIATIONS:

CARAMEL-NUT STICKY ROLLS: Generously grease 13x9-inch pan. In small bowl, combine ½ cup firmly packed brown sugar, ½ cup softened margarine or butter and 2 tablespoons light corn syrup; blend well. Drop mixture by spoonfuls into prepared pan; spread evenly. Sprinkle with ¼ cup chopped nuts. On lightly floured surface, roll out ½ recipe Basic Sweet Dough to 20x12-inch rectangle. Spread with 2 tablespoons softened margarine or butter. In small bowl, combine ¼ cup sugar and 1 teaspoon cinnamon; blend well. Sprinkle over dough. Starting with 20-inch side, roll up jelly-roll fashion; pinch edges firmly to seal seams. Cut into twenty 1-inch slices; place cut side down in prepared pan.

Cover; let rise in warm place (80 to 85°F.) until light and doubled in size, about 35 to 45 minutes. Heat oven to 375°F. Bake 25 to 30 minutes or until deep golden brown. Cool in pan 1 minute; invert onto wire rack. **20 rolls.**

NUTRIENTS PER 1 ROLL

Calories	210	Dietary Fiber	1 g
Protein	3 g	Sodium	210 mg
Carbohydrate	29 g	Potassium	70 mg
Fat	9 g	Calcium	2% U.S. RDA
Cholesterol	6 mg	Iron	8% U.S. RDA

CINNAMON ROLLS: Generously grease 13x9-inch pan. On lightly floured surface, roll out ½ recipe Basic Sweet Dough to 20x12-inch rectangle. Spread with ¼ cup softened margarine or butter. In small bowl, combine ½ cup sugar and 2 teaspoons cinnamon; blend well. Sprinkle over dough. Starting with 20-inch side, roll up jelly-roll fashion; pinch edges firmly to seal seams. Cut into twenty 1-inch slices; place cut side down in prepared pan.

Cover; let rise in warm place (80 to 85°F.) until light and doubled in size, about 35 to 45 minutes. Heat oven to 375°F. Bake 25 to 30 minutes or until golden brown. Remove from pan immediately. In small bowl, combine ¾ cup powdered sugar, 1 tablespoon softened margarine or butter, 1 to 2 tablespoons milk and ¼ teaspoon vanilla; mix well. Drizzle over warm rolls. Serve warm. **20 rolls.**

NUTRIENTS PER 1 ROLL

Calories	180	Dietary Fiber	1 g
Protein	3 g	Sodium	170 mg
Carbohydrate	28 g	Potassium	45 mg
Fat	6 g	Calcium	<2% U.S. RDA
Cholesterol	6 mg	Iron	6% U.S. RDA

EASY FRUIT-FILLED BRAID: Grease 2 cookie sheets. In small bowl, combine ¼ cup sugar, ¼ to ½ cup chopped nuts and ¾ teaspoon cinnamon; set aside. Divide ½ recipe Basic Sweet Dough in half again. On lightly floured surface, roll each half to 12x6-inch rectangle; place on prepared cookie sheets. Spread each with ½ tablespoon softened margarine or butter, 3 tablespoons apricot or peach preserves and half of cinnamon-sugar mixture lengthwise down center third of rectangle. Cut 1-inch wide strips along both sides of filling. Fold strips at an angle across filling, alternating from side to side.

Cover; let rise in warm place (80 to 85°F.) until doubled in size, about 45 minutes. Heat oven to 350°F. Bake for 25 to 30 minutes or until deep golden brown. Remove from cookie sheets immediately; cool. In small bowl, combine ½ cup powdered sugar and 3 to 4 teaspoons milk until smooth; drizzle over braids. **2 braids; 12 servings each.**

NUTRIENTS PER ¹/₂₄ OF RECIPE

Calories	150	Dietary Fiber	1 g
Protein	3 g	Sodium	125 mg
Carbohydrate	25 g	Potassium	45 mg
Fat	4 g	Calcium	<2% U.S. RDA
Cholesterol	6 mg	Iron	4% U.S. RDA

FRUIT-FILLED SWEET ROLLS: Lightly grease cookie sheets. On lightly floured surface, divide ½ recipe Basic Sweet Dough into 16 equal pieces. Roll each piece into 15-inch rope. Beginning at center, make a loose swirl with each rope; tuck end under. Place on prepared cookie sheets. Cover; let rise in warm place (80 to 85°F.) until light and doubled in size, about 20 to 25 minutes.

Heat oven to 375°F. Carefully brush rolls with 1 to 2 table-spoons melted margarine or butter. Make deep thumbprint in center of each roll; fill each with 1 teaspoon any flavor fruit preserves. Bake at 375°F. for 12 to 16 minutes or until light golden brown. Remove from pan immediately; brush with 1 to 2 tablespoons melted margarine or butter. In small bowl, combine ¾ cup powdered sugar, 1 tablespoon softened margarine or butter, 1 to 2 tablespoons milk and ¼ teaspoon vanilla; mix well. Drizzle over warm rolls. Serve warm. **16 rolls.**

NUTRIENTS PER 1 ROLL

Calories	210	Dietary Fiber	1 g
Protein	4 g	Sodium	210 mg
Carbohydrate	34 g	Potassium	60 mg
Fat	6 g	Calcium	2% U.S. RDA
Cholesterol	8 mg	Iron	8% U.S. RDA

FRESH APPLE COFFEE CAKE: Generously grease 13x9-inch pan. Press ½ recipe Basic Sweet Dough in prepared pan. Arrange 4 cups sliced, peeled apples (¼-inch thick slices) in rows on top of dough. In small bowl, blend ¾ cup sugar, 3 tablespoons flour, ½ teaspoon cinnamon and 2 tablespoons softened margarine or butter with fork until crumbly. Sprinkle evenly over apples. Cover; let rise in warm place (80 to 85°F.) until light and doubled in size, about 40 to 45 minutes.

Heat oven to 375°F. Bake 30 to 40 minutes or until golden brown around edges and apples are tender. In small bowl, combine ½ cup powdered sugar and 2 to 4 teaspoons milk; blend well. Drizzle over warm coffee cake. Serve warm. **15 servings.**

NUTRIENTS PER ⅟₁₅ OF RECIPE

Calories	250	Dietary Fiber	2 g
Protein	4 g	Sodium	200 mg
Carbohydrate	47 g	Potassium	110 mg
Fat	5 g	Calcium	2% U.S. RDA
Cholesterol	10 mg	Iron	8% U.S. RDA

HOT CROSS BUNS: Grease cookie sheet. Stir ½ cup raisins into ½ recipe Basic Sweet Dough before kneading. After dough has rested 15 minutes, divide into 15 pieces. Shape each piece into a ball making sure raisins are covered. Place 2 inches apart on prepared cookie sheet.

Cover; let rise in warm place (80 to 85°F.) until doubled in size, 40 to 50 minutes. Brush balls with mixture of 1 egg yolk and 2 tablespoons water. Heat oven to 375°F. Bake 15 to 20 minutes or until deep golden brown. Immediately remove from cookie sheets; cool. If desired, form a cross on each bun with powdered sugar frosting. **15 rolls.**

NUTRIENTS PER 1 ROLL

Calories	170	Dietary Fiber	2 g
Protein	4 g	Sodium	190 mg
Carbohydrate	30 g	Potassium	90 mg
Fat	4 g	Calcium	2% U.S. RDA
Cholesterol	30 mg	Iron	8% U.S. RDA

SWEDISH TEA RING: Grease cookie sheet. On floured surface, roll ½ recipe Basic Sweet Dough to 18x15-inch rectangle. Brush dough with ¼ cup melted margarine or butter, leaving ½ inch on one 18-inch side free of margarine for ease in sealing edge. Combine ½ cup firmly packed brown sugar or sugar and 2 teaspoons cinnamon; sprinkle over margarine. Starting with 18-inch side, roll up jelly-roll fashion toward ungreased edge. Pinch edge to seal. Place seam side down on prepared cookie sheet, joining ends to form a circle; pinch to seal. With scissors, make cuts at 1-inch intervals to within ½ inch of inside of ring. Turn each slice on its side, cut side up. Cover; let rise in warm place (80 to 85°F.) until doubled in size, about 45 minutes.

Bake at 350°F. for 25 to 30 minutes. If desired, glaze with powdered sugar glaze. **16 servings.**

NUTRIENTS PER ¹⁄₁₆ OF RECIPE

Calories	200	Dietary Fiber	2 g
Protein	4 g	Sodium	210 mg
Carbohydrate	31 g	Potassium	75 mg
Fat	6 g	Calcium	2% U.S. RDA
Cholesterol	8 mg	Iron	8% U.S. RDA

STREUSEL COFFEE CAKE: Grease 13x9-inch pan. Press ½ recipe Basic Sweet Dough in prepared pan. Cover; let rise in warm place (80 to 85°F.) until light and doubled in size, 45 to 60 minutes.

In small bowl, combine ½ cup all purpose flour, ⅓ cup firmly packed brown sugar, 1 teaspoon cinnamon and ¼ cup margarine or butter until crumbly. Stir in ½ cup chopped nuts. Sprinkle topping over dough. Heat oven to 375°F. Bake 20 to 25 minutes or until golden brown. Serve warm. **15 servings.**

NUTRIENTS PER ¹⁄₁₅ OF RECIPE

Calories	240	Dietary Fiber	2 g
Protein	5 g	Sodium	220 mg
Carbohydrate	35 g	Potassium	95 mg
Fat	9 g	Calcium	2% U.S. RDA
Cholesterol	10 mg	Iron	10% U.S. RDA

TROPICAL TREAT COFFEE CAKE: Grease 13x9-inch pan. Press ½ recipe Basic Sweet Dough in prepared pan. Cover; let rise in warm place until light and doubled in size, 45 to 60 minutes.

In small bowl, combine 10-oz. jar peach or apricot preserves and 2 tablespoons melted margarine; spread over dough. Sprinkle with ½ cup coconut and, if desired, ¼ cup chopped nuts. Cover loosely with greased plastic wrap and cloth towel. Let rise in warm place (80 to 85°F.) until light and doubled in size, about 40 to 45 minutes.

Heat oven to 375°F. Bake 30 to 40 minutes or until golden brown around edges. Serve warm. **15 servings.**

NUTRIENTS PER ¹⁄₁₅ OF RECIPE

Calories	250	Dietary Fiber	2 g
Protein	4 g	Sodium	210 mg
Carbohydrate	41 g	Potassium	90 mg
Fat	8 g	Calcium	2% U.S. RDA
Cholesterol	10 mg	Iron	8% U.S. RDA

Cakes, Frostings & Fillings

Cakes, Frostings & Fillings

Cakes

First choice in any culinary language for marking special events, cakes are also a popular selection for family desserts and snacks. With enough variety to satisfy any appetite or occasion, cakes can range from simple one-bowl, single-pan styles to elaborate layered tortes. Hearty fruit- and nut-filled gems contrast with airy chiffon and angel food beauties. Old-fashioned jelly rolls and cupcakes hold their own alongside sophisticated liqueur-laced batters and show-off meringue cakes.

The countless number of cake variations fall into two major categories—*shortening types* and *foam* or *sponge* cakes. As the name indicates, shortening cakes contain shortening in some form. Foam cakes depend mainly on air beaten into egg whites for leavening. They include angel food and sponge, which do not use shortening, and chiffon cakes, which use oil.

Keys to Successful Cakes

• Measure all ingredients accurately. Combine ingredients in order specified in recipe. Do not over- or underbeat, which can cause problems in the cake texture and structure.

• Egg whites should be brought to room temperature before beating for greater volume.

• Use pan size and preparation recommended in recipe. Use shiny metal cake pans for delicate browning and a tender exterior.

• Preheat oven to temperature stated in recipe. Place one pan in center of oven unless otherwise indicated. For even heat circulation, stagger several pans on one or more racks so pans do not touch.

• Use doneness test suggested and check cake at minimum bake time given.

• Follow recipe instructions for cooling and removal from pan. Cake can stick if left in pan too long after baking. If this happens, heat in oven 1 minute; remove from pan. Wire racks are useful for cooling because of unrestricted air flow.

• Do not add filling or frosting until cake is completely cooled (about 1 to 2 hours), unless recipe indicates otherwise.

• Shortening cakes should be cut in a gentle back-and-forth sawing motion with a thin, sharp knife. A long, serrated knife works best for foam cakes.

• Store cakes only after they are completely cooled. All cakes containing dairy products in filling or frosting must be refrigerated. Store layer or tube cakes under a cake cover or similar device.

• Fluffy frostings tend to be absorbed into the cake after a day or so; cakes with these toppings should be served as soon as possible. Leftovers can be placed under a cake cover, but slip a knife under the edge so the container is not airtight.

• Freeze unfrosted cakes, properly wrapped with plastic wrap or foil, up to 6 months; add frosting and decorative touches after thawing. Freeze frosted cakes uncovered until the frosting becomes firm; then wrap. Cakes with cream or fruit filling or with whipped cream or fluffy-type frosting will not freeze well.

• Thaw unfrosted cakes, wrapped, at room temperature. Frosted cakes should be unwrapped immediately when taken from the freezer, and allowed to stand at room temperature until thawed.

Hints for Shortening Cakes

• Shortening cakes include the basic white, yellow, chocolate and pound cakes. When margarine is called for in a recipe, use only stick-type margarine, not whipped. Shortening-type cakes depend mainly on baking powder or baking soda for leavening. Cake texture, volume and moistness are affected by the method of mixing. Follow specific directions given for each recipe.

Simple White Cake

   2 cups all purpose flour
1½ cups sugar
   3 teaspoons baking powder
   1 teaspoon salt
   1 cup milk
  ½ cup shortening
   2 teaspoons vanilla or ½ teaspoon almond extract
   4 egg whites

Heat oven to 350°F. Grease and flour two 9-inch round cake pans. In large bowl, combine flour, sugar, baking powder, salt, milk and shortening at low speed until moistened; beat 2 minutes at medium speed. Add vanilla and egg whites; continue beating an additional 2 minutes. Pour into prepared pans. Bake at 350°F. for 20 to 30 minutes or until toothpick inserted in center comes out clean. Cool 10 minutes; remove from pans. Cool completely. If desired, fill cake with Lemon Filling, Lord Baltimore or Lady Baltimore Filling; spread top and sides with White Cloud Frosting or Lord Baltimore Frosting (see Index). **12 servings.**

TIP: Cake can be baked in 13x9-inch pan. Grease and flour bottom only. Bake 25 to 35 minutes or until toothpick inserted in center comes out clean. Cool completely. Frost as desired.

HIGH ALTITUDE: Increase flour to 2 cups plus 3 table-spoons. Bake at 375°F. for 20 to 30 minutes.

VARIATIONS:

CHERRY NUT CAKE: Stir ½ cup each chopped maraschino cherries and nuts into batter before pouring into prepared pans.

COCONUT CAKE: Stir 1 cup flaked coconut into batter before pouring into prepared pans. Sprinkle additional coconut over frosting.

POPPY SEED CAKE: Combine ¼ cup poppy seed with an additional ¼ cup milk; allow to stand 30 minutes. Add to batter with egg whites and vanilla.

NUTRIENTS PER ¹⁄₁₂ OF RECIPE WITHOUT FROSTING

Calories	260	Dietary Fiber	1 g
Protein	4 g	Sodium	280 mg
Carbohydrate	42 g	Potassium	70 mg
Fat	9 g	Calcium	8% U.S. RDA
Cholesterol	0 mg	Iron	4% U.S. RDA

Cookies 'n Cream Cake

CAKE

1 pkg. pudding-included white cake mix
1¼ cups water
⅓ cup oil
3 egg whites
1 cup coarsely crushed cream-filled chocolate sandwich cookies

FROSTING

3 cups powdered sugar
¾ cup shortening
1 teaspoon vanilla
2 egg whites

Heat oven to 350°F. Grease and flour two 9 or 8-inch round cake pans. In large bowl, combine all cake ingredients except crushed cookies at low speed until moistened; beat 2 minutes at highest speed. Gently stir in crushed cookies. Pour batter into prepared pans. Bake at 350°F. for 25 to 35 minutes or until toothpick inserted in center comes out clean. Cool 10 minutes; remove from pans. Cool completely.

In small bowl, combine ½ cup of the powdered sugar, shortening, vanilla and 2 egg whites; blend well. Beat in remaining powdered sugar until frosting is smooth and creamy. Fill and frost cake. **12 servings.**

HIGH ALTITUDE: Add 3 tablespoons flour to dry cake mix. Increase water to 1⅓ cups. Bake at 375°F. for 20 to 30 minutes.

NUTRIENTS PER ½₂ OF RECIPE

Calories 490	Dietary Fiber ....1 g
Protein ....4 g	Sodium ....330 mg
Carbohydrate..........................63 g	Potassium ....45 mg
Fat ....25 g	Calcium ....4% U.S. RDA
Cholesterol ....2 mg	Iron ....4% U.S. RDA

Basic Yellow Cake

2½ cups all purpose flour
1½ cups sugar
3 teaspoons baking powder
1 teaspoon salt
1¼ cups milk
⅔ cup shortening
2 teaspoons vanilla
2 egg yolks
2 eggs

Heat oven to 350°F. Generously grease and lightly flour bottom only of 13x9-inch pan. In large bowl, blend all ingredients except vanilla, egg yolks and eggs, at low speed until moistened. Beat 2 minutes at medium speed. Add vanilla, egg yolks and eggs; beat 2 more minutes at medium speed. Pour batter into prepared pan. Bake at 350°F. for 40 to 45 minutes or until toothpick inserted in center comes out clean. Cool completely. Frost as desired. **12 servings.**

TIP: Cake can be baked in 2 well-greased and lightly floured 9-inch or three 8-inch round cake pans. Bake 35 to 40 minutes. Cool 10 minutes; remove from pans. Cool completely. 2 or 3-layer cake.

HIGH ALTITUDE: Increase flour 2 tablespoons and milk to 1½ cups; use 3 whole eggs. Bake at 375°F. for 30 to 40 minutes.

NUTRIENTS PER ¹⁄₁₂ OF RECIPE WITHOUT FROSTING

Calories	330	Dietary Fiber	1 g
Protein	5 g	Sodium	280 mg
Carbohydrate	46 g	Potassium	80 mg
Fat	14 g	Calcium	8% U.S. RDA
Cholesterol	90 mg	Iron	8% U.S. RDA

Peanut Butter Crunch Cake

    1 pkg. pudding-included yellow cake mix
    ½ cup firmly packed brown sugar
    1 cup chunky peanut butter
    1 cup water
    ¼ cup oil
    3 eggs
    ½ cup semi-sweet chocolate chips
    ½ cup peanut butter chips*
    ½ cup chopped peanuts

Heat oven to 350°F. Grease and flour 13x9-inch pan. In large bowl, combine cake mix, brown sugar and peanut butter at low speed until crumbly. Reserve ½ cup peanut butter mixture; set aside. To remaining peanut butter mixture, add water, oil and eggs. Mix at low speed until moistened; beat 2 minutes at highest speed. Fold ¼ cup of the chocolate chips and ¼ cup of the peanut butter chips into batter. Pour batter into prepared pan. In small bowl, combine reserved ½ cup peanut butter mixture, remaining chocolate chips and peanuts; sprinkle evenly over batter.

Bake at 350°F. for 40 to 50 minutes or until toothpick inserted in center comes out clean. Immediately sprinkle with remaining peanut butter chips; gently press into top of cake. Cool completely. **12 to 15 servings.**

TIP: *Semi-sweet chocolate chips can be substituted for the peanut butter chips.

HIGH ALTITUDE: Add 3 tablespoons flour to dry cake mix. Bake at 375°F. for 40 to 50 minutes.

NUTRIENTS PER ¹⁄₁₅ OF RECIPE

Calories	420	Dietary Fiber	2 g
Protein	10 g	Sodium	350 mg
Carbohydrate	44 g	Potassium	240 mg
Fat	23 g	Calcium	6% U.S. RDA
Cholesterol	50 mg	Iron	8% U.S. RDA

Delicious Devil's Food Cake

1½ cups all purpose flour
1¼ cups sugar
½ cup unsweetened cocoa
1¼ teaspoons baking soda
1 teaspoon salt
1 cup buttermilk*
⅔ cup oil
1 teaspoon vanilla
2 eggs

Heat oven to 350°F. Grease and lightly flour bottoms only of two 8-inch round cake pans.** In large bowl, blend all ingredients at low speed until moistened; beat 3 minutes at medium speed. Pour batter into prepared pans. Bake at 350°F. for 25 to 30 minutes or until toothpick inserted in center comes out clean. Cool 5 minutes; remove from pans. Cool completely. Frost as desired. **12 servings.**

TIPS: *To substitute for buttermilk, use 1 tablespoon vinegar or lemon juice plus milk to make 1 cup.

**Cake can be baked in greased and lightly floured 13x9-inch pan. Bake 30 to 35 minutes.

HIGH ALTITUDE: Increase flour to 1½ cups plus 3 tablespoons. Bake at 375°F. for 25 to 30 minutes.

NUTRIENTS PER ¹⁄₁₂ OF RECIPE WITHOUT FROSTING

Calories	280	Dietary Fiber	1 g
Protein	4 g	Sodium	350 mg
Carbohydrate	35 g	Potassium	80 mg
Fat	14 g	Calcium	2% U.S. RDA
Cholesterol	45 mg	Iron	6% U.S. RDA

German Chocolate Cake

    4-oz. bar sweet cooking chocolate
      ½ cup hot water
      1 cup margarine or butter, softened
      2 cups sugar
      4 eggs
    2½ cups all purpose flour
      1 teaspoon baking soda
      ½ teaspoon salt
      1 cup buttermilk*
      1 teaspoon vanilla
         Coconut Pecan Frosting (see Index)

Heat oven to 350°F. Grease and lightly flour three 9-inch round cake pans. In small saucepan over low heat, melt chocolate with water; set aside. In large bowl, cream margarine and sugar until light and fluffy. Add eggs, one at a time, beating well after each. Add remaining ingredients except frosting; blend at low speed just until combined. Pour batter into prepared pans. Bake at 350°F. for 35 to 45 minutes or until toothpick inserted in center comes out clean. Cool 5 minutes; remove from pans. Cool completely. Spread Coconut Pecan Frosting between layers and on top, leaving sides plain or spread with whipped cream. **12 servings.**

TIP: *To substitute for buttermilk, use 1 tablespoon vinegar or lemon juice plus milk to make 1 cup.

HIGH ALTITUDE: Decrease sugar to 1¾ cups and baking soda to ¾ teaspoon. Bake at 375°F. for 25 to 30 minutes.

NUTRIENTS PER ¹⁄₁₂ OF RECIPE WITH FROSTING

Calories	730	Dietary Fiber	3 g
Protein	10 g	Sodium	540 mg
Carbohydrate	84 g	Potassium	270 mg
Fat	39 g	Calcium	10% U.S. RDA
Cholesterol	160 mg	Iron	10% U.S. RDA

Chocolate Zucchini Cake

1 pkg. pudding-included devil's food cake mix
1 teaspoon cinnamon
⅛ teaspoon cloves
2 cups shredded, unpeeled zucchini
½ cup buttermilk*
½ cup oil
3 eggs
½ cup chopped nuts
½ cup semi-sweet chocolate chips

Heat oven to 350°F. Grease and flour 13x9-inch pan. In large bowl, blend cake mix, cinnamon, cloves, zucchini, buttermilk, oil and eggs at low speed until moistened; beat 2 minutes at highest speed. Pour into prepared pan; sprinkle with nuts and chocolate chips. Bake at 350°F. for 35 to 45 minutes or until toothpick inserted in center comes out clean. Serve plain or frost as desired. **12 servings.**

TIP: *To substitute for buttermilk, use 1½ teaspoons vinegar or lemon juice plus milk to make ½ cup.

HIGH ALTITUDE: Add 4 tablespoons flour to dry cake mix. Bake at 375°F. for 35 to 45 minutes.

NUTRIENTS PER ½ OF RECIPE

Calories	360	Dietary Fiber	1 g
Protein	5 g	Sodium	380 mg
Carbohydrate	38 g	Potassium	180 mg
Fat	21 g	Calcium	10% U.S. RDA
Cholesterol	70 mg	Iron	8% U.S. RDA

Tunnel of Fudge Cake

CAKE

    1¾ cups margarine or butter, softened
    1¾ cups granulated sugar
     6 eggs
     2 cups powdered sugar
    2¼ cups all purpose flour
     ¾ cup unsweetened cocoa
     2 cups chopped nuts*

GLAZE

     ¾ cup powdered sugar
     ¼ cup unsweetened cocoa
    1½ to 2 tablespoons milk

Heat oven to 350°F. Grease and flour 12-cup fluted tube pan or 10-inch tube pan. In large bowl, beat margarine and granulated sugar until light and fluffy. Add eggs one at a time, beating well after each addition. Gradually add powdered sugar; blend well. By hand, stir in remaining cake ingredients until well blended. Spoon batter into prepared pan; spread evenly. Bake at 350°F. for 58 to 62 minutes.** Cool upright in pan on wire rack 1 hour; invert onto serving plate. Cool completely.

In small bowl, combine glaze ingredients until well blended. Spoon over top of cake, allowing some to run down sides. Store tightly covered. **16 servings.**

TIPS: *Nuts are essential for the success of the recipe.

**Since this cake has a soft tunnel of fudge, ordinary doneness tests cannot be used. Accurate oven temperature and bake time are essential.

HIGH ALTITUDE: Increase flour to 2¼ cups plus 3 tablespoons.

NUTRIENTS PER ¹⁄₁₆ OF RECIPE

Calories	540	Dietary Fiber	2 g
Protein	8 g	Sodium	300 mg
Carbohydrate	58 g	Potassium	160 mg
Fat	33 g	Calcium	4% U.S. RDA
Cholesterol	100 mg	Iron	10% U.S. RDA

Chocolate Praline Layer Cake

CAKE

- ½ cup butter or margarine
- ¼ cup whipping cream
- 1 cup firmly packed brown sugar
- ¾ cup coarsely chopped pecans
- 1 pkg. pudding-included devil's food cake mix
- 1¼ cups water
- ⅓ cup oil
- 3 eggs

TOPPING

- 1¾ cups whipping cream
- ¼ cup powdered sugar
- ¼ teaspoon vanilla

Whole pecans, if desired
Chocolate curls, if desired

Heat oven to 325°F. In small heavy saucepan, combine butter, ¼ cup whipping cream and brown sugar. Cook over low heat just until butter is melted, stirring occasionally. Pour into two 9 or 8-inch round cake pans; sprinkle evenly with chopped pecans. In large bowl, combine cake mix, water, oil and eggs at low speed until moistened; beat 2 minutes at highest speed. Carefully spoon batter over pecan mixture. Bake at 325°F. for 35 to 45 minutes or until cake springs back when touched lightly in center. Cool 5 minutes. Remove from pans. Cool completely.

In small bowl, beat 1¾ cups whipping cream until soft peaks form. Blend in powdered sugar and vanilla; beat until stiff peaks form. To assemble cake, place 1 layer on serving plate, praline side up. Spread with ½ of whipped cream. Top with second layer, praline side up; spread top with remaining whipped cream. Garnish with whole pecans and chocolate curls, if desired. Store in refrigerator. **12 servings.**

HIGH ALTITUDE: Add 2 tablespoons flour to dry cake mix. Increase water to 1⅓ cups. Bake at 350°F. for 30 to 35 minutes. Immediately remove from pans.

NUTRIENTS PER ¹⁄₁₂ OF RECIPE

Calories	610	Dietary Fiber	1 g
Protein	5 g	Sodium	470 mg
Carbohydrate	56 g	Potassium	230 mg
Fat	41 g	Calcium	15% U.S. RDA
Cholesterol	140 mg	Iron	10% U.S. RDA

Double Chocolate
Cream Cheese Cake

CAKE

   3 cups all purpose flour
   2 cups sugar

½ cup unsweetened cocoa
2 teaspoons baking soda
½ teaspoon salt
2 cups hot coffee
⅔ cup oil
2 tablespoons vinegar
2 teaspoons vanilla
2 eggs

FILLING

⅓ cup sugar
8-oz. pkg. cream cheese, softened
½ teaspoon vanilla
1 egg
6-oz. pkg. (1 cup) semi-sweet chocolate chips
1 cup finely chopped nuts
¼ cup sugar

Heat oven to 350°F. Grease and flour bottom only of 13x9-inch pan. In large bowl, combine all cake ingredients at low speed until moistened; beat 1 minute at medium speed (batter will be thin). Pour batter into prepared pan. In small bowl, beat ⅓ cup sugar, cream cheese, ½ teaspoon vanilla and 1 egg until fluffy; stir in chocolate chips and nuts. Spoon teaspoonfuls of filling evenly over batter; sprinkle with ¼ cup sugar. Bake at 350°F. for 45 to 60 minutes or until toothpick inserted in center comes out clean. Cool completely. Store in refrigerator. **16 servings.**

HIGH ALTITUDE: Decrease baking soda to 1½ teaspoons. Bake at 375°F. for 60 to 70 minutes.

NUTRIENTS PER ¹⁄₁₆ OF RECIPE

Calories	490	Dietary Fiber	2 g
Protein	7 g	Sodium	250 mg
Carbohydrate	59 g	Potassium	165 mg
Fat	25 g	Calcium	2% U.S. RDA
Cholesterol	70 mg	Iron	10% U.S. RDA

Banana Snack Cake

    1 cup sugar
    1 cup margarine or butter, softened
    2 eggs
    ½ cup buttermilk
    1 cup (2 medium) mashed bananas
    1 teaspoon vanilla
    2 cups all purpose flour
    1 cup quick-cooking rolled oats
 1½ teaspoons baking soda
    ½ teaspoon salt
 6-oz. pkg (1 cup) semi-sweet chocolate chips
    ½ cup chopped nuts

Heat oven to 350°F. Grease 13x9-inch pan. In large bowl, combine sugar, margarine and eggs; mix well. Stir in buttermilk, bananas and vanilla; blend thoroughly. Stir in flour, oats, baking soda and salt; mix well. Stir in chocolate chips. Spread batter in prepared pan. Sprinkle nuts evenly over top. Bake at 350°F. for 30 to 35 minutes or until toothpick inserted in center comes out clean. **16 servings.**

NUTRIENTS PER ¹⁄₁₆ OF RECIPE

Calories	340	Dietary Fiber	2 g
Protein	5 g	Sodium	370 mg
Carbohydrate	38 g	Potassium	170 mg
Fat	19 g	Calcium	6% U.S. RDA
Cholesterol	35 mg	Iron	10% U.S. RDA

Anytime Oatmeal Cake

 1½ cups quick-cooking rolled oats
 1¼ cups boiling water
    1 cup sugar
    1 cup firmly packed brown sugar
    ½ cup margarine or butter, softened
    1 teaspoon vanilla

>   3 eggs
> 1½ cups all purpose flour
>   1 teaspoon baking soda
>   ½ teaspoon baking powder
>   ½ teaspoon salt
> 1½ teaspoons cinnamon
>   ½ teaspoon nutmeg
>   Broiled Coconut Topping (see Index)

Heat oven to 350°F. Grease and flour 13x9-inch pan. In small bowl, combine rolled oats and boiling water; let stand 20 minutes. In large bowl, beat sugar, brown sugar and margarine until well combined. Add vanilla and eggs; blend well. Add oatmeal, flour, baking soda, baking powder, salt, cinnamon and nutmeg; mix until well combined. Pour batter into prepared pan. Bake at 350°F. for 35 to 45 minutes or until toothpick inserted in center comes out clean. Top with Broiled Coconut Topping. **16 servings.**

HIGH ALTITUDE: Decrease brown sugar to ¾ cup; increase flour to 1½ cups plus 3 tablespoons. Bake at 375°F. for 30 to 40 minutes.

NUTRIENTS PER ¹⁄₁₆ OF RECIPE WITH TOPPING

Calories	360	Dietary Fiber	3 g
Protein	4 g	Sodium	270 mg
Carbohydrate	52 g	Potassium	170 mg
Fat	15 g	Calcium	4 % U.S. RDA
Cholesterol	60 mg	Iron	10% U.S. RDA

Orange Carrot Cake

>   3 cups all purpose flour
>   2 cups sugar
>   1 cup coconut
> 2½ teaspoons baking soda
>   1 teaspoon salt
> 2½ teaspoons cinnamon

    2   cups (4 medium) shredded carrots
 1¼   cups oil
    2   teaspoons vanilla
    1   teaspoon grated orange peel
    3   eggs
11-oz. can mandarin orange segments, undrained
        Cream Cheese Frosting (see Index)

Heat oven to 350°F. Grease 13x9-inch pan. In large bowl, combine all ingredients except frosting at low speed until moistened; beat 2 minutes at highest speed. Pour batter into prepared pan. Bake at 350°F. for 45 to 55 minutes or until toothpick inserted in center comes out clean. Cool completely. If desired, frost with Cream Cheese Frosting. **16 servings.**

HIGH ALTITUDE: Decrease baking soda to 2 teaspoons. Bake at 350°F. for 40 to 45 minutes.

NUTRIENTS PER ¹⁄₁₆ OF RECIPE WITH FROSTING

Calories	530	Dietary Fiber	2 g
Protein	5 g	Sodium	390 mg
Carbohydrate	68 g	Potassium	150 mg
Fat	27 g	Calcium	2% U.S. RDA
Cholesterol	70 mg	Iron	10% U.S. RDA

Gingerbread

 1⅓   cups all purpose flour*
  ¾   teaspoon cinnamon
  ¾   teaspoon ginger
  ½   teaspoon baking powder
  ½   teaspoon baking soda
  ½   teaspoon allspice
  ¼   teaspoon salt
  ½   cup firmly packed brown sugar
  ½   cup shortening or margarine
  ½   cup boiling water
  ½   cup molasses
   1   egg, slightly beaten

Heat oven to 350°F. Grease bottom only of 9 or 8-inch square pan.** In large bowl, combine first 7 ingredients. Add remaining ingredients; blend well. Pour batter into prepared pan. Bake at 350°F. for 25 to 35 minutes or until toothpick inserted in center comes out clean. Serve slightly warm with whipped cream, whipped cream cheese, lemon sauce or applesauce, if desired. **9 servings.**

MICROWAVE DIRECTIONS: Prepare batter as directed above. Pour into ungreased 8-inch round microwave-safe dish. Microwave on HIGH for 6 to 7½ minutes or until toothpick inserted in center comes out clean. Cool directly on counter 10 minutes.

TIPS: *If desired, ⅔ cup whole wheat flour and ½ cup all purpose flour can be used.

**If desired, 11x7-inch pan or 12 muffin cups lined with paper baking cups can be substituted. Bake at 350°F. for 25 to 30 minutes.

HIGH ALTITUDE: Decrease baking powder to ¼ teaspoon. Bake at 375°F. for about 30 minutes.

NUTRIENTS PER ⅑ OF RECIPE

Calories 260	Dietary Fiber............................1 g
Protein.......................................3 g	Sodium.............................150 mg
Carbohydrate.........................37 g	Potassium.........................260 mg
Fat ....12 g	Calcium................8% U.S. RDA
Cholesterol..........................30 mg	Iron.....................15% U.S. RDA

Dixie Spice Cake

2¼ cups all purpose flour
1¼ cups firmly packed brown sugar
½ cup sugar
1 teaspoon baking soda
½ teaspoon salt
½ teaspoon nutmeg
½ teaspoon allspice

    1   cup buttermilk*
    ⅔   cup shortening
    1   teaspoon vanilla
    3   eggs
    1   cup chopped walnuts or pecans
        Caramel Frosting (see Index)

Heat oven to 350°F. Generously grease and flour bottom
only of 13x9-inch pan.** In large bowl, combine all ingredients except nuts at low speed until moistened; beat 3 minutes at medium speed. Stir in nuts. Pour batter into prepared
pan. Bake at 350°F. for 40 to 45 minutes or until cake
springs back when touched lightly in center. Cool completely. Frost. **12 servings.**

TIPS: *To substitute for buttermilk, use 1 tablespoon vinegar or lemon juice plus milk to make 1 cup.

**For cupcakes, fill 24 to 30 paper-lined muffin cups ⅔ full.
Bake at 350°F. for 20 to 25 minutes.

HIGH ALTITUDE: Increase flour to 2¼ cups plus 3 tablespoons. Decrease brown sugar to 1 cup. Bake at 375°F. for
35 to 40 minutes.

NUTRIENTS PER ½ OF RECIPE WITH FROSTING

Calories	640	Dietary Fiber	2 g
Protein	6 g	Sodium	320 mg
Carbohydrate	94 g	Potassium	270 mg
Fat	27 g	Calcium	8% U.S. RDA
Cholesterol	70 mg	Iron	15% U.S. RDA

Swiss Almond Apple Cake

CAKE
    ⅔   cup sugar
    ½   cup butter or margarine, softened
    2   eggs
    2   tablespoons lemon juice

2   cups all purpose flour
2   teaspoons baking powder
¼   teaspoon salt
¼   cup red raspberry preserves
4   (3½ cups) apples, peeled, thinly sliced

TOPPING
1   cup ground almonds
½   cup sugar
½   cup dairy sour cream
2   eggs, beaten
2   tablespoons flour
1   teaspoon grated lemon peel

GLAZE
¼   cup powdered sugar
1 to 2   teaspoons lemon juice

Heat oven to 350°F. Grease and flour 9 or 10-inch spring-form pan. In large bowl, combine ⅔ cup sugar and butter; beat until light and fluffy. Add 2 eggs and 2 tablespoons lemon juice; beat until well blended. In small bowl, combine 2 cups flour, baking powder and salt; blend well. Add to egg mixture; beat at low speed until well blended. Spread in prepared pan. Spoon preserves over batter; carefully spread to cover. Top with apple slices; slightly press into batter. In medium bowl, combine all topping ingredients; blend well. Pour over apples.

Bake at 350°F. for 55 to 65 minutes or until apples are tender, edges are light golden brown and toothpick inserted in center comes out clean. Cool 10 minutes. Carefully remove sides of pan. In small bowl, blend all glaze ingredients until smooth; drizzle over cake. Serve warm or cool. **16 servings.**

NUTRIENTS PER ¹⁄₁₆ OF RECIPE

Calories	280	Dietary Fiber	2 g
Protein	5 g	Sodium	150 mg
Carbohydrate	39 g	Potassium	125 mg
Fat	12 g	Calcium	6% U.S. RDA
Cholesterol	90 mg	Iron	6% U.S. RDA

Nutty Graham Picnic Cake

CAKE

- 2 cups all purpose flour
- 1 cup (14 squares) graham cracker crumbs
- 1 cup firmly packed brown sugar
- ½ cup sugar
- 1 teaspoon salt
- 1 teaspoon baking powder
- 1 teaspoon baking soda
- ½ teaspoon cinnamon
- 1 cup margarine or butter, softened
- 1 cup orange juice
- 1 tablespoon grated orange peel
- 3 eggs
- 1 cup chopped nuts

GLAZE

- 2 tablespoons brown sugar
- 5 teaspoons milk
- 1 tablespoon margarine or butter
- ¾ cup powdered sugar
- ¼ cup chopped nuts

Heat oven to 350°F. Generously grease and flour 12-cup fluted tube pan or 10-inch tube pan. In large bowl, combine all cake ingredients except nuts at low speed until moistened; beat 3 minutes at medium speed. Stir in 1 cup nuts. Pour into prepared pan. Bake at 350°F. for 40 to 60 minutes or until toothpick inserted in center comes out clean. Cool upright in pan 15 minutes; invert onto serving plate. Cool completely.

In small saucepan, heat 2 tablespoons brown sugar, milk and 1 tablespoon margarine just until melted. Remove from heat; add powdered sugar and blend until smooth. Drizzle over cake; sprinkle with ¼ cup nuts. **12 to 16 servings.**

HIGH ALTITUDE: Bake at 350°F. for 50 to 55 minutes.

NUTRIENTS PER ¹⁄₁₆ OF RECIPE

Calories	370	Dietary Fiber	2 g
Protein	5 g	Sodium	420 mg
Carbohydrate	44 g	Potassium	180 mg
Fat	20 g	Calcium	4% U.S. RDA
Cholesterol	50 mg	Iron	10% U.S. RDA

Lots o' Apple Cake

1⅓ cups all purpose flour
1 cup whole wheat flour
1¼ cups sugar
2 teaspoons baking soda
1 teaspoon salt
1 teaspoon cinnamon
5 cups (5 medium) thinly sliced, peeled apples
½ cup oil
¼ cup honey
1 teaspoon vanilla
2 eggs
½ cup chopped nuts

Heat oven to 350°F. Grease and flour bottom only of 13x9-inch pan. In large bowl, combine all ingredients except nuts at low speed until moistened; beat 2 minutes at medium speed. Stir in nuts. Spread batter in prepared pan. Bake at 350°F. for 40 to 50 minutes or until toothpick inserted in center comes out clean. Serve warm or cool with whipped cream, ice cream, butter sauce or caramel sauce, if desired. **12 servings.**

HIGH ALTITUDE: Increase all purpose flour to 1⅓ cups plus 2 tablespoons. Bake as directed.

NUTRIENTS PER ½ OF RECIPE

Calories	350	Dietary Fiber	3 g
Protein	5 g	Sodium	375 mg
Carbohydrate	53 g	Potassium	145 mg
Fat	14 g	Calcium	2% U.S. RDA
Cholesterol	45 mg	Iron	6% U.S. RDA

Lemon Meringue Cake

CAKE

1 pkg. pudding-included lemon or yellow cake mix
1 cup water
⅓ cup oil
3 eggs

LEMON FILLING

1 cup sugar
3 tablespoons cornstarch
¼ teaspoon salt
½ cup water
¼ cup lemon juice
4 teaspoons margarine or butter
1 teaspoon grated lemon peel
4 egg yolks

MERINGUE

4 egg whites
¼ teaspoon cream of tartar
¾ cup sugar

Heat oven to 350°F. Grease and flour two 8 or 9-inch round cake pans. In large bowl, combine all cake ingredients at low speed until moistened; beat 2 minutes at highest speed. Pour batter into prepared pans. Bake at 350°F. for 25 to 35 minutes or until cake springs back when touched lightly in center. Cool 15 minutes; remove from pans. Cool completely.

Meanwhile, in medium-size heavy saucepan combine 1 cup sugar, cornstarch and salt. Gradually stir in water, lemon juice, margarine and lemon peel. Cook over medium heat until mixture boils and thickens, stirring constantly; remove from heat. In small bowl, beat egg yolks slightly; gradually blend about ¼ of hot lemon mixture into egg yolks. Return egg yolk mixture to saucepan; cook 2 to 3 minutes, stirring constantly. Cool.

Heat oven to 450°F. In large bowl, beat egg whites and cream of tartar until foamy. Gradually add ¾ cup sugar, beating until stiff peaks form. To assemble cake, split each layer in half horizontally to form 4 layers. Place 1 layer on ovenproof serving plate; spread with ⅓ of filling. Repeat with remaining layers and filling. Spread meringue over sides and top of cake. Bake frosted cake at 450°F. for 4 to 5 minutes or until meringue is light golden brown. Cool completely. Store in refrigerator. **12 servings.**

HIGH ALTITUDE: Add 3 tablespoons flour to dry cake mix. Bake at 375°F. for 25 to 35 minutes.

NUTRIENTS PER ¹⁄₁₂ OF RECIPE

Calories	410	Dietary Fiber	1 g
Protein	5 g	Sodium	370 mg
Carbohydrate	66 g	Potassium	60 mg
Fat	14 g	Calcium	4% U.S. RDA
Cholesterol	160 mg	Iron	8% U.S. RDA

Pineapple Upside Down Cake

- ½ cup firmly packed brown sugar
- ¼ cup margarine or butter, melted
- 6 canned pineapple slices, drained
- 6 maraschino cherries
- 2 eggs, separated

½ cup sugar
¾ cup all purpose flour
½ teaspoon baking powder
¼ teaspoon salt
¼ cup pineapple juice
  Whipped cream

Heat oven to 350°F. In small bowl, combine brown sugar and margarine; blend well. Spread in bottom of 9-inch round cake pan. Arrange pineapple slices and maraschino cherries over brown sugar mixture. Set aside.

In small bowl, beat egg yolks until thick and lemon colored. Gradually add sugar; beat well. Add flour, baking powder, salt and pineapple juice to egg yolk mixture; mix well. In another small bowl, beat egg whites until stiff peaks form; fold into batter. Pour batter into prepared pan, covering pineapple slices and cherries.

Bake at 350°F. for 30 to 35 minutes or until toothpick inserted in center comes out clean. Cool upright in pan 2 minutes; invert onto serving plate. Serve warm with whipped cream. **6 servings.**

HIGH ALTITUDE: Increase flour to ¾ cup plus 3 tablespoons. Bake at 375°F. for 30 to 35 minutes.

NUTRIENTS PER ¼ OF RECIPE

Calories 350	Dietary Fiber ....1 g
Protein ....4 g	Sodium ....230 mg
Carbohydrate ....54 g	Potassium ....200 mg
Fat ....13 g	Calcium ....6% U.S. RDA
Cholesterol ....100 mg	Iron ....10% U.S. RDA

Sour Cream Pound Cake

2¾ cups sugar
1½ cups butter or margarine, softened
1 teaspoon vanilla

6 eggs
3 cups all purpose flour
½ teaspoon baking powder
½ teaspoon salt
1 teaspoon grated orange or lemon peel
1 cup dairy sour cream

Heat oven to 350°F. Generously grease and lightly flour 12-cup fluted tube pan. In large bowl, cream together sugar and butter until light and fluffy. Add vanilla and eggs, one at a time, beating until well blended after each addition. Combine flour, baking powder, salt and orange peel; add alternately with sour cream, beating well after each addition. Pour batter into prepared pan.

Bake at 350°F. for 55 to 65 minutes or until toothpick inserted in center comes out clean. Cool 15 minutes; invert onto serving plate. Cool completely. **16 servings.**

HIGH ALTITUDE: Decrease sugar to 2½ cups. Bake at 375°F. for 55 to 65 minutes.

NUTRIENTS PER ¹⁄₁₆ OF RECIPE

Calories 440	Dietary Fiber..........................1 g
Protein.....................................5 g	Sodium............................290 mg
Carbohydrate........................53 g	Potassium...........................75 mg
Fat ....23 g	Calcium................4% U.S. RDA
Cholesterol.......................160 mg	Iron.......................8% U.S. RDA

Lemon Delight Pound Cake

CAKE

2½ cups all purpose flour
1½ cups sugar
3 teaspoons baking powder
½ teaspoon salt
¾ cup apricot nectar or orange juice
¾ cup cooking oil
2 teaspoons lemon extract
4 eggs

GLAZE
  1½ cups powdered sugar
  ½ cup lemon juice

Heat oven to 325°F. Generously grease and flour 12-cup fluted tube pan. In large bowl, combine cake ingredients. Blend on low speed until ingredients are moistened; beat 3 minutes at medium speed. Pour into prepared pan.

Bake at 325°F. for 40 to 50 minutes or until toothpick inserted in center comes out clean. Remove cake from oven. Prick deeply every inch with fork. In small bowl, blend glaze ingredients until smooth. Spoon half of glaze over hot cake in pan. Let stand 10 minutes; invert onto serving plate. Spoon remaining glaze over cake. **16 servings.**

HIGH ALTITUDE: Reduce baking powder to 2½ teaspoons. Bake at 350°F. for 40 to 50 minutes.

NUTRIENTS PER ⅟₁₆ OF RECIPE

Calories	300	Dietary Fiber	1 g
Protein	4 g	Sodium	140 mg
Carbohydrate	45 g	Potassium	60 mg
Fat	12 g	Calcium	4% U.S. RDA
Cholesterol	70 mg	Iron	6% U.S. RDA

Foam Cakes

Hints for Foam Cakes

• Foam cakes depend on several factors for their texture and distinctive appearance—proper beating of egg whites (at room temperature) for full volume, folding of ingredients according to recipe, baking in an ungreased tube pan at the correct oven temperature and inverting the pan immediately after baking. Cool completely before removing from pan. To remove from pan, run a thin-bladed knife in an up-and-down motion between pan and cake sides. Invert onto serving plate.

How to Prepare Foam Cakes

For best volume, start with egg whites at room temperature. Make sure no yolk is present in egg whites and utensils are grease-free. Beat egg whites until stiff peaks form. Egg whites will form sharp straight peaks when beaters are removed.

To fold, using rubber spatula, insert edge vertically down through center of beaten egg whites. Slide spatula across bottom of bowl, bring up side with some of the mixture, then fold gently over top; rotate bowl ¼ turn. Repeat just until well blended. Do not overfold.

To prevent cake from collapsing, immediately invert hot cake onto funnel or bottle to cool.

Angel Food Cake

 ¾ cup all purpose flour
 ¾ cup sugar
1½ cups (about 12) egg whites, room temperature
1½ teaspoons cream of tartar
 ¼ teaspoon salt
1½ teaspoons vanilla
 ½ teaspoon almond extract
 ¾ cup sugar

Heat oven to 375°F. In small bowl, combine flour with ¾ cup sugar. In large bowl, beat egg whites with cream of tartar, salt, vanilla and almond extract until mixture forms soft peaks. Add ¾ cup sugar, 2 tablespoons at a time, beating at highest speed until stiff peaks form. Spoon flour-sugar mixture ¼ cup at a time over beaten egg whites; fold in gently *just* until blended. Pour batter into ungreased 10-inch tube pan. With knife, cut gently through batter to remove large air bubbles.

Bake at 375°F. on lowest oven rack for 30 to 40 minutes or until crust is golden brown and cracks are very dry. Immediately invert pan onto funnel or soft drink bottle; let hang until completely cool. Remove cooled cake from pan. If desired, drizzle with glaze or serve topped with fresh fruit. **12 servings.**

TIP: To make loaves, bake in 2 ungreased 9x5-inch loaf pans for 25 to 30 minutes.

HIGH ALTITUDE: Increase flour to 1 cup; increase egg whites to 1¾ cups (about 13). Bake at 400°F. for 30 to 35 minutes.

VARIATION:

CHOCOLATE-CHERRY ANGEL CAKE: Fold ½ cup well-drained, chopped maraschino cherries and 2 squares grated semi-sweet chocolate into batter.

NUTRIENTS PER ¹⁄₁₂ OF RECIPE WITHOUT GLAZE

Calories	140	Dietary Fiber	<1g
Protein	4 g	Sodium	90 mg
Carbohydrate	31 g	Potassium	55 mg
Fat	0 g	Calcium	<2% U.S. RDA
Cholesterol	0 mg	Iron	2% U.S. RDA

Sponge Cake

    6 eggs, separated
    ¾ teaspoon cream of tartar
 1½ cups sugar
 1½ cups all purpose flour
    1 tablespoon grated orange peel
    1 teaspoon baking powder
    ½ teaspoon salt
    ½ cup apricot nectar or water
    1 teaspoon rum extract or vanilla

Heat oven to 350°F. Separate eggs, placing whites in large bowl and yolks in small bowl. Add cream of tartar to egg whites; beat until mixture forms soft peaks. *Gradually* add ¾ cup of the sugar, 2 tablespoons at a time, beating at highest speed until stiff peaks form. To egg yolks, add flour, remaining ¾ cup sugar, orange peel, baking powder, salt, apricot nectar and rum extract. Blend at low speed until moistened; beat 1 minute at medium speed. Pour over egg whites; fold in gently *just* until blended. Pour batter into ungreased 10-inch tube pan. Bake at 350°F. for 35 to 45 minutes or until cake springs back when touched lightly. Invert pan on funnel or soft drink bottle; let hang until completely cool. Remove cooled cake from pan. If desired, serve with fruit, sherbet or whipped cream, or split cake horizontally into 3 layers and fill with Lemon Filling and frost with Seven-Minute Frosting (see Index). **12 servings.**

HIGH ALTITUDE: Decrease sugar to 1¼ cups (using ½ cup plus 2 tablespoons for first addition). Bake at 375°F. for 35 to 45 minutes.

NUTRIENTS PER ¹⁄₁₂ OF RECIPE WITHOUT FILLING OR FROSTING

Calories	200	Dietary Fiber	1 g
Protein	5 g	Sodium	150 mg
Carbohydrate	39 g	Potassium	60 mg
Fat	3 g	Calcium	2% U.S. RDA
Cholesterol	140 mg	Iron	6% U.S. RDA

Choffee Chiffon Cake

CAKE

   7 eggs, separated
   1 teaspoon cream of tartar
  ½ teaspoon salt
   1 cup sugar
   1 tablespoon instant coffee granules or crystals
  ⅓ cup water
   1 cup all purpose flour

2 oz. (2 squares) semi-sweet chocolate, grated
2 teaspoons vanilla

FROSTING

2 cups whipping cream
2 oz. (2 squares) semi-sweet chocolate, grated
⅓ cup powdered sugar
1½ teaspoons instant coffee granules or crystals
1 teaspoon vanilla

Heat oven to 325°F. In large bowl, beat egg whites, cream of tartar and salt until mixture forms soft peaks. Gradually add ½ cup of the sugar, beating until *very stiff peaks* form. In small bowl, beat egg yolks until very thick and lemon colored. Gradually add remaining ½ cup sugar, beating until thick. Dissolve 1 tablespoon instant coffee in water. Blend coffee mixture, flour, 2 oz. grated chocolate and 2 teaspoons vanilla into egg yolk mixture. Beat 1 minute at low speed or just until blended. Fold egg yolk mixture into egg whites. Pour into ungreased 10-inch tube pan. Bake at 325°F. for 50 to 60 minutes or until cake springs back when touched lightly in center. Invert cake on funnel or soft drink bottle; let hang until completely cool. Remove cooled cake from pan.

In large bowl, beat whipping cream until slightly thickened. Reserve 1 tablespoon grated chocolate for top. Add remaining grated chocolate, powdered sugar, 1½ teaspoons instant coffee and 1 teaspoon vanilla to cream; beat until stiff peaks form (do not overbeat). Slice cake into 2 layers. Fill and frost sides and top of cake; sprinkle reserved 1 tablespoon grated chocolate over top. Store in refrigerator. **20 servings.**

HIGH ALTITUDE: Increase flour to 1 cup plus 3 tablespoons. Bake at 350°F. for 45 to 55 minutes.

NUTRIENTS PER ¹⁄₂₀ OF RECIPE

Calories	220	Dietary Fiber	<1 g
Protein	4 g	Sodium	85 mg
Carbohydrate	19 g	Potassium	100 mg
Fat	14 g	Calcium	2% U.S. RDA
Cholesterol	130 mg	Iron	4% U.S. RDA

Jelly Roll

    4 eggs
  ¾ cup sugar
  ¼ cup cold water
    1 teaspoon vanilla
    1 cup all purpose flour
    1 teaspoon baking powder
  ¼ teaspoon salt
       Powdered sugar

Heat oven to 375°F. Generously grease and lightly flour
15x10-inch jelly roll pan. In large bowl, beat eggs at highest
speed until thick and lemon-colored, about 5 minutes.
Gradually add sugar, beating until light and fluffy. Stir in
water and vanilla. Add flour, baking powder and salt; blend
at low speed *just* until dry ingredients are moistened. Pour
batter into prepared pan; spread evenly. Bake at 375°F. for 8
to 12 minutes or until cake springs back when touched
lightly in center. Loosen edges; immediately turn onto towel
dusted with powdered sugar. Starting at narrow end, roll up
cake in towel; place on rack to cool completely. When cake
is cooled, unroll; remove towel. Spread cake with desired
filling; roll up again, rolling loosely to incorporate filling.
Wrap in foil or waxed paper; refrigerate. If desired, sprinkle
with powdered sugar to serve. **8 to 10 servings.**

TIP: For filling, spread cake with ¾ cup raspberry preserves or favorite jelly before rolling up. Or fill with Lemon
Filling or Coconut Cream Filling (see Index).

NUTRIENTS PER ¹⁄₁₀ OF RECIPE WITHOUT FILLING

Calories	140	Dietary Fiber	1 g
Protein	4 g	Sodium	110 mg
Carbohydrate	25 g	Potassium	40 mg
Fat	2 g	Calcium	2% U.S. RDA
Cholesterol	110 mg	Iron	4% U.S. RDA

Black Bottom Cups

    2 (3-oz.) pkg. cream cheese, softened
   ⅓ cup sugar
    1 egg
6-oz. pkg. (1 cup) chocolate chips
  1½ cups all purpose flour
    1 cup sugar
   ¼ cup unsweetened cocoa
    1 teaspoon baking soda
   ½ teaspoon salt
    1 cup water
   ⅓ cup oil
    1 tablespoon vinegar
    1 teaspoon vanilla
    2 tablespoons sugar
   ½ cup chopped nuts

Heat oven to 350°F. Line 18 medium muffin cups with paper baking cups. In small bowl, combine cream cheese, ⅓ cup sugar and egg; mix well. Stir in chocolate chips; set aside. In large bowl, combine flour, 1 cup sugar, cocoa, baking soda and salt. Add water, oil, vinegar and vanilla; beat 2 minutes at medium speed. Fill prepared muffin cups half full; top each with tablespoonful of cream cheese mixture. Sprinkle with 2 tablespoons sugar and nuts. Bake at 350°F. for 20 to 30 minutes or until cream cheese mixture is light golden brown. Cool 15 minutes; remove from pans. Cool completely. Refrigerate leftovers. **18 cupcakes.**

NUTRIENTS PER 1 CUPCAKE

Calories	250	Dietary Fiber	1 g
Protein	3 g	Sodium	145 mg
Carbohydrate	31 g	Potassium	85 mg
Fat	14 g	Calcium	<2% U.S. RDA
Cholesterol	25 mg	Iron	4% U.S. RDA

Peanut Butter Cups

- 1¾ cups all purpose flour
- 1¼ cups firmly packed brown sugar
- 3 teaspoons baking powder
- 1 teaspoon salt
- 1 cup milk
- ⅓ cup shortening
- ⅓ cup peanut butter
- 1 teaspoon vanilla
- 2 eggs
- 24 miniature milk chocolate-covered peanut butter cups

Heat oven to 350°F. Line 24 muffin cups with paper baking cups. In large bowl, combine all ingredients except peanut butter cups at low speed until moistened; beat 2 minutes at medium speed. Fill prepared muffin cups ⅔ full. Press a peanut butter cup into batter until top edge is even with batter. Bake at 350°F. for 18 to 28 minutes or until cupcakes spring back when touched lightly. **24 cupcakes.**

NUTRIENTS PER 1 CUPCAKE

Calories	170	Dietary Fiber	1 g
Protein	4 g	Sodium	185 mg
Carbohydrate	23 g	Potassium	120 mg
Fat	7 g	Calcium	4% U.S. RDA
Cholesterol	25 mg	Iron	4% U.S. RDA

Sweet Fruitcake

2	eggs
2	cups water
2	pkg. date or nut bread mix
2	cups pecans (halves or chopped)
2	cups raisins
12 to 13	oz. (2 cups) candied cherries*
1	cup cut-up candied pineapple*
	Corn syrup, if desired

Heat oven to 350°F. Grease and flour bottom and sides of 12-cup fluted tube or 10-inch tube pan.** In large bowl, combine eggs and water. Add remaining ingredients except corn syrup; stir by hand until combined. Pour into prepared pan. Bake at 350°F. for 75 to 85 minutes or until toothpick inserted in center comes out clean. Cool in pan 30 minutes; loosen edges and remove from pan. Cool completely. Wrap in plastic wrap or foil and store in refrigerator. Glaze with warm corn syrup before serving. Decorate with additional candied fruits and nuts, if desired. **24 to 36 servings.**

TIP: *If desired, substitute 2 lb. (4 cups) mixed candied fruit for candied cherries and pineapple.

HIGH ALTITUDE: Add 2 tablespoons flour to dry bread mix. For 12-cup fluted tube or 10-inch tube pan, bake at 375°F. for 60 to 70 minutes.

VARIATIONS:

**If desired, recipe can be baked in the following pans:

MUFFIN CUPS: Line cups with paper baking cups; fill ⅔ full. Bake 20 to 25 minutes. **About 3½ dozen.**

TWO (6 TO 8-CUP) RING MOLDS: Grease and flour molds. Bake 40 to 50 minutes. **2 rings.**

FLUTED MUFFIN CUPS: Grease and flour cups; fill ⅔ full. Bake 15 to 20 minutes. **About 3½ dozen.**

TWO (8x4 or 9x5-INCH) LOAF PANS: Grease and flour bottom and sides of pans. Bake 65 to 75 minutes. **2 loaves.**

NUTRIENTS PER ⅓₆ OF RECIPE

Calories 240	Dietary Fiber...........................2 g
Protein......................................3 g	Sodium.............................100 mg
Carbohydrate..........................41 g	Potassium.........................210 mg
Fat ....7 g	Calcium.................2% U.S. RDA
Cholesterol.........................15 mg	Iron......................6% U.S. RDA

Delicious White Fruitcake

1¾ cups all purpose flour
1 cup sugar
½ teaspoon salt
½ teaspoon baking powder
1½ cups margarine or butter, softened
1 tablespoon vanilla
1 tablespoon lemon extract
5 eggs
1 lb. (4 cups) pecan halves
1 lb. (2 cups) cut-up candied pineapple
¾ lb. (1½ cups) candied cherries, whole or cut up

Heat oven to 300°F. Generously grease and lightly flour two 8x4-inch loaf pans. In large bowl, blend all ingredients except nuts and fruits at low speed until moistened; beat 2 minutes at medium speed. Stir in nuts and fruits. Spoon batter into prepared pans. Bake at 300°F. for 1¼ to 2 hours or until toothpick inserted in center comes out clean. Cool; remove from pans. Wrap tightly in plastic wrap or foil; store in refrigerator up to 6 months. **2 loaves; 20 slices each.**

TIP: Fruitcake can be wrapped in cheesecloth that has been soaked in brandy or fruit juice. Overwrap with foil. Store in refrigerator. Moisten cloth every 2 weeks.

NUTRIENTS PER 1 SLICE

Calories	260	Dietary Fiber	1 g
Protein	3 g	Sodium	125 mg
Carbohydrate	28 g	Potassium	85 mg
Fat	16 g	Calcium	<2% U.S. RDA
Cholesterol	35 mg	Iron	2% U.S. RDA

French Walnut Torte

CAKE

1½ cups sugar
1 tablespoon vanilla
3 eggs
1¾ cups all purpose flour
2 teaspoons baking powder
½ teaspoon salt
1 cup ground walnuts
1½ cups whipping cream, whipped

GLAZE

½ cup apricot or peach preserves
1 tablespoon sugar

FROSTING

2 cups powdered sugar
½ cup margarine or butter, softened
½ teaspoon vanilla
3-oz. pkg. cream cheese, softened
½ cup ground walnuts

Heat oven to 350°F. Grease and flour two 9-inch round cake pans. In large bowl, beat 1½ cups sugar, 1 tablespoon vanilla and eggs 5 minutes at highest speed. Combine flour, baking powder and salt; stir in 1 cup ground walnuts. Add flour mixture and whipped cream alternately to sugar mixture, beginning and ending with flour mixture. Pour into prepared pans. Bake at 350°F. for 25 to 30 minutes or until cake springs back when touched lightly in center. Cool 15 minutes; remove from pans.

In small saucepan, combine preserves and 1 tablespoon sugar; heat until warm and sugar dissolves, stirring occasionally. Reserve ¼ cup glaze. Spread remaining glaze over top of warm layers. Refrigerate glazed layers and reserved glaze for 30 minutes.

In medium bowl, beat all frosting ingredients except ½ cup ground walnuts 2 minutes at medium speed. Using half of frosting, frost top only of 1 glazed layer. Place other layer over frosting; spread remaining frosting over top. (Do not frost sides.) Sprinkle with ½ cup ground walnuts. Refrigerate 30 minutes. Spread reserved ¼ cup glaze on sides of cake; if desired, press an additional ½ cup ground walnuts into glaze. Refrigerate at least 1 hour or until served. **16 servings.**

HIGH ALTITUDE: Decrease sugar in cake to 1⅓ cups; decrease baking powder to 1¾ teaspoons. Bake at 375°F. for 25 to 30 minutes.

NUTRIENTS PER ⅟₁₆ OF RECIPE

Calories	440	Dietary Fiber	1 g
Protein	6 g	Sodium	235 mg
Carbohydrate	52 g	Potassium	105 mg
Fat	24 g	Calcium	4% U.S. RDA
Cholesterol	90 mg	Iron	6% U.S. RDA

Almond Raspberry Torte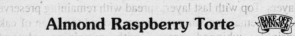

CAKE

    2 eggs, separated
    1 cup whipping cream
    1 cup sugar
  ½ teaspoon almond extract
1½ cups all purpose flour
1½ teaspoons baking powder
  ½ teaspoon salt

TOPPING
   1 cup whipping cream
   1 tablespoon powdered sugar
   1 cup red raspberry preserves
   ½ cup sliced almonds

Heat oven to 350°F. Grease and flour two 8 or 9-inch round cake pans. In small bowl, beat egg whites until soft peaks form. In a second small bowl, beat 1 cup whipping cream until soft peaks form. Fold whipped cream into beaten egg whites. In same bowl used for whipping cream, combine egg yolks, sugar and almond extract; beat 3 minutes at medium speed, scraping down sides of bowl frequently. Combine flour, baking powder and salt. Add to egg yolk mixture; blend well. (Mixture will be dry.) Fold egg white mixture thoroughly into flour mixture. Spoon thick batter into prepared pans; spread evenly.

Bake at 350°F. for 20 to 30 minutes or until toothpick inserted in center comes out clean. (Cake does not rise high.) Cool 10 minutes; remove from pans. Cool completely.

In small bowl, beat 1 cup whipping cream and powdered sugar until stiff peaks form. To assemble cake, slice each cake layer in half horizontally to make 4 layers. Place 1 layer on serving plate. Spread with ¼ cup of the raspberry preserves; sprinkle with 1 tablespoonful of the almonds. Spread with ¼ of the whipped cream. Repeat with 2 more layers. Top with last layer; spread with remaining preserves. Spoon remaining whipped cream around top edge of cake; sprinkle whipped cream with remaining almonds. Refrigerate until serving time. Store in refrigerator. **16 servings.**

HIGH ALTITUDE: Decrease sugar to 1 cup minus 2 tablespoons. Decrease baking powder to 1 teaspoon. Bake as directed above.

NUTRIENTS PER ¹⁄₁₆ OF RECIPE

Calories 280	Dietary Fiber ....1 g
Protein ....3 g	Sodium ....120 mg
Carbohydrate ....37 g	Potassium ....80 mg
Fat ....13 g	Calcium ....4% U.S. RDA
Cholesterol ....80 mg	Iron ....4% U.S. RDA

Apricot Petits Fours

CAKE

- 1 pkg. pudding-included yellow cake mix
- 1 cup apricot nectar
- ⅓ cup oil
- 1 teaspoon grated orange peel
- 3 eggs

GLAZE

- ¾ cup apricot preserves

ICING

- 6 cups powdered sugar
- ¼ cup corn syrup
- 3 tablespoons margarine or butter, melted
- 1 teaspoon vanilla
- ½ to ¾ cup apricot nectar
  Decorator icing

Heat oven to 350°F. Grease and flour 15x10-inch jelly roll pan. In large bowl, combine all cake ingredients at low speed until moistened; beat 2 minutes at highest speed. Pour batter into prepared pan. Bake at 350°F. for 18 to 22 minutes or until cake springs back when touched lightly in center.

In small saucepan, heat preserves. Press through strainer, if desired. Spread preserves over warm cake. Cool completely. To avoid cake crumbs, freeze cake 1 hour before cutting.

In large bowl, combine powdered sugar, corn syrup, margarine, vanilla and ¼ cup of the apricot nectar; blend at low speed until moistened. Continue beating, adding apricot nectar a tablespoon at a time until desired consistency.

Cut cake into diamond shapes by cutting diagonal lines 2 inches apart. Remove cake pieces from pan; set on wire rack over cookie sheet. Spoon icing evenly over top and sides of cake pieces. (Icing which drips off can be reused.) Allow icing to set 1 to 2 hours. Decorate with decorator icing, as desired. **24 to 30 petits fours.**

HIGH ALTITUDE: Add 3 tablespoons flour to dry cake mix. Bake at 375°F. for 18 to 22 minutes.

NUTRIENTS PER ⅟₃₀ OF RECIPE

Calories 230	Dietary Fiber....................<1 g
Protein.............................1 g	Sodium............................135 mg
Carbohydrate.......................43 g	Potassium..........................40 mg
Fat ....6 g	Calcium................2% U.S. RDA
Cholesterol.........................25 mg	Iron.......................2% U.S. RDA

Confetti Balloon Cake

CAKE
- 1 pkg. pudding-included white cake mix
- ¾ cup water
- ½ cup dairy sour cream
- 2 eggs
- ¼ cup multi-colored candy sprinkles

FROSTING
- ¾ cup margarine or butter, softened
- ¾ cup shortening
- 1 teaspoon vanilla
- 6 cups powdered sugar
- 4 to 5 tablespoons milk
- 1 tablespoon unsweetened cocoa
  Food coloring
  Colored decorator icing
  Red or black string licorice

Heat oven to 350°F. Grease and flour two 9-inch round cake pans and one 8x4-inch loaf pan. In large bowl, combine cake mix, water, sour cream and eggs at low speed until moistened; beat 2 minutes at highest speed. Gently fold in candy sprinkles. Pour scant 1 cup batter into prepared loaf pan. Divide remaining batter evenly between 2 prepared round pans. Bake at 350°F. for 20 to 30 minutes or until toothpick inserted in center comes out clean. Cool 10 minutes; remove from pans. Cool completely.

In large bowl, combine margarine, shortening and vanilla; blend well. Gradually add powdered sugar, beating at medium speed until creamy. Add milk; beat at highest speed until light and fluffy. Cover; set aside.

Cover 20x12-inch heavy cardboard with foil. Trim cake layers if necessary to obtain straight sides and level tops. Cut loaf cake in half, forming two 4x4-inch squares. Position cakes on foil-covered cardboard, with 1 round cake centered about 6 inches from 1 cake square.

Measure 3 cups frosting; place in medium bowl and cover. Spread remaining frosting between layers and on sides of round cake. From reserved 3 cups frosting, measure 1 cup and place in small bowl; add cocoa, stirring until well blended. Fill and frost sides and top of square cake with cocoa-flavored frosting. (Using fork dipped in water, make basket weave design on square cake, if desired.) Divide remaining 2 cups frosting into 3 portions. Color each with desired food coloring; cover. Frost top of round cake with stripes of colored frosting. Using colored decorator icing, pipe stars around edge of balloon and basket. Attach string licorice from bottom of balloon to top of basket. **16 servings.**

HIGH ALTITUDE: Add 2 tablespoons flour to dry cake mix. Bake at 375°F. for 20 to 25 minutes.

NUTRIENTS PER ¹⁄₁₆ OF RECIPE

Calories 490	Dietary Fiber............................1 g
Protein...3 g	Sodium.............................330 mg
Carbohydrate..........................66 g	Potassium...........................45 mg
Fat ....24 g	Calcium.................4% U.S. RDA
Cholesterol........................50 mg	Iron.......................4% U.S. RDA

Antique Satin Wedding Cake

Basic Recipe (4½ cups batter)
- 1 pkg. pudding-included white cake mix
- 1¼ cups water
- 2 tablespoons oil
- 3 egg whites

Heat oven to 350°F. Generously grease and flour 2-inch-deep cake pans. In large bowl, combine cake mix, water, oil and egg at low speed until moistened; beat 2 minutes at **medium** speed. To save time, mix a double batch of cake batter. Beating time is the same: 2 minutes at **medium** speed.

Fill cake pans half full or use amounts listed in chart. Bake at 350°F. as directed or until toothpick inserted in center comes out clean or when top springs back when touched lightly in center. Top will be golden brown. (Do not over-bake.) Cool 15 to 20 minutes on rack; carefully remove cake from pan. Be sure cooling racks are large enough to support each layer to avoid cracking. Cool completely. **4½ cups cake batter.**

Pan Size	Cake Batter	Bake Time
6-inch round layer	1¾ cups	30 to 40 minutes
8-inch round layer	2¼ cups	25 to 35 minutes
10-inch round layer	4½ cups	30 to 40 minutes
12-inch round layer	6 cups	35 to 45 minutes
14-inch round layer	9 cups	40 to 50 minutes
18x12x1-inch sheetcake (Foil pan)	9 cups	25 to 35 minutes

Each tier of this cake is made up of 2 layers frosted together; these 12-inch, 10-inch and 6-inch tiers require six packages of cake mix. About 1½ cups of batter will be left over.

Cake layers can be baked in advance, cooled, wrapped in foil and frozen. Unwrap and thaw at room temperature for 3 to 4 hours before frosting and decorating. Layers must be level on top; trim with a sharp knife if necessary.

HIGH ALTITUDE: Above 3500 Feet: For each package of dry cake mix, add ¼ cup flour.

NUTRIENTS: Variables in this recipe make it impossible to calculate nutrition information.

Cutting and Serving Tips

• To cut a tiered wedding cake, set aside the top tier. Cut a circle 2 inches from the outside edge of the second tier. Slice the circle into 1-inch-wide pieces. Move in 2 more inches from the outside edge and cut a second circle; slice it into 1-inch-wide pieces. Cut center core into pieces. Continue this method with each remaining tier.

• Approximate Number of 2 x 2-inch Servings from Layers:
   6x4-inch round layer   15 servings
   8x4-inch round layer   25 servings
   10x4-inch round layer   40 servings
   12x4-inch round layer   65 servings
   14x4-inch round layer   90 servings

Buttercream Decorating Icing and Frosting

   ½   cup butter
   ½   cup vegetable shortening
   1   teaspoon vanilla
   ⅛   teaspoon salt
   4   cups powdered sugar
   3   tablespoons milk

Cream butter and shortening together. Add vanilla and salt. Beat in sugar, 1 cup at a time, scraping sides and bottom of bowl often. Add milk; beat at high speed until light and fluffy. Keep icing covered in refrigerator when not in use. **3 cups.**

Frosting Required for a pair of:	Between Layers	Sides & Top
6-inch round layers	⅓ cup	2 cups
8-inch round layers	¾ cup	2½ cups
10-inch round layers	1¼ cups	3½ cups
12-inch round layers	1¾ cups	4½ cups
14-inch round layers	2 cups	6 cups

TIPS: Thin above recipe with an additional 2 tablespoons milk to use for frosting.

Frosting and decorating a 12-inch, 10-inch and 6-inch tiered cake requires about 5 times this recipe.

Plan design and color of decorations on paper as a guide.

Smooth frosting on cake by dipping metal spatula in hot water, pressing against cake and slowly turning cake until sides and top are smooth.

Heat from your hands may cause icing in decorating tube to soften. If this happens, refrigerate until correct consistency.

Store frosted cake in cool place or refrigerate.

NUTRIENTS: Variables in this recipe make it impossible to calculate nutrition information.

How to Frost a Two Layer Cake

1. Cool cake layers completely; brush loose crumbs from sides.

2. Place 1 cake layer top side down on serving plate. If desired, arrange strips of waxed paper under edge of cake layer

to keep serving plate clean. Spread about ¼ of frosting evenly over first layer to within ½ inch of edge.

3. Place remaining cake layer top side up on frosted layer. Spread sides of cake with a very thin coat of frosting to seal in crumbs.

4. Use about ⅔ of remaining frosting to spread a thicker layer over sides. For best-shaped frosted cake, use upward strokes, bringing frosting up high on sides of cake.

5. Spread remaining frosting over top of cake just to edge of frosted sides. Carefully remove waxed paper strips.

Decorating with Pastry Tubes and Tips

Simple to elaborate decorations can be made using pastry tubes and tips. Either whipped cream or frosting can be used to make designs on desserts and cakes. For whipped cream decorations, use larger pastry tubes and tips. After decorating, refrigerate cake or dessert until serving.

To decorate with frosting, use recipe for Buttercream Frosting. The following suggestions will be helpful as you begin to decorate:

• Sift powdered sugar for frosting. Small lumps present in unsifted powdered sugar may clog pastry tip.

• Frosting must be correct consistency for decorations to hold their shape. Adjust consistency with a small amount of powdered sugar or water.

• When tinting frosting, always mix enough of each color before decorating. Frosting will darken slightly as it dries.

• Cover frosting bowl with a damp cloth to prevent drying.

• Pack frosting to the end of the tube to prevent air bubbles. Squeeze out a little frosting before starting to decorate.

• Make sure frosted surface where decorations will be made is smooth and even.

• Draw design with a toothpick on cake before beginning to decorate.

• Frosting made with butter or margarine may soften from the heat of your hand when decorating. If frosting becomes too soft, chill for a few minutes.

Frostings & Fillings

When you top your cake with a frosting or glaze or fill it with a luscious filling, you have truly added that final touch which says you care to make the very best. Many of our cake recipes have suggestions for a complementary frosting or filling. However, there are no strict rules. Feel free to experiment with different flavor and texture combinations.

Buttercream Frosting

  ⅔ cup butter, softened
  4 cups powdered sugar
3 to 5 tablespoons half-and-half or milk
  1 teaspoon vanilla

In large bowl, cream butter until light and fluffy. Gradually add powdered sugar, beating well after each addition. Add vanilla and half-and-half a tablespoon at a time; beat to desired spreading consistency. **Frosts 2-layer or 13x9-inch cake.**

VARIATIONS:

BROWNED BUTTER FROSTING: Brown butter in large heavy saucepan over medium heat until light golden brown, stirring constantly. Blend in remaining ingredients; beat until smooth.

CHOCOLATE BUTTERCREAM FROSTING: Blend ⅓ cup unsweetened cocoa or 2 envelopes premelted unsweetened baking chocolate flavor or 2 oz. (2 squares) melted unsweetened chocolate into creamed butter.

CHOCOLATE-CHERRY BUTTERCREAM FROSTING: Blend 3 tablespoons drained chopped maraschino cherries into Chocolate Buttercream Frosting.

COFFEE BUTTERCREAM FROSTING: Add 1½ teaspoons instant coffee granules or crystals with the sugar. (The coffee can be dissolved in the milk for a smooth, no fleck appearance.)

DECORATOR FROSTING: Substitute shortening for softened butter. Pipe frosting from a pastry tube.

MOCHA BUTTERCREAM FROSTING: Blend 3 tablespoons unsweetened cocoa and 1 teaspoon instant coffee granules or crystals into creamed butter.

NUT BUTTERCREAM FROSTING: Stir in ¼ cup chopped nuts.

ORANGE OR LEMON BUTTERCREAM FROSTING: Substitute 2 to 3 tablespoons orange or lemon juice for the milk and 1 teaspoon grated orange or lemon peel for the vanilla.

PEANUT BUTTER FROSTING: Cream 3 tablespoons peanut butter with the butter.

NUTRIENTS PER ½₂ OF RECIPE

Calories	230	Dietary Fiber	0 g
Protein	0 g	Sodium	105 mg
Carbohydrate	33 g	Potassium	10 mg
Fat	11 g	Calcium	<2% U.S. RDA
Cholesterol	30 mg	Iron	<2% U.S. RDA

Fudgy Cocoa Pecan Frosting

$\frac{1}{2}$ cup margarine or butter
$\frac{1}{2}$ cup unsweetened cocoa
3 cups powdered sugar
$\frac{1}{4}$ cup milk
1 teaspoon vanilla
$\frac{1}{2}$ cup chopped pecans

In small saucepan over medium heat, melt margarine. Blend in cocoa and heat just until mixture comes to a boil, stirring constantly. Pour into large bowl; cool.

Blend in powdered sugar, milk and vanilla at low speed until smooth. Add additional milk a tablespoon at a time until desired spreading consistency. Stir in nuts. **2 cups.**

NUTRIENTS PER $\frac{1}{12}$ OF RECIPE

Calories	220	Dietary Fiber	0 g
Protein	1 g	Sodium	120 mg
Carbohydrate	28 g	Potassium	55 mg
Fat	12 g	Calcium	<2% U.S. RDA
Cholesterol	0 mg	Iron	2% U.S. RDA

Cream Cheese Chocolate Frosting

3-oz. pkg. cream cheese, softened
2 cups powdered sugar
6-oz. pkg. (1 cup) semi-sweet chocolate chips, melted, cooled
3 tablespoons milk
1 teaspoon vanilla

In small bowl, blend cream cheese and powdered sugar at medium speed until light and fluffy. Blend in chocolate, milk and vanilla at low speed until smooth. If necessary, add additional milk a teaspoon at a time until desired spreading consistency. Frost cake or bars; store in refrigerator. **1¾ cups; frosts 2-layer or 13x9-inch cake.**

NUTRIENTS PER ½ OF RECIPE

Calories	160	Dietary Fiber	0 g
Protein	1 g	Sodium	25 mg
Carbohydrate	25 g	Potassium	60 mg
Fat	8 g	Calcium	<2% U.S. RDA
Cholesterol	8 mg	Iron	2% U.S. RDA

Sour Cream Chocolate Frosting

```
   2  cups powdered sugar
  ½  cup dairy sour cream
   1  tablespoon margarine or butter, softened
6-oz.  pkg. (1 cup) semi-sweet chocolate chips, melted,
       cooled
   1  teaspoon vanilla
      Milk
```

In small bowl, blend powdered sugar, sour cream and margarine at medium speed until light and fluffy. Blend in chocolate and vanilla at low speed until smooth. If necessary, add milk a teaspoon at a time until desired spreading consistency. Frost cake or bars; store in refrigerator. **2 cups; frosts 2-layer or 13x9-inch cake.**

NUTRIENTS PER ½ OF RECIPE

Calories	170	Dietary Fiber	0 g
Protein	1 g	Sodium	15 mg
Carbohydrate	25 g	Potassium	60 mg
Fat	8 g	Calcium	<2% U.S. RDA
Cholesterol	4 mg	Iron	2% U.S. RDA

Chocolate Cream Frosting

In small bowl, beat 1 cup whipping cream at highest speed just until it begins to thicken. Gradually add ⅓ cup chocolate flavored syrup and continue beating until soft peaks form. Frost cake and serve immediately; store in refrigerator. **2¼ cups; frosts 2-layer or 13x9-inch cake.**

NUTRIENTS PER ¹⁄₁₂ OF RECIPE

Calories	90	Dietary Fiber	0 g
Protein	1 g	Sodium	10 mg
Carbohydrate	6 g	Potassium	40 mg
Fat	8 g	Calcium	<2% U.S. RDA
Cholesterol	25 mg	Iron	<2% U.S. RDA

Almond Bark Buttercream Frosting

6 oz.	(3 cubes) almond bark or vanilla-flavored candy coating, cut into pieces
3 to 4	tablespoons chocolate-flavored liqueur
¾	cup butter, softened
¼	cup powdered sugar

In small saucepan over low heat, melt almond bark, stirring constantly. Remove from heat; stir in chocolate liqueur. Cool 30 minutes.

In small bowl, cream butter and powdered sugar until light and fluffy. Gradually beat in cooled almond bark mixture until smooth. **About 2 cups; frosts 2-layer or 13x9-inch cake.**

NUTRIENTS PER ¹⁄₁₂ OF RECIPE

Calories	200	Dietary Fiber	0 g
Protein	1 g	Sodium	115 mg
Carbohydrate	10 g	Potassium	90 mg
Fat	19 g	Calcium	<2% U.S. RDA
Cholesterol	35 mg	Iron	4% U.S. RDA

Caramel Frosting

½ cup margarine or butter
1 cup firmly packed brown sugar
¼ cup milk
3 cups powdered sugar
½ teaspoon vanilla

In medium saucepan, melt margarine; add brown sugar. Cook over low heat 2 minutes, stirring constantly. Add milk; continue cooking until mixture comes to a rolling boil. Remove from heat. Gradually add powdered sugar and vanilla; mix well. If needed, add a few drops of milk for desired spreading consistency. **Frosts 2-layer or 13x9-inch cake.**

NUTRIENTS PER ½ OF RECIPE

Calories	240	Dietary Fiber	0 g
Protein	0 g	Sodium	95 mg
Carbohydrate	43 g	Potassium	75 mg
Fat	8 g	Calcium	2% U.S. RDA
Cholesterol	0 mg	Iron	2% U.S. RDA

Fudge Frosting

2 cups sugar
¾ cup half-and-half
2 oz. (2 squares) unsweetened chocolate or 2 envelopes premelted unsweetened baking chocolate flavor
2 tablespoons light corn syrup
⅛ teaspoon salt
2 tablespoons margarine or butter
1 teaspoon vanilla

In heavy saucepan, combine sugar, half-and-half, chocolate, corn syrup and salt. Heat slowly, stirring just until sugar is dissolved. Cover; cook over medium heat for 2 minutes. Uncover; cook until candy thermometer reaches soft ball stage (234°F.), about 5 minutes. Do not stir while cooking.

Remove from heat; add margarine. Cool to lukewarm (110°F.). Additional cooling may cause frosting to harden too soon. Add vanilla; beat until frosting begins to thicken and loses its gloss. If necessary, thin with a few drops of cream. **2¼ cups; frosts 2-layer or 13x9-inch cake.**

VARIATIONS:

MARSHMALLOW NUT FUDGE FROSTING: Add 1 cup miniature marshmallows and ½ cup chopped nuts to frosting just before spreading.

PEANUT BUTTER FUDGE FROSTING: Add ¼ cup creamy peanut butter with margarine.

NUTRIENTS PER ½₂ OF RECIPE

Calories	240	Dietary Fiber	0 g
Protein	1 g	Sodium	55 mg
Carbohydrate	38 g	Potassium	55 mg
Fat	10 g	Calcium	<2% U.S. RDA
Cholesterol	20 mg	Iron	2% U.S. RDA

Cream Cheese Frosting

    3 cups powdered sugar
8-oz. pkg. cream cheese, softened
    2 tablespoons margarine or butter, melted
    1 teaspoon vanilla

In large bowl, combine all ingredients; beat until smooth. **Frosts 2-layer or 13x9-inch cake.**

NUTRIENTS PER ½₂ OF RECIPE

Calories	180	Dietary Fiber	0 g
Protein	1 g	Sodium	80 mg
Carbohydrate	25 g	Potassium	25 mg
Fat	8 g	Calcium	<2% U.S. RDA
Cholesterol	20 mg	Iron	<2% U.S. RDA

Basic Powdered Sugar Glaze

2 cups powdered sugar
2 tablespoons margarine or butter, softened
1 teaspoon vanilla
3 to 4 tablespoons milk or light cream

In medium bowl, combine powdered sugar, margarine, vanilla and milk until mixture has consistency of a glaze. Use to glaze cakes, coffee cakes or pastries. **1½ cups.**

VARIATIONS:

CHOCOLATE GLAZE: Add 2 oz. (2 squares) melted unsweetened chocolate or 2 envelopes premelted unsweetened baking chocolate flavor.

COFFEE GLAZE: Substitute hot water for milk. Dissolve 1 teaspoon instant coffee granules or crystals in the hot water.

LEMON GLAZE: Substitute 2 tablespoons lemon juice for part of milk and add 1 teaspoon grated lemon peel.

MAPLE GLAZE: Add ½ teaspoon maple extract.

ORANGE GLAZE: Substitute orange juice for milk and add 1 teaspoon grated orange peel.

SPICE GLAZE: Combine ¼ teaspoon cinnamon and ⅛ teaspoon nutmeg with powdered sugar.

NUTRIENTS PER ¹⁄₁₂ OF RECIPE

Calories 96	Dietary Fiber...........................0 g	
Protein......................................0 g	Sodium...............................25 mg	
Carbohydrate.........................20 g	Potassium.............................7 mg	
Fat..2 g	Calcium...............<2% U.S. RDA	
Cholesterol...........................0 mg	Iron ....<2% U.S. RDA	

Coconut Pecan Frosting

    1   cup sugar
    1   cup evaporated milk
    ½   cup margarine or butter
    3   eggs, beaten
    1⅓ cups flaked coconut
    1   cup chopped pecans or almonds
    1   teaspoon vanilla

In medium saucepan, combine sugar, milk, margarine and eggs. Cook over medium heat until mixture starts to bubble, stirring constantly. Stir in remaining ingredients. Cool until of spreading consistency. **Frosts 3-layer or 13x9-inch cake.**

NUTRIENTS PER ½ OF RECIPE

Calories	290	Dietary Fiber	2 g
Protein	4 g	Sodium	135 mg
Carbohydrate	25 g	Potassium	160 mg
Fat	19 g	Calcium	8% U.S. RDA
Cholesterol	70 mg	Iron	4% U.S. RDA

Broiled Coconut Topping

    ¼   cup margarine or butter
    1   cup flaked or shredded coconut
    ⅔   cup firmly packed brown sugar
    ½   cup chopped nuts
    3   tablespoons cream or milk

In small saucepan, melt margarine. Stir in remaining ingredients. Spread on warm cake. Broil about 5 inches from heat for 1 to 2 minutes or until bubbly and light golden brown. (Watch carefully, mixture burns easily.) **Frosts 13x9-inch cake.**

NUTRIENTS PER ¹⁄₁₂ OF RECIPE

Calories	150	Dietary Fiber	1 g
Protein	1 g	Sodium	50 mg
Carbohydrate	16 g	Potassium	95 mg
Fat	10 g	Calcium	2% U.S. RDA
Cholesterol	0 mg	Iron	4% U.S. RDA

Seven-Minute Frosting

1½ cups sugar
¼ teaspoon cream of tartar
¼ teaspoon salt
⅓ cup water
2 teaspoons light corn syrup
2 egg whites
1 teaspoon vanilla

In top of double boiler, combine all ingredients except vanilla. Place over rapidly boiling water (water should not touch bottom of pan); beat at highest speed until mixture stands in peaks, about 7 minutes. (Do not overcook.) Remove from heat; add vanilla. Continue beating until frosting holds deep swirls, about 2 minutes. **Frosts 2-layer or 13x9-inch cake.**

VARIATIONS:

SEVEN-MINUTE CHERRY FROSTING: Substitute ⅓ cup maraschino cherry juice for water. Fold ⅓ cup drained chopped maraschino cherries into finished frosting.

SEVEN-MINUTE CHOCOLATE REVEL FROSTING: Add ⅓ cup semi-sweet chocolate chips to finished frosting. Let stand 1 to 2 minutes. Chocolate will swirl through frosting when spread on cake.

SEVEN-MINUTE LEMON OR ORANGE FROSTING: Fold 3 teaspoons grated lemon or orange peel into finished frosting.

SEVEN-MINUTE MAPLE FROSTING: Substitute ½ to 1 teaspoon maple extract for vanilla.

SEVEN-MINUTE NESSELRODE FROSTING: Substitute 1 teaspoon rum extract for vanilla. Place 1 cup frosting in small bowl; stir in ½ cup chopped mixed candied fruit and ½ cup toasted coconut. Spread between layers. Frost sides and top with remaining plain frosting.

SEVEN-MINUTE PEPPERMINT FROSTING: Substitute 3 to 5 drops peppermint extract for vanilla. Fold ½ cup crushed hard peppermint candy into finished frosting.

NUTRIENTS PER ½ OF RECIPE

Calories 102	Dietary Fiber ....0 g
Protein......................................0 g	Sodium.................................54 mg
Carbohydrate.........................26 g	Potassium...............................8 mg
Fat ....0 g	Calcium...............<2% U.S. RDA
Cholesterol...........................0 mg	Iron ....<2% U.S. RDA

White Cloud Frosting

    2 egg whites
    ¼ teaspoon salt
 1½ teaspoons vanilla
    ¼ cup sugar
    ¾ cup light corn syrup

In small deep bowl, beat egg whites, salt and vanilla at medium speed until foamy. Gradually add sugar, 1 tablespoon at a time, beating at highest speed until soft peaks form and sugar is dissolved. In small saucepan over medium heat, bring corn syrup just to a boil. Pour in thin stream over egg whites, beating at highest speed until mixture is stiff. **4 cups; frosts 2-layer or 13x9-inch cake.**

NUTRIENTS PER ¹⁄₁₂ OF RECIPE

Calories 80	Dietary Fiber..........................0 g
Protein.......................................1 g	Sodium..............................65 mg
Carbohydrate.........................20 g	Potassium...........................10 mg
Fat ....0 g	Calcium...............<2% U.S. RDA
Cholesterol ....0 mg	Iron......................4% U.S. RDA

Lord Baltimore Frosting

   2 egg whites
 ¹⁄₄ teaspoon salt
1¹⁄₄ teaspoons vanilla
 ¹⁄₄ cup firmly packed brown sugar
 ³⁄₄ cup light corn syrup

In small deep bowl, beat egg whites, salt and vanilla at medium speed until foamy. Gradually add sugar, 1 tablespoon at a time, beating at highest speed until soft peaks form and sugar is dissolved. In small saucepan over medium heat, bring corn syrup just to a boil. Pour in thin stream over egg whites, beating at highest speed until mixture is stiff. **4 cups; frosts 2-layer or 13x9-inch cake.**

NUTRIENTS PER ¹⁄₁₂ OF RECIPE

Calories 80	Dietary Fiber..........................0 g
Protein.......................................1 g	Sodium..............................65 mg
Carbohydrate.........................20 g	Potassium...........................25 mg
Fat ....0 g	Calcium...............< 2% U.S. RDA
Cholesterol ....0 mg	Iron......................6% U.S. RDA

Lord Baltimore Filling

   1 cup Lord Baltimore Frosting (above)
 ¹⁄₂ cup chopped pecans
 ¹⁄₂ cup crumbled soft macaroon cookies
  10 candied cherries, chopped (¹⁄₄ cup)

In small bowl, combine all ingredients; mix well. **1½ cups; fills 2-layer cake.**

NUTRIENTS PER ½2 OF RECIPE

Calories	90	Dietary Fiber	1 g
Protein	1 g	Sodium	20 mg
Carbohydrate	11 g	Potassium	60 mg
Fat	5 g	Calcium	<2% U.S. RDA
Cholesterol	4 mg	Iron	2% U.S. RDA

Lady Baltimore Filling

⅓ cup golden or dark raisins
⅓ cup chopped pitted dates or dried figs
⅓ cup chopped pecans
2 tablespoons cream sherry
1 cup White Cloud Frosting (page 231)

In small bowl, combine raisins, dates, pecans and sherry; mix well. Cover; let stand at least 1 hour at room temperature to blend flavors, stirring occasionally. Stir frosting into fruit. **1⅓ cups; fills 2-layer cake.**

NUTRIENTS PER ½2 OF RECIPE

Calories	70	Dietary Fiber	1 g
Protein	1 g	Sodium	15 mg
Carbohydrate	12 g	Potassium	85 mg
Fat	2 g	Calcium	<2% U.S. RDA
Cholesterol	0 mg	Iron	2% U.S. RDA

Basic Cream Filling

½ cup sugar
3 tablespoons flour
¼ teaspoon salt
1¼ cups milk
2 egg yolks or 1 egg, slightly beaten
1 tablespoon margarine or butter
1 teaspoon vanilla

In small saucepan, combine sugar, flour and salt. Gradually add milk; mix well. Cook over medium heat until mixture boils, stirring constantly; boil 1 minute. Blend small amount (about ¼ cup) hot mixture into egg. Return egg mixture to saucepan; mix well. Cook until mixture starts to bubble, stirring constantly. Stir in margarine and vanilla. Cover and cool. **1⅓ cups; fills 2-layer cake or 1 jelly roll.**

VARIATIONS:

CHOCOLATE CREAM FILLING: Increase sugar to ¾ cup and add 1 oz. (1 square) melted unsweetened chocolate or 1 envelope premelted unsweetened baking chocolate flavor with the sugar. **1⅔ cups.**

COCONUT CREAM FILLING: Stir in ⅓ cup flaked coconut with vanilla. **1⅔ cups.**

BUTTERSCOTCH CREAM FILLING: Substitute ⅔ cup firmly packed brown sugar for sugar. **1⅔ cups.**

NUTRIENTS PER ¹⁄₁₂ OF RECIPE

Calories 70	Dietary Fiber ....0 g
Protein ....2 g	Sodium ....65 mg
Carbohydrate ....11 g	Potassium ....45 mg
Fat ....2 g	Calcium ....2% U.S. RDA
Cholesterol ....45 mg	Iron ....<2% U.S. RDA

Lemon Filling

    ¾ cup sugar
    3 tablespoons cornstarch
    ¼ teaspoon salt
    ¾ cup cold water
    2 egg yolks
    1 tablespoon margarine or butter
    2 teaspoons grated lemon peel
    3 tablespoons lemon juice

In small saucepan, combine sugar, cornstarch and salt; mix well. Gradually stir in cold water until smooth. Cook over medium heat, stirring constantly, until mixture boils; boil 1 minute, stirring constantly. Remove from heat.

In small bowl, beat egg yolks; stir about ¼ cup of hot mixture into egg yolks. Gradually stir yolk mixture into hot mixture. Cook over low heat, stirring constantly, until mixture boils; boil 1 minute, stirring constantly. Remove from heat; stir in margarine, lemon peel and lemon juice. Cool. **1⅓ cups; fills 2-layer cake or 1 jelly roll.**

VARIATIONS:

ORANGE FILLING: Omit lemon peel and lemon juice; substitute orange juice for water and add 1 tablespoon grated orange peel with margarine.

PINEAPPLE FILLING: Omit lemon peel and lemon juice. Drain liquid from 8-oz. can (1 cup) crushed pineapple; add water to liquid to measure ¾ cup. Substitute pineapple liquid for cold water. Add pineapple after stirring yolk mixture into hot mixture. Continue as directed above. **1½ cups.**

NUTRIENTS PER ⅟₁₂ OF RECIPE

Calories 80	Dietary Fiber...........................0 g
Protein......................................0 g	Sodium...............................55 mg
Carbohydrate........................15 g	Potassium...........................10 mg
Fat ....2 g	Calcium..............<2% U.S. RDA
Cholesterol........................45 mg	Iron ....<2% U.S. RDA

Cookies &
Candies

Cookies & Candies

Our affection for cookies and confections is unlimited by age, time of day or season. They're great for lunch box, backpack, picnic basket and mailing carton . . . or for giving with an unmistakable personal touch . . . from scratch or made in minutes with mixes . . . cooked conventionally or in the microwave . . . hot from the oven or fresh-tasting from the freezer. As you bake and cook your way through this special collection of cookie and candy recipes, you will delight in their variety and versatility.

Cookies

Cookies come in all shapes and sizes and are generally categorized by preparation method. Main classifications are: *drop, molded (or shaped), pressed, rolled, refrigerator, and bar.*

Cookie Baking Hints

• Measure as accurately as you can so that cookies and bars are not dry and crumbly or so soft that they spread during baking.

• Use baking powder before the expiration date printed on the bottom of the can.

• Our recipes usually call for butter or margarine. For easy measuring, cut off the amount needed from a refrigerated block or stick. When softened butter or margarine is called for, it should be soft enough to blend smoothly with other ingredients. Do not soften by melting and do not substitute oils or whipped butter or margarine products. If a recipe calls for shortening, use solid shortening from a can.

• Use the correct pan size and shiny cookie sheets that are flat or have only slightly raised edges. Pans and baking sheets with dark, nonstick coating may cause cookies to brown more quickly.

• Space unbaked dough carefully to avoid unattractive, run-together results.

• Cool pans of bars on wire cooling racks. Cool cookies on brown paper, waxed paper or paper toweling. A wire rack may be used for firm-textured cookies that will not bend or break. If cookies stick to the cookie sheet before they can be removed, return them to the hot oven to warm slightly.

• Cool baking sheets between baking times to prevent cookie dough from spreading unnecessarily.

• Store cookies according to type and only when completely cooled.

  • Crisp and soft cookies should be stored in separate containers with tight-fitting lids.

  • Cardboard containers are not recommended for storage unless lined with foil or plastic wrap to keep cookies from absorbing any cardboard flavor or aroma.

  • Frosted or filled thumbprint cookies should be stored in a single layer in a tightly covered container. If space is limited, allow frosting or filling to become firm before storing; layer cookies between waxed paper to protect appearance.

  • Bar cookies may be stored, tightly covered, in the baking pan. For food safety, some frostings, fillings or other ingredients may require refrigerator storage, as stated in the recipe.

  • Store cookies or cookie dough no longer than 6 months in freezer. Meringue-type cookies do not freeze well.

Keys to Successful Cookies

• **Drop Cookies:** For even baking and attractive results, drop cookies should be uniform in size; two regular teaspoons, or one regular teaspoon and a spatula or a commercially made cookie dropper work well.

• **Shaped Cookies:** These cookies require dough that is firm enough to hold its shape. Chill dough for easier handling, dust hands lightly with flour to help prevent sticking and roll each cookie smoothly between palms of hands. For "flattened" cookies, press each mound of dough with a thumb, with a fork or with the bottom of a glass dipped in sugar or flour. For maximum flavor and attractive appearance, cookies to be rolled in powdered sugar should be coated once while still warm and again after cooling.

• **Pressed Cookies:** These are tender cookies made from soft and pliable dough that passes easily through a press. Use room-temperature margarine, butter or shortening, creaming with other ingredients just until light and fluffy. Test consistency by pressing a small amount of dough through the press. A too-soft dough may benefit from a brief period of refrigeration or the addition of 1 to 2 tablespoons of flour. Dough that is too stiff may be remedied with the addition of 1 egg yolk. Using a cool baking sheet, hold press so tip rests on the sheet; force dough onto sheet, raising press only when correct form is achieved.

• **Rolled Cookies:** Roll out dough thinly for a crisp texture or more thickly for a softer texture. For tender cookies, roll out small amounts of dough from center to edges with light, even strokes. A floured pastry cloth and stockinette-covered rolling pin are helpful. Using cutters dipped in flour, cut out cookies as close together as possible. To prevent breaking, move cookies to and from baking sheets with a wide spatula or pancake turner.

• **Refrigerator Cookies:** This dough is chilled thoroughly before slicing and baking. For firm and smoothly shaped rolls, wrap rolls of dough securely in plastic wrap, foil or waxed paper to chill. Unwrap and slice evenly with a thin, sharp knife.

• **Bar Cookies:** These cookies vary greatly. Use pan and doneness tests specified in recipe to avoid under- or over-baking. For best appearance, cool in pan completely before cutting into pieces unless recipe states otherwise.

Chewy Granola Cookies

        3   cups rolled oats
    1½   cups all purpose flour
        1   cup wheat germ
        1   teaspoon baking powder
      ½   teaspoon salt
        1   cup firmly packed brown sugar
        1   cup margarine or butter, softened
      ½   cup honey
    1½   teaspoons vanilla
        2   eggs
      ½   cup raisins
      ½   cup chopped almonds
      ¼   cup sesame seeds
      ¼   cup sunflower nuts

Heat oven to 375°F. Lightly grease cookie sheets. In medium bowl, combine oats, flour, wheat germ, baking powder and salt; mix well. Set aside. In large bowl, beat brown sugar, margarine and honey until light and fluffy. Add vanilla and eggs; blend well. Stir in flour mixture. Add raisins, almonds, sesame seeds and sunflower nuts; mix well. Drop by rounded teaspoonfuls onto prepared cookie sheets. Bake at 375°F. for 7 to 8 minutes or until edges are light golden brown. Immediately remove from cookie sheets. **5 dozen cookies.**

TIP: For large-sized cookies, place ¼ cup of dough 4 inches apart on prepared cookie sheets. Using metal spoon, flatten into 3-inch circles. Bake at 375°F. for 12 to 14 minutes.

NUTRIENTS PER 1 COOKIE

Calories	100	Dietary Fiber	1 g
Protein	2 g	Sodium	60 mg
Carbohydrate	13 g	Potassium	70 mg
Fat	5 g	Calcium	2% U.S. RDA
Cholesterol	8 mg	Iron	4% U.S. RDA

Chocolate Brownie Cookies

4 oz.	(4 squares) semi-sweet chocolate, chopped
2 oz.	(2 squares) unsweetened chocolate, chopped
⅓	cup margarine or butter
¾	cup sugar
1½	teaspoons instant coffee granules
2	eggs
½	cup all purpose flour
¼	teaspoon baking powder
¼	teaspoon salt
¾	cup milk chocolate chips
¾	cup chopped walnuts

Heat oven to 350°F. Cover cookie sheets with parchment paper. In small saucepan over low heat, melt semi-sweet chocolate, unsweetened chocolate and margarine, stirring constantly until smooth. Remove from heat; cool. In large bowl, beat sugar, instant coffee and eggs at highest speed for 2 to 3 minutes. Blend in melted chocolate. Stir in flour, baking powder and salt; mix well. Stir in milk chocolate chips and walnuts; mix well.

Drop dough by teaspoonfuls 2 inches apart onto prepared cookie sheets. Bake at 350°F. for 7 to 11 minutes or until tops of cookies are cracked. DO NOT OVERBAKE. Cool 1 minute; remove from parchment paper. **36 cookies.**

NUTRIENTS PER 1 COOKIE

Calories	110	Dietary Fiber	<1 g
Protein	1 g	Sodium	40 mg
Carbohydrate	10 g	Potassium	55 mg
Fat	7 g	Calcium	<2% U.S. RDA
Cholesterol	15 mg	Iron	2% U.S. RDA

Chocolate Chip Cookies

- ¾ cup firmly packed brown sugar
- ½ cup sugar
- ½ cup margarine or butter, softened
- ½ cup shortening
- 1½ teaspoons vanilla
- 1 egg
- 1¾ cups all purpose flour
- 1 teaspoon baking soda
- ½ teaspoon salt
- 6-oz. pkg. (1 cup) chocolate chips
- ½ cup chopped nuts or sunflower nuts, if desired

Heat oven to 375°F. In large bowl, beat brown sugar, sugar, margarine and shortening until light and fluffy. Add vanilla and egg; beat well. Add flour, baking soda and salt; mix well. Stir in chocolate chips and nuts. Drop by teaspoonfuls 2 inches apart onto ungreased cookie sheets. Bake at 375°F. for 8 to 10 minutes or until light golden brown. Cool 1 minute; remove from cookie sheets. **4 dozen cookies.**

NUTRIENTS PER 1 CHOCOLATE CHIP COOKIE

Calories	100	Dietary Fiber	<1 g
Protein	1 g	Sodium	70 mg
Carbohydrate	11 g	Potassium	35 mg
Fat	6 g	Calcium	<2% U.S. RDA
Cholesterol	6 mg	Iron	2% U.S. RDA

VARIATIONS:

CHOCOLATE CHOCOLATE CHIP COOKIES: One cup margarine or butter, softened, can be substituted for the ½ cup margarine and ½ cup shortening. Decrease vanilla to 1 teaspoon. Add ¼ cup unsweetened cocoa with flour, baking soda and salt. Bake at 375°F. for 7 to 11 minutes or until set. **4 dozen cookies.**

CHOCOLATE CHUNK COOKIES: Substitute 8 oz. coarsely chopped chocolate for chocolate chips. Drop dough by tablespoonfuls 3 inches apart onto ungreased cookie sheets. Bake at 375°F. for 9 to 12 minutes or until light golden brown. **3 dozen cookies.**

CHOCOLATE CHIP COOKIE BARS: Spread dough in ungreased 13x9-inch pan. Bake at 375°F. for 15 to 25 minutes or until light golden brown. Cool completely. Cut into bars. **36 bars.**

PEANUT BUTTER FILLED CHOCOLATE CHIP COOKIES: Prepare chocolate chip cookies as directed in recipe using a teaspoonful of dough for each cookie. Spread 1 heaping teaspoon of peanut butter between 2 cooled cookies. **2 dozen sandwich cookies.**

KID-SIZED COOKIES: Prepare dough as directed in recipe omitting ½ cup sugar, 1 cup semi-sweet chocolate chips and ½ cup chopped nuts. Increase vanilla to 2 teaspoons. Stir 1 cup candy-coated chocolate pieces and ½ cup sunflower nuts into prepared dough. (If necessary, refrigerate dough for easier handling.) Shape into 2-inch balls. Place 4 inches apart on ungreased cookie sheets. Press an additional ½ cup candy-coated chocolate pieces into balls to decorate tops of cookies. Bake at 350°F. for 15 to 20 minutes or until light golden brown. Cool 2 minutes; remove from cookie sheets. **14 large cookies.**

CHOCOLATE CHIP ICE CREAM COOKIEWICHES: Drop dough by heaping teaspoonfuls 3 inches apart onto ungreased cookie sheets. Bake at 375°F. for 9 to 14 minutes or until light golden brown. Cool completely. For each cookiewich, place scoop of favorite ice cream on bottom side of 1 cookie; flatten ice cream slightly. Place another cookie bottom side down on top of ice cream. Gently press cookies together in center to form ice cream sandwich. Quickly wrap in foil. Freeze. **12 cookiewiches.**

CLOVERLEAF COOKIES: Prepare dough as directed in recipe omitting chocolate chips and nuts. Divide dough into 3 parts; place in small bowls. Add ½ cup miniature semi-sweet chocolate chips to first part, ¼ cup chunky peanut butter to second; 1 oz. (1 square) unsweetened chocolate, melted, cooled to third; blend each well. Refrigerate dough ½ hour for easier handling. Shape ½ teaspoon of each dough into ball. Form each cookie by placing 1 of each flavor ball cloverleaf-style on ungreased cookie sheets. Bake at 375°F. for 10 to 12 minutes or until set. **3½ dozen cookies.**

MAXI CHIPPERS: For each cookie, place ⅓ cup of the dough 4 inches apart on ungreased cookie sheets. Bake at 375°F. for 12 to 18 minutes or until golden brown. **10 cookies.**

Double Peanut Scotchies

¾	cup firmly packed brown sugar
½	cup margarine or butter, softened
½	cup peanut butter
2	eggs
1½	cups all purpose flour
1	teaspoon baking soda
1	cup peanuts
6-oz.	pkg. (1 cup) butterscotch chips

Heat oven to 350°F. In large bowl, cream brown sugar and margarine until light and fluffy. Add peanut butter and eggs; mix well. Stir in flour and baking soda; mix well. Stir in peanuts and butterscotch chips. Drop by rounded teaspoonfuls 2 inches apart onto ungreased cookie sheets. Bake at 350°F. for 9 to 12 minutes or until golden brown. Immediately remove from cookie sheets. **4 dozen cookies.**

NUTRIENTS PER 1 COOKIE

Calories 100	Dietary Fiber.........................<1 g
Protein.......................................2 g	Sodium................................65 mg
Carbohydrate.........................10 g	Potassium...........................55 mg
Fat ....6 g	Calcium..............<2% U.S. RDA
Cholesterol..........................10 mg	Iron.........................2% U.S. RDA

Orange and Oat Chewies

        2 cups firmly packed brown sugar
        1 cup shortening
        3 tablespoons frozen orange juice concentrate,
           thawed
        1 tablespoon grated orange peel
        2 eggs
        2 cups all purpose flour
        1 teaspoon baking soda
      ¾ teaspoon salt
        2 cups rolled oats
        1 cup chopped nuts
      ⅓ cup coconut

Heat oven to 350°F. Grease cookie sheets. In large bowl, combine brown sugar, shortening, orange juice, orange peel and eggs; mix well. Add flour, baking soda and salt; mix well. By hand, stir in oats, nuts and coconut. Drop by rounded teaspoonfuls 2 inches apart onto prepared cookie sheets. Bake at 350°F. for 10 to 12 minutes or until light golden brown. Cool 1 minute before removing from cookie sheets. **5 dozen cookies.**

HIGH ALTITUDE: Increase flour to 2½ cups. Bake at 375°F. for 9 to 12 minutes.

NUTRIENTS PER 1 COOKIE

Calories 100	Dietary Fiber.........................<1 g
Protein.......................................1 g	Sodium................................50 mg
Carbohydrate.........................13 g	Potassium...........................55 mg
Fat ....5 g	Calcium..............<2% U.S. RDA
Cholesterol............................8 mg	Iron.........................2% U.S. RDA

Good-For-You Cookies

    1   cup margarine or butter, softened
    ½   cup firmly packed brown sugar
    ½   cup honey
    1   tablespoon molasses
    2   tablespoons milk
    ½   teaspoon salt
    1   egg
    1½ cups whole wheat flour
    1½ cups rolled oats
    ½   cup chopped nuts
    1   cup coconut
    1   cup raisins

Heat oven to 350°F. Lightly grease cookie sheets. In large bowl, combine margarine, brown sugar, honey, molasses, milk, salt and egg; blend well. Stir in remaining ingredients. Drop by rounded teaspoonfuls 2 inches apart onto prepared cookie sheets. Bake at 350°F. for 12 to 14 minutes or until golden brown. Cool 1 minute; remove from cookie sheets. Store in loosely covered container. **3 to 4 dozen cookies.**

NUTRIENTS PER 1 COOKIE

Calories	100	Dietary Fiber	1 g
Protein	1 g	Sodium	95 mg
Carbohydrate	13 g	Potassium	75 mg
Fat	5 g	Calcium	2% U.S. RDA
Cholesterol	6 mg	Iron	4% U.S. RDA

Frosted Carrot Drops

    ¾   cup sugar
    1   cup margarine or butter, softened
    1   teaspoon vanilla
    1   egg
    2   cups all purpose flour
    1   teaspoon baking powder

  ½ teaspoon salt
   1 cup finely shredded carrots
  ½ cup chopped walnuts
  ½ cup raisins

FROSTING
  ½ cup margarine or butter, melted
   2 cups powdered sugar
   1 tablespoon grated orange peel
2 to 3 tablespoons orange juice

Heat oven to 350°F. In large bowl, cream sugar and margarine until light and fluffy. Add vanilla and egg; beat well. Add flour, baking powder and salt; blend well. Stir in carrots, walnuts and raisins. Drop by teaspoonfuls 2 inches apart onto ungreased cookie sheets. Bake at 350°F. for 8 to 12 minutes or until edges are light golden brown. Remove from cookie sheets; cool completely.

In small bowl, combine all frosting ingredients; beat until smooth. Frost cooled cookies. **4½ dozen cookies.**

NUTRIENTS PER 1 COOKIE

Calories	100	Dietary Fiber	<1 g
Protein	1 g	Sodium	85 mg
Carbohydrate	12 g	Potassium	30 mg
Fat	6 g	Calcium	<2% U.S. RDA
Cholesterol	4 mg	Iron	<2% U.S. RDA

Ginger Creams

  ½ cup sugar
  ¼ cup shortening
  ½ cup molasses
  ½ cup hot water
   1 egg
   2 cups all purpose flour
   1 teaspoon baking soda

½ teaspoon salt
½ teaspoon ginger
½ teaspoon nutmeg
½ teaspoon cloves

FROSTING
 2 tablespoons margarine or butter, softened
 2 cups powdered sugar
    Dash salt
½ teaspoon vanilla
2 to 3 tablespoons milk

Heat oven to 375°F. Grease cookie sheets. In large bowl, combine sugar, shortening, molasses, water and egg; beat well. Add flour, baking soda, salt, ginger, nutmeg and cloves; stir just until blended. Drop by teaspoonfuls 2 inches apart onto prepared cookie sheets. Bake at 375°F. for 10 to 15 minutes or until edges are light golden brown. Immediately remove from cookie sheets.

In small bowl, combine all frosting ingredients; beat until smooth. Frost cooled cookies. **3 dozen cookies.**

NUTRIENTS PER 1 COOKIE

Calories	90	Dietary Fiber	<1 g
Protein	1 g	Sodium	80 mg
Carbohydrate	16 g	Potassium	60 mg
Fat	2 g	Calcium	<2% U.S. RDA
Cholesterol	8 mg	Iron	2% U.S. RDA

Raspberry Meringues

 3 egg whites, room temperature
¼ teaspoon cream of tartar
    Dash salt
¾ cup sugar
¼ cup raspberry preserves
5 to 6 drops red food coloring

Heat oven to 225°F. Cover cookie sheets with brown paper. In small bowl, beat egg whites, cream of tartar and salt until soft peaks form. Gradually add sugar, beating until *very* stiff peaks form, about 10 minutes. Add preserves and food coloring; beat 1 minute at *highest* speed. Drop meringue from teaspoon or pipe with pastry tube into 1-inch mounds onto paper-lined cookie sheets. Bake at 225°F. for 2 hours. Cool completely. Remove from paper. **36 cookies.**

NUTRIENTS PER 1 COOKIE

Calories	25	Dietary Fiber	<1 g
Protein	0 g	Sodium	10 mg
Carbohydrate	6 g	Potassium	5 mg
Fat	0 g	Calcium	<2% U.S. RDA
Cholesterol	0 mg	Iron	<2% U.S. RDA

Coconut Meringue Macaroons

      2 egg whites
    ⅛ teaspoon salt
    ½ cup sugar
      1 teaspoon vanilla or ½ teaspoon almond extract
  1½ cups flaked coconut

Heat oven to 350°F. Grease cookie sheets. In medium bowl, beat egg whites and salt until foamy. *Gradually* add sugar, beating continuously until stiff peaks form. Do not overbeat. By hand, fold in remaining ingredients. Drop by teaspoonfuls 2 inches apart onto prepared cookie sheets. Bake at 350°F. for 12 to 15 minutes or until lightly browned. Cool 1 minute; remove from cookie sheets. **24 cookies.**

VARIATIONS:

CEREAL MERINGUE MACAROONS: 1½ cups flaked cereal can be substituted for coconut.

CHEWY CHOCOLATE MERINGUE MACAROONS: Reduce vanilla to ½ teaspoon and coconut to ½ cup. In small saucepan, melt ½ cup semi-sweet chocolate chips over low heat, stirring constantly; cool. Fold melted chocolate and an additional ½ cup semi-sweet chocolate chips into egg whites with vanilla and coconut. Bake at 350°F. for 8 to 12 minutes or until set. **2½ dozen cookies.**

NUTRIENTS PER 1 COOKIE

Calories	45	Dietary Fiber	<1 g
Protein	0 g	Sodium	15 mg
Carbohydrate	7 g	Potassium	20 mg
Fat	2 g	Calcium	<2% U.S. RDA
Cholesterol	0 mg	Iron	<2% U.S. RDA

Chewy Date Drops

    2 cups chopped dates
    ½ cup sugar
    ½ cup water
    1 cup firmly packed brown sugar
    ½ cup sugar
    1 cup margarine or butter, softened
    1 teaspoon vanilla
    3 eggs
    4 cups all purpose flour
    1 teaspoon baking soda
    1 teaspoon salt
    1 cup chopped walnuts

In medium saucepan, combine dates, ½ cup sugar and water. Cook over medium heat until thickened, stirring occasionally. Cool.

Heat oven to 375°F. Grease cookie sheets. In large bowl, beat brown sugar, ½ cup sugar and margarine until light and fluffy. Add vanilla and eggs; blend well. Stir in flour, baking soda and salt; mix well. Stir in date mixture and nuts. Drop by rounded teaspoonfuls 2 inches apart onto prepared cookie sheets. Bake at 375°F. for 8 to 10 minutes or until light golden brown. Immediately remove from cookie sheets. **6 dozen cookies.**

HIGH ALTITUDE: Decrease sugar beaten with margarine to ¼ cup. Bake as directed above.

NUTRIENTS PER 1 COOKIE

Calories	100	Dietary Fiber	<1 g
Protein	1 g	Sodium	80 mg
Carbohydrate	15 g	Potassium	65 mg
Fat	4 g	Calcium	2% U.S. RDA
Cholesterol	10 mg	Iron	2% U.S. RDA

Thumbprints

½ cup sugar
1 cup margarine or butter, softened
1 teaspoon vanilla
2 egg yolks
2¼ cups all purpose flour
1 teaspoon baking powder

In medium bowl, cream sugar, margarine, vanilla and egg yolks until light and fluffy. Gradually add flour and baking powder; mix well. Refrigerate 30 minutes.

Heat oven to 350°F. Shape dough into 1-inch balls; place 2 inches apart on ungreased cookie sheets. With thumb, make imprint in center of each cookie. Fill cookies before or after baking as directed in the following filling recipes. Bake at 350°F. for 11 to 14 minutes or until golden brown around edges. **3½ dozen cookies.**

CUSTARD FILLING: In small saucepan, combine 1 tablespoon sugar, 1 tablespoon flour and ¼ teaspoon almond extract. Gradually add ½ cup whipping cream or half-and-half; cook over low heat until smooth and thickened, stirring constantly. In small bowl, blend 2 tablespoons hot mixture into 1 slightly beaten egg yolk. Return to saucepan; blend well.

Cook just until mixture bubbles, stirring constantly. Cool. Spoon ½ teaspoon filling into each *unbaked* cookie. Bake as directed above. Store cookies in refrigerator.

JAM FILLING: Spoon ¼ teaspoon any flavor jam or preserves into each *baked* cookie.

LEMON FILLING: In medium saucepan, combine 1 beaten egg, ⅔ cup sugar, 2 to 3 teaspoons grated lemon peel, 1 teaspoon cornstarch, ¼ teaspoon salt, 3 tablespoons lemon juice and 1 tablespoon margarine or butter. Cook over low heat until smooth and thickened, stirring constantly. Cool filling slightly. Spoon ¼ teaspoon filling into each *baked* cookie. Sprinkle with powdered sugar or coconut.

NUTRIENTS PER 1 COOKIE WITH CUSTARD FILLING

Calories ...90	Dietary Fiber ...<1 g
Protein ...1 g	Sodium ...60 mg
Carbohydrate ...8 g	Potassium ...10 mg
Fat ...6 g	Calcium ...<2% U.S. RDA
Cholesterol ...25 mg	Iron ...2% U.S. RDA

Snappy Turtle Cookies

- ½ cup firmly packed brown sugar
- ½ cup margarine or butter, softened
- ¼ teaspoon vanilla
- ⅛ teaspoon maple flavoring, if desired
- 1 egg
- 1 egg, separated
- 1½ cups all purpose flour
- ¼ teaspoon baking soda
- ¼ teaspoon salt
- 1½ to 2 cups pecan halves, split in half lengthwise

FROSTING

- ⅓ cup semi-sweet chocolate chips
- 3 tablespoons milk
- 1 tablespoon margarine or butter
- 1 cup powdered sugar

In medium bowl, cream brown sugar and ½ cup margarine. Add vanilla, maple flavoring, 1 whole egg and 1 egg yolk; beat well. By hand, stir in flour, baking soda and salt; mix well. Refrigerate dough for easier handling.

Heat oven to 350°F. Grease cookie sheets. Arrange pecan pieces in groups of 5 on prepared cookie sheets to resemble head and legs of turtle. Beat reserved egg white. Shape rounded teaspoonfuls of dough into balls. Dip bottoms into egg white and press lightly onto pecans. Tips of pecans should show. Bake at 350°F. for 10 to 12 minutes or until light golden brown around edges. (Do not overbake.) Immediately remove from cookie sheets. Cool.

In small saucepan, melt chocolate chips, milk and 1 table-spoon margarine over low heat; stir until smooth. Remove from heat; stir in powdered sugar. If necessary, add additional powdered sugar for spreading consistency. Frost cookies. **3 to 4 dozen cookies.**

NUTRIENTS PER 1 COOKIE

Calories	90	Dietary Fiber	<1 g
Protein	1 g	Sodium	45 mg
Carbohydrate	9 g	Potassium	50 mg
Fat	6 g	Calcium	<2% U.S. RDA
Cholesterol	10 mg	Iron	2% U.S. RDA

Peanut Butter Cookies

½ cup sugar
½ cup firmly packed brown sugar
½ cup margarine or butter, softened
½ cup peanut butter
2 tablespoons milk
1 teaspoon vanilla
1 egg
1¾ cups all purpose flour
1 teaspoon baking soda
½ teaspoon salt

Heat oven to 375°F. In large bowl, cream sugar, brown sugar and margarine. Blend in peanut butter, milk, vanilla and egg. Stir in flour, baking soda and salt. Shape dough into 1-inch balls. Place 2 inches apart on ungreased cookie sheets; flatten balls in crisscross pattern with fork dipped in sugar. Bake at 375°F for 10 to 12 minutes or until golden brown. **3½ dozen cookies.**

VARIATION:

PEANUT BLOSSOMS: Shape dough into 1-inch balls; roll in sugar. Bake as directed above. Immediately top each cookie with a milk chocolate candy kiss, pressing down firmly so cookie cracks around edge.

NUTRIENTS PER 1 COOKIE

Calories	80	Dietary Fiber	<1 g
Protein	2 g	Sodium	100 mg
Carbohydrate	10 g	Potassium	40 mg
Fat	4 g	Calcium	<2% U.S. RDA
Cholesterol	6 mg	Iron	2% U.S. RDA

Snickerdoodles

1½ cups sugar
½ cup margarine or butter, softened
1 teaspoon vanilla
2 eggs
2¾ cups all purpose flour
1 teaspoon cream of tartar
½ teaspoon baking soda
¼ teaspoon salt
2 tablespoons sugar
2 teaspoons cinnamon

Heat oven to 400°F. In large bowl, combine 1½ cups sugar and margarine until light and fluffy. Blend in vanilla and eggs. Blend flour, cream of tartar, baking soda and salt into creamed mixture. Combine 2 tablespoons sugar and cinnamon. Shape dough into 1-inch balls; roll balls in sugar-cinnamon mixture. Place 2 inches apart onto ungreased cookie sheets. Bake at 400°F. for 8 to 10 minutes or until set. Remove from cookie sheets immediately. **4 dozen cookies.**

VARIATIONS:

CHOCOLATE SNICKERDOODLES: One-half cup unsweetened cocoa can be substituted for ½ cup of all purpose flour. Bake at 400°F. for 6 to 9 minutes or until set. **5½ dozen cookies.**

WHOLE WHEAT SNICKERDOODLES: A combination of 1 cup whole wheat flour and 1 cup all purpose flour can be substituted for all purpose flour. Bake at 350°F. for 10 to 14 minutes or until set. **4 to 5 dozen cookies.**

NUTRIENTS PER 1 COOKIE

Calories	70	Dietary Fiber	<1 g
Protein	1 g	Sodium	45 mg
Carbohydrate	12 g	Potassium	10 mg
Fat	2 g	Calcium	<2% U.S. RDA
Cholesterol	10 mg	Iron	2% U.S. RDA

No-Roll Sugar Cookies

    1 cup sugar
    1 cup powdered sugar
    1 cup margarine or butter, softened
    1 cup oil
    1 teaspoon vanilla
    2 eggs
 4¼ cups all purpose flour
    1 teaspoon baking soda
    1 teaspoon cream of tartar
    1 teaspoon salt

In large bowl, cream sugar, powdered sugar and margarine until light and fluffy. Add oil, vanilla and eggs; mix well.

Stir in flour, baking soda, cream of tartar and salt until well blended. Refrigerate at least 2 hours or overnight for easier handling.

Heat oven to 375°F. Shape dough into 1-inch balls; place 2 inches apart on ungreased cookie sheets. Flatten with bottom of glass dipped in sugar. Bake at 375°F. for 5 to 8 minutes or until set but not brown. **9 to 10 dozen cookies.**

VARIATIONS:

ALMOND SUGAR COOKIES: Add 1 teaspoon almond extract in addition to the vanilla.

ORANGE SUGAR COOKIES: Add 2 teaspoons grated orange peel and 1 teaspoon cinnamon with the dry ingredients.

NUTRIENTS PER 1 COOKIE

Calories	60	Dietary Fiber	<1 g
Protein	1 g	Sodium	45 mg
Carbohydrate	6 g	Potassium	5 mg
Fat	3 g	Calcium	<2% U.S. RDA
Cholesterol	4 mg	Iron	<2% U.S. RDA

Chocolate Truffle Cookies

      1 cup butter or margarine, softened
    ½ cup powdered sugar
    1½ teaspoons vanilla
1 oz. (1 square) unsweetened chocolate, melted
   2¼ cups all purpose flour
    ¼ teaspoon salt
6-oz. pkg. (1 cup) chocolate chips
    ¼ cup powdered sugar
      2 tablespoons unsweetened cocoa

Heat oven to 375°F. Lightly grease cookie sheets. In large bowl, cream butter and ½ cup powdered sugar. Blend in vanilla and chocolate. At low speed, blend in flour and salt. By hand, stir in chocolate chips. Shape into 1-inch balls;

place on prepared cookie sheets. Bake at 375°F. for 10 to 12 minutes; cool.

In small bowl, combine ¼ cup powdered sugar and cocoa. Roll cooled cookies in cocoa mixture. **4 dozen cookies.**

NUTRIENTS PER 1 COOKIE

Calories	80	Dietary Fiber	<1 g
Protein	1 g	Sodium	50 mg
Carbohydrate	8 g	Potassium	25 mg
Fat	5 g	Calcium	<2% U.S. RDA
Cholesterol	10 mg	Iron	2% U.S. RDA

No-Bake Honey Crispies

       3 cups crisp rice cereal
       1 cup powdered sugar
       1 cup honey
       1 cup peanut butter
       1 cup raisins
  1¾ to 2 cups shredded coconut

Line cookie sheet with waxed paper. In large bowl, combine all ingredients except coconut; mix well. Shape into 1¼-inch balls. Roll in shredded coconut. Place on prepared cookie sheet. Refrigerate 1 to 2 hours or until firm. Store in tightly covered container. **4 dozen cookies.**

NUTRIENTS PER 1 COOKIE

Calories	100	Dietary Fiber	1 g
Protein	2 g	Sodium	55 mg
Carbohydrate	15 g	Potassium	75 mg
Fat	4 g	Calcium	<2% U.S. RDA
Cholesterol	0 mg	Iron	2% U.S. RDA

Starlight Mint Surprise Cookies

- 1 cup sugar
- ½ cup firmly packed brown sugar
- ¾ cup margarine or butter, softened
- 2 eggs
- 2 tablespoons water
- 1 teaspoon vanilla
- 3 cups all purpose flour
- 1 teaspoon baking soda
- ½ teaspoon salt
- 2 (6-oz.) pkg. solid chocolate mint candy wafers, unwrapped
- 60 walnut halves

In large bowl, combine sugar, brown sugar, margarine, eggs, water and vanilla; mix well. Stir in flour, soda and salt; mix well. Chill dough at least 2 hours.

Heat oven to 375°F. Enclose each wafer completely in about 1 tablespoonful of dough; place 2 inches apart on ungreased cookie sheets. Top each with walnut half. Bake at 375°F. for 7 to 9 minutes or until light golden brown. **5 dozen cookies.**

NUTRIENTS PER 1 COOKIE

Calories	100	Dietary Fiber	<1 g
Protein	1 g	Sodium	65 mg
Carbohydrate	13 g	Potassium	40 mg
Fat	5 g	Calcium	<2% U.S. RDA
Cholesterol	8 mg	Iron	2% U.S. RDA

Lemon Kiss Cookies

- 1½ cups butter or margarine, softened
- ¾ cup sugar
- 1 tablespoon lemon extract
- 2¾ cups all purpose flour
- 1½ cups finely chopped almonds
- 14-oz. pkg. milk chocolate candy kisses

      Powdered sugar
½ cup semi-sweet chocolate chips
1 tablespoon shortening

In large bowl, beat butter, sugar and lemon extract until light and fluffy. Add flour and almonds; beat at low speed until well blended. Cover; refrigerate at least 1 hour for easier handling.

Heat oven to 375°F. Shape scant tablespoonful dough around each candy kiss, covering completely. Roll in hands to form ball. Place on ungreased cookie sheets. Bake at 375°F. for 8 to 12 minutes or until set and bottom edges are light golden brown. Cool 1 minute; remove from cookie sheets. Cool completely.

Lightly sprinkle cooled cookies with powdered sugar. In small saucepan over low heat, melt chocolate chips and shortening, stirring until smooth. Drizzle over each cookie. **About 6 dozen cookies.**

HIGH ALTITUDE: Decrease margarine to 1¼ cups. Bake as directed above.

NUTRIENTS PER 1 COOKIE

Calories	120	Dietary Fiber	<1 g
Protein	2 g	Sodium	45 mg
Carbohydrate	10 g	Potassium	50 mg
Fat	8 g	Calcium	2% U.S. RDA
Cholesterol	10 mg	Iron	2% U.S. RDA

Rosettes

2 eggs
1 tablespoon sugar
¼ teaspoon salt
1 cup all purpose flour
1 cup milk
¼ teaspoon vanilla
      Oil for deep frying

In medium bowl, beat eggs slightly. Add sugar and salt; blend well. Add flour and 1 cup milk alternately; blend until smooth. Stir in vanilla.

In deep fryer or heavy saucepan, heat 3 to 4 inches oil to 365°F. Place rosette iron in hot oil for about 30 to 60 seconds or until iron is hot. Gently dip hot iron into batter; DO NOT ALLOW TO RUN OVER TOP OF IRON. Return iron to hot oil, immersing completely for 25 to 30 seconds or until rosette is crisp and lightly browned.* Remove from oil; allow oil to drip off. Gently slip rosette off iron onto paper towel. Cool completely. Store in tightly covered container. **5 dozen rosettes.**

TIP: *If rosettes drop from mold, oil is too hot. If rosettes are soft, increase frying time. If rosettes have blisters, eggs are over beaten.

VARIATION:

ICED ROSETTES: In small bowl, combine 1 cup powdered sugar, 3 to 4 tablespoons milk and 5 to 6 drops food coloring; blend until smooth. Icing should be quite thin. Gently dip top edges of rosettes (not rounded edges) into icing. Allow to dry icing side up. Store in tightly covered container making sure sides do not touch.

NUTRIENTS PER 1 ROSETTE

Calories 50	Dietary Fiber.........................<1 g
Protein ....1 g	Sodium ....15 mg
Carbohydrate............................2 g	Potassium ....10 mg
Fat ....5 g	Calcium...............<2% U.S. RDA
Cholesterol ....8 mg	Iron ....<2% U.S. RDA

Cashew Tassies

    1 cup all purpose flour
   ½ cup margarine or butter, softened
3-oz. pkg. cream cheese, softened

FILLING

- ¾ cup coarsely chopped cashews
- ½ cup firmly packed brown sugar
- 1 teaspoon vanilla
- 1 egg

Heat oven to 350°F. In small bowl, combine flour, margarine and cream cheese; blend well. Divide dough into 24 pieces. Press dough in bottom and up sides of 24 ungreased miniature muffin cups. Divide cashews evenly into unbaked shells. In small bowl, beat brown sugar, vanilla and egg until well blended. Spoon 1 teaspoon filling over cashews. Bake at 350°F. for 20 to 25 minutes or until filling is set and crusts are light golden brown. Cool 1 minute; remove from pans. **24 cookies.**

NUTRIENTS PER 1 COOKIE

Calories	110	Dietary Fiber	<1 g
Protein	2 g	Sodium	60 mg
Carbohydrate	10 g	Potassium	50 mg
Fat	7 g	Calcium	<2% U.S. RDA
Cholesterol	15 mg	Iron	2% U.S. RDA

Shortbread

BASIC DOUGH

- 2 cups powdered sugar
- 2 cups butter or margarine, softened
- 2 egg yolks
- 4 cups all purpose flour
- 1 cup cornstarch

In large bowl, combine powdered sugar and butter; beat until light and fluffy. Add egg yolks; blend well. Add flour and cornstarch; stir until mixture forms a smooth dough. Shape and flavor dough as directed below.

VARIATIONS:

SHORTBREAD TRIANGLES:
½ recipe basic dough

Shape ½ recipe dough into a 12-inch roll, 1½ inches in diameter. Wrap in waxed paper. Press sides of roll with palm of hand to make 3 even sides forming triangular shape. Press roll against countertop to smooth and flatten sides. Refrigerate until firm. Heat oven to 350°F. Slice dough into ¼-inch slices. Place on ungreased cookie sheets. Bake at 350°F. for 8 to 13 minutes or until lightly browned and set. Prick tops of cookies with fork; remove from cookie sheets. **About 4 dozen cookies.**

NUTRIENTS PER 1 SHORTBREAD TRIANGLE COOKIE

Calories	70	Dietary Fiber	<1 g
Protein	1 g	Sodium	40 mg
Carbohydrate	7 g	Potassium	5 mg
Fat	4 g	Calcium	<2% U.S. RDA
Cholesterol	15 mg	Iron	<2% U.S. RDA

ORANGE-NUT SHORTBREAD COOKIES:
½ recipe basic dough
¾ cup chopped walnuts
1 tablespoon grated orange peel
   Sugar
2 cups powdered sugar
3 tablespoons butter or margarine, softened
2 to 3 tablespoons orange juice
1 teaspoon grated orange peel

Combine ½ recipe dough, walnuts and 1 tablespoon orange peel; knead to blend. Shape dough into 1-inch balls. Place 2 inches apart on ungreased cookie sheets. Flatten balls with glass dipped in sugar. Bake at 350°F. for 8 to 13 minutes or until lightly browned and set. Immediately remove from cookie sheets; cool.

In small bowl, combine powdered sugar, butter, orange juice and 1 teaspoon grated orange peel; beat until smooth. Frost cooled cookies. **About 4½ to 5 dozen cookies.**

NUTRIENTS PER 1 ORANGE-NUT SHORTBREAD

Calories	90	Dietary Fiber	<1 g
Protein	1 g	Sodium	35 mg
Carbohydrate	7 g	Potassium	15 mg
Fat	5 g	Calcium	<2% U.S. RDA
Cholesterol	15 mg	Iron	<2% U.S. RDA

Swedish Tea Cakes

½ cup powdered sugar
1 cup margarine or butter, softened
2 teaspoons vanilla
2 cups all purpose flour
1 cup finely chopped or ground almonds or pecans
¼ teaspoon salt
Powdered sugar

Heat oven to 325°F. In large bowl, combine ½ cup powdered sugar, margarine and vanilla; blend well. Stir in flour, almonds and salt until dough holds together. Shape into 1-inch balls. Place 1 inch apart on ungreased cookie sheets. Bake at 325°F. for 15 to 20 minutes or until set but not brown. Immediately remove from cookie sheets. Cool slightly; roll in powdered sugar. Cool completely; roll again in powdered sugar. **5 dozen cookies.**

NUTRIENTS PER 1 COOKIE

Calories	70	Dietary Fiber	<1 g
Protein	1 g	Sodium	45 mg
Carbohydrate	8 g	Potassium	25 mg
Fat	4 g	Calcium	<2% U.S. RDA
Cholesterol	0 mg	Iron	<2% U.S. RDA

Chocolate-Nut Wafers

```
    1  cup sugar
   ¾  cup margarine or butter, softened
2 oz.  (2 squares) unsweetened chocolate, melted
    1  teaspoon vanilla
    1  egg
  2¼  cups all purpose flour
   ¼  teaspoon salt
   ¼  teaspoon baking soda
   ¼  teaspoon cinnamon
   ½  cup chopped nuts
```

In large bowl, combine sugar, margarine, chocolate, vanilla and egg; blend well. Stir in remaining ingredients until well blended. Divide dough in half on 2 sheets of waxed paper; shape each half into roll 2 inches in diameter. Wrap; refrigerate about 3 hours or until firm.

Heat oven to 400°F. Cut dough into ¼-inch slices; place 2 inches apart on ungreased cookie sheets. Bake at 400°F. for 6 to 8 minutes or until set. (Do not overbake.) Immediately remove from cookie sheets. **5 to 6 dozen cookies.**

NUTRIENTS PER 1 COOKIE

Calories	50	Dietary Fiber	<1 g
Protein	1 g	Sodium	35 mg
Carbohydrate	6 g	Potassium	15 mg
Fat	3 g	Calcium	<2% U.S. RDA
Cholesterol	4 mg	Iron	<2% U.S. RDA

Basic Refrigerator Cookies

```
   ¾  cup sugar
   ¾  cup firmly packed brown sugar
    1  cup margarine or butter, softened
  1½  teaspoons vanilla
    2  eggs
```

    3 cups all purpose flour
 1½ teaspoons baking powder
   ¾ teaspoon salt
    1 cup finely chopped nuts

In large bowl, combine sugar, brown sugar, margarine, vanilla and eggs; blend well. Stir in flour, baking powder and salt; blend well. Stir in nuts. Divide dough into thirds on 3 sheets of waxed paper; shape each third into roll 1½ inches in diameter. Wrap; refrigerate at least 2 hours or until firm.

Heat oven to 425°F. Cut dough into ¼-inch slices. Place 1 inch apart on ungreased cookie sheets. Bake at 425°F. for 5 to 7 minutes or until light brown. Immediately remove from cookie sheets. **7½ dozen cookies.**

TIP: Cookie dough keeps up to 2 weeks in refrigerator and up to 6 weeks in freezer. Slice and bake frozen dough same as directed above.

HIGH ALTITUDE: Add 3 tablespoons milk with eggs. Prepare and bake as directed.

VARIATIONS:

ORANGE OR LEMON REFRIGERATOR COOKIES: Add 1 tablespoon grated peel with flour.

SPICE REFRIGERATOR COOKIES: Add 1 teaspoon cinnamon, ½ teaspoon nutmeg and ¼ to ½ teaspoon cloves with flour.

COCONUT REFRIGERATOR COOKIES: Add 1 cup coconut with nuts.

NUTRIENTS PER 1 COOKIE

Calories	60	Dietary Fiber	<1 g
Protein	1 g	Sodium	50 mg
Carbohydrate	7 g	Potassium	20 mg
Fat	3 g	Calcium	<2% U.S. RDA
Cholesterol	6 mg	Iron	<2% U.S. RDA

Oatmeal Refrigerator Cookies

      1 cup sugar
      1 cup firmly packed brown sugar
      1 cup margarine or butter, softened
      2 eggs
      2 cups all purpose flour
      1 teaspoon baking powder
      1 teaspoon baking soda
      1 teaspoon salt
      2 cups quick-cooking rolled oats
      1 cup coconut
½ to 1 cup chopped nuts

In large bowl, combine sugar, brown sugar, margarine and
eggs; beat well. Add flour, baking powder, baking soda and
salt; mix well. Stir in oats, coconut and nuts. Divide dough
in half. On waxed paper, shape each half into a roll 2 inches
in diameter. Wrap; refrigerate at least 2 hours or until firm.

Heat oven to 375°F. Cut dough into ¼-inch slices. Place 2
inches apart on ungreased cookie sheets. Bake at 375°F. for
8 to 11 minutes or until golden brown. Immediately remove
from cookie sheets. **6 dozen cookies.**

NUTRIENTS PER 1 COOKIE

Calories	80	Dietary Fiber	<1 g
Protein	1 g	Sodium	80 mg
Carbohydrate	11 g	Potassium	35 mg
Fat	4 g	Calcium	<2% U.S. RDA
Cholesterol	8 mg	Iron	2% U.S. RDA

Cream Cheese Sugar Cookies

      1 cup sugar
      1 cup margarine or butter, softened
  3-oz. pkg. cream cheese, softened
     ½ teaspoon salt

½ teaspoon almond extract
½ teaspoon vanilla
1 egg yolk (reserve white)
2 cups all purpose flour
   Colored sugar, if desired

In large bowl, combine sugar, margarine, cream cheese, salt, almond extract, vanilla and egg yolk; blend well. Stir in flour until well blended. Refrigerate dough 2 hours.

Heat oven to 375°F. On lightly floured surface, roll out dough one-third at a time to ⅛-inch thickness. Cut into desired shapes with lightly-floured cookie cutters. Place 1 inch apart on ungreased cookie sheets. Leave cookie plain or if desired, brush with slightly beaten egg white and sprinkle with colored sugar. Bake at 375°F. for 7 to 10 minutes or until light golden brown. Cool completely. If desired, frost and decorate plain cookies. **5 to 6 dozen cookies.**

NUTRIENTS PER 1 COOKIE

Calories	50	Dietary Fiber	<1 g
Protein	1 g	Sodium	50 mg
Carbohydrate	6 g	Potassium	5 mg
Fat	3 g	Calcium	<2% U.S. RDA
Cholesterol	4 mg	Iron	<2% U.S. RDA

Frosted Ginger Cut-Outs

COOKIES

1 cup shortening
1 cup molasses
3 cups all purpose flour
2 teaspoons baking soda
1 teaspoon salt
½ teaspoon ginger
¼ teaspoon nutmeg
¼ teaspoon cloves

FROSTING

- ¾ cup water
- 1 envelope unflavored gelatin
- ¾ cup sugar
- ¾ cup powdered sugar
- 1 teaspoon baking powder
- 1 teaspoon vanilla

In large bowl, combine shortening and molasses; blend well. Add flour and remaining cookie ingredients to molasses mixture; mix well. Cover with plastic wrap; refrigerate at least 2 hours for easier handling.

Heat oven to 350°F. On well-floured surface, roll dough to ¼-inch thickness; cut with floured cookie cutter. Place 1 inch apart on ungreased cookie sheets. Bake at 350°F. for 8 to 10 minutes or until set. Cool completely.

In 2-quart saucepan, combine water and gelatin; let stand 5 minutes. Stir in sugar; bring to a boil. Reduce heat and simmer 10 minutes. Stir in powdered sugar; beat until foamy. Stir in baking powder and vanilla; beat at highest speed until thick. Turn cookies over and spread frosting over underside to within ⅛ inch of edge. Decorate, if desired. Let stand until frosting is dry. **3 dozen cookies.**

VARIATION:

GINGERBREAD MEN: Roll dough ¼-inch thick for soft cookies or ⅛-inch thick for crisp cookies. Cut dough with floured gingerbread men cookie cutter. Bake as directed above. To decorate, pipe frosting on cooled cookies.

NUTRIENTS PER 1 COOKIE

Calories 130	Dietary Fiber.........................<1 g
Protein.......................................1 g	Sodium..............................130 mg
Carbohydrate..........................20 g	Potassium ....110 mg
Fat...6 g	Calcium................2% U.S. RDA
Cholesterol...........................0 mg	Iron.......................6% U.S. RDA

Fattimand

8 egg yolks
2 eggs
¾ cup sugar
3 tablespoons rum
1 cup whipping cream
5 cups all purpose flour
1 teaspoon cardamom
Oil for deep frying
1 cup sifted powdered sugar
½ teaspoon cinnamon

In large bowl, combine egg yolks, eggs, sugar and rum; beat until thick and lemon colored, about 5 minutes. Add cream until well blended. By hand, stir in flour and cardamom to form a soft dough. Wrap dough in plastic wrap; refrigerate overnight.

In deep fryer or heavy saucepan, heat 3 to 4 inches oil to 365°F. Meanwhile, divide dough into 4 parts; refrigerate 3 parts of dough. On lightly floured surface, roll out 1 part dough to ⅟₁₆-inch thickness. Cut dough into diamond shapes about 5x2½ inches as shown in diagram. Make a lengthwise slit in center of each diamond and pull 1 pointed end through slit.

Drop dough pieces into hot oil, about 3 or 4 at a time. Fry 1 to 1½ minutes or until deep golden brown and puffed. Drain on paper towel; cool. Repeat with remaining dough. In small bowl, combine powdered sugar and cinnamon; mix well. Sprinkle lightly over cooled cookies just before serving. Store in tightly covered container in cool dry place. **8 dozen cookies.**

NUTRIENTS PER 1 COOKIE

Calories	70	Dietary Fiber	<1 g
Protein	1 g	Sodium	0 mg
Carbohydrate	8 g	Potassium	10 mg
Fat	3 g	Calcium	<2% U.S. RDA
Cholesterol	30 mg	Iron	2% U.S. RDA

Spritz

1   cup powdered sugar
1   cup butter or margarine, softened
½   teaspoon vanilla
1   egg
2⅓   cups all purpose flour
¼   teaspoon salt

Heat oven to 400°F. In large bowl, cream powdered sugar, butter, vanilla and egg until light and fluffy. Stir in flour and salt; blend well. Fill cookie press; press dough into desired shapes onto ungreased cookie sheets. Bake at 400°F. for 5 to 7 minutes or until lightly browned on edges. Immediately remove from cookie sheets. **5 dozen cookies.**

VARIATIONS:

CHOCOLATE SPRITZ: Add 2 oz. melted unsweetened chocolate to creamed mixture.

EGGNOG SPRITZ: One teaspoon rum flavoring can be substituted for vanilla. Add ¼ teaspoon nutmeg with dry ingredients.

ORANGE SPRITZ: Add 1 tablespoon grated orange peel with dry ingredients.

NUTRIENTS PER 1 COOKIE

Calories	50	Dietary Fiber	<1 g
Protein	1 g	Sodium	45 mg
Carbohydrate	5 g	Potassium	5 mg
Fat	3 g	Calcium	<2% U.S. RDA
Cholesterol	4 mg	Iron	<2% U.S. RDA

"Dip-a-Cookie" Treats

8 oz.   chocolate, vanilla or butterscotch-flavored candy
        coating
        Any of the following cookies can be used:

creme-filled vanilla, chocolate or peanut butter
    sandwich cookies
vanilla wafers
shortbread cookies
sugar wafers
coconut bar cookies
fig bars
round buttery crackers filled with peanut butter
any purchased cookie

In small saucepan, melt candy coating over low heat, stirring constantly. Dip cookies halfway into coating; allow excess to drip off. Place on waxed paper to dry. Decorate as
desired. **¾ cup cookie coating.**

MICROWAVE DIRECTIONS: Place candy coating in
small microwave-safe bowl. Microwave on HIGH for 1½ to
2 minutes or until smooth, stirring once halfway through
cooking. Continue as directed above.

NUTRIENTS: Variables in this recipe make it impossible to calculate
nutrition information.

Peanut Butter 'n Fudge Brownies

BROWNIES

    2 cups sugar
    1 cup margarine or butter, softened
    4 eggs
    2 teaspoons vanilla
  1½ cups all purpose flour
   ¾ cup unsweetened cocoa
    1 teaspoon baking powder
   ½ teaspoon salt
    1 cup peanut butter chips
   ¾ cup peanut butter
   ⅓ cup margarine or butter, softened
   ⅓ cup sugar

2   tablespoons flour
¾   teaspoon vanilla
2   eggs

FROSTING

3 oz.   (3 squares) unsweetened chocolate
3   tablespoons margarine or butter
2⅔   cups powdered sugar
¼   teaspoon salt
¾   teaspoon vanilla
4 to 5   tablespoons water

Heat oven to 350°F. Grease 13x9-inch pan. In large bowl, beat 2 cups sugar and 1 cup margarine until light and fluffy. Add 4 eggs, one at a time, beating well after each addition. Stir in 2 teaspoons vanilla. In small bowl, combine 1½ cups flour, cocoa, baking powder and ½ teaspoon salt. Gradually add flour mixture to sugar mixture; mix well. Stir in peanut butter chips.

In small bowl, beat peanut butter and ⅓ cup margarine until smooth. Add ⅓ cup sugar and 2 tablespoons flour; blend well. Add ¾ teaspoon vanilla and 2 eggs; beat until smooth. Spread half of chocolate mixture in prepared pan. Spread peanut butter mixture over chocolate mixture. Spread remaining chocolate mixture over peanut butter mixture. Gently cut through layers with knife to marble. Bake at 350°F. for 40 to 50 minutes or until top springs back when touched lightly in center and brownies begin to pull away from sides of pan. Cool completely.

In medium saucepan, melt chocolate and 3 tablespoons margarine over low heat, stirring constantly until well blended. Remove from heat. Stir in powdered sugar, ¼ teaspoon salt, ¾ teaspoon vanilla and enough water for desired frosting consistency; blend until smooth. Frost cooled brownies. Cut into bars. **36 bars.**

NUTRIENTS PER 1 BAR

Calories	260	Dietary Fiber	2 g
Protein	5 g	Sodium	210 mg
Carbohydrate	30 g	Potassium	105 mg
Fat	14 g	Calcium	2% U.S. RDA
Cholesterol	45 mg	Iron	4% U.S. RDA

Favorite Fudge Brownies

BARS

5 oz.	(5 squares) unsweetened chocolate, cut into pieces
¾	cup butter or margarine
1	tablespoon vanilla
2¼	cups sugar
4	eggs
1⅓	cups all purpose flour
1½	cups coarsely chopped nuts

FROSTING

1½	cups powdered sugar
2	tablespoons unsweetened cocoa
¼	cup butter or margarine, softened
2	tablespoons milk
½	teaspoon vanilla
	Whole pecans or walnuts, if desired

Heat oven to 375°F. Grease 13x9-inch pan. In small saucepan over low heat, melt chocolate and ¾ cup butter, stirring constantly. Remove from heat. Stir in 1 tablespoon vanilla; set aside.

In large bowl, beat sugar and 4 eggs about 7 minutes or until sugar is dissolved. Fold chocolate mixture, flour and nuts into egg mixture just until blended. Pour batter into prepared pan. Bake at 375°F. for 25 to 35 minutes. (Do not overbake.) Cool.

In small bowl, blend all frosting ingredients until smooth. Spread over bars. Refrigerate 1 hour; cut into bars. Garnish each bar with whole pecan. Store in refrigerator. **36 bars.**

NUTRIENTS PER 1 BAR

Calories 190	Dietary Fiber ....1 g
Protein ....2 g	Sodium ....65 mg
Carbohydrate ....22 g	Potassium ....75 mg
Fat ....11 g	Calcium ....<2% U.S. RDA
Cholesterol ....44 mg	Iron ....4% U.S. RDA

Butterscotch Squares

1½ cups firmly packed brown sugar
½ cup margarine or butter, softened
2 teaspoons vanilla
2 eggs
2 cups all purpose flour
2 teaspoons baking powder
½ teaspoon salt
½ cup chopped nuts
Powdered sugar

Heat oven to 350°F. Grease 13x9-inch pan. In large bowl, combine brown sugar and margarine. Add vanilla and eggs, mixing well. Add flour, baking powder, salt and nuts to sugar mixture; blend well. Spread in prepared pan. Bake at 350°F. for 15 to 20 minutes or until edges are light brown. (Do not overbake.) Cool; sprinkle with powdered sugar. **24 bars.**

FOOD PROCESSOR DIRECTIONS: In food processor bowl with metal blade, combine brown sugar and margarine (no need to soften). Cover; process until well blended. Add vanilla and eggs. Cover; process about 10 seconds or until blended. Add flour, baking powder and salt. Cover; process 10 to 20 seconds until well combined. Add nuts. Cover; process 5 seconds. Continue as directed above.

NUTRIENTS PER 1 BAR

Calories	150	Dietary Fiber	<1 g
Protein	2 g	Sodium	125 mg
Carbohydrate	22 g	Potassium	75 mg
Fat	6 g	Calcium	2% U.S. RDA
Cholesterol	25 mg	Iron	6% U.S. RDA

Crispy Date Bars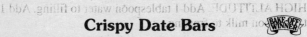

CRUST
1 cup all purpose flour
½ cup firmly packed brown sugar
½ cup margarine or butter, softened

FILLING
1 cup chopped pitted dates
½ cup sugar
½ cup margarine or butter
1 egg, well beaten
2 cups crisp rice cereal
1 cup chopped nuts
1 teaspoon vanilla

FROSTING
2 cups powdered sugar
½ teaspoon vanilla
3-oz. pkg. cream cheese, softened

Heat oven to 375°F. In small bowl, combine crust ingredients; mix until crumbly. Press in bottom of ungreased 9-inch square pan. Bake at 375°F. for 10 to 12 minutes or until golden brown.

In medium saucepan, combine dates, sugar and ½ cup margarine. Cook over medium heat until mixture boils, stirring constantly; simmer 3 minutes. Blend about ¼ cup hot mixture into beaten egg; return to saucepan. Cook until mixture bubbles, stirring constantly. Remove from heat; stir in cereal, nuts and 1 teaspoon vanilla. Spread over baked crust; cool.

In small bowl, combine frosting ingredients; beat at low speed until smooth. Spread over filling. Cut into bars. **24 bars.**

HIGH ALTITUDE: Add 1 tablespoon water to filling. Add 1 tablespoon milk to frosting.

NUTRIENTS PER 1 BAR

Calories 230	Dietary Fiber...........................1 g
Protein.....................................2 g	Sodium...........................130 mg
Carbohydrate.........................29 g	Potassium...........................105 mg
Fat ....12 g	Calcium...............<2% U.S. RDA
Cholesterol.........................15 mg	Iron.......................4% U.S. RDA

Candy Bar Cookies

BASE

- 2 cups all purpose flour
- ¾ cup powdered sugar
- ¾ cup margarine or butter, softened
- 2 tablespoons whipping cream
- 1 teaspoon vanilla

FILLING

- 28 caramels
- ¼ cup whipping cream
- ¼ cup margarine or butter
- 1 cup powdered sugar
- 1 cup chopped pecans

GLAZE

- ½ cup semi-sweet chocolate chips
- 2 tablespoons whipping cream
- 1 tablespoon margarine or butter
- ¼ cup powdered sugar
- 1 teaspoon vanilla

Heat oven to 325°F. In large bowl, blend all base ingredients until crumbly. Press mixture into ungreased 15x10-inch jelly roll pan. Bake at 325°F. for 15 to 20 minutes or until lightly browned.

In small saucepan, melt caramels with ¼ cup cream and ¼ cup margarine, stirring constantly, until smooth. Remove from heat; stir in 1 cup powdered sugar and pecans. (Add additional cream if needed for spreading consistency.) Spread over base.

In small saucepan over low heat, melt chocolate chips with 2 tablespoons cream and 1 tablespoon margarine, stirring constantly, until smooth. Remove from heat; stir in ¼ cup powdered sugar and vanilla. Drizzle glaze over bars. **48 bars.**

NUTRIENTS PER 1 BAR

Calories	130	Dietary Fiber	<1 g
Protein	1 g	Sodium	60 mg
Carbohydrate	14 g	Potassium	40 mg
Fat	8 g	Calcium	<2% U.S. RDA
Cholesterol	2 mg	Iron	2% U.S. RDA

Easy Toffee Bars

15 graham crackers (2½-inch squares)
 1 cup firmly packed brown sugar
 1 cup butter or margarine
6-oz. pkg. (1 cup) milk chocolate chips
 ¼ cup chopped nuts

Heat oven to 400°F. Line 13x9-inch pan with foil; butter foil. Arrange graham crackers in prepared pan. (Some graham crackers may need to be broken apart so that entire pan bottom is covered.) In medium saucepan, combine brown sugar and butter; bring to boil. Remove from heat; pour over graham crackers. Bake at 400°F. for 5 minutes. Remove from oven; immediately sprinkle with chocolate chips.

When chips are soft, spread over top; sprinkle with nuts. Refrigerate about 30 minutes until chocolate is set. Cut into bars or break into pieces. Store in refrigerator. **24 bars.**

NUTRIENTS PER 1 BAR

Calories	160	Dietary Fiber	1 g
Protein	1 g	Sodium	130 mg
Carbohydrate	16 g	Potassium	85 mg
Fat	11 g	Calcium	2% U.S. RDA
Cholesterol	20 mg	Iron	2% U.S. RDA

Chocolate Caramel Bars

BASE
- 1 pkg. pudding-included devil's food cake mix
- ½ cup quick-cooking rolled oats
- ⅓ cup margarine or butter, softened
- 1 egg

TOPPING
- 6-oz. pkg. (1 cup) semi-sweet chocolate chips
- ¾ cup caramel ice cream topping
- 3 tablespoons flour
- ½ cup chopped nuts

Heat oven to 350°F. Grease and flour 13x9-inch pan. In large bowl, combine all base ingredients at low speed until crumbly. Reserve 1 cup crumb mixture for topping. Press remaining crumb mixture in bottom of prepared pan. Bake at 350°F. for 8 to 10 minutes or until base is slightly puffy.

Sprinkle warm base with chocolate chips. In small bowl, combine caramel topping and flour; pour evenly over chocolate chips. In small bowl, combine 1 cup reserved crumb mixture and nuts; sprinkle over caramel topping. Return to oven and bake an additional 10 to 20 minutes or until set in center. Cool completely. Cut into bars. **36 bars.**

NUTRIENTS PER 1 BAR

Calories	140	Dietary Fiber	1 g
Protein	2 g	Sodium	160 mg
Carbohydrate	20 g	Potassium	60 mg
Fat	6 g	Calcium	4% U.S. RDA
Cholesterol	8 mg	Iron	2% U.S. RDA

Sunburst Lemon Bars

CRUST

    2   cups all purpose flour
   ½   cup powdered sugar
    1   cup margarine or butter, softened

FILLING

    4   eggs, slightly beaten
    2   cups sugar
   ¼   cup flour
    1   teaspoon baking powder
   ¼   cup lemon juice

GLAZE

    1   cup powdered sugar
 2 to 3   tablespoons lemon juice

Heat oven to 350°F. In large bowl, combine 2 cups flour, ½ cup powdered sugar and margarine at low speed until crumbly. Press mixture evenly in bottom of ungreased 13x9-inch pan. Bake at 350°F. for 20 to 30 minutes or until light golden brown.

In large bowl, combine eggs, sugar, ¼ cup flour and baking powder; blend well. Stir in lemon juice. Pour mixture over warm crust. Return to oven and bake 25 to 30 minutes or until top is light golden brown. Cool completely.

In small bowl, combine powdered sugar and enough lemon juice for desired glaze consistency; blend until smooth. Drizzle over cooled bars. Cut into bars. **36 bars.**

NUTRIENTS PER 1 BAR

Calories	150	Dietary Fiber	<1 g
Protein	2 g	Sodium	75 mg
Carbohydrate	22 g	Potassium	20 mg
Fat	6 g	Calcium	<2% U.S. RDA
Cholesterol	30 mg	Iron	2% U.S. RDA

Cheesecake Bars

BASE

    1/3 cup margarine or butter, softened
    1/3 cup firmly packed brown sugar
     1 cup all purpose flour
    1/2 cup finely chopped walnuts

FILLING

    1/4 cup sugar
  8-oz. pkg. cream cheese, softened
     2 tablespoons milk
     1 tablespoon lemon juice
    1/2 teaspoon vanilla
     1 egg

Heat oven to 350°F. In small bowl, beat margarine and brown sugar until light and fluffy. Combine flour and walnuts with creamed mixture. Reserve 1 cup for topping. Press remainder into bottom of ungreased 8 or 9-inch square pan. Bake at 350°F. for 9 to 11 minutes or until lightly browned.

In small bowl, blend sugar and cream cheese until smooth. Add milk, lemon juice, vanilla and egg; beat well. Spread over baked crust. Sprinkle with reserved crumb mixture. Bake at 350°F. for 23 to 27 minutes or until lightly browned. Cool; cut into bars. Store in refrigerator. **24 bars.**

NUTRIENTS PER 1 BAR

Calories 120	Dietary Fiber.........................<1 g
Protein...2 g	Sodium.......................................60 mg
Carbohydrate........................10 g	Potassium..............................40 mg
Fat ....8 g	Calcium.................<2% U.S. RDA
Cholesterol........................20 mg	Iron...........................2% U.S. RDA

Chewy Granola Bars

1 cup firmly packed brown sugar
⅔ cup peanut butter
½ cup light corn syrup
½ cup margarine or butter, melted
2 teaspoons vanilla
3 cups quick-cooking rolled oats
½ cup coconut
½ cup sunflower nuts
½ cup raisins
⅓ cup wheat germ
2 tablespoons sesame seed
6-oz. pkg. (1 cup) semi-sweet chocolate or carob chips,
  if desired

Heat oven to 350°F. Grease 13x9-inch pan. In large bowl, combine brown sugar, peanut butter, corn syrup, margarine and vanilla; blend well. Stir in remaining ingredients. Press mixture evenly in prepared pan. Bake at 350°F. for 15 to 20 minutes or until light golden brown. Cool completely. Cut into bars. **24 bars.**

NUTRIENTS PER 1 BAR

Calories 240	Dietary Fiber............................3 g
Protein...5 g	Sodium.......................................95 mg
Carbohydrate........................30 g	Potassium..............................200 mg
Fat ....12 g	Calcium.................2% U.S. RDA
Cholesterol............................0 mg	Iron...........................10% U.S. RDA

Glazed Fruitcake Squares

2 cups powdered sugar
½ cup margarine or butter, softened
¼ cup brandy*
2 eggs
2 cups all purpose flour
1 tablespoon baking powder
1 teaspoon salt
2 cups chopped candied fruit
1 cup coarsely chopped walnuts

GLAZE
1 cup powdered sugar
3 to 4 tablespoons brandy*
1 tablespoon margarine or butter, softened

Heat oven to 375°F. Grease 15x10-inch jelly roll pan. In large bowl, combine 2 cups powdered sugar, ½ cup margarine, ¼ cup brandy and eggs; blend well. By hand, stir in flour, baking powder, salt, candied fruit and walnuts; press into prepared pan. Bake at 375°F. for 15 to 25 minutes or until light golden brown; cool. In small bowl, combine all glaze ingredients; beat until smooth. Drizzle glaze over top. When glaze is set, cut into bars. **48 bars.**

TIPS: *To substitute for brandy, use ¼ cup water or orange juice and 1 teaspoon brandy extract.

**To substitute for brandy in the glaze, combine 1 to 2 tablespoons water with ½ teaspoon brandy extract.

NUTRIENTS PER 1 BAR

Calories	100	Dietary Fiber	<1 g
Protein	1 g	Sodium	85 mg
Carbohydrate	16 g	Potassium	20 mg
Fat	4 g	Calcium	<2% U.S. RDA
Cholesterol	10 mg	Iron	<2% U.S. RDA

Spicy Zucchini Bars

½ cup firmly packed brown sugar
½ cup sugar
¾ cup margarine or butter, softened
1¾ cups all purpose flour
1½ teaspoons baking powder
1 teaspoon cinnamon
½ teaspoon nutmeg
2 eggs
1 teaspoon vanilla
2 cups shredded zucchini, patted dry with paper towel
1 cup chopped nuts
½ cup coconut

FROSTING

3 cups powdered sugar
1 teaspoon cinnamon
3 tablespoons milk
3 tablespoons margarine or butter, softened
1 teaspoon vanilla

Heat oven to 350°F. Grease 15x10-inch jelly roll pan. In large bowl, cream brown sugar, sugar and ¾ cup margarine. Blend flour, baking powder, 1 teaspoon cinnamon, nutmeg, eggs and 1 teaspoon vanilla into creamed mixture. Stir in zucchini, nuts and coconut. Spread dough evenly in prepared pan. Bake at 350°F. for 30 to 35 minutes or until light golden brown. Cool.

In large bowl, blend all frosting ingredients until smooth and creamy. Spread over bars. **48 bars.**

NUTRIENTS PER 1 BAR

Calories	115	Dietary Fiber	<1 g
Protein	1 g	Sodium	55 mg
Carbohydrate	15 g	Potassium	45 mg
Fat	6 g	Calcium	<2% U.S. RDA
Cholesterol	10 mg	Iron	2% U.S. RDA

Pumpkin Bars

BARS

2 cups all purpose flour
2 cups sugar
2 teaspoons baking powder
1 teaspoon baking soda
1 teaspoon cinnamon
1 teaspoon nutmeg
½ teaspoon cloves
½ teaspoon salt
1 cup oil
16-oz. can pumpkin
4 eggs

FROSTING

2 cups powdered sugar
⅓ cup margarine or butter, softened
3-oz. pkg. cream cheese, softened
1 tablespoon milk
1 teaspoon vanilla

Heat oven to 350°F. Grease 15x10-inch jelly roll pan. In large bowl, blend all bar ingredients at low speed until moistened. Beat 2 minutes at medium speed. Pour into prepared pan. Bake at 350°F. for 25 to 30 minutes or until toothpick inserted in center comes out clean. Cool.

In small bowl, combine frosting ingredients; beat until smooth. Spread over cooled bars. Refrigerate leftovers. **48 bars.**

HIGH ALTITUDE: Decrease baking soda to ½ teaspoon; bake at 375°F. for 30 to 35 minutes.

VARIATION:

CURRANT PUMPKIN BARS: Add ½ cup dried currants or raisins.

NUTRIENTS PER 1 BAR

Calories 140	Dietary Fiber........................<1 g
Protein...................................1 g	Sodium.................................85 mg
Carbohydrate.......................17 g	Potassium............................40 mg
Fat..7 g	Calcium.................<2% U.S. RDA
Cholesterol.......................25 mg	Iron..........................2% U.S. RDA

Chocolate Mint Parfait Bars

BASE

    1   pkg. pudding-included devil's food cake mix
   1/3 cup margarine or butter, softened
    1   egg

FILLING

    1   envelope unflavored gelatin
   1/4 cup boiling water
    4   cups powdered sugar
   1/2 cup margarine or butter, softened
   1/2 cup shortening
   1/4 teaspoon peppermint extract
2 to 3 drops green food coloring

FROSTING

6-oz. pkg. (1 cup) semi-sweet chocolate chips
   3   tablespoons margarine or butter

Heat oven to 350°F. Grease 15x10x1-inch jelly roll pan. In large bowl, combine all base ingredients at low speed until crumbly. Press in bottom of prepared pan. Bake at 350°F. for 10 minutes. Cool completely.

Dissolve gelatin in boiling water; cool. In large bowl, combine dissolved gelatin and 2 cups of the powdered sugar. Add 1/2 cup margarine, shortening, peppermint extract and food coloring; beat 1 minute at medium speed or until smooth and creamy. Blend in remaining 2 cups powdered sugar until smooth. Spread filling evenly over cooled base.

In small saucepan over low heat, melt chocolate chips and 3 tablespoons margarine, stirring constantly until well blended. Spoon frosting evenly over filling, carefully spreading to cover. Refrigerate until firm; cut into bars. Store in refrigerator. **48 bars.**

TIP: For easier cutting, remove from refrigerator 20 minutes before serving.

NUTRIENTS PER 1 BAR

Calories	150	Dietary Fiber	<1 g
Protein	1 g	Sodium	135 mg
Carbohydrate	18 g	Potassium	30 mg
Fat	8 g	Calcium	2% U.S. RDA
Cholesterol	6 mg	Iron	<2% U.S. RDA

Raspberry Chocolate Supremes

CRUST
- 1 cup all purpose flour
- ¼ cup powdered sugar
- ½ cup margarine or butter

FILLING
- ½ cup raspberry jam
- 3-oz. pkg. cream cheese, softened
- 2 tablespoons milk
- 1 cup vanilla milk chips, or 4 oz. white chocolate, melted

GLAZE
- 2 oz. (2 squares) semi-sweet chocolate, cut into pieces
- 1 tablespoon shortening

Heat oven to 375°F. In medium bowl, combine flour and powdered sugar. Using pastry blender or fork, cut in margarine until crumbly. Press mixture in ungreased 9-inch square pan. Bake at 375°F. for 15 to 17 minutes or until lightly browned.

Spread jam evenly over baked crust. In small bowl, beat cream cheese and milk until smooth. Add melted vanilla chips to cream cheese mixture; beat until smooth. Drop mixture by teaspoonfuls evenly over jam; carefully spread to cover. Refrigerate until set.

In small saucepan over low heat, melt chocolate with shortening, stirring constantly. Spread over white chocolate layer. Cool completely; cut into bars. Store in refrigerator. **25 bars.**

NUTRIENTS PER 1 BAR

Calories	140	Dietary Fiber	<1 g
Protein	1 g	Sodium	55 mg
Carbohydrate	14 g	Potassium	50 mg
Fat	9 g	Calcium	<2% U.S. RDA
Cholesterol	4 mg	Iron	2% U.S. RDA

Salted Peanut Chews

CRUST

   1½ cups all purpose flour
   ⅔ cup firmly packed brown sugar
   ½ teaspoon baking powder
   ½ teaspoon salt
   ¼ teaspoon baking soda
   ½ cup margarine or butter, softened
   1 teaspoon vanilla
   2 egg yolks
   3 cups miniature marshmallows

TOPPING

   ⅔ cup corn syrup
   ¼ cup margarine or butter
   2 teaspoons vanilla
12-oz. pkg. (2 cups) peanut butter chips
   2 cups crisp rice cereal
   2 cups salted peanuts

Heat oven to 350°F. In large bowl, combine all crust ingredients except marshmallows on low speed until crumbly. Press firmly in bottom of ungreased 13x9-inch pan. Bake at 350°F. for 12 to 15 minutes or until light golden brown. Immediately sprinkle with marshmallows. Return to oven for 1 to 2 minutes or until marshmallows just begin to puff. Cool while preparing topping.

In large saucepan, heat corn syrup, ¼ cup margarine, 2 teaspoons vanilla and peanut butter chips just until chips are melted and mixture is smooth, stirring constantly. Remove from heat; stir in cereal and nuts. Immediately spoon and spread warm topping over marshmallows to cover. Refrigerate until firm; cut into bars. **36 bars.**

MICROWAVE DIRECTIONS: Combine crust ingredients as directed above. Press in bottom of ungreased 13x9-inch (3-quart) microwave-safe dish. Microwave on HIGH for 4 to 5½ minutes, rotating dish ½ turn halfway through cooking. Immediately sprinkle with marshmallows and continue to microwave on HIGH for 1 to 1½ minutes or until marshmallows begin to puff.

In 2-quart microwave-safe casserole, combine corn syrup, ¼ cup margarine, 2 teaspoons vanilla and peanut butter chips. Microwave on HIGH for 2 to 2½ minutes or until chips are melted, stirring once. Stir in cereal and nuts. Immediately spoon warm topping over marshmallows and spread to cover. Refrigerate until firm; cut into bars.

NUTRIENTS PER 1 BAR

Calories 210	Dietary Fiber............................1 g
Protein.......................................5 g	Sodium............................170 mg
Carbohydrate..........................23 g	Potassium......................125 mg
Fat ....11 g	Calcium.................2% U.S. RDA
Cholesterol........................15 mg	Iron.........................6% U.S. RDA

Pecan Pie Surprise Bars

BASE

 1 pkg. pudding-included yellow or butter cake mix
 ⅓ cup margarine or butter, softened
 1 egg

FILLING

 ½ cup firmly packed brown sugar
 1½ cups dark corn syrup
 1 teaspoon vanilla
 3 eggs
 1 cup chopped pecans

Heat oven to 350°F. Grease 13x9-inch pan. Reserve ⅔ cup dry cake mix for filling. In large bowl, combine remaining dry cake mix, margarine and 1 egg at low speed until well blended. Spread in prepared pan. Bake at 350°F. for 15 to 20 minutes or until light golden brown.

In large bowl, combine reserved cake mix, brown sugar, corn syrup, vanilla and 3 eggs at low speed until moistened. Beat at medium speed about 1 minute or until well blended. Pour filling over base; sprinkle with pecans. Return to oven and bake 30 to 35 minutes or until filling is set. Cool completely. Cut into bars. Store in refrigerator. **36 bars.**

HIGH ALTITUDE: Decrease brown sugar by 1 tablespoon. Bake base at 375°F. for 15 to 20 minutes and filling for 30 to 35 minutes.

NUTRIENTS PER 1 BAR

Calories	160	Dietary Fiber	<1 g
Protein	2 g	Sodium	130 mg
Carbohydrate	25 g	Potassium	45 mg
Fat	6 g	Calcium	2% U.S. RDA
Cholesterol	30 mg	Iron	6% U.S. RDA

Candies

Homemade candy of all kinds is almost as much fun to prepare as it is to eat. Candy mixtures can be a bit temperamental and close attention must be paid to recipe instructions, but with an assist from a candy thermometer, guesswork and the possibility of failure are greatly reduced. With microwave directions, timing is streamlined and chances of scorching are minimized. Candies that require no cooking are practically foolproof and can be easily prepared by young, inexperienced candy makers.

Candy Cooking Hints

• Have all ingredients ready to use and premeasured if possible, so there is no delay when preparation steps must be done quickly. We do not recommend doubling candy recipes; make only one recipe at a time.

• Use a heavy saucepan large enough to allow space for candy to bubble up when boiling. Too large or too small a saucepan may affect the cooking time.

• A good candy thermometer is almost a necessity. The investment is small and the rewards are great. When using the thermometer, make sure its ball is completely covered with boiling liquid and does not touch the bottom of the pan. The cold water test (see Candy Cooking Stages) may be used if you do not have a thermometer.

• During humid weather or rainy days, cook candy to a point 1 or 2 degrees higher than you would on a normal day.

• To prevent sugaring, carefully follow directions about stirring and covering. Also use moderate heat so candy does not come to the boiling point too rapidly.

• For candies that are poured into a greased pan after cooking, prepare pan in advance to prevent candy from hardening in saucepan.

Keys to Cooking with Chocolate

• Facilitate melting by breaking chocolate blocks, bars or chunks into smaller uniform pieces.

• Place chocolate pieces for melting in pan or dish that is completely dry and use thoroughly dry utensils for stirring.

• For stove-top melting, place chocolate pieces in heavy saucepan. Avoid scorching and stiffening by stirring constantly over low, even heat not exceeding a temperature of 110°F. Melted chocolate should feel lukewarm, not hot, to the touch.

• If chocolate should harden or stiffen during stove-top melting, add 1 teaspoon shortening or oil (not butter) for each ounce of chocolate and stir until texture returns to normal.

• For microwave oven melting, place chocolate pieces in microwave-safe container. A 1-ounce square will take 1 to 2 minutes at MEDIUM setting to become soft enough to stir to smooth consistency. Add 10 seconds per each additional ounce. Six ounces, (1 cup) chocolate chips need 2½ to 3½ minutes of MEDIUM microwave heat to become soft enough to stir. Add 2 to 3 minutes for each additional cup of chips. Most chocolates melted by microwave method will retain original shape even when softened to proper consistency. Look for *glossy appearance,* and *stir* before cooking additional time.

Candy Cooking Stages

Stage of hardness	Temperature of syrup	Description of syrup when dropped into very cold water
Thread	230° to 234°F.	Syrup forms a 2-inch thread.
Soft ball	234° to 240°F.	Syrup forms a soft ball that flattens on removal from water.
Firm ball	244° to 248°F.	Syrup forms a firm ball that does not flatten on removal from water.
Hard ball	250° to 266°F.	Syrup forms a ball that is hard enough to hold its shape, yet pliable.
Crack	270° to 290°F.	Syrup separates into threads that are hard but not brittle.
Hard crack	300° to 310°F.	Syrup separates into threads that are hard and brittle.

Chocolate Fudge

2½ cups sugar
½ cup margarine or butter
5-oz. can (⅔ cup) evaporated milk
7-oz. jar (2 cups) marshmallow creme
12-oz. pkg. (2 cups) semi-sweet chocolate chips
¾ cup chopped walnuts
1 teaspoon vanilla

Line 9-inch square or 13x9-inch pan with foil so that foil extends over sides of pan; butter foil. In large saucepan, combine sugar, margarine and milk. Bring to a boil, stirring constantly. Continue boiling 5 minutes over medium heat, stirring constantly. Remove from heat. Add marshmallow creme and chocolate chips; blend until smooth. Stir in walnuts and vanilla. Pour into prepared pan. Cool to room temperature. Score fudge into 36 or 48 squares. Refrigerate until firm. Remove fudge from pan by lifting foil; remove foil from fudge. Using large knife, cut through scored lines. Store in refrigerator. **About 3 lb.**

MICROWAVE DIRECTIONS: In 2-quart microwave-safe bowl, combine margarine, sugar and evaporated milk. Microwave on HIGH for 6 to 8 minutes or until rolling boil, stirring twice during cooking. Stir in marshmallow creme and chocolate chips; blend until smooth. Stir in walnuts and vanilla. Pour into prepared pan.

VARIATIONS:

CONFETTI FUDGE: Substitute 2 cups candy-coated chocolate pieces for walnuts. Stir 1½ cups of the chocolate pieces into fudge. Sprinkle remaining ½ cup over top; press lightly into warm fudge. Cool to room temperature; do not refrigerate before cutting. Continue as directed above. Serve at room temperature.

TURTLE FUDGE: Substitute cashews for walnuts. Stir in 24 caramels, quartered, with cashews and vanilla. Cool to room temperature; do not refrigerate before cutting. Continue as directed above. Serve at room temperature.

ROCKY ROAD FUDGE: Stir in 2 cups miniature marshmallows after walnuts and vanilla. (Marshmallows should not melt completely.) Quickly spread in prepared pan.

NUTRIENTS PER 1 OZ.

Calories	130	Dietary Fiber	<1 g
Protein	1 g	Sodium	30 mg
Carbohydrate	18 g	Potassium	45 mg
Fat	6 g	Calcium	<2% U.S. RDA
Cholesterol	0 mg	Iron	<2% U.S. RDA

Vanilla Fudge

  2½ cups sugar
  ½ cup margarine or butter
5-oz. can (⅔ cup) evaporated milk
7-oz. jar (2 cups) marshmallow creme
8 oz. almond bark or vanilla-flavored candy coating,
       coarsely chopped
  ¾ cup chopped walnuts
  1 teaspoon vanilla

Line 9-inch square or 13x9-inch pan with foil so that foil extends over sides of pan; butter foil. In large saucepan, combine sugar, margarine and milk. Bring to a boil, stirring constantly. Continue boiling 5 minutes over medium heat, stirring constantly. Remove from heat. Add marshmallow creme and almond bark; blend until smooth. Stir in walnuts and vanilla. Pour into prepared pan. Cool to room temperature. Score fudge into 36 or 48 squares. Refrigerate until firm. Remove fudge from pan by lifting foil; remove foil from fudge. Using large knife, cut through scored lines. Store in refrigerator. **About 2½ lb.**

VARIATIONS:

EGGNOG FUDGE: Substitute ⅔ cup eggnog for evaporated milk and ½ to 1 teaspoon rum extract for vanilla.

PEANUT BUTTER FUDGE: Decrease almond bark to 6 ounces. Add ½ cup peanut butter with marshmallow creme and almond bark. Substitute ¾ cup chopped dry roasted peanuts for walnuts.

CHRISTMAS FUDGE: Substitute ½ cup chopped almonds for walnuts and ¼ teaspoon almond extract for vanilla. Stir in ½ cup chopped dates and ½ cup chopped red candied cherries with almonds and almond extract.

PEPPERMINT CANDY FUDGE: Omit walnuts and vanilla. Substitute ½ cup finely crushed peppermint candy for nuts and add desired amount of red food coloring.

PISTACHIO FUDGE: Substitute pistachios for walnuts and add desired amount of green food coloring.

NUTRIENTS PER 1 OZ.

Calories	130	Dietary Fiber	<1 g
Protein	1 g	Sodium	35 mg
Carbohydrate	20 g	Potassium	45 mg
Fat	6 g	Calcium	<2% U.S. RDA
Cholesterol	0 mg	Iron	<2% U.S. RDA

Peanut Brittle

2 cups sugar
1 cup light corn syrup
1 cup water
1 tablespoon margarine or butter
2 cups peanuts
1 teaspoon vanilla
1 teaspoon baking soda

Generously butter 2 cookie sheets. In large heavy saucepan, combine sugar, corn syrup and water. Cook until sugar dissolves, stirring constantly. Continue cooking until candy thermometer reaches hard crack stage (300°F.), stirring occasionally. Stir in margarine and peanuts. Remove from heat; stir in vanilla and baking soda. Pour onto prepared cookie sheets; spread as thin as possible. Cool completely; break into pieces. Store in airtight container in cool dry place. **2 lb.**

VARIATION:

MIXED NUT BRITTLE: Substitute 2 cups mixed nuts for the peanuts. Brazil nuts and other large nuts can be cut in smaller pieces for a more uniform appearance.

NUTRIENTS PER 1 OZ.

Calories 140	Dietary Fiber........................<1 g
Protein.....................................2 g	Sodium ....85 mg
Carbohydrate..........................22 g	Potassium...........................60 mg
Fat ....5 g	Calcium..............<2% U.S. RDA
Cholesterol...........................0 mg	Iron.....................2% U.S. RDA

Microwave Peanut Brittle

    1 cup sugar
  ½ cup light corn syrup
    1 cup roasted salted peanuts
    1 teaspoon margarine or butter
    1 teaspoon vanilla
    1 teaspoon baking soda

Butter cookie sheet. In 1½-quart microwave-safe casserole, combine sugar and corn syrup. Microwave on HIGH for 4 minutes. Stir in peanuts. Microwave on HIGH for 3 to 5 minutes or until light brown. Stir in margarine and vanilla; blend well. Microwave on HIGH for 1 to 2 minutes. (Peanuts should be lightly browned.) Add baking soda and stir gently until light and foamy. Pour onto prepared cookie sheet. Let cool 30 minutes; break into pieces. **1 lb.**

NUTRIENTS PER 1 OZ.

Calories 140	Dietary Fiber........................<1 g
Protein.....................................2 g	Sodium ....115 mg
Carbohydrate..........................22 g	Potassium...........................60 mg
Fat ....5 g	Calcium..............<2% U.S. RDA
Cholesterol...........................0 mg	Iron.....................2% U.S. RDA

Quick Fondant

        1 tablespoon light corn syrup
      ⅔ cup sweetened condensed milk (not evaporated)
  4½ to 5 cups powdered sugar

In large bowl, combine corn syrup and condensed milk. Add powdered sugar gradually, stirring to form a stiff, smooth dough. (If all powdered sugar cannot be stirred in, place fondant on cookie sheet and knead in sugar.)

VARIATIONS:

CLASSIC NEAPOLITAN SLICES

- ½ recipe prepared Quick Fondant
- ⅛ teaspoon peppermint extract
- 2 drops red food color
- 2 tablespoons finely chopped almonds
- 2 tablespoons semi-sweet chocolate chips, melted

Divide ½ recipe fondant into 3 equal parts. To 1 part, add peppermint extract and red food coloring; knead on cookie sheet until well blended. To second part, add almonds; knead gently to distribute almonds. In small bowl, combine third part with melted chocolate chips; stir or knead until blended.

Sprinkle powdered sugar on counter or cookie sheet. Using rolling pin, roll each part fondant to a 12x1-inch strip, about ½-inch thick. Moisten top of pink strip with water; place white strip on top. Moisten top of white strip with water; place chocolate strip on top. Using rolling pin, lightly roll lengthwise over sandwiched strips. Set candy on edge so that the 3 layers are visible on top. Roll again lengthwise with rolling pin, so that candy is 1-inch high and 1-inch wide. Cut candy into ¼-inch slices; place on cookie sheet. Cover with waxed paper; allow to dry several hours. Store in tightly covered container in cool dry place. **4½ dozen candies.**

NUTRIENTS PER 1 CANDY

Calories	45	Dietary Fiber	<1 g
Protein	0 g	Sodium	0 mg
Carbohydrate	11 g	Potassium	10 mg
Fat	0 g	Calcium	<2% U.S. RDA
Cholesterol	0 mg	Iron	<2% U.S. RDA

CHERRY ALMOND CREAMS

 ½ recipe prepared Quick Fondant
 ⅓ cup chopped candied cherries
 ¼ teaspoon almond extract
 1 drop red food color
    Toasted, sliced almonds

In medium bowl, combine ½ recipe fondant, cherries, almond extract and food color; knead on cookie sheet until well blended. Roll fondant into rope about 1-inch thick. Slice into ¼-inch slices. Place on cookie sheet. Cover with waxed paper; allow to dry several hours. Garnish with toasted almond slices, if desired. Store in tightly covered container in cool dry place. **4 dozen candies.**

NUTRIENTS PER 1 CANDY

Calories	35	Dietary Fiber	<1 g
Protein	0 g	Sodium	0 mg
Carbohydrate	8 g	Potassium	15 mg
Fat	0 g	Calcium	<2% U.S. RDA
Cholesterol	0 mg	Iron	<2% U.S. RDA

Old-Fashioned Caramels

 1 cup margarine or butter
 2¼ cups firmly packed brown sugar
 1 cup light corn syrup
 14-oz. can sweetened condensed milk (not evaporated)
 1½ teaspoons vanilla

Line 9-inch square pan with foil; butter lightly. In heavy 3-quart saucepan, melt margarine. Add brown sugar; mix well. Stir in corn syrup; cook over medium-low heat, until sugar dissolves and mixture is well blended. Remove pan from heat; stir in sweetened condensed milk. Cook over medium heat, stirring constantly, until candy thermometer reaches firm ball stage (244°F.), about 20 to 30 minutes. Remove from heat; stir in vanilla. Pour hot mixture into prepared pan. Cool to room temperature. When candy has completely set, carefully remove from pan. Using a thin bladed knife, cut caramel into pieces, using a light sawing motion. Wrap individual pieces in waxed paper. Store in refrigerator. **2¾ lb.**

VARIATION:

CHOCOLATE CARAMELS: After stirring in sweetened condensed milk, cook over medium heat, stirring constantly, until mixture reaches 230°F. on candy thermometer, about 20 to 30 minutes. Stir in 2 oz. (2 squares) unsweetened chocolate, coarsely chopped; continue cooking until mixture reaches 240°F., about 15 minutes. Continue as directed above.

NUTRIENTS PER 1 OZ.

Calories	130	Dietary Fiber	0 g
Protein	1 g	Sodium	70 mg
Carbohydrate	21 g	Potassium	70 mg
Fat	5 g	Calcium	4% U.S. RDA
Cholesterol	4 mg	Iron	4% U.S. RDA

Peppermint Taffy

1½	cups sugar
2	cups light corn syrup
¼	cup margarine or butter
½	teaspoon salt
2	teaspoons peppermint extract
4 to 6	drops red food coloring

Grease 15x10-inch jelly roll pan. In large heavy saucepan, combine sugar and syrup. Bring to a boil, stirring constantly. Add margarine; stir until melted. Cook, without stirring, until candy thermometer reaches hard ball stage (250°F.). Remove from heat; stir in salt, extract and food coloring. Pour into prepared pan. Cool slightly; fold edges toward center to cool evenly.

When taffy is just cool enough to handle, divide into 4 or 5 pieces. With buttered hands, pull and fold taffy for 10 to 20 minutes or until taffy turns opaque and stiff. (If candy becomes too stiff to work with, warm briefly in oven at 350°F.) Pull into long rope about ½-inch wide and cut into 1-inch pieces while still warm. Wrap individual pieces in waxed paper and store in cool dry place. **1½ lb.**

NUTRIENTS PER 1 OZ.

Calories	150	Dietary Fiber	0 g
Protein	0 g	Sodium	85 mg
Carbohydrate	33 g	Potassium	0 mg
Fat	2 g	Calcium	<2% U.S. RDA
Cholesterol	0 mg	Iron	6% U.S. RDA

Nut Goodie Bars

12-oz.   pkg. (2 cups) semi-sweet chocolate chips
12-oz.   pkg. (2 cups) butterscotch chips
   2   cups peanut butter
   2   cups peanuts
   1   cup margarine or butter
   ½   cup evaporated milk
3⅛-oz.   pkg. vanilla pudding and pie filling mix (not instant)
   2   lb. (7½ cups) powdered sugar
   1   teaspoon vanilla

Butter 15x10-inch jelly roll pan. In large saucepan over low heat, melt chocolate and butterscotch chips, stirring constantly. Remove from heat; stir in peanut butter. Mix well. Spread half of mixture in prepared pan; refrigerate. Stir peanuts into remaining mixture; set aside.

In large saucepan over low heat, melt margarine; slowly add evaporated milk. Stir in pudding mix. Cook, stirring constantly, until mixture is slightly thickened. (Do not boil.) Remove from heat. Stir in powdered sugar and vanilla; cool slightly. Carefully spread mixture over chilled chocolate layer. Refrigerate 30 minutes. Drop reserved chocolate-peanut mixture by tablespoonfuls over chilled pudding layer; spread to cover. Refrigerate until firm; cut into bars. Store tightly covered in refrigerator. **48 bars.**

NUTRIENTS PER 1 BAR

Calories	290	Dietary Fiber	2 g
Protein	5 g	Sodium	125 mg
Carbohydrate	33 g	Potassium	145 mg
Fat	17 g	Calcium	2% U.S. RDA
Cholesterol	0 mg	Iron	2% U.S. RDA

Apricot-Coconut Balls

    4 cups finely chopped dried apricots
    4 cups coconut
    2 cups chopped walnuts
14-oz. can sweetened condensed milk (not evaporated)
       Powdered sugar, if desired

In large bowl, combine apricots, coconut, walnuts and condensed milk. Form into 1-inch balls. Roll in powdered sugar. Store in refrigerator. **8 to 10 dozen candies.**

NUTRIENTS PER 1 CANDY

Calories	50	Dietary Fiber	<1 g
Protein	1 g	Sodium	5 mg
Carbohydrate	6 g	Potassium	70 mg
Fat	3 g	Calcium	<2% U.S. RDA
Cholesterol	0 mg	Iron	<2% U.S. RDA

Fudgy Brandied Truffles

12-oz. pkg. (2 cups) semi-sweet chocolate chips
    ¾ cup sweetened condensed milk (not evaporated)
    1 teaspoon brandy extract
    ¾ cup ground walnuts or ¼ cup cocoa

In top of double boiler or in heavy saucepan over low heat, melt chocolate chips, stirring occasionally. Add condensed milk and brandy extract; stir until well blended. Remove from heat. Refrigerate mixture about 30 minutes or until easy to handle. With buttered hands, shape mixture into 1-inch balls. Roll in nuts or cocoa. Store in tightly covered container in refrigerator. **4 dozen candies.**

NUTRIENTS PER 1 CANDY

Calories	60	Dietary Fiber	<1 g
Protein	1 g	Sodium	5 mg
Carbohydrate	7 g	Potassium	45 mg
Fat	4 g	Calcium	<2% U.S. RDA
Cholesterol	2 mg	Iron	<2% U.S. RDA

Peanut Clusters

12 oz.	(6 cubes) almond bark or vanilla-flavored candy coating, cut into pieces
12-oz.	pkg. (2 cups) chocolate chips
4	cups dry roasted peanuts

Line cookie sheets with waxed paper. In medium saucepan over low heat, melt almond bark and chocolate chips, stirring until smooth.* Stir in peanuts. Drop by teaspoonfuls onto prepared cookie sheets. Refrigerate until set. Store in airtight container in cool dry place. **8 dozen candies.**

MICROWAVE DIRECTIONS: In medium microwave-safe bowl, combine candy coating and chocolate chips. Microwave on HIGH for 2 to 3 minutes or until melted, stirring once halfway through coating. Continue as directed.

TIP: *Moisture can cause coating to thicken; keep utensils and coating free from moisture.

NUTRIENTS PER 1 CANDY

Calories 70	Dietary Fiber.........................<1 g
Protein.....................................2 g	Sodium ....0 mg
Carbohydrate............................5 g	Potassium............................65 mg
Fat ....5 g	Calcium..............<2% U.S. RDA
Cholesterol ....0 mg	Iron ....<2% U.S. RDA

Cashew Clusters

12-oz. pkg. (2 cups) semi-sweet chocolate chips
 1 oz. (1 square) unsweetened chocolate
 2 cups cashews

Line cookie sheets with waxed paper. In large saucepan over low heat, melt chips and chocolate; stir until smooth. Stir in cashews. Drop candy by teaspoonfuls onto prepared cookie sheets. Refrigerate until set. Store in tightly covered container in refrigerator. **3 dozen candies.**

MICROWAVE DIRECTIONS: In 1-quart microwave-safe casserole, combine chocolate chips and unsweetened chocolate. Microwave on HIGH for 2½ to 3½ minutes or until melted, stirring once halfway during cooking. Continue as directed above.

NUTRIENTS PER 1 CANDY

Calories 100	Dietary Fiber.........................2 g
Protein.....................................2 g	Sodium ....0 mg
Carbohydrate............................8 g	Potassium............................80 mg
Fat ....8 g	Calcium..............<2% U.S. RDA
Cholesterol ....0 mg	Iron ....4% U.S. RDA

Divinity

 2 cups sugar
 ¼ teaspoon salt
 ½ cup hot water
 ⅓ cup light corn syrup

2 egg whites
1 teaspoon vanilla
½ to 1 cup chopped nuts

In medium-size heavy saucepan, combine sugar, salt, water and corn syrup. Cook until mixture boils, stirring constantly. Cook uncovered without stirring until candy thermometer reaches hard ball stage (250°F.). In large bowl, beat egg whites until stiff peaks form. Pour syrup over egg whites in steady fine stream and continue beating until mixture holds its shape and loses gloss. Stir in vanilla and nuts. Drop by teaspoonfuls onto waxed paper. **1 lb.**

NUTRIENTS PER 1 OZ.

Calories	170	Dietary Fiber	<1 g
Protein	1 g	Sodium	45 mg
Carbohydrate	31 g	Potassium	45 mg
Fat	5 g	Calcium	<2% U.S. RDA
Cholesterol	0 mg	Iron	2% U.S. RDA

Toffee Chocolate Crunch

1 cup butter
1¼ cups sugar
2 tablespoons water
4 teaspoons corn syrup
1½ cups chopped almonds, toasted*
1 teaspoon vanilla
6-oz. pkg. (1 cup) semi-sweet chocolate chips

Butter 15x10-inch jelly roll pan. In medium-size heavy saucepan over low heat, melt butter. Stir in sugar, water and corn syrup. Cook over medium heat until candy thermometer reaches soft crack stage (270°F.), stirring constantly. Remove from heat; stir in 1 cup of the almonds and vanilla. Immediately pour mixture into prepared pan; quickly spread evenly. Cool 2 minutes. Sprinkle chips over warm toffee; let stand 2 minutes to soften. Spread chocolate evenly. Sprinkle chocolate with remaining ½ cup almonds. Refrigerate until chocolate is set; break into pieces. Store covered in refrigerator. **1¾ lb.**

TIP: *To toast almonds, bake at 350°F. for 8 to 10 minutes or until golden brown.

NUTRIENTS PER 1 OZ.

Calories	170	Dietary Fiber	1 g
Protein	2 g	Sodium	80 mg
Carbohydrate	14 g	Potassium	75 mg
Fat	12 g	Calcium	2% U.S. RDA
Cholesterol	20 mg	Iron	2% U.S. RDA

After-Dinner Peppermints

3½	cups powdered sugar
3	tablespoons water
3	tablespoons light corn syrup
⅛ to ¼	teaspoon peppermint extract
2 to 3	drops any color food coloring, if desired

In top of double boiler, combine powdered sugar, water and corn syrup. Cook over simmering water until sugar dissolves and mixture is smooth. (DO NOT ALLOW WATER TO BOIL.) Remove from heat; stir in peppermint extract and food coloring. Keep mixture over hot water; quickly drop by teaspoonfuls onto ungreased cookie sheet forming ¾-inch patties. Let stand until firm. Store in tightly covered container. **5 to 6 dozen candies.**

NUTRIENTS PER 1 CANDY

Calories	20	Dietary Fiber	0 g
Protein	0 g	Sodium	0 mg
Carbohydrate	5 g	Potassium	0 mg
Fat	0 g	Calcium	<2% U.S. RDA
Cholesterol	0 mg	Iron	<2% U.S. RDA

Sugared 'n Spiced Nuts

3 cups pecan or walnut halves
1 cup sugar
⅓ cup water
1 tablespoon cinnamon
½ teaspoon cloves
½ teaspoon salt
1½ teaspoons vanilla

Heat oven to 275°F. Grease cookie sheet. Spread nuts on prepared cookie sheet; bake 10 minutes. In medium saucepan, combine sugar, water, cinnamon, cloves and salt. Bring to boil; continue cooking for 2 minutes, stirring occasionally. Remove from heat; stir in vanilla and nuts. Using slotted spoon, remove nuts to foil or waxed paper. Separate with fork; let dry. Store in airtight container in cool dry place. **4½ cups.**

NUTRIENTS PER 1 TABLESPOON

Calories	40	Dietary Fiber	<1 g
Protein	1 g	Sodium	15 mg
Carbohydrate	4 g	Potassium	20 mg
Fat	3 g	Calcium	<2% U.S. RDA
Cholesterol	0 mg	Iron	<2% U.S. RDA

Sherried Pecan Pralines

2¼ cups firmly packed brown sugar
1 cup whipping cream
1 tablespoon butter or margarine
2 tablespoons sherry
1½ cups pecan pieces, lightly toasted

In heavy 2-quart saucepan, cook brown sugar, whipping cream and butter until bubbly, stirring occasionally. Cook uncovered without stirring, until candy thermometer reaches soft ball stage (234°F.). Remove from heat; let stand 5 minutes. Add sherry; beat with a wooden spoon until thick and creamy. Quickly stir in pecans. Drop by teaspoonfuls onto waxed paper to form candies 2 inches in diameter. Allow pralines to dry at room temperature until firm. Store in airtight container in a cool dry place. **48 pralines.**

NUTRIENTS PER 1 PRALINE

Calories 90	Dietary Fiber.........................<1 g
Protein......................................0 g	Sodium...............................10 mg
Carbohydrate.........................11 g	Potassium..........................65 mg
Fat ....5 g	Calcium...............<2% U.S. RDA
Cholesterol............................6 mg	Iron........................2% U.S. RDA

Desserts
& Pies

Desserts & Pies

For many, the sweet ending of a meal is the best part and the most eagerly anticipated. And no wonder. A delicious dessert, such as a wedge of homemade pie or cheesecake or warm-from-the-oven fruit crisp, can transform the simplest of meals into a special occasion. Even in bad economic times, enterprising cooks have managed to create memorable desserts from inexpensive, on-hand ingredients and economical fruits of the season.

Desserts

Fruit with Caramel Cream

      6 cups fresh fruit, whole or cut into bite-size pieces*
      2 tablespoons orange-flavored liqueur, if desired
      1 cup dairy sour cream
      2 tablespoons brown sugar
      2 (3-oz.) pkg. cream cheese, softened
     ¼ cup firmly packed brown sugar

Place fruit in 1½-quart shallow broiler-proof casserole or au gratin dish. Sprinkle with liqueur. In small bowl, beat sour cream, 2 tablespoons brown sugar and cream cheese until smooth and creamy. Spoon evenly over fruit. Sprinkle or sift ¼ cup brown sugar evenly over cream cheese mixture. Broil 4 to 5 inches from heat for about 2 minutes or until brown sugar melts slightly and is golden brown. **8 servings.**

FOOD PROCESSOR DIRECTIONS: Prepare fruit mixture as directed above. In food processor bowl with metal blade, place sour cream, 2 tablespoons brown sugar and cream cheese, cut into 1-inch pieces (no need to soften).

Cover; process just until smooth and creamy. Continue as directed above.

TIP: *Select 1 or a combination of fruit such as green or red seedless grapes, blueberries, raspberries, strawberries, nectarines or peaches.

NUTRIENTS PER ⅛ OF RECIPE

Calories	250	Dietary Fiber	2 g
Protein	3 g	Sodium	85 mg
Carbohydrate	29 g	Potassium	310 mg
Fat	14 g	Calcium	8% U.S. RDA
Cholesterol	35 mg	Iron	6% U.S. RDA

Orange Poached Pears

- ½ cup firmly packed brown sugar
- 1 cinnamon stick
- 1½ cups orange juice
- 4 firm, ripe large pears, peeled, halved and cored

In large saucepan, combine brown sugar, cinnamon and orange juice. Cook over medium heat until sugar is dissolved, stirring constantly. Add pear halves; cover and simmer 15 to 20 minutes or until just tender. Remove from heat; cool in liquid. Spoon poaching liquid over pears to serve. **8 servings.**

VARIATION:

ORANGE POACHED PEACHES: Substitute peaches for the pears.

NUTRIENTS PER ⅛ OF RECIPE

Calories	130	Dietary Fiber	1 g
Protein	1 g	Sodium	0 mg
Carbohydrate	32 g	Potassium	250 mg
Fat	0 g	Calcium	2% U.S. RDA
Cholesterol	0 mg	Iron	4% U.S. RDA

Broiled Grapefruit

3 medium grapefruit, room temperature
2 tablespoons butter
⅓ cup firmly packed brown sugar
Dairy sour cream
Cinnamon

Cut each grapefruit in half. Remove seeds and cut around sections to loosen. In small bowl, combine butter and brown sugar. Spread heaping tablespoon of mixture around outer edge of each grapefruit half. Place on broiler pan. Broil 4 to 6 inches from heat about 3 to 5 minutes or until topping is bubbly. Top each half with sour cream and dash of cinnamon. **6 servings.**

NUTRIENTS PER ⅙ OF RECIPE

Calories	130	Dietary Fiber	2 g
Protein	1 g	Sodium	45 mg
Carbohydrate	20 g	Potassium	190 mg
Fat	6 g	Calcium	2% U.S. RDA
Cholesterol	15 mg	Iron	2% U.S. RDA

Baked Apples

6 large baking apples
2 tablespoons lemon juice
½ cup raisins
½ teaspoon cinnamon
1 cup maple or maple-flavored syrup
¼ cup water

Heat oven to 350°F. Core apples and cut a 1-inch strip of peel around top to prevent splitting. Brush tops and insides with lemon juice. Place apples in 8-inch (2-quart) square baking dish. In small bowl, combine raisins and cinnamon; fill center of each apple with mixture. Pour maple syrup over apples. Add ¼ cup water to baking dish. Bake at 350°F.

for 45 to 50 minutes or until apples are tender, spooning syrup mixture over apples occasionally. Serve warm. **6 servings.**

MICROWAVE DIRECTIONS: Prepare and fill apples as directed above; place in 12x8-inch (2-quart) microwave-safe dish. Pour maple syrup over apples. Add ¼ cup water to dish; cover with waxed paper. Microwave on HIGH for 10 to 12 minutes or until apples are tender, spooning syrup mixture over apples twice during cooking.

NUTRIENTS PER ¼ OF RECIPE

Calories	320	Dietary Fiber	5 g
Protein	1 g	Sodium	5 mg
Carbohydrate	77 g	Potassium	430 mg
Fat	1 g	Calcium	8% U.S. RDA
Cholesterol	0 mg	Iron	6% U.S. RDA

Apple Crisp

6 cups sliced, peeled apples
1 teaspoon cinnamon, if desired
1 tablespoon water
1 teaspoon lemon juice
1 cup rolled oats
¾ cup all purpose flour
¾ cup firmly packed brown sugar
½ cup margarine or butter, softened

Heat oven to 375°F. Place apples in ungreased 2-quart casserole. Sprinkle with cinnamon, water and lemon juice. In large bowl, combine remaining ingredients; mix with pastry blender or fork until crumbly. Sprinkle crumb mixture evenly over apples. Bake at 375°F. for 25 to 35 minutes or until fruit is tender and topping is golden brown. Serve warm with cream, ice cream or whipped cream. **12 servings.**

MICROWAVE DIRECTIONS: Place apples in 8-inch (2-quart) square microwave-safe dish. Sprinkle with cinnamon, water and lemon juice. Combine remaining ingredients; mix until crumbly. Sprinkle over apples. Microwave on HIGH for 12 to 14 minutes or until fruit is tender, rotating dish ¼ turn once during cooking.

VARIATIONS:

BLUEBERRY CRISP: Substitute blueberries for the apples.

PEACH CRISP: Substitute sliced, peeled peaches for the apples.

NUTRIENTS PER ½ OF RECIPE

Calories	210	Dietary Fiber	3 g
Protein	2 g	Sodium	95 mg
Carbohydrate	32 g	Potassium	150 mg
Fat	8 g	Calcium	2% U.S. RDA
Cholesterol	0 mg	Iron	6% U.S. RDA

Applesauce

```
6 to 8   medium apples, peeled, quartered
   ½     cup water
½ to ¾   cup sugar or brown sugar
   1     teaspoon cinnamon, if desired
```

In large saucepan, combine apples and water. Bring to a boil. Cover; simmer over low heat, 15 to 20 minutes or until tender, stirring occasionally. Stir in sugar and cinnamon; cook until thoroughly heated. **6 servings.**

TIP: To retain the apple pieces, combine sugar and water. Add sliced apples; simmer covered 15 to 20 minutes or until tender. Stir in cinnamon. (Most fruits keep their shape when cooked in a sugar-water mixture, but become sauce-like when cooked without sugar.)

NUTRIENTS PER ⅙ OF RECIPE

Calories	200	Dietary Fiber	4 g
Protein	0 g	Sodium	0 mg
Carbohydrate	51 g	Potassium	200 mg
Fat	1 g	Calcium	<2% U.S. RDA
Cholesterol	0 mg	Iron	<2% U.S. RDA

Baked Fruit Ambrosia

   2   tablespoons margarine or butter
  ¼   cup flour
  ¼   cup firmly packed brown sugar
  ¼   teaspoon salt
29-oz.   can sliced peaches, drained
20-oz.   can pineapple chunks, drained
16-oz.   can pitted dark cherries, drained
¾ to 1   cup coconut

Heat oven to 400°F. While heating oven, melt margarine in 1½-quart casserole; remove from oven. Stir in flour, brown sugar and salt; mix thoroughly. Add peaches, pineapple and cherries; toss lightly to combine. Bake at 400°F. for 20 minutes. Sprinkle with coconut and bake an additional 10 to 15 minutes or until hot and bubbly. Serve warm with ice cream or whipped cream, if desired. **10 servings.**

NUTRIENTS PER ⅒ OF RECIPE

Calories	210	Dietary Fiber	3 g
Protein	2 g	Sodium	85 mg
Carbohydrate	38 g	Potassium	290 mg
Fat	6 g	Calcium	2% U.S. RDA
Cholesterol	0 mg	Iron	6% U.S. RDA

Raspberry Delight

   3   cups fresh raspberries or strawberries
⅓ to ½   cup sugar
      Dash salt

1 egg white
1 envelope unflavored gelatin
½ cup cold water
½ cup whipping cream, whipped

In large bowl, combine 2 cups of the raspberries, sugar, salt and egg white. In small saucepan, soften gelatin in cold water; stir over low heat until dissolved. Add to raspberry mixture; mix well. Refrigerate mixture until thickened but not set; beat 1 minute at medium speed. Fold in whipped cream, then remaining raspberries. Spoon into dessert dishes. Refrigerate until firm. If desired, garnish with whipped cream and mint leaves. **8 servings.**

Tip: If desired, serve mixture in Meringue Tarts (see Index).

NUTRIENTS PER ½ CUP

Calories 130	Dietary Fiber...........................2 g
Protein.....................................2 g	Sodium..............................30 mg
Carbohydrate.........................18 g	Potassium...........................90 mg
Fat ....6 g	Calcium.................2% U.S. RDA
Cholesterol ....20 mg	Iron ....<2% U.S. RDA

Sliced Oranges in Strawberry Sauce

3 to 4 large seedless oranges
2 tablespoons orange-flavored liqueur, if desired
1 pint (2 cups) fresh strawberries, sliced
2 tablespoons sugar
½ cup currant jelly
¼ teaspoon lemon juice

Peel oranges; cut each into 4 or 5 round slices. Place in individual dessert dishes or shallow serving bowl; drizzle with liqueur. Refrigerate. In small bowl, combine strawberries and sugar. Let stand at room temperature for 30 minutes.

Melt jelly; add lemon juice. Pour over strawberries; mix well. Spoon strawberries over oranges. Refrigerate at least 1 hour or until serving time. **6 to 8 servings.**

NUTRIENTS PER ⅛ OF RECIPE

Calories	120	Dietary Fiber	3 g
Protein	1 g	Sodium	0 mg
Carbohydrate	30 g	Potassium	190 mg
Fat	0 g	Calcium	2% U.S. RDA
Cholesterol	0 mg	Iron	2% U.S. RDA

Peach Melba

    2 teaspoons cornstarch
   ½ cup currant jelly
10-oz. pkg. frozen sweetened raspberries, thawed, drained
29-oz. can peach halves, drained or 6 fresh peach halves
    1 quart (4 cups) vanilla ice cream

In medium saucepan, combine cornstarch, jelly and raspberries. Cook over medium heat until mixture boils and thickens, stirring frequently. If desired, strain to remove seeds; cool. Place peach half in each serving dish. Top with ice cream; spoon cooled raspberry sauce over ice cream. **6 servings.**

NUTRIENTS PER ⅙ OF RECIPE

Calories	340	Dietary Fiber	2 g
Protein	4 g	Sodium	85 mg
Carbohydrate	60 g	Potassium	380 mg
Fat	10 g	Calcium	10% U.S. RDA
Cholesterol	40 mg	Iron	6% U.S. RDA

Cherries Jubilee

    1 tablespoon cornstarch
16-oz. can (2 cups) pitted dark sweet cherries, undrained
   ¼ cup brandy
    1 quart (4 cups) French vanilla or vanilla ice cream

In chafing dish or skillet, combine cornstarch and cherries. Heat until mixture boils and thickens, stirring occasionally. Heat brandy in small saucepan or ladle; carefully ignite. Quickly pour over cherries. Serve over ice cream. **6 to 8 servings.**

NUTRIENTS PER ⅛ OF RECIPE

Calories	190	
Protein	3 g	
Carbohydrate	27 g	
Fat	7 g	
Cholesterol	30 mg	
Dietary Fiber	1 g	
Sodium	60 mg	
Potassium	210 mg	
Calcium	8% U.S. RDA	
Iron	<2% U.S. RDA	

Peaches Flambe

1 quart (4 cups) vanilla ice cream
½ cup peach preserves
3 tablespoons orange juice
16-oz. pkg. frozen sliced peaches, thawed
⅓ to ½ cup brandy

Spoon ice cream into 6 dessert dishes; place in freezer until serving time. Just before serving, in chafing dish or medium skillet, combine preserves and orange juice; cook over medium heat until bubbly. Add peaches; heat thoroughly. To flame, heat brandy in small saucepan or ladle; carefully ignite. Quickly pour over peach mixture; serve immediately over ice cream. **6 servings.**

NUTRIENTS PER ⅙ OF RECIPE

Calories	360	
Protein	5 g	
Carbohydrate	55 g	
Fat	10 g	
Cholesterol	40 mg	
Dietary Fiber	2 g	
Sodium	60 mg	
Potassium	290 mg	
Calcium	15% U.S. RDA	
Iron	4% U.S. RDA	

Winter Fruit Deep-Dish Pie

FILLING

29-oz. can sliced peaches, undrained
16-oz. can purple plums, drained, pitted, quartered
½ cup coarsely chopped nuts
½ cup dark or golden raisins
½ cup firmly packed brown sugar
2 tablespoons cornstarch
¼ teaspoon cinnamon
¼ teaspoon nutmeg

BISCUIT PASTRY

2 cups all purpose flour
1 tablespoon sugar
3 teaspoons baking powder
1 teaspoon salt
⅓ cup shortening
1 cup dairy sour cream
Milk
Sugar

Heat oven to 400°F. In ungreased 2½-quart shallow oval baking dish or casserole, combine all filling ingredients.

In medium bowl, combine flour, 1 tablespoon sugar, baking powder and salt. Using pastry blender, cut in shortening until mixture resembles coarse crumbs. Stir in sour cream until blended. On floured surface, toss dough lightly to coat with flour. Knead 8 to 10 times. Roll lightly until in shape of and slightly smaller than casserole, about ½-inch thick. Trim to even edges. Flute edge, if desired. Using biscuit cutter, cut 1 or 2-inch circle in center of pastry or cut a decorative design using small cookie cutters. Top fruit mixture with pastry. (Edge of pastry should not touch sides of casserole.) Brush pastry lightly with milk; sprinkle with sugar. Bake at 400°F. for 35 to 45 minutes or until pastry is dark golden brown. Cool at least 20 to 30 minutes before serving; serve with cream or ice cream, if desired. **8 servings.**

HIGH ALTITUDE: Bake at 400°F. for 30 to 40 minutes.

NUTRIENTS PER ⅛ OF RECIPE

Calories	520	Dietary Fiber	4 g
Protein	6 g	Sodium	420 mg
Carbohydrate	79 g	Potassium	445 mg
Fat	20 g	Calcium	10% U.S. RDA
Cholesterol	10 mg	Iron	15% U.S. RDA

Baked Pears

6 firm, ripe pears
3 tablespoons sugar
6 teaspoons margarine or butter
⅓ cup firmly packed brown sugar
1 tablespoon flour
½ teaspoon cinnamon
1 tablespoon water
Whipped cream cheese, if desired*

Heat oven to 375°F. Core pears and peel 1-inch strip of skin around top to prevent splitting. Place pears upright in 12x8-inch or 8-inch square (2-quart) baking dish. Place ½ table-spoon sugar and 1 teaspoon margarine in cavity of each pear. Bake at 375°F. for 25 minutes. Combine remaining ingredients except cream cheese; mix well. Spoon over baked pears. Return to oven and bake an additional 10 minutes or until tender. Serve warm or cool with whipped cream cheese. **6 servings.**

MICROWAVE DIRECTIONS: Prepare pears as directed. Place pears upright in 8-inch round microwave-safe dish. Place ½ tablespoon sugar and 1 teaspoon margarine in cavity of each pear. Cover with microwave-safe plastic wrap. Microwave on HIGH for 8 to 12 minutes or until tender, rotating dish ¼ turn halfway through cooking. Combine remaining ingredients except cream cheese; mix well. Spoon over pears. Cover; microwave on HIGH for 2 minutes.

TIP: *To make whipped cream cheese, beat softened cream cheese until light and fluffy.

NUTRIENTS PER ⅙ OF RECIPE

Calories	210	Dietary Fiber	4 g
Protein	1 g	Sodium	55 mg
Carbohydrate	44 g	Potassium	255 mg
Fat	4 g	Calcium	2% U.S. RDA
Cholesterol	10 mg	Iron	4% U.S. RDA

Lemon Pudding Cake

3 eggs, separated
½ cup milk
¼ cup lemon juice
1 teaspoon grated lemon peel
½ cup sugar
⅓ cup all purpose flour
⅛ teaspoon salt

Heat oven to 350°F. Grease 1-quart casserole. In small bowl, beat egg yolks (reserve whites in small bowl). Blend in milk, lemon juice and lemon peel. Add sugar, flour and salt; beat until smooth. Beat reserved egg whites until stiff. Fold in yolk mixture gently but thoroughly. Pour into prepared casserole. Place casserole in 13x9-inch pan; pour hot water into pan, about 1 inch deep. Bake at 350°F. for 25 to 35 minutes or until light golden brown. Serve warm or cool. Garnish with whipped cream, if desired. **6 servings.**

NUTRIENTS PER ⅙ OF RECIPE

Calories	150	Dietary Fiber	<1 g
Protein	5 g	Sodium	85 mg
Carbohydrate	24 g	Potassium	85 mg
Fat	4 g	Calcium	4% U.S. RDA
Cholesterol	140 mg	Iron	4% U.S. RDA

Bread Pudding

    2 cups (about 2 slices) soft or dry bread cubes
   ¼ cup raisins
    2 eggs, slightly beaten
   ¼ cup sugar
   ¼ teaspoon cinnamon
   ⅛ teaspoon salt
 1⅓ cups milk
    1 teaspoon vanilla

Heat oven to 350°F. Lightly grease 1-quart casserole. Place bread cubes in casserole; sprinkle with raisins. In small bowl, combine remaining ingredients; beat well. Pour over bread cubes. Place casserole in baking pan filled with about 1 inch hot water. Bake at 350°F. for 55 to 65 minutes or until knife inserted near center comes out clean. Serve warm with cream, if desired. **4 to 5 servings.**

NUTRIENTS PER ⅕ OF RECIPE

Calories	170	Dietary Fiber	1 g
Protein	6 g	Sodium	210 mg
Carbohydrate	28 g	Potassium	200 mg
Fat	4 g	Calcium	10% U.S. RDA
Cholesterol	120 mg	Iron	6% U.S. RDA

Steamed Plum Pudding

    1 cup all purpose flour
    3 tablespoons brown sugar
    1 teaspoon cinnamon
   ½ teaspoon baking powder
   ½ teaspoon allspice
   ½ teaspoon cloves
   ¼ teaspoon baking soda
   ½ cup milk
    3 tablespoons oil
    2 tablespoons molasses

    1 egg
    1 cup candied fruit
    ½ cup raisins
    ½ cup chopped nuts

Using shortening, generously grease 1-quart mold or casserole. In medium bowl, combine all ingredients except fruit, raisins and nuts. Mix until dry ingredients are moistened. Fold in fruit, raisins and nuts. Spoon into prepared mold. Cover with lid or foil. Place on wire rack in large steamer or kettle. Pour boiling water, 3 to 4 inches deep, into steamer; cover. Keep water boiling gently over low heat. If necessary, add water to maintain steam. Steam 1½ to 2 hours or until pudding springs back when touched lightly in center. Serve hot with Hard Sauce (See Index). **6 to 8 servings.**

NUTRIENTS PER ⅛ OF RECIPE

Calories	300	Dietary Fiber	3 g
Protein	4 g	Sodium	135 mg
Carbohydrate	46 g	Potassium	250 mg
Fat	11 g	Calcium	8% U.S. RDA
Cholesterol	35 mg	Iron	10% U.S. RDA

Shortcake

    2 cups all purpose flour*
    2 tablespoons sugar
    3 teaspoons baking powder
    ½ teaspoon salt
    ½ cup margarine, butter or shortening
    ¾ cup milk
       Sweetened fruit
       Whipped cream

Heat oven to 425°F. Grease 9-inch round cake or 8-inch square pan. In large bowl, combine flour, sugar, baking powder and salt. Using pastry blender, cut in margarine until consistency of coarse meal. Add milk; stir *just* until dry ingredients are moistened. Spread dough in prepared pan. Bake at 425°F. for 20 to 25 minutes or until golden brown. Cool 5 minutes; remove from pan. Serve warm or cool, split and filled with sweetened fruit and whipped cream. **8 servings.**

FOOD PROCESSOR DIRECTIONS: In food processor bowl with metal blade, combine flour, sugar, baking powder and salt. Cover; process with 5 on/off turns to mix. Add margarine to flour mixture. Process until mixture resembles coarse crumbs. Add ½ to ⅔ cup milk; process with on/off turns *just* until ball starts to form. Continue as directed above.

TIPS: *Self-rising flour can be substituted for all purpose flour. Omit baking powder and salt.

Shortcake can be cut into wedges or squares before splitting. Fill each individual piece with sweetened fruit and whipped cream.

For individual shortcakes, drop dough by rounded tablespoons, 2 inches apart, onto greased cookie sheet. Bake at 450°F. for 10 to 12 minutes or until golden brown.

NUTRIENTS PER ⅛ OF RECIPE

Calories	390	Dietary Fiber	4 g
Protein	5 g	Sodium	400 mg
Carbohydrate	41 g	Potassium	240 mg
Fat	23 g	Calcium	15% U.S. RDA
Cholesterol	40 mg	Iron	10% U.S. RDA

Baked Custard

```
    3  eggs, slightly beaten
   ¼  cup sugar
   ⅛  teaspoon salt
    1  teaspoon vanilla
 2½  cups milk
       Dash nutmeg
```

Heat oven to 350°F. In large bowl, combine eggs, sugar, salt and vanilla; blend well. Gradually stir in milk. Pour into six 6-oz. custard cups. Sprinkle with nutmeg. Place in 13x9-inch pan; fill pan with about 1 inch hot water. Bake at 350°F. for 45 to 55 minutes or until knife inserted near center comes out clean. Serve warm or cold. Store in refrigerator. **6 servings.**

TIP: If desired, pour mixture into 1 to 1 ½-quart casserole. Place in 13x9-inch pan; fill pan with about 1 inch hot water. Bake at 350°F. for 50 to 60 minutes.

NUTRIENTS PER ⅙ OF RECIPE

Calories	120	Dietary Fiber	0 g
Protein	6 g	Sodium	130 mg
Carbohydrate	13 g	Potassium	190 mg
Fat	5 g	Calcium	15% U.S. RDA
Cholesterol	150 mg	Iron	2% U.S. RDA

Soft Custard

      3 eggs, well beaten or 6 egg yolks
    ¼ cup sugar
    ¼ teaspoon salt
  1¼ cups half-and-half or milk
      2 tablespoons orange juice

In top of double boiler or heavy saucepan, combine eggs, sugar and salt. Gradually add half-and-half. Cook over low heat, stirring constantly, until mixture coats metal spoon, about 6 minutes. *Do not boil.* Remove from heat; stir in 2 tablespoons orange juice. Cover; refrigerate until cool. **4 servings.**

VARIATION:

FLOATING ISLAND CUSTARD: Pour soft custard into 4 individual baking dishes or custard cups. To prepare meringues, beat 2 egg whites and ⅛ teaspoon salt until foamy. Gradually add ¼ cup sugar, beating continuously until stiff peaks form. Float spoonfuls of meringue on each custard. Broil 1 to 2 minutes or until peaks of meringue are golden brown.

NUTRIENTS PER ¼ OF RECIPE

Calories	210	Dietary Fiber	0 g
Protein	7 g	Sodium	210 mg
Carbohydrate	17 g	Potassium	160 mg
Fat	13 g	Calcium	10% U.S. RDA
Cholesterol	230 mg	Iron	4% U.S. RDA

Creme Caramel

- ¼ cup sugar
- ⅓ cup sugar
- ¼ teaspoon salt
- 1 teaspoon vanilla
- 2 eggs, slightly beaten
- 1⅔ cups milk
- 1 teaspoon grated orange peel

Heat oven to 350°F. In saucepan, heat *¼ cup* sugar over very low heat until sugar melts, stirring frequently. Evenly divide caramelized sugar into four 6-oz. custard cups; rotate to coat bottom of cups.

In medium bowl, combine *⅓ cup* sugar, salt, vanilla and eggs; gradually stir in milk. Blend in orange peel. Pour custard into prepared cups; place in 8 or 9-inch square pan. Pour very hot water into pan to within ½ inch of tops of cups. Bake at 350°F. for 50 to 60 minutes or until knife inserted near center comes out clean. Serve chilled or warm. Invert custard cups to unmold. **4 servings.**

MICROWAVE DIRECTIONS: In small microwave-safe bowl, melt ¼ cup sugar; microwave on HIGH for 10 to 12 minutes, stirring every 3 minutes until melted. Pour caramelized sugar into four 6-oz. custard cups. In medium bowl, combine ⅓ cup sugar, salt, vanilla, eggs and milk; mix well. Pour custard into prepared cups. Microwave on MEDIUM for 5 minutes. Rotate each cup ½ turn; repeat. Microwave on MEDIUM for an additional 2 minutes or until custard is set.

NUTRIENTS PER ¼ OF RECIPE

Calories	210	Dietary Fiber	0 g
Protein	6 g	Sodium	210 mg
Carbohydrate	35 g	Potassium	190 mg
Fat	5 g	Calcium	15% U.S. RDA
Cholesterol	150 mg	Iron	2% U.S. RDA

Vanilla Pudding

⅓ cup sugar
2 tablespoons cornstarch
⅛ teaspoon salt
2 cups milk
2 egg yolks, slightly beaten
1 tablespoon margarine or butter
1 teaspoon vanilla

In medium saucepan, combine sugar, cornstarch and salt. Gradually stir in milk. Cook over medium heat until mixture boils and thickens, stirring constantly. Boil 1 minute. In small bowl, blend about ⅓ of hot mixture into egg yolks. Return yolk mixture to hot mixture; blend well. Cook until mixture bubbles, stirring constantly. Remove from heat; add margarine and vanilla. Cool slightly before serving. Store in refrigerator. **4 servings.**

MICROWAVE DIRECTIONS: In 2-quart microwave-safe casserole, combine sugar, cornstarch and salt. Gradually stir in milk. Microwave on HIGH for 7 to 9 minutes or until thickened, stirring twice during cooking. Stir about ⅓ of hot mixture into egg yolks. Return yolk mixture to hot mixture; beat well with wire whisk. Microwave on HIGH for 30 to 60 seconds or until thickened; beat well. Stir in margarine and vanilla.

VARIATIONS:

CHOCOLATE PUDDING: Increase sugar to ½ cup and cornstarch to 3 tablespoons. Add 1 oz. (1 square) unsweetened chocolate with milk. After cooking pudding, beat with rotary beater until smooth. Omit margarine.

BUTTERSCOTCH PUDDING: Substitute ½ cup firmly packed brown sugar for sugar.

NUTRIENTS PER ¼ OF RECIPE

Calories	200	Dietary Fiber	0 g
Protein	5 g	Sodium	160 mg
Carbohydrate	26 g	Potassium	200 mg
Fat	8 g	Calcium	15% U.S. RDA
Cholesterol	150 mg	Iron	2% U.S. RDA

Rice Pudding

     2 cups milk
  1½ cups cooked rice
    ½ cup raisins, if desired
    ⅓ cup sugar
     1 teaspoon cinnamon
     1 teaspoon vanilla
     2 eggs, beaten

Heat oven to 350°F. In medium saucepan, heat milk to very warm. *Do not boil.* Remove from heat; add remaining ingredients; mix well. Pour into ungreased 1½-quart casserole. Place casserole in baking pan with about 1 inch hot water. Bake at 350°F. for 30 minutes. Carefully stir pudding; bake an additional 15 to 20 minutes or until knife inserted near center comes out clean. Serve warm or cold with cream, if desired. **12 servings.**

NUTRIENTS PER ¹⁄₁₂ OF RECIPE

Calories	110	Dietary Fiber	1 g
Protein	3 g	Sodium	35 mg
Carbohydrate	19 g	Potassium	125 mg
Fat	2 g	Calcium	6% U.S. RDA
Cholesterol	50 mg	Iron	2% U.S. RDA

Glorified Rice

```
   3  cups cold cooked rice*
   1  cup (1 large) chopped tart apple
 ¹⁄₃  cup sugar
 ¹⁄₂  teaspoon salt
   1  pint (2 cups) whipping cream, whipped, or 4 cups
      frozen whipped topping, thawed
   1  teaspoon vanilla
 ¹⁄₂  teaspoon almond extract
20-oz. can crushed pineapple, drained
10-oz. jar (1 cup) maraschino cherries, drained, quartered
```

In large bowl, combine all ingredients; mix well. Cover and refrigerate until serving time. **10 servings.**

TIP: *For lighter, fluffier rice, add 1 teaspoon lemon juice to the cooking water.

NUTRIENTS PER ¹⁄₁₀ OF RECIPE

Calories	220	Dietary Fiber	2 g
Protein	2 g	Sodium	115 mg
Carbohydrate	34 g	Potassium	90 mg
Fat	9 g	Calcium	2% U.S. RDA
Cholesterol	70 mg	Iron	4% U.S. RDA

Tapioca Pudding

```
 ¹⁄₄  cup sugar
   2  tablespoons quick-cooking tapioca
      Dash salt
```

      2 cups milk
      2 eggs, separated
      1 teaspoon vanilla
      2 tablespoons sugar

In medium saucepan, combine ¼ cup sugar, tapioca and salt; stir in milk and egg yolks. Cook over medium heat, stirring constantly, until mixture comes to a full boil, about 10 to 15 minutes. Remove from heat; blend in vanilla. Beat egg whites until foamy. Gradually add 2 tablespoons sugar, beating until stiff peaks form. Fold into tapioca mixture. Spoon into serving dishes. Refrigerate to chill. **8 servings.**

MICROWAVE DIRECTIONS: In 2-quart microwave-safe casserole, combine ¼ cup sugar, tapioca and salt; stir in milk and egg yolks. Microwave on MEDIUM for 14 to 18 minutes or until mixture boils and slightly thickens, beating with wire whisk twice during cooking. Continue as directed above.

TIP: If desired, fold in ½ cup finely chopped dates, peaches, apricots, strawberries, raspberries or other desired fruit.

NUTRIENTS PER ⅛ OF RECIPE

Calories 100	Dietary Fiber.........................<1 g
Protein.....................................4 g	Sodium................................65 mg
Carbohydrate........................14 g	Potassium ....110 mg
Fat ....3 g	Calcium................8% U.S. RDA
Cholesterol........................70 mg	Iron ....<2% U.S. RDA

Rich Orange Flan

      ¾ cup sugar
      3 tablespoons boiling water
      6 eggs
14-oz. can sweetened condensed milk
15-oz. can evaporated milk
      ¼ cup orange juice
      2 tablespoons finely grated orange peel
      1 teaspoon vanilla

Heat oven to 325°F. Spread sugar evenly over bottom of heavy skillet. Cook over medium heat, stirring constantly, until sugar melts and turns light caramel color. Add 3 tablespoons boiling water, stirring until sugar is dissolved. Pour into 8-inch (2-quart) square baking dish or 10-inch glass deep dish pie pan. Tilt to evenly cover bottom; set aside.

In medium bowl, combine remaining ingredients; beat at medium speed 1 to 2 minutes or until thoroughly blended. Pour over caramelized sugar. Place baking dish in large pan (broiler pan) with 1 inch hot water. Bake at 325°F. for 40 to 45 minutes or until mixture is almost set and knife inserted in center comes out clean. Cool; refrigerate. Loosen edges; invert onto serving plate. **10 to 12 servings.**

NUTRIENTS PER ¹⁄₁₂ OF RECIPE

Calories	240	Dietary Fiber	<1 g
Protein	8 g	Sodium	110 mg
Carbohydrate	34 g	Potassium	255 mg
Fat	8 g	Calcium	20% U.S. RDA
Cholesterol	150 mg	Iron	4% U.S. RDA

Cheesy Cherry Blintzes

   10   Easy Crepes (see Index)

FILLING

   1½   cups ricotta cheese
   1   egg, slightly beaten
   1   tablespoon sugar
   ¼ to ½   teaspoon almond extract
   2   tablespoons margarine or butter, melted

   Dark Cherry Sauce (see Index)

Prepare crepes. Butter 12x8-inch (2-quart) baking dish. In small bowl, combine ricotta cheese, egg, sugar and ¼ to ½ teaspoon almond extract; blend well. Spoon 2 tablespoons filling in center of each crepe; fold 2 opposite edges to overlap filling. Fold in remaining edges forming a square packet. Place seam side down in prepared dish. Cover; refrigerate overnight.

Heat oven to 400°F. Remove cover; brush blintzes with melted margarine. Bake at 400°F. for 18 to 22 minutes or until light golden brown. Prepare Dark Cherry Sauce. Serve over blintzes. Garnish as desired. **5 servings.**

NUTRIENTS PER ⅕ OF RECIPE

Calories	380	Dietary Fiber	<1 g
Protein	15 g	Sodium	560 mg
Carbohydrate	45 g	Potassium	250 mg
Fat	15 g	Calcium	30% U.S. RDA
Cholesterol	170 mg	Iron	15% U.S. RDA

Crepes Suzette

CREPES

½ cup (4 oz.) creamed cottage cheese
½ cup all purpose flour
1½ teaspoons sugar
1½ teaspoons grated orange peel
½ cup dairy sour cream
4 teaspoons orange juice
2 eggs

ORANGE HONEY SAUCE

½ cup honey
⅓ cup margarine or butter
2 teaspoons grated orange peel
¼ teaspoon cinnamon
2 tablespoons orange juice

2 tablespoons brandy, if desired

In blender container, blend cottage cheese until smooth. Add remaining crepe ingredients; blend at high speed until well mixed. Heat 6-inch crepe pan or skillet over medium-high heat (375°F.). A few drops of water sprinkled on the pan sizzle and bounce when heat is just right. Grease pan lightly. Pour 3 tablespoons batter into pan, tilting pan to spread evenly. When crepe is light brown and set, turn to brown other side. Fold warm crepes in quarters; arrange in chafing or oblong serving dish.

In small saucepan, blend all sauce ingredients. Heat until hot, stirring occasionally. Pour hot sauce over crepes. To flame, warm brandy in small saucepan just until small bubbles form; ignite with match. Immediately pour over crepes. If desired, serve with whipped cream. **5 to 6 servings.**

TIP: To make ahead, prepare crepes; stack between paper towels. Wrap and store in refrigerator or freezer.

NUTRIENTS PER ⅙ OF RECIPE

Calories	310	Dietary Fiber	<1 g
Protein	5 g	Sodium	190 mg
Carbohydrate	35 g	Potassium	110 mg
Fat	17 g	Calcium	4% U.S. RDA
Cholesterol	100 mg	Iron	6% U.S. RDA

Cream Puffs

½ cup water
¼ cup margarine or butter
½ cup all purpose flour
¼ teaspoon salt
2 eggs

Heat oven to 425°F. In medium saucepan, heat water and margarine to boiling. Stir in flour and salt. Cook over medium heat, stirring vigorously until mixture leaves sides of pan in smooth compact ball, about 2 minutes. Remove from heat. Add eggs, one at a time, beating vigorously after each until mixture is smooth and glossy. Spoon 6 mounds of dough about 3 inches apart onto ungreased cookie sheet. Bake at 425°F. for 30 to 40 minutes or until puffed and golden brown. Cool completely. Split; remove any filaments of soft dough. Fill as desired.* **6 cream puffs.**

TIP: *Fill with ice cream, whipped cream, mousse or pudding; top with glaze, sauce or powdered sugar. Or fill with chicken or seafood salad.

VARIATIONS:

ECLAIRS: Drop cream puff dough into 12 long ovals about 1-inch wide. Bake as directed above. When cool, fill with Vanilla Pudding and glaze with Chocolate Glaze (see Index).

SNACK CREAM PUFFS: Drop by tablespoons, making about 20 small cream puffs. Bake as directed.

NUTRIENTS PER 1 UNFILLED CREAM PUFF

Calories	130	Dietary Fiber	4 g
Protein	3 g	Sodium	200 mg
Carbohydrate	8 g	Potassium	35 mg
Fat	10 g	Calcium	<2% U.S. RDA
Cholesterol	90 mg	Iron	4% U.S. RDA

Strawberry Cream Puff Ring

PUFF
- 6 tablespoons margarine
- ¾ cup water
- ¾ cup all purpose flour
- ¼ teaspoon salt
- 3 eggs

FILLING
3⅛-oz. pkg. vanilla pudding and pie filling mix
(not instant)
1½ cups milk

    2 teaspoons grated orange peel
 ½ cup whipping cream, whipped or 1 cup frozen
    whipped topping, thawed

    1 pint (2 cups) fresh strawberries, sliced

GLAZE
 2 oz. semi-sweet chocolate
    2 tablespoons margarine or butter
 ⅔ cup powdered sugar
    2 tablespoons milk

Heat oven to 400°F. Grease cookie sheet. In medium saucepan, combine margarine and water; bring to a boil over medium heat. Stir in flour and salt; cook, stirring constantly, until mixture leaves sides of pan in smooth ball. Remove from heat. Add eggs one at a time, beating vigorously after each, until mixture is smooth and glossy. Form ring by placing 8 to 10 spoonfuls of batter, sides touching, on prepared cookie sheet to form an 8-inch circle. Bake at 400°F. for 40 to 50 minutes or until golden brown. Remove from oven; prick puff with sharp knife. Cool.

In medium saucepan, combine pudding mix, milk and orange peel. Bring to a boil over medium heat, stirring constantly. Boil 1 minute; remove from heat. Cover; cool 1 hour. Fold whipped cream into cooled pudding.

To assemble, place puff on serving plate; slice in half horizontally. Spoon pudding mixture into bottom half of puff. Top with strawberries. Replace top of puff. In small saucepan, combine chocolate and margarine; cook over medium heat until melted. Stir in powdered sugar and milk; blend until smooth. Drizzle over puff. Refrigerate leftovers. **8 to 10 servings.**

HIGH ALTITUDE: Bake at 400°F. for 35 to 45 minutes.

NUTRIENTS PER ¹⁄₁₀ OF RECIPE

Calories	300	Dietary Fiber	2 g
Protein	5 g	Sodium	240 mg
Carbohydrate	29 g	Potassium	200 mg
Fat	19 g	Calcium	8% U.S. RDA
Cholesterol	100 mg	Iron	6% U.S. RDA

Strawberry Meringue Torte

MERINGUE

     6 egg whites
   ½ teaspoon cream of tartar
       Dash salt
  1½ cups sugar
   ½ teaspoon vanilla

FILLING

     3 cups half-and-half
6-oz. pkg. instant vanilla pudding and pie filling mix
     1 teaspoon almond extract

TOPPING

     3 cups strawberries, halved
     3 tablespoons currant jelly, melted

Heat oven to 275°F. Line 2 cookie sheets with brown or parchment paper. In large bowl, beat egg whites, cream of tartar and salt until frothy. Gradually add sugar, beating continuously until stiff peaks form, about 10 minutes. Beat in vanilla. Spoon half of meringue onto each prepared pan. Shape into two 9-inch circles, building up sides slightly with back of spoon.

Bake at 275°F. for 1¼ hours. Turn off oven; leave meringues in closed oven for 2 hours. Remove from oven; cool completely. Remove meringues from paper.

To prepare filling, in medium bowl combine half-and-half and pudding mix; beat at low speed 1 minute. Stir in almond extract.

To assemble, place 1 meringue on large serving plate. Spread pudding mixture to edges of meringue; top with remaining meringue. Arrange strawberries over top. Brush melted jelly over berries. Refrigerate at least 2 hours to soften meringues. **12 servings.**

TIP: Meringues can be made a day ahead. Cover loosely; store at room temperature. Fill and top with berries; refrigerate at least 2 hours before serving.

NUTRIENTS PER ¹⁄₁₂ OF RECIPE

Calories	270	Dietary Fiber	1 g
Protein	4 g	Sodium	120 mg
Carbohydrate	47 g	Potassium	200 mg
Fat	7 g	Calcium	10% U.S. RDA
Cholesterol	20 mg	Iron	2% U.S. RDA

Peach Praline Meringues

      3 egg whites
    ¼ teaspoon cream of tartar
    ½ cup firmly packed brown sugar
    ½ cup finely chopped pecans
10-oz. pkg. frozen peach slices, thawed and drained, or
        16-oz. can peach slices, drained
      1 pint (2 cups) vanilla ice milk or ice cream

Heat oven to 250°F. Line cookie sheet with brown paper. In small bowl, beat egg whites with cream of tartar until foamy; gradually add brown sugar, beating continuously until stiff peaks form. Fold in pecans. Form individual meringue shells by spooning about ⅓ cup meringue onto lined cookie sheet. Make a deep well in center of each shell, gently building up sides with back of spoon forming 3-inch circles.

Bake at 250°F. for 1 hour. Turn oven off, letting meringues *cool in oven with door closed* for an additional 2 hours. Remove from oven. Let cool completely on paper; remove from paper. To serve, place peach slices in meringue shells; top with ice milk. **8 servings.**

TIP: Peaches can be pureed in blender or food processor. Fill meringue shells with ice milk; top with pureed peaches.

NUTRIENTS PER ⅛ OF RECIPE

Calories	190	Dietary Fiber	1 g
Protein	3 g	Sodium	50 mg
Carbohydrate	30 g	Potassium	220 mg
Fat	7 g	Calcium	6% U.S. RDA
Cholesterol	4 mg	Iron	4% U.S. RDA

Chocolate Lace Cheesecake

CRUST
- 1½ cups chocolate wafer crumbs
- ½ cup finely chopped almonds
- ¼ cup margarine or butter, melted

FILLING
- 2 (8-oz.) pkg. cream cheese, softened
- ⅔ cup sugar
- 3 eggs
- 12-oz. pkg. (2 cups) semi-sweet chocolate chips, melted
- 1 cup whipping cream
- 2 tablespoons margarine or butter, melted
- 1 teaspoon vanilla

TOPPING
- 1 cup dairy sour cream
- 1½ teaspoons vanilla
- 1 teaspoon sugar
- ½ oz. (½ square) unsweetened chocolate, melted

Heat oven to 325°F. Butter 9-inch springform pan. In large bowl, blend crust ingredients. Press into bottom and up sides of prepared pan; refrigerate. In large bowl, beat cream cheese and ⅔ cup sugar until smooth. Add eggs one at a time, beating well after each addition. Add melted chocolate chips; beat well. Add whipping cream, 2 tablespoons margarine and 1 teaspoon vanilla; beat until smooth. Pour into prepared crust. Bake at 325°F. for 65 to 80 minutes or until center is set. Center of cheesecake will be soft. (To minimize cracking, place shallow pan half full of water on lower oven rack during baking.) Cool in pan 5 minutes; carefully remove sides of pan. Cool completely.

In small bowl, combine sour cream, 1½ teaspoons vanilla and 1 teaspoon sugar; stir until smooth. Spread over cooled cheesecake. Drizzle with ½ oz. melted chocolate in lace pattern. Refrigerate several hours or overnight before serving. Garnish as desired. **16 servings.**

NUTRIENTS PER ¹⁄₁₆ OF RECIPE

Calories	470	Dietary Fiber	3 g
Protein	7 g	Sodium	180 mg
Carbohydrate	31 g	Potassium	200 mg
Fat	36 g	Calcium	8% U.S. RDA
Cholesterol	110 mg	Iron	8% U.S. RDA

Cheesecake

CRUST

    2 cups graham cracker crumbs
    ½ cup margarine or butter, melted

FILLING

    3 eggs
    2 (8-oz.) pkg. cream cheese, softened
    1 cup sugar
    ¼ teaspoon salt
    2 teaspoons vanilla
    3 cups dairy sour cream

Heat oven to 350°F. In medium bowl, combine crust ingredients; blend well. Press in bottom and 1½ inches up sides of ungreased 10-inch springform pan. In large bowl, beat eggs. Add cream cheese, sugar, salt and vanilla; beat until smooth. Add sour cream; blend well. Pour into crust-lined pan.

Bake at 350°F. for 60 to 70 minutes or until set.* Cool in pan 5 minutes; remove sides of pan. Cool completely. Store in refrigerator. If desired, serve with Dark Cherry Sauce (see Index). **16 servings.**

TIP: *To prevent cracks on top of cheesecake, place pan of water on rack below cheesecake while baking.

NUTRIENTS PER ¹⁄₁₆ OF RECIPE

Calories	360	Dietary Fiber	<1 g
Protein	6 g	Sodium	290 mg
Carbohydrate	23 g	Potassium	150 mg
Fat	27 g	Calcium	8% U.S. RDA
Cholesterol	100 mg	Iron	4% U.S. RDA

Cream Cheese Cherry Strudel

3-oz. pkg. cream cheese, softened
   ¼ cup sugar
   ¼ teaspoon almond extract
   6 (13x9-inch) frozen fillo (phyllo) pastry sheets, thawed
   ¼ cup margarine or butter, melted
   3 tablespoons plain bread crumbs
16-oz. can pitted tart or dark sweet cherries, well drained
   ¼ cup sliced almonds
   1 teaspoon sugar

Heat oven to 375°F. Grease cookie sheet. In medium bowl, combine cream cheese, ¼ cup sugar and almond extract; set aside.

Unroll fillo sheets; cover with plastic wrap or towel. Place 1 fillo sheet on large sheet of plastic wrap. Brush with melted margarine and 1 tablespoon bread crumbs. Repeat layering 5 more times, using melted margarine on each sheet and 1 tablespoon bread crumbs on alternating sheets. (Top fillo sheet should be brushed with margarine only.) Spread cream cheese mixture over fillo to 1½ inches from each edge. Top with cherries and almonds. Fold shorter sides of fillo 1 inch over filling. Starting with longer side and using plastic wrap, lift fillo and carefully roll up jelly-roll fashion. Place on prepared cookie sheet. Brush with remaining melted margarine and sprinkle with 1 teaspoon sugar. Bake at 375°F. for 25 to 30 minutes or until golden brown. **6 to 8 servings.**

NUTRIENTS PER ⅛ OF RECIPE

Calories	200	Dietary Fiber	<1 g
Protein	2 g	Sodium	150 mg
Carbohydrate	23 g	Potassium	100 mg
Fat	11 g	Calcium	2% U.S. RDA
Cholesterol	10 mg	Iron	6% U.S. RDA

Cherries 'n Cream Squares

CRUST

  1½ cups vanilla wafer or graham cracker crumbs
    2 tablespoons powdered sugar
  ⅓ cup margarine or butter, melted

FILLING

8-oz. pkg. cream cheese, softened
    1 cup powdered sugar
    1 teaspoon vanilla
    2 cups miniature marshmallows
    1 cup whipping cream, whipped
21-oz. can cherry fruit pie filling
  ¼ teaspoon almond extract

In medium bowl, combine all crust ingredients; blend well. Press in bottom of ungreased 13x9-inch pan; refrigerate. In large bowl, beat cream cheese, 1 cup powdered sugar and vanilla until light and fluffy. Fold in marshmallows and whipped cream. Spread mixture over crust. In small bowl, combine pie filling and almond extract. Spread over cream layer. Refrigerate several hours or until firm. **16 servings.**

NUTRIENTS PER ⅟₁₆ OF RECIPE

Calories	300	Dietary Fiber	1 g
Protein	2 g	Sodium	120 mg
Carbohydrate	37 g	Potassium	65 mg
Fat	16 g	Calcium	2% U.S. RDA
Cholesterol	35 mg	Iron	2% U.S. RDA

Raspberry Trifle

3⅛-oz. pkg. vanilla pudding and pie filling mix
　　　(not instant)
　2　cups milk
　1　cup whipping cream, whipped
　12　ladyfingers
　½　cup raspberry preserves
8-oz. pkg. soft macaroons, crumbled (2 cups)
　3　tablespoons dry sherry
　　　Whipped cream
　　　Sliced almonds

In medium saucepan, combine pudding and milk. Bring to a boil over medium heat; boil 1 minute, stirring constantly. Remove from heat. Cover with plastic wrap; refrigerate 1 hour. In small bowl, beat 1 cup whipping cream until soft peaks form; fold into cooled pudding.

Split ladyfingers lengthwise and spread each cut side with raspberry preserves. Arrange 8 ladyfinger halves, preserves side up, in bottom of 2½-quart glass bowl. Reserve 2 tablespoons of the crumbled macaroons for garnish. Sprinkle ⅓ of the remaining macaroons over ladyfingers; sprinkle 1 tablespoon sherry over macaroons. Top with ⅓ of the pudding mixture. Repeat layering 2 more times. Cover; refrigerate at least 4 hours or overnight. Garnish with additional whipped cream, almonds and reserve macaroon crumbs. **10 to 12 servings.**

NUTRIENTS PER ½ OF RECIPE

Calories	320	Dietary Fiber	1 g
Protein	4 g	Sodium	80 mg
Carbohydrate	39 g	Potassium	210 mg
Fat	17 g	Calcium	8% U.S. RDA
Cholesterol	100 mg	Iron	4% U.S. RDA

Strawberry Margarita Dessert

Pretzel Crust (see Index for Crumb Crusts)

FILLING

14-oz. can sweetened condensed milk (not evaporated)
  ¼ cup lime juice
  2 tablespoons tequila
  2 tablespoons orange-flavored liqueur
10-oz. pkg. frozen strawberries, thawed
  1 cup whipping cream, whipped

Prepare crust in ungreased 10-inch springform pan. Refrigerate.

In large bowl, combine sweetened condensed milk, lime juice, tequila and liqueur; beat until smooth. Add strawberries; beat at low speed until well blended. Fold in whipped cream. Pour over crust. Freeze until firm. Let stand at room temperature about 15 minutes before serving. If desired, garnish with lime slices and fresh strawberries. **8 to 10 servings.**

NUTRIENTS PER ⅒ OF RECIPE

Calories	410	Dietary Fiber	<1 g
Protein	5 g	Sodium	385 mg
Carbohydrate	48 g	Potassium	205 mg
Fat	22 g	Calcium	10% U.S. RDA
Cholesterol	50 mg	Iron	2% U.S. RDA

Chilled Lemon Souffle

  ½ cup sugar
  ¼ teaspoon salt
  1 envelope unflavored gelatin
  1 cup water
  3 eggs, separated
  1 tablespoon grated lemon peel
3 to 4 tablespoons lemon juice
  ⅓ cup sugar
  1 cup whipping cream, whipped

Prepare 3 or 4-cup souffle dish by forming a collar of waxed paper around top of dish that extends about 1 inch above edge of dish. Tape or tie paper to hold in place. Do not grease.

In medium saucepan, combine ½ cup sugar, salt and gelatin. Stir in water. Beat egg yolks; add to gelatin mixture, blending well. Cook over medium heat just until mixture begins to bubble, stirring constantly. Remove from heat. If mixture is not smooth, beat with wire whisk or rotary beater. Stir in lemon peel and lemon juice. Refrigerate until mixture is thickened but not set.

In small bowl, beat egg whites until foamy. Gradually add ⅓ cup sugar, beating until stiff peaks form. Fold beaten egg whites and whipped cream into gelatin mixture; blend well. Pour into prepared dish. Refrigerate until set. Carefully remove collar from dish before serving. Garnish with lemon slices. **10 servings.**

NUTRIENTS PER ½ CUP

Calories 290	Dietary Fiber.........................<1 g
Protein ....5 g	Sodium ....135 mg
Carbohydrate.........................30 g	Potassium ....80 mg
Fat ....17 g	Calcium ....4% U.S. RDA
Cholesterol ....120 mg	Iron ....2% U.S. RDA

Chocolate Souffle

> ½ cup sugar
> 2 tablespoons cornstarch
> ¼ teaspoon salt
> ¾ cup milk
> 2 oz. (2 squares) unsweetened chocolate or 2 envelopes premelted unsweetened baking chocolate flavor
> 3 tablespoons margarine or butter
> 1 teaspoon vanilla
> 4 eggs, separated
> ¼ teaspoon cream of tartar
> Whipped cream or topping, if desired

Heat oven to 350°F. Prepare a 4 to 5-cup souffle dish or casserole with foil band by cutting 3-inch strip of foil to go around top of dish. Lightly grease dish and strip of foil. With greased side toward inside of dish, secure foil band around top of dish, letting it extend 2 inches above edge of dish.

In medium saucepan, combine sugar, cornstarch and salt. Stir in milk. Cook over medium heat, stirring constantly, until mixture boils and thickens. Remove from heat; stir in chocolate and margarine until melted. Stir in vanilla. Add egg yolks one at a time, beating well after each addition. In medium bowl, beat egg whites with cream of tartar until soft peaks form. Gently fold in chocolate mixture. Pour into prepared souffle dish.*

Bake at 350°F. for 45 to 50 minutes or until knife inserted near center comes out clean. Remove foil band; immediately serve souffle with whipped cream or topping. **10 servings.**

TIP: *Souffle can stand at room temperature, loosely covered, up to 1 hour before baking.

VARIATION:

CHOCOLATE MOCHA SOUFFLE: Add 1 teaspoon instant coffee to cornstarch.

NUTRIENTS PER ¹⁄₁₀ OF RECIPE

Calories 170	Dietary Fiber.......................<1 g
Protein....................................4 g	Sodium.............................130 mg
Carbohydrate........................15 g	Potassium...........................95 mg
Fat ....11 g	Calcium.................4% U.S. RDA
Cholesterol.......................120 mg	Iron........................4% U.S. RDA

Vanilla Custard Ice Cream

    ¾ cup sugar
     2 cups milk
     2 eggs, slightly beaten
     1 pint (2 cups) whipping cream
2 to 3 teaspoons vanilla

In medium saucepan, combine sugar, milk and eggs. Cook over medium heat until mixture coats a metal spoon, stirring constantly. Cool.* When ready to freeze, add cream and vanilla. Prepare ice cream freezer and freeze according to manufacturer's directions. **16 servings.**

TIPS: To make ahead, prepare to *, cover and refrigerate up to 2 days. When ready to freeze, continue from *.

To prepare without ice cream freezer, prepare to *. Pour into 2 ice cube trays or loaf pans. Freeze until edges are set. In small bowl, beat whipping cream until thickened. In large bowl, beat partially frozen custard mixture until smooth and light. Fold whipped cream into custard mixture. Return to trays and freeze until firm. (Store covered in foil.)

VARIATIONS:

CHOCOLATE CUSTARD ICE CREAM: Increase sugar to 1 cup and add 2 oz. (2 squares) melted unsweetened chocolate or 2 envelopes premelted unsweetened baking chocolate flavor before cooking. Beat with rotary beater until smooth before adding cream.

STRAWBERRY CUSTARD ICE CREAM: Wash, hull and crush 1 pint (2 cups) fresh strawberries. Stir in ¼ cup sugar and strawberries with cream; omit vanilla.

NUTRIENTS PER ¹⁄₁₆ OF RECIPE

Calories	160	Dietary Fiber	0 g
Protein	2 g	Sodium	35 mg
Carbohydrate	12 g	Potassium	80 mg
Fat	12 g	Calcium	6% U.S. RDA
Cholesterol	80 mg	Iron	<2% U.S. RDA

Orange-Lemon Sorbet

    2 cups water
    1 cup sugar
    1 cup orange juice
    ¼ cup lemon juice
    1 tablespoon grated orange peel
    1 tablespoon grated lemon peel

In medium saucepan, bring water and sugar to a boil; boil 5 minutes. Cool to room temperature; add juices and peels. Pour into 8-inch square pan. Freeze 3 to 4 hours, stirring every half hour. (Volume increases as it is stirred.) **12 servings.**

NUTRIENTS PER ¹⁄₁₂ OF RECIPE

Calories	80	Dietary Fiber	<1 g
Protein	0 g	Sodium	0 mg
Carbohydrate	20 g	Potassium	50 mg
Fat	0 g	Calcium	<2% U.S. RDA
Cholesterol	0 mg	Iron	<2% U.S. RDA

Pies

Keys to Successful Pastries and Pie Crusts

• Measure and blend ingredients carefully. Accurate measuring and mixing of ingredients can ensure pastry and filling of highest quality.

• Stir together the flour and salt thoroughly before adding shortening and water. Using a pastry blender or two knives, cut in the shortening until the mixture forms coarse crumbs. Distributing shortening particles evenly throughout the flour produces a flaky crust. Ice-cold water and a light touch of the hand are also important for flaky pastry. Guard against overmixing, which can toughen pastry.

• For easier handling, chill dough for ½ hour before rolling out.

• A floured surface is essential for rolling out dough without sticking, but the less flour used, the flakier the pastry. A lightly floured pastry-cloth-covered surface and stockinet-covered rolling pin are best.

• Ovenproof glass plates or aluminum pans with dull finish are preferred for even baking and browning. We achieved the most evenly baked and highest-quality pastry using 9-inch glass pie pans.

• Heat circulation in ovens varies. If edges of crust are browning before the center is done, cover those edges with 2-inch strips of foil. If the whole top is overbrowning, loosely drape a sheet of foil over the pie.

• For crumb crusts, to crush crumbs finely use a food processor or place broken cookies or crackers in a plastic bag and roll with a rolling pin.

• Crumb crusts may be baked or chilled to set the crumb mixture. Baked crusts usually release from pan easily when pie is cut. To release an unbaked crust, press warm towel around outside of pan to soften margarine before cutting.

Toppings for Pies

For an added touch, choose a topping that will complement the filling.

Special Touches for Two-Crust Pies:

• For a shiny top, brush with slightly beaten egg whites. If desired, sprinkle with sugar.

• For a golden-brown crust, brush with milk, cream or a mixture of 1 egg yolk and 1 tablespoon water. If desired, sprinkle with sugar.

• For pastry cutouts, roll out scraps of leftover dough. Cut out shapes with cookie cutters or knife. With water, moisten back of the cutout and place design, moistened side down, on top crust.

• For cut-out designs, use a knife or canape cutter before placing top crust over filling.

Special Touches for Cream Pies:

• Top cream pies with Meringue Topping (see Index) or, after the pie has been chilled, with whipped cream.

• Add a complementary garnish such as banana slices, chocolate curls or toasted coconut.

Storing Pies and Tarts

Food safety is a concern for pies containing eggs and dairy products (milk, sour cream, whipped cream or topping, ice cream, yogurt and cream cheese). These pies should be refrigerated or frozen following preparation. Baked fruit pies can be safely stored at room temperature for 24 to 48 hours unless room temperature is excessively warm; in that case,

refrigerate. It is possible to freeze pastry and some pies. See
Special Helps for specific details on freezer storage.

How to Make Pastry (see recipe p. 351)

After shortening is cut evenly into flour mixture, ice-cold
water is added a tablespoon at a time. Toss lightly and as little as possible to moisten mixture. (Do not use stirring motion as shortening will melt, causing tough pastry.) Add cold
water until dough is just moist enough to form a ball when
lightly pressed together.

Flatten ball of dough to ½-inch thickness, rounding and
smoothing edges. Roll out on surface rubbed with small
amount of flour. Using light, even strokes with rolling pin,
roll dough from center to edge, lifting rolling pin as it
reaches the edge. Continue to roll from center to edges
maintaining the circle shape, until reaching desired size. Lift
pastry occasionally, giving it a quarter turn, to prevent sticking.

Roll pastry into a circle 1½ inches larger than inverted pie
pan you are using. **Fold dough in half or quarters;** place
fold in center of pan. Unfold, easing pastry into pan without
stretching. Use fingertips to gently press pastry into pan and
to eliminate air bubbles. Trim edge as directed for the pie
you are making.

For two-crust pie, trim bottom pastry even with pan edge
and fill with desired filling. Cover filling with top pastry, allowing a 1-inch overlap of top pastry around the edge. Press
well to seal and form a standing rim of pastry to flute. To
finish your pie, cut slits to release steam during baking. For
one-crust pie, trim edge of pastry 1 inch from edge of pan.
For fluting techniques, see below.

Lattice Crust & Fluting Techniques

Lattice Crust: Prepare pastry for two-crust pie. Roll out
bottom crust as directed. Place in pie pan, leaving ½ inch of

bottom crust extending beyond edge of pan. Roll out remaining dough as if making top crust. Cut into strips ½ inch wide. For a decorative edge, use a fluted pastry wheel. Lay part of strips across filling in parallel rows, about ¾ inch apart, twisting if desired. Place more strips at right angles, forming a crisscross pattern. (For a woven lattice top, lift every other strip as the cross strips are added.) Trim ends even with edge of dough. Form a stand-up rim; flute.

Fork Edge: Flatten pastry on rim of pie pan. Dip fork tines in flour; press pastry firmly around edge on rim of pie pan.

Pinch Edge: Place index finger on inside rim of pastry. Make flutes about ½ inch apart by pushing pastry into the V shaped by the right thumb and index finger on the outside of the rim. Pinch points to make definite edges.

Rope Edge: Place thumb on stand-up rim at an angle; press pastry against thumb with knuckle of index finger. Repeat pattern diagonally around edge on rim of pie pan.

Scalloped Edge: Roll tip of a teaspoon around edge of crust, forming scalloped edge.

Pastry

ONE-CRUST PIE

1	cup all purpose flour
½	teaspoon salt
⅓	cup shortening
2 to 4	tablespoons ice water

TWO-CRUST PIE

2	cups all purpose flour
1	teaspoon salt
⅔	cup shortening
5 to 7	tablespoons ice water

In medium bowl, combine flour and salt. Using fork or pastry blender, cut shortening into flour until mixture resembles coarse crumbs. Sprinkle flour mixture with water, 1 tablespoon at a time, while tossing and mixing lightly with fork. Add water until dough is just moist enough to form a ball when lightly pressed together. (Too much water causes dough to become sticky and tough; too little water causes edges to crack and pastry to tear easily while rolling.)

Shape dough into 1 ball for one-crust pie (2 balls for two-crust pie). Flatten ball to ½-inch thickness, rounding and smoothing edges. Roll 1 ball lightly on floured surface from center to edge into circle 1½ inches larger than inverted 9-inch pie pan. Fold pastry in half; place in pie pan. Unfold; fit evenly into pan. Do not stretch.

FOR FILLED ONE-CRUST PIE: Fold edge under to form a stand-up rim of pastry; flute. Do not prick pastry. Continue as directed in recipe.

FOR UNFILLED ONE-CRUST PIE: Fold edge under to form a stand-up rim of pastry; flute. Prick bottom and sides of pastry generously with fork to prevent shell from puffing as it bakes. Bake at 450°F. for 9 to 12 minutes or until light golden brown; cool. Continue as directed in recipe.

FOR TWO-CRUST PIE: Trim bottom pastry even with pan edge. Roll out remaining pastry; set aside. Continue as directed in recipe.

FOOD PROCESSOR DIRECTIONS: Place flour, salt and shortening in processor bowl fitted with metal blade. Process 20 to 30 seconds until mixture resembles coarse crumbs. With machine running, add *minimum* amount ice water all at once through feed tube. Process 20 to 30 seconds or just until ball forms. (If ball does not form in 30 seconds, shape into ball with hands.) Wrap dough in plastic wrap; refrigerate 30 minutes or freeze 10 minutes before continuing as directed above.

HIGH ALTITUDE: When preparing pastry in food processor, increase water to 3 tablespoons for one-crust or 6 tablespoons for two-crust pie.

VARIATIONS:

CHEESE PASTRY: Add shredded Cheddar or American cheese to flour. Use ¼ to ½ cup for one-crust pie; ½ to 1 cup for two-crust pie. Omit salt.

EXTRA FLAKY PASTRY: Add sugar with flour and vinegar with water. Use 1 teaspoon sugar and 1 teaspoon vinegar for one-crust pie; 2 teaspoons sugar and 2 teaspoons vinegar for two-crust pie.

WHOLE WHEAT PASTRY: Whole wheat flour can be substituted for up to half of the all purpose flour, adding a little more water if necessary.

NUTRIENTS PER ⅛ OF ONE-CRUST PIE

Calories	130	Dietary Fiber	<1g
Protein	2 g	Sodium	130 mg
Carbohydrate	12 g	Potassium	15 mg
Fat	8 g	Calcium	<2% U.S. RDA
Cholesterol	0 mg	Iron	4% U.S. RDA

NUTRIENTS PER ⅛ OF TWO-CRUST PIE

Calories	260	Dietary Fiber	2 g
Protein	3 g	Sodium	270 mg
Carbohydrate	24 g	Potassium	30 mg
Fat	17 g	Calcium	<2% U.S. RDA
Cholesterol	0 mg	Iron	8% U.S. RDA

Oil Pastry

  1¾ cups all purpose flour
    1 teaspoon sugar
    1 teaspoon salt
  ½ cup oil
  ¼ cup milk

Heat oven to 425°F. In medium bowl, combine flour, sugar and salt. In small bowl, combine oil and milk; pour over flour mixture. Stir with fork until well mixed. Press in bottom and up sides of 9-inch pan; flute edge. pie* Prick bottom and sides of pastry generously with fork. Bake at 425°F. for 12 to 17 minutes or until light golden brown. Cool. Fill with desired filling. **9-inch baked pastry.**

TIP: *Crust can be rolled out between 2 sheets of waxed paper.

NUTRIENTS PER ⅛ OF RECIPE

Calories	230	Dietary Fiber	2 g
Protein	3 g	Sodium	270 mg
Carbohydrate	22 g	Potassium	40 mg
Fat	14 g	Calcium	<2% U.S. RDA
Cholesterol	0 mg	Iron	6% U.S. RDA

Meringue Crust

Heat oven to 275°F. Generously butter 9-inch metal pie pan. (Crust may stick in glass pie pan.) In large bowl, beat 4 egg whites and ½ teaspoon cream of tartar until frothy. Add 1 cup sugar, 2 tablespoons at a time, beating continuously until sugar is dissolved and stiff glossy peaks form, about 8 to 10 minutes. *Do not underbeat.* (To determine whether sugar is dissolved, rub small amount of meringue between thumb and forefinger.) Spread evenly over bottom and up sides of prepared pan. Bake at 275°F. for 1 hour. Turn oven off, letting meringue *cool in oven with door closed* for an additional 2 hours. Fill with desired filling. Overnight refrigeration allows crust to soften for easier cutting and serving. Avoid preparing meringue in humid weather. **8 servings.**

VARIATIONS:

LARGE MERINGUE SHELL: Line cookie sheet with brown paper. Spoon meringue onto prepared cookie sheet. Shape into a 9 to 10-inch circle, building up sides with back of spoon. Bake at 275°F. for 1 to 1¼ hours. Turn oven off, letting meringue *cool in oven with door closed* for an additional 2 hours. Fill with desired filling. **10 servings.**

MERINGUE TARTS: Line cookie sheet with brown paper. Spoon about ⅓ cup meringue onto prepared cookie sheet. Make a deep well in center of each shell, building up sides with back of spoon, shaping into 4-inch circles. Bake at 275°F. for 40 to 50 minutes or until crisp and lightly browned. Turn oven off, letting meringues *cool in oven with door closed* for an additional 2 hours. Fill with desired filling. **10 to 12 tarts.**

NUTRIENTS PER ⅛ OF RECIPE

Calories	110	Dietary Fiber	0 g
Protein	2 g	Sodium	25 mg
Carbohydrate	25 g	Potassium	25 mg
Fat	0 g	Calcium	<2% U.S. RDA
Cholesterol	0 mg	Iron	<2% U.S. RDA

Crumb Crust

In small bowl, combine crumbs, sugar and melted margarine. Press mixture in bottom and up sides of 8 or 9-inch pie pan or in bottom of 9-inch springform pan. Refrigerate 10 to 15 minutes or bake at 375°F. for 8 to 10 minutes or until golden brown. Cool; fill as desired.

Kind	Amount of Crumbs	Sugar	Margarine or Butter, Melted
Chocolate Wafer	1¼ cups (20 wafers)	¼ cup	¼ cup
Creme-filled Choc./Vanilla Cookie	1½ cups (15 cookies)	—	¼ cup
Crisp Macaroon Cookie	1½ cups	—	¼ cup
Gingersnap Cookie	1½ cups	—	¼ cup
Graham Cracker*	1½ cups (21 squares)	¼ cup	⅓ cup
Granola	1½ cups (coarsely crushed)	—	¼ cup
Pretzel**	1¼ cups	¼ cup	½ cup
Vanilla Wafer	1½ cups (30 wafers)	—	¼ cup

TIPS: *One-half teaspoon cinnamon can be added, if desired.
**For easier serving, butter pan before preparing crust.

VARIATION:

ICE CREAM PIE: Fill crust with ice cream; freeze until solid. Wrap carefully and store in freezer. When ready to serve, remove pie from freezer 5 to 10 minutes before serving. Dip knife into warm water for easier cutting.

Apple Nut Lattice Tart

15-oz. pkg. refrigerated pie crust
1 teaspoon flour

FILLING
3 to 3½ cups (3 to 4 medium) thinly sliced,
peeled apples
½ cup sugar
3 tablespoons golden raisins
3 tablespoons chopped walnuts or pecans
½ teaspoon cinnamon
¼ to ½ teaspoon grated lemon peel
2 teaspoons lemon juice
1 egg yolk, beaten
1 teaspoon water

GLAZE
¼ cup powdered sugar
1 to 2 teaspoons lemon juice

Prepare pie crust according to package directions for two-crust pie using 10-inch tart pan with removable bottom or 9-inch pie pan. Heat oven to 400°F. Place prepared crust in bottom and up sides of pan. Trim edges.

In large bowl, combine apples, sugar, raisins, walnuts, cinnamon, lemon peel and 2 teaspoons lemon juice; mix lightly. Spoon into pie crust-lined pan.

To make a lattice top, cut remaining crust into ½-inch wide strips. Arrange strips in lattice design over apple mixture. Trim and seal edges. In small bowl, combine egg yolk and water; gently brush over lattice. Bake at 400°F. for 40 to 60 minutes or until golden brown and apples are tender. Cool 1 hour.

In small bowl, combine glaze ingredients; drizzle over slightly warm tart. Cool; remove sides of pan. **8 servings.**

TIP: Cover tart with foil during last 15 to 20 minutes of baking if necessary to prevent excessive browning.

NUTRIENTS PER ⅛ OF RECIPE

Calories 380	Dietary Fiber..........................2 g
Protein.....................................2 g	Sodium.............................330 mg
Carbohydrate........................50 g	Potassium........................125 mg
Fat ....19 g	Calcium..............<2% U.S. RDA
Cholesterol........................35 mg	Iron.........................2% U.S. RDA

Perfect Apple Pie

Pastry for two-crust pie

FILLING

- 6 cups thinly sliced, peeled apples
- ¾ cup sugar
- 2 tablespoons flour
- ¾ teaspoon cinnamon
- ¼ teaspoon salt
- ⅛ teaspoon nutmeg
- 1 tablespoon lemon juice

Prepare pastry for two-crust pie using 9-inch pie pan.

Heat oven to 425°F. In large bowl, combine all filling ingredients; mix lightly. Spoon into pastry-lined pan. Top with remaining pastry; fold edge of top pastry under bottom pastry. Press together to seal; flute edge. Cut slits in several places in top of pastry. Bake at 425°F. for 40 to 45 minutes or until apples are tender and crust is golden brown. (Place pan on foil or cookie sheet during baking to guard against spillage.) **8 servings.**

NUTRIENTS PER ⅛ OF RECIPE

Calories 400	Dietary Fiber..........................4 g
Protein.....................................4 g	Sodium.............................330 mg
Carbohydrate........................58 g	Potassium........................140 mg
Fat ....17 g	Calcium..............<2% U.S. RDA
Cholesterol..........................0 mg	Iron.........................8% U.S. RDA

Pear Tart Elegante

PASTRY

¼ cup margarine or butter, softened
2 tablespoons sugar
Dash salt
½ teaspoon grated lemon peel
½ teaspoon vanilla
1 egg yolk
¾ cup all purpose flour
¼ cup finely ground blanched almonds

FILLING

2 tablespoons red currant jelly
½ cup all purpose flour
3 tablespoons sugar
¼ cup margarine or butter, softened
½ teaspoon grated lemon peel
½ teaspoon almond extract
3-oz. pkg. cream cheese, softened
1 egg
5 canned pear halves, well drained
2 tablespoons red currant jelly
1 cup fresh or frozen whole raspberries or
strawberries, slightly thawed

Heat oven to 375°F. In medium bowl, combine ¼ cup margarine; 2 tablespoons sugar and salt; beat at medium speed until fluffy. Add ½ teaspoon lemon peel, vanilla and egg yolk; beat until smooth. Stir in ¾ cup flour and almonds; blend well. Press pastry in bottom and up sides of ungreased 10-inch tart pan or 9-inch springform pan. Bake at 375°F. for 10 minutes; cool.

Brush baked pastry with 2 tablespoons currant jelly. In medium bowl, combine ½ cup flour, 3 tablespoons sugar, ¼ cup margarine, ½ teaspoon grated lemon peel, almond extract, cream cheese and egg; beat 1 minute at medium speed.

Pour filling over pastry. Arrange pear halves on filling, rounded-sides-up and narrow ends pointing toward center. If desired, score pears, making ⅛-inch deep cuts crosswise at ¼-inch intervals on each side of pear half. Bake at 375°F. for 25 to 35 minutes or until center is set. Cool.

In small saucepan, heat 2 tablespoons currant jelly over medium heat until melted. Arrange berries in rows between pear halves. Brush mixture lightly over pears, berries and filling. Garnish as desired. Store in refrigerator. **8 servings.**

NUTRIENTS PER ⅛ OF RECIPE

Calories 320	Dietary Fiber ....3 g
Protein ....5 g	Sodium ....195 mg
Carbohydrate ....35 g	Potassium ....125 mg
Fat ....19 g	Calcium ....2% U.S. RDA
Cholesterol ....80 mg	Iron ....6% U.S. RDA

Old-Fashioned Pumpkin Pie

Pastry for filled one-crust pie

FILLING

    ¾ cup sugar
    1½ teaspoons pumpkin pie spice
    ½ teaspoon salt
16-oz. can (2 cups) pumpkin
    1½ cups evaporated milk
    2 eggs, beaten

Prepare pastry for filled one-crust pie using 9-inch pie pan.

Heat oven to 425°F. In large bowl, combine all filling ingredients; blend well. Pour into pastry-lined pan. Bake at 425°F. for 15 minutes. Reduce oven temperature to 350°F.; continue baking for 40 to 50 minutes or until knife inserted near center comes out clean. Cool; refrigerate until serving time. If desired, serve topped with whipped cream. **8 servings.**

NUTRIENTS PER ⅛ OF RECIPE WITHOUT WHIPPED CREAM

Calories 280	Dietary Fiber...........................2 g
Protein......................................7 g	Sodium..............................340 mg
Carbohydrate..........................41 g	Potassium..........................330 mg
Fat ....10 g	Calcium...............15% U.S. RDA
Cholesterol..........................70 mg	Iron........................8% U.S. RDA

Cherry Pie

Pastry for two-crust pie

FILLING

    2 (16-oz.) cans pitted red tart cherries, drained*
 1¼ cups sugar
  ¼ cup flour
    2 tablespoons margarine or butter

Prepare pastry for two-crust pie using 9-inch pie pan.

Heat oven to 425°F. In large bowl, combine cherries, sugar and flour; toss lightly to mix. Spoon into pastry-lined pan. Dot with margarine. Top with remaining pastry**; fold edge of top pastry under bottom pastry. Press together to seal; flute edge. Cut slits in several places in top pastry. Bake at 425°F. for 35 to 45 minutes or until juice begins to bubble through slits in crust. **8 servings.**

TIPS: *Four cups fresh red tart pitted cherries can be substituted for the canned cherries.

If desired, sprinkle cherries with ¼ teaspoon almond extract before dotting with margarine.

**If desired, top with lattice crust; brush with beaten egg white and sprinkle with sugar.

NUTRIENTS PER ⅛ OF RECIPE

Calories 470	Dietary Fiber...........................3 g
Protein......................................5 g	Sodium..............................310 mg
Carbohydrate..........................68 g	Potassium..........................150 mg
Fat ....20 g	Calcium.................2% U.S. RDA
Cholesterol............................0 mg	Iron......................15% U.S. RDA

Golden Pecan Pie

Pastry for filled one-crust pie

FILLING
- ⅓ cup firmly packed brown sugar
- 1½ teaspoons flour
- 1¼ cups light corn syrup
- 3 eggs
- 1¼ teaspoons vanilla
- 2 tablespoons butter or margarine, melted
- 1 cup pecan halves or broken pecans

Prepare pastry for filled one-crust pie using 9-inch pie pan.

Heat oven to 375°F. In large bowl, combine brown sugar, flour, corn syrup, eggs and vanilla; beat well. Stir in butter and pecans. Pour into pastry-lined pan. Bake at 375°F. for 40 to 50 minutes or until center of pie is puffed and golden brown. **8 servings.**

NUTRIENTS PER ⅛ OF RECIPE

Calories	480	Dietary Fiber	2 g
Protein	5 g	Sodium	230 mg
Carbohydrate	62 g	Potassium	160 mg
Fat	24 g	Calcium	6% U.S. RDA
Cholesterol	110 mg	Iron	20% U.S. RDA

Lemon Meringue Pie

Pastry for unfilled one-crust pie

FILLING
- 1 cup sugar
- ¼ cup cornstarch
- ½ teaspoon salt
- 1⅔ cups cold water
- 3 egg yolks

> 2 tablespoons margarine or butter
> 1½ teaspoons grated lemon peel
> ⅓ cup *fresh* lemon juice

MERINGUE

> 3 egg whites
> ¼ teaspoon cream of tartar
> ½ teaspoon vanilla
> ¼ cup sugar

Prepare and bake pastry for unfilled one-crust pie using 9-inch pie pan.

In medium saucepan, combine 1 cup sugar, cornstarch and salt; mix well. Gradually stir in cold water until smooth. Cook over medium heat, stirring constantly, until mixture boils; boil 1 minute, stirring constantly. Remove from heat.

In small bowl, beat egg yolks; stir about ¼ cup of hot mixture into egg yolks. Gradually stir yolk mixture into hot mixture. Cook over low heat, stirring constantly, until mixture boils; boil 1 minute, stirring constantly. Remove from heat; stir in margarine, lemon peel and lemon juice. Cool slightly, about 15 minutes. Pour into cooled, baked crust.

Reduce oven temperature to 350°F. In small deep bowl, beat egg whites, cream of tartar and vanilla at medium speed until soft peaks form, about 1 minute. Add ¼ cup sugar, 1 tablespoon at a time, beating at highest speed until stiff glossy peaks form and sugar is dissolved. Spoon meringue onto hot filling; spread to edge of crust to seal well and prevent shrinkage. Use narrow spatula or knife to swirl meringue. Bake at 350°F. for 12 to 15 minutes or until light golden brown. Cool on wire rack; refrigerate 3 hours or until filling is set. Store in refrigerator. **8 servings.**

VARIATION:

SOUTHERN-STYLE LEMON MERINGUE PIE: Spread ½ cup blackberry or raspberry preserves in bottom of cooled, baked crust. Continue as directed above.

NUTRIENTS PER ⅛ OF RECIPE

Calories	320	Dietary Fiber	<1 g
Protein	4 g	Sodium	320 mg
Carbohydrate	48 g	Potassium	55 mg
Fat	13 g	Calcium	<2% U.S. RDA
Cholesterol	100 mg	Iron	6% U.S. RDA

Fresh Strawberry-Rhubarb Pie

15-oz. pkg. refrigerated pie crusts
   1   teaspoon flour

FILLING
   1   pint fresh strawberries, washed and stemmed
   3   cups chopped fresh rhubarb*
   1   cup sugar
   ¼   cup cornstarch

Prepare pie crust according to package directions for two-crust pie using 9-inch pie pan. Heat oven to 400°F.

In large bowl, combine all filling ingredients; mix lightly. Spoon into pie crust-lined pan; top with second crust. Fold edge of top crust under bottom crust; flute edge. Cut deep slits in several places. Bake at 400°F. for 45 to 60 minutes or until golden brown. (Place pan on foil or cookie sheet during last 15 minutes of baking to guard against spillage.) If desired, serve with whipped cream and additional strawberries. **8 servings.**

TIPS: *16-oz. pkg. frozen sliced rhubarb, thawed and well drained, can be substituted for fresh rhubarb.

Cover edge of pie crust with strip of foil during last 10 to 15 minutes of baking if necessary to prevent excessive browning.

NUTRIENTS PER ⅛ OF RECIPE

Calories	380	Dietary Fiber	6 g
Protein	2 g	Sodium	330 mg
Carbohydrate	57 g	Potassium	220 mg
Fat	16 g	Calcium	4% U.S. RDA
Cholesterol	0 mg	Iron	<2% U.S. RDA

Fresh Strawberry Pie

Pastry for unfilled one-crust pie

FILLING
  3 pints (6 cups) strawberries, hulled, washed and drained
  1 cup sugar
  3 tablespoons cornstarch
  ½ cup water
4 to 5 drops red food coloring, if desired
     Whipped cream

Prepare and bake pastry for unfilled one-crust pie using 9-inch pie pan.

In small bowl, crush enough strawberries to make 1 cup. In medium saucepan, combine sugar and cornstarch. Add crushed strawberries and water. Cook until mixture boils and thickens, stirring constantly; stir in food coloring. Cool. Spoon remaining whole or sliced strawberries into cooled pie shell; pour cooked strawberry mixture over top. Refrigerate 3 hours or until set. To serve, top with whipped cream. **6 to 8 servings.**

VARIATIONS:

FRESH PEACH PIE: Substitute sliced peaches for strawberries. Omit red food coloring.

FRESH RASPBERRY PIE: Substitute raspberries for strawberries.

NUTRIENTS PER ⅛ OF RECIPE WITHOUT WHIPPED CREAM

Calories	300	Dietary Fiber	3 g
Protein	2 g	Sodium	135 mg
Carbohydrate	47 g	Potassium	210 mg
Fat	12 g	Calcium	2% U.S. RDA
Cholesterol	10 mg	Iron	6% U.S. RDA

Streusel Top Peach Pie

Pastry for filled one-crust pie

FILLING

    4 cups sliced, peeled peaches*
    ½ cup powdered sugar
    ⅓ cup flour
    ½ teaspoon cinnamon

TOPPING

    ¾ cup all purpose flour
    ½ cup firmly packed brown sugar
    ½ teaspoon cinnamon
    ⅓ cup margarine or butter

Prepare pastry for filled one-crust pie using 9-inch pie pan.

Heat oven to 375°F. In large bowl, combine all filling ingredients; blend well. Spoon into pastry-lined pan. In medium bowl, blend topping ingredients with fork until crumbly. Sprinkle over filling. Bake at 375°F. for 40 to 45 minutes or until peaches are tender and topping is golden brown. **8 servings.**

TIP: *Two 29-oz. cans peach slices, well drained, or 4 cups frozen sliced peaches, thawed and well drained, can be substituted for the fresh peaches.

VARIATIONS:

STREUSEL TOP APRICOT PIE: Substitute 4 cups fresh apricot halves or 2 (29-oz.) cans apricot halves, well drained, for the peaches. Continue as directed above.

STREUSEL TOP BLUEBERRY PIE: Substitute 4 cups fresh or unsweetened frozen blueberries, partially thawed and drained, for the peaches. Well drained, canned blueberries can also be used. Continue as directed above.

NUTRIENTS PER ⅛ OF RECIPE

Calories	370	Dietary Fiber	2 g
Protein	4 g	Sodium	230 mg
Carbohydrate	54 g	Potassium	250 mg
Fat	16 g	Calcium	2% U.S. RDA
Cholesterol	0 mg	Iron	10% U.S. RDA

Rhubarb Cream Pie

Pastry for filled one-crust pie

FILLING

    2 cups diced fresh rhubarb
    3 egg yolks
    ½ cup half-and-half
    1 cup sugar
    2 tablespoons flour
    ½ teaspoon salt

MERINGUE

    3 egg whites
    ¼ teaspoon cream of tartar
    ½ teaspoon vanilla
    6 tablespoons sugar

Prepare pastry for filled one-crust pie using 9-inch pie pan.

Heat oven to 400°F. Place rhubarb in pastry-lined pan. In small bowl, beat egg yolks until thick and lemon colored. Blend in half-and-half. Add 1 cup sugar, flour and salt; mix well. Pour egg mixture over rhubarb. Bake at 400°F. for 10 minutes. Cover edge of pie crust with strip of foil. Reduce oven temperature to 350°F. and bake an additional 40 minutes.

In small bowl, beat egg whites, cream of tartar and vanilla until soft peaks form. Gradually add 6 tablespoons sugar, beating until stiff peaks form, about 3 minutes. Spread over hot filling; seal to edge of crust. Bake at 350°F. for 12 to 15 minutes or until lightly browned. **8 servings.**

NUTRIENTS PER ⅛ OF RECIPE

Calories	320	Dietary Fiber	2 g
Protein	5 g	Sodium	300 mg
Carbohydrate	50 g	Potassium	150 mg
Fat	12 g	Calcium	6% U.S. RDA
Cholesterol	110 mg	Iron	6% U.S. RDA

Sour Cream Raisin Pie

Pastry for unfilled one-crust pie

FILLING

1½ cups raisins
¾ cup sugar
¼ cup cornstarch
½ teaspoon cinnamon
¼ teaspoon salt
¼ teaspoon nutmeg
2 cups milk
3 egg yolks, beaten
1 cup dairy sour cream
1 tablespoon lemon juice
1 cup whipping cream, whipped

Prepare and bake pastry for unfilled one-crust pie using 9-inch pie pan.

In medium saucepan, combine raisins, sugar, cornstarch, cinnamon, salt and nutmeg. Stir in milk, blending until smooth. Cook over medium heat until mixture boils, stirring constantly. Boil 1 minute; remove from heat. Blend small amount of hot raisin mixture into egg yolks; return yolk mixture to hot mixture. Add sour cream; mix well. Cook just until mixture starts to bubble, stirring constantly. Remove from heat; stir in lemon juice. Cool slightly; pour into cooled, baked crust. Refrigerate 2 hours or until set. Top with whipped cream. **8 servings.**

NUTRIENTS PER ⅛ OF RECIPE

Calories	530	Dietary Fiber	3 g
Protein	7 g	Sodium	260 mg
Carbohydrate	61 g	Potassium	390 mg
Fat	29 g	Calcium	15% U.S. RDA
Cholesterol	160 mg	Iron	8% U.S. RDA

Black Forest Pie

15-oz. pkg. refrigerated pie crusts
1 teaspoon flour

FILLING
¾ cup sugar
⅓ cup unsweetened cocoa
2 tablespoons flour
¼ cup margarine or butter
⅓ cup milk
2 eggs, beaten
21-oz. can cherry fruit pie filling

TOPPING
9-oz. container frozen whipped topping, thawed
1 oz. (1 square) unsweetened chocolate, coarsely grated

Prepare pie crust according to package directions for filled one-crust pie using 9-inch pie pan. (Refrigerate remaining crust for later use.) Heat oven to 350°F.

In medium saucepan, combine sugar, cocoa and flour. Stir in margarine and milk. Cook over medium heat until mixture begins to boil, stirring constantly. Remove from heat. Blend small amount of hot mixture into eggs. Return to saucepan; blend well. Fold half of cherry pie filling into chocolate mixture; reserve remaining pie filling for topping. Pour chocolate mixture into pie crust-lined pan. Bake at 350°F. for 35 to 45 minutes or until center is set but still shiny. Cool. Refrigerate 1 hour.

Combine 2 cups of the whipped topping and grated chocolate; spread over cooled pie. Top with reserved pie filling and remaining whipped topping. Decorate with chocolate curls or as desired. Refrigerate at least 30 minutes before serving time. **8 to 10 servings.**

NUTRIENTS PER ⅒ OF RECIPE

Calories	450	Dietary Fiber	4 g
Protein	4 g	Sodium	230 mg
Carbohydrate	61g	Potassium	135 mg
Fat	21 g	Calcium	2% U.S. RDA
Cholesterol	60 mg	Iron	6% U.S. RDA

Fruit and Custard Tart

Pastry for unfilled one-crust pie

FILLING

⅓ cup sugar
3 tablespoons flour
¼ teaspoon salt
1¼ cups milk
4 egg yolks, well beaten
2 tablespoons margarine or butter
1½ teaspoons vanilla
2 tablespoons almond-flavored liqueur or
   ½ teaspoon almond extract
½ cup whipping cream, whipped

TOPPING AND GLAZE
  1½ to 2 cups fresh strawberries, halved
  1 to 1½ cups seedless green grapes, halved
      2 tablespoons apricot preserves
      2 teaspoons almond-flavored liqueur or orange
          juice

Heat oven to 450°F. Prepare pastry for unfilled one-crust pie using ungreased 10-inch tart pan with removable bottom or 10-inch springform pan. Place prepared pastry in bottom and ¾ inch up sides of pan. Generously prick crust with fork. Bake at 450°F. for 9 to 11 minutes or until lightly browned. Cool completely.

In small saucepan, combine sugar, 3 tablespoons flour and salt. Gradually add milk; mix well. Cook over medium heat until mixture boils and thickens, stirring constantly. Boil slowly 1 minute. Remove from heat. Blend small amount of the hot mixture into egg yolks. Return yolk mixture to hot mixture; blend well. Cook just until mixture begins to bubble, stirring constantly. Boil 1 minute. Remove from heat. Stir in margarine and vanilla. Cover with plastic wrap; refrigerate 30 minutes. Stir in 2 tablespoons liqueur; fold in whipped cream. Pour into cooled, baked crust.

Remove sides of pan; arrange fresh fruit over filling. In small saucepan, heat preserves and 2 teaspoons liqueur just until warm; brush over fruit. Refrigerate at least 2 hours before serving. **8 servings.**

NUTRIENTS PER ⅛ OF RECIPE

Calories	370	Dietary Fiber	3 g
Protein	5 g	Sodium	260 mg
Carbohydrate	40 g	Potassium	220 mg
Fat	21 g	Calcium	8% U.S. RDA
Cholesterol	160 mg	Iron	8% U.S. RDA

Custard Pie

Pastry for filled one-crust pie

FILLING
   3 eggs
   ¾ cup sugar
   ¼ teaspoon salt
   ¼ teaspoon nutmeg or cinnamon
   1 teaspoon vanilla
   2½ cups milk, scalded

Prepare pastry for filled one-crust pie using 9-inch pie pan.

Heat oven to 400°F. In large bowl, beat eggs. Add sugar, salt, nutmeg and vanilla; mix well. Blend in hot milk. Pour into pastry-lined pan. Bake at 400°F. for 25 to 30 minutes or until knife inserted near center comes out clean. Cool. Serve warm or chilled. **8 servings.**

NUTRIENTS PER ⅛ OF RECIPE

Calories	270	Dietary Fiber	<1 g
Protein	6 g	Sodium	260 mg
Carbohydrate	34 g	Potassium	160 mg
Fat	12 g	Calcium	10% U.S. RDA
Cholesterol	110 mg	Iron	6% U.S. RDA

Angel Pie

Meringue Crust (see Index)

FILLING
   ½ cup sugar
   1 tablespoon grated lemon peel
   3 tablespoons lemon juice
   3 egg yolks
   1 cup whipping cream, whipped

Prepare and bake crust in greased 9-inch pie pan.

In small saucepan, combine all filling ingredients except whipped cream. Cook over low heat until thickened, about 10 minutes, stirring constantly. Cool. Fold into whipped cream. Pour into meringue crust. Refrigerate overnight. If desired, garnish with thin lemon slices or grated lemon peel. **8 servings.**

NUTRIENTS PER ⅛ OF RECIPE

Calories 280	Dietary Fiber..........................<1 g
Protein.....................................3 g	Sodium..............................40 mg
Carbohydrate.........................39 g	Potassium...........................60 mg
Fat ....13 g	Calcium................2% U.S. RDA
Cholesterol.......................140 mg	Iron........................2% U.S. RDA

Vanilla Cream Pie

Pastry for unfilled one-crust pie

FILLING
- ¾ cup sugar
- ¼ cup cornstarch
- ¼ teaspoon salt
- 3 cups milk
- 3 egg yolks, slightly beaten
- 2 tablespoons margarine or butter
- 2 teaspoons vanilla

Prepare and bake pastry for unfilled one-crust pie using 9-inch pie pan.

In medium saucepan, combine sugar, cornstarch and salt. Stir in milk, blending until smooth. Cook over medium heat until mixture boils and thickens, stirring constantly. Boil 2 minutes; remove from heat. Blend a small amount of hot mixture into egg yolks. Return yolk mixture to hot mixture, blending well. Cook until mixture just begins to bubble, stirring constantly. Remove from heat; stir in margarine and vanilla. Pour into cooled, baked crust. Refrigerate 3 hours or until set. If desired, serve with whipped cream. **8 servings.**

VARIATIONS:

BANANA CREAM PIE: Cool filling in saucepan to luke-warm. Slice 2 or 3 bananas into cooled, baked crust; pour filling over bananas.

BUTTERSCOTCH CREAM PIE: Substitute firmly packed brown sugar for sugar.

CHOCOLATE CREAM PIE: Increase sugar to 1 cup and add 2 oz. (2 squares) unsweetened chocolate to filling mixture before cooking.

COCONUT CREAM PIE: Stir 1 cup coconut into cooked filling with margarine and vanilla.

NUTRIENTS PER ⅛ OF RECIPE WITHOUT WHIPPED CREAM

Calories	330	Dietary Fiber	<1 g
Protein	6 g	Sodium	290 mg
Carbohydrate	38 g	Potassium	160 mg
Fat	17 g	Calcium	10% U.S. RDA
Cholesterol	110 mg	Iron	6% U.S. RDA

Sweetened Whipped Cream

    1   cup whipping cream
    2   tablespoons powdered sugar
    ½   teaspoon vanilla

In small bowl, beat cream until soft peaks form. Blend in sugar and vanilla; beat until stiff peaks form. **2 cups.**

TIP: One to 2 tablespoons brandy, rum or flavored liqueur can be substituted for vanilla.

VARIATIONS:

CHOCOLATE WHIPPED CREAM: Add 2 tablespoons unsweetened cocoa and dash salt to cream before beating; increase powdered sugar to 4 tablespoons.

SPICY WHIPPED CREAM: Add ¼ teaspoon cinnamon (or ⅛ teaspoon cinnamon and ⅛ teaspoon nutmeg) with powdered sugar and vanilla.

NUTRIENTS PER 1 TABLESPOON

Calories	25	Dietary Fiber	0 g
Protein	0 g	Sodium	0 mg
Carbohydrate	1 g	Potassium	5 mg
Fat	3 g	Calcium	<2% U.S. RDA
Cholesterol	10 mg	Iron	<2% U.S. RDA

Easy Creme Fraiche

    2 tablespoons brown sugar
       Dash salt
    1 cup dairy sour cream
  ½ cup whipping cream

In small bowl, sprinkle brown sugar and salt over sour cream; let stand 2 minutes. Gently fold in cream, 1 tablespoon at a time, until thoroughly blended. Cover; refrigerate until served. Spoon onto fresh fruit tarts. **1½ cups.**

NUTRIENTS PER 1 TABLESPOON

Calories	40	Dietary Fiber	0 g
Protein	0 g	Sodium	15 mg
Carbohydrate	2 g	Potassium	25 mg
Fat	4 g	Calcium	<2% U.S. RDA
Cholesterol	10 mg	Iron	<2% U.S. RDA

Hot Butter Rum Sauce

    1 cup firmly packed brown sugar
    ½ cup whipping cream
    ¼ cup dark corn syrup
    2 tablespoons butter
       Dash salt
    ½ teaspoon rum extract
    ½ cup chopped pecans

In medium saucepan, combine brown sugar, cream, corn syrup, butter and salt. Cook over medium heat, stirring constantly, until mixture boils and thickens. Reduce heat to low and simmer 5 minutes, stirring constantly. Stir in rum extract and pecans. Serve warm over ice cream. **2 cups.**

NUTRIENTS PER 1 TABLESPOON

Calories 60	Dietary Fiber........................<1 g
Protein ....0 g	Sodium ....15 mg
Carbohydrate ....9 g	Potassium ....40 mg
Fat ....3 g	Calcium...............<2% U.S. RDA
Cholesterol ....6 mg	Iron ....<2% U.S. RDA

Hot Caramel Sauce

    1½ cups sugar
     1 cup half-and-half
     ½ cup light corn syrup
     6 tablespoons butter or margarine
     ½ teaspoon vanilla

In medium saucepan, combine sugar, ½ cup of the half-and-half, corn syrup and butter. Bring to a full rolling boil. Gradually add remaining half-and-half. *Be sure boiling does not stop.* Cook over medium heat to soft ball stage (230°F.), stirring occasionally. Remove from heat; stir in vanilla. Serve warm over ice cream. **2 cups.**

NUTRIENTS PER 1 TABLESPOON

Calories 80	Dietary Fiber............................0 g
Protein......................................0 g	Sodium.................................35 mg
Carbohydrate.........................13 g	Potassium............................10 mg
Fat ....3 g	Calcium...............<2% U.S. RDA
Cholesterol............................8 mg	Iron ....<2% U.S. RDA

Velvet Fudge Sauce

      2 cups powdered sugar
      1 cup evaporated milk
    ½ cup margarine or butter
      1 tablespoon corn syrup
  6-oz. pkg. (1 cup) semi-sweet chocolate chips
      1 teaspoon vanilla

In medium saucepan, combine powdered sugar, milk, margarine, corn syrup and chocolate chips. Cook over medium heat until mixture boils, stirring constantly. Reduce heat to low; cook 8 minutes, stirring constantly. Remove from heat; stir in vanilla. Serve warm over ice cream or dessert. Cover; store in refrigerator. **2⅔ cups.**

MICROWAVE DIRECTIONS: In medium microwave-safe bowl, combine all ingredients except vanilla; mix well. Microwave on HIGH for 4½ to 6 minutes or until mixture begins to bubble, stirring twice during cooking. Microwave on DEFROST for 3 to 4 minutes, stirring once halfway through cooking. Stir in vanilla.

VARIATIONS:

MARSHMALLOW CREME FUDGE SAUCE: Stir 7-oz. jar marshmallow creme into chocolate mixture with vanilla.

MOCHA FUDGE SAUCE: Add 3 teaspoons instant coffee granules or crystals to chocolate chip mixture before cooking.

ORANGE FUDGE SAUCE: Reduce evaporated milk to ⅔ cup and add ⅓ cup frozen orange juice concentrate.

NUTRIENTS PER 1 TABLESPOON

Calories	70	Dietary Fiber	<1 g
Protein	1 g	Sodium	35 mg
Carbohydrate	8 g	Potassium	35 mg
Fat	4 g	Calcium	<2% U.S. RDA
Cholesterol	0 mg	Iron	<2% U.S. RDA

Hot Fudge Sauce

3 oz. (3 squares) semi-sweet chocolate
⅔ cup sugar
Dash salt
5⅓-oz. can evaporated milk

In small saucepan, melt chocolate over very low heat, stirring constantly. Stir in sugar and salt. Gradually add milk, stirring constantly. Heat until thickened and hot, stirring constantly. Serve warm or cool. **1 cup.**

MICROWAVE DIRECTIONS: In small microwave-safe bowl, microwave chocolate on MEDIUM for 4 minutes or until melted. Stir in sugar and salt; mix well. Add half of the evaporated milk; beat with fork. Microwave on HIGH for 1 minute; stir. Add remaining milk; microwave on HIGH for 2 to 3 minutes. Sauce will be thin, but will thicken as it stands.

NUTRIENTS PER 1 TABLESPOON

Calories	70	Dietary Fiber	<1 g
Protein	1 g	Sodium	20 mg
Carbohydrate	11 g	Potassium	70 mg
Fat	3 g	Calcium	2% U.S. RDA
Cholesterol	0 mg	Iron	2% U.S. RDA

Lemon Sauce

½ cup sugar
1 tablespoon cornstarch
⅛ teaspoon salt
1 cup boiling water
2 tablespoons margarine or butter
1 teaspoon grated lemon peel
3 tablespoons lemon juice

In medium saucepan, combine sugar, cornstarch and salt; mix well. Gradually stir in boiling water. Bring to a boil; cook, stirring constantly, 5 minutes or until thickened. Remove from heat. Add margarine, lemon peel and lemon juice; mix well. Serve warm or cool. **1¼ cups.**

NUTRIENTS PER 1 TABLESPOON

Calories 30	Dietary Fiber............................0 g
Protein.....................................0 g	Sodium...............................25 mg
Carbohydrate..........................6 g	Potassium.............................0 mg
Fat ....1 g	Calcium..............<2% U.S. RDA
Cholesterol..........................0 mg	Iron ....<2% U.S. RDA

White Chocolate Sauce

1½ cups whipping cream
¼ cup powdered sugar
4 oz. white chocolate or almond bark, cut
into pieces
2 tablespoons rum

In medium saucepan, combine cream and powdered sugar. Cook over medium heat until mixture boils, stirring constantly. Reduce heat; simmer 3 to 4 minutes. Add white chocolate and rum, stirring until chocolate is melted and sauce is smooth. Serve warm or cool. Store in refrigerator. **2 cups.**

NUTRIENTS PER 2 TABLESPOONS

Calories 120	Dietary Fiber ....0 g
Protein ....1 g	Sodium ....10 mg
Carbohydrate ....6 g	Potassium ....40 mg
Fat ....11 g	Calcium ....<2% U.S. RDA
Cholesterol ....30 mg	Iron ....<2% U.S. RDA

Dark Cherry Sauce

     2 tablespoons sugar
     5 teaspoons cornstarch
       Dash salt
  ¼ cup water
16-oz. pkg. frozen dark sweet cherries, partially thawed, undrained*
4 to 5 tablespoons almond-flavored liqueur

In medium saucepan, combine sugar, cornstarch and salt; mix well. Stir in water until combined. Add cherries; cook over medium heat until mixture becomes clear and thickened, about 7 to 8 minutes. Stir in liqueur. Cool to room temperature. **2 cups.**

TIP: *Three cups fresh bing cherries, pitted, can be substituted for the frozen cherries. Increase water to ½ cup.

NUTRIENTS PER ¼ CUP

Calories 80	Dietary Fiber ....<1 g
Protein ....1 g	Sodium ....15 mg
Carbohydrate ....19 g	Potassium ....100 mg
Fat ....0 g	Calcium ....<2% U.S. RDA
Cholesterol ....0 mg	Iron ....<2% U.S. RDA

Ruby Raspberry Sauce

10-oz. pkg. frozen raspberries with syrup, thawed
     2 tablespoons sugar
     2 tablespoons orange-flavored liqueur

In blender container or food processor bowl with metal blade, combine raspberries, sugar and liqueur. Cover; blend until smooth. Strain to remove seeds. Refrigerate to chill. **1½ cups.**

NUTRIENTS PER 2 TABLESPOONS

Calories	40	Dietary Fiber	<1 g
Protein	0 g	Sodium	0 mg
Carbohydrate	10 g	Potassium	25 mg
Fat	0 g	Calcium	<2% U.S. RDA
Cholesterol	0 mg	Iron	<2% U.S. RDA

Creme Anglaise

    1 cup whipping cream
    2 egg yolks
  ⅓ cup sugar

In medium saucepan, bring cream just to a boil. In small bowl, combine egg yolks and sugar. Blend a small amount of cream into yolks. Blend yolk mixture into cream and cook over low heat about 10 minutes or until custard coats a spoon, stirring constantly. DO NOT BOIL. Remove from heat. Cool to room temperature and refrigerate.

NUTRIENTS PER 1 TABLESPOON

Calories	80	Dietary Fiber	0 g
Protein	1 g	Sodium	5 mg
Carbohydrate	5 g	Potassium	15 mg
Fat	6 g	Calcium	<2% U.S. RDA
Cholesterol	50 mg	Iron	<2% U.S. RDA

Butter Sauce

      1 cup sugar
    ¾ cup half-and-half or evaporated milk
    ½ cup butter
¼ to ½ teaspoon rum extract, if desired

In small saucepan, combine all ingredients; heat just to boiling, stirring occasionally. Serve warm. **1½ cups.**

NUTRIENTS PER 1 TABLESPOON

Calories	80	Dietary Fiber	0 g
Protein	0 g	Sodium	40 mg
Carbohydrate	9 g	Potassium	10 mg
Fat	5 g	Calcium	<2% U.S. RDA
Cholesterol	15 mg	Iron	<2% U.S. RDA

Hard Sauce

    2 cups powdered sugar
    ½ cup butter or margarine, softened
    1 tablespoon hot water
    2 teaspoons rum or brandy extract or 2 tablespoons
       rum or brandy
    1 teaspoon vanilla

In small bowl, combine all ingredients. Beat at highest speed until well blended. Cover; refrigerate until serving time. **1½ cups.**

NUTRIENTS PER 1 TABLESPOON

Calories	70	Dietary Fiber	0 g
Protein	0 g	Sodium	40 mg
Carbohydrate	8 g	Potassium	0 mg
Fat	4 g	Calcium	<2% U.S. RDA
Cholesterol	10 mg	Iron	<2% U.S. RDA

Eggs, Cheese, Pasta & Rice

Eggs, Cheese, Pasta & Rice

Eggs

Convenient, economical, versatile and nutritious—each describes a cook's best friend, the egg. Nutritionally, eggs are a rich source of high-quality protein and important vitamins and minerals, making them acceptable as a replacement for meat, fish and poultry in fulfilling basic food group requirements. And, depending on preparation, eggs generally are low in calories as well. Because of their cholesterol content, eggs are restricted on some special diets; however, for the average person they may be eaten in moderation like all other foods.

Purchasing Eggs

• Purchase eggs that have been kept under refrigeration and are clean, with unbroken shells. There are two main guidelines for purchasing eggs—size and grade. Egg sizes include jumbo, extra large, large, medium and small. Our recipes were tested with large eggs. Correct size can be important in recipes having exacting measurement requirements, like cakes. Differences in size, shell and yolk color have no effect on quality.

Egg grading takes into account the quality and appearance of the egg. Nutritional content is the same with all grades. Grade AA is the best from an appearance standpoint, particularly for poached, fried and deviled eggs, because the yolk is round and evenly centered and the white is thick and firm. Grade A is another excellent choice, although the white may be a little thinner and the yolk may be off center. Grade B has a flatter yolk, but is excellent for baking. Grade C, acceptable only for baking purposes, is seldom available in markets.

Storing Eggs

• Store eggs in the refrigerator, large end up to keep yolk centered, for up to a month. Eggs are best stored in their original carton because they can absorb odors from other foods. Eggs are highly perishable and should be refrigerated after cooking.

Do not use an uncooked egg with a broken or cracked shell or an off odor. Fresh eggs have a high-standing yolk and a thick, cloudy white.

Leftover whites and yolks may be stored in tightly sealed containers in the refrigerator, up to 10 days for whites and 2 days for yolks.

Hints for Handling Eggs

• Eggs will separate best when cold from the refrigerator. To avoid getting a little yolk in a bowl of whites, separate each egg into a small bowl, then combine with other separated whites and yolks.

• To beat egg whites to highest volume, bring whites to room temperature and prevent the presence of any fat.

• To bring eggs to room temperature, remove from refrigerator 1 hour before using or cover eggs for 1 to 2 minutes with hot tap water.

• To prevent the presence of fat which reduces foaming action, make sure the whites contain no specks of yolk and that the bowl and beaters are free of any oil residue. Avoid using plastic bowls because they tend to retain fat.

• Cream of tartar may be added to increase the stability of beaten egg whites. Sugar also increases the stability but decreases the volume, therefore it is added gradually during the latter part of beating.

• Overbeaten egg whites cannot be corrected.

• Eggshell fragments that accidentally fall into egg mixture can be removed using another piece of eggshell.

• To keep beaten eggs from curdling when combining with a hot mixture, stir a small amount of the hot mixture into the eggs. Gradually add egg mixture to remaining hot portion.

• Eggs can be microwaved in a variety of ways. However, never attempt to microwave an egg in its shell as it may burst. Eggs microwave rapidly, with the yolks cooking more quickly than the whites.

Hard and Soft-Cooked Eggs

Place whole eggs in saucepan; cover with cold water. Heat to boiling; reduce heat and allow to barely simmer about 15 minutes for hard-cooked eggs or 2 to 3 minutes (depending on desired doneness) for soft-cooked eggs. To stop cooking, place eggs under cold water a few seconds. Cut soft-cooked eggs in half; spoon out of shell. Serve in egg cups, if desired. Peel hard-cooked eggs and use in casseroles, salads, deviled eggs, etc.

TIPS: If water boils hard, the egg white will toughen.

Eggs a few days old are easier to remove from the shell than very fresh eggs. For ease in shelling, crack and peel eggs under cold water, beginning at larger end.

NUTRIENTS PER 1 COOKED EGG

Calories 80	Dietary Fiber ....0 g
Protein ....6 g	Sodium ....70 mg
Carbohydrate ....1 g	Potassium ....65 mg
Fat ....6 g	Calcium ....2% U.S. RDA
Cholesterol ....270 mg	Iron ....6% U.S. RDA

Scrambled Eggs

For each egg, allow 1 tablespoon milk, cream or water, ⅛ teaspoon salt and 1 teaspoon margarine. In bowl, break eggs; add milk and salt. Beat slightly with fork until uniform in color. In skillet, melt margarine over medium heat; tilt pan to coat. Add egg mixture. Reduce heat to low; stir occasionally from outside edge to center, allowing uncooked egg to flow to bottom of skillet. Cook until eggs are set but still moist.

TIP: Dress up scrambled eggs by adding one of the following near end of cooking: chopped chives, parsley or pimiento, hot pepper sauce, shredded or cubed cheese, diced cooked ham, crumbled cooked bacon, sliced cooked sausage links, drained canned seafood (flaked crab meat, tuna, salmon or shrimp), mushrooms, cubed cream cheese, chopped tomato, green pepper or green chiles, catsup.

NUTRIENTS PER 1 SCRAMBLED EGG

Calories 120	Dietary Fiber ....0 g
Protein ....7 g	Sodium ....390 mg
Carbohydrate ....1 g	Potassium ....90 mg
Fat ....10 g	Calcium ....4% U.S. RDA
Cholesterol ....280 mg	Iron ....6% U.S. RDA

Fried Eggs

In skillet, heat 1 to 2 tablespoons of margarine, butter or bacon drippings until hot. Break eggs, one at a time, into custard cup or saucer; carefully slip each egg into skillet. Reduce heat to low and cook until of desired doneness.

VARIATIONS:

EGGS OVER EASY: Cook eggs 2 to 3 minutes or until set on the bottom. Carefully turn eggs over to cook other side; cook until of desired doneness.

SUNNY-SIDE-UP BASTED EGGS: Spoon hot fat over eggs until whites are set and white film forms over yolk.

SUNNY-SIDE-UP STEAMED EGGS: Add 1 to 2 teaspoons water and cover skillet until whites are set and a white film forms over yolk, 3 to 5 minutes.

TIP: To eliminate the need for margarine, butter or drippings, use a skillet coated with a non-stick surface. Add 1 tablespoon water with the eggs. Cook covered until of desired doneness.

NUTRIENTS PER 1 FRIED EGG

Calories	280	Dietary Fiber	0 g
Protein	6 g	Sodium	340 mg
Carbohydrate	1 g	Potassium	75 mg
Fat	28 g	Calcium	2% U.S. RDA
Cholesterol	270 mg	Iron	6% U.S. RDA

Baked Eggs

Heat oven to 325°F. Butter 6-oz. custard cups or large muffin cups. Break an egg into each prepared cup. If desired, add 1 tablespoon cream or milk to each. Sprinkle with salt and pepper; dot with margarine. Bake uncovered at 325°F. for 12 to 15 minutes or until eggs are set.

VARIATIONS:

BAKED BACON AND EGGS: Partially cook slices of bacon and place a slice around inside edge of each cup before adding egg. Continue as directed above.

BAKED EGGS AND HASH: Line each dish with about ¼ cup corned beef hash, making a well in the center. Top with egg and continue as directed above.

BAKED EGGS IN TOAST CUPS: Remove crust from bread slices; butter both sides and cut in half. Fit into cups. Top with eggs and continue as directed above. If desired, serve with Cheese Sauce (see Index).

BAKED EGGS SUISSE: Sprinkle about 2 tablespoons shredded Swiss cheese on each egg after baking; return to oven a few minutes or until cheese melts.

BAKED HAM AND EGGS: Carefully fit square ham slice in bottom and up sides of each cup. Top with egg, salt and pepper. Cover loosely with foil. Bake as directed above. After baking remove foil; sprinkle with 1 tablespoon shredded Cheddar cheese. Replace foil; let stand until cheese has melted.

NUTRIENTS PER 1 BAKED EGG

Calories	150	Dietary Fiber	0 g
Protein	6 g	Sodium	230 mg
Carbohydrate	1 g	Potassium	80 mg
Fat	13 g	Calcium	4% U.S. RDA
Cholesterol	300 mg	Iron	6% U.S. RDA

Basic Omelet

    4 eggs
    ¼ cup milk or water
    ¼ teaspoon salt
       Dash pepper
    4 teaspoons margarine or butter

In small bowl, combine eggs, milk, salt and pepper; beat with fork until uniform in color. In 9 or 10-inch skillet or omelet pan, melt margarine over medium-high heat; tilt pan to coat. Pour eggs into skillet; reduce heat to low. Cook without stirring. As edges set, run spatula around edge of skillet and lift egg mixture to allow uncooked egg to flow to the bottom of skillet. Cook until mixture is set but top is still moist looking. If desired, add filling to omelet. With spatula, loosen edge of omelet and fold in half as omelet slides from pan to serving platter. **2 servings.**

TIP: For other size omelets, use 1 tablespoon milk or water and about 1 teaspoon margarine for each egg.

VARIATIONS:

FILLED OMELET: Fill omelet with sauteed mushrooms, crumbled cooked bacon, chopped cooked ham, shredded cheese, cottage cheese, diced tomato, jelly or marmalade, sweetened strawberries or raspberries. Add filling just before folding in half.

ORIENTAL OMELET: Cook 2 tablespoons onion and 1 tablespoon green pepper in 1 tablespoon margarine or butter until tender. Add ⅓ cup fresh bean sprouts, ⅓ cup cooked chopped shrimp, ½ teaspoon soy sauce and dash ginger. Heat thoroughly. Spoon part of shrimp mixture on omelet before folding and spoon remaining mixture over omelet on serving platter.

SPANISH OMELET: Cook 3 tablespoons chopped onion in 4 teaspoons margarine or butter until tender. Blend in 2 teaspoons flour. Stir in 1 cup chopped, peeled tomatoes, ⅓ cup sliced ripe olives, ¼ teaspoon salt and dash pepper. Simmer covered, about 15 minutes, stirring occasionally. Prepare omelet; spoon part of tomato mixture on omelet before folding and spoon remaining mixture over omelet on serving platter.

NUTRIENTS PER ½ OF RECIPE

Calories	240	Dietary Fiber	0 g
Protein	13 g	Sodium	490 mg
Carbohydrate	3 g	Potassium	180 mg
Fat	19 g	Calcium	10% U.S. RDA
Cholesterol	550 mg	Iron	10% U.S. RDA

Poached Eggs

In deep, buttered or non-stick surface skillet, heat 2 to 3 inches water with 1 tablespoon vinegar just to boiling. Break each egg into a shallow dish. Slip eggs gently into water. Quickly spoon hot water over each egg until film forms over yolk. Reduce heat to keep water just simmering; simmer 3 to 4 minutes until eggs are to desired doneness. Remove eggs with slotted spoon. Season to taste with salt and pepper. Serve on buttered toast.

TIPS: To make ahead, prepare as directed above omitting salt and pepper. Cover with cold water; store covered in refrigerator for up to 24 hours. To reheat, cover eggs with very hot (not boiling) water for 5 to 8 minutes or until thoroughly heated.

Eggs can be poached in milk or in bouillon-flavored water.

NUTRIENTS PER 1 EGG ON 1 SLICE TOAST

Calories	200	Dietary Fiber	0 g
Protein	9 g	Sodium	400 mg
Carbohydrate	14 g	Potassium	95 mg
Fat	12 g	Calcium	4% U.S. RDA
Cholesterol	290 mg	Iron	10% U.S. RDA

Eggs Benedict

Prepare Hollandaise Sauce. Keep warm over hot (not boiling) water. Broil or fry 6 slices Canadian bacon. Split and toast 3 English muffins while preparing 6 Poached Eggs. Spread each toasted muffin half with margarine or butter; place on serving plate. Top with slice of hot Canadian bacon, poached egg and hollandaise sauce. **6 servings.**

TIP: Hollandaise sauce mix prepared according to package directions can be used.

NUTRIENTS PER ⅙ OF RECIPE

Calories	400	Dietary Fiber	0 g
Protein	16 g	Sodium	700 mg
Carbohydrate	17 g	Potassium	170 mg
Fat	30 g	Calcium	8% U.S. RDA
Cholesterol	330 mg	Iron	10% U.S. RDA

Hollandaise Sauce

    3 egg yolks
    ⅛ teaspoon salt, if desired
       Dash white pepper
    4 teaspoons lemon juice
    ½ cup margarine or butter, softened

In small saucepan or top of double boiler, slightly beat egg yolks. Add salt, pepper, lemon juice and ¼ cup of the margarine; blend well. Cook over low heat or over hot (not boiling) water until margarine is melted, stirring constantly. Gradually add remaining margarine, 1 tablespoon at a time, beating well after each addition. Continue beating until mixture is smooth and thickened. Remove from heat; serve immediately or keep warm over hot (not boiling) water. **¾ cup.**

TIP: If sauce curdles, add hot water 1 teaspoon at a time; beat until sauce is smooth.

VARIATIONS:

BLENDER HOLLANDAISE SAUCE: In blender container, combine egg yolks, salt, pepper and lemon juice. Cover; blend at medium speed 30 seconds. In small saucepan, heat margarine until bubbly but not brown. Slowly pour margarine into egg yolk mixture while blending at low speed. Blend just until smooth and thickened.

MICROWAVE HOLLANDAISE SAUCE: In medium-size microwave-safe bowl, combine egg yolks, salt, pepper and lemon juice; blend well. In small microwave-safe bowl, microwave margarine on HIGH for 30 to 40 seconds or until melted. Add to egg yolk mixture in a slow steady stream, stirring constantly. Microwave on HIGH about 1 minute, stirring every 15 seconds, or until sauce becomes smooth and thickened.

NUTRIENTS PER 1 TABLESPOON

Calories	80	Dietary Fiber	0 g
Protein	1 g	Sodium	115 mg
Carbohydrate	0 g	Potassium	10 mg
Fat	9 g	Calcium	<2% U.S. RDA
Cholesterol	70 mg	Iron	<2% U.S. RDA

Deviled Eggs

12 small eggs, hard-cooked
⅓ cup mayonnaise, salad dressing or dairy sour cream
 1 tablespoon vinegar
½ teaspoon Worcestershire sauce
½ teaspoon dry mustard or 1 teaspoon prepared mustard
¼ teaspoon salt
¼ teaspoon onion powder
   Dash pepper

Remove shells from eggs and halve lengthwise or crosswise. Carefully remove yolks and place in medium bowl. Mash yolks with fork. Add remaining ingredients; mix well. Lightly spoon mixture back into egg white halves, or pipe filling mixture through pastry bag. Refrigerate until served; garnish as desired. **24 servings.**

TIP: If desired, add one of the following to filling:
¼ cup crumbled blue cheese
½ cup shredded Cheddar cheese
½ cup chopped ripe olives
 2 teaspoons chopped chives

4 green onions, chopped
3 tablespoons anchovy paste (omit salt)
½ cup drained, flaked tuna, salmon, shrimp or crab meat
½ cup deviled ham (omit salt)
½ teaspoon curry powder

NUTRIENTS PER ¼ OF RECIPE

Calories	60	Dietary Fiber	0 g
Protein	3 g	Sodium	75 mg
Carbohydrate	0 g	Potassium	35 mg
Fat	5 g	Calcium	<2% U.S. RDA
Cholesterol	120 mg	Iron	2% U.S. RDA

Fancy Baked Egg Scramble

EGGS

3 tablespoons margarine or butter
¼ cup chopped onion
¼ cup chopped green pepper
2 cups cubed cooked ham
12 eggs, beaten
4.5-oz. jar sliced mushrooms, drained

MORNAY SAUCE

2 tablespoons margarine or butter
2 tablespoons flour
1 teaspoon chicken-flavor instant bouillon
1½ cups milk
2 oz. (½ cup) shredded Swiss cheese
¼ cup grated Parmesan cheese

TOPPING

2 cups soft bread crumbs
¼ cup grated Parmesan cheese
¼ cup margarine or butter, melted
2 tablespoons chopped fresh parsley

Heat oven to 350°F. Grease 12x8-inch (2-quart) baking dish. In large skillet, melt 3 tablespoons margarine; saute onion and green pepper in margarine until onion is crisp-tender. Add ham and eggs; cook and stir just until eggs are set. Fold in mushrooms.

In medium saucepan, melt 2 tablespoons margarine. Blend in flour and bouillon; cook until smooth and bubbly, stirring constantly. Gradually add milk; cook until mixture boils and thickens, stirring constantly. Add Swiss cheese and ¼ cup Parmesan cheese; stir until smooth. Fold scrambled eggs into sauce. Pour into prepared pan. Combine all topping ingredients; sprinkle over eggs. Bake at 350°F. for 25 to 30 minutes or until light golden brown. **10 to 12 servings.**

TIP: To make ahead, prepare, cover and refrigerate up to 3 hours before baking. Bake uncovered as directed above.

NUTRIENTS PER ¹⁄₁₂ OF RECIPE

Calories 280	Dietary Fiber........................<1 g
Protein................................18 g	Sodium......................245 mg
Carbohydrate..........................8 g	Potassium.......................225 mg
Fat ....20 g	Calcium...............15% U.S. RDA
Cholesterol.......................300 mg	Iron.....................10% U.S. RDA

Swiss Eggs in Crepe Cups

```
     6  Easy Crepes (see Index)
1½ oz. (6 tablespoons) shredded Swiss cheese
     6  eggs
        Salt
        Pepper
1½ oz. (6 tablespoons) shredded Swiss cheese
```

Heat oven to 350°F. Generously grease six 6 or 10-oz. custard cups; place on cookie sheet. Fit crepes into prepared custard cups (edges will be ruffled); sprinkle 1 tablespoon shredded cheese on bottom of each crepe. Break 1 egg into each cup; sprinkle with salt and pepper. Bake uncovered at

350°F. for 15 to 20 minutes or until set. Sprinkle 1 tablespoon cheese over each egg; return to oven and bake an additional 2 to 3 minutes or until cheese melts. Serve immediately. **6 servings.**

NUTRIENTS PER ¼ OF RECIPE

Calories	200	Dietary Fiber	<1 g
Protein	13 g	Sodium	405 mg
Carbohydrate	9 g	Potassium	115 mg
Fat	12 g	Calcium	20% U.S. RDA
Cholesterol	330 mg	Iron	10% U.S. RDA

Vegetable Scrambled Eggs

      2 tablespoons margarine or butter
      1 cup (1 medium) coarsely chopped zucchini
    ½ cup (1 medium) shredded carrot
    ¼ cup chopped onion
      8 eggs, beaten
    ½ teaspoon salt
    ¼ teaspoon pepper
 2 oz. (½ cup) shredded Cheddar cheese

In large skillet, melt margarine. Stir in zucchini, carrot and onion. Cover; cook 2 minutes. Uncover; cook an additional 1 to 2 minutes or until vegetables are crisp-tender. Stir in eggs, salt and pepper. Reduce heat to low; cook until eggs are set but still moist, stirring occasionally from outside edge to center of pan. Stir in cheese. Serve immediately. **4 to 6 servings.**

NUTRIENTS PER ¼ OF RECIPE

Calories	190	Dietary Fiber	<1 g
Protein	11 g	Sodium	380 mg
Carbohydrate	3 g	Potassium	190 mg
Fat	14 g	Calcium	10% U.S. RDA
Cholesterol	380 mg	Iron	8% U.S. RDA

Eggs Foo Yong

6 eggs
½ cup finely chopped onion
2 tablespoons chopped green pepper
½ teaspoon salt
Dash pepper
16 oz. can bean sprouts, drained, rinsed
2 tablespoons oil

SAUCE
1 tablespoon cornstarch
2 teaspoons sugar
1 chicken-flavor bouillon cube
Dash ginger
1 cup water
2 tablespoons soy sauce

Heat oven to 300°F. In large bowl, beat eggs well. Add onion, green pepper, salt, pepper and bean sprouts; mix well. In large skillet, heat oil. Drop egg mixture by tablespoons into skillet; fry until golden. Turn and brown other side. Drain on paper towels. If necessary, add additional oil to skillet and continue to cook the remaining egg mixture. Keep patties warm in 300°F. oven while preparing sauce.

In small saucepan, combine cornstarch, sugar, bouillon cube and ginger. Stir in water and soy sauce. Cook until mixture boils and thickens, stirring constantly. Serve patties with sauce. **5 servings.**

TIP: Diced, cooked pork or ham can be added, if desired.

NUTRIENTS PER ⅕ OF RECIPE

Calories 180	Dietary Fiber............................2 g
Protein ....10 g	Sodium............................1020 mg
Carbohydrate.............................9 g	Potassium.........................220 mg
Fat ....12 g	Calcium.................4% U.S. RDA
Cholesterol.......................330 mg	Iron......................10% U.S. RDA

Egg Salad Breakfast Muffins

6   eggs, hard-cooked, chopped
½   cup salad dressing or mayonnaise
2   tablespoons sweet pickle relish
¼   teaspoon prepared mustard
4   English muffins, split, toasted*
8   slices Canadian style bacon or ham
2 oz.   (½ cup) shredded Cheddar cheese, if desired

Heat oven to 350°F. In small bowl, combine eggs, salad dressing, relish and mustard; blend well. Top each muffin half with a slice of the Canadian bacon. Top Canadian bacon with about ¼ cup of egg mixture. Place on ungreased cookie sheet; sprinkle each with 1 tablespoon cheese. Bake at 350°F. for 6 to 8 minutes or until thoroughly heated and cheese is melted. **8 sandwiches.**

TIP: *Four bagels can be substituted for the English muffins; do not toast.

MICROWAVE DIRECTIONS: Prepare as directed above. Place on microwave-safe plate lined with paper towel. Microwave one muffin on HIGH for 45 to 60 seconds or until thoroughly heated and cheese is melted. Microwave four muffins on HIGH for 2 to 2½ minutes, rotating plate ½ turn halfway through cooking.

NUTRIENTS PER 1 SANDWICH

Calories	270	Dietary Fiber	<1 g
Protein	15 g	Sodium	560 mg
Carbohydrate	21 g	Potassium	150 mg
Fat	14 g	Calcium	10% U.S. RDA
Cholesterol	230 mg	Iron	10% U.S. RDA

Bacon and Egg Lasagne

 12 uncooked lasagne noodles
  1 lb. bacon, cut into 1-inch strips
 1/3 cup bacon drippings
  1 cup chopped onion
 1/3 cup flour
 1/2 teaspoon salt
 1/4 teaspoon pepper
  4 cups milk
 12 eggs, hard-cooked, sliced
 8 oz. (2 cups) shredded Swiss cheese
 1/3 cup grated Parmesan cheese
  2 tablespoons chopped fresh parsley

Cook lasagne noodles to desired doneness as directed on package. Drain; rinse with hot water.

In large skillet, cook bacon until crisp; drain, reserving 1/3 cup drippings. Set bacon aside. Cook onions in bacon drippings until tender. Add flour, salt and pepper; stir until smooth and bubbly. Gradually add milk; cook until mixture boils and thickens, stirring constantly.

Heat oven to 350°F. Grease 13x9-inch (3-quart) baking dish. Spoon a small amount of sauce into bottom of pan. Divide lasagne noodles, bacon, sauce, eggs and Swiss cheese into thirds; layer in pan. Sprinkle with Parmesan cheese. Bake at 350°F. for 25 to 30 minutes or until thoroughly heated. Sprinkle with parsley. Let stand 10 minutes before serving. **12 servings.**

NUTRIENTS PER 1/12 OF RECIPE

Calories	420	Dietary Fiber	<1 g
Protein	22 g	Sodium	465 mg
Carbohydrate	25 g	Potassium	310 mg
Fat	25 g	Calcium	35% U.S. RDA
Cholesterol	320 mg	Iron	15% U.S. RDA

Cheese Souffle

6 tablespoons margarine or butter
⅔ cup all purpose flour
½ teaspoon dry mustard
¼ teaspoon salt
1½ cups milk
1½ cups (6 oz.) shredded Cheddar cheese
1 teaspoon Worcestershire sauce
6 eggs, separated

Heat oven to 350°F. Grease and lightly flour 1½-quart souffle dish or casserole. Make a 4-inch band of double thickness foil 2 inches longer than the circumference of dish; grease one side. Extend depth of dish by wrapping foil, greased side in, around top edge of dish. Secure foil with clear tape.

In large saucepan, melt margarine. Blend in flour, mustard and salt. Heat until bubbly, stirring occasionally. Add milk; cook over medium heat until mixture is very thick and smooth, stirring constantly. Add cheese and Worcestershire sauce; stir until cheese melts. Remove from heat; blend in egg yolks, one at a time, beating well after each. Beat egg whites until stiff peaks form. (Do not overbeat.) Fold into cheese mixture. Carefully pour into souffle dish. Bake at 350°F. for 55 to 60 minutes or until knife inserted near center comes out clean. Remove foil band. Serve immediately. **6 servings.**

TIP: To halve recipe, use half the ingredient amounts and bake in 1-quart souffle dish or casserole for 35 to 40 minutes.

VARIATIONS:

BACON OR HAM SOUFFLE: Add 6 to 8 slices crumbled, cooked bacon or 1 cup finely chopped cooked ham with cheese.

TUNA OR CHICKEN SOUFFLE: Add 1 cup finely chopped canned tuna or cooked chicken with cheese.

NUTRIENTS PER ¼ OF RECIPE

Calories	380	Dietary Fiber	<1 g
Protein	17 g	Sodium	500 mg
Carbohydrate	15 g	Potassium	210 mg
Fat	28 g	Calcium	30% U.S. RDA
Cholesterol	310 mg	Iron	10% U.S. RDA

Baked Broccoli Frittata

- 1 cup sliced onions
- ½ cup sliced red or green bell pepper
- 1 garlic clove, minced
- 2 tablespoons margarine or butter
- 6 eggs
- ⅓ cup half-and-half
- ½ teaspoon basil leaves
- ½ teaspoon thyme leaves
- ½ teaspoon seasoned salt or lemon pepper seasoning
- 1 to 1½ cups frozen broccoli cuts, cooked crisp-tender, drained
- 4 oz. (1 cup) shredded Monterey jack cheese
- ½ cup grated Parmesan cheese

Heat oven to 425°F. Generously butter a 2-quart shallow casserole or 4 individual baking dishes. In large skillet over medium-low heat, saute onions, red pepper and garlic in margarine until tender; cool slightly. In large bowl, beat eggs, half-and-half and seasonings until well mixed. Stir in onion-pepper mixture and broccoli. Pour into casserole. Sprinkle with cheeses. Bake at 425°F. for 15 to 20 minutes or until mixture is set (top will remain moist). Let stand 5 minutes before serving. **4 servings.**

NUTRIENTS PER ¼ OF RECIPE

Calories 400	Dietary Fiber..........................3 g
Protein......................................24 g	Sodium.............................980 mg
Carbohydrate...........................12 g	Potassium.........................360 mg
Fat..28 g	Calcium...............30% U.S. RDA
Cholesterol.........................450 mg	Iron......................15% U.S. RDA

Skillet Corn Frittata

6	tablespoons margarine or butter
16-oz.	pkg. (3 cups) frozen corn
¼	cup sliced green onions
10	eggs, well beaten
½	cup whipping cream
1	teaspoon basil leaves
½	teaspoon salt
⅛	teaspoon pepper
2	tomatoes, peeled, sliced
1	green pepper, cut into rings
4 oz.	(1 cup) shredded Swiss cheese

In large skillet over medium heat, melt margarine; saute corn and onions until tender, about 5 minutes. Remove from heat. In large bowl, combine eggs, cream, basil, salt and pepper; mix well. Pour over vegetables. Cook over low heat 6 minutes. As edges set, run spatula around edge of skillet and lift vegetable mixture to allow uncooked egg to flow to bottom of skillet. Cover; cook an additional 6 minutes or until top is almost set (top will be moist). Arrange tomato slices and green pepper rings around outer edge of skillet; sprinkle with cheese. Cover; cook an additional 5 minutes or until cheese is melted. Remove from heat; let stand 5 minutes. Cut into wedges. **8 servings.**

NUTRIENTS PER ⅛ OF RECIPE

Calories 350	Dietary Fiber..........................3 g
Protein......................................14 g	Sodium.............................370 mg
Carbohydrate...........................16 g	Potassium.........................320 mg
Fat ....26 g	Calcium...............20% U.S. RDA
Cholesterol.........................380 mg	Iron......................10% U.S. RDA

Quiche Lorraine

Pastry for filled one-crust pie (see Index)

FILLING

8 oz.	(2 cups) Swiss cheese, cut into thin strips
2	tablespoons flour
4	eggs
1½	cups half-and-half
¼	cup chopped onion
8	slices crisply cooked, crumbled bacon
	Dash pepper

Prepare pastry for filled one-crust pie using 9-inch pie pan.

Heat oven to 350°F. Toss cheese with flour. In large bowl, beat eggs slightly. Add half-and-half, onion, bacon, pepper and cheese; mix well. Pour into pastry-lined pan. Bake at 350°F. for 40 to 45 minutes or until knife inserted just off center comes out clean. Cool 10 minutes before serving. Store in refrigerator. **6 servings.**

NUTRIENTS PER ⅙ OF RECIPE

Calories	520	Dietary Fiber	1 g
Protein	22 g	Sodium	500 mg
Carbohydrate	23 g	Potassium	250 mg
Fat	37 g	Calcium	45% U.S. RDA
Cholesterol	250 mg	Iron	10% U.S. RDA

Vegetable Strata Supreme

16-oz.	pkg. frozen broccoli, cauliflower and carrots
7	slices white or wheat bread, cut into ½-inch cubes
1	cup chopped cooked ham
8	eggs
1½	cups milk
1	teaspoon dry mustard
½	teaspoon garlic powder
½	teaspoon onion powder
6 oz.	(1½ cups) shredded Cheddar cheese

Grease 13x9-inch (3-quart) baking dish. Arrange frozen vegetables in bottom of prepared dish; sprinkle with bread cubes and ham. In medium bowl, combine eggs, milk, mustard, garlic powder and onion powder; mix well. Pour egg mixture over vegetables; sprinkle with cheese. Cover with plastic wrap. Refrigerate 6 hours or overnight.

Heat oven to 350°F. Uncover; bake for 40 to 50 minutes or until knife inserted near center comes out clean. **8 to 10 servings.**

NUTRIENTS PER ⅒ OF RECIPE

Calories 240
Protein.....................................16 g
Carbohydrate.........................14 g
Fat ....13 g
Cholesterol.......................250 mg

Dietary Fiber...........................3 g
Sodium.............................510 mg
Potassium.........................320 mg
Calcium...............20% U.S. RDA
Iron......................10% U.S. RDA

Sundance Eggs

    4 flour tortillas (8-inch diameter)
    8 eggs
    2 teaspoons water
   ¼ teaspoon salt
    1 tablespoon margarine or butter
   ½ cup chopped green onions
    2 medium tomatoes, peeled, seeded, chopped
4-oz. can chopped green chiles, drained
4-oz. (1 cup) shredded Monterey jack cheese
    4 tablespoons taco sauce
       Dairy sour cream, if desired

Heat oven to 350°F. Wrap tortillas in foil; bake about 5 minutes or until warm.* While tortillas are baking, combine eggs, water and salt in medium bowl; beat well. In large skillet, melt margarine. Add egg mixture and cook, stirring occasionally, until eggs are almost set. Remove from heat.

Place warm tortillas on large ungreased cookie sheet. Top each tortilla with ¼ of the eggs, onion, tomato, green chiles and cheese. Bake at 350°F. for 5 to 10 minutes or until very warm and cheese is melted. Top each with 1 tablespoon taco sauce and sour cream. **4 servings.**

TIP: *For crisper tortillas, fry each in small amount of oil, turning frequently, until light golden brown.

NUTRIENTS PER ¼ OF RECIPE

Calories 430	Dietary Fiber............................3 g
Protein....................................22 g	Sodium.............................730 mg
Carbohydrate........................26 g	Potassium.........................380 mg
Fat ....26 g	Calcium...............15% U.S. RDA
Cholesterol.......................580 mg	Iron......................20% U.S. RDA

Cheese

Eaten as is or combined with other ingredients, cheese offers flavors from mild to sharp, textures from soft and creamy to hard and coarse, and aromas from mild to pungent. This favorite food is appealing for appetizers, entrees or menu finales.

The *nutrients* in cheese place it on a protein level with meat, poultry, fish and eggs. In addition, cheese is a concentrated source of the nutrients in milk—calcium, vitamin A and riboflavin. Soft and/or white cheeses generally are lower in fat and cholesterol than firm yellow cheeses.

Types of Cheese

• **Natural cheeses** are made directly from milk. Milk is co-agulated, then the curds are separated from the liquid portion and pressed into various forms. General classifications for natural cheeses are soft, semi-soft, firm, hard and blue-veined.

• **Pasteurized process cheeses** are a blend of fresh and aged natural cheeses that have been melted, pasteurized and mixed with an emulsifier. Process cheeses are often used in cooked foods because they melt easily.

• **Cold-pack cheeses** are a combination of natural cheeses which have been ground and blended so that they are soft and spreadable at room temperature. Often wine, fruit or vegetables are added for variety.

• **Unripened cheeses** such as cream cheese and cottage cheese are soft-textured and mild-flavored and are not aged.

Storing Cheese

Cheese is perishable; it should be wrapped and stored in the refrigerator. The length of storage varies considerably with type of cheese. In general, the harder the cheese, the longer it will keep. Natural and process cheeses can be refrigerated several months, cream and other soft cheeses about two weeks and cottage and ricotta cheeses about one week. Mold that may develop on the surface of harder natural cheeses should be cut away.

Cooking with Cheese

Cooking with cheese usually requires low heat and brief cooking time to avoid a tough, stringy texture. Some recipes for casseroles will advise adding a cheese topping at the very end of the cooking time to allow cheese to melt into a smooth topping without toughening. When cheese is added to a sauce, it should be diced or shredded so it blends quickly into other ingredients without prolonged cooking.

Cheese is easier to shred when cold from the refrigerator. Process cheese can be placed in the freezer for a few minutes before shredding. Four ounces of cheese will yield 1 cup of shredded cheese.

One cheese can be substituted for another in a recipe if similar in flavor and consistency.

Serving Cheese

Serving cheese at room temperature brings out its full flavor and improves its consistency for cutting or spreading. Exceptions are cream cheese and cottage cheese, which should be kept refrigerated until serving to avoid spoilage. When selecting varieties for appetizers, snacks or dessert, choose different colors, shapes, textures and flavors for an interesting combination. Crackers and fresh fruits like pears, apples and grapes are favorite complementary accompaniments.

Selection Guide for Natural Cheeses

Type	Cheese (Origins)	Characteristics	Uses
Soft	Cottage Cheese (Unknown)	Unripened; moist; available plain or creamed; large or small curds; white; mild, slightly acidic flavor.	Appetizer; dips; salad; cooking
	Cream Cheese (U.S.A.)	Unripened; smooth texture; white; mild, slightly acidic flavor.	Appetizer; dips; spreads; sandwiches; cooking; dessert
	Neufchâtel (France)	Unripened; smooth texture; white; mild, buttery flavor; similar to cream cheese, but lower in fat.	Appetizer; dips; spreads; cooking
	Ricotta (Italy)	Unripened; moist; grainy texture; drier than cottage cheese; white; bland, sweet flavor.	Cooking, especially pasta main dishes; dessert
	Brie (France)	Creamy texture; pale yellow interior with edible white crust; mild to pungent flavor; sharper than Camembert.	Appetizer; dessert
	Camembert (France)	Creamy texture; light cream-colored interior with edible white crust; mild to pungent flavor.	Appetizer; dessert
	Limburger (Belgium)	Smooth texture; creamy white interior with yellow-orange rind; robust flavor, highly aromatic.	Sandwiches; snack; dessert

Selection Guide for Natural Cheeses (cont.)

Type	Cheese (Origins)	Characteristics	Uses
Soft (cont.)	Chèvre (France)	Goat cheese; creamy texture; very pungent flavor.	Appetizer; salad; cooking
Semi-Soft	Bel Paese (Italy)	Smooth waxy texture, creamy yellow interior with gray surface; mild to robust flavor.	Appetizer; snack; cooking; dessert
	Brick (U.S.A.)	Smooth, waxy, open texture; creamy white; mild to moderately sharp flavor.	Appetizer; sandwiches
	Feta (Greece)	Made from sheep or goat milk; crumbly; white; salty; tangy flavor.	Appetizer; salad; cooking
	Havarti (Denmark)	Rich, creamy, open texture; creamy white; mild flavor.	Appetizer; sandwiches; dessert
	Monterey jack (U.S.A.)	Smooth, open texture; creamy white; mild flavor.	All-purpose cheese. Appetizer; sandwiches; sauces; cooking
	Mozzarella (Italy)	Unripened; plastic texture; creamy white; mild flavor.	Pizza; cooking
	Muenster (Germany)	Open texture; creamy white interior with orange rind; mild to mellow flavor.	Appetizer; sandwiches; dessert

Selection Guide for Natural Cheeses (cont.)

Type	Cheese (Origins)	Characteristics	Uses
Semi-Soft (cont.)	Port du Salut (France)	Smooth, buttery, open texture; creamy white interior with reddish brown surface; mellow to robust flavor.	Appetizer; sandwiches; sauces; cooking
Firm	Cheddar (England)	Open texture; creamy white to orange; mild to sharp flavor depending on aging.	All-purpose cheese. Appetizer; sandwiches; sauces; salad; cooking; dessert; especially good with fruit
	Colby (U.S.A.)	Softer and more open than cheddar; light yellow to orange; mild flavor.	Appetizer; sandwiches; sauces; salad; dessert
	Edam (Netherlands)	Open texture; creamy yellow; mild, nut-like flavor.	Appetizer; sandwiches; salad; cooking; dessert
	Gouda (Netherlands)	Open texture; creamy yellow; mild, nut-like flavor.	Appetizer; sandwiches; salad; cooking; dessert
	Fontina (Italy)	Yellow interior; bland to nutty flavor.	Appetizer; eggs; sandwiches; cooking; dessert
	Gruyere (Switzerland)	Open texture; light yellow; mild, sweet, nut-like flavor.	Appetizer; fondues; cooking; dessert

Selection Guide for Natural Cheeses (cont.)

Type	Cheese (Origins)	Characteristics	Uses
Firm (cont.)	Gjetost (Norway)	Unripened; smooth texture; caramel-colored; sweet flavor.	Appetizer; sandwiches; dessert
	Jarlsberg (Norway)	Similar in appearance to Swiss cheese; mild, nutty flavor.	Appetizer; sandwiches; snack; cooking; salad
	Provolone (Italy)	Dense, flaky texture; light creamy yellow to golden brown; mellow to sharp flavor, usually smoked and salted.	Appetizer; pasta; cooking; dessert
	Swiss (U.S.A.)	Smooth texture with large holes; creamy white; mild, sweet flavor.	Appetizer; fondues; sandwiches; sauces; salad; cooking; dessert
Hard	Parmesan (Italy)	Brittle; creamy yellow with brown or black coating; sharp, pungent flavor.	Pasta; soups; sauces; salad; cooking; grated
	Romano (Italy)	Brittle; creamy yellow with greenish black coating; sharp, very pungent flavor.	Pasta; sauces; cooking; grated
Blue-Veined	Blue (France)	Semi-soft, pasty, somewhat crumbly texture; white marbled with blue-green mold; tangy, sharp flavor.	Appetizer; salad; salad dressing; dessert

Selection Guide for Natural Cheeses (cont.)

Type	Cheese (Origins)	Characteristics	Uses
Blue-Veined (cont.)	Gorgonzola (Italy)	Firm; white marbled with blue-green mold; piquant, salty flavor; has most pungent flavor of blues.	Appetizer; dips; spreads; salad; dessert
	Roquefort (France)	Semi-soft, moist, crumbly texture; white marbled with blue-green mold; salty flavor.	Appetizer; salad; salad dressing; cooking; dessert
	Stilton (England)	Semi-soft, crumbly texture; creamy white marbled with blue-green mold; piquant flavor but mellow.	Appetizer; snack; salad; dessert

Garden Fresh Rarebit

½ cup finely chopped lettuce
½ cup finely chopped carrots
½ cup finely chopped green pepper
½ cup finely chopped celery
½ cup finely chopped radishes
6 slices whole wheat bread, toasted
6 oz. (1½ cups) shredded American cheese
6 oz. (1½ cups) shredded Monterey jack cheese
¼ cup beer or water
Alfalfa sprouts
Paprika

In small bowl, combine lettuce, carrots, green pepper, celery and radishes. Place toast on ungreased jelly roll pan or cookie sheet; top each with scant ½ cup vegetable mixture.

In medium saucepan, combine cheeses and beer. Cook over low heat, stirring until cheese is melted. Spoon cheese sauce over sandwiches. Broil 4 inches from heat for 3 to 5 minutes or until cheese is light golden brown and bubbly. Top with alfalfa sprouts and sprinkle with paprika. **6 servings.**

TIP: To speed preparation time, use food processor or blender to finely chop vegetables.

NUTRIENTS PER 1 SANDWICH

Calories	280	Dietary Fiber	2 g
Protein	16 g	Sodium	675 mg
Carbohydrate	16 g	Potassium	245 mg
Fat	17 g	Calcium	25% U.S. RDA
Cholesterol	50 mg	Iron	6% U.S. RDA

Welsh Rarebit

3	tablespoons margarine or butter
12 oz.	(3 cups) cubed American cheese
12-oz.	can (1½ cups) beer
3	eggs, slightly beaten
1½	teaspoons dry mustard
1	teaspoon Worcestershire sauce
6	drops hot pepper sauce, if desired
6	slices toast

In medium saucepan, melt margarine over low heat. Add cheese and beer. Cook over very low heat until cheese is melted, stirring constantly. In small bowl, combine eggs, mustard, Worcestershire sauce and hot pepper sauce. Slowly add to melted cheese, beating with a wire whisk or rotary beater. Continue cooking about 10 minutes, stirring occasionally until thickened. Serve over toast. **6 servings.**

NUTRIENTS PER ¼ OF RECIPE

Calories	400	Dietary Fiber	<1 g
Protein	18 g	Sodium	1060 mg
Carbohydrate	17 g	Potassium	170 mg
Fat	27 g	Calcium	40% U.S. RDA
Cholesterol	190 mg	Iron	8% U.S. RDA

Grilled Cheese a la Veggies

8	slices whole wheat or rye bread
16	thin slices zucchini
8	thin slices peeled tomato
4	thin slices onion
8 oz.	(8 slices) Monterey jack or Muenster cheese
½	teaspoon dill weed
	Margarine or butter, softened

Heat griddle or skillet to medium heat (340°F.). To assemble sandwiches, top each of 4 slices of bread with ¼ of the zucchini, tomato, onion and cheese; sprinkle with dill weed. Cover with remaining slices of bread. Spread margarine on outside of each slice of bread. Place sandwiches on griddle; grill on each side until golden brown and cheese is melted. **4 sandwiches.**

TIP: If desired, crisply cooked bacon strips can be added.

NUTRIENTS PER 1 SANDWICH

Calories	426	Dietary Fiber	3 g
Protein	19 g	Sodium	750 mg
Carbohydrate	30 g	Potassium	330 mg
Fat	25 g	Calcium	6% U.S. RDA
Cholesterol	50 mg	Iron	10% U.S. RDA

Cheesy Egg Strata

      8   slices white bread, crusts removed
  8 oz.   (2 cups) shredded mozzarella cheese
  8 oz.   (2 cups) shredded Cheddar cheese
      8   slices bacon, crisply cooked, crumbled
      6   eggs
      3   cups milk
    ½   teaspoon salt
         Dash pepper

Heat oven to 350°F. Butter 13x9-inch (3-quart) baking dish;
line bottom with bread slices. Layer mozzarella cheese,
Cheddar cheese and bacon. In large bowl, beat eggs. Add
milk, salt and pepper; beat until well blended. Pour over
cheese-bacon mixture in dish.* Bake at 350°F. for 45 to 50
minutes or until knife inserted near center comes out clean.
8 servings.

TIPS: *Recipe can be made ahead to this point; cover and
refrigerate overnight. Bake uncovered as directed above.

To reheat, cover loosely with foil; heat at 350°F. for 15 to 20
minutes.

NUTRIENTS PER ⅛ OF RECIPE

Calories	460	Dietary Fiber	<1 g
Protein	22 g	Sodium	705 mg
Carbohydrate	18 g	Potassium	270 mg
Fat	33 g	Calcium	60% U.S. RDA
Cholesterol	270 mg	Iron	10% U.S. RDA

Swiss Cheese Fondue

      1   garlic clove
    ¾   cup sauterne or Chablis white wine
 12 oz.   (3 cups) shredded Swiss cheese
      2   tablespoons flour
    ¼   teaspoon salt

⅛ teaspoon nutmeg
Dash pepper
1 to 2 tablespoons cherry-flavored liqueur, if desired
1 loaf French bread, cut into bite-size pieces

Rub inside of saucepan or fondue pot with cut garlic clove. Add wine and heat until bubbly. In medium bowl, combine cheese, flour, salt, nutmeg and pepper. Add about ¼ cup of the cheese mixture to wine; stir vigorously. Continue adding cheese mixture in small amounts and stirring until all cheese is melted and mixture is thoroughly blended. Stir in liqueur. Keep hot while serving. Each guest uses fondue fork to dip bread into fondue. **4 servings.**

TIP: If fondue becomes too thick during serving, stir in a little more warm wine.

NUTRIENTS PER ¼ OF RECIPE

Calories	720	Dietary Fiber	3 g
Protein	35 g	Sodium	1010 mg
Carbohydrate	75 g	Potassium	240 mg
Fat	27 g	Calcium	90% U.S. RDA
Cholesterol	80 mg	Iron	20% U.S. RDA

Cheese Sauce

2 tablespoons margarine or butter
2 tablespoons flour
¼ teaspoon salt
⅛ teaspoon pepper
2 cups milk
8 oz. (2 cups) shredded American or Cheddar cheese
1 teaspoon Worcestershire sauce
Dash hot pepper sauce

In medium saucepan over low heat, melt margarine. Stir in flour, salt and pepper. Cook 1 minute, stirring constantly, until smooth and bubbly. Gradually stir in milk. Cook over medium heat, stirring constantly, until bubbly and slightly thickened, about 7 minutes. Remove from heat. Add cheese, Worcestershire sauce and hot pepper sauce; stir until cheese is melted. **2¼ cups.**

NUTRIENTS PER 1 TABLESPOON

Calories 40	Dietary Fiber...........................0 g
Protein.......................................2 g	Sodium..............................120 mg
Carbohydrate............................1 g	Potassium.............................30 mg
Fat ....3 g	Calcium.................6% U.S. RDA
Cholesterol............................6 mg	Iron ....<2% U.S. RDA

Baked Brie on French Bread

Heat oven to 325°F. Cut 12 to 14-inch loaf of crusty French bread into 1-inch thick slices. Cut 8-oz. round Brie cheese into 12 to 14 pieces. Place each piece of cheese on slice of bread; place on ungreased cookie sheet. Bake at 325°F. for 9 to 12 minutes or until cheese melts. **12 to 14 servings.**

NUTRIENTS PER ¼ OF RECIPE

Calories 160	Dietary Fiber.........................<1 g
Protein.......................................7 g	Sodium..............................300 mg
Carbohydrate..........................19 g	Potassium.............................55 mg
Fat ....6 g	Calcium.................4% U.S. RDA
Cholesterol..........................15 mg	Iron......................6% U.S. RDA

Pizza Deluxe

1	recipe Thick Crust Pizza Dough
¾	cup Pizza Sauce
3½-oz.	pkg. sliced pepperoni
2.5-oz.	jar sliced mushrooms, drained
¼	cup chopped green pepper
6 oz.	(1½ cups) shredded mozzarella cheese
4 oz.	(1 cup) shredded provolone cheese

Grease 12-inch pizza pan. With greased fingers, press dough into prepared pan, forming ½-inch rim. Cover; let rise in warm place (80 to 85°F.) until light and doubled in size, 15 to 30 minutes.

Heat oven to 400°F. Bake crust 8 to 10 minutes or until set and very light golden brown. Spread sauce over partially baked crust. Arrange pepperoni, mushrooms and green pepper over sauce. Combine mozzarella and provolone cheeses; sprinkle over pizza. Bake at 400°F. for an additional 18 to 25 minutes or until crust is deep golden brown. **8 servings.**

TIP: Any combination of pizza toppings can be substituted for pepperoni, mushrooms and green pepper.

NUTRIENTS PER ⅛ OF RECIPE

Calories	320	Dietary Fiber	2 g
Protein	16 g	Sodium	960 mg
Carbohydrate	29 g	Potassium	280 mg
Fat	16 g	Calcium	25% U.S. RDA
Cholesterol	20 mg	Iron	10% U.S. RDA

Pizza Sauce

½ cup chopped onion
3 garlic cloves, minced
2 tablespoons oil
1 cup chopped fresh tomatoes or halved cherry tomatoes
8-oz. can (1 cup) tomato sauce
6-oz. can tomato paste
1 teaspoon salt
2 teaspoons oregano leaves
2 teaspoons basil leaves
⅛ teaspoon pepper

In large skillet, saute onion and garlic in oil until tender. Stir in remaining ingredients; simmer 30 minutes, stirring occasionally. **2¼ cups.**

NUTRIENTS PER 1 TABLESPOON

Calories 16	Dietary Fiber..........................<1 g
Protein......................................0 g	Sodium.............................130 mg
Carbohydrate............................2 g	Potassium...........................85 mg
Fat ....1 g	Calcium...............<2% U.S. RDA
Cholesterol ....0 mg	Iron ....<2% U.S. RDA

Thick Crust Pizza Dough

        1½ to 2 cups all purpose flour
            1 teaspoon salt
           ½ teaspoon sugar
            1 pkg. active dry yeast
           ¾ cup water
            1 tablespoon oil

In large bowl, combine ¾ cup flour, salt, sugar and yeast;
blend well. In small saucepan, heat water and oil until very
warm (120 to 130°F.); add to flour mixture. Blend at low
speed until moistened; beat 2 minutes at medium speed. Stir
in ½ to ¾ cup flour to form a stiff dough.

On floured surface, knead in ¼ to ½ cup flour until dough
is smooth and elastic, about 3 to 5 minutes. Place dough in
greased bowl; cover loosely with plastic wrap and cloth
towel. Let rise in warm place (80 to 85°F.) until light and
doubled in size, about 30 to 40 minutes.

Punch down dough several times to remove all air bubbles.
Prepare as directed in Pizza Deluxe or for your favorite
pizza recipe. **1 thick crust.**

VARIATIONS:

THIN CRUST PIZZA DOUGH: Prepare dough as directed
above; divide in half. Press each half into greased 12-inch
pizza pan. Top with pizza toppings. Bake at 400°F. for 18 to
25 minutes or until crust is golden brown. **2 thin crust piz-
zas.**

WHOLE WHEAT PIZZA DOUGH: Substitute ½ cup whole wheat flour for part of the all purpose flour. Prepare as directed above.

NUTRIENTS PER ⅛ OF RECIPE

Calories	130	Dietary Fiber	1 g
Protein	4 g	Sodium	270 mg
Carbohydrate	24 g	Potassium	45 mg
Fat	2 g	Calcium	<2% U.S. RDA
Cholesterol	0 mg	Iron	8% U.S. RDA

Veggie-Cheese Stuffed Pizza

2¼ to 3	cups all purpose flour
2	teaspoons salt
1	teaspoon sugar
2	pkg. active dry yeast
1½	cups water
2	tablespoons oil
1	cup whole wheat flour
1	tablespoon cornmeal
12 oz.	(3 cups) shredded mozzarella cheese
1	cup frozen broccoli cuts, thawed, drained
1	cup frozen cauliflower florets, thawed, drained
5 oz.	pepperoni, chopped
½ to 1	teaspoon oregano leaves
	Beaten egg
8-oz.	can tomato sauce, if desired
1	teaspoon basil leaves, if desired

In large bowl, combine 1½ cups all purpose flour, salt, sugar and yeast; blend well. In small saucepan, heat 1½ cups water and oil until very warm (120 to 130°F.); add to flour mixture. Blend at low speed until moistened; beat 2 minutes at medium speed. Stir in whole wheat flour and an additional ½ to 1 cup all purpose flour to form a stiff dough.

On floured surface, knead in ¼ to ½ cup all purpose flour until dough is smooth and elastic, about 3 to 5 minutes. Place dough in greased bowl; cover loosely with plastic wrap and cloth towel. Let rise in warm place (80 to 85°F.) until light and doubled in size, about 30 to 40 minutes.

Heat oven to 375°F. Grease a 12-inch pizza pan; sprinkle with cornmeal. Punch down dough several times to remove all air bubbles. On lightly floured surface, roll ⅔ of dough into a 14-inch circle; place in prepared pan. In large bowl, combine cheese, broccoli, cauliflower, pepperoni and oregano; spoon over dough. Roll remaining dough into a 14-inch circle; place on top of filling. Fold edge of crust under bottom; flute to seal. Make 5 slits with tip of knife for steam to escape. Brush with beaten egg. Bake at 375°F. for 25 to 35 minutes or until crust is golden brown.

Meanwhile, in small saucepan combine tomato sauce and basil; simmer 3 to 5 minutes or until thoroughly heated. Serve over pizza. **8 servings**.

NUTRIENTS PER ⅛ OF RECIPE

Calories 500	Dietary Fiber ....3 g
Protein......................................25 g	Sodium............................1310 mg
Carbohydrate.........................54 g	Potassium ....430 mg
Fat ....20 g	Calcium...............35% U.S. RDA
Cholesterol ....70 mg	Iron.....................20% U.S. RDA

Crazy Crust Pizza

- 1½ lb. ground beef or bulk sausage
- 1 cup all purpose flour
- 1 teaspoon Italian seasoning or oregano leaves
- ½ teaspoon salt
- ⅛ teaspoon pepper
- ⅔ cup milk
- 2 eggs
- ¼ cup chopped onion
- 1 cup mushroom pieces and stems, well drained

8-oz. can tomato sauce
1 to 2 teaspoons oregano leaves
4 oz. (1 cup) shredded mozzarella cheese

Heat oven to 425°F. (Place oven rack at lowest position.) Lightly grease 12-inch pizza pan; sprinkle with flour or cornmeal. In large skillet, brown meat; drain. In small bowl, combine flour, Italian seasoning, salt, pepper, milk and eggs; blend until smooth. Pour batter into prepared pan, tilting pan so batter covers bottom. Spoon meat mixture over batter; top with onion and mushrooms.

Bake at 425°F. on lowest oven rack for 25 to 30 minutes or until pizza is deep golden brown. Combine tomato sauce and oregano; spoon over pizza. Sprinkle with cheese. Bake an additional 10 to 15 minutes. **6 servings.**

NUTRIENTS PER ⅙ OF RECIPE

Calories	410	Dietary Fiber	3 g
Protein	30 g	Sodium	720 mg
Carbohydrate	23 g	Potassium	520 mg
Fat	22 g	Calcium	20% U.S. RDA
Cholesterol	170 mg	Iron	20% U.S. RDA

Pasta

The pleasures of pasta are as numerous as the hundreds of shapes and sizes available and the endless ways they can be prepared. Although Americans may not consume as much pasta as people in some other countries, we are quickly learning to appreciate the virtues of this versatile food. With nutritional value, convenience, endless culinary possibilities and low cost to its credit, pasta has become a favorite in home and restaurant kitchens.

Nutritionally, pasta is far more than just a filler or extender food. The enriched varieties are excellent sources of B vitamins, iron, protein and complex carbohydrates. Low in sodium and fat, pasta is not only wholesome, but is easily

Pasta Cooking Reference

Pasta	Dry Measurement (approximately)	Cooked Measurement (approximately)
Spaghetti	8 ounces	4 cups
Macaroni		
elbow	1¾ cups	3⅔ cups
ring	2 cups	2⅔ cups
orzo	1¼ cups	2¾ cups
rigatoni	2 cups	4 cups
medium shells	2¾ cups	4 cups
spiral	3⅔ cups	4 cups
Egg Noodles		
bow ties	4½ cups	4 cups
fine	4 cups	4 cups
medium	5 cups	4 cups
spinach	3¼ cups	3¾ cups

Homemade Egg Pasta

    2 cups all purpose flour*
    ½ teaspoon salt
    5 tablespoons water
    2 teaspoons oil
    2 eggs, beaten

In small bowl, combine flour and salt; blend well. Make a well in center; add water, oil and eggs. Gradually work flour into liquid to form dough. On floured surface, knead until dough is smooth, about 2 to 3 minutes. Wrap dough in plastic bag; rest at room temperature 1 hour.**

On floured surface, roll half of dough out as thin as possible into rectangle (about 18x15 inches). Sprinkle lightly with flour. Starting at shortest side, loosely fold dough over into thirds. Cut into ¼-inch slices for fettuccine or ⅛-inch slices for linguine. Unfold slices; cut into desired lengths. Repeat with remaining half of dough.

Bring 12 cups water and 1 tablespoon salt to a boil. Drop pasta into boiling water; after water returns to a boil, cook uncovered for 5 to 10 minutes or until pasta is tender, stirring occasionally. Drain. Use as desired. **About 1 lb. uncooked pasta; 6 cups cooked pasta.**

FOOD PROCESSOR DIRECTIONS: In food processor bowl with metal blade, combine flour and salt. In measuring cup, combine water, oil and eggs. With machine running, add egg mixture all at once. Process until dough forms a ball. (If ball does not form quickly, add cold water through feed tube, 1 teaspoon at a time; process with about 10 on/off turns until ball forms.) Continue as directed above.

TIPS: *Whole wheat flour can be used for half of the all purpose flour. Use 1 additional tablespoon water.

**To roll and cut pasta using manual or electric pasta-rolling machine, follow manufacturer's directions. (Electric extrusion-type pasta machines are not recommended for this recipe.)

Pasta dough or fresh pasta can be stored in plastic bags in refrigerator for up to 3 days or freezer for up to 1 month.

VARIATION:

SPINACH-FLAVORED EGG PASTA: Using the food processor, add 1 cup firmly-packed, thoroughly-dry, torn spinach leaves with the flour. Process until very finely chopped. Continue as directed above using only 1 to 2 tablespoons water. (Spinach pasta color will fade slightly if not cooked or frozen immediately.)

NUTRIENTS PER 1 CUP

Calories	190	Dietary Fiber	2 g
Protein	6 g	Sodium	200 mg
Carbohydrate	32 g	Potassium	60 mg
Fat	4 g	Calcium	<2% U.S. RDA
Cholesterol	90 mg	Iron	10% U.S. RDA

Quick Spaghetti Sauce

         1   lb. ground beef
       ½   cup chopped onion
         2   (15-oz.) cans tomato sauce
   4-oz.   can mushroom pieces and stems, drained
       ½   teaspoon oregano leaves
       ½   teaspoon basil leaves
       ¼   teaspoon garlic powder
 ⅛ to ¼   teaspoon cayenne pepper
       ⅛   teaspoon pepper

In large skillet or Dutch oven, brown ground beef and onion; drain. Add remaining ingredients; mix well. Simmer 15 minutes, stirring occasionally. **5 cups.**

MICROWAVE DIRECTIONS: In 2-quart microwave-safe casserole, crumble ground beef; add onion. Microwave on HIGH for 4 to 5 minutes or until meat is no longer pink, stirring once halfway through cooking; drain well. Add remaining ingredients. Microwave on HIGH for 8 to 10 minutes or until hot.

NUTRIENTS PER ½ CUP

Calories 130	Dietary Fiber..........................2 g
Protein.....................................10 g	Sodium.............................500 mg
Carbohydrate............................7 g	Potassium.........................530 mg
Fat ....7 g	Calcium...............<2% U.S. RDA
Cholesterol........................30 mg	Iron......................10% U.S. RDA

Pesto Sauce

         1   cup grated Parmesan cheese*
         1   cup fresh basil leaves*
   6 to 8   tablespoons olive or vegetable oil
         2   tablespoons lemon juice

In food processor bowl with metal blade or blender container, blend Parmesan cheese and basil; gradually add oil a tablespoon at a time until a smooth thick paste is formed. Blend in lemon juice. To store pesto sauce, place in jar. Cover with thin layer of olive oil; cover tightly. Refrigerate. **¾ cup.**

TIP: *One cup grated Parmesan cheese and ¼ cup dry basil leaves can be substituted for freshly grated Parmesan cheese and fresh basil.

NUTRIENTS PER 1 TABLESPOON

Calories	120	Dietary Fiber	<1 g
Protein	4 g	Sodium	160 mg
Carbohydrate	1 g	Potassium	60 mg
Fat	12 g	Calcium	15% U.S. RDA
Cholesterol	6 mg	Iron	4% U.S. RDA

Italian Spaghetti Sauce

½	cup finely chopped onion
1	garlic clove, minced
2	tablespoons olive or vegetable oil
3	cups water
28-oz.	can tomatoes, cut up
2	(6-oz.) cans tomato paste
1	tablespoon sugar
2	teaspoons salt
1	teaspoon oregano leaves
½	teaspoon basil leaves
½	teaspoon pepper
1	large bay leaf

In Dutch oven, cook onion and garlic in oil until tender. Stir in remaining ingredients. Heat to boiling, stirring occasionally. Reduce heat; simmer uncovered 1 to 1½ hours or until sauce is thickened. **5 cups.**

TIP: For a meaty sauce, add Basic Meatballs (see Index) or 1 lb. ground beef that has been browned and drained.

NUTRIENTS PER ½ CUP

Calories	80	Dietary Fiber	2 g
Protein	2 g	Sodium	800 mg
Carbohydrate	12 g	Potassium	500 mg
Fat	3 g	Calcium	2% U.S. RDA
Cholesterol	0 mg	Iron	10% U.S. RDA

Scallops Linguine

1 lb. frozen or fresh scallops
8 oz. uncooked linguine
2 tablespoons lemon juice
1 garlic clove, minced
1 tablespoon chopped fresh parsley
½ teaspoon dill weed
¼ teaspoon salt
¼ teaspoon pepper
⅓ cup margarine or butter
½ cup whipping cream
¼ cup grated Parmesan cheese, if desired

Thaw frozen scallops. Cook linguine to desired doneness as directed on package. Drain; rinse with hot water. Rinse scallops with cold water; drain. Cut large scallops in half crosswise, if desired. In large bowl, combine scallops, lemon juice and garlic. Sprinkle with parsley, dill weed, salt and pepper; toss gently. Cover; refrigerate 10 to 15 minutes to blend flavors.

In large saucepan, melt margarine. Drain scallops; saute over medium heat in margarine for 3 to 4 minutes, stirring constantly. Add cream; cook until thoroughly heated, about 1 minute. Add linguine to scallop mixture, tossing gently to distribute scallops and heat thoroughly. Sprinkle with Parmesan cheese. **6 servings.**

MICROWAVE DIRECTIONS: Prepare scallops as directed above. Cook linguine as directed above. In 2-quart microwave-safe bowl, microwave margarine on HIGH for 45 to 60 seconds or until melted. Add drained scallops. Microwave on HIGH for 3 to 4½ minutes, stirring once halfway through cooking. Add cream. Microwave on HIGH for 1½ to 2 minutes; stir. Add linguine; toss gently to distribute scallops. Microwave on MEDIUM for 4 to 5½ minutes or until thoroughly heated, stirring once halfway through cooking. Sprinkle with Parmesan cheese.

NUTRIENTS PER ¼ OF RECIPE

Calories	380	Dietary Fiber	<1 g
Protein	19 g	Sodium	480 mg
Carbohydrate	33 g	Potassium	420 mg
Fat	19 g	Calcium	10% U.S. RDA
Cholesterol	60 mg	Iron	15% U.S. RDA

Tortellini with Pepper Sauce

8-oz. pkg. fresh or frozen cheese tortellini

SAUCE
- 1 tablespoon olive or vegetable oil
- 3 large (3 cups) red bell peppers, chopped
- 1 tablespoon chopped onion
- 1 garlic clove, minced
- 1 cup chicken broth
- 1 tablespoon tomato paste
- ½ teaspoon thyme leaves
- Dash hot pepper sauce

Cook tortellini to desired doneness as directed on package. Drain; rinse with hot water. Keep warm.

In medium saucepan, heat oil. Saute red peppers, onions and garlic until tender, about 5 minutes. Add remaining sauce ingredients. Simmer 10 to 15 minutes or until thickened. In food processor with metal blade or blender container, process until smooth. Serve over cooked tortellini. **4 servings.**

NUTRIENTS PER ¼ OF RECIPE

Calories	220	Dietary Fiber	3 g
Protein	11 g	Sodium	440 mg
Carbohydrate	24 g	Potassium	410 mg
Fat	9 g	Calcium	10% U.S. RDA
Cholesterol	70 mg	Iron	20% U.S. RDA

Savory Chicken Rigatoni

SAUCE

- 2 tablespoons cornstarch
- 1 teaspoon sugar
- 2 teaspoons instant chicken bouillon granules
- 1 cup water
- 1 teaspoon grated lemon peel
- 3 tablespoons lemon juice

3½ oz. (1½ cups) uncooked rigatoni
- 2 tablespoons oil
- 1 medium (1 cup) yellow bell pepper, cut into strips
- 1 medium (1 cup) green bell pepper, cut into strips
- 2 whole chicken breasts (about 1 lb.) skinned, boned, cut into thin strips
- 2 medium tomatoes, cut into wedges
- 1 tablespoon chopped fresh basil or ½ teaspoon dried basil leaves
- ½ cup freshly grated Romano cheese

In small bowl, combine cornstarch, sugar and bouillon granules; blend well. Stir in remaining sauce ingredients; set aside. Cook rigatoni to desired doneness as directed on package. Drain; rinse with hot water. Keep warm.

In large skillet or wok, heat 1 tablespoon oil. Stir-fry peppers 2 minutes or until crisp-tender. Remove from pan. Heat remaining 1 tablespoon oil; add chicken. Stir-fry 5 minutes or until chicken is tender and no longer pink. Add sauce mixture, peppers, tomatoes and basil; cook until thoroughly heated and slightly thickened, stirring occasionally. Spoon over cooked rigatoni; toss lightly. Sprinkle with cheese. **4 to 6 servings.**

MICROWAVE DIRECTIONS: Prepare rigatoni as directed above. Place chicken in 9-inch microwave-safe glass pie pan. Cover with waxed paper. Microwave on HIGH for 5 to 6 minutes or until chicken is no longer pink, stirring once halfway through cooking. Drain; set aside. Keep warm.

Place peppers in 3-quart microwave-safe bowl. *Omit oil.* Cover with microwave-safe plastic wrap. Microwave on HIGH for 3½ to 4 minutes or until crisp-tender, stirring once halfway through cooking. Keep warm.

In 2-cup glass measure, combine cornstarch, sugar and bouillon granules; blend well. Stir in remaining sauce ingredients. Microwave on HIGH for 2½ to 3½ minutes, stirring with wire whisk after first minute and then after every 30 seconds until thickened. Add chicken, sauce, tomatoes and basil to peppers; toss to coat. Spoon over cooked rigatoni; toss lightly. Sprinkle with cheese.

NUTRIENTS PER ¼ OF RECIPE

Calories	260	Dietary Fiber	1 g
Protein	23 g	Sodium	270 mg
Carbohydrate	20 g	Potassium	330 mg
Fat	9 g	Calcium	10% U.S. RDA
Cholesterol	60 mg	Iron	8% U.S. RDA

Linguine Vegetable Supreme

6 oz. uncooked linguine
  2 tablespoons margarine or butter
  2 cups (2 medium) shredded zucchini
  ½ cup (1 small) shredded carrot
  ½ cup chopped onion
4 oz. (1 cup) shredded mozzarella cheese
  ½ cup half-and-half or milk
  2 tablespoons dry white wine, if desired
  ½ teaspoon salt
  ⅛ teaspoon garlic powder
  ⅛ teaspoon basil leaves

Cook linguine to desired doneness as directed on package. Drain; rinse with hot water.

In large skillet, melt margarine. Add zucchini, carrot and onion; cook over medium heat for 3 minutes, stirring occasionally. Add cooked linguine and remaining ingredients to vegetables; toss mixture until cheese is melted. Serve immediately. **6 servings.**

NUTRIENTS PER ⅙ OF RECIPE

Calories 230	Dietary Fiber ....2 g
Protein......................................9 g	Sodium.............................320 mg
Carbohydrate.........................26 g	Potassium.......................230 mg
Fat ....10 g	Calcium...............15% U.S. RDA
Cholesterol.........................20 mg	Iron.......................6% U.S. RDA

Cheese & Veggie Pasta Toss

8 oz. (½ recipe) Homemade Egg Pasta, cooked* (see Index)
  1 cup pea pods or sugar snap peas, cooked briefly, drained
  1 cup (1 medium) chopped cucumber
  2 green onions, thinly sliced

    1   tablespoon minced fresh parsley
  1½ teaspoons chopped fresh dill or ½ teaspoon dill
       weed
12-oz. carton (1½ cups) small-curd creamed cottage
       cheese
       Salt and pepper, if desired

Prepare Homemade Egg Pasta. In large bowl, combine pea pods, cucumber, onions, parsley, dill and cottage cheese; mix well. Toss with warm pasta or serve sauce over warm pasta. Season to taste with salt and pepper. Serve immediately. **4 servings.**

TIP: *Six to 8 ounces packaged fettuccine or linguine, or 1½ cups spiral macaroni, cooked and drained, can be substituted for Homemade Egg Pasta.

NUTRIENTS PER ¼ OF RECIPE

Calories	250	Dietary Fiber	3 g
Protein	17 g	Sodium	490 mg
Carbohydrate	31 g	Potassium	240 mg
Fat	7 g	Calcium	10% U.S. RDA
Cholesterol	80 mg	Iron	15% U.S. RDA

Noodles Primavera

  7 oz. (4 cups) uncooked wide egg noodles
    ¼ cup margarine or butter
    1 cup chopped onion
    1 garlic clove, minced
  1½ cups broccoli florets, cut into 1-inch pieces*
    1 cup thinly sliced carrots
    1 cup sliced fresh mushrooms
    ½ teaspoon basil leaves
    ¼ teaspoon seasoned salt
    1 medium zucchini, cut into 1½-inch lengths and
       quartered
    1 cup frozen peas
       Grated Parmesan cheese, if desired

Cook noodles to desired doneness as directed on package. Drain; rinse with hot water.

In large skillet or wok, melt margarine over medium heat. Add onions and garlic; stir-fry 2 minutes. Add broccoli, carrots, mushrooms, basil and seasoned salt. Cover; cook 3 to 4 minutes or until vegetables are crisp-tender. Add zucchini and peas; stir-fry about 4 minutes or until vegetables are crisp-tender. Toss with cooked noodles. Sprinkle with Parmesan cheese. **8 servings.**

TIP: *One 9-oz. pkg. frozen cut broccoli, thawed and drained, can be substituted for fresh broccoli.

NUTRIENTS PER ⅛ OF RECIPE

Calories 180	Dietary Fiber............................3 g
Protein.....................................6 g	Sodium.............................170 mg
Carbohydrate........................23 g	Potassium.......................310 mg
Fat ....7 g	Calcium.................6% U.S. RDA
Cholesterol........................30 mg	Iron.......................8% U.S. RDA

Fresh Tomato and Basil with Vermicelli

- 6 oz. uncooked vermicelli
- 2 tablespoons olive oil
- 1 cup sliced zucchini
- 2 garlic cloves, crushed
- 2 cups (2 medium) tomatoes, peeled, seeded, chopped
- ¼ cup fresh chopped basil or 1½ teaspoons basil leaves
- ¼ teaspoon fresh ground pepper
- ½ cup grated Parmesan cheese or 1 cup freshly grated Parmesan cheese

Cook vermicelli to desired doneness as directed on package. Drain; rinse with hot water. Keep warm.

In large skillet heat oil; lightly saute zucchini and garlic. Stir in tomatoes, basil and pepper. Cook until thoroughly heated and slightly thickened, stirring occasionally. In four individual serving dishes, place ¼ of the hot vermicelli; top each with ¼ of tomato mixture. Sprinkle with cheese. Serve immediately. **4 servings.**

NUTRIENTS PER ¼ OF RECIPE

Calories	290	Dietary Fiber	2 g
Protein	12 g	Sodium	240 mg
Carbohydrate	37 g	Potassium	330 mg
Fat	11 g	Calcium	20% U.S. RDA
Cholesterol	10 mg	Iron	10% U.S. RDA

Italian Spaghetti Pie

6 oz.	uncooked spaghetti
1 lb.	ground beef
¼ cup	chopped celery
15½-oz.	jar prepared spaghetti sauce
2.5-oz.	jar sliced mushrooms, drained
2	eggs, slightly beaten
½ cup	grated Parmesan cheese
½ teaspoon	garlic salt

Cook spaghetti to desired doneness as directed on package. Drain; rinse with hot water.

Heat oven to 350°F. Grease 10-inch pie pan or 9-inch square pan. In large skillet, brown ground beef with celery; drain. Stir in prepared spaghetti sauce and mushrooms. Simmer 15 minutes, stirring occasionally.

Combine cooked spaghetti, eggs, ¼ cup of the Parmesan cheese and garlic salt; toss lightly. Place spaghetti mixture in prepared pan. Press evenly in bottom and up sides of pan, forming a crust. Pour meat mixture over spaghetti. Sprinkle with remaining Parmesan cheese. Bake at 350°F. for 25 to

30 minutes or until crust is set and top edge is lightly browned. Let stand 5 minutes before serving. **6 servings.**

MICROWAVE DIRECTIONS: Cook spaghetti as directed above. Lightly grease 10-inch microwave-safe pie pan. In medium bowl, combine cooked spaghetti and *1* egg. Sprinkle *½ cup* Parmesan cheese and garlic salt over spaghetti; toss gently. Place spaghetti mixture in prepared pie pan. Press evenly in bottom and up sides of pan, forming a crust. Microwave on HIGH for 2 to 3 minutes or until crust is slightly set.

In 1½-quart microwave-safe casserole, crumble ground beef; stir in celery. Microwave on HIGH for 4 to 6 minutes or until beef is no longer pink, stirring once halfway through cooking; drain. Add spaghetti sauce, mushrooms and *⅓ cup dry bread crumbs;* stir until well blended. Spoon meat mixture over prepared crust; cover with microwave-safe plastic wrap. Microwave on HIGH for 9 to 12 minutes or until thoroughly heated, rotating ½ turn halfway through cooking. Let stand 10 minutes before serving.

NUTRIENTS PER ⅙ OF RECIPE

Calories 390	Dietary Fiber............................2 g
Protein.....................................24 g	Sodium.............................920 mg
Carbohydrate...........................33 g	Potassium.........................270 mg
Fat ....17 g	Calcium...............15% U.S. RDA
Cholesterol.......................140 mg	Iron.....................20% U.S. RDA

Manicotti Italian Style

8 oz.	uncooked manicotti shells
2	eggs, beaten
2	tablespoons finely chopped onion
½	cup grated Parmesan cheese
½	teaspoon nutmeg
2	(12-oz.) cartons (3 cups) creamed cottage cheese
9-oz.	pkg. frozen chopped spinach, thawed, squeezed to drain

4 oz.   (1 cup) shredded mozzarella cheese
32-oz. jar prepared spaghetti sauce with meat
   ¼ cup grated Parmesan cheese

Cook manicotti shells to desired doneness as directed on package. Drain; place in cold water.

Heat oven to 350°F. Grease 13x9-inch (3-quart) baking dish. In large bowl, combine eggs, onion, ½ cup Parmesan cheese, nutmeg, cottage cheese, spinach and mozzarella cheese; mix well. Drain manicotti. Fill shells with cheese mixture. Place side by side in dish. Pour spaghetti sauce over manicotti; sprinkle with ¼ cup Parmesan cheese. Bake at 350°F. for 35 to 40 minutes or until bubbly. **6 to 7 servings.**

NUTRIENTS PER ⅓ OF RECIPE

Calories 440	Dietary Fiber...........................1 g
Protein.....................................32 g	Sodium...........................1700 mg
Carbohydrate..........................48 g	Potassium.........................350 mg
Fat ....13 g	Calcium...............40% U.S. RDA
Cholesterol.........................110 mg	Iron.....................15% U.S. RDA

Classic Lasagne

9   uncooked lasagne noodles

MEAT SAUCE

   1 lb. bulk Italian sausage or ground beef
   ½ cup chopped onion
16-oz. can tomatoes, undrained, chopped
   2 (6-oz.) cans tomato paste
   1 cup water
   2 teaspoons basil leaves
   1 garlic clove, minced

CHEESE MIXTURE

12-oz.	carton (1½ cups) creamed cottage cheese
½	cup grated Parmesan cheese
1	tablespoon chopped fresh parsley
¼ to ½	teaspoon pepper
2	eggs, beaten
12 oz.	sliced or 3 cups shredded mozzarella cheese

Cook lasagne noodles to desired doneness as directed on package. Drain; rinse with hot water.

In large saucepan or Dutch oven, brown sausage and onion; drain. Add remaining meat sauce ingredients. Simmer 30 minutes, stirring occasionally. In small bowl, combine all cheese mixture ingredients; stir until well blended.

Heat oven to 350°F. In ungreased 13x9-inch (3-quart) baking dish, layer ⅓ of noodles, ⅓ of meat sauce, ⅓ of cheese mixture and ⅓ of mozzarella cheese; repeat layers ending with mozzarella on top. Bake at 350°F. for 30 to 35 minutes. Let stand 10 to 15 minutes before serving. **8 servings.**

NUTRIENTS PER ⅛ OF RECIPE

Calories	420	Dietary Fiber	1 g
Protein	31 g	Sodium	1160 mg
Carbohydrate	33 g	Potassium	760 mg
Fat	18 g	Calcium	45% U.S. RDA
Cholesterol	120 mg	Iron	20% U.S. RDA

Lazy-Day Overnight Lasagne

1	lb. mild Italian sausage or ground beef
32-oz.	jar prepared spaghetti sauce
1	cup water
15-oz.	carton ricotta cheese
2	tablespoons chopped fresh chives
½	teaspoon oregano leaves
1	egg
8 oz.	uncooked lasagne noodles

16-oz. pkg. sliced mozzarella cheese
  2 tablespoons grated Parmesan cheese

In large skillet, brown sausage; drain well. Add spaghetti sauce and water; blend well. Simmer 5 minutes. In medium bowl, combine ricotta cheese, chives, oregano and egg; mix well. In ungreased 13x9-inch (3-quart) baking dish or lasagne pan, spread 1½ cups of meat sauce; top with ½ of uncooked noodles, ½ of ricotta cheese mixture and ½ of mozzarella cheese. Repeat layers; top with remaining meat sauce. Sprinkle with Parmesan cheese. Cover and refrigerate overnight.

Heat oven to 350°F. Uncover baking dish; bake 50 to 60 minutes or until noodles are tender and casserole is bubbly. Let stand 15 minutes before serving. **12 servings.**

NUTRIENTS PER ¹⁄₁₂ OF RECIPE

Calories	350	Dietary Fiber	<1 g
Protein	22 g	Sodium	920 mg
Carbohydrate	28 g	Potassium	180 mg
Fat	16 g	Calcium	40% U.S. RDA
Cholesterol	70 mg	Iron	10% U.S. RDA

Fettuccine Alfredo

12 oz. uncooked fettuccine
  ¾ cup margarine or butter
  1 cup whipping cream
  ¼ teaspoon white pepper
1¼ cups grated Parmesan cheese
  2 teaspoons chopped fresh parsley, if desired
  ¼ teaspoon nutmeg, if desired

Cook fettuccine to desired doneness as directed on package. Drain; rinse with hot water.

In Dutch oven, melt margarine. Stir in cream and pepper. Cook over low heat for about 5 minutes or until mixture thickens slightly, stirring frequently. Stir in Parmesan cheese and cook over low heat just until cheese is melted, stirring constantly. Immediately stir in cooked fettuccine; toss to coat with sauce. Stir in parsley and nutmeg. If sauce begins to separate, stir in a little more cream and cook over low heat until smooth. **6 servings.**

MICROWAVE DIRECTIONS: Cook fettuccine as directed above. Meanwhile, in 3-quart microwave-safe casserole, microwave margarine on HIGH for 2 to 3 minutes or until melted. Add cream and pepper; beat with fork. Microwave on MEDIUM for 4 to 6 minutes or until very slightly thickened, stirring once halfway through cooking. Stir in Parmesan cheese. Microwave on HIGH for 1 to 1½ minutes or until cheese is melted. Immediately stir in cooked fettuccine; toss to coat with sauce. Stir in parsley and nutmeg. Microwave on HIGH for 4 to 5½ minutes or until thoroughly heated, stirring once halfway through cooking.

NUTRIENTS PER ¼ OF RECIPE

Calories 650	Dietary Fiber...........................1 g
Protein...................................17 g	Sodium.............................670 mg
Carbohydrate........................45 g	Potassium........................180 mg
Fat ....44 g	Calcium...............35% U.S. RDA
Cholesterol.......................70 mg	Iron.....................10% U.S. RDA

Easy Noodles Romanoff

4 oz. (2½ cups) uncooked wide egg noodles
   1 cup creamed cottage cheese
   1 cup dairy sour cream
   2 tablespoons chopped green onions
   ¼ teaspoon garlic salt

TOPPING

   ¼ cup bread crumbs
   2 tablespoons margarine or butter, melted
   1 tablespoon dried parsley
   1 teaspoon Worcestershire sauce

Heat oven to 350°F. Grease 1½-quart casserole. Cook noodles to desired doneness as directed on package. Drain; rinse with hot water. In prepared casserole, combine noodles, cottage cheese, sour cream, green onions and garlic salt; blend well.

In small bowl, combine all topping ingredients; mix well. Spoon over noodles. Bake at 350°F. for 25 to 35 minutes or until thoroughly heated and crumbs are golden brown. **6 servings.**

MICROWAVE DIRECTIONS: Prepare topping. Place margarine in 1-cup microwave-safe measuring cup; microwave on HIGH for 30 to 45 seconds or until melted. Stir in bread crumbs; microwave on HIGH for 1 to 1½ minutes or until bread crumbs are lightly browned, stirring twice during cooking. Stir in parsley and Worcestershire; set aside.

Prepare casserole as directed above. Cover; microwave on MEDIUM for 12 to 13 minutes or until thoroughly heated, stirring twice during cooking. Uncover. Spoon topping over noodles; microwave on MEDIUM for 2 minutes or until topping is thoroughly heated.

NUTRIENTS PER ⅙ OF RECIPE

Calories 250	Dietary Fiber .... <1 g
Protein .... 9 g	Sodium .... 340 mg
Carbohydrate .... 20 g	Potassium .... 140 mg
Fat .... 14 g	Calcium .... 8% U.S. RDA
Cholesterol .... 40 mg	Iron .... 4% U.S. RDA

Creamy Mac 'n Cheese

8 oz. (1¾ cups) uncooked elbow macaroni
¼ cup all purpose flour
2 cups milk
8 oz. (2 cups) shredded American cheese
⅛ teaspoon pepper

Cook macaroni to desired doneness as directed on package.
Drain; rinse with hot water.

In jar with tight-fitting lid, combine flour and 1 cup of the
milk; shake until well blended. Pour into medium saucepan;
add remaining milk. Cook over medium heat, stirring constantly, until mixture boils and thickens. Add cheese; continue cooking until cheese is melted, stirring constantly. Add
cooked macaroni and pepper. Heat thoroughly. **8 servings.**

NUTRIENTS PER ⅛ OF RECIPE

Calories	260	Dietary Fiber	<1 g
Protein	12 g	Sodium	440 mg
Carbohydrate	28 g	Potassium	200 mg
Fat	10 g	Calcium	25% U.S. RDA
Cholesterol	30 mg	Iron	6% U.S. RDA

Gnocchi

1 cup water
2 tablespoons margarine or butter
½ cup milk
2 egg yolks
1½ cups mashed potato flakes
1½ cups all purpose flour
¼ teaspoon nutmeg
2 tablespoons margarine or butter
4 oz. (1 cup) shredded mozzarella, Swiss or fontina
cheese
2 cups Homemade Tomato Sauce (see Index)

Heat oven to 400°F. Generously butter 13x9-inch pan or shallow 3-quart casserole. In medium saucepan, bring water and 2 tablespoons margarine to a boil. Remove saucepan from heat. Stir in milk, egg yolks and potato flakes. Add 1 cup of the flour and nutmeg; stir until stiff dough forms. On lightly floured surface, knead in remaining ½ cup flour until no longer sticky.

Divide potato mixture into 3 equal parts. Shape each part into a 12-inch long rope. Cut each rope into eight 1½-inch pieces; flatten slightly. Make indention with thumb in center of each piece. Arrange in prepared pan. Melt 2 tablespoons margarine; drizzle over dumplings. Bake at 400°F. for 15 to 20 minutes or until dumplings are firm. Remove from oven; sprinkle with shredded cheese. Return to oven for 1 to 2 minutes until cheese is melted or broil about 4 inches from heat until bubbly and light golden brown. Serve hot accompanied with Homemade Tomato Sauce. **4 servings.**

NUTRIENTS PER ¼ OF RECIPE

Calories	550	Dietary Fiber	8 g
Protein	12 g	Sodium	435 mg
Carbohydrate	56 g	Potassium	660 mg
Fat	31 g	Calcium	30% U.S. RDA
Cholesterol	150 mg	Iron	20% U.S. RDA

Spätzle

1½	cups all purpose flour
¼	teaspoon salt
	Dash nutmeg, if desired
2	eggs, slightly beaten
½ to ¾	cup milk
8	cups water
¼	teaspoon salt

In large bowl, combine flour, ¼ teaspoon salt and nutmeg. By hand, beat eggs into flour mixture. Gradually add milk, stirring constantly until mixture forms a smooth, soft, moist dough. If dough is too thick, add additional milk 1 tablespoon at a time; dough should easily flow through holes in colander when pressed with spoon.

In large saucepan, bring water and remaining ¼ teaspoon salt to a boil. Press spätzle dough, a small amount at a time, through colander with large holes (not slits) or spätzle maker or drop by ¼ teaspoonfuls into boiling salted water. After water returns to a boil, cook uncovered for 5 to 7 minutes or until tender, stirring occasionally. Remove with slotted spoon; drain. Repeat with remaining dough. Use as desired in soups, stews, vegetables or buttered as a side dish. **2⅓ cups.**

TIP: Spätzle can be prepared a day ahead. Cool; cover and refrigerate until ready to use.

NUTRIENTS PER ⅓ CUP

Calories	130	Dietary Fiber	1 g
Protein	6 g	Sodium	185 mg
Carbohydrate	22 g	Potassium	85 mg
Fat	2 g	Calcium	4% U.S. RDA
Cholesterol	80 mg	Iron	6% U.S. RDA

Rice

In this country, rice comes to the table mainly as a side dish or combined with other ingredients. It is valued for its flavor and texture, which team well with a wide variety of accompaniments and seasonings. Rice is also valued for its nutrients, relatively low cost, ease of preparation and lengthy shelf life.

Nutritionally, rice is a valuable source of complex carbohydrates, protein and nutrients. It contains only a trace amount of fat, is low in sodium and supplies B vitamins and iron. Brown rice offers vitamin E and fiber. To retain vitamins, do not rinse rice, unless specified on package, before or after cooking, and use only the amount of water that will be absorbed during cooking.

Types of Rice

Shoppers are offered a wide selection of rice products from dry to frozen; plain or combined with other ingredients.

• **Regular White Rice** has been milled to remove the hull and entire bran coating. Almost all commercially available white rice has been enriched to restore the nutrients lost in processing. Regular rice comes in long, medium and short grains. Shorter-grained rice tends to be softer, stickier and more moist. Long-grain rice is the best for all-purpose use.

• **Parboiled or Converted Rice** has been specially treated before milling, to enable it to retain much of the natural vitamin and mineral content. It takes slightly longer to cook than regular rice.

• **Precooked or Quick-Cooking Rice** has been cooked and then commercially dried. Cooking time is short and preparation easy.

• **Brown Rice** has had only the outer hull removed, leaving the brown bran layer surrounding the rice. It has a firmer texture, more nutlike flavor and takes longer to cook than regular white rice.

• **Wild Rice** is really a grain but is usually prepared and served like rice or mixed with rice. Wild rice needs a longer cooking time.

• Other grains prepared and served in ways similar to rice and even at times in combination with rice include grits, barley, cracked wheat, bulgur and couscous.

Storing Rice

Store dry, uncooked rice in a cool, dry place tightly sealed in its package or other covered container. Use before expiration date marked on package. Cooked rice can be stored, covered, in the refrigerator up to a week or frozen up to 8 months.

Basic Rice Recipe

Rice (1 cup uncooked)	Water	Salt	Simmering Time	Yield
Regular White Rice	2 cups	1 teaspoon	14 minutes	3 cups
Brown Rice	2½ cups	1 teaspoon	30 to 40 minutes	3 cups
Wild Rice	2½ cups	1 teaspoon	40 to 50 minutes	3 cups
Parboiled Rice	Follow package directions			3 to 4 cups
Precooked Rice	Follow package directions			2 cups

To Cook Rice

• In medium saucepan, combine rice, salt and water. Bring to a boil, stirring occasionally. Cover tightly; reduce heat and simmer according to Basic Rice Recipe.

• Remove from heat and fluff with fork; cover and let stand 5 minutes.

• Lifting the lid during cooking and overcooking can cause gummy, unattractive results.

• If possible, follow package directions for specifics about cooking each type of rice. One type of rice may be substituted for another, but adjustments must be made in the amount of liquid and the cooking time.

Reheating Rice

To reheat, place in saucepan with 2 to 3 tablespoons water (thaw first if frozen). Simmer uncovered until heated through, about 5 to 10 minutes. To reheat in oven, place in covered casserole with 2 to 3 tablespoons water at 350°F. for 20 to 25 minutes. For microwave reheating, cover and cook on HIGH, allowing about 1 minute per cup.

Brown and Wild Rice Bake

- ½ cup uncooked wild rice
- 1 cup uncooked brown rice
- ¼ teaspoon thyme leaves
- ¼ teaspoon sage
- ¼ teaspoon pepper
- 1 cup dry white wine
- ¼ cup margarine or butter
- 2 (10¾-oz.) cans condensed chicken broth

4.5-oz. jar sliced mushrooms, undrained

Heat oven to 350°F. Wash and drain wild rice. In ungreased 2-quart casserole, combine all ingredients. Cover; bake at 350°F. for 1 hour. Remove cover; bake an additional 45 to 60 minutes or until rice is tender and liquid is absorbed. **12 servings.**

NUTRIENTS PER ¹⁄₁₂ OF RECIPE

Calories	140	Dietary Fiber .... 1 g
Protein	4 g	Sodium .... 400 mg
Carbohydrate	19 g	Potassium .... 80 mg
Fat	4 g	Calcium .... <2% U.S. RDA
Cholesterol	0 mg	Iron .... 6% U.S. RDA

Golden Rice

½ cup thinly sliced green onions
½ cup (1 medium) shredded carrot
2 tablespoons margarine or butter
1 cup orange or apple juice
1 cup water
1 cup uncooked regular long grain rice
½ cup golden raisins
1 tablespoon brown sugar
½ teaspoon salt
½ teaspoon curry powder
¼ teaspoon cinnamon
¼ teaspoon ginger
½ cup chopped peanuts, almonds or cashews

In medium saucepan, saute onions and carrot in margarine until crisp-tender. Stir in orange juice, water and remaining ingredients except peanuts; heat to boiling. Reduce heat; cover and simmer until rice is tender and liquid is absorbed, 20 to 30 minutes. Stir in peanuts just before serving. Garnish with additional green onions and peanuts, if desired. **4 servings.**

NUTRIENTS PER ¼ OF RECIPE

Calories	330	Dietary Fiber	7 g
Protein	7 g	Sodium	540 mg
Carbohydrate	43 g	Potassium	490 mg
Fat	15 g	Calcium	4% U.S. RDA
Cholesterol	0 mg	Iron	10% U.S. RDA

Cracked Wheat-Rice Pilaf

¼ cup margarine or butter
½ cup chopped celery
½ cup chopped onion
3 cups water

  3   chicken-flavor bouillon cubes or 3 teaspoons
       chicken-flavor instant bouillon
¾   cup cracked wheat or bulgur
¾   cup uncooked regular long grain rice
  2   tablespoons chopped fresh parsley

Heat oven to 350°F. In large skillet, melt margarine. Add
celery and onion; cook until tender. Stir in water and bouillon; heat until bouillon is dissolved. Add remaining ingredients; mix well. Pour into ungreased 2-quart casserole; cover.
Bake at 350°F. for 50 to 60 minutes or until wheat and rice
are tender. **10 servings.**

MICROWAVE DIRECTIONS: In 2-quart microwave-
safe bowl or casserole, combine margarine, celery, onion,
wheat and rice. Microwave on HIGH for 5 minutes, stirring
once halfway through cooking. Add water, bouillon and
parsley; blend well. Cover with waxed paper. Microwave on
HIGH for 16 to 22 minutes or until wheat and rice are tender, stirring once halfway through cooking.

NUTRIENTS PER ⅒ OF RECIPE

Calories	140	Dietary Fiber	<1 g
Protein	3 g	Sodium	350 mg
Carbohydrate	22 g	Potassium	95 mg
Fat	5 g	Calcium	<2% U.S. RDA
Cholesterol	0 mg	Iron	6% U.S. RDA

Cashew-Rice Pilaf

¼   cup margarine or butter
⅓   cup finely chopped onion
  1   cup uncooked regular long grain rice
  2   cups chicken broth
½ to 1   teaspoon salt
½   cup cashews, coarsely chopped
¼   cup chopped fresh parsley

In large saucepan, melt margarine. Saute onion until soft. Add rice; stir until coated. Stir in broth and salt. Cover; simmer 25 to 30 minutes or until rice is tender and liquid is absorbed. Stir in cashews and parsley. **6 servings.**

NUTRIENTS PER ¼ OF RECIPE

Calories	260	Dietary Fiber	2 g
Protein	6 g	Sodium	710 mg
Carbohydrate	29 g	Potassium	185 mg
Fat	14 g	Calcium	2% U.S. RDA
Cholesterol	0 mg	Iron	8% U.S. RDA

Rice and Vegetable Stir-Fry

  2 tablespoons oil
  4 eggs, beaten
  1 cup frozen broccoli cuts
  ½ cup coarsely chopped onion
  ⅓ cup coarsely chopped green pepper
  2 celery stalks, cut diagonally into ¼-inch slices
     (1 cup)
  1 tablespoon water
  1 cup frozen corn
  1 tablespoon chopped pimiento
  ½ teaspoon salt
  ½ teaspoon garlic powder
  ½ teaspoon oregano leaves
  2 cups cooked rice

In small skillet, heat 1 tablespoon of the oil over medium heat; add beaten eggs. Cook eggs until hard without stirring, gently lifting edges to allow uncooked egg to flow to bottom of skillet; cut into chunks. Set aside.

Heat large skillet or wok over medium-high heat until hot. Add remaining 1 tablespoon oil; heat until it ripples. Add broccoli, onion, green pepper and celery; stir-fry 2 minutes. Add water; cover and cook 2 to 3 minutes or until vegetables are crisp-tender. Add corn, pimiento, salt, garlic powder and oregano leaves. Stir-fry about 2 minutes or until most of cooking liquid has evaporated and vegetables are crisp-tender. Add rice and egg chunks. Stir-fry 2 minutes or until thoroughly heated. **4 servings.**

NUTRIENTS PER ¼ OF RECIPE

Calories	310	Dietary Fiber	4 g
Protein	11 g	Sodium	630 mg
Carbohydrate	38 g	Potassium	380 mg
Fat	13 g	Calcium	6% U.S. RDA
Cholesterol	270 mg	Iron	15% U.S. RDA

Fried Pork 'n Rice

3	tablespoons oil
4	eggs
1	tablespoon water
10 oz.	(1½ cups) slivered lean raw pork
1½	cups fresh bean sprouts
¼	teaspoon ginger
3	cups cooked rice
3	tablespoons soy sauce
½	cup sliced green onions

In wok or large skillet, heat 1 tablespoon of the oil. In small bowl, beat eggs with water; cook eggs in hot oil, stirring constantly to scramble. Remove eggs from wok; chop into small pieces. Set aside. Add remaining 2 tablespoons oil to wok; fry pork. Add bean sprouts and ginger. When thoroughly heated, add rice. Return eggs to rice mixture and toss constantly while adding soy sauce. Cook until thoroughly heated, stirring occasionally. Scatter green onions over top. Serve immediately. **6 servings.**

NUTRIENTS PER ⅙ OF RECIPE

Calories 330	Dietary Fiber...........................2 g
Protein....................................18 g	Sodium............................1010 mg
Carbohydrate........................28 g	Potassium.........................180 mg
Fat ....16 g	Calcium................4% U.S. RDA
Cholesterol.....................230 mg	Iron......................20% U.S. RDA

Zesty Onion Couscous

    2   tablespoons margarine or butter
    ½   cup chopped carrot
    ½   cup sliced green onions
    1½ cups water
    1   teaspoon chicken-flavor instant bouillon
    ½   teaspoon sugar
    ⅛   teaspoon cayenne pepper
    1   cup uncooked couscous
    ¼   cup chopped fresh parsley

In medium skillet, melt margarine over medium-high heat.
Saute carrot and onions until tender. Stir in water, bouillon,
sugar and cayenne pepper. Bring to a boil; remove from
heat. Stir in couscous. Cover; let stand 5 minutes. Stir in
parsley. **8 servings.**

MICROWAVE DIRECTIONS: In 1½-quart microwave-
safe casserole, place margarine. Microwave on HIGH for 30
to 45 seconds or until melted. Stir in carrot and onions.
Cover tightly. Microwave on HIGH for 2 to 2½ minutes or
until vegetables are crisp-tender. Stir in water, bouillon,
sugar and cayenne pepper. Microwave on HIGH for 3½ to
4½ minutes or until boiling. Stir in couscous. Cover; let
stand 5 minutes. Stir in parsley.

NUTRIENTS PER ⅛ OF RECIPE

Calories 80	Dietary Fiber...........................2 g
Protein......................................2 g	Sodium...............................85 mg
Carbohydrate..........................10 g	Potassium...........................70 mg
Fat ....3 g	Calcium...............<2% U.S. RDA
Cholesterol..........................0 mg	Iron........................2% U.S. RDA

Vegetable Confetti Rice

    2 cups water
    1 tablespoon margarine or butter
    1 chicken-flavor bouillon cube
    ¾ cup uncooked regular long grain rice
    ½ cup coarsely grated carrot
    ½ cup sliced celery
    1 tablespoon finely chopped onion
    ½ cup frozen peas, thawed

In medium saucepan, heat water, margarine and bouillon cube to boiling. Stir to dissolve bouillon cube. Add rice, carrot, celery and onion; mix well. Bring to a boil; cover and simmer 20 minutes or until rice is tender and liquid is absorbed. Add peas; cook an additional 5 minutes. **6 servings.**

NUTRIENTS PER ⅙ OF RECIPE

Calories 120	Dietary Fiber ....2 g
Protein ....2 g	Sodium ....215 mg
Carbohydrate ....22 g	Potassium ....110 mg
Fat ....2 g	Calcium...............<2% U.S. RDA
Cholesterol ....0 mg	Iron.......................6% U.S. RDA

Grits 'n Cheese

       1 cup quick grits
       4 cups milk
       ¾ cup margarine or butter
    6 oz. (1½ cups) shredded Swiss cheese
    2 oz. (½ cup) grated Parmesan cheese

Heat oven to 350°F. Lightly grease 12x8-inch (2-quart) baking dish. Cook grits *in milk* following package directions. Remove from heat; add ½ cup of the margarine. With electric mixer, beat 5 minutes at medium speed. Pour half of grits mixture into prepared baking dish. Top with half of the Swiss cheese. Repeat, using remaining grits mixture and

Swiss cheese. Dot with remaining ¼ cup margarine; sprinkle with Parmesan cheese. Bake at 350°F. for 50 to 55 minutes or until golden brown. **10 servings.**

NUTRIENTS PER ⅒ OF RECIPE

Calories	320	Dietary Fiber	0 g
Protein	11 g	Sodium	455 mg
Carbohydrate	18 g	Potassium	180 mg
Fat	23 g	Calcium	35% U.S. RDA
Cholesterol	25 mg	Iron	2% U.S. RDA

Fish & Shellfish

Fish & Shellfish

Seafood, which includes both fish and shellfish, is enjoying a historic surge in popularity for a variety of tasty, healthful and practical reasons. Refrigerated air transportation has made a wide selection of fresh seafood from all over the world readily available. Most types are quick and easy to prepare in a multitude of ways. And they are congenial with a host of marinades, sauces, side dishes and other accompaniments. Fish refers to both freshwater and saltwater varieties, and shellfish includes such popular choices as shrimp, crabs, lobsters, scallops, clams and oysters.

Although the nutritive value of fish and shellfish varies according to variety and origin, they are all good choices for lighter eating. Both are excellent sources of easily digestible protein and are rich in numerous vitamins and minerals, especially B vitamins, potassium and iodine. Shellfish in particular provide calcium, phosphorus and magnesium. Fat content will vary according to type and the season of the year, but all fish and shellfish are relatively low in calories. Even "fat fish" contain less fat than most meats, and most of the fat is unsaturated.

Storing Fish & Shellfish

Seafood of all types is highly perishable and can quickly lose quality. Wrap fresh fish or shellfish loosely in plastic wrap, place in coldest area of refrigerator and use within twenty-four hours of purchasing. If you do not plan to cook fish immediately, wrap securely in aluminum foil or freezer paper and freeze. Properly wrapped lean fish freezes well and keeps up to six months at 0°F. or lower. Fish with high fat content should be frozen no longer than three months to retain optimum flavor and texture. Seafood purchased frozen can be stored in the original wrappings. Frozen seafood should remain solidly frozen until thawing. Thaw in the refrigerator or place under cold running water. Room-temperature thawing is unsafe and can produce a mushy texture. Once thawed, it must be used immediately and never refrozen unless cooked first. Cooked seafood, securely wrapped, can be refrigerated for two to three days.

Purchasing Fish

Fish can be purchased fresh, frozen, canned or smoked.

- **Fresh or Frozen Market Forms:**

  - **Whole or round,** correctly speaking, refers to the fish simply as it comes from the water. However, most recipes that use whole fish actually mean whole dressed fish.
  - **Drawn** indicates a whole fish minus internal organs.
  - **Dressed or pan-dressed** refers to fish that has been eviscerated and scaled if necessary. Often the head, tail and fins are removed. This form is ready to cook.
  - **Fillets** refer to the sides of the fish removed from the backbone in lengthwise cuts. They are boneless and may have skin on one side.
  - **Steaks** are cross-section slices of large dressed fish and may have a section of the backbone still remaining.

- **Selection:** When buying fresh fish, look for fresh and mild odor, flesh that is firm and elastic, bright, clear and bulging eyes if head remains, reddish gills and scales with a high sheen. Avoid products that appear dull with cloudy, sunken eyes, dry spots or strong "fishy" odor. If the fish looks as if it could be alive, it is probably as fresh-tasting as it looks.

When buying frozen fish, make sure the package is tightly sealed and solidly frozen. Contents should have little or no odor and no discoloration or ice crystals.

When buying canned fish, consult the label for helpful purchasing information like quantity, type of fish or seafood, place of origin, style—whole, chunks or flakes—and whether packed in oil or water.

• How Much to Buy

This depends on the weight of fish, size of appetites and number of other dishes to be served. Use the following guidelines:

- Whole or Drawn Fish—Allow 1 lb. per serving.
- Dressed or Pan-dressed Fish—Allow ½ lb. per serving.
- Steaks or Fillets—Allow ⅓ to ½ lb. per serving.

Preparing Fish

The best method for cooking a particular type of fish depends on its fat content. Fish are generally classified as fat or lean. Fat fish contain more than 5% fat; lean, less than 5%. Fat fish are preferred for baking, broiling and grilling as their natural oils help keep them moist as they cook. Lean fish requires preparation methods that retain moisture, such as steaming, poaching and microwaving. Lean fish can be baked or broiled if basted frequently or cooked with a sauce. Both lean and fat fish are suitable for frying. Knowing the fat classification of a fish is helpful in selecting appropriate substitutions, or a type where the recipe does not specify a particular fish.

Cooking must be timed carefully to avoid a dry texture and strong flavor. Fish is by nature tender, as there are no tough connective tissues to be tenderized by long, slow cooking. Follow recipe instructions for testing fish for doneness. Generally, if flesh flakes or slides apart along natural divisions when tines of fork are inserted, and looks milky white or opaque in the thickest portion, it is ready to eat. If flesh resists flaking and is translucent or gray-white in color, additional cooking is required.

Fish Fillets Primavera

    2 tablespoons margarine or butter
    4 (4 to 5-oz.) orange roughy fish fillets*
    2 tablespoons lemon juice
       Dash salt and pepper
    1 garlic clove, minced
    ¼ cup oil
 1½ cups fresh broccoli florets
    1 cup fresh cauliflower florets
    1 cup julienne-cut carrots
    1 cup sliced fresh mushrooms or 2.5-oz. jar sliced
       mushrooms, drained
    ½ cup diagonally sliced celery
    ¼ teaspoon salt
    ¼ teaspoon basil leaves
    ¼ cup grated Parmesan cheese

Heat oven to 450°F. Melt margarine in 13x9-inch (3-quart) baking dish. Place fish in melted margarine; turn to coat. Sprinkle with lemon juice, salt and pepper. Bake at 450°F. for 5 minutes.

Meanwhile, in large skillet saute garlic in oil over high heat. Add remaining ingredients except Parmesan cheese; toss to coat with oil. Stir-fry until vegetables are crisp-tender, about 2 to 3 minutes. Spoon hot vegetables evenly over top of each fish fillet; sprinkle with Parmesan cheese. Return to oven and bake an additional 3 to 5 minutes or until fish flakes easily with fork. **4 servings.**

TIP: *Any white-fleshed, mild-flavored fish such as haddock, sole or white fish can be substituted for orange roughy.

NUTRIENTS PER ¼ OF RECIPE

Calories	360	Dietary Fiber	3 g
Protein	30 g	Sodium	510 mg
Carbohydrate	10 g	Potassium	970 mg
Fat	23 g	Calcium	20% U.S. RDA
Cholesterol	70 mg	Iron	10% U.S. RDA

Fish Creole

 1   lb. fish fillets
 1   tablespoon margarine or butter
⅓   cup chopped onion
¼   cup chopped celery
 2   tablespoons finely chopped green pepper
 1   tablespoon sugar
¼   teaspoon oregano leaves
⅛   teaspoon pepper
8-oz. can (1-cup) stewed tomatoes, cut into pieces

Heat oven to 350°F. Arrange fish fillets in ungreased 12x8-inch or 8-inch square (2-quart) baking dish. In medium skillet, melt margarine; saute onion, celery and green pepper until tender. Stir in remaining ingredients. Spoon over fish. Bake at 350°F. for 15 to 20 minutes or until fish flakes easily with fork. **4 servings.**

MICROWAVE DIRECTIONS: In 12x8-inch (2-quart) microwave-safe dish, microwave margarine on HIGH for 30 to 40 seconds or until melted. Stir in onion, celery, and green pepper. Microwave on HIGH for 3 to 4 minutes or until tender, stirring every minute. Add sugar, oregano leaves, pepper and stewed tomatoes; blend well. Arrange fish fillets in dish, placing thickest pieces on outside edge of dish. Spoon sauce over fish. Microwave on HIGH for 7 to 9 minutes or until fish flakes easily with fork, rearranging fish once halfway through cooking.

NUTRIENTS PER ¼ OF RECIPE

Calories 150	Dietary Fiber.........................<1 g
Protein.....................................21 g	Sodium ....200 mg
Carbohydrate...........................7 g	Potassium.........................620 mg
Fat ....3 g	Calcium.................2% U.S. RDA
Cholesterol ....50 mg	Iron.......................4% U.S. RDA

Microwave Fish Amandine

¼ cup margarine or butter
1 lb. fish fillets
¼ cup slivered or sliced almonds
2 tablespoons dry white wine or sherry, if desired
2 teaspoons lemon juice
   Salt and pepper

Place margarine in 1½-quart shallow microwave-safe dish. Microwave on HIGH for 1 minute or until melted. Arrange fish in dish with thickest parts to outside; cover with microwave-safe plastic wrap. Microwave for 6 to 8 minutes or until fish flakes easily with fork, rotating dish ½ turn halfway through cooking. Remove fish to serving platter. Add almonds, wine and lemon juice to pan drippings. Microwave on HIGH for 1 minute or until thoroughly heated; pour over fish. Salt and pepper to taste. **4 servings.**

NUTRIENTS PER ¼ OF RECIPE

Calories	230	Dietary Fiber	<1 g
Protein	19 g	Sodium	470 mg
Carbohydrate	2 g	Potassium	450 mg
Fat	15 g	Calcium	2% U.S. RDA
Cholesterol	50 mg	Iron	4% U.S. RDA

Favorite Fish Fillets

1½ lb. fresh or frozen fish fillets, about ½-inch thick, thawed*
6 slices bacon, crisply cooked
6 oz. (1 cup) fresh or frozen peeled, cooked shrimp, thawed
3 tablespoons margarine or butter, melted
1 tablespoon lemon juice
1½ teaspoons Worcestershire sauce
½ teaspoon prepared mustard
6 tomato slices

3 oz. (3 slices) American cheese, cut into 6 strips each,
or ½ cup shredded American cheese
2 teaspoons chopped chives or fresh parsley

Heat oven to 350°F. Arrange fillets in single layer (skin side
down, if necessary) in 12x8-inch (2-quart) baking dish. Place
cooked bacon on fillets; top evenly with shrimp. In small
bowl, combine margarine, lemon juice, Worcestershire sauce
and mustard. Spoon half of sauce mixture over fillets. Bake
at 350°F. for 10 to 15 minutes. Arrange tomato and cheese
strips over fillets. Spoon remaining sauce mixture over fillets; continue baking 10 to 15 minutes or until cheese melts
and fish flakes easily with fork. Sprinkle with chopped
chives. **6 servings.**

MICROWAVE DIRECTIONS: Arrange fillets in single
layer (skin side down, if necessary) in 12x8-inch (2-quart)
microwave-safe baking dish. Place cooked bacon on fillets;
top evenly with shrimp. In glass measuring cup, microwave
unmelted margarine on HIGH for 30 to 45 seconds or until
melted. Stir in lemon juice, Worcestershire sauce and mustard. Spoon half of sauce mixture over fillets. Arrange
tomato and cheese slices over fillets. Spoon remaining sauce
mixture over fillets. Cover with microwave-safe plastic
wrap. Microwave on HIGH for 5 to 7 minutes or until
cheese melts and fish flakes easily with fork. Let stand covered 2 minutes before serving. Sprinkle with chives.

TIP: *Fillets of grouper, haddock, lemon sole, pike, red
snapper, sea bass, scrod or other lean fish, ½-inch thick, can
be used for this recipe.

NUTRIENTS PER ¼ OF RECIPE

Calories	300	Dietary Fiber	<1 g
Protein	34 g	Sodium	530 mg
Carbohydrate	1 g	Potassium	980 mg
Fat	17 g	Calcium	15% U.S. RDA
Cholesterol	100 mg	Iron	8% U.S. RDA

Orange Roughy with Dill

     3 tablespoons butter or margarine
     1 lb. orange roughy fish fillets
    ½ teaspoon dill weed
       Dash salt and pepper
  1½ teaspoons butter or margarine
     2 tablespoons dry bread crumbs

Heat oven to 350°F. In 12x8-inch or 8-inch square (2-quart) baking dish, melt 3 tablespoons butter in oven. Place fish fillets in baking dish; turn to coat with melted butter. Sprinkle with dill weed, salt and pepper. Bake at 350°F. for 15 to 20 minutes or until fish flakes easily with fork.

Meanwhile, in small skillet or saucepan over medium heat, melt 1½ teaspoons butter. Add bread crumbs; cook, stirring constantly, until crumbs are light golden brown. Sprinkle over fish during last 3 minutes of baking time. **4 servings.**

MICROWAVE DIRECTIONS: To prepare bread crumbs, in small microwave-safe bowl, microwave 1½ teaspoons butter on HIGH for 30 seconds or until melted. Stir in bread crumbs and *¼ teaspoon paprika.* Microwave on HIGH for 45 to 60 seconds or until mixture is crumbly, stirring twice during cooking.

In 12x8-inch (2-quart) microwave-safe dish, microwave 3 tablespoons butter on HIGH for 40 to 50 seconds or until melted. Place fish fillets in baking dish; turn to coat with melted butter. Sprinkle with dill weed, salt and pepper; cover with microwave-safe plastic wrap. Microwave on HIGH for 7 to 9 minutes or until fish flakes easily with fork. Remove cover; sprinkle with bread crumbs. Microwave on HIGH for 1 minute or until thoroughly heated.

NUTRIENTS PER ¼ OF RECIPE

Calories	190	Dietary Fiber	<1 g
Protein	20 g	Sodium	250 mg
Carbohydrate	2 g	Potassium	450 mg
Fat	10 g	Calcium	2% U.S. RDA
Cholesterol	80 mg	Iron	2% U.S. RDA

Salmon-Filled Flounder

4 medium or 8 small flounder or sole fillets (about 1 to 1½ lb.)
½ teaspoon salt
¼ teaspoon pepper
1 tablespoon chopped fresh dill or tarragon
1 tablespoon thinly sliced green onions
1 tablespoon chopped fresh parsley
1 tablespoon lemon juice
7½-oz. can salmon, drained, flaked

SAUCE
½ cup dairy sour cream
½ cup finely chopped cucumber
1 tablespoon chopped fresh parsley
1 teaspoon chopped fresh dill or tarragon
1 teaspoon lemon juice

Heat over to 400°F. Sprinkle fillets with salt and pepper. Turn fillets skin side up; place on waxed paper. In small bowl, combine 1 tablespoon each dill, green onions, parsley and lemon juice with salmon; mix well. Place spoonful of salmon filling evenly on each fillet; roll up firmly with filling inside. Place seam side down in ungreased 8-inch (2-quart) square baking dish; cover with foil. Bake at 400°F. for 10 minutes. Remove foil. Return to oven; bake 5 to 10 minutes longer or until fish flakes easily with fork. Serve fish immediately or refrigerate until thoroughly chilled.

Meanwhile in small bowl, combine all sauce ingredients. Refrigerate until serving time. To serve, top each portion with spoonful of sauce. (Fish portions can be cut in half to serve 1½ roll-ups per person. When chilled, fish is firm enough to cut into slices.) **4 to 6 servings.**

MICROWAVE DIRECTIONS: Prepare fillets as directed above. Place prepared fillets in 8-inch (2-quart) square microwave-safe dish; cover with microwave-safe plastic wrap. Microwave on HIGH for 7 to 9½ minutes or until fish flakes easily with fork, rotating dish ½ turn halfway through cooking. Drain off liquid. Continue as directed above.

NUTRIENTS PER ¼ OF RECIPE

Calories 250	Dietary Fiber.........................<1 g
Protein.......................................30 g	Sodium..............................520 mg
Carbohydrate............................2 g	Potassium.........................630 mg
Fat...13 g	Calcium...............15% U.S. RDA
Cholesterol.........................70 mg	Iron.....................10% U.S. RDA

Mushroom-Lemon Fillets

         2 tablespoons margarine or butter
    1½ cups sliced fresh mushrooms
         2 green onions, chopped
         2 tablespoons flour
         2 teaspoons chopped fresh parsley
      ½ teaspoon salt
           Dash pepper
      ½ cup milk
      ½ teaspoon grated lemon peel
         1 lb. fish fillets

Heat oven to 350°F. Lightly grease 12x8-inch or 8-inch square (2-quart) baking dish. In large skillet, melt margarine; saute mushrooms and onions until tender. Reduce heat to low. Stir in flour, parsley, salt and pepper. Cook 1 minute, stirring constantly, until smooth and bubbly.

Gradually stir in milk. Cook over medium heat, stirring constantly, until thickened and bubbly. Stir in lemon peel.

Place fish fillets in baking dish. Spoon sauce over fish. Bake at 350°F. for 15 to 20 minutes or until fish flakes easily with fork. **4 servings.**

MICROWAVE DIRECTIONS: Lightly grease 12x8-inch (2-quart) microwave-safe dish. In 4-cup microwave-safe measuring cup, microwave margarine on HIGH for 30 to 40 seconds or until melted. Stir in mushrooms and green onions. Microwave on HIGH for 2½ to 3½ minutes or until tender, stirring once every minute. Stir in flour, parsley, salt, pepper, milk and lemon peel, blending well. Microwave on HIGH for 2 to 3 minutes or until thickened, stirring once every minute. Place fish fillets in prepared dish; cover with microwave-safe plastic wrap. Microwave on HIGH for 5 minutes. Remove cover; drain well. Spoon sauce over fish. Microwave on HIGH for an additional 1 to 3 minutes or until fish flakes easily with fork.

NUTRIENTS PER ¼ OF RECIPE

Calories	180	Dietary Fiber	<1 g
Protein	22 g	Sodium	430 mg
Carbohydrate	7 g	Potassium	620 mg
Fat	7 g	Calcium	6% U.S. RDA
Cholesterol	50 mg	Iron	4% U.S. RDA

Baked Fish-Stuffed Tomatoes

      4   large tomatoes
      ½   cup sliced fresh mushrooms
      ½   cup chopped water chestnuts, celery or jicama
      2   tablespoons chopped green or red bell pepper
      1   tablespoon margarine or butter
  3-oz.   pkg. cream cheese, softened
1 to 1½   cups cubed, cooked fish*
      ½   cup frozen peas, thawed
           Salt and pepper, if desired

¼ cup soft bread crumbs
2 teaspoons finely chopped fresh parsley
2 teaspoons margarine or butter, melted

Heat oven to 400°F. Cut thin slices from tops of tomatoes; remove pulp. If desired, cut decorative edge on tomatoes. Turn upside down on paper towels to drain while preparing filling. In medium skillet, saute mushrooms, water chestnuts and green pepper in 1 tablespoon margarine until crisptender. Stir in cream cheese; blend well. Gently stir in fish and peas. Season to taste with salt and pepper. Place tomatoes in ungreased 8-inch (2-quart) square baking dish. Spoon fish mixture evenly into tomato shells. In small bowl, combine bread crumbs, parsley and melted margarine. Sprinkle topping over tomatoes. Bake at 400°F. for 5 to 10 minutes or until thoroughly heated. **4 servings.**

MICROWAVE DIRECTIONS: Prepare tomatoes as directed above. In 1-quart microwave-safe casserole, microwave 1 tablespoon margarine on HIGH for 30 to 45 seconds or until melted. Add mushrooms, water chestnuts and green pepper; stir. Microwave on HIGH for 2 to 3 minutes or until peppers are tender. Add cream cheese, fish and peas; stir gently to blend. Season to taste with salt and pepper. Microwave on MEDIUM for 3 to 4 minutes or until thoroughly heated, stirring once halfway through cooking. Place tomatoes on microwave-safe tray or in 8-inch (2-quart) microwave-safe dish. Spoon fish mixture evenly into tomato shells. In small bowl, combine bread crumbs, parsley and melted margarine. Sprinkle topping over tomatoes. Microwave on HIGH for 3 to 4½ minutes or until thoroughly heated.

TIP: *About ½ to ¾ lb. cooked fish fillets from any firm-textured white fish (cod, orange roughy, snapper) or salmon can be used.

NUTRIENTS PER ¼ OF RECIPE

Calories	310	Dietary Fiber	4 g
Protein	21 g	Sodium	260 mg
Carbohydrate	22 g	Potassium	900 mg
Fat	16 g	Calcium	6% U.S. RDA
Cholesterol	70 mg	Iron	15% U.S. RDA

Catch of the Day Croissants

1	tablespoon lemon juice
12-oz.	pkg. frozen cod or fish fillets
3	slices bacon
½	cup sliced fresh mushrooms
1	cup (1 large) chopped tomato, drained
2	tablespoons sliced green onions
¼	cup mayonnaise or salad dressing
¼	cup dairy sour cream
½ to 1	teaspoon dry mustard
	Salt and pepper,if desired
6	large or 9 small whole wheat croissants
	Lettuce leaves
1	avocado, peeled, sliced

Place 1 to 1½ inches of water in large skillet. Bring to a boil; add lemon juice. Place frozen fish fillets in boiling water. Reduce heat; cover and simmer 10 to 12 minutes or until fish flakes easily with fork. Drain; cut fish into bite-size pieces; refrigerate.

In same skillet, cook bacon until crisp. Remove bacon; drain, reserving drippings in skillet. Crumble bacon; set aside. Saute mushrooms in reserved drippings; drain.

In medium bowl, combine fish, bacon, mushrooms, tomato, green onions, mayonnaise, sour cream, dry mustard, salt and pepper. Slice croissants in half lengthwise. Arrange lettuce on bottom half of each croissant; top each with ½ cup fish mixture and avocado slices.* Cover each with top half of croissant. **6 sandwiches.**

TIP: *If using small croissants, use ⅓ cup of fish mixture in each.

NUTRIENTS PER 1 SANDWICH

Calories	390	Dietary Fiber	3 g
Protein	15 g	Sodium	380 mg
Carbohydrate	24 g	Potassium	580 mg
Fat	26 g	Calcium	2% U.S. RDA
Cholesterol	40 mg	Iron	10% U.S. RDA

Oven-Fried Fish

    3 tablespoons margarine or butter
    1 egg, slightly beaten
    1 tablespoon water
    1 tablespoon lemon juice
    ¼ cup all purpose flour
 ½ to 1 teaspoon onion salt
         Dash pepper
 ½ to ¾ cup crushed cereal flakes, crackers or bread
         crumbs
    1 lb. fish fillets

Heat oven to 350°F. In 13x9-inch (3-quart) baking dish, melt margarine in oven. In medium bowl, combine egg, water and lemon juice. In shallow pan, combine flour, onion salt and pepper. Coat fish fillets with flour mixture; dip in egg mixture. Roll in cereal flakes. Place fish in baking dish; turn to coat with melted margarine. Bake at 350°F. for 15 to 20 minutes or until fish flakes easily with fork. **4 servings.**

MICROWAVE DIRECTIONS: In shallow microwave-safe bowl, microwave margarine on HIGH for 45 to 60 seconds or until melted. In medium bowl, combine egg, water and lemon juice. In shallow pan, combine flour, onion salt, pepper and ½ *teaspoon paprika*. Coat fish fillets with flour mixture; dip in egg mixture. Roll in cereal flakes. Dip in melted margarine. Place fish on microwave-safe roasting or bacon rack. Microwave on HIGH for 6½ to 8 minutes or until fish flakes easily with fork.

NUTRIENTS PER ¼ OF RECIPE

Calories	260	Dietary Fiber	<1 g
Protein	23 g	Sodium	730 mg
Carbohydrate	16 g	Potassium	480 mg
Fat	10 g	Calcium	2% U.S. RDA
Cholesterol	120 mg	Iron	10% U.S. RDA

Batter-Fried Fish

```
 1  lb. fish fillets*
    Oil for frying
½  cup milk
 1  egg
½  cup all purpose flour
½  teaspoon salt
    Dash hot pepper sauce
```

Cut fish into serving size pieces. Heat 1 to 1½ inches oil in skillet or saucepan to 375°F. In small bowl, beat milk and egg. Add flour, salt and hot pepper sauce; beat until smooth. Dip fish in batter, draining off excess. Fry at 375°F. for 3 to 4 minutes or until golden brown and fish flakes easily with fork. Drain on paper towels. Serve with tartar sauce. **4 servings.**

TIP: *Fish may be fresh or frozen. If frozen, thaw and drain before frying.

NUTRIENTS PER ¼ OF RECIPE

Calories	230	Dietary Fiber	<1 g
Protein	22 g	Sodium	360 mg
Carbohydrate	13 g	Potassium	460 mg
Fat	9 g	Calcium	6% U.S. RDA
Cholesterol	120 mg	Iron	8% U.S. RDA

Pan-Fried Trout

  1 egg
 ⅓ cup all purpose flour
  2 tablespoons grated lemon peel
  2 teaspoons dill weed
 ½ teaspoon salt
 ¼ teaspoon pepper
  4 (8-oz.) brook or rainbow trout, dressed
  2 tablespoons margarine or butter
  3 tablespoons oil
  1 tablespoon lemon juice

In pie pan, beat egg. On waxed paper, combine flour, lemon peel, dill weed, salt and pepper. Dip trout in egg; coat with flour mixture.

In large skillet, heat margarine, oil and lemon juice. Add trout. Fry over medium-high heat for 10 to 12 minutes, turning once, or until fish flakes easily with fork. **4 servings.**

NUTRIENTS PER ¼ OF RECIPE

Calories	400	Dietary Fiber	<1 g
Protein	41 g	Sodium	350 mg
Carbohydrate	9 g	Potassium	55 mg
Fat	22 g	Calcium	2% U.S. RDA
Cholesterol	180 mg	Iron	6% U.S. RDA

Pan-Fried Fish

     1 egg, slightly beaten
    ¼ cup milk
 2-lb. dressed fish or 1 lb. fish fillets
    ½ cup all purpose flour, cornmeal or buttermilk
        pancake and waffle mix
    ¼ cup oil or shortening
        Salt and pepper

In small bowl, combine egg and milk. Dip fish in egg mixture; coat with flour. In large skillet, fry in hot oil over medium-high heat about 5 to 7 minutes or until golden brown and fish flakes easily with fork, turning fish only once. Salt and pepper to taste. **3 to 4 servings.**

NUTRIENTS PER ¼ OF RECIPE

Calories	375	Dietary Fiber	<1 g
Protein	24 g	Sodium	216 mg
Carbohydrate	13 g	Potassium	373 mg
Fat	25 g	Calcium	3% U.S. RDA
Cholesterol	150 mg	Iron	7% U.S. RDA

Poached Fish

2 lb. dressed whole fish or fish fillets
1 tablespoon salt
4 peppercorns
2 stalks celery, cut into pieces
2 carrots, cut into pieces
2 slices lemon
2 bay leaves
1 medium onion, sliced
1 quart (4 cups) water

Wrap fish in cheesecloth for ease in transferring fish after cooking. In large skillet, combine all ingredients except fish. Heat to boiling; simmer covered about 10 minutes. Carefully place fish in liquid; simmer covered about 20 minutes or until fish flakes easily with fork. If liquid does not cover fish, turn fish over after 10 minutes for even cooking. Lift fish from liquid; carefully remove cheesecloth and place on platter. **4 servings.**

TIP: If desired, use ½ cup dry white wine for part of liquid.

NUTRIENTS PER ¼ OF RECIPE

Calories 120	Dietary Fiber ....0 g
Protein ....26 g	Sodium ....120 mg
Carbohydrate ....0 g	Potassium ....530 mg
Fat ....1 g	Calcium ....<2% U.S. RDA
Cholesterol ....80 mg	Iron ....6% U.S. RDA

Broiled Fish Fillets

Cut 2 lb. fish fillets (¼ to ½-inch thick) into serving size pieces. Arrange on broiler pan (if fish has skin, place skin side up); brush both sides of fish with ¼ cup melted margarine or butter. Broil 2 to 3 inches from heat for 5 to 8 minutes or until fish flakes easily with fork, turning fish once and basting with margarine. Salt and pepper to taste. **6 servings.**

VARIATION:

FISH STEAKS (½ to 1-inch thick): Broil 2 to 3 inches from heat for 10 to 12 minutes, turning once, basting with margarine.

NUTRIENTS PER ⅙ OF RECIPE

Calories 170	Dietary Fiber ....0 g
Protein ....24 g	Sodium ....360 mg
Carbohydrate ....0 g	Potassium ....510 mg
Fat ....8 g	Calcium ....<2% U.S. RDA
Cholesterol ....70 mg	Iron ....2% U.S. RDA

Baked Stuffed Fish

2 to 3 lb. dressed whole fish*
        Salt
    2 cups stuffing (see Bread Stuffing for Fish)
    2 tablespoons margarine or butter, melted

Heat oven to 400°F. Lightly sprinkle inside of fish with salt. Fill cavity with stuffing; secure edges of fish together with skewers or toothpicks. Place in greased shallow baking pan; brush with melted margarine. Bake at 400°F. for 45 minutes or until fish flakes easily with fork, basting occasionally with margarine.** Remove skewers before serving. To serve, cut sections by slicing through backbone and spoon out dressing. **6 servings.**

TIPS: *Smaller fish can also be stuffed. Allow ½ cup stuffing per 12 to 16-oz. fish.

**If desired, omit basting. Top fish with uncooked bacon slices; or pour 1 cup half-and-half or evaporated milk over fish before baking.

NUTRIENTS PER ¼ OF RECIPE

Calories	270	Dietary Fiber	<1 g
Protein	27 g	Sodium	770 mg
Carbohydrate	8 g	Potassium	570 mg
Fat	13 g	Calcium	4% U.S. RDA
Cholesterol	80 mg	Iron	10% U.S. RDA

Baked Whole Fish

Heat oven to 350°F. Grease shallow roasting pan. Rub inside of 2½ to 3-lb. dressed whole fish with salt. Place in prepared pan; brush with about 1 tablespoon margarine. Bake at 350°F. for 40 to 45 minutes or until fish flakes easily with fork, basting occasionally with an additional tablespoon melted margarine. **5 to 6 servings.**

NUTRIENTS PER ¼ OF RECIPE

Calories	160	Dietary Fiber	0 g
Protein	26 g	Sodium	520 mg
Carbohydrate	0 g	Potassium	530 mg
Fat	5 g	Calcium	2% U.S. RDA
Cholesterol	80 mg	Iron	6% U.S. RDA

Bread Stuffing for Fish

¼ cup chopped celery
2 tablespoons chopped onion
¼ cup margarine or butter
2 cups (2 slices) soft bread cubes
¼ teaspoon salt
¼ teaspoon thyme
⅛ teaspoon pepper

In medium skillet, saute celery and onion in margarine until tender. Stir in remaining ingredients. **2 cups stuffing.**

VARIATIONS:

CRAB STUFFING: Add ½ cup cooked crab meat with bread.

DILL STUFFING: Add ¼ cup chopped dill pickle with bread or ¼ teaspoon dill weed.

LEMON STUFFING: Add 2 teaspoons grated lemon peel and 2 tablespoons lemon juice with bread.

MUSHROOM STUFFING: Saute ½ cup sliced fresh mushrooms with onion and celery.

SHRIMP STUFFING: Add ½ cup cooked shrimp with bread.

NUTRIENTS PER ¼ OF RECIPE

Calories	170	Dietary Fiber	<1 g
Protein	2 g	Sodium	390 mg
Carbohydrate	12 g	Potassium	60 mg
Fat	12 g	Calcium	2% U.S. RDA
Cholesterol	0 mg	Iron	4% U.S. RDA

Flounder en Papillote

  2   tablespoons margarine or butter
 ½   cup chopped red bell pepper
 ¼   cup sliced green onions
4.5-oz.   jar sliced mushrooms, drained
  2   tablespoons flour
 ¼   teaspoon salt
 ⅛   teaspoon white pepper
 ⅓   cup lowfat milk
  2   tablespoons white wine or sherry
      Kitchen parchment paper*
  1   lb. flounder, sole or orange roughy fillets

Heat oven to 425°F. In medium saucepan, melt margarine; saute red pepper, onions and mushrooms for 2 minutes. Stir in flour, salt and pepper; cook until mixture is bubbly, stirring constantly. Gradually add milk and wine. Cook until mixture boils and thickens, stirring constantly. Remove from heat.

Cut four 10x12-inch heart-shaped pieces from parchment paper. Divide fish into 4 equal portions; place each portion on left half of a heart-shaped parchment. Spoon sauce over fish. Bring right side of parchment over fish to meet left side of parchment; seal open edges securely with tight double folds. Place on ungreased cookie sheet. Bake at 425°F. for 10 to 12 minutes or until paper begins to turn golden brown. To serve, cut X-shaped slit on top of parchment; tear back to expose fish. **4 servings.**

TIP: *Foil can be substituted for parchment paper. Bake for 10 to 12 minutes or until fish flakes easily with fork.

NUTRIENTS PER ¼ OF RECIPE

Calories	190	Dietary Fiber .... 1 g
Protein .... 21 g		Sodium .... 380 mg
Carbohydrate .... 7 g		Potassium .... 520 mg
Fat .... 7 g		Calcium .... 4% U.S. RDA
Cholesterol .... 50 mg		Iron .... 8% U.S. RDA

Saucy Baked Fillets

1 lb. sole or haddock fish fillets
Salt and pepper
1 small green pepper, cut into strips
1 small onion, sliced
8 tablespoons catsup
1 tablespoon margarine or butter
4 tablespoons grated Parmesan cheese

Heat oven to 350°F. Grease 8-inch (2-quart) square baking dish. Divide fish into 4 portions; place in prepared pan. Sprinkle with salt and pepper. Top each fish portion with green pepper, onion and 2 tablespoons catsup; dot with margarine. Sprinkle each portion with 1 tablespoon Parmesan cheese. Cover with foil; bake at 350°F. for 20 minutes. Remove foil and continue baking an additional 5 minutes or until fish flakes easily with fork. **4 servings.**

NUTRIENTS PER ¼ OF RECIPE

Calories	270	Dietary Fiber	<1 g
Protein	24 g	Sodium	490 mg
Carbohydrate	11 g	Potassium	535 mg
Fat	14 g	Calcium	6% U.S. RDA
Cholesterol	50 mg	Iron	4% U.S. RDA

Savory Marinated Fish

1½ lb. fish fillets
½ cup dry white wine
¼ cup lemon juice
1 garlic clove, minced
½ teaspoon savory or thyme leaves
Lemon, if desired

Arrange fish in single layer in glass baking dish. In small bowl, combine wine, lemon juice, garlic and savory; pour over fish. Cover with plastic wrap; refrigerate 1 to 4 hours, turning occasionally. Place fish on broiler pan, skin side down. Broil 6 inches from heat for 4 to 8 minutes or until fish flakes easily with fork, brushing occasionally with remaining marinade. Garnish with lemon. **4 to 6 servings.**

VARIATIONS:

ITALIAN MARINADE: Combine 1 cup prepared Italian salad dressing, 1 tablespoon lemon juice and ½ teaspoon salt.

LEMON MARINADE: Combine ¼ cup lemon juice, ¼ cup oil, 2 teaspoons chopped onion or minced fresh parsley, 2 teaspoons anchovy paste, 1 teaspoon prepared horseradish and ½ teaspoon basil leaves.

WINE MARINADE: Combine ¼ cup dry white wine, ¼ cup oil, 1 lemon, thinly sliced and 1 tablespoon minced fresh parsley.

NUTRIENTS PER ¼ OF RECIPE

Calories	160	Dietary Fiber	0 g
Protein	19 g	Sodium	50 mg
Carbohydrate	0 g	Potassium	300 mg
Fat	8 g	Calcium	2% U.S. RDA
Cholesterol	50 mg	Iron	2% U.S. RDA

Barbecued Whole Fish

Fill the cavity of a whole dressed fish with about 2 cups favorite stuffing. Fasten edges together with metal skewers or sew opening closed with heavy thread. Brush both sides of fish with melted margarine or butter; place on piece of heavy duty foil. (If grill does not have cover, wrap fish in foil.) Place foil on grill 6 to 8 inches from hot coals. Cover; cook, allowing 15 to 20 minutes per pound of fish, turning several times. Brush occasionally with melted margarine. **Allow about ½ lb. of whole fish per serving.**

NUTRIENTS: Variables in this recipe make it impossible to calculate nutrition information.

Grilled Fillets of Fish

SAUCE

1½	cups chopped tomato
1	avocado, chopped
¼	cup chopped green onions
4-oz.	can diced green chiles, drained
2	tablespoons white wine vinegar
1	tablespoon oil
½	teaspoon salt
1	tablespoon chopped fresh cilantro or parsley, if desired
1½	lb. fresh or frozen cod, pollack, halibut or other firm fish, thawed
1 to 2	tablespoons oil or butter

In medium bowl, combine all ingredients for sauce; mix well. Cover; refrigerate. When ready to barbecue, place fish on oiled grill 4 to 6 inches from medium coals. Brush lightly with 1 tablespoon oil. Cook 12 to 15 minutes or until fish flakes easily with fork, turning once and brushing lightly with remaining oil. To serve, top with sauce. **6 servings**.

BROILER METHOD: Prepare sauce as directed. Brush fish lightly with 1 tablespoon oil. Broil fish 4 to 6 inches from heat for 15 to 18 minutes or until fish flakes easily, turning once and brushing lightly with remaining oil.

NUTRIENTS PER ⅙ OF RECIPE

Calories	220	Dietary Fiber	1 g
Protein	19 g	Sodium	250 mg
Carbohydrate	6 g	Potassium	670 mg
Fat	13 g	Calcium	2% U.S. RDA
Cholesterol	50 mg	Iron	6% U.S. RDA

Sweet and Sour Fish Kabobs

MARINADE
- ½ cup catsup
- ¼ cup sugar
- 3 tablespoons vinegar
- 2 tablespoons pineapple juice
- 2 tablespoons soy sauce

- 1 lb. fresh or frozen red snapper, swordfish or cod, thawed, cut into bite-size pieces (1½ to 2-inch cubes)
- 8-oz. can whole water chestnuts, drained, if desired
- ½ fresh pineapple, cut into 1-inch pieces or 8-oz. can pineapple chunks, drained
- 1 red bell pepper, cut into 1½-inch pieces
- 1 green pepper, cut into 1½-inch pieces

In medium non-metal bowl, combine all marinade ingredients; mix well. Add fish, turning to coat all sides. Cover; refrigerate 30 minutes to 2 hours.

Drain fish, reserving marinade. On metal skewers, arrange fish, water chestnuts, pineapple and peppers. When ready to barbecue, place kabobs on grill 4 to 6 inches from medium-high coals. Brush with marinade; cook 16 to 20 minutes or until fish flakes easily with fork, turning once and brushing frequently with marinade. **4 servings.**

BROILER METHOD: Prepare kabobs as directed above. Broil 4 to 6 inches from heat for 20 to 25 minutes, turning once and brushing frequently with marinade.

NUTRIENTS PER ¼ OF RECIPE

Calories	250	Dietary Fiber	3 g
Protein	23 g	Sodium	960 mg
Carbohydrate	39 g	Potassium	850 mg
Fat	1 g	Calcium	4% U.S. RDA
Cholesterol	60 mg	Iron	10% U.S. RDA

Salmon Loaf

15½-oz. can (2 cups) salmon, undrained
2 eggs
2 cups (2 slices) soft bread cubes or ⅓ cup dry bread crumbs
2 tablespoons finely chopped fresh parsley
¼ teaspoon salt
⅛ teaspoon pepper
1 small onion, chopped
2 tablespoons lemon juice

Heat oven to 350°F. In large bowl, flake salmon, removing bones and skin. With a fork, beat in eggs. Add remaining ingredients; mix well. Place in well-greased 8x4-inch loaf pan or 8-inch square pan forming into loaf shape. Bake at 350°F. for 50 to 60 minutes or until golden brown and knife inserted in center comes out clean. Loosen edges and lift out of pan. To serve, cut into slices. **6 servings.**

TIP: To make ahead, prepare, cover and refrigerate up to 24 hours. Bake as directed.

VARIATIONS:

BAKED SALMON RING: Press mixture in well-greased 5-cup ring mold. Place mold in pan of hot water. Bake for 50 to 60 minutes.

MICROWAVE SALMON RING: Place mixture in 8-inch round microwave-safe baking dish. Move mixture away from center; place microwave-safe glass or custard cup in center to make a ring shape. Microwave on HIGH for 8 to 9 minutes or until mixture is set around glass. Remove glass; invert onto serving plate.

SALMON PATTIES: Form mixture into 8 patties. Dip each patty into dry bread crumbs. Fry patties in oil over low heat until golden brown on both sides, about 10 minutes.

NUTRIENTS PER ⅙ OF RECIPE

Calories	190	Dietary Fiber	<1 g
Protein	18 g	Sodium	550 mg
Carbohydrate	9 g	Potassium	310 mg
Fat	9 g	Calcium	20% U.S. RDA
Cholesterol	120 mg	Iron	10% U.S. RDA

Salmon Quiche

Pastry for one-crust pie (see Index)

FILLING

1	tablespoon margarine or butter
⅓	cup thinly sliced green onions
4	eggs
½	cup half-and-half or milk
¾	teaspoon salt
¼	teaspoon paprika
⅛	teaspoon pepper
15½-oz.	can salmon, drained, flaked, reserving liquid
6 oz.	(1½ cups) shredded Swiss cheese
	Fresh parsley, if desired

Prepare pastry for filled one-crust pie using 9-inch pie pan.*

Heat oven to 375°F. In small skillet, melt margarine; saute onions until crisp-tender. In large bowl, combine eggs and half-and-half; beat until smooth. Add salt, paprika, pepper and onions; mix well. Stir in salmon and all reserved liquid. Sprinkle cheese in bottom of pastry-lined pan. Pour salmon mixture over cheese. Bake at 375°F. for 45 to 50 minutes or until knife inserted in center comes out clean. Let stand 10 minutes before serving. Garnish with fresh parsley. **8 servings.**

TIPS: *Use 9-inch pie pan only.

Cover edge of pie crust with strip of foil during last 10 to 15 minutes of baking if necessary to prevent excessive browning.

NUTRIENTS PER ⅛ OF RECIPE

Calories	470	Dietary Fiber	1 g
Protein	22 g	Sodium	1040 mg
Carbohydrate	25 g	Potassium	305 mg
Fat	31 g	Calcium	35% U.S. RDA
Cholesterol	180 mg	Iron	6% U.S. RDA

Lemon Poached Salmon

    4 cups water
    ¼ cup sliced green onions
    1 lemon, sliced
    ¼ teaspoon salt
    ⅛ teaspoon pepper
    4 (6-oz.) salmon steaks
       Lemon wedges and fresh dill, if desired

In large skillet, combine water, onions, lemon slices, salt and pepper. Bring to a boil; simmer 5 minutes to blend flavors. Add salmon. Cover; simmer 7 to 10 minutes or until salmon flakes easily with fork. Lift salmon out of liquid onto serving platter; garnish with lemon wedges and dill. **4 servings.**

NUTRIENTS PER ¼ OF RECIPE

Calories	280	Dietary Fiber	<1 g
Protein	31 g	Sodium	140 mg
Carbohydrate	0 g	Potassium	590 mg
Fat	16 g	Calcium	20% U.S. RDA
Cholesterol	70 mg	Iron	10% U.S. RDA

Layered Salmon and Egg Pie

Pastry for two-crust pie (see Index)

FILLING

    ½ cup sliced green onions
    ¼ cup margarine or butter
    ⅓ cup flour
    1 cup milk
    ¼ cup chopped fresh parsley
15½-oz. can salmon, drained, flaked
    3 eggs, hard-cooked, sliced
    ¼ cup sliced stuffed green olives

Prepare pastry for two-crust pie using 9-inch pie pan.

Heat oven to 425°F. In medium saucepan, saute onions in margarine until tender. Stir in flour; cook until mixture is smooth and bubbly, stirring constantly. Gradually add milk. Cook until mixture boils and thickens, stirring constantly. Remove from heat; stir in parsley. Sprinkle salmon into bottom of pastry-lined pan. Pour sauce over salmon; layer egg slices over sauce. Sprinkle with olives. Top with second crust and flute; cut slits in several places. Bake at 425°F. for 35 to 45 minutes or until golden brown. Let stand 10 minutes before serving. **8 servings.**

TIPS: If desired, make decorative fish-shaped cut-outs in second crust before topping filled pie; omit slits.

Cover edge of pie crust with strip of foil during last 10 to 15 minutes of baking if necessary to prevent excessive browning.

NUTRIENTS PER ⅛ OF RECIPE

Calories	430	Dietary Fiber	2 g
Protein	15 g	Sodium	705 mg
Carbohydrate	30 g	Potassium	290 mg
Fat	30 g	Calcium	15% U.S. RDA
Cholesterol	120 mg	Iron	6% U.S. RDA

Salmon with Spinach Sauce

    2 cups chicken broth
    3 tablespoons finely chopped onion
    3 tablespoons finely chopped fresh parsley
  ¼ teaspoon salt
    1 bay leaf
    6 salmon steaks (about 2 lb.)
  ¾ cup whipping cream
    3 egg yolks, beaten
9-oz. pkg. frozen chopped spinach, cooked, well drained
    1 tablespoon lemon juice

In large skillet, combine chicken broth, onion, parsley, salt and bay leaf; bring to a boil. Add salmon; cover and simmer over low heat 8 to 10 minutes or until salmon flakes easily with fork. Remove salmon to serving plate; keep warm. Remove bay leaf.

Boil broth mixture until reduced to about 1 cup. In small bowl, combine cream and egg yolks; blend well. Slowly stir about half of broth mixture into cream mixture. Stir cream mixture into remaining broth mixture. Cook over low heat, stirring constantly, until thickened and bubbly. Stir in spinach and lemon juice; heat thoroughly. If desired, blend sauce in food processor or blender until smooth. Serve with salmon steaks. **6 servings.**

NUTRIENTS PER ⅙ OF RECIPE

Calories	370	Dietary Fiber	1 g
Protein	30 g	Sodium	475 mg
Carbohydrate	4 g	Potassium	270 mg
Fat	26 g	Calcium	10% U.S. RDA
Cholesterol	220 mg	Iron	20% U.S. RDA

Dill Marinated Salmon Steaks

  2   tablespoons lemon juice
  1   tablespoon oil
  1   teaspoon dill weed
  ¼   teaspoon salt
  ⅛   teaspoon pepper
  4   medium-size salmon steaks, cut 1-inch thick

In small bowl, combine all ingredients except salmon steaks; mix well. Pour over fish in shallow non-metal container or plastic bag, turning to coat both sides. Cover; marinate 1 hour at room temperature or several hours in refrigerator. Remove fish steaks from marinade; place each on sheet of heavy-duty foil. Wrap securely with double-fold seal.

When ready to barbecue, place fish packets on grill 4 to 6 inches from hot coals. Cook 10 to 15 minutes or until fish flakes easily with fork, turning once. **4 servings.**

BROILER METHOD: Marinate salmon steaks as directed above. Line broiler pan with foil; place fish on prepared pan. Broil 4 to 6 inches from heat for 10 to 15 minutes or until fish flakes easily with fork, turning once.

NUTRIENTS PER ¼ OF RECIPE

Calories	270	Dietary Fiber	0 g
Protein	26 g	Sodium	190 mg
Carbohydrate	1 g	Potassium	520 mg
Fat	17 g	Calcium	15% U.S. RDA
Cholesterol	40 mg	Iron	8% U.S. RDA

Salmon a la King

10 oz.   (4 cups) uncooked spinach egg noodles
  1   tablespoon chopped onion
  ⅓   cup margarine or butter
  ⅓   cup all purpose flour

>   1 teaspoon salt
>   Dash pepper
>   3 cups milk
>   3 eggs, hard-cooked, sliced
>   1 tablespoon chopped pimiento
> 15½-oz. can salmon, drained and flaked

Cook spinach noodles to desired doneness as directed on package. Drain; rinse with hot water.

In large saucepan, saute onion in margarine until tender. Add flour, salt and pepper; blend well. Add milk. Cook over medium heat until mixture thickens and boils, stirring constantly. Stir in egg slices, pimiento and salmon; cook until thoroughly heated. Serve over cooked spinach noodles. **6 servings.**

MICROWAVE DIRECTIONS: Cook spinach noodles as directed above. Meanwhile, in 2-quart microwave-safe casserole, microwave onion and margarine on HIGH for 1 to 2 minutes or until onion is tender. Stir in flour, salt and pepper, microwave on HIGH for 30 seconds or until bubbly. Add milk. Microwave on HIGH for 6 to 9 minutes or until mixture thickens and boils, stirring twice during cooking. Stir in egg slices, pimiento and salmon; microwave on HIGH for 2 to 3½ minutes or until thoroughly heated. Serve over cooked spinach noodles.

NUTRIENTS PER ⅙ OF RECIPE

Calories	470	Dietary Fiber	4 g
Protein	25 g	Sodium	880 mg
Carbohydrate	39 g	Potassium	490 mg
Fat	23 g	Calcium	35% U.S. RDA
Cholesterol	220 mg	Iron	15% U.S. RDA

Tuna Asparagus Casserole

4 oz.	(2 cups) uncooked fine egg noodles
½	cup chopped green pepper
3	tablespoons margarine or butter
3	tablespoons flour
	Dash pepper
4.5-oz.	jar sliced mushrooms, drained, reserving liquid
	Milk (about 1¼ cups)
4-oz.	(1 cup) shredded American cheese
6½-oz.	can tuna, drained, flaked
15-oz.	can asparagus spears, drained
½	cup fresh bread crumbs
1	tablespoon margarine or butter, melted

Cook noodles to desired doneness as directed on package. Drain; rinse with hot water.

Heat oven to 350°F. In medium saucepan, saute green pepper in 3 tablespoons margarine until tender. Stir in flour and pepper; cook until mixture is smooth and bubbly. Add milk to reserved mushroom liquid to make 1½ cups. Gradually add milk mixture to green peppers. Heat until mixture boils and thickens, stirring constantly. Add cheese; stir until melted. Remove from heat; combine with cooked noodles, tuna and mushrooms. Pour into 12x8-inch (2-quart) baking dish. Arrange asparagus spears evenly down center of tuna-noodle mixture. Combine bread crumbs and melted margarine; sprinkle over asparagus. Bake at 350°F. for 20 to 25 minutes or until heated. **4 to 5 servings.**

NUTRIENTS PER ⅕ OF RECIPE

Calories	320	Dietary Fiber	3 g
Protein	17 g	Sodium	385 mg
Carbohydrate	28 g	Potassium	280 mg
Fat	15 g	Calcium	8% U.S. RDA
Cholesterol	70 mg	Iron	15% U.S. RDA

Tuna Broccoli Pie

       1 cup frozen cut broccoli, thawed, drained
       2 teaspoons lemon juice
     ¾ cup uncooked long grain rice
6½-oz. can tuna, drained, flaked
  6 oz. (1½ cups) shredded American or Swiss cheese
     ¼ cup finely chopped onion
       1 cup milk
       4 eggs
     ¼ teaspoon salt
     ¼ teaspoon pepper

Heat oven to 350°F. Generously grease 10-inch pie pan or 9-inch square pan. Pour lemon juice over chopped broccoli; set aside. Cook rice according to package directions. With fork, lightly press hot rice evenly over bottom and up sides of pan, forming crust. Layer tuna, cheese, broccoli and onion over crust.

In small bowl, combine milk, eggs, salt and pepper; beat well. Pour over tuna mixture. Bake at 350°F. for 45 to 50 minutes or until knife inserted near center comes out clean. Let stand 10 minutes before serving. **4 to 6 servings.**

VARIATION:

HAM BROCCOLI PIE: Substitute 1 cup cubed, cooked ham for tuna.

NUTRIENTS PER ⅙ OF RECIPE

Calories 340	Dietary Fiber ....1 g
Protein ....24 g	Sodium ....750 mg
Carbohydrate ....25 g	Potassium ....280 mg
Fat ....16 g	Calcium ....30% U.S. RDA
Cholesterol ....230 mg	Iron ....15% U.S. RDA

Old-Time Tuna Bake

7 oz.	(4 cups) uncooked wide egg noodles
12-oz.	can (1½ cups) evaporated milk or half-and-half
1	tablespoon instant minced onion
2	teaspoons seasoned salt
2	(6½-oz.) cans tuna, drained, flaked
9-oz.	pkg. frozen peas, thawed, drained
2.8-oz.	can french fried onion rings

Cook noodles to desired doneness as directed on package. Drain; rinse with hot water.

Heat oven to 350°F. In ungreased 2-quart casserole, combine evaporated milk, onion and salt. Add cooked egg noodles, tuna and peas; mix well. Cover; bake at 350°F. for 30 minutes. Remove from oven; stir well. Sprinkle with french fried onions and bake uncovered an additional 5 minutes. **6 servings.**

MICROWAVE DIRECTIONS: Cook noodles as directed above. In 2-quart microwave-safe casserole, combine evaporated milk, onion and salt. Add cooked noodles, tuna and peas; mix well. Microwave on HIGH for 15 to 17 minutes or until hot and bubbly, stirring once halfway through cooking. Stir; sprinkle with french fried onions. Microwave on HIGH for 2 minutes or until onions are hot.

NUTRIENTS PER ⅙ OF RECIPE

Calories	350	Dietary Fiber	3 g
Protein	24 g	Sodium	790 mg
Carbohydrate	42 g	Potassium	450 mg
Fat	9 g	Calcium	20% U.S. RDA
Cholesterol	70 mg	Iron	15% U.S. RDA

Tuna Salad Buns

4 oz. (1 cup) cubed or shredded American or Cheddar cheese
 ¼ cup sliced stuffed green olives
 2 tablespoons chopped onion
 2 tablespoons chopped green pepper
 2 tablespoons pickle relish, drained
 ⅓ cup mayonnaise or salad dressing
6½-oz. can tuna, drained, flaked
 6 hamburger or hot dog buns, sliced

Heat oven to 350°F. In bowl, combine all ingredients except buns; mix well. Fill buns with mixture. Wrap each in foil. Bake at 350°F. for 15 minutes or until cheese melts. **6 sandwiches.**

TIP: For open-faced sandwiches, spread filling on bun halves or toasted bread. Broil 3 to 5 minutes or until cheese melts.

NUTRIENTS PER 1 SANDWICH

Calories	330	Dietary Fiber	1 g
Protein	16 g	Sodium	730 mg
Carbohydrate	24 g	Potassium	180 mg
Fat	19 g	Calcium	15% U.S. RDA
Cholesterol	45 mg	Iron	10% U.S. RDA

Tuna Casserole

 9 oz. (2 cups) uncooked elbow macaroni
 1 cup milk
 4 oz. (1 cup) shredded Cheddar cheese
10¾-oz. can condensed cream of mushroom soup
6½-oz. can tuna, drained, flaked
 4-oz. can mushroom pieces and stems, drained
 2 tablespoons chopped pimiento
 2 teaspoons instant minced onion
 ½ teaspoon dry mustard
 ½ cup crushed potato chips

Cook macaroni to desired doneness as directed on package. Drain; rinse with hot water.

Heat oven to 350°F. Butter 2-quart casserole. In large bowl, combine cooked macaroni and remaining ingredients except crushed potato chips. Pour mixture into prepared casserole; sprinkle with potato chips. Bake at 350°F. for 25 to 35 minutes or until thoroughly heated. **6 servings.**

NUTRIENTS PER ¼ OF RECIPE

Calories	370	Dietary Fiber	2 g
Protein	20 g	Sodium	625 mg
Carbohydrate	42 g	Potassium	360 mg
Fat	14 g	Calcium	20% U.S. RDA
Cholesterol	40 mg	Iron	10% U.S. RDA

Creamed Tuna on Toast

½	cup milk
½	teaspoon instant minced onion
10¾-oz.	can condensed cream of celery soup
1	tablespoon chopped pimiento
17-oz.	can peas, drained
6½-oz.	can tuna, drained, flaked
6 to 8	slices toast, buttered

In medium saucepan, combine milk, onion and soup; cook until smooth. Stir in pimiento, peas and tuna; continue cooking until thoroughly heated. Serve over toast. **4 to 6 servings.**

NUTRIENTS PER ⅙ OF RECIPE

Calories	270	Dietary Fiber	2 g
Protein	14 g	Sodium	760 mg
Carbohydrate	32 g	Potassium	240 mg
Fat	9 g	Calcium	8% U.S. RDA
Cholesterol	35 mg	Iron	15% U.S. RDA

Velvet Tuna Quiche

PASTRY

    1 cup whole wheat flour
3 oz. (¾ cup) shredded Cheddar cheese
    ¼ cup chopped almonds
    ¼ teaspoon paprika
    ⅓ cup oil

FILLING

    1 cup dairy sour cream
    ½ cup dry white wine
    ¼ cup mayonnaise or salad dressing
    3 eggs, well beaten
6½-oz. can tuna, drained, flaked
  2 oz. (½ cup) shredded Cheddar cheese
    1 tablespoon finely chopped onion
    ¼ teaspoon dill weed
2 to 3 drops hot pepper sauce

Heat oven to 400°F. In small bowl, combine all pastry ingredients just until crumbly and mixture holds together. Press in bottom and up sides of 10-inch pie pan or quiche pan. Bake at 400°F. for 8 to 10 minutes or until light golden brown.

In large bowl, combine sour cream, wine, mayonnaise and eggs; mix well. Stir in tuna, ½ cup cheese, onion, dill weed and hot pepper sauce until well blended. Pour into partially baked crust. Reduce oven temperature to 325°F.; bake an additional 40 to 45 minutes or until knife inserted near center comes out clean. Let stand 5 minutes before serving. **6 servings.**

NUTRIENTS PER ⅙ OF RECIPE

Calories	570	Dietary Fiber	3 g
Protein	23 g	Sodium	455 mg
Carbohydrate	19 g	Potassium	255 mg
Fat	44 g	Calcium	25% U.S. RDA
Cholesterol	200 mg	Iron	15% U.S. RDA

Crescent Tuna Melt

¼ cup salad dressing or mayonnaise
2 tablespoons chopped dill pickle
1 tablespoon prepared mustard
1 tablespoon instant minced onion or ¼ cup chopped onion
9¼-oz. can water-packed tuna, drained, flaked
2 eggs, hard-cooked, chopped
8-oz. can refrigerated crescent dinner rolls
4 oz. (1 cup) shredded Cheddar or Swiss cheese
1 tablespoon sesame seeds, toasted

Heat oven to 375°F. In medium bowl, combine salad dressing, dill pickle, mustard and onion. Stir in tuna and eggs. Unroll dough into 2 long rectangles. Place on ungreased cookie sheet with long sides overlapping ½ inch; firmly press edges and perforations to seal. Press or roll to form 14x9-inch rectangle. Spoon tuna mixture in 3-inch strip lengthwise down center of dough. Sprinkle ½ cup cheese over filling. Make cuts 1 inch apart on each side of rectangle just to edge of filling. To give braided appearance, fold strips of dough at an angle halfway across filling, alternating from side to side.

Bake at 357°F. for 17 to 24 minutes or until deep golden brown. Remove from oven; sprinkle with remaining ½ cup cheese and sesame seeds. Return to oven and bake until cheese melts, about 2 to 3 minutes. Cool 5 minutes. **8 servings.**

TIPS: To make ahead, prepare, cover and refrigerate up to 2 hours; bake at 375°F. for 24 to 29 minutes. Sprinkle with cheese; bake 2 to 3 minutes.

To reheat, cover loosely with foil; heat at 350°F. for 15 to 20 minutes.

NUTRIENTS PER ⅛ OF RECIPE

Calories 270	Dietary Fiber...........................1 g
Protein......................................15 g	Sodium..............................520 mg
Carbohydrate.........................13 g	Potassium.........................135 mg
Fat ....17 g	Calcium...............15% U.S. RDA
Cholesterol ....110 mg	Iron.....................10% U.S. RDA

Shellfish

Purchasing Shellfish

• **Shrimp:** Shrimp are available fresh, frozen and canned. Fresh and frozen can be purchased raw or cooked, both in the shell and with shells removed. Canned shrimp always comes cooked and shelled. Since all the meat is located in the tail, shrimp is usually marketed with heads removed. Shrimp comes in various sizes and is sold by size or count per pound. The smaller the count, the larger and more expensive the shrimp will be.

When buying fresh shrimp, look for mild odor and firm flesh. Uncooked shrimp is translucent and may appear green to slightly pink in color with small areas of black discoloration on the shells. Cooked shrimp is an opaque pinkish red color.

When buying frozen shrimp, make sure the package is tightly sealed. Contents should be solidly frozen and free from ice crystals or white spots.

Fresh, frozen and canned shrimp can generally be used interchangeably in recipes; however, it is best to use the form stated in the recipe when appearance or size of shrimp is important to the final product.

For fresh shrimp, raw shrimp in the shell are the best buy. Shrimp can be cooked before or after peeling and deveining but the sand vein is easier to remove before cooking. Follow recipe instructions to avoid overcooking. Overcooked shrimp will be tough and rubbery.

Two pounds raw shrimp will yield about one pound peeled, deveined and cooked shrimp.

• **Scallops:** Scallops are available both fresh and frozen and usually with their shells removed. The two most common varieties are sea scallops, which are as large as 2 inches in diameter, and bay scallops, which are about ½ inch in diameter. Bay scallops are usually more tender with a sweeter, more delicate taste. They can be used interchangeably in recipes but the cooking time will vary.

Fresh scallops should have a slightly sweet odor and creamy pink to tan color. They should be moist and shiny with little liquid around them. Rinse well before using to remove any sand. As with other shellfish, follow recipe instructions carefully to avoid overcooking.

Allow 3 to 4 oz. per serving.

• **Crabs:** Crab varieties differ from region to region. The most commonly marketed varieties are Blue, Dungeness, King, Stone and Snow Crabs. Soft-shell crabs are not a different variety but are blue crabs that have shed their hard shells. Their availability is limited to May, June, July and August.

Experts insist that for the finest and freshest flavor, crabs should be purchased alive. Live crabs should be active and fresh-smelling.

Cooked whole crabs in the shell are also sold both fresh and frozen. Cooked crabs should have bright red shells with no disagreeable odor. Alaska king crab is most often marketed as cooked frozen crab legs.

Cooked crabmeat is available frozen and canned. Lump meat refers to choice meat from the body of the crab, flaked meat consists of small pieces from the rest of the body, and claw meat is darker than the meat from the body. Flakes and claw meat are less expensive than lump meat.

Since crab can easily be overcooked, watch timing carefully.

4 lb. crab in the shell yields about 1 lb. cooked crabmeat. Both one 6-oz. package frozen crabmeat and one 6½-oz. can cooked flaked crabmeat are equivalent to 1 cup cooked lump crabmeat.

• **Lobster:** Fresh lobsters must be shipped and purchased live, for they quickly spoil. Live lobsters should be active and their tails should curl down and not just hang when the lobster is picked up. Be sure the claws are banded. Live lobsters may be kept in the refrigerator a few hours if necessary before cooking.

Whole cooked lobster in the shell may be purchased fresh or frozen. Cooked lobster should have a bright orange-red shell, curled tail and a fresh smell.

Cooked lobster meat can also be purchased canned. Cooked lobster need not be reheated before eating, only thawed if frozen.

A whole lobster will weigh 1 to 2 lb.; allow one lobster per serving. Allow ½ lb. lobster tail per serving. One 8 oz. tail or a 1 lb. whole lobster will yield 4 to 5 oz. or 1 cup cooked lobster meat.

Lobster tail may be purchased frozen, cooked or uncooked. Uncooked, the shells will be a black-green color.

• **Oysters/Clams:** Oysters and clams are available live in the shell or shucked. Shucked oysters may be purchased fresh, frozen, canned or smoked. Shucked clams may be purchased fresh or canned.

When purchased live, oysters and clams should have their shells tightly closed or if open they should close when touched. Discard any with shells that do not close.

Shucked oysters and clams should be plump and fresh-smelling with a small amount of slightly milky liquid. Do not wash shucked meat before cooking or discard liquid. This liquid is very flavorful and can be consumed with the raw shellfish or used for adding flavor to cooked dishes.

Purchase oysters and clams in the shell by the dozen and shucked oysters or clams by the pint. About 24 oysters in the shell will yield 1 pint shucked oysters; about 18 small clams, such as littleneck or cherrystone, will yield 1 pint shucked clams.

Batter-Fried Shrimp or Scallops

- 1 lb. fresh or frozen shrimp or scallops*
- ½ cup milk
- 1 egg
- ½ cup all purpose flour
- ½ teaspoon salt
  Dash hot pepper sauce

Rinse and drain shrimp well. In skillet or heavy saucepan, heat 1 to 1½ inches oil to 375°F. In small bowl, beat milk and egg. Add flour, salt and hot pepper sauce; beat until smooth. Dip shrimp in batter, draining off excess. Fry shrimp at 375°F. for 3 to 4 minutes or until golden brown. Drain slightly on paper towel. Serve with Tartar Sauce or Seafood Cocktail Sauce (see Index). **4 servings.**

TIP: *If shrimp are in shell, peel and devein before dipping into batter.

VARIATION:

BUTTERFLIED SHRIMP: Remove shell except for tail portion. With sharp knife, cut almost all the way through back of shrimp lengthwise to form butterfly shape; keep tail intact and remove black vein. Spread to open. Dip in batter; fry as directed.

NUTRIENTS PER ¼ OF RECIPE

Calories	170	Dietary Fiber	1 g
Protein	20 g	Sodium	420 mg
Carbohydrate	15 g	Potassium	270 mg
Fat	3 g	Calcium	10% U.S. RDA
Cholesterol	200 mg	Iron	10% U.S. RDA

Cooking Fresh Raw Shrimp

In saucepan, bring enough water to cover shrimp to a boil. Add shrimp; immediately reduce heat. Simmer for 3 to 5 minutes or until shrimp are firm and pink; *do not boil.* Shrimp will become tough if overcooked. Drain, peel and devein; serve warm or refrigerate.

NUTRIENTS PER ⅓ LB. RAW SHRIMP, COOKED

Calories	100	Dietary Fiber	0 g
Protein	21 g	Sodium	160 mg
Carbohydrate	2 g	Potassium	250 mg
Fat	1 g	Calcium	6% U.S. RDA
Cholesterol	170 mg	Iron	10% U.S. RDA

Elegant Shrimp and Broccoli

6	eggs, hard-cooked
⅓ cup	mayonnaise or salad dressing
½ teaspoon	prepared mustard
¼ teaspoon	salt
¼ teaspoon	onion powder
⅛ teaspoon	hot pepper sauce
	Paprika
¼ cup	margarine or butter
¼ cup	all purpose flour
⅛ teaspoon	oregano leaves
1 cup	milk
4 oz.	(1 cup) shredded Cheddar cheese
4.5-oz.	jar sliced mushrooms, drained
9-oz.	pkg. frozen cut broccoli, thawed
10-oz.	pkg. frozen shrimp, thawed, rinsed, drained
⅓ cup	grated Parmesan cheese
4 cups	hot cooked rice

Cut eggs in half lengthwise; remove egg yolks from whites. Place yolks in small bowl; mash. Add mayonnaise, mustard, salt, onion powder and hot pepper sauce; blend well. Fill egg white centers with yolk mixture. Sprinkle lightly with paprika; refrigerate.

Heat oven to 350°F. In large saucepan over medium heat, melt margarine. Stir in flour and oregano; cook until mixture is smooth and bubbly, stirring constantly. Gradually add milk. Cook until mixture boils and thickens, stirring constantly. Add Cheddar cheese; stir until melted. Add mushrooms, broccoli and shrimp to cheese sauce; cook 2 to 3 minutes, stirring constantly. Pour into ungreased 10-inch deep dish pie pan, quiche pan or 12x8-inch (2-quart) baking dish. Arrange prepared eggs around edge of dish. Sprinkle entire casserole with Parmesan cheese. Bake at 350°F. for 15 to 20 minutes or until thoroughly heated. Serve over hot cooked rice. **6 servings.**

NUTRIENTS PER ¼ OF RECIPE

Calories 430	Dietary Fiber..........................3 g
Protein.....................................25 g	Sodium.............................700 mg
Carbohydrate.........................10 g	Potassium.........................370 mg
Fat ....32 g	Calcium...............35% U.S. RDA
Cholesterol......................380 mg	Iron.....................15% U.S. RDA

Shrimp Asparagus Pasta Toss

6 oz. uncooked angel hair pasta

SAUCE

    2 tablespoons margarine or butter
    2 tablespoons flour
    1 teaspoon instant chicken bouillon granules
1½ cups milk
2 oz. (½ cup) shredded Swiss cheese
  ¼ cup grated Parmesan cheese
  ½ lb. fresh or frozen cooked shrimp
8 oz. (18 spears) fresh asparagus, cooked and cut into 1-inch pieces*
2 oz. (1 cup) sliced fresh mushrooms

Cook angel hair pasta to desired doneness as directed on package. Drain; rinse with hot water. Keep warm.

In medium saucepan, melt margarine. Blend in flour and bouillon granules; cook until smooth and bubbly. Gradually add milk; cook until mixture boils and thickens, stirring constantly. Add cheeses; stir until smooth. Stir in shrimp, asparagus and mushrooms; cook until thoroughly heated. Serve over pasta. **4 servings.**

MICROWAVE DIRECTIONS: Prepare pasta as directed above. Place asparagus and ¼ *cup water* in 9-inch microwave-safe pie plate. Cover with microwave-safe plastic wrap. Microwave on HIGH for 3½ to 4 minutes or until crisp-tender. Drain.

Place margarine in 3-quart microwave-safe bowl. Microwave on HIGH for 30 seconds or until melted. Stir in flour and bouillon granules. Microwave on HIGH for 30 seconds. Using wire whisk, gradually stir in milk. Microwave on HIGH for 3 to 4 minutes or until thickened, stirring once halfway through cooking. Stir in cheeses. Microwave on HIGH for 30 to 45 seconds or until cheese is melted. Stir in shrimp, asparagus and mushrooms. Microwave on HIGH for 1 to 1½ minutes or until thoroughly heated. Serve over cooked pasta.

TIP: *10-oz. pkg. frozen asparagus cuts, thawed, can be substituted for fresh asparagus.

NUTRIENTS PER ¼ OF RECIPE

Calories 430	Dietary Fiber............................2 g
Protein.....................................29 g	Sodium...............................430 mg
Carbohydrate..........................44 g	Potassium...........................640 mg
Fat ....15 g	Calcium...............40% U.S. RDA
Cholesterol.......................100 mg	Iron.....................15% U.S. RDA

Jambalaya

         2 tablespoons margarine or butter
         1 medium onion, coarsely chopped
         1 medium green pepper, coarsely chopped
         1 lb. cooked Polish sausage, cut into ½-inch slices
         1 lb. frozen large shrimp
    16-oz. can tomatoes, undrained, cut up
   10¾-oz. can condensed chicken broth
     6-oz. can tomato paste
        ¾ cup uncooked regular rice
         2 teaspoons sugar
         1 teaspoon thyme leaves
        ½ teaspoon garlic powder
        ⅛ teaspoon cayenne pepper
        ⅛ teaspoon pepper
         1 bay leaf

In large Dutch oven, melt margarine; saute onion for 2 to 3 minutes or just until tender. Stir in remaining ingredients; blend well. Cover; simmer for 20 to 30 minutes until rice is tender and liquis has been absorbed, stirring occasionally. Remove bay leaf. **8 servings.**

NUTRIENTS PER ⅛ OF RECIPE

Calories	380	Dietary Fiber	1 g
Protein	23 g	Sodium	1090 mg
Carbohydrate	25 g	Potassium	710 mg
Fat	20 g	Calcium	6% U.S. RDA
Cholesterol	130 mg	Iron	20% U.S. RDA

Shrimp Creole

         1 medium green pepper, sliced into thin strips
         2 medium onions, thinly sliced
        ½ cup chopped celery
         1 garlic clove, minced
        ¼ cup oil

½ cup slivered almonds
¼ cup raisins
¼ cup chopped fresh parsley
¼ cup chili sauce
1 bay leaf
¼ teaspoon salt
¼ teaspoon pepper
¼ teaspoon thyme leaves
¼ teaspoon curry powder
1 teaspoon lemon juice
¼ to ½ teaspoon hot pepper sauce
16-oz. can (2 cups) whole tomatoes, cut up
1 lb. cooked shrimp, peeled and deveined
Hot cooked rice, if desired

In large skillet, saute green pepper, onions, celery and garlic in oil until crisp-tender. Add remaining ingredients except shrimp. Cover; simmer 40 to 50 minutes or until flavors are blended, stirring occasionally. Add shrimp. Simmer an additional 10 minutes or until thoroughly heated. Serve with hot cooked rice. **5 to 6 servings.**

NUTRIENTS PER ⅙ OF RECIPE

Calories	390	Dietary Fiber	5 g
Protein	22 g	Sodium	470 mg
Carbohydrate	42 g	Potassium	640 mg
Fat	15 g	Calcium	15% U.S. RDA
Cholesterol	90 mg	Iron	20% U.S. RDA

Shrimp in Garlic Butter

½ cup margarine or butter
3 garlic cloves, minced
1 tablespoon finely chopped fresh parsley
2 tablespoons lemon juice
¼ teaspoon salt
1½ to 2 lb. fresh shrimp,* peeled and deveined

Melt margarine; add garlic, parsley, lemon juice and salt; set aside. Thread shrimp on 4 to 6 skewers.

Place shrimp on greased grill, 4 to 6 inches from hot coals. Cook 15 to 20 minutes or until done, turning and brushing occasionally with garlic butter. **4 to 6 servings.**

TIP: *Two 12-oz. pkg. frozen large shrimp, thawed, can be substituted for fresh.

NUTRIENTS PER ⅙ OF RECIPE

Calories 240	Dietary Fiber ....0 g
Protein.....................................21 g	Sodium.............................420 mg
Carbohydrate...........................3 g	Potassium.........................280 mg
Fat ....16 g	Calcium.................8% U.S. RDA
Cholesterol.......................170 mg	Iron.....................10% U.S. RDA

Lemon-Basil Shrimp Kabobs

MARINADE

- ⅔ cup lemon juice
- ⅓ cup oil
- 2 tablespoons finely chopped onion
- 2 tablespoons finely chopped fresh parsley
- 2 teaspoons basil leaves, crushed
- 1 teaspoon grated lemon peel
- 1 teaspoon salt

- 24 to 30 (1¼ to 1½ lb.) large fresh shrimp, peeled, deveined, tails left on
- 24 large mushrooms
- 12 thin lemon slices
- 1 large red bell pepper, cut into 1-inch pieces
- 3 small zucchini, cut into ½-inch pieces

In medium bowl, combine marinade ingredients; mix well. Add shrimp; stir to coat. Cover; refrigerate 1 to 3 hours.

Drain shrimp, reserving marinade. On each of 12 skewers, arrange 2 to 3 shrimp, 2 mushrooms, 1 lemon slice, red pepper pieces and zucchini pieces. When ready to barbecue, place kabobs on grill 4 to 6 inches from medium-high coals. Cook 15 to 20 minutes or until shrimp are pink and vegetables are crisp-tender, turning once and brushing frequently with marinade. **6 servings.**

BROILER METHOD: Prepare kabobs as directed above. Broil kabobs about 4 to 6 inches from heat for 7 to 10 minutes, turning once and brushing frequently with marinade.

NUTRIENTS PER ⅙ OF RECIPE

Calories 260	Dietary Fiber..........................2 g
Protein...................................23 g	Sodium.............................520 mg
Carbohydrate........................11 g	Potassium........................670 mg
Fat ....14 g	Calcium...............10% U.S. RDA
Cholesterol......................170 mg	Iron.....................20% U.S. RDA

Butter Scallops

   3 tablespoons margarine or butter
   2 teaspoons chicken-flavor instant bouillon
  ½ teaspoon dill weed
   1 lb. fresh small scallops
   1 tablespoon dry sherry

MICROWAVE DIRECTIONS: Place margarine in 1-quart microwave-safe casserole. Microwave on HIGH for 1 minute or until melted. Stir in bouillon and dill. Add scallops. Cover with microwave-safe plastic wrap. Microwave on HIGH for 6 to 7 minutes or until thoroughly heated and scallops are opaque. Stir in sherry. **4 servings.**

VARIATION:

BUTTER SHRIMP: Substitute 1 lb. uncooked shrimp for scallops.

NUTRIENTS PER ¼ OF RECIPE

Calories	180	Dietary Fiber	0 g
Protein	18 g	Sodium	580 mg
Carbohydrate	4 g	Potassium	460 mg
Fat	9 g	Calcium	2% U.S. RDA
Cholesterol	40 mg	Iron	10% U.S. RDA

Scallops en Casserole

2 oz. uncooked spaghetti, broken
8 oz. fresh small scallops, or large scallops cut in half
  3 tablespoons margarine or butter
  2 tablespoons flour
  ¼ teaspoon salt
    Dash pepper
  1 cup half-and-half
  2 tablespoons white wine, if desired
2.5-oz. jar sliced mushrooms, drained
  ½ cup frozen peas
  2 tablespoons grated Parmesan cheese

Cook spaghetti to desired doneness as directed on package. Drain; rinse with hot water.

Heat oven to 375°F. Lightly grease 2 individual casseroles (about 2 cups each). Thoroughly rinse scallops in cold water; drain. In 8-inch skillet, melt *1 tablespoon* margarine. Add scallops; saute scallops over medium-high heat 6 to 8 minutes or until opaque. Remove scallops; set aside. In same pan, melt remaining 2 tablespoons margarine. Add flour, salt and pepper; blend well. Add half-and-half all at once. Cook until mixture thickens, about 5 minutes, stirring constantly. Add scallops, wine, mushrooms and peas; heat, stirring constantly, until thoroughly heated. Spoon hot spaghetti evenly into prepared dishes. Spoon scallop mixture on top of spaghetti; sprinkle with Parmesan cheese. Bake at 375°F. for 20 to 25 minutes or until light brown and bubbly around the edges. **2 servings.**

NUTRIENTS PER ½ OF RECIPE

Calories	640	Dietary Fiber	2 g
Protein	39 g	Sodium	1005 mg
Carbohydrate	39 g	Potassium	855 mg
Fat	35 g	Calcium	35% U.S. RDA
Cholesterol	90 mg	Iron	30% U.S. RDA

Coquilles St. Jacques

¼ cup chopped celery
4 oz. (1½ cups) sliced fresh mushrooms
2 medium green onions, sliced, or 2 tablespoons chopped onion
¼ cup margarine or butter
2 tablespoons chopped green pepper
2 tablespoons flour
¼ teaspoon salt
⅛ teaspoon pepper
½ bay leaf
½ cup dry white wine
1 lb. fresh or frozen scallops, cut in half if large
¼ cup whipping cream or evaporated milk
1 egg yolk
1 tablespoon chopped pimiento
2 tablespoons margarine or butter, melted
3 tablespoons dry bread crumbs
3 tablespoons grated Parmesan cheese

In large saucepan, saute celery, mushrooms and onions in margarine until tender. Stir in green pepper, flour, salt, pepper, bay leaf and wine; mix well. Add scallops. Cook over medium heat until mixture boils and thickens, stirring occasionally. Cover; simmer 5 minutes (10 to 15 minutes if scallops are frozen) or until scallops are opaque. Combine cream and egg yolk; beat well. Stir into scallops along with pimiento. Cook until mixture begins to bubble.

Remove bay leaf. Spoon mixture into 4 lightly greased shells (8 small appetizer shells), individual baking dishes, or 1½-quart shallow casserole. Combine 2 tablespoons melted margarine, bread crumbs and cheese. Sprinkle over each serving. Broil 2 to 3 inches from heat until heated through and crumbs are browned. **4 main course or 8 appetizer servings.**

TIP: To make ahead, prepare, cover and refrigerate up to 12 hours before broiling. Remove cover and broil as directed above.

NUTRIENTS PER ¼ OF RECIPE

Calories 400	Dietary Fiber ....1 g
Protein ....22 g	Sodium ....760 mg
Carbohydrate ....14 g	Potassium ....670 mg
Fat ....26 g	Calcium ....10% U.S. RDA
Cholesterol ....130 mg	Iron ....20% U.S. RDA

Maryland Deviled Crab

    2 tablespoons chopped onion
    2 tablespoons chopped green pepper
    3 tablespoons margarine or butter
    2 tablespoons flour
   ¾ cup milk
    2 cups (about ½ lb.) cooked crab meat, drained,
       flaked*
    1 tablespoon chopped parsley
   ½ teaspoon dry mustard
    2 teaspoons lemon juice
   ½ teaspoon Worcestershire sauce
   ½ teaspoon hot pepper sauce
    1 egg, slightly beaten
   ½ cup fresh bread crumbs
    2 tablespoons margarine or butter, melted

Heat oven to 400°F. Lightly grease 1-quart casserole or 4 individual baking dishes or shells. In medium saucepan, saute onion and green pepper in 3 tablespoons margarine until tender. Stir in flour. Gradually add milk. Cook until mixture boils and thickens, stirring constantly. Add remaining ingredients except bread crumbs and 2 tablespoons margarine; mix well. Spoon into prepared casserole. In small bowl, combine bread crumbs and 2 tablespoons margarine. Sprinkle evenly over crab mixture. Bake at 400°F. for 15 to 20 minutes or until thoroughly heated. **4 servings.**

TIP: *A combination of cooked crab meat and fish or an 8-oz. pkg. Pacific fish and crab meat blend can be substituted for crab meat.

NUTRIENTS PER ¼ OF RECIPE

Calories 270	Dietary Fiber.........................<1 g
Protein......................................14 g	Sodium.............................825 mg
Carbohydrate...........................10 g	Potassium.........................190 mg
Fat ....19 g	Calcium...............10% U.S. RDA
Cholesterol......................130 mg	Iron.......................6% U.S. RDA

Boiled Live Crab

Purchase live Dungeness crab, allowing 1 crab for 2 servings. In large saucepan, heat salted water to boiling. Pick up live crab from the rear, holding the last 1 or 2 legs on either side. Drop crabs into boiling water. Return to boil; simmer covered about 15 minutes. Remove from water; crack claws and legs and serve with Seasoned Butter, Clarified Butter or Tartar Sauce (see Index).

NUTRIENTS PER ½ WHOLE CRAB

Calories 80	Dietary Fiber...........................0 g
Protein......................................14 g	Sodium.............................170 mg
Carbohydrate...............................0 g	Potassium.........................150 mg
Fat ....2 g	Calcium.................2% U.S. RDA
Cholesterol........................80 mg	Iron.......................2% U.S. RDA

Broiled Lobster Tails

Allow ½ lb. per serving for lobster tails.* Prepare fresh lobster for broiling by cutting along underside of tail with shears; clip off fins along edges. Peel back soft undershell and discard. To prevent curling, bend tail back to crack shell or insert skewer between meat and shell. Lay cut side up on broiler pan. Brush with mixture of ¼ cup melted butter, ½ teaspoon salt and ¼ teaspoon paprika. Broil 4 inches from heat for 10 to 15 minutes or until lobster meat is firm. Serve with Clarified Butter (see Index).

VARIATION:

BUTTERFLIED LOBSTER TAILS: Cut lobster lengthwise through center of hard top shell with shears, then cut through the meat with a sharp knife without cutting through soft undershell. Spread open; cook as directed.

TIP: *If desired, frozen lobster tail can be simmered, covered, in salted boiling water for about 15 minutes. Prepare as directed for broiling. Broil for 2 to 3 minutes.

NUTRIENTS PER ½ LB. RAW LOBSTER TAIL, COOKED WITH 1T. BUTTER

Calories	210	Dietary Fiber	0 g
Protein	21 g	Sodium	620 mg
Carbohydrate	0 g	Potassium	210 mg
Fat	13 g	Calcium	8% U.S. RDA
Cholesterol	130 mg	Iron	4% U.S. RDA

Boiled Live Lobster

In large saucepan, bring to a boil enough salted water to cover lobster generously. With long tongs, pick up lobster just behind eyes. Plunge live lobster, head first, into boiling water. Return to a boil. Reduce heat. Cover; simmer about 7 minutes for 1-lb. lobster or 10 minutes for 2-lb. lobster or until lobster turns bright red. Remove from water; plunge into cold water to stop cooking. Drain; turn on back. With sharp knife or shears, cut lobster in half lengthwise. Remove sac near back of head and dark vein which runs along underside of tail. Dark roe and green liver are edible parts. Crack claws using claw or nut cracker. Serve with Clarified Butter (see Index). **1 serving.**

NUTRIENTS PER 1 LB. RAW WHOLE LOBSTER, COOKED

Calories	100	Dietary Fiber	0 g
Protein	20 g	Sodium	220 mg
Carbohydrate	0 g	Potassium	190 mg
Fat	2 g	Calcium	6% U.S. RDA
Cholesterol	90 mg	Iron	4% U.S. RDA

Lobster Thermidor

10¾-oz. can condensed cream of shrimp or mushroom soup
8 oz. (2 cups) cooked lobster meat, cut into chunks*
¼ teaspoon dry mustard
Dash cayenne pepper
¼ cup milk
4.5-oz. jar sliced mushrooms, drained
Grated Parmesan cheese
Paprika

In medium saucepan, heat soup over low heat, stirring occasionally. Stir in lobster, mustard, pepper, milk and mushrooms. Cook over low heat until thoroughly heated, stirring occasionally. Spoon into 4 lightly greased individual baking dishes or shells.** Sprinkle with Parmesan cheese and paprika. Broil 3 to 4 inches from heat 2 to 3 minutes or until hot and bubbly. **4 servings.**

TIPS: *Two 5-oz. cans lobster, drained, can be substituted for the cooked lobster.

**With careful handling, lobster tail shells can be used as individual baking dishes.

NUTRIENTS PER ¼ OF RECIPE

Calories	150	Dietary Fiber	<1 g
Protein	15 g	Sodium	940 mg
Carbohydrate	8 g	Potassium	170 mg
Fat	6 g	Calcium	10% U.S. RDA
Cholesterol	50 mg	Iron	4% U.S. RDA

Lobster Newburg

 ¼ cup margarine or butter
 4½ teaspoons flour
8 oz. (2 cups) cooked lobster meat, cut into chunks
 ½ teaspoon salt
  Dash paprika
 ¼ cup dry sherry or dry white wine
 2 egg yolks, slightly beaten
 1½ cups light cream

In medium saucepan, melt margarine. Stir in flour; cook 1 minute. Add lobster, salt, paprika and sherry. In small bowl, combine beaten egg yolks and cream. Gradually add yolk mixture to lobster mixture; blend well. Cook over very low heat until thickened, stirring frequently. Serve over toast points or patty shells. **4 servings.**

VARIATIONS:

CRAB NEWBURG: Substitute cooked crab meat for lobster.

SHRIMP NEWBURG: Substitute cooked shrimp for lobster.

NUTRIENTS PER ¼ OF RECIPE

Calories	400	Dietary Fiber	0 g
Protein	18 g	Sodium	680 mg
Carbohydrate	7 g	Potassium	270 mg
Fat	33 g	Calcium	15% U.S. RDA
Cholesterol	260 mg	Iron	6% U.S. RDA

Scalloped Oysters

¼ cup margarine or butter
2 cups (2 slices) soft bread crumbs
¼ cup grated Parmesan cheese
¼ teaspoon salt
   Dash mace, if desired
1 pint fresh shucked oysters, drained*
¼ cup dry sherry or dry white wine**

Heat oven to 375°F. In 8 or 9-inch square pan, melt margarine in oven. Stir in bread crumbs, cheese, salt and mace. Remove about half of crumbs; arrange remaining crumbs evenly in pan. Place oysters over crumbs; pour sherry over top. Sprinkle with remaining crumbs. Bake at 375°F. for 20 to 25 minutes or until lightly browned. **4 servings.**

TIPS: *Two 8-oz. cans oysters, drained, can be substituted for fresh. Omit salt.

**Oysters or clams packed in light cream can be substituted for the fresh oysters and sherry.

VARIATION:

SCALLOPED CLAMS: Substitute fresh shucked or canned clams for oysters.

NUTRIENTS PER ¼ OF RECIPE

Calories 280	Dietary Fiber....................<1 g
Protein....................14 g	Sodium............................570 mg
Carbohydrate....................17 g	Potassium..........................180 mg
Fat ....16 g	Calcium...............20% U.S. RDA
Cholesterol....................60 mg	Iron.....................40% U.S. RDA

Fried Oysters

⅓ cup all purpose flour
1 teaspoon salt
⅛ teaspoon pepper

    1 egg
    1 tablespoon water
    1 pint fresh shucked oysters, drained
    ⅔ cup cracker or bread crumbs
    ¼ cup oil or butter

In small bowl, combine flour, salt and pepper. In another small bowl, beat egg and water. In medium skillet, heat oil. Dip oysters in flour mixture to coat, then dip in egg mixture. Roll in crumbs. Fry oysters until golden brown, about 5 minutes on each side, turning once. Serve with lemon wedges or Tartar Sauce (see Index). **4 servings.**

TIP: If desired, fry in deep fryer (375°F.) for about 2 to 3 minutes.

NUTRIENTS PER ¼ OF RECIPE

Calories	300	Dietary Fiber	<1 g
Protein	13 g	Sodium	760 mg
Carbohydrate	20 g	Potassium	170 mg
Fat	18 g	Calcium	12% U.S. RDA
Cholesterol	120 mg	Iron	40% U.S. RDA

VARIATIONS:

FRIED CLAMS: Substitute shucked fresh clams for oysters.

NUTRIENTS PER ¼ OF RECIPE

Calories	320	Dietary Fiber	<1 g
Protein	16 g	Sodium	910 mg
Carbohydrate	23 g	Potassium	390 mg
Fat	18 g	Calcium	8% U.S. RDA
Cholesterol	130 mg	Iron	50% U.S. RDA

FRIED FROG LEGS: Substitute 3 lb. frog legs for oysters. Fry about 10 minutes on each side or until golden brown. If they are large, add a little water. Cover; simmer 10 minutes. Remove cover; continue frying until crisp.

NUTRIENTS PER ¼ OF RECIPE

Calories 390	Dietary Fiber........................<1 g
Protein.....................................40 g	Sodium.............................810 mg
Carbohydrate.........................16 g	Potassium.........................670 mg
Fat ....17 g	Calcium.................4% U.S. RDA
Cholesterol.......................180 mg	Iron.....................25% U.S. RDA

Clam Bake in Foil

```
    6  clams
    1  lb. lobster
½ to ¾  lb. frying chicken pieces
    2  medium potatoes, unpeeled
    2  small onions
    2  unhusked ears of corn, silks removed
    ½  cup water
```

Clams should be scrubbed and lobster freshly killed. Place all ingredients on large square of double thickness heavy duty foil. Seal packet carefully but securely (wrap loosely as lobster may puncture foil). Place about 4 inches from hot coals. Cook about 1 hour, turning packet frequently while cooking. Serve with melted butter or margarine and fresh lemon wedges. **2 servings.**

NUTRIENTS PER ½ OF RECIPE

Calories 460	Dietary Fiber..........................8 g
Protein.....................................46 g	Sodium.............................320 mg
Carbohydrate.........................40 g	Potassium.......................1340 mg
Fat ....14 g	Calcium...............15% U.S. RDA
Cholesterol.......................150 mg	Iron.....................60% U.S. RDA

Clam Sauce with Linguine

```
6 oz.  uncooked linguine
    ¼  cup finely chopped onion
    1  garlic clove, minced
    2  tablespoons olive or cooking oil
```

2 tablespoons chopped fresh parsley
½ teaspoon oregano leaves
½ teaspoon basil leaves
⅛ teaspoon pepper
¼ cup dry white wine
6½-oz. can minced clams, drained, reserving liquid
Grated Parmesan cheese, if desired

Cook linguine to desired doneness as directed on package. Drain; rinse with hot water.

In medium skillet, saute onion and garlic in oil until tender. Stir in parsley, oregano, basil, pepper, wine and reserved clam liquid. Cook 5 minutes, stirring constantly. Add clams; cook until thoroughly heated. Serve sauce over cooked linguine in bowls; sprinkle with Parmesan cheese. **3 servings.**

NUTRIENTS PER ⅓ OF RECIPE

Calories 370	Dietary Fiber.........................<1 g
Protein......................................14 g	Sodium.............................430 mg
Carbohydrate.........................48 g	Potassium..........................260 mg
Fat ....11 g	Calcium...............10% U.S. RDA
Cholesterol ....20 mg	Iron.....................25% U.S. RDA

Steamed Clams

Select soft-shelled "steamer" clams, allowing about one dozen clams per serving. Wash thoroughly. Let stand in salt water 15 minutes; drain. In large saucepan, bring ½ inch water to boil. Add clams. Cover tightly; steam over medium heat for 5 to 10 minutes or until shells open. Discard any clams whose shells do not open. Remove any sand from cooking broth by straining through several layers of cheesecloth. Serve clams with cups of cooking broth and melted butter.

NUTRIENTS PER DOZEN CLAMS WITHOUT BUTTER

Calories 180	Dietary Fiber..........................0 g
Protein....................................30 g	Sodium............................130 mg
Carbohydrate..........................6 g	Potassium.......................760 mg
Fat ....1 g	Calcium...............12% U.S. RDA
Cholesterol........................80 mg	Iron....................100% U.S. RDA

Cucumber-Dill Sauce

1 small cucumber, peeled, seeded, finely chopped
   (1 cup)
1 cup dairy sour cream
2 tablespoons brown sugar
2 tablespoons white vinegar
1 tablespoon prepared mustard
2 teaspoons dill weed
½ teaspoon salt

In small bowl, combine all ingredients; mix well. Cover; refrigerate to chill. **1½ cups.**

NUTRIENTS PER 1 TABLESPOON

Calories 25	Dietary Fiber..........................0 g
Protein......................................0 g	Sodium..............................55 mg
Carbohydrate..........................2 g	Potassium.........................30 mg
Fat ....2 g	Calcium...............<2% U.S. RDA
Cholesterol..........................4 mg	Iron ....<2% U.S. RDA

Hot Dill Sauce

2 tablespoons margarine or butter
1 tablespoon finely chopped onion
2 tablespoons flour
1 teaspoon salt
1 teaspoon dill weed
⅛ teaspoon pepper
1½ cups milk

In small saucepan, saute onion in margarine until tender. Add flour, salt, dill weed and pepper; blend well. Gradually add milk. Cook until mixture boils and thickens, stirring constantly. Serve warm over fish. **1½ cups.**

NUTRIENTS PER 1 TABLESPOON

Calories 18	Dietary Fiber...........................0 g
Protein.......................................1 g	Sodium ....110 mg
Carbohydrate............................1 g	Potassium............................25 mg
Fat ....1 g	Calcium.................2% U.S. RDA
Cholesterol...........................0 mg	Iron ....<2% U.S. RDA

Mustard and Dill Sauce

In small bowl, combine ½ cup mayonnaise or salad dressing, 1 teaspoon prepared mustard and ¼ teaspoon dill weed; mix well. Cover; refrigerate to chill. **½ cup.**

NUTRIENTS PER 1 TABLESPOON

Calories 100	Dietary Fiber...........................0 g
Protein.......................................0 g	Sodium ....85 mg
Carbohydrate............................0 g	Potassium..............................5 mg
Fat ....11 mg	Calcium...............<2% U.S. RDA
Cholesterol...........................8 mg	Iron ....<2% U.S. RDA

Tartar Sauce

    1   cup mayonnaise or salad dressing
   ¼   cup finely chopped dill pickle or pickle relish
    1   tablespoon lemon juice
    2   tablespoons finely chopped fresh parsley
    1   tablespoon chopped pimiento
   ½   teaspoon finely chopped onion
   ¼   teaspoon Worcestershire sauce

In small bowl, combine all ingredients; mix well. Cover, refrigerate to chill. **1½ cups.**

VARIATION:

QUICK TARTAR SAUCE: In small bowl, combine ½ cup mayonnaise or salad dressing, 1 tablespoon sweet pickle relish and ½ teaspoon instant minced onion; mix well.

NUTRIENTS PER 1 TABLESPOON

Calories	70	Dietary Fiber	0 g
Protein	0 g	Sodium	75 mg
Carbohydrate	1 g	Potassium	5 mg
Fat	7 g	Calcium	<2% U.S. RDA
Cholesterol	4 mg	Iron	<2% U.S. RDA

Curry-Sour Cream Sauce

In small bowl, combine 1 cup dairy sour cream, 1 teaspoon curry powder, ¼ teaspoon salt and dash hot pepper sauce; mix well. Cover; refrigerate to chill. **1 cup.**

NUTRIENTS PER 1 TABLESPOON

Calories	29	Dietary Fiber	0 g
Protein	0 g	Sodium	40 mg
Carbohydrate	0 g	Potassium	2 mg
Fat	3 g	Calcium	<2% U.S. RDA
Cholesterol	6 mg	Iron	<2% U.S. RDA

Seafood Cocktail Sauce

  ½ cup chili sauce
  ½ teaspoon celery seed
  2 tablespoons lemon juice
  1 teaspoon prepared horseradish
  ½ teaspoon Worcestershire sauce

In small bowl, combine all ingredients; mix well. Cover and chill. **¾ cup.**

NUTRIENTS PER 1 TABLESPOON

Calories	12	Dietary Fiber	<1 g
Protein	0 g	Sodium	155 mg
Carbohydrate	3 g	Potassium	45 mg
Fat	0 g	Calcium	<2% U.S. RDA
Cholesterol	0 mg	Iron	<2% U.S. RDA

Creamy Herb Sauce

- ¼ cup mayonnaise or salad dressing
- ¼ teaspoon salt
  Dash garlic powder
- 2 tablespoons dairy sour cream
- 1 tablespoon chopped fresh parsley
- 1½ teaspoons lemon juice

In small bowl, combine all ingredients; mix well. Refrigerate to chill. **⅓ cup.**

NUTRIENTS PER 1 TABLESPOON

Calories	90	Dietary Fiber	0 g
Protein	0 g	Sodium	170 mg
Carbohydrate	1 g	Potassium	20 mg
Fat	10 g	Calcium	<2% U.S. RDA
Cholesterol	8 mg	Iron	<2% U.S. RDA

Cucumber Sauce

- 1 cup dairy sour cream or yogurt
- 2 teaspoons chopped fresh parsley
- ½ teaspoon chopped chives
- ½ medium cucumber, peeled, finely chopped or shredded
- 2 teaspoons lemon juice

In small bowl, combine all ingredients; mix well. Serve warm or cold. To serve warm, spoon over cooked fish. Bake at 350°F. for 5 minutes to heat sauce. **1½ cups.**

NUTRIENTS PER 1 TABLESPOON

Calories 25	Dietary Fiber..........................0 g
Protein.....................................0 g	Sodium....................................5 mg
Carbohydrate..........................1 g	Potassium............................30 mg
Fat ....2 g	Calcium..............<2% U.S. RDA
Cholesterol............................4 mg	Iron ....<2% U.S. RDA

Clarified Butter

In saucepan, slowly melt desired amount of butter. Remove from heat; let stand a few minutes until clear part can be spooned off into serving dish, discarding the milky portion that is left. Serve warm.

VARIATION:

LEMON BUTTER: Add 1 tablespoon lemon juice to ¼ cup clarified butter.

NUTRIENTS PER 1 TABLESPOON

Calories 110	Dietary Fiber..........................0 g
Protein.....................................0 g	Sodium............................115 mg
Carbohydrate..........................0 g	Potassium...............................0 mg
Fat ....12 g	Calcium..............<2% U.S. RDA
Cholesterol........................30 mg	Iron ....<2% U.S. RDA

Meats

Meats

Meats continue to play a starring role in most American menus and bring to our diet a valuable source of protein, an essential nutrient required for growth and for repair of body tissues. Because meat is often the most expensive item in the food budget, it is important to shop wisely, considering both quality and quantity, and to store and prepare all types and cuts carefully to gain maximum nutritional value and finest flavor and texture.

Purchasing

The following general guidelines can be useful when purchasing meat, although there may be variations according to how meat is cut or ground.

Meats, especially beef, veal and lamb, may be graded for quality; prime, choice and good are the grades most commonly available at retail. Although all contain the same proteins, minerals and vitamins, the top-quality meats usually have more marbling and are more tender as well as more costly. Marbling refers to the flecks and streaks of fat distributed through the lean portion of meat cuts. The presence of this fat contributes to the meat's juiciness, flavor and tenderness.

- **Fresh Meats**
  - **Beef** should be red with fat content creamy white in color. Texture should be fine-grained and firm. Vacuum-packed beef will have a darker, bluish-red color until packaging is removed.The red color of ground beef decreases as amount of fat increases. Be alert to labeling indicating lean-fat ratio. Increased fat means a lower price; however, since the fat melts away during cooking, proportionate shrinkage can be expected.
  - **Veal** should be virtually fat-free with lean, pink meat.

Texture should be fine-grained and firm. Any fat covering on larger cuts should be firm and white. Red meat indicates age and may mean diminished quality, flavor and tenderness.

• **Pork** should be light pink to rose in color with firm, fine-grained texture. Fat should be firm and white in color and bones should be pink. Modern technology is bringing leaner, more tender pork cuts to market.

• **Lamb** should be pink to light red in color with a fat covering or trim that is firm and white. Dark red flesh usually indicates older meat. The parchment-like covering found on a leg of lamb (called the "fell") is usually left on to help retain juices. It should be trimmed from steaks and chops before cooking for best appearance and even cooking.

• Frozen Meats

Most guidelines for selecting fresh meat apply. Frozen meats should be in well-sealed packages and feel solid to the touch. Avoid packages with tears, freezer burn, or frost crystals.

• Canned Meats

Avoid any cans that are bulging or leaking. Consult the label for information on nutrition, quantity and approximate number of servings, water and/or fat content, processing method, and additives. Although canned meats are cooked before packing, heating often increases flavor.

• How Much to Buy

This depends on cut, amount of bone and fat, size of appetites, other items on the menu and whether leftovers are desired for other meals. When meat is not combined with other ingredients, plan on ¼ to ⅓ pound per serving for boneless meat with little fat. Meat with minimal amount of bone and fat, ⅓ to ½ pound per serving; for meat with larger amounts of bone and fat, you may need as much as ¾ to 1 pound per serving.

• **Figuring Cost**

Since the number of servings that can be obtained from 1 pound will depend upon the amount of bone and fat waste, the best way to figure the value of your meat is on the basis of cost per serving, not cost per pound.

Meat costs can be reduced by shopping for advertised specials, by purchasing less tender cuts and by preparing meat in the most suitable method to achieve tender results. Leftover meat can be utilized in sandwich spreads, salads, soups, casseroles, stir-fry combinations and other dishes where the addition of complementary ingredients act as extenders.

Storing

• **Fresh meats** are highly perishable and should be stored in the coldest part of your refrigerator. Since air circulation is necessary during refrigerator storage, meat that has not been prepackaged should be loosely wrapped. Prepackaged meats may be kept in their store wrappings for 1 or 2 days. Ground meats deteriorate more quickly than other cuts and should be used promptly. Avoid using any meat that has become gray in color, slippery to the touch, or has an off odor.

• **Cooked meats** may be refrigerated in a tightly covered container 4 to 5 days or frozen, properly wrapped, up to 3 months.

• **Cured meats** should be lightly wrapped or covered, refrigerated and used within 5 days.

• **Canned meats** should be stored in a cool, dry place, unopened. After opening, remove to a more suitable container or wrap and refrigerate. Use product before expiration date on can.

Hints for Handling Meats

• Thoroughly clean countertop, cutting board, slicer, knives, hands and dishes that come in contact with meat with hot, soapy water after each use.

• Once cooking is started, continue until meat is cooked, because bacteria can thrive in a warm, moist environment. If cooking is divided between microwave and grill, have grill heated and ready to receive partially cooked meat.

• If meats are to be transported, keep hot meats hot (above 140°F.) and cold meats chilled (below 40°F.).

• It is important to refrigerate leftovers as soon as possible after cooking to prevent spoilage.

Cooking Guidelines for Meats

There are two basic methods for cooking meat—moist heat and dry heat. Less tender cuts require cooking that will help break down tough connective tissues; moist heat methods like braising and cooking in liquid are preferred. Tender cuts, which do not require moisture and long, slow cooking, are usually cooked with a dry heat method—roasting, broiling, panbroiling, grilling and panfrying.

The method you choose should relate directly to the inherent tenderness of the cut of meat. Tenderness is determined by where on the animal the meat comes from, degree of marbling, age of animal and how meat was stored and prepared for market. In general, cuts from the loin section are the most tender. As the cuts get farther from this section, they are usually less tender. Tenderness can be enhanced by the butcher or consumer in a number of ways—forcing meat through a mechanical tenderizer, pounding with meat mallet, marinating, scoring and slicing across the grain perpendicular to muscle fibers. These techniques make it possible to cook less tender cuts with methods usually used for tender cuts of meats.

A meat thermometer is the most accurate way to determine doneness of larger cuts of meat. Insert meat thermometer so tip reaches the center of the thickest part of meat, but do not let it rest in fat or on bone. Refer to timetables for roasting to determine meat temperature for desired doneness. Piercing or making a small cut in meat to check for a color change is appropriate for steaks and small cuts of meat.

Basic Cooking Methods

Use to help you select the appropriate cooking methods for the cut of meat you plan to prepare. If no specific recipe is given, follow these general instructions:

- **Roasting**
  - Place meat fat side up on rack in shallow roasting pan.
  - Season as desired.
  - Insert meat thermometer so tip does not rest in fat or on bone.
  - Do not add water or cover.
  - Roast at 325°F. until thermometer reaches desired doneness.

- **Broiling**
  - Place meat on rack in broiler pan.
  - Place pan 2 to 5 inches from heat. The thicker the cut, the farther the meat should be placed from the heating unit to assure even cooking.
  - Broil one side until browned.
  - Season cooked side, if desired.
  - Turn meat; cook second side to desired doneness and until meat is browned.
  - Season second side, if desired.

- **Panbroiling**
  - Place meat in preheated heavy frypan.
  - Do not add oil or water. Do not cover.
  - Cook slowly, turn occasionally and pour off fat as it accumulates.

- Cook to desired doneness and until both sides are browned.
- Season if desired.

- **Panfrying**
  - Heat small amount of oil in skillet over medium heat.
  - When oil is hot, add meat. Do not cover.
  - Turn occasionally until done as desired and browned on both sides.
  - Season if desired.

- **Braising**
  - In heavy pan, brown meat in small amount of oil; pour off fat.
  - Season if desired.
  - Add a small amount of liquid to meat; cover pan tightly.
  - Simmer on top of range or in oven until tender.

- **Cooking in Liquid**
  - In Dutch oven or heavy pan, brown meat in a small amount of oil; pour off fat.
  - Season if desired.
  - Add enough liquid to cover meat completely; cover pan tightly.
  - Simmer on top of range or in oven until tender.

- **Grilling**
  - Preheat gas grill or start coals 30 to 40 minutes in advance. Start cooking when coals are partially covered with gray ash.
  - Rub grill with oil to prevent meat from sticking.
  - Adjust grill up or down to control intensity of heat.
  - Place meat on grill. Cook first side until browned.
  - Season cooked side before turning, if desired.
  - Turn with tongs; cook second side to desired doneness and until meat is browned.
  - Season second side, if desired.
  - For additional grilling information see Special Helps—Barbecuing.

Beef

Beef Roast

Allow ⅓ to ½ lb. per serving for bone-in roast and ¼ to ⅓ lb. per serving for boneless roast. Heat oven to 325°F. Sprinkle meat with salt and pepper. Place roast fat side up on rack in shallow roasting pan. Insert meat thermometer. Do not add water or cover. Roast to desired degree of doneness using Timetable for Roasting Beef.

AU JUS GRAVY: After removing roast from pan, skim off fat from meat juices. Add water to meat juice, about ⅓ to ½ cup. Cook over medium-high heat, stirring and scraping bottom of pan until mixture begins to boil. If desired, strain. Salt and pepper to taste. Serve with meat.

NUTRIENTS PER ½ LB. RAW RIB ROAST WITH BONE, COOKED

Calories	270	Dietary Fiber	0 g
Protein	31 g	Sodium	85 mg
Carbohydrate	0 g	Potassium	430 mg
Fat	16 g	Calcium	<2% U.S. RDA
Cholesterol	90 mg	Iron	22% U.S. RDA

Timetable for Roasting Beef

(Oven Temperature 325°F.)

Roast	Weight (pounds)	Thermometer Reading (°F.)	Cooking Time* (Minutes Per Pound)
Rib (Bone in)	6 to 8	140°F. (rare) 160°F. (med.) 170°F. (well)	23 to 25 27 to 30 32 to 35
Boneless or Rolled Rib	4 to 6	140°F. (rare) 160°F. (med.) 170°F. (well)	26 to 32 34 to 38 40 to 42
Rib Eye**	4 to 6	140°F. (rare) 160°F. (med.) 170°F. (well)	18 to 20 20 to 22 22 to 24
Boneless or Rolled Rump	4 to 6	150° to 170°F.	25 to 30
Sirloin Tip	3½ to 4 6 to 8	140° to 170°F. 140° to 170°F.	35 to 40 30 to 35
Top Round	4 to 6	140° to 170°F.	25 to 30

*Based on meat taken directly from refrigerator.
**Roast at 350°F.

Beef Tenderloin

Allow approximately ¼ to ⅓ lb. beef tenderloin per serving. Heat oven to 425°F. Remove excess surface fat and connective tissue from tenderloin; sprinkle with salt and pepper. Place roast on rack in shallow roasting pan. Turn thin ends under; brush with oil or melted margarine. Insert meat thermometer so the tip reaches the center of the thickest part of meat. Do not add water or cover. Roast 45 to 60 minutes or until meat thermometer registers 140°F. To serve, cut into slices across grain of meat.

NUTRIENTS PER ⅓ LB. RAW TENDERLOIN, COOKED

Calories	190	Dietary Fiber	0 g
Protein	26 g	Sodium	55 mg
Carbohydrate	0 g	Potassium	380 mg
Fat	8 g	Calcium	<2% U.S. RDA
Cholesterol	80 mg	Iron	20% U.S. RDA

Marinated Rolled Rib Roast

¼ cup	oil
¼ cup	wine vinegar
3 tablespoons	chopped fresh parsley
1 teaspoon	seasoned salt
1 teaspoon	thyme leaves
½ teaspoon	pepper
1 tablespoon	soy sauce
2	garlic cloves, crushed
3 to 4-lb.	rolled beef rib roast

In small bowl, combine oil, vinegar, parsley, seasoned salt, thyme, pepper, soy sauce and garlic. Place roast in non-metal bowl or plastic bag; pour marinade over roast. Cover bowl or seal bag; marinate 8 to 12 hours in refrigerator, turning several times to season.

Heat oven to 350°F. Drain roast; place on rack in shallow roasting pan. (Reserve marinade for basting.) Insert meat thermometer. Roast uncovered at 350°F. until meat thermometer registers 160°F., about 1½ to 2 hours, basting with marinade every 20 to 30 minutes.* Let stand 15 minutes before slicing. **8 to 10 servings.**

TIP: *For rare roast beef, cook to 140°F.; for well-done roast beef, cook to 170°F.

NUTRIENTS PER ⅒ OF RECIPE

Calories	260	Dietary Fiber	0 g
Protein	28 g	Sodium	140 mg
Carbohydrate	0 g	Potassium	390 mg
Fat	15 g	Calcium	<2% U.S. RDA
Cholesterol	80 mg	Iron	15% U.S. RDA

Steak Marinades

BURGUNDY MARINADE

½ teaspoon salt
¼ teaspoon pepper
1 garlic clove, minced
½ cup oil
½ cup Burgundy or dry red wine
2 tablespoons catsup
2 tablespoons molasses

In small bowl, combine all ingredients; mix well. **1¼ cups.**

SOY MARINADE

½ teaspoon ginger
1 green onion, chopped, if desired
1 garlic clove, minced
¾ cup oil
¼ cup soy sauce
3 tablespoons honey or sugar
2 tablespoons vinegar or lemon juice

In small bowl, combine all ingredients; mix well. **1⅓ cups.**

LEMON-LIME MARINADE
    2 limes
    1 lemon
    ½ cup oil

Cut limes and lemon into ½-inch slices. In medium saucepan, combine all ingredients. Cool over medium heat about 5 minutes or until hot, pressing fruit with back of spoon as it heats. Pour hot mixture over steak. **1 cup.**

Grilling Steak

Steaks for grilling should be at least ¾-inch thick. For less tender cuts such as chuck and top round steak, use high-quality beef or marinate meat to tenderize before grilling. Trim excess fat from steaks so drippings will not catch fire. Without cutting into the meat, slash the fat edge at 1-inch intervals to prevent curling. Low to moderate temperature is best for grilling beef. Coals are ready when your hand can be held about 4 to 5 inches from the coals for 4 to 5 seconds. Spread coals apart to lower temperature; move coals together for more heat.

Timetable for Grilling Steak

Steak	Thickness	Total Cooking Time in Minutes (Rare to Medium)
Rib, Rib Eye or Top Loin Sirloin, Porterhouse, T-Bone, Top Sirloin	¾ inch 1 inch 1½ inches	12 to 16 minutes 15 to 20 minutes 22 to 30 minutes
Chuck	¾ to 1 inch 1½ inches	14 to 20 minutes 18 to 24 minutes
Top Round	¾ to 1 inch 1½ inches	22 to 26 minutes 28 to 35 minutes
Tenderloin	1 inch 1½ inches 2 inches	6 to 8 minutes 8 to 10 minutes 10 to 12 minutes

Timetable for Broiling Steak

Steak	Thickness	Total Cooking Time in Minutes (Rare to Medium)
Rib, Rib Eye or Top Loin	¾ inch 1 inch 1½ inches	8 to 12 15 to 20 25 to 30
Sirloin, Porterhouse or T-Bone	¾ inch 1 inch 1½ inches	10 to 15 20 to 25 30 to 35
Tenderloin (Filet Mignon)	1 inch 2 inches	10 to 15 15 to 20
Chuck Steak	¾ inch 1 inch 1½ inches	14 to 20 20 to 25 30 to 35
Top Round Steak	1 inch 1½ inches	20 to 30 30 to 35

Broiled Steak

Allow ⅓ to ½ lb. per serving of bone-in steak or ¼ to ⅓ lb. per serving of boneless steak. Place steak on broiler pan. Place or adjust broiler pan so the top of a ¾-inch-thick steak is 2 to 3 inches from the heat, a 1-inch-thick steak is 3 to 4 inches from the heat and a 1½ to 2-inch-thick steak is 4 to 5 inches from the heat. When one side is browned, turn and finish cooking on the second side. Broil to desired doneness using Timetable for Broiling Steak. Sprinkle with salt and pepper.

NUTRIENTS PER ½ LB. RAW BEEF STEAK WITH BONE, COOKED

Calories	240	Dietary Fiber	0 g
Protein	34 g	Sodium	75 mg
Carbohydrate	0 g	Potassium	460 mg
Fat	10 g	Calcium	<2% U.S. RDA
Cholesterol	100 mg	Iron	20% U.S. RDA

Trafalgar Steak

Broil or grill steak. In small saucepan, combine ½ teaspoon garlic salt, ½ cup dairy sour cream and 2 to 3 teaspoons prepared horseradish. Cook, stirring constantly, until thoroughly heated. *Do not boil.* Serve warm. **4 servings.**

NUTRIENTS PER ¼ OF SAUCE SERVED WITH 4 OZ. COOKED STEAK

Calories	300	Dietary Fiber	0 g
Protein	35 g	Sodium	330 mg
Carbohydrate	2 g	Potassium	510 mg
Fat	16 g	Calcium	4% U.S. RDA
Cholesterol	110 mg	Iron	<2% U.S. RDA

Steak Champignon

In large skillet, fry 1 to 1½-inch thick steak in 1 to 2 tablespoons margarine or butter until desired doneness. Remove steak to platter; keep warm. Add ½ cup dairy sour cream, ¼ cup dry red wine or milk and 4.5-oz. jar sliced mushrooms, drained, to pan drippings. Cook over low heat, stirring constantly, until thoroughly heated. *Do not boil.* Spoon over steak. **4 servings.**

NUTRIENTS PER ¼ OF SAUCE SERVED WITH 4 OZ. COOKED STEAK

Calories	370	Dietary Fiber	<1 g
Protein	36 g	Sodium	280 mg
Carbohydrate	3 g	Potassium	560 mg
Fat	22 g	Calcium	4% U.S. RDA
Cholesterol	110 mg	Iron	25% U.S. RDA

Stuffed Flank Steak

1½ lb. flank steak

MARINADE
¼ cup oil
¼ cup red wine vinegar
1 tablespoon soy sauce
¼ teaspoon seasoned salt
¼ teaspoon thyme leaves, crushed
¼ teaspoon pepper

FILLING
2 tablespoons margarine or butter
½ cup chopped onion
½ cup shredded carrots
½ cup shredded mozzarella cheese
9-oz. pkg. frozen chopped spinach in a pouch, thawed, well drained

1 teaspoon Dijon mustard
⅛ teaspoon pepper

Score steak on both sides diagonally in a criss-cross pattern; pound meat lightly with meat mallet or rolling pin. Place in shallow glass dish. In small bowl, combine marinade ingredients; pour over meat. Cover; marinate in refrigerator 8 to 24 hours.

Heat oven to 325°F. In medium skillet, melt margarine over medium heat. Saute onion in margarine until tender. Remove from heat. Stir in remaining filling ingredients; blend well. Remove meat from marinade; discard marinade. Spoon filling evenly over meat. Roll tightly starting with narrow end; tie securely with string if necessary. Place beef roll in 10x6-inch (1-quart) baking dish.* Roast at 325°F. for 1½ hours or until desired doneness. Cover; let stand 5 to 10 minutes before slicing. **8 servings.**

TIP: *Stuffed Flank Steak can be made ahead. To make ahead, prepare as above to *; cover and refrigerate no longer than 8 hours. Bake as directed above.

NUTRIENTS PER ⅛ OF RECIPE

Calories	200	Dietary Fiber	2 g
Protein	17 g	Sodium	200 mg
Carbohydrate	3 g	Potassium	320 mg
Fat	13 g	Calcium	10% U.S. RDA
Cholesterol	40 mg	Iron	15% U.S. RDA

Brown Sauce

2 tablespoons margarine or butter
2 tablespoons flour
¾ teaspoon salt
⅛ teaspoon pepper
2 beef-flavor bouillon cubes or 2 teaspoons beef-flavor instant bouillon
2 cups water

In small saucepan, melt margarine. Add flour; cook until golden brown, stirring constantly. Add remaining ingredients. Cook until mixture boils and thickens, stirring constantly. **2 cups.**

TIP: One 10-½ oz. can condensed beef broth with enough water added to make 2 cups liquid can be substituted for bouillon cubes and water. If desired, use ½ cup red wine or sherry for part of the water.

VARIATIONS:

BORDELAISE SAUCE: Saute 2 tablespoons minced green onion, 1 garlic clove, minced, 1 carrot, finely chopped, 1 small bay leaf and 4 peppercorns in margarine before adding flour. Prepare sauce as directed. Strain to remove vegetables and spices before serving. If desired, stir in ½ teaspoon chopped parsley and dash thyme. Serve warm.

MADEIRA SAUCE: Substitute ½ cup madeira wine for ½ cup of the water.

MUSHROOM SAUCE: After mixture comes to a boil, stir in 4.5-oz. jar whole or sliced mushrooms, drained. Cook until thoroughly heated.

NUTRIENTS PER 1 TABLESPOON

Calories ...8	Dietary Fiber ...0 g
Protein ...0 g	Sodium ...115 mg
Carbohydrate ...0 g	Potassium ...0 mg
Fat ...1 g	Calcium ...<2% U.S. RDA
Cholesterol ...0 mg	Iron ...<2% U.S. RDA

Pan Gravy

3 tablespoons flour
3 tablespoons meat or poultry drippings
2 cups liquid (water or broth)
  Salt and pepper

In skillet or roasting pan, add flour to drippings. Blend over low heat until smooth and browned. Add liquid; cook until mixture boils and thickens, stirring constantly. Salt and pepper to taste. **2 cups.**

TIP: Flour and drippings can be decreased to 2 tablespoons each for thin gravy or increased to 4 tablespoons for thick gravy.

VARIATION:

MUSHROOM GRAVY: Add 4.5-oz. jar whole or sliced mushrooms, drained, to gravy after it comes to a boil and thickens. Cook until mixture returns to a boil, stirring occasionally.

NUTRIENTS: Variables in this recipe make it impossible to calculate nutrition information.

Bearnaise Sauce

  ½ cup margarine or butter
  1 tablespoon finely chopped onion
  1 teaspoon tarragon leaves
  ½ teaspoon chervil leaves
  ¼ teaspoon salt
    Dash pepper
  ¼ cup hot water
  4 egg yolks
  2 tablespoons white wine
  4 teaspoons lemon juice

In small saucepan or top of double boiler, combine margarine, onion, tarragon, chervil, salt, pepper and hot water. Cook until margarine is melted, stirring frequently. In small bowl, beat egg yolks slightly. Blend small amount of margarine mixture into beaten egg yolks; add to remaining margarine mixture. Cook over low heat or place top of double boiler over hot but not boiling water. Beat mixture with rotary beater or briskly with spoon until thick and smooth. Add white wine and lemon juice; blend well. Serve immediately. **1 cup.**

NUTRIENTS PER 1 TABLESPOON

Calories 70	Dietary Fiber...........................0 g
Protein......................................1 g	Sodium............................100 mg
Carbohydrate............................0 g	Potassium...........................10 mg
Fat ....7 g	Calcium..............<2% U.S. RDA
Cholesterol........................70 mg	Iron ....<2% U.S. RDA

Honey-Spice Glaze

Heat oven to 350°F. In small bowl, combine ¼ cup barbecue sauce, ¼ cup soy sauce and 2 tablespoons honey; mix well. Place cooked beef brisket in shallow baking pan; spread brisket with glaze mixture. Bake at 350°F. for 30 to 40 minutes, basting occasionally with pan juices. **½ cup.**

NUTRIENTS PER 1 TABLESPOON

Calories 25	Dietary Fiber...........................0 g
Protein......................................1 g	Sodium............................580 mg
Carbohydrate............................6 g	Potassium...........................50 mg
Fat ....0 g	Calcium..............<2% U.S. RDA
Cholesterol..........................0 mg	Iron ....<2% U.S. RDA

Pot Roast and Gravy

2	tablespoons oil
3 to 4-lb.	beef chuck arm, blade or 7-bone pot roast
½	teaspoon pepper
4	medium onions, quartered
4	stalks celery, cut into pieces
1	bay leaf
2	beef-flavor bouillon cubes or 2 teaspoons beef-flavor instant bouillon
1½	cups hot water

6 medium potatoes, halved
6 medium carrots, cut into pieces
3 tablespoons flour
¼ cup cold water
   Salt to taste

Heat oven to 325°F. In 5-quart Dutch oven or roasting pan, heat oil over medium-high heat; brown meat about 5 minutes on each side. Drain excess fat, if desired. Sprinkle pepper on all sides of meat. Add 1 onion, 1 stalk celery and bay leaf to meat. Dissolve bouillon in hot water; pour ¾ cup of the bouillon around meat, reserving ¾ cup. Bring to a boil; cover. Bake at 325°F. for 60 minutes. Add remaining vegetables; cover and bake an additional 60 to 75 minutes or until meat and vegetables are fork-tender.

To prepare gravy, place meat and vegetables on warm platter; cover loosely to keep warm. Measure drippings from Dutch oven. Skim off fat, if desired. Add reserved bouillon to drippings to make 3 cups; return to Dutch oven. In small jar with lid, add flour to cold water; shake well. Gradually stir into drippings. Cook over medium heat, stirring constantly, until mixture thickens and boils. Salt to taste. Serve with meat and vegetables. **6 servings.**

NUTRIENTS PER ⅙ OF RECIPE

Calories	540	Dietary Fiber	7 g
Protein	50 g	Sodium	630 mg
Carbohydrate	42 g	Potassium	1580 mg
Fat	19 g	Calcium	6% U.S. RDA
Cholesterol	140 mg	Iron	40% U.S. RDA

Beef Brisket

Allow approximately ⅓ to ½ lb. uncooked boneless beef brisket per serving. In large saucepan, cover brisket with water. Add 1 bay leaf, 1½ teaspoons salt and 1 teaspoon peppercorns to the water. Cover; simmer 3 to 3½ hours or until tender. After cooking, drain; serve plain or with Honey-Spice Glaze (see Index). The brisket can be cooked one day, then glazed and heated the following day.

NUTRIENTS PER ½ LB. RAW BEEF BRISKET, COOKED

Calories	260	Dietary Fiber	0 g
Protein	31 g	Sodium	NA
Carbohydrate	0 g	Potassium	310 mg
Fat	14 g	Calcium	<2% U.S. RDA
Cholesterol	100 mg	Iron	15% U.S. RDA

New England Boiled Dinner

3-lb. corned beef
1 teaspoon peppercorns or ¼ teaspoon pepper
6 whole cloves
1 bay leaf
6 potatoes, peeled and quartered
6 carrots, halved lengthwise
1 medium head cabbage, cut into 6 wedges

In large saucepan, cover corned beef with water. Add peppercorns, cloves and bay leaf. Cover; simmer 3 to 3½ hours or until tender. Add potatoes and carrots. Cover; simmer 15 minutes longer. Add cabbage; cook an additional 15 minutes or until vegetables are tender. Remove bay leaf. Cut meat into pieces. Serve with cooking liquid and vegetables. **6 to 8 servings.**

TIP: If corned beef is packaged with spice packet, omit peppercorns, cloves and bay leaf.

NUTRIENTS PER ⅛ OF RECIPE

Calories	440	Dietary Fiber	7 g
Protein	26 g	Sodium	1410 mg
Carbohydrate	32 g	Potassium	1240 mg
Fat	23 g	Calcium	8% U.S. RDA
Cholesterol	120 mg	Iron	20% U.S. RDA

Swiss Steak

2 to 2½-lb. beef round steak, cut ½ to ¾-inch thick
¼ cup all purpose flour
1 teaspoon salt
¼ teaspoon pepper
1 to 2 tablespoons oil
1 large onion, sliced
8-oz. can (1 cup) tomatoes, undrained, cut up
8-oz. can (1 cup) tomato sauce

Cut meat into serving pieces. In small bowl, combine flour, salt and pepper. Coat meat with seasoned flour (use all the flour). In large skillet, brown meat in hot oil. Add remaining ingredients. Cover, simmer 1¼ to 1½ hours or until meat is tender. Serve with potatoes or noodles. **6 servings.**

TIPS: If desired, substitute one 10½-oz. can condensed tomato soup and ½ cup water for tomatoes and tomato sauce.

Vegetables such as peas, beans or mushrooms can be added to Swiss Steak. Add peas and beans toward end of cooking; add mushrooms with onion.

NUTRIENTS PER ⅙ OF RECIPE

Calories	290	Dietary Fiber	1 g
Protein	32 g	Sodium	710 mg
Carbohydrate	10 g	Potassium	710 mg
Fat	13 g	Calcium	2% U.S. RDA
Cholesterol	90 mg	Iron	20% U.S. RDA

Beef Stroganoff

¼ cup all purpose flour
½ teaspoon salt
⅛ teaspoon pepper
2½ lb. beef sirloin steak, cut into 3x½-inch strips
¼ cup oil or shortening

10½-oz. can condensed beef broth
  ½ cup water
  3 tablespoons tomato juice
  1 tablespoon Worcestershire sauce
  2 teaspoons prepared mustard
  1½ cups dairy sour cream
  Hot cooked rice or noodles

In plastic bag, combine flour, salt and pepper. Add beef; shake to coat. In large skillet, heat oil. Add meat, cooking until browned; drain. Add beef broth, water, tomato juice, Worcestershire sauce and mustard; mix well. Cover, simmer for 20 to 30 minutes or until meat is tender. Stir in sour cream; heat thoroughly. *Do not boil*. Serve over hot cooked rice or noodles. **8 servings.**

NUTRIENTS PER ⅛ OF RECIPE

Calories	450	Dietary Fiber	2 g
Protein	28 g	Sodium	460 mg
Carbohydrate	31 g	Potassium	460 mg
Fat	23 g	Calcium	8% U.S. RDA
Cholesterol	90 mg	Iron	20% U.S. RDA

Beef Oriental with Rice

MARINADE
  ¼ cup soy sauce
  1 tablespoon sugar
  2 tablespoons dry sherry
  2 tablespoons oil
  ½ to ¾ teaspoon ginger
  2 garlic cloves, minced

  1 lb. beef top sirloin steak, cut into thin strips*
  2 tablespoons oil
  2 medium carrots, cut into julienne strips 1-inch long (1 cup)

2 stalks celery, cut diagonally into ¼-inch slices
(1 cup)
1 medium onion, cut into wedges
6-oz. pkg. frozen pea pods, thawed, drained
8-oz. can sliced water chestnuts, drained
1 tablespoon cornstarch
½ cup cold water
Hot cooked rice

In large bowl, combine marinade ingredients. Add meat; stir to coat evenly with marinade. Cover; let stand at least 30 minutes. Drain, reserving marinade.

Heat large skillet or wok over medium-high heat until hot. Add 2 tablespoons oil; heat until it ripples. Add meat; stir-fry 2 minutes. Add reserved marinade; stir-fry 2 minutes. (Marinade should be bubbling vigorously.) Add carrots; cover and cook 2 to 3 minutes or until carrots are crisp-tender. Add celery, onion, pea pods and water chestnuts; stir-fry 1 minute. Combine cornstarch and cold water; stir into meat-vegetable mixture. Cook, stirring constantly, until sauce is thickened. Serve over hot cooked rice. **4 to 5 servings.**

TIP: *For easier slicing, place meat in freezer for 30 to 45 minutes or until firm but not frozen; slice thinly.

NUTRIENTS PER ⅕ OF RECIPE

Calories	400	Dietary Fiber	5 g
Protein	19 g	Sodium	880 mg
Carbohydrate	45 g	Potassium	610 mg
Fat	15 g	Calcium	4% U.S. RDA
Cholesterol	45 mg	Iron	20% U.S. RDA

Burgundy Beef

3 slices bacon, cut into 2-inch pieces
3-lb. beef round steak, cut into 1-inch cubes
2 cups Burgundy or dry red wine

       ½ cup water
10½-oz. can condensed beef broth
       ½ teaspoon thyme leaves
        1 garlic clove, minced
        1 bay leaf
       16 small boiling onions or 16-oz. can small onions, drained
       16 baby carrots or 5 carrots, cut into 2-inch pieces
        2 tablespoons margarine or butter, softened
        2 tablespoons flour
        2 tablespoons chopped fresh parsley, if desired
           Hot cooked rice

Heat oven to 350°F. In ovenproof Dutch oven, fry bacon until crisp. Remove bacon; drain on paper towel, reserving drippings. Brown beef in bacon drippings. Stir in wine, water, beef broth, thyme, garlic and bay leaf. Cover; bake at 350°F. for 2 hours, stirring occasionally. Add bacon, onions and carrots. Cover; continue baking 1 to 1½ hours or until meat and vegetables are tender, stirring occasionally.

Remove from oven; remove bay leaf. Remove meat and vegetables; keep warm. In small bowl, combine margarine and flour. Gradually add about ½ cup of the cooking liquid, stirring until smooth. Add flour mixture to remaining liquid; cook over medium heat until mixture thickens, stirring constantly. Add meat and vegetables; heat thoroughly. Spoon into serving dish; sprinkle with parsley. Serve over rice. **8 servings.**

NUTRIENTS PER ⅛ OF RECIPE

Calories 420	Dietary Fiber...........................4 g
Protein......................................33 g	Sodium..............................350 mg
Carbohydrate..........................34 g	Potassium.........................730 mg
Fat ....12 g	Calcium................4% U.S. RDA
Cholesterol.........................80 mg	Iron......................25% U.S. RDA

Beef Fondue

For each serving, allow about ½ lb. boneless sirloin or tenderloin, cut into 1-inch cubes.* Arrange cubes of meat in individual dishes lined with lettuce leaves; place at each setting. Prepare 3 or 4 sauces. (Make your own or try prepared steak sauce, horseradish sauce, cocktail dips, mustard sauce, teriyaki sauce or blue cheese salad dressing.) Place fondue pot base in center of table. In fondue pot, heat cooking oil over medium heat to about 375°F. or until it browns a cube of bread quickly. Place fondue pot over base. (If using electric fondue pot, use electric base to heat oil in fondue pot.)

With fondue fork, spear meat. Cook in hot oil until of desired doneness. Remove to plate; eat with dinner fork, dipping meat into desired sauces. (The fondue fork becomes very hot in the oil.)

TIPS: *Try other types of fondue—cubes of lamb served with chutney, sweet-sour and curry sauces; fresh or thawed and well-drained frozen shrimp served with cocktail, sweet-sour and curry sauces; or cubes of boneless chicken breast served with sweet-sour, chive-butter and curry sauces.

For vegetables with fondue, add whole fresh mushrooms or thick sliced zucchini to dishes of meat. Cook vegetables along with meat.

Leftover oil can be strained and stored in refrigerator to be used the next time fondue is served or for other frying.

NUTRIENTS PER ½ LB. RAW BEEF, COOKED

Calories	310	Dietary Fiber	0 g
Protein	45 g	Sodium	100 mg
Carbohydrate	0 g	Potassium	600 mg
Fat	13 g	Calcium	<2% U.S. RDA
Cholesterol	130 mg	Iron	30% U.S. RDA

Barbecued Beef Sandwiches

    2 tablespoons brown sugar
 ¼ teaspoon dry mustard
    1 garlic clove, minced or ⅛ teaspoon garlic powder
      Dash pepper
1½ cups catsup
 ½ cup water
    2 tablespoons chopped onion
    2 tablespoons lemon juice
    1 tablespoon vinegar
    1 tablespoon Worcestershire sauce
    3 cups thinly sliced cooked beef, cut into strips
    6 sandwich buns, split

In medium saucepan, combine all ingredients except beef
and sandwich buns; bring to a boil. Reduce heat; simmer 30
minutes, stirring occasionally. Stir in beef; cover and simmer an additional 15 minutes. Spoon about ½ cup mixture
onto each bun. **6 sandwiches.**

NUTRIENTS PER 1 SANDWICH

Calories	350	Dietary Fiber	<1 g
Protein	25 g	Sodium	990 mg
Carbohydrate	44 g	Potassium	610 mg
Fat	8 g	Calcium	4% U.S. RDA
Cholesterol	60 mg	Iron	20% U.S. RDA

Baked Ribs and Sauerkraut

      3 lb. ribs
  1½ teaspoons salt
   ¼ teaspoon pepper
32-oz. jar (4 cups) sauerkraut, undrained
    2 tablespoons brown sugar
    2 tart apples, peeled, chopped
    1 small onion, chopped
 ¼ cup water

Heat oven to 450°F. Cut ribs into serving pieces. Place in ungreased 13x9-inch pan; sprinkle with salt and pepper. Bake at 450°F. for 20 minutes. Reduce oven temperature to 350°F. Remove ribs; drain fat from pan. In same pan, combine sauerkraut, brown sugar, apples, onion and water; spread evenly. Arrange ribs on top; bake at 350°F. for an additional 1½ to 2 hours or until ribs are tender, stirring occasionally. **5 to 6 servings.**

NUTRIENTS PER ⅙ OF RECIPE

Calories	410	Dietary Fiber	6 g
Protein	27 g	Sodium	1302 mg
Carbohydrate	15 g	Potassium	490 mg
Fat	27 g	Calcium	8% U.S. RDA
Cholesterol	110 mg	Iron	10% U.S. RDA

Basic Meat Loaf

    2 lb. lean ground beef
    ½ cup chili sauce or catsup
    2 eggs
    ⅓ cup dry bread crumbs
    ½ teaspoon thyme leaves
    ½ teaspoon onion salt
    ⅛ teaspoon pepper

Heat oven to 350°F. In large bowl, combine all ingredients; mix well. Press meat mixture in ungreased 8x4-inch loaf pan. Bake at 350°F. for 65 to 70 minutes or until meat is well browned and firm. **8 servings.**

VARIATION:

SAUCY MEAT LOAF: In small saucepan, combine 8¼-oz. can crushed pineapple in heavy syrup undrained, ½ cup catsup, 2 tablespoons brown sugar and 2 teaspoons cornstarch. Cook over medium heat until mixture boils and thickens, stirring frequently. Spoon over baked meat loaf; bake an additional 15 to 20 minutes.

NUTRIENTS PER ⅙ OF RECIPE

Calories	270	Dietary Fiber	<1 g
Protein	22 g	Sodium	440 mg
Carbohydrate	8 g	Potassium	330 mg
Fat	17 g	Calcium	2% U.S. RDA
Cholesterol	140 mg	Iron	10% U.S. RDA

Basic Meatballs

1 lb. ground beef
¼ cup dry bread or cracker crumbs
½ teaspoon salt
⅛ teaspoon pepper
1 small onion, chopped
1 egg
1 tablespoon oil

In medium bowl, combine all ingredients except oil; mix well. Shape into 1½ to 2-inch balls. In large skillet, brown meatballs in hot oil; drain. Add desired sauce to meatballs; cook as directed in recipe. **4 servings.**

TIP: To brown in oven, arrange in ungreased shallow baking pan; bake at 400°F. for 15 minutes or until browned.

VARIATIONS:

COCKTAIL MEATBALLS: Shape into 1-inch balls; continue as directed above. **24 meatballs.**

SPEEDY SWEDISH MEATBALLS: In large skillet, combine browned meatballs with one 10¾-oz. can condensed cream of mushroom or chicken soup, ¼ cup water or milk and ⅛ teaspoon nutmeg or allspice. Cover; simmer for 15 minutes, stirring occasionally. **4 servings.**

NUTRIENTS PER ¼ OF RECIPE

Calories	300	Dietary Fiber	<1 g
Protein	21 g	Sodium	390 mg
Carbohydrate	6 g	Potassium	270 mg
Fat	21 g	Calcium	2% U.S. RDA
Cholesterol	140 mg	Iron	10% U.S. RDA

Stuffed Green Peppers

     4 large green peppers
     1 lb. ground beef
    ¼ cup chopped celery
     2 tablespoons chopped onion
     1 cup cooked rice
    ½ teaspoon salt
        Dash pepper
    ¼ cup catsup
     1 medium tomato, chopped
 8-oz. can (1 cup) tomato sauce
     1 teaspoon sugar
    ¼ teaspoon basil leaves
     1 oz. (¼ cup) shredded Cheddar cheese

Heat oven to 350°F. Cut tops from peppers; remove membrane and seeds. Place in large saucepan; cover with water. Bring to a boil; boil 5 minutes. Drain; set aside. In large skillet, brown ground beef, celery and onion; drain. Add rice, salt, pepper, catsup and tomato; mix well.

Spoon mixture into peppers. Place peppers in ungreased shallow baking pan. In small bowl, combine tomato sauce, sugar and basil; mix well. Spoon half of sauce over peppers. Bake at 350°F. for 30 to 40 minutes or until peppers are tender. Spoon on remaining sauce and sprinkle with cheese during last 5 minutes of baking. **4 servings.**

NUTRIENTS PER ¼ OF RECIPE

Calories	390	Dietary Fiber	5 g
Protein	24 g	Sodium	910 mg
Carbohydrate	32 g	Potassium	920 mg
Fat	19 g	Calcium	8% U.S. RDA
Cholesterol	80 mg	Iron	30% U.S. RDA

VARIATION:

STUFFED CABBAGE LEAVES: In large saucepan, cook 12 large cabbage leaves in boiling water for 5 minutes.

Drain; set aside. Prepare filling as directed above, adding *1 egg* with rice. Divide meat mixture equally on each cabbage leaf. Fold edges in; roll filling inside each leaf. Secure with toothpicks. Place rolls in ungreased 13x9-inch (2-quart) baking dish.

In small bowl, combine tomato sauce, sugar and basil; spoon over cabbage rolls. Cover with foil; bake at 350°F. for 40 to 50 minutes or until heated. Remove foil; sprinkle with 1 cup shredded Cheddar or American cheese. Return to oven; bake until cheese melts. **6 servings.**

NUTRIENTS PER ⅙ OF RECIPE

Calories	320	Dietary Fiber	3 g
Protein	20 g	Sodium	710 mg
Carbohydrate	19 g	Potassium	540 mg
Fat	18 g	Calcium	20% U.S. RDA
Cholesterol	110 mg	Iron	15% U.S. RDA

Tostados

1½	lb. ground beef
½	cup chopped onion
16-oz.	can (2 cups) tomatoes, undrained, cut up
8-oz.	can (1 cup) tomato sauce
1	teaspoon salt
1 to 3	teaspoons chili powder
½	teaspoon oregano leaves
¼	teaspoon cumin
¼	cup oil
8	(8-inch) flour tortillas
	Refried Beans (see Index)
	Shredded lettuce
	Chopped tomatoes
	Classic Guacamole (see Index)
	Salsa (see Index)

In large skillet, brown ground beef and onion; drain. Add tomatoes, tomato sauce, salt, chili powder, oregano leaves and cumin; mix well. Simmer 25 to 30 minutes, stirring occasionally, until thoroughly heated and flavors are well blended.

In 10-inch skillet, heat ¼ cup oil over medium heat. Fry tortillas in hot oil for 5 to 10 seconds on each side until lightly browned and blistered; drain well on paper towels.*

To serve, spread refried beans over each tortilla. Spoon meat mixture onto center of each tortilla. Top with lettuce, tomato, guacamole and salsa. **8 servings.**

TIP: *For soft tortillas, wrap in foil. Bake at 350°F. for about 5 minutes or until warm.

NUTRIENTS PER ⅛ OF RECIPE

Calories	480	Dietary Fiber	7 g
Protein	21 g	Sodium	1420 mg
Carbohydrate	39 g	Potassium	690 mg
Fat	27 g	Calcium	8% U.S. RDA
Cholesterol	50 mg	Iron	20% U.S. RDA

Beef Enchiladas

ENCHILADA SAUCE

    2 tablespoons oil
   ⅓ cup finely chopped onion
    1 garlic clove, minced
    1 beef-flavor bouillon cube or 1 teaspoon beef-flavor instant bouillon
   ½ cup hot water
    2 (8-oz.) cans tomato sauce
1 to 2 tablespoons chili powder
    1 teaspoon sugar
   ¼ teaspoon salt
   ¼ teaspoon cumin
   ½ cup cold water
    1 tablespoon cornstarch

BEEF FILLING
    2 tablespoons oil
   ¼ cup chopped onion
    1 garlic clove, minced
 2½ cups shredded cooked beef
4-oz. can diced green chiles, drained
   ½ teaspoon salt

  12 (6-inch) corn tortillas
   4 oz. (1 cup) shredded Cheddar cheese
   4 oz. (1 cup) shredded Monterey jack cheese

To prepare enchilada sauce, in medium saucepan heat oil; saute ⅓ cup onion and 1 garlic clove until tender. Dissolve bouillon in ½ cup hot water; add to onion mixture. Stir in tomato sauce, chili powder, sugar, salt and cumin. Combine ½ cup cold water and cornstarch; gradually stir into tomato sauce mixture. Simmer 10 to 15 minutes or until slightly thickened, stirring occasionally.

To prepare beef filling, in large skillet heat oil; saute ¼ cup onion and 1 garlic clove until tender. Stir in remaining filling ingredients and ¾ cup of the enchilada sauce; simmer 10 to 15 minutes or until thickened.

Heat oven to 375°F. Spread ½ cup of the enchilada sauce evenly over bottom of 12x8-inch (2-quart) baking dish. Set aside. In ungreased skillet, heat 1 tortilla over medium-high heat about 15 seconds or until warm, turning frequently. Fill each tortilla with 2 tablespoons beef filling; roll up. Place seam side down in prepared dish. Pour remaining 1¼ cups enchilada sauce over filled tortillas. Bake at 375°F. for 10 minutes. Sprinkle with cheese; bake an additional 3 to 5 minutes or until cheese is melted and enchiladas are heated. **6 servings.**

NUTRIENTS PER ⅙ OF RECIPE

Calories	530	Dietary Fiber	4 g
Protein	31 g	Sodium	1330 mg
Carbohydrate	39 g	Potassium	670 mg
Fat	28 g	Calcium	45% U.S. RDA
Cholesterol	80 mg	Iron	25% U.S. RDA

Tacos

1 lb. ground beef
1 small onion, chopped
1 teaspoon chili powder
½ teaspoon salt
½ teaspoon garlic powder
8-oz. can (1 cup) tomato sauce
4-oz. pkg. taco shells or 10 corn tortillas*
4 oz. (1 cup) shredded American or Cheddar cheese
2 cups shredded lettuce
2 tomatoes, chopped
   Taco sauce
½ cup dairy sour cream, if desired

Heat oven to 250°F. In medium skillet, brown ground beef
and onion; drain. Stir in chili powder, salt, garlic powder and
tomato sauce. Cover; simmer 10 minutes, stirring occasionally. Heat taco shells in oven at 250°F. for 5 minutes.
Assemble tacos by layering meat mixture, cheese, lettuce
and tomatoes in each shell. Serve with taco sauce; top with
sour cream. **10 servings.**

TIPS: *If tortillas are used, fry in ¼-inch hot oil for 5 to 10
seconds on each side to soften. Remove from oil; drain on
paper towels and fold in half.

If desired, refried beans can be added to meat mixture after
simmering. Cook until thoroughly heated.

NUTRIENTS PER ¹⁄₁₀ OF RECIPE

Calories	230	Dietary Fiber	2 g
Protein	12 g	Sodium	630 mg
Carbohydrate	13 g	Potassium	340 mg
Fat	15 g	Calcium	10% U.S. RDA
Cholesterol	45 mg	Iron	8% U.S. RDA

Tri-Bean Burger Bake

        1 lb. ground beef
        4 slices bacon, cut into 1-inch pieces
      ½ cup chopped onion
  16-oz. can diagonal-cut green beans, drained
  16-oz. can baked beans
15½-oz. can kidney beans, drained
      ½ cup firmly packed brown sugar
        1 teaspoon salt
      ½ cup catsup
        1 tablespoon vinegar
        1 teaspoon prepared mustard

Heat oven to 350°F. In large skillet, brown ground beef, bacon and onion; drain. Add all remaining ingredients; mix well. Pour into ungreased 2-quart casserole. Cover; bake at 350°F. for 30 minutes or until bubbly. **6 servings.**

MICROWAVE DIRECTIONS: In 2-quart microwave-safe casserole, microwave bacon on HIGH for 4 to 5 minutes or until crisp; remove and drain. Crumble ground beef into casserole; stir in onion. Microwave on HIGH for 4 to 5 minutes or until meat is no longer pink; drain. Stir in bacon and remaining ingredients. Microwave on HIGH for 8 to 10 minutes or until fully heated, stirring once halfway through cooking.

VARIATION:

TRI-BEAN BAKE: Omit ground beef. Pour into 1½-quart casserole. Bake at 350°F. for 30 minutes or until bubbly. **10 servings.**

NUTRIENTS PER ⅙ OF RECIPE

Calories 420	Dietary Fiber........................12 g
Protein......................................22 g	Sodium ....1140 mg
Carbohydrate..........................53 g	Potassium........................800 mg
Fat ....14 g	Calcium................8% U.S. RDA
Cholesterol.........................50 mg	Iron.....................25% U.S. RDA

Main Dish Spanish Rice

         1   lb. ground beef
         6   slices bacon
         1   medium onion, thinly sliced
       ¼   cup chopped green pepper
       ¾   cup uncooked regular long grain rice
       ½   teaspoon salt
       ⅛   teaspoon pepper
       ¼   cup catsup
16-oz.   can tomatoes, undrained, cut up
  8-oz.   can tomato sauce
         2   drops hot pepper sauce

In large skillet, brown ground beef; drain well. Remove meat from skillet and set aside. In same skillet, cook bacon until crisp. Remove bacon; drain, reserving 2 tablespoons drippings in skillet. Crumble bacon; set aside. Saute onion and green pepper in reserved drippings until crisp-tender. Stir in ground beef, crumbled bacon and remaining ingredients. Bring to a boil; cover and simmer for 30 to 40 minutes or until rice is tender. **5 servings.**

NUTRIENTS PER ⅕ OF RECIPE

Calories 390	Dietary Fiber...........................3 g
Protein.....................................21 g	Sodium..............................970 mg
Carbohydrate.........................35 g	Potassium........................710 mg
Fat ....18 g	Calcium.................4% U.S. RDA
Cholesterol ....60 mg	Iron.....................20% U.S. RDA

Sloppy Joes

       1   lb. ground beef
     ½   cup chopped green pepper or celery
       1   medium onion, chopped (½ cup)
       1   tablespoon brown sugar
       1   teaspoon dry mustard
     ¼   teaspoon salt

⅛ teaspoon pepper
8-oz. can tomato sauce
½ cup catsup
1 tablespoon Worcestershire sauce
1 tablespoon vinegar
6 sandwich buns

In large skillet, brown ground beef, green pepper and onion; drain well. Stir in remaining ingredients. Cover; simmer 15 to 20 minutes, stirring occasionally, until thoroughly heated. Serve on buns. **6 servings.**

MICROWAVE DIRECTIONS: In 2-quart microwave-safe casserole, crumble ground beef; add green pepper and onion. Cover loosely with waxed paper. Microwave on HIGH for 5 to 7 minutes or until browned, stirring once halfway through cooking; drain well. Stir in remaining ingredients; cover loosely with waxed paper. Microwave on HIGH for 7 to 9 minutes or until thoroughly heated.

NUTRIENTS PER ⅙ OF RECIPE

Calories	320	Dietary Fiber	2 g
Protein	17 g	Sodium	830 mg
Carbohydrate	34 g	Potassium	470 mg
Fat	13 g	Calcium	4% U.S. RDA
Cholesterol	50 mg	Iron	15% U.S. RDA

French Dip

In medium saucepan, add 1½ lb. cooked sliced beef to 1½ cups water and beef pan drippings or 2 beef-flavor bouillon cubes. Cook until thoroughly heated. Stir in ½ teaspoon soy sauce and 1 teaspoon instant minced onion. Simmer 2 to 3 minutes. Remove beef slices. Serve between slices of crusty French bread. Individual portions of meat juices can be served for dipping sandwiches. **6 servings.**

NUTRIENTS PER ¼ OF RECIPE

Calories	560	Dietary Fiber	1 g
Protein	26 g	Sodium	820 mg
Carbohydrate	39 g	Potassium	390 mg
Fat	32 g	Calcium	4% U.S. RDA
Cholesterol	80 mg	Iron	20% U.S. RDA

Reuben Sandwiches

     8 slices pumpernickel, rye or other dark bread
     ½ lb. thinly sliced corned beef
  8-oz. can (1 cup) sauerkraut, well-drained
2 to 3 tablespoons prepared Thousand Island dressing
     4 slices Swiss cheese
     2 tablespoons margarine or butter, softened

Heat griddle or skillet to medium heat (340°F.). To assemble sandwiches, top each of 4 slices of bread with ¼ of the corned beef, sauerkraut, dressing and cheese. Cover with remaining bread slices. Spread margarine on outside of each sandwich. Place sandwiches on griddle; grill on each side until golden brown and cheese is melted. **4 sandwiches.**

TIPS: For thoroughly drained sauerkraut, drain liquid. Place drained sauerkraut in 2 or 3 layers of paper towels; squeeze out excess liquid.

If desired, ½ teaspoon prepared mustard and ¼ teaspoon caraway seed can be added with dressing.

VARIATION:

OPEN-FACED REUBEN SANDWICHES: Toast bread and arrange filling on bread, ending with cheese. Broil until cheese melts. Garnish each with cherry tomato.

NUTRIENTS PER 1 SANDWICH

Calories	480	Dietary Fiber	5 g
Protein	23 g	Sodium	1430 mg
Carbohydrate	31 g	Potassium	410 mg
Fat	29 g	Calcium	35% U.S. RDA
Cholesterol	90 mg	Iron	15% U.S. RDA

Veal

Veal Roast

Allow ⅓ to ½ lb. per serving for bone-in roast and ¼ to ⅓ lb. per serving for boneless roast. Heat oven to 325°F. Place roast fat side up in a shallow roasting pan. Sprinkle with salt and pepper. Insert meat thermometer. Do not add water or cover. Roast to 170°F. using Timetable for Roasting Veal. Roast can be basted occasionally with additional margarine or pan drippings to add moistness.

NUTRIENTS PER ½ LB. RAW VEAL ROAST WITH BONE, COOKED

Calories 270	Dietary Fiber............................0 g
Protein.....................................33 g	Sodium..............................80 mg
Carbohydrate...........................0 g	Potassium.........................370 mg
Fat ....14 g	Calcium..............<2% U.S. RDA
Cholesterol.......................120 mg	Iron.....................20% U.S. RDA

Timetable for Roasting Veal

(Oven Temperature 325°F./
Meat Thermometer Reading 170°F.)

Roast	Weight (Pounds)	Cooking Time (Minutes per Pound)
Rib	3 to 5	35 to 40
Loin	4 to 6	30 to 35
Shoulder (boneless)	4 to 6	40 to 45
Rump Roast	5 to 8	25 to 35

*Based on meat taken directly from the refrigerator.

Veal Scallopini

¼ cup all purpose flour
1 teaspoon salt
⅛ teaspoon pepper
6 boneless veal cutlets*
2 tablespoons oil
½ cup dry white wine
3 tomatoes, coarsely chopped
1 beef-flavor bouillon cube or 1 teaspoon beef-flavor instant bouillon
⅓ cup margarine or butter
12 oz. (4 cups) sliced fresh mushrooms
1 small onion, chopped
1 green pepper, sliced
1 garlic clove, minced
8 oz. (5 cups) uncooked egg noodles
Grated Parmesan cheese

In small bowl, combine flour, salt and pepper. Coat meat with flour mixture. In large skillet, brown veal in hot oil for 5 to 7 minutes. Stir in wine, tomatoes and bouillon. Cover; simmer 15 minutes. In another large skillet, melt margarine. Saute mushrooms, onion, green pepper and garlic in margarine until tender. Cook noodles to desired doneness as directed on package. Drain; rinse with hot water. Add vegetables to meat. Simmer about 10 minutes to blend flavors. Serve over noodles; sprinkle with Parmesan cheese. **6 servings.**

TIP: *If desired, 1½-lb. veal round steak cut into 6 pieces can be substituted for the veal cutlets. Pound round steak with flat side of meat mallet or rolling pin until about ¼-inch thick. Continue as directed.

NUTRIENTS PER ⅙ OF RECIPE

Calories 620	Dietary Fiber ....4 g
Protein ....41 g	Sodium ....830 mg
Carbohydrate ....39 g	Potassium ....770 mg
Fat ....31 g	Calcium ....10% U.S. RDA
Cholesterol ....150 mg	Iron ....35% U.S. RDA

Veal Parmigiana

⅓ cup grated Parmesan cheese
2 tablespoons cornflake or dry bread crumbs
1 to 1½ lb. boneless veal cutlets or veal round steak, cut into 4 serving pieces
1 egg, slightly beaten
2 tablespoons oil
1 medium onion, chopped
¼ teaspoon salt
⅛ teaspoon pepper
⅛ teaspoon oregano leaves or Italian seasoning
8-oz. can (1 cup) tomato sauce
4 oz. (1 cup) shredded mozzarella cheese
Grated Parmesan cheese

Heat oven to 375°F. In small bowl, combine ⅓ cup Parmesan cheese and crumbs. Dip veal in egg; coat with cheese-crumb mixture. In large skillet, brown veal in hot oil. Remove veal to ungreased 8-inch square or round pan. Add onion to skillet; saute until tender. Stir in salt, pepper, oregano and tomato sauce. Top pieces of veal with mozzarella cheese. Pour tomato mixture over cheese, spreading to cover. Sprinkle with additional Parmesan cheese. Bake at 375°F. for 30 minutes until bubbly. **4 servings.**

NUTRIENTS PER ¼ OF RECIPE

Calories	500	Dietary Fiber	1 g
Protein	47 g	Sodium	1010 mg
Carbohydrate	10 g	Potassium	650 mg
Fat	30 g	Calcium	45% U.S. RDA
Cholesterol	210 mg	Iron	25% U.S. RDA

Wiener Schnitzel

        6 boneless veal cutlets, ⅜-inch thick
        2 tablespoons flour
       ½ teaspoon salt
       ¼ teaspoon pepper
        2 eggs, slightly beaten
        1 tablespoon milk
1 to 1½ cups dry bread crumbs
        6 tablespoons oil

Place 1 veal cutlet between 2 pieces of plastic wrap. Working from the center, lightly pound cutlet with flat side of meat mallet or rolling pin until about ⅛-inch thick; remove wrap. Repeat with remaining cutlets.

In small bowl, combine flour, salt and pepper. In another small bowl, combine egg and milk. Coat cutlets with seasoned flour; dip in egg mixture, then coat with crumbs. In large skillet, heat 3 tablespoons of the oil over medium-high heat. Fry 3 cutlets on both sides until golden brown, about 5 to 7 minutes. Place cutlets on platter in warm oven. Using remaining 3 tablespoons oil, fry remaining 3 cutlets. Serve immediately. **6 servings.**

TIP: To make ahead, coat cutlets as directed above. Refrigerate up to 3 hours before frying.

NUTRIENTS PER ¼ OF RECIPE

Calories	450	Dietary Fiber	<1 g
Protein	28 g	Sodium	440 mg
Carbohydrate	21 g	Potassium	320 mg
Fat	28 g	Calcium	4% U.S. RDA
Cholesterol	210 mg	Iron	25% U.S. RDA

Veal with Asparagus and Fennel

    1 tablespoon oil
 1½ lb. boneless veal, cut into paper-thin strips
    1 lb. fresh asparagus, cut into 1-inch pieces
   ¼ cup chopped red bell pepper
   ½ teaspoon salt
   ¼ teaspoon sugar
   ¼ teaspoon fennel seed, crushed
   ⅛ teaspoon onion powder
   ⅛ teaspoon pepper
    2 tablespoons dry white wine

In large skillet or wok, heat oil over high heat. Add veal; stir-fry until lightly browned. Stir in remaining ingredients. Cover; reduce heat. Simmer for 4 to 6 minutes or until asparagus is crisp-tender. **6 servings.**

VARIATION:

CHICKEN WITH ASPARAGUS AND FENNEL: Substitute 2 whole chicken breasts, skinned, boned, cut into thin strips for the veal.

NUTRIENTS PER ¼ OF RECIPE

Calories	220	Dietary Fiber	1 g
Protein	24 g	Sodium	230 mg
Carbohydrate	3 g	Potassium	490 mg
Fat	11 g	Calcium	2% U.S. RDA
Cholesterol	80 mg	Iron	20% U.S. RDA

Veal Marengo

  1 lb. lean veal steak, cut into thin strips
  1 tablespoon margarine or butter
  1 cup sliced fresh mushrooms
  1 large onion, thinly sliced
  1 clove garlic, minced
  1 teaspoon thyme leaves
  1/8 teaspoon pepper
  3 medium tomatoes, peeled, cut into wedges or
    16-oz. can whole tomatoes, drained, cut into
    wedges
  1/2 cup dry white wine or beef broth
  12 oz. (6¾ cups) wide egg noodles
  1 tablespoon flour
    Chopped fresh parsley, if desired

In large skillet, cook veal in margarine over medium-high heat until no longer pink. Remove veal from pan; cover to keep warm. To drippings in skillet, add mushrooms, onions, garlic, thyme and pepper. Cook over medium-high heat until onions are tender. Stir in tomatoes and wine. Simmer 15 minutes to blend flavors, stirring occasionally.

Meanwhile, cook noodles to desired doneness as directed on package. Drain; rinse with hot water. Toss veal with flour; add to tomato mixture. Cook and stir until thickened. Serve over hot cooked noodles; sprinkle with parsley. **6 servings.**

NUTRIENTS PER ⅙ OF RECIPE

Calories 370	Dietary Fiber.............................3 g
Protein......................................20 g	Sodium..................................60 mg
Carbohydrate.........................47 g	Potassium.........................430 mg
Fat ....9 g	Calcium................4% U.S. RDA
Cholesterol.........................90 mg	Iron.....................25% U.S. RDA

Liver, Bacon and Onions

1 lb. beef, veal, lamb or pork liver
¼ cup all purpose flour
½ teaspoon salt
⅛ teaspoon pepper
4 slices bacon
2 medium onions, sliced

Cut liver into serving pieces. Combine flour, salt and pepper; mix well. Coat liver with flour mixture. In large skillet, fry bacon until crisp. Remove bacon; drain on paper towel, reserving drippings. Brown liver with onions in bacon drippings for 2 to 3 minutes on each side. Serve topped with crisp bacon. **4 servings.**

NUTRIENTS PER ¼ OF RECIPE

Calories	250	Dietary Fiber	1 g
Protein	26 g	Sodium	470 mg
Carbohydrate	16 g	Potassium	480 mg
Fat	8 g	Calcium	2% U.S. RDA
Cholesterol	410 mg	Iron	45% U.S. RDA

Broiled Liver

Arrange slices of baby beef, veal or lamb liver on broiler pan. Broil 4 to 5 inches from heat for 3 minutes. Season with salt and pepper. Turn and broil second side 2 to 3 minutes or until meat just loses red color. (Overcooking will toughen liver.)

NUTRIENTS PER ¼ LB. COOKED BEEF LIVER

Calories	180	Dietary Fiber	0 g
Protein	28 g	Sodium	80 mg
Carbohydrate	4 g	Potassium	270 mg
Fat	6 g	Calcium	<2% U.S. RDA
Cholesterol	440 mg	Iron	45% U.S. RDA

Pork

Timetable for Roasting Fresh Pork

(Oven Temperature 325°F./
Meat Thermometer Reading 165°F.)

Roast	Weight (Pounds)	Cooking Time* (Minutes per Pound)
Loin		
Center	3 to 5	30 to 35
Half	5 to 7	35 to 40
Blade or Sirloin End	3 to 4	40 to 45
Top (double)	3 to 5	35 to 40
Top (boneless)	2 to 4	30 to 35
Crown	6 to 10	25 to 30
Arm Picnic Shoulder		
Bone-in	5 to 8	30 to 35
Boneless	3 to 5	35 to 40
Blade Boston Shoulder	4 to 6	40 to 45
Leg		
Whole (bone in)	12 to 16	22 to 24
Whole (boneless)	10 to 14	24 to 28
Half (bone in)	5 to 8	35 to 40
Tenderloin	½ to 1	45 to 60

*Based on meat taken directly from the refrigerator.

Timetable for Roasting Smoked Pork

Cut	Approximate Weight (Pounds)	Thermometer Reading °F.	Cooking Time* (Minutes Per Pound)
Ham—Cook before eating		165°F.	
Whole (boneless)	8 to 12		17 to 21
Whole (bone in)	14 to 16		18 to 20
Half (bone in)	7 to 8		22 to 25
Portion (boneless)	3 to 5		35 to 40
Ham—Fully cooked		130 to 140°F.	
Whole (boneless)	8 to 12		15 to 18
Whole (bone in)	14 to 16		15 to 18
Half (boneless)	4 to 6		18 to 25
Half (bone in)	7 to 8		18 to 25
Portion (bone in)	3 to 4		27 to 33
Arm Picnic Shoulder			
Cook before eating	5 to 8	165°F.	30 to 35
Fully cooked	5 to 8	140°F.	25 to 30

*Based on meat taken directly from refrigerator.

Pork Roast

Allow ⅓ to ½ lb. per serving for bone-in roast and ¼ to ⅓ lb. per serving for boneless roast. Heat oven to 325°F. Place roast fat side up on a rack in a shallow roasting pan. Sprinkle with salt and pepper. Insert meat thermometer. Do not add water or cover. Roast until meat thermometer registers 165°F. using Timetable for Roasting Fresh Pork.

NUTRIENTS PER ½ LB. RAW PORK ROAST WITH BONE, COOKED

Calories	270	Dietary Fiber	0 g
Protein	28 g	Sodium	85 mg
Carbohydrate	0 g	Potassium	390 mg
Fat	16 g	Calcium	<2% U.S. RDA
Cholesterol	110 mg	Iron	8% U.S. RDA

Carving a Pork Loin Roast

Remove backbone by cutting close along bone. Place roast with bone side up facing carver. Make slices by cutting close along each side of the rib bone. One slice will contain the rib bone; the next will be boneless.

Carving a Whole Ham or Leg of Lamb

Place meat fat side up; remove a few slices from thin side, forming a base on which to set meat. Turn meat onto base. Cut slices down to leg bone. To release slices, run knife horizontally along bone. For additional servings, turn over to original position and slice in a similar manner.

Pork and Stir-Fried Vegetables

3 to 4-lb. center cut pork loin roast
Garlic powder
Pepper
2 tablespoons oil
1 garlic clove, minced
¼ teaspoon ginger
2 cups julienne-cut carrots
2 cups julienne-cut green or red bell pepper
2 cups julienne-cut zucchini
¼ cup water
¼ to ½ teaspoon salt

Heat oven to 325°F. Rub roast with garlic powder and pepper; place on rack in shallow roasting pan. Insert meat thermometer in center of roast. Roast at 325°F. until meat thermometer registers 170°F., about 1½ to 2 hours.

When meat is done, remove from oven. Cover; let stand while preparing vegetables. In wok or large skillet, heat oil over high heat; add garlic and ginger. Stir-fry carrots, green pepper and zucchini for 2 minutes. Add water; cover and simmer 2 to 3 minutes or until crisp-tender. Sprinkle vegetables with salt. Serve immediately with roast. **6 to 8 servings.**

NUTRIENTS PER ⅛ OF RECIPE

Calories	350	Dietary Fiber	2 g
Protein	36 g	Sodium	230 mg
Carbohydrate	6 g	Potassium	700 mg
Fat	20 g	Calcium	2% U.S. RDA
Cholesterol	110 mg	Iron	10% U.S. RDA

Wine Marinade for Pork Roast

2 tablespoons chopped fresh parsley
2 teaspoons salt
¼ teaspoon pepper
2 garlic cloves, sliced
1 cup dry white wine

In small bowl, combine all ingredients; mix well. Place 4 to 6-lb. pork roast in plastic bag or non-metal container. Pour marinade over meat. Seal bag or cover bowl. Marinate at least 2 hours at room temperature or overnight in refrigerator, stirring once or twice. **1 cup.**

NUTRIENTS PER 1 TABLESPOON

Calories	14	Dietary Fiber	0 g
Protein	0 g	Sodium	270 mg
Carbohydrate	1 g	Potassium	20 mg
Fat	0 g	Calcium	<2% U.S. RDA
Cholesterol	0 mg	Iron	<2% U.S. RDA

Stuffed Crown Roast of Pork

7-lb. pork crown roast
1½ teaspoons salt
¼ teaspoon pepper

Purchase roast with backbone removed. Heat oven to 325°F. Place meat in roasting pan, rib bones up. Sprinkle with salt and pepper. Wrap tips of bones in foil to prevent excess browning. Insert meat thermometer so bulb reaches center of thickest part of meat, but does not rest in fat or on bone. (Do not add water; do not cover.) Roast on lowest oven rack at 325°F. for 2 hours. Meanwhile, prepare 1 quart of favorite Bread or Rice Stuffing (see Index). Fill center of roast with stuffing; roast 1½ to 2 hours longer, until meat thermometer registers 170°F. Cover stuffing with foil if top becomes too brown. To serve, remove foil and cover bone ends with paper frills or spiced crab apples. **6 to 8 servings.**

NUTRIENTS PER ⅛ OF RECIPE WITHOUT STUFFING

Calories	410	Dietary Fiber	0 g
Protein	49 g	Sodium	120 mg
Carbohydrate	0 g	Potassium	620 mg
Fat	22 g	Calcium	<2% U.S. RDA
Cholesterol	160 mg	Iron	10% U.S. RDA

Breaded Pork Cutlets

       2 tablespoons flour
      ½ teaspoon salt
      ½ teaspoon paprika
      ⅛ teaspoon pepper
       1 egg, slightly beaten
 1 to 2 teaspoons Worcestershire sauce
       4 boneless pork chops or steaks*
      ½ cup dry bread crumbs
 2 to 3 tablespoons oil

In small bowl, combine first 4 ingredients. In another small bowl, combine egg and Worcestershire sauce. Coat pork chops with seasoned flour; dip in egg mixture and coat with crumbs. In large skillet, brown chops in hot oil until golden brown. Continue cooking over medium heat 5 to 7 minutes or until done. **4 servings.**

TIP: *If desired, use pork tenderloin, allowing about ¼ lb. per serving. Cut into ½-inch slices and flatten to ¼-inch thickness by placing between sheets of plastic wrap and pounding with flat side of meat mallet or rolling pin.

VARIATIONS:

CHEESE-TOPPED PORK CUTLETS: Decrease bread crumbs to ¼ cup. Mix crumbs with ¼ cup grated Parmesan cheese. After turning browned cutlets, top each with slice of mozzarella cheese and tomato slice. Cover; heat until tomato is hot and cheese begins to melt.

OVEN-BAKED BREADED PORK CUTLETS: Prepare as directed above. Place in ungreased shallow roasting pan. Bake at 425°F. for 30 to 35 minutes or until done.

NUTRIENTS PER ¼ OF RECIPE

Calories	350	Dietary Fiber	<1 g
Protein	25 g	Sodium	390 mg
Carbohydrate	6 g	Potassium	340 mg
Fat	24 g	Calcium	2% U.S. RDA
Cholesterol	150 mg	Iron	8% U.S. RDA

Broiled/Grilled Pork Chops

Combine 1 tablespoon oil, ¼ teaspoon salt and ¼ teaspoon garlic salt. Brush 4 pork chops, about 1-inch thick, with oil mixture. Broil or grill 4 to 6 inches from heat for 15 to 20 minutes or until pork is done, turning once during cooking. **4 servings.**

NUTRIENTS PER ¼ OF RECIPE

Calories	300	Dietary Fiber	0 g
Protein	30 g	Sodium	320 mg
Carbohydrate	0 g	Potassium	410 mg
Fat	19 g	Calcium	<2% U.S. RDA
Cholesterol	100 mg	Iron	6% U.S. RDA

Pork Chops in Sour Cream

6 loin pork chops
½ cup water
2 tablespoons brown sugar
2 tablespoons finely chopped onion
2 tablespoons catsup
1 garlic clove, minced

1 beef-flavor bouillon cube or 1 teaspoon beef-flavor
   instant bouillon
2 tablespoons flour
¼ cup water
½ cup dairy sour cream

In large skillet, brown pork chops. Add ½ cup water, brown
sugar, onion, catsup, garlic and bouillon cube. Cover; simmer 30 to 40 minutes or until tender. Remove chops to serving platter; keep warm.

In small bowl, combine flour with ¼ cup water; slowly add
to cooking liquid, stirring constantly. Cook until thickened,
stirring constantly. Stir in sour cream; heat thoroughly. *Do
not boil.* Serve sauce over chops. **6 servings.**

NUTRIENTS PER ⅙ OF RECIPE

Calories	230	Dietary Fiber	0 g
Protein	15 g	Sodium	270 mg
Carbohydrate	9 g	Potassium	270 mg
Fat	15 g	Calcium	4% U.S. RDA
Cholesterol	60 mg	Iron	6% U.S. RDA

Spareribs on the Grill

Purchase about ¾ to 1 lb. of pork spareribs for each serving
desired. Cut ribs into sections. Precooking ribs will render
out some fat and save time on the grill. Choose one of these
precooking methods.

Foil-Wrapped: Wrap uncooked ribs securely in heavy-duty
foil. Grill 30 minutes, turning once, or bake at 350°F. for 30
minutes. Unwrap; place ribs on grill. Cook about 20 to 30
minutes or until browned, turning frequently and basting
with barbecue sauce often.

Microwave: Arrange ribs in 12x8-inch (2-quart) microwave-safe baking dish. Cover with waxed paper.

Microwave on HIGH for 20 minutes, rearranging and turning over ribs once during cooking. Place ribs on grill. Cook about 20 to 30 minutes or until browned, turning frequently and basting often.

Conventional Oven: In 13x9-inch pan with rack, or on broiler pan, bake ribs at 350°F. for 1 hour. Place ribs on grill. Cook about 20 to 30 minutes or until browned, turning frequently and basting with barbecue sauce often.

NUTRIENTS PER 1 LB. PORK SPARERIBS WITH BONE, COOKED WITHOUT BARBECUE SAUCE

Calories	340	Dietary Fiber	0 g
Protein	37 g	Sodium	85 mg
Carbohydrate	0 g	Potassium	570 mg
Fat	19 g	Calcium	<2% U.S. RDA
Cholesterol	120 mg	Iron	6% U.S. RDA

Honey-Mustard Rib Glaze

- 1 cup honey
- 1 cup vinegar
- ⅔ cup prepared Dijon mustard
- ½ cup chopped onion
- 2 garlic cloves, minced
- 2 teaspoons celery salt
- 1 teaspoon paprika

In medium saucepan, combine all ingredients. Bring to a boil, stirring until well blended. **2⅓ cups.**

NUTRIENTS PER 1 TABLESPOON

Calories	35	Dietary Fiber	0 g
Protein	0 g	Sodium	220 mg
Carbohydrate	8 g	Potassium	15 mg
Fat	0 g	Calcium	<2% U.S. RDA
Cholesterol	0 mg	Iron	<2% U.S. RDA

Deluxe Barbecue Sauce

    1 cup catsup
    1 cup chili sauce
    ½ cup finely chopped onion
    ¼ cup firmly packed brown sugar
    1 teaspoon celery seed
    1 teaspoon salt
    ¼ teaspoon instant minced garlic
    2 tablespoons Worcestershire sauce
    2 tablespoons lemon juice
    1 teaspoon prepared mustard

In medium saucepan, combine all ingredients. Bring to a
boil, stirring until well blended. Simmer 15 minutes, stirring
occasionally. **3 cups; covers 12 lb. ribs.**

NUTRIENTS PER 1 TABLESPOON

Calories 18	Dietary Fiber........................<1 g
Protein......................................0 g	Sodium..............................190 mg
Carbohydrate...........................4 g	Potassium.............................50 mg
Fat ....0 g	Calcium...............<2% U.S. RDA
Cholesterol............................0 mg	Iron ....<2% U.S. RDA

Creamy Mustard Sauce

    1 cup dairy sour cream
    2 tablespoons prepared mustard
    2 tablespoons apple cider
    1 teaspoon prepared horseradish

In small bowl, combine all ingredients. Cover; refrigerate
several hours to blend flavors. **About 1¼ cups.**

NUTRIENTS PER 1 TABLESPOON

Calories 35	Dietary Fiber............................0 g
Protein......................................1 g	Sodium................................30 mg
Carbohydrate...........................1 g	Potassium.............................25 mg
Fat ....3 g	Calcium...............<2% U.S. RDA
Cholesterol............................6 mg	Iron ....<2% U.S. RDA

Sweet-Sour Pork

- 1 tablespoon shortening
- 1 lb. boneless pork, cut into 1½-inch pieces
- 1 teaspoon paprika
- 3 tablespoons brown sugar
- 2 tablespoons cornstarch
- ½ teaspoon salt
- 15¼-oz. can pineapple chunks, drained, reserving ⅔ cup liquid
- ⅓ cup vinegar
- ⅓ cup water
- 1 tablespoon soy sauce
- 1 teaspoon Worcestershire sauce
- 1 green pepper, cut into ¼-inch strips
- 1 small onion, thinly sliced
- 2 cups hot cooked rice or egg noodles

In large skillet over medium heat, melt shortening. Add pork; sprinkle with paprika. Brown well. Cover; simmer about 20 to 25 minutes or until tender, stirring occasionally.

In medium bowl, combine brown sugar, cornstarch and salt. Gradually add reserved ⅔ cup pineapple liquid, vinegar, water, soy sauce and Worcestershire sauce; mix well. Gradually stir into meat. Cook over low heat until thickened; stirring constantly. Stir in green pepper, onion and pineapple. Cover; simmer over low heat 6 to 8 minutes or until vegetables are crisp-tender. Serve over hot cooked rice. **4 servings.**

NUTRIENTS PER ¼ OF RECIPE

Calories 420	Dietary Fiber ....3 g
Protein ....20 g	Sodium ....580 mg
Carbohydrate ....59 g	Potassium ....530 mg
Fat ....12 g	Calcium ....4% U.S. RDA
Cholesterol ....35 mg	Iron ....15% U.S. RDA

Quick Pork Chow Mein

    2 cups cooked pork, cut into thin strips
    1 cup sliced celery
  ½ cup chopped onion
  ½ cup coarsely chopped red or green pepper
    1 teaspoon chicken-flavor instant bouillon
    1 teaspoon sugar
  ⅛ teaspoon pepper
 1½ cups water
    2 tablespoons soy sauce
16-oz. can bean sprouts, drained, rinsed
    2 tablespoons cornstarch
  ¼ cup cold water
        Chow mein noodles or hot cooked rice

In large skillet, combine pork, celery, onion, red pepper, bouillon, sugar, pepper, 1½ cups water and soy sauce; cover. Bring to a boil; simmer 10 minutes or until vegetables are tender. Stir in bean sprouts. In small bowl, combine cornstarch and ¼ cup water until smooth. Over medium-high heat, carefully add to skillet mixture, stirring constantly until thickened. Serve over noodles. **4 servings.**

MICROWAVE DIRECTIONS: In 2-quart microwave-safe casserole, combine celery, onion and red pepper; cover with microwave-safe plastic wrap or glass cover. Microwave on HIGH for 2½ to 3 minutes or until vegetables are tender, stirring once halfway through cooking. Stir in pork, bouillon, sugar, pepper, 1½ cups water and soy sauce; cover. Microwave on HIGH for 7 to 8 minutes or until mixture comes to a boil, stirring once halfway through cooking. Stir in bean sprouts. In small bowl, combine cornstarch and ¼ cup water; stir into pork mixture. Microwave on HIGH for 3 to 4 minutes or until thickened; stir once halfway through cooking.

NUTRIENTS PER ¼ OF RECIPE

Calories	340	Dietary Fiber	4 g
Protein	25 g	Sodium	930 mg
Carbohydrate	26 g	Potassium	570 mg
Fat	15 g	Calcium	4% U.S. RDA
Cholesterol	70 mg	Iron	10% U.S. RDA

Ham and Sweet Potatoes

        1 tablespoon margarine or butter
    1½ lb. fully-cooked center cut ham slice, 1-inch thick
      ½ cup apricot preserves
        2 tablespoons lemon juice
        2 tablespoons raisins
      ⅛ teaspoon allspice
17-oz. can sweet potatoes, drained

In large skillet, melt margarine over medium-high heat; brown ham slice on both sides. In small bowl, combine apricot preserves, lemon juice, raisins and allspice; spoon over ham slice, spreading evenly. Cover; simmer 10 minutes. Arrange sweet potatoes around ham; spoon apricot sauce over sweet potatoes. Cover; simmer an additional 5 minutes or until thoroughly heated. Place ham and sweet potatoes on serving platter; spoon any remaining sauce over top. **6 servings.**

NUTRIENTS PER ¼ OF RECIPE

Calories	350	Dietary Fiber	2 g
Protein	26 g	Sodium	1430 mg
Carbohydrate	44 g	Potassium	540 mg
Fat	8 g	Calcium	4% U.S. RDA
Cholesterol	60 mg	Iron	15% U.S. RDA

Microwave Glazed Ham

3 lb. fully cooked boneless ham

GLAZE

½ cup orange marmalade or apricot preserves
¼ teaspoon ginger
1 tablespoon orange-flavored liqueur or orange juice
Whole cloves

MICROWAVE DIRECTIONS: Place ham, fat side down, on microwave-safe roasting rack; cover with microwave-safe plastic wrap. Microwave on HIGH for 5 minutes. Rotate ½ turn; microwave on MEDIUM for 20 minutes. Turn ham over, fat side up; cover with microwave-safe plastic wrap. Microwave on MEDIUM for 10 to 15 minutes. Meanwhile, in small bowl combine all glaze ingredients except cloves; mix well. With sharp knife, score top of ham; insert cloves. Brush ham with marmalade mixture. Microwave on MEDIUM for 5 minutes or until thoroughly heated. Let stand 5 to 10 minutes before serving. Serve with remaining glaze. **14 to 16 servings.**

NUTRIENTS PER ¹⁄₁₆ OF RECIPE

Calories	150	Dietary Fiber	0 g
Protein	18 g	Sodium	1030 mg
Carbohydrate	9 g	Potassium	250 mg
Fat	5 g	Calcium	<2% U.S. RDA
Cholesterol	45 mg	Iron	6% U.S. RDA

Baked Ham

Heat oven to 325°F. Place ham fat side up on rack in shallow roasting pan. Insert meat thermometer so the bulb reaches the center of the thickest part of meat, but does not rest in fat or on bone. Bake using Timetable for Roasting Smoked Pork (see Index).

To glaze baked ham, pour drippings from pan. If necessary, trim fat, leaving only a thin layer on ham. Score ham by cutting diamond shapes about ¼-inch deep through the fat. If desired, insert a whole clove in each diamond. Spoon one of the suggested glazes over ham. Return to oven; bake an additional 15 to 20 minutes.

NUTRIENTS PER ¼ LB. COOKED HAM

Calories	200	Dietary Fiber	0 g
Protein	26 g	Sodium	1700 mg
Carbohydrate	0 g	Potassium	460 mg
Fat	10 g	Calcium	<2% U.S. RDA
Cholesterol	70 mg	Iron	8% U.S. RDA

Glazes for Baked Ham

Allow ⅓ to ½ lb. of ham per serving. Score ham before spreading on glaze. Glaze will not run off as easily and flavor will penetrate more.

BROWN SUGAR GLAZE: Combine 1 cup firmly packed brown sugar, 2 tablespoons flour, ½ teaspoon dry or prepared mustard, ⅛ teaspoon cinnamon and 3 tablespoons dry sherry, vinegar or water; mix well. Spread on ham.

JELLY GLAZE: Heat 1 cup currant or apple jelly until melted. Spread on ham.

ORANGE MARMALADE GLAZE: Use 1 cup orange marmalade to spread on ham.

PINEAPPLE GLAZE: Combine 1 cup firmly packed brown sugar with ¾ cup drained crushed pineapple. Spread on ham.

Spicy Raisin Sauce

½ cup firmly packed brown sugar
1 tablespoon cornstarch
¼ teaspoon cinnamon
¼ cup raisins
1 tablespoon margarine or butter
1 cup water
2 tablespoons lemon juice

In small saucepan, combine brown sugar, cornstarch and cinnamon. Add remaining ingredients; stir to combine. Heat until mixture boils and thickens, stirring occasionally. Simmer about 10 minutes or until flavors have blended. **1 cup.**

NUTRIENTS PER 1 TABLESPOON

Calories 40	Dietary Fiber...........................0 g
Protein.....................................0 g	Sodium...............................10 mg
Carbohydrate...........................9 g	Potassium............................45 mg
Fat ....1 g	Calcium...............<2% U.S. RDA
Cholesterol..........................0 mg	Iron ....<2% U.S. RDA

Ham Rolls with Zippy Sauce

HAM ROLLS

1 lb. ground cooked ham
½ lb. ground pork
1 lb. lean ground beef
1½ cups graham cracker crumbs
1 cup milk
1 egg, well beaten
¼ teaspoon salt
¼ teaspoon pepper

ZIPPY SAUCE

10¾-oz. can condensed tomato soup
 1 cup firmly packed brown sugar
 ⅓ cup cider vinegar
 1 teaspoon dry mustard

Heat oven to 350°F. In large bowl, combine all ham roll ingredients; mix well. Using about ⅓ cup mixture for each,
shape into 24 rolls, each about 4 inches long. Place in 13x9-
inch (3-quart) baking dish.

In medium bowl, combine all sauce ingredients; pour over
rolls. Bake at 350°F. for 50 to 60 minutes or until fully
heated. **12 servings.**

TIP: Ham rolls can be prepared ahead, unbaked and frozen.
Thaw slightly and proceed as directed above.

NUTRIENTS PER ½ OF RECIPE

Calories	300	Dietary Fiber	1 g
Protein	20 g	Sodium	800 mg
Carbohydrate	31 g	Potassium	430 mg
Fat	11 g	Calcium	6% U.S. RDA
Cholesterol	80 mg	Iron	15% U.S. RDA

Au Gratin Potatoes and Ham

 6 medium (about 2 lb.) potatoes, peeled, sliced
  (6 cups)
 1 medium onion, coarsely chopped (½ cup)
 8 oz. (1½ cups) cooked ham, cubed
 4 oz. (1 cup) shredded American cheese
10¾-oz. can condensed cream of mushroom soup
 ½ cup milk
 ¼ to ½ teaspoon thyme leaves

In slow cooker, layer ½ of the potatoes, onion, ham and
cheese; repeat layers. In small bowl, combine soup, milk
and thyme; pour over top. Cover; cook on high setting for 3

hours. Reduce to low setting; cook for 2 to 2½ hours or until potatoes are tender. **6 servings.**

NUTRIENTS PER 1 CUP

Calories	280	Dietary Fiber	4 g
Protein	16 g	Sodium	1150 mg
Carbohydrate	26 g	Potassium	690 mg
Fat	12 g	Calcium	15% U.S. RDA
Cholesterol	40 mg	Iron	10% U.S. RDA

Danish Ham and Tomato Sandwiches

½ cup mayonnaise or salad dressing
½ cup dairy sour cream
2 teaspoons lemon juice
1 teaspoon dill weed
8 slices white, wheat or rye bread, toasted
4 cups shredded or leaf lettuce
¼ cup sliced green onions
1 large tomato, thinly sliced
8 oz. thinly sliced cooked ham
¼ cup sliced radishes

In small bowl, combine mayonnaise, sour cream, lemon juice and dill weed; blend well. Spread 1 tablespoon dill mixture on each bread slice. Place 2 bread slices, side by side, dill side up, on each of 4 salad plates. Cover evenly with lettuce; sprinkle with onions. Top with tomato slices. Evenly distribute ham and radishes on top of tomatoes. Spoon remaining dill mixture over sandwiches. **8 sandwiches.**

NUTRIENTS PER 1 SANDWICH

Calories	310	Dietary Fiber	1 g
Protein	11 g	Sodium	475 mg
Carbohydrate	17 g	Potassium	445 mg
Fat	22 g	Calcium	6% U.S. RDA
Cholesterol	30 mg	Iron	10% U.S. RDA

Cranberry Glazed Ham Loaf

       2 lb. ground cooked ham
     ¾ lb. ground beef
       1 cup soft bread crumbs
       1 cup cranberry juice cocktail
       2 eggs, slightly beaten

GLAZE
     ½ cup cranberry juice cocktail
     ⅓ cup firmly packed brown sugar
     ½ teaspoon dry mustard

Heat oven to 350°F. In large bowl, combine ham, ground beef, bread crumbs, 1 cup cranberry juice cocktail and eggs; mix well. Form into 2 loaves; place side by side in ungreased 9-inch square pan. Bake at 350°F. for 1 hour; drain.

Meanwhile, in small saucepan combine ½ cup cranberry juice cocktail, brown sugar and mustard; bring to a boil. Simmer 1 minute or until brown sugar is dissolved, stirring constantly. Baste ham loaf with glaze, continue baking for 25 to 30 minutes or until meat is firm, basting often. Let stand 5 minutes before serving. **2 loaves; 10 servings.**

NUTRIENTS PER ¹⁄₁₀ OF RECIPE

Calories 190	Dietary Fiber ....0 g
Protein.................................13 g	Sodium.............................265 mg
Carbohydrate.......................16 g	Potassium........................230 mg
Fat ....8 g	Calcium.................2% U.S. RDA
Cholesterol......................120 mg	Iron......................10% U.S. RDA

Hot Ham and Swiss on Rye

     ½ cup margarine or butter, softened
     ¼ cup prepared horseradish mustard
     ¼ cup chopped onion
       4 teaspoons poppy seed

8 rye hamburger buns, sliced
8 thin slices boiled ham
8 slices (3½x3½-inch) Swiss cheese

Heat oven to 350°F. In small bowl, combine margarine, mustard, onion and poppy seed. Spread mixture on both cut surfaces of sliced buns. Fill each bun with 1 slice ham and 1 slice cheese. Wrap each sandwich in foil; place on cookie sheet. Bake at 350°F. for 15 to 20 minutes or until thoroughly heated. **8 sandwiches.**

NUTRIENTS PER 1 SANDWICH

Calories	380	Dietary Fiber	3 g
Protein	17 g	Sodium	870 mg
Carbohydrate	23 g	Potassium	125 mg
Fat	25 g	Calcium	30% U.S. RDA
Cholesterol	35 mg	Iron	10% U.S. RDA

Hot Italian Sandwiches

SAUCE

8-oz. can (1 cup) tomato sauce
¼ teaspoon basil leaves
⅛ to ¼ teaspoon crushed red pepper
⅛ teaspoon garlic powder

SANDWICH

1 lb. ground Italian pork sausage
1 medium onion, thinly sliced
8 slices French bread, cut diagonally, ¾-inch thick
6 oz. mozzarella cheese, sliced
2 tablespoons margarine or butter, softened

In small saucepan, combine sauce ingredients. Bring to a boil; simmer 15 minutes, stirring occasionally.

Shape pork sausage into 4 large thin oval patties, about 4½ inches long. In large skillet, fry over medium heat about 10 minutes or until done, turing frequently; remove sausage patties from skillet. In same skillet, cook onion until tender; set aside. Remove all grease and drippings from skillet.

To assemble sandwiches, top each of 4 slices of bread with ¼ of the cheese slices, 1 sausage patty and ¼ of the cooked onion. Cover with remaining slices of bread. Spread margarine on outside of each sandwich. Place in skillet over medium heat. Grill sandwiches on both sides until bread begins to brown and sandwich is thoroughly heated. Serve each sandwich with about ¼ cup sauce for dipping. **4 sandwiches.**

NUTRIENTS PER 1 SANDWICH

Calories	560	Dietary Fiber	<1 g
Protein	29 g	Sodium	1465 mg
Carbohydrate	47 g	Potassium	565 mg
Fat	28 g	Calcium	35% U.S. RDA
Cholesterol	70 mg	Iron	20% U.S. RDA

Beer and Bratwurst

1	lb. (about 4) bratwurst or other smoked sausage
12-oz.	can beer
1	medium onion, sliced
10	whole black peppercorns

In large saucepan, combine all ingredients. Cook until almost boiling. Cover; simmer 10 minutes. Remove bratwurst. Continue simmering onions until tender. Broil or grill bratwurst 3 to 5 inches from heat about 3 to 5 minutes on each side. To serve, drain onions and serve with sausage. **4 servings.**

NUTRIENTS PER ¼ OF RECIPE

Calories	240	Dietary Fiber	<1 g
Protein	11 g	Sodium	430 mg
Carbohydrate	3 g	Potassium	190 mg
Fat	20 g	Calcium	4% U.S. RDA
Cholesterol	45 mg	Iron	6% U.S. RDA

Beans 'n Wieners

1   lb. wieners, cut into fourths
3   (16-oz.) cans pork and beans in tomato sauce
½   cup catsup
¼   cup chopped onion
¼   cup molasses
2   teaspoons prepared mustard

In slow cooker, combine all ingredients. Cover; cook on low setting for 3 to 4 hours. **8 servings.**

TIPS: Four slices bacon, crisply cooked and crumbled, can be added last hour of cooking.

If desired, combine ingredients in ungreased 3-quart casserole. Cover; bake at 350°F. for 30 to 35 minutes or until thoroughly heated. For thicker sauce, bake 15 minutes longer.

NUTRIENTS PER 1 CUP

Calories	420	Dietary Fiber	13 g
Protein	16 g	Sodium	1480 mg
Carbohydrate	46 g	Potassium	800 mg
Fat	19 g	Calcium	15% U.S. RDA
Cholesterol	45 mg	Iron	25% U.S. RDA

Hot Dog Ideas

Prepare wieners or frankfurters as desired. Place in buns. Top with one of the following:

Chili
Sloppy Joe filling
Barbecue sauce and chopped green pepper
Chili sauce, chopped lettuce and shredded cheese
Catsup and pineapple

Sauerkraut
Sauerkraut and baked beans
Sauerkraut and shredded Swiss cheese; broil
Shredded cheese and crumbled cooked bacon
Cottage cheese and sliced green onions; broil

Lamb

Timetable for Roasting Lamb

(Oven Temperature 325°F.)

Roast	Weight (Pounds)	Thermometer Reading °F.	Cooking Time* (Minutes Per Pound)
Leg (bone in)	5 to 7	140°F. (rare)	20 to 25
		160°F. (med.)	25 to 30
		170°F. (well)	30 to 35
	7 to 9	140°F. (rare)	15 to 20
		160°F. (med.)	20 to 25
		170°F. (well)	25 to 30
Leg (boneless)	4 to 7	140°F. (rare)	25 to 30
		160°F. (med.)	30 to 35
		170°F. (well)	35 to 40
Leg Half (shank or sirloin)	3 to 4	140°F. (rare)	25 to 35
		160°F. (med.)	35 to 45
		170°F. (well)	45 to 50
Shoulder (boneless)	3½ to 5	140°F. (rare)	30 to 35
		160°F. (med.)	35 to 40
		170°F. (well)	40 to 45

*Based on meat taken directly from refrigerator.

Glazes for Lamb Roasts

GARLIC GLAZE: Combine 1 tablespoon paprika, ½ teaspoon basil leaves, 3 garlic cloves, minced, ⅓ cup water, ⅓ cup sherry, 2 tablespoons oil and 2 tablespoons soy sauce. Brush on lamb every 30 minutes during roasting.

JELLY GLAZE: Melt ¾ cup mint, currant or apricot jelly over low heat. Brush on lamb during last hour of roasting.

PLUM GLAZE: In blender container, combine 16-oz. can (2 cups) pitted purple plums, drained (reserve ¼ cup liquid), reserved liquid, 2 tablespoons lemon juice, 1 tablespoon soy sauce, 1 teaspoon basil leaves and 1 teaspoon Worcestershire sauce. Blend at medium speed until smooth. Brush lamb with glaze very 30 minutes during roasting.

SPICY GLAZE: Combine ¼ cup firmly packed brown sugar, 1½ teaspoons salt, ½ teaspoon dry mustard, ½ teaspoon chili powder, ¼ teaspoon ginger, ¼ teaspoon cloves, 1 garlic clove, minced and 1 tablespoon lemon juice. Brush on lamb during last hour of roasting.

Lamb Roast

Heat oven to 325°F. Place roast fat side up on rack in shallow roasting pan. Sprinkle with salt and pepper unless using glaze with salt or soy sauce added. Insert meat thermometer so the bulb reaches the center of the thickest part of meat, but does not rest in fat or on bone. Roast to desired degree of doneness using Timetable for Roasting Lamb. For ease in carving, allow roast to stand 15 minutes to set juices.

NUTRIENTS PER ½ LB. LAMB ROAST WITHOUT BONE, COOKED

Calories	240	Dietary Fiber	0 g
Protein	32 g	Sodium	1140 mg
Carbohydrate	0 g	Potassium	360 mg
Fat	12 g	Calcium	<2% U.S. RDA
Cholesterol	120 mg	Iron	13% U.S. RDA

Savory Lamb Shish Kabobs

1½ to 2-lb.	boned leg of lamb, cut into 1½-inch cubes
⅓ cup	oil
¼ cup	lemon juice
1½ teaspoons	salt
1 teaspoon	mint leaves
1 teaspoon	rosemary
½ teaspoon	pepper
1	garlic clove, minced

Place lamb cubes in plastic bag or non-metal bowl. Combine remaining ingredients to make marinade. Pour over lamb; stir to coat cubes. Seal bag or cover bowl; marinate at least 2 hours at room temperature or overnight in refrigerator, stirring once or twice. Drain lamb; reserve marinade for basting sauce. Thread lamb cubes onto 4 to 6 skewers.

When ready to barbecue, place skewers on grill 3 to 4 inches from hot coals. Brush with reserved marinade. Cook about 20 minutes, turning and brushing with marinade, until browned and desired doneness. **6 to 8 servings.**

TIP: Kabobs can be broiled as directed in oven.

NUTRIENTS PER ⅛ OF RECIPE

Calories	180	Dietary Fiber	0 g
Protein	14 g	Sodium	435 mg
Carbohydrate	1 g	Potassium	15 mg
Fat	13 g	Calcium	<2% U.S. RDA
Cholesterol	70 mg	Iron	6% U.S. RDA

Gyro Sandwich

½ lb. lean ground lamb
½ lb. ground beef
1 teaspoon salt
¼ teaspoon allspice
1 garlic clove, minced
5 pocket breads (6-inch diameter)
   Shredded lettuce
1 medium onion, cut into 5 slices
1 medium tomato, cut into 5 slices

DRESSING
1 cup plain yogurt
¼ teaspoon salt
¼ teaspoon dill weed
1 garlic clove, minced
1 tablespoon lemon juice

In large bowl, combine ground lamb, beef, salt, allspice and 1 garlic clove; mix well. Shape into five 4-inch patties. In large skillet, fry patties over medium heat 3 to 5 minutes. Reduce heat; turn and cook until done as desired.

In small bowl, combine all dressing ingredients; mix well. Warm pocket breads. Place shredded lettuce in bottom of pocket. Layer meat patty, onion and tomato in pocket and drizzle with dressing. **5 sandwiches.**

NUTRIENTS PER ⅕ OF RECIPE

Calories	460	Dietary Fiber	2 g
Protein	28 g	Sodium	610 mg
Carbohydrate	58 g	Potassium	370 mg
Fat	12 g	Calcium	20% U.S. RDA
Cholesterol	60 mg	Iron	25% U.S. RDA

Broiled Lamb Chops

Place lamb rib, loin or shoulder chops on broiler pan. Place or adjust broiler pan so tops of 1-inch thick chops are 2 inches from heat and 2-inch thick chops are 3 inches from heat. Broil 1-inch thick chops 10 to 12 minutes; 2-inch thick chops 20 to 22 minutes, turning once during cooking. Sprinkle with salt and pepper unless using glaze or marinade containing salt or soy sauce.

TIPS: Other seasonings for lamb chops include a dash of garlic salt, paprika or curry powder.

Serve Zesty Onion Couscous (see Index) as a sidedish accompaniment.

NUTRIENTS PER 1 THICK RIB CHOP, COOKED

Calories	190	Dietary Fiber	0 g
Protein	27 g	Sodium	65 mg
Carbohydrate	0 g	Potassium	300 mg
Fat	8 g	Calcium	<2% U.S. RDA
Cholesterol	100 mg	Iron	10% U.S. RDA

Lamb Chop Marinade

In small bowl, combine ⅓ cup oil, 1 tablespoon vinegar, 1 teaspoon salt, 2 garlic cloves, minced and 1 bay leaf, crushed. Place 4 to 6 lamb chops in plastic bag or non-metal bowl. Pour marinade over chops. Seal bag or cover bowl. Marinate at least 2 hours at room temperature or overnight in refrigerator, stirring once or twice. Drain well; broil as directed.

NUTRIENTS: Variables in this recipe make it impossible to calculate nutrition information.

Lamb Patties

In medium bowl, combine 1 lb. ground lamb, 2 tablespoons chopped onion, ½ teaspoon salt and ⅛ teaspoon pepper; shape into 4 patties. Broil or grill 3 to 4 inches from heat for 6 to 8 minutes on each side. If desired, brush with one of Glazes for Lamb Roasts during broiling or grilling (see Index). **4 servings.**

NUTRIENTS PER ¼ OF RECIPE

Calories	120	
Protein	19 g	
Carbohydrate	0 g	
Fat	5 g	
Cholesterol	70 mg	
Dietary Fiber	0 g	
Sodium	310 mg	
Potassium	220 mg	
Calcium	<2% U.S. RDA	
Iron	8% U.S. RDA	

Poultry

Poultry

Poultry

In many homes, chicken used to be reserved for company dinners or the big Sunday meal. And turkey was definitely a special-occasion treat. Today, thanks to ingenious poultry raising methods, both have become increasingly available and two of the most popular items on weekly shopping lists. Cooks and diners alike praise poultry for its mild flavor, versatility and all-around appeal.

Poultry is a noted source of high-quality protein along with thiamine, riboflavin, niacin and calcium. Chicken is rich in vitamin A and essential amino acids and turkey is high in B vitamins and iron. Depending on preparation methods, poultry can be significantly lower in calories and saturated fats than most meats.

Purchasing Poultry

• **Types of Poultry:** Poultry includes chickens, turkeys, game hens, ducks and geese.
  • **Frying chickens,** also referred to as fryers, broilers or broiler-fryers, are young tender chickens weighing from 1½ to 4 lb. This all-purpose chicken is good for broiling, frying, roasting, braising, stewing, barbecuing and poaching.
  • **Roasters and Capons,** weighing from 4 to 6 lb., are best roasted.
  • **Stewing chickens or hens** are very meaty, older birds; they are best simmered or used in stews or soups.
  • **Turkeys** on the market are young and labeled that way. Fresh and frozen turkeys have equal quality. Whole turkeys are usually roasted. They range in size from 4 to 30 lb.; the larger the bird the more meat in proportion to bone.
  • **Game hens** are small birds weighing 1 to 1½ lb. They can be broiled, grilled, microwaved or roasted.

- **Ducks and geese** have all dark meat and are usually sold frozen. Compared to most poultry, the proportion of meat to bone is lower and the amount of fat higher; plan on at least 1 lb. per serving.

- **Cuts of Poultry**
Chicken comes ready to cook in a variety of ways including whole, halved, quartered, in serving pieces, and in boneless cuts. Turkey can be purchased whole or in parts, ground, and in roasts, steaks, cutlets, fresh or frozen or processed in smoked and cured forms.

- **Fresh Poultry**
Fresh uncooked chicken should be firm, moist and creamy yellow in color. Skin color may vary but it is not a factor in quality or freshness. Turkey should have the same qualities, with a white skin. All poultry should be free of skin tears and bruises and have a fresh odor.

- **Frozen Poultry**
It should be solid to the touch, free of ice crystals and freezer burn, and the package should be tightly sealed.

- **How Much to Buy**
For whole turkeys, allow about a pound per serving and for steaks and cutlets, 4 to 6 ounces per serving. With ground turkey, 4 ounces may be appropriate per serving, but this can fluctuate depending on preparation method. For chicken, allow ½ pound uncooked with bone in, ½ breast, 2 drumsticks or 4 wings per serving. Most cooks plan on one Cornish hen per person. These guidelines are general and amounts purchased depend upon appetites, preparation and accompaniment dishes.

Storing and Thawing Poultry

Highly perishable, uncooked poultry should be stored in the coldest section of the refrigerator no longer than 2 days. Wrap loosely to allow air circulation; remove and store liver and giblets separately.

Store fresh poultry in moisture-and vapor-proof wrap at 0°F. up to 3 months. Wrap giblets separately and use within 3 months. Do not freeze stuffed poultry.

Room temperature thawing is not recommended. Thaw poultry under refrigerated conditions for optimum food safety. Or immerse wrapped poultry completely in cold water, changing water frequently until poultry is thawed but still cold. Large turkeys take up to 3 days to thaw in the refrigerator. Do not thaw commercially stuffed birds; follow label directions. Cook as soon as possible after thawing. Never refreeze thawed, uncooked poultry.

Cooked poultry should be cooled quickly, covered and refrigerated for no more than several days.

Orange Burgundy Chicken

2½ to 3-lb. frying chicken, cut up
   2 tablespoons margarine or butter
  ½ teaspoon seasoned salt or salt
  ⅛ teaspoon pepper, if desired
   2 tablespoons firmly packed brown sugar
   2 tablespoons cornstarch
  ¼ teaspoon salt
  ⅛ teaspoon ginger, if desired
  ½ cup orange marmalade
  ½ cup orange juice
   1 tablespoon lemon juice
  ½ cup Burgundy or dry red wine*
   1 orange thinly sliced, if desired

In large skillet, brown chicken in margarine. Sprinkle with ½ teaspoon salt and pepper. In small bowl, combine remaining ingredients, except Burgundy wine and orange slices. Pour over chicken. Cover; simmer 25 to 35 minutes or until tender, stirring occasionally. Add wine and orange slices. Continue simmering 10 minutes. **4 to 6 servings.**

MICROWAVE DIRECTIONS: Cut larger pieces of chicken in half for uniform size. Arrange chicken skin side up in 12x8-inch (2-quart) microwave-safe dish. *Omit margarine.* Sprinkle with ½ teaspoon salt and pepper. In small bowl, combine remaining ingredients. Pour over chicken. Cover with microwave-safe plastic wrap. Microwave on HIGH for 10 minutes. Rearrange chicken and stir sauce. Cover; microwave on HIGH for 14 to 18 minutes or until chicken is tender and no longer pink, spooning sauce occasionally over chicken.

TIPS: *One-third cup additional orange juice can be substituted for wine.

To bake in oven, brown chicken. Sprinkle with ½ teaspoon salt and pepper. Arrange chicken in ungreased 13x9-inch pan. Combine remaining ingredients except wine and orange slices. Pour over chicken. Cover with foil. Bake at 350°F. for 1 hour, adding wine and orange slices during last 15 minutes of baking time.

Peach or apricot preserves can be substituted for orange marmalade.

NUTRIENTS PER ¼ OF RECIPE

Calories	430	Dietary Fiber	0 g
Protein	31 g	Sodium	360 mg
Carbohydrate	29 g	Potassium	340 mg
Fat	19 g	Calcium	2% U.S. RDA
Cholesterol	100 mg	Iron	10% U.S. RDA

Oven-Crisp Chicken

     1   cup mashed potato flakes
     1   teaspoon salt
     ¼   teaspoon pepper
     ¼   teaspoon rosemary, crushed, or ⅛ teaspoon poultry
         seasoning
     1   egg, slightly beaten

1   teaspoon lemon juice
2-lb. frying chicken, cut up

Heat oven to 375°F. In plastic bag, combine potato flakes and seasonings. In shallow bowl, combine egg and lemon juice. Dip chicken pieces in egg mixture; shake in plastic bag to coat with potato flake mixture. Place chicken skin side up in ungreased 15x10-inch jelly roll pan. Bake at 375°F. for 60 to 75 minutes or until chicken is tender. **6 servings.**

TIP: Tarragon, basil, marjoram or thyme leaves, or paprika can be added to potato flakes mixture. Onion, garlic or seasoned salt can be substituted for plain salt.

NUTRIENTS PER ⅙ OF RECIPE

Calories 170	Dietary Fiber .... 1 g
Protein .... 21 g	Sodium .... 375 mg
Carbohydrate .... 7 g	Potassium .... 135 mg
Fat .... 6 g	Calcium .... 2% U.S. RDA
Cholesterol .... 110 mg	Iron .... 10% U.S. RDA

Savory Baked Chicken

2½ to 3-lb. frying chicken, cut up
3   tablespoons margarine or butter, melted
1   tablespoon lemon juice
¼   teaspoon salt
¼   teaspoon tarragon leaves
¼   teaspoon paprika
⅛   teaspoon pepper

Heat oven to 325°F. Place chicken pieces in 13x9-inch pan. Combine margarine and lemon juice; pour over chicken. Sprinkle with salt, tarragon, paprika and pepper. Cover with foil. Bake at 325°F. for 45 minutes. Uncover; bake another 15 minutes or until tender. **4 servings.**

NUTRIENTS PER ¼ OF RECIPE

Calories	490	Dietary Fiber	0 g
Protein	47 g	Sodium	370 mg
Carbohydrate	1 g	Potassium	400 mg
Fat	32 g	Calcium	2% U.S. RDA
Cholesterol	150 mg	Iron	10% U.S. RDA

Chicken Cacciatore

¼ cup	all purpose flour
2½ to 3-lb.	frying chicken, cut up, skinned
2	tablespoons oil
1	medium onion, sliced
1	medium green pepper, sliced
1	teaspoon Italian seasoning
½	teaspoon sugar
½	teaspoon salt
⅛	teaspoon pepper
16-oz.	can (2 cups) tomatoes, undrained, cut up
	Hot cooked egg noodles

Place flour in shallow dish; coat chicken pieces with flour. In large skillet, brown chicken in hot oil; drain excess oil from skillet. Add remaining ingredients except spaghetti; mix well. Cover; simmer 30 to 40 minutes or until chicken is fork tender, stirring occasionally. Serve over hot cooked noodles. **4 to 6 servings.**

MICROWAVE DIRECTIONS: *Omit flour and oil.* Arrange chicken in 12x8-inch (2-quart) microwave-safe dish. In medium bowl, combine remaining ingredients except noodles; pour over chicken. Cover with microwave-safe plastic wrap. Microwave on HIGH for 22 to 26 minutes or until chicken is tender and no longer pink, rotating dish ½ turn and spooning sauce over chicken once during cooking. Serve as directed.

NUTRIENTS PER ⅙ OF RECIPE

Calories	490	Dietary Fiber .... 2 g
Protein	45 g	Sodium .... 350 mg
Carbohydrate	53 g	Potassium .... 820 mg
Fat	9 g	Calcium .... 4% U.S. RDA
Cholesterol	80 mg	Iron .... 20% U.S. RDA

Fried Chicken

⅓ cup all purpose flour
½ to 1 teaspoon salt
1 teaspoon paprika
½ teaspoon pepper
2½ to 3-lb. frying chicken, cut up
1 cup oil or shortening

In paper or plastic bag, combine flour, salt, paprika and pepper. Shake chicken, a few pieces at a time, in flour mixture to coat. In large skillet over medium heat, heat oil. Brown chicken. Reduce heat. Cover; simmer 30 minutes or until chicken is tender. Remove cover last 10 minutes to crisp chicken. If gravy is desired, drain oil except for about 3 tablespoons. See Index for Chicken Gravy. **4 to 6 servings.**

TIP: After browning, chicken can be placed in ungreased shallow baking pan and baked uncovered at 350°F. for about 45 minutes.

VARIATIONS:

CRUSTY CHICKEN: Dip chicken in mixture of 1 egg beaten with 2 tablespoons water and then in flour mixture, increasing flour to ½ cup.

ONION CHICKEN: Shake chicken pieces in mixture of ½ cup dry bread crumbs, 2 tablespoons dry onion soup mix, ½ teaspoon salt and ⅛ teaspoon pepper. Fry as directed.

SEASONED CHICKEN: Add any one of the following to

flour mixture: ½ teaspoon poultry seasoning, ½ teaspoon lemon-pepper seasoning or ⅛ teaspoon garlic or onion powder.

SOUTHERN-FRIED CHICKEN: Omit paprika from flour mixture. Prepare chicken as directed above. *Milk Gravy:* Add 2 cups hot milk to drippings. Combine ¼ cup all-purpose flour and ¼ cup cold milk; mix until smooth. Add flour mixture to hot liquid. Cook until mixture boils and thickens, stirring constantly. Season with salt and pepper. **2 cups.**

NUTRIENTS PER ⅙ OF RECIPE

Calories 540	Dietary Fiber........................<1 g
Protein.....................................32 g	Sodium.............................450 mg
Carbohydrate............................6 g	Potassium.........................270 mg
Fat ....43 g	Calcium.................2% U.S. RDA
Cholesterol.........................100 mg	Iron.....................10% U.S. RDA

Italian Oven-Fried Chicken

½ cup margarine or butter
1 garlic clove, minced
1 cup dry bread crumbs
¼ cup grated Parmesan cheese
¼ cup finely chopped almonds
2 tablespoons chopped fresh parsley
1 teaspoon salt
¼ teaspoon thyme leaves or poultry seasoning
⅛ teaspoon pepper
2½ to 3-lb. frying chicken, cut up or quartered

Heat oven to 400°F. In 13x9-inch pan, melt margarine with garlic. In medium bowl or shallow pan, combine bread crumbs, cheese, almonds, parsley, salt, thyme and pepper; mix well. Dip chicken pieces in garlic butter; coat with crumb mixture. Place skin side up in pan containing garlic butter. Bake at 400°F. for 1 hour or until chicken is tender, basting occasionally with pan drippings. **4 to 6 servings.**

VARIATIONS:

CREAMY MUSHROOM FRIED CHICKEN: In 13x9-inch pan, melt ¼ cup margarine. Crush 3 cups croutons to 1½ cups. Dip chicken in 1 can (10¾ oz.) condensed cream of mushroom soup. Roll in crushed croutons or crumb mixture, if desired. Place skin side up in 13x9-inch pan containing margarine. Bake as directed above.

OVEN-FRIED SESAME CHICKEN: Dip chicken in mixture of ⅓ cup honey, 1 tablespoon lemon juice, 1 tablespoon soy sauce and ¼ cup melted margarine. Roll lightly in ⅔ cup sesame seed. Place skin side up in ungreased 13x9-inch pan; sprinkle with salt. Bake as directed above.

NUTRIENTS PER ¼ OF RECIPE

Calories	530	Dietary Fiber	<1 g
Protein	36 g	Sodium	830 mg
Carbohydrate	14 g	Potassium	340 mg
Fat	36 g	Calcium	10% U.S. RDA
Cholesterol	100 mg	Iron	15% U.S. RDA

Oven-Barbecued Chicken

          1 garlic clove, minced
          2 tablespoons margarine or butter
          1 cup catsup
         ¼ cup water
          2 tablespoons brown sugar
         ½ teaspoon salt
         ⅛ teaspoon pepper
          1 tablespoon Worcestershire sauce
    2½ to 3-lb. frying chicken, cut up, skinned
          3 small onions, sliced, separated into rings

Heat oven to 375°F. In small saucepan over medium heat, saute garlic in margarine about 1 minute. Stir in catsup, water, brown sugar, salt, pepper and Worcestershire sauce; bring to a boil. Reduce heat. Cover; simmer 5 minutes, stirring occasionally. Arrange chicken pieces in ungreased 12x8-inch (2-quart) baking dish. Place onion rings over chicken; pour sauce over top. Bake at 375°F. for 1 hour or until chicken is tender, basting occasionally. **4 servings.**

NUTRIENTS PER ¼ OF RECIPE

Calories	460	Dietary Fiber	1 g
Protein	55 g	Sodium	1220 mg
Carbohydrate	28 g	Potassium	750 mg
Fat	14 g	Calcium	6% U.S. RDA
Cholesterol	150 mg	Iron	15% U.S. RDA

Spicy Barbecued Chicken

2½ to 3-lb.	frying chicken, quartered
1	teaspoon salt
½	cup chopped onion
1	garlic clove, minced
1	tablespoon oil
8-oz.	can (1 cup) tomato sauce
3	tablespoons brown sugar
2	teaspoons chili powder
⅓	cup vinegar
2 to 3	drops hot pepper sauce
1	tomato, peeled, chopped

Place chicken in large saucepan or Dutch oven. Add salt and enough water to cover. Bring to a boil; reduce heat. Cover; simmer 10 minutes. Drain. In small saucepan, saute onion and garlic in oil until tender. Stir in remaining ingredients. Bring to a boil; simmer 5 minutes, stirring occasionally. Brush chicken with about ½ cup sauce.

Place chicken bone side down on grill 4 to 6 inches from medium coals. Brush with sauce. Cook 15 to 20 minutes or until tender. Baste chicken with sauce last 10 minutes of cooking time. Serve remaining sauce with chicken. **4 servings.**

VARIATION:

OVEN-BAKED SPICY BARBECUED CHICKEN: After cooking chicken in water, place in greased 13x9-inch pan. Brush with ½ cup sauce. Bake at 350°F. for 30 to 40 minutes or until tender, basting chicken occasionally with sauce.

NUTRIENTS PER ¼ OF RECIPE

Calories	290	Dietary Fiber	1 g
Protein	34 g	Sodium	980 mg
Carbohydrate	19 g	Potassium	790 mg
Fat	9 g	Calcium	4% U.S. RDA
Cholesterol	150 mg	Iron	15% U.S. RDA

Chicken a l'Orange

```
3-lb.  frying chicken, cut up
    2  tablespoons margarine or butter
    1  teaspoon salt
  ⅛  teaspoon pepper, if desired
    3  tablespoons brown sugar
    1  tablespoon cornstarch
  ⅛  teaspoon ginger, if desired
  ⅔  cup orange juice
  ⅓  cup orange marmalade
    1  tablespoon lemon juice
    3  large peeled carrots, cut into 2½x¼-inch strips
    1  large green pepper, cut into pieces
```

In large skillet, brown chicken in margarine. Season with salt and pepper. Cover; simmer 20 minutes. Remove chicken; drain. In small bowl, combine brown sugar, cornstarch, ginger, orange juice, marmalade and lemon juice. Add to skillet; bring to a boil, stirring constantly until bubbly and thickened. Reduce heat. Add chicken and carrots; stir to coat. Cover; simmer for 10 minutes. Add green pepper; simmer uncovered 5 minutes or until vegetables are crisp-tender. **4 to 6 servings.**

NUTRIENTS PER ¼ OF RECIPE

Calories 280	Dietary Fiber...........................2 g
Protein....................................22 g	Sodium............................480 mg
Carbohydrate.........................29 g	Potassium........................430 mg
Fat..9 g	Calcium.................4% U.S. RDA
Cholesterol........................60 mg	Iron.......................4% U.S. RDA

Fresh Herb-Grilled Chicken

4 whole chicken breasts, skinned, halved, pierced with fork
⅓ cup lemon juice
¼ cup oil
2 teaspoons chopped fresh rosemary or ½ teaspoon rosemary
1½ teaspoons chopped fresh thyme or ½ teaspoon thyme leaves
1 garlic clove, minced
⅛ teaspoon pepper
Salt, if desired

MICROWAVE-TO-GRILL DIRECTIONS: In 12x8-inch (2-quart) microwave-safe baking dish, arrange chicken breasts thickest portions to outside. In small bowl, combine remaining ingredients; pour over chicken. Cover with microwave-safe plastic wrap; refrigerate 6 to 8 hours.

Prepare charcoal fire for grilling. Just before grilling, remove chicken from refrigerator; do not uncover. Microwave chicken on HIGH for 5 to 7 minutes or until edges of chicken begin to cook. Drain; reserve marinade. Immediately place chicken on grill 4 to 6 inches from medium coals. Cook 20 to 25 minutes or until no longer pink, turning once and brushing frequently with marinade. **8 servings.**

VARIATION:

HERB-BROILED CHICKEN: Arrange raw chicken bone side up on broiler pan. In small bowl, combine remaining ingredients; brush over chicken. Broil about 4 inches from heat for 8 minutes, brushing frequently with sauce. Turn chicken; continue broiling, brushing frequently with sauce, for 6 to 8 minutes or until chicken is tender. Serve warm or cold.

NUTRIENTS PER ⅛ OF RECIPE

Calories	190	Dietary Fiber	0 g
Protein	25 g	Sodium	60 mg
Carbohydrate	1 g	Potassium	220 mg
Fat	10 g	Calcium	<2% U.S. RDA
Cholesterol	70 mg	Iron	4% U.S. RDA

French Dressing Chicken Grill

½ cup low calorie creamy French dressing
¼ cup dry white wine
2½ to 3-lb. frying chicken, cut up, skinned*

MICROWAVE-TO-GRILL DIRECTIONS: Combine dressing and wine in 12x8-inch (2-quart) microwave-safe baking dish. Add chicken pieces; turn to coat. Cover; refrigerate 1 to 2 hours.

Prepare charcoal fire for grilling. Drain chicken; reserve marinade. Cover marinade; refrigerate. Arrange chicken in same baking dish with thickest pieces to outside. Cover with microwave-safe plastic wrap. Microwave on HIGH for 8 to 12 minutes or until outer edges of chicken begin to cook; drain. Immediately place chicken on grill 4 to 6 inches from medium coals. Cook 15 to 20 minutes or until chicken is tender, turning once and brushing with marinade the last 5 minutes. **4 to 5 servings.**

TIP: *If desired, skin may be left on chicken.

NUTRIENTS PER ⅕ OF RECIPE

Calories	240	Dietary Fiber	0 g
Protein	34 g	Sodium	190 mg
Carbohydrate	1 g	Potassium	310 mg
Fat	10 g	Calcium	<2% U.S. RDA
Cholesterol	100 mg	Iron	8% U.S. RDA

Herb-Lemon Basting Sauce

⅓ cup lemon juice
¼ cup oil
1 teaspoon rosemary, crushed
½ teaspoon thyme leaves
¼ teaspoon garlic powder
Dash pepper
Dash paprika

In small bowl, combine all ingredients. **½ cup.**

NUTRIENTS PER 1 TABLESPOON

Calories	60	Dietary Fiber	0 g
Protein	0 g	Sodium	0 mg
Carbohydrate	1 g	Potassium	15 mg
Fat	7 g	Calcium	<2% U.S. RDA
Cholesterol	0 mg	Iron	<2% U.S. RDA

Southern Barbecue Basting Sauce

¾ cup catsup
¼ cup finely chopped onion
¼ cup water
¼ cup margarine or butter
2 tablespoons vinegar
1 tablespoon Worcestershire sauce
1 teaspoon lemon pepper seasoning*
1 teaspoon dry mustard
¼ teaspoon cayenne pepper
Few drops hot pepper sauce

In small saucepan over low heat, combine all ingredients. Simmer 10 minutes. Use while warm or store, covered, in refrigerator; reheat before using. **1½ cups.**

TIP: *One teaspoon seasoned salt plus 1 tablespoon lemon juice can be substituted for lemon pepper seasoning.

VARIATION:

SWEET SPICY BASTING SAUCE: Substitute 10-oz. jar peach preserves for catsup.

NUTRIENTS PER 1 TABLESPOON

Calories	30	Dietary Fiber	0 g
Protein	0 g	Sodium	170 mg
Carbohydrate	3 g	Potassium	35 mg
Fat	2 g	Calcium	<2% U.S. RDA
Cholesterol	0 mg	Iron	<2% U.S. RDA

Chicken with Pineapple Glaze

  2 (2½ to 3-lb.) frying chickens, quartered or halved
  2 tablespoons margarine or butter
      Salt
      Pepper
      Paprika
  1 cup firmly packed brown sugar
  2 tablespoons lemon juice
  2 tablespoons prepared mustard or 1 teaspoon dry
      mustard
      Dash salt
8-oz. can (1 cup) crushed pineapple, undrained

Rub chicken with margarine. Sprinkle with salt, pepper and paprika. In small bowl, combine remaining ingredients; mix well.

Place chicken on grill skin side up 6 to 8 inches from hot coals. Cook 30 to 45 minutes, turning once to brown both sides. Brush with pineapple glaze during last 10 to 15 minutes. If desired, heat any remaining glaze and serve with chicken. **8 servings.**

NUTRIENTS PER ⅛ OF RECIPE

Calories 560	Dietary Fiber........................<1 g
Protein.....................................47 g	Sodium..............................380 mg
Carbohydrate.........................32 g	Potassium..........................520 mg
Fat ....26 g	Calcium................5% U.S. RDA
Cholesterol.......................150 mg	Iron.....................26% U.S. RDA

Sauteed Chicken Livers

    8 oz. chicken livers
    2 tablespoons margarine or butter
 ¼ cup chopped onion
 ¼ teaspoon salt
 ⅛ teaspoon pepper

Rinse livers; pat dry. In large skillet, melt margarine. Add livers and remaining ingredients. Saute 8 to 10 minutes or until tender. **4 servings.**

NUTRIENTS PER ¼ OF RECIPE

Calories 130	Dietary Fiber...........................0 g
Protein.....................................10 g	Sodium..............................240 mg
Carbohydrate...........................3 g	Potassium..........................150 mg
Fat ....8 g	Calcium...............<2% U.S. RDA
Cholesterol.......................250 mg	Iron.....................25% U.S. RDA

How to Bone a Chicken Breast

Remove skin. Lay breast bone side up. Using a sharp knife, run blade down center to cut thin membrane and expose keel bone (dark spoon-shaped bone) and white cartilage.

To remove keel bone, place a thumb at base of rib cage just above top of keel bone and the other thumb at lower tip of bone. Bend back until keel bone breaks through membrane.

Run finger under edge of keel bone; pull partially away from breast and then pull down to remove white cartilage.

To remove rib bones, insert point of knife under long first rib on one side of breast. Resting knife against bones, gradually scrape meat away from bones. Cut rib away. Cut through shoulder joint; run point of knife under joint. Remove shoulder joint. Repeat with other side of breast. Locate wishbone at top center of breast; run point of knife close to bone. Remove wishbone.

Lay breast flat; cut in half along cleft that contained the keel bone. Remove white tendon. Trim off fat.

Poaching Chicken Breasts

    2 (1½-lb.) whole chicken breasts, skinned, boned,
       halved
       Cold water
    1 stalk celery, sliced
    1 medium carrot, sliced
    1 small onion, quartered
    1 teaspoon chopped fresh parsley
  ¼ teaspoon salt
  ⅛ teaspoon thyme leaves
  ⅛ teaspoon pepper
    1 bay leaf
    1 garlic clove, sliced

Place chicken breasts in large saucepan. Add cold water to just cover chicken. Bring to a boil. Reduce heat. Simmer partially covered 10 minutes. Skim off any scum that rises to surface. Add remaining ingredients. Simmer partially covered an additional 30 to 40 minutes or until chicken is tender.

Remove chicken from broth; cool. Strain broth. Cool broth uncovered in refrigerator. Cut chicken into desired size pieces. Cover; refrigerate or freeze until ready to use. After broth is completely cooled, cover and store in refrigerator or freezer. Skim fat from broth before using in recipe. **3 cups cut-up, cooked chicken and 4 to 4½ cups broth.**

NUTRIENTS PER ½ CUP CUT-UP, COOKED CHICKEN

Calories	120	Dietary Fiber	<1 g
Protein	18 g	Sodium	135 mg
Carbohydrate	0 g	Potassium	160 mg
Fat	5 g	Calcium	<2% U.S. RDA
Cholesterol	50 mg	Iron	4% U.S. RDA

Gourmet Chicken and Artichokes

14½-oz.	can chicken broth or 1¾ cups chicken broth
3	whole chicken breasts, skinned, boned, halved
¼	cup margarine or butter
¼	cup chopped onion
1	garlic clove, minced
¼	cup all purpose flour
¼	teaspoon salt
⅛	teaspoon pepper
¾	cup half-and-half
½	cup grated Parmesan cheese
2	tablespoons dry white wine
½	teaspoon rosemary, crushed
14-oz.	can artichoke hearts, drained
2	tablespoons margarine or butter
12 oz.	fresh mushrooms, sliced (2 cups)

In large skillet, bring chicken broth to a boil; add boned chicken breasts. Cover; simmer 20 minutes or until chicken is tender (reserve ¾ cup chicken broth). Cool chicken. In medium saucepan over medium heat, melt ¼ cup margarine. Add onion and garlic; saute until tender. Reduce heat to low. Stir in flour, salt and pepper. Cook 1 minute until mixture is smooth and bubbly, stirring constantly. Gradually stir in reserved chicken broth and half-and-half. Cook over medium heat until mixture boils and thickens, stirring constantly. Remove from heat. Add Parmesan cheese, wine and rosemary; stir until cheese is melted.

Heat oven to 325°F. Place chicken breasts in ungreased 12x8-inch (2-quart) baking dish. Cut artichokes in half; arrange around chicken. Pour sauce evenly over chicken and artichokes. Bake at 325°F. for 25 to 35 minutes or until thoroughly heated. In medium skillet over medium heat, melt 2 tablespoons margarine; lightly saute mushrooms. Spoon over sauce. Serve over hot cooked rice, if desired. **6 servings.**

NUTRIENTS PER ⅙ OF RECIPE

Calories	370	Dietary Fiber	2 g
Protein	33 g	Sodium	680 mg
Carbohydrate	11 g	Potassium	550 mg
Fat	21 g	Calcium	15% U.S. RDA
Cholesterol	80 mg	Iron	10% U.S. RDA

Chicken Teriyaki

3 whole chicken breasts, skinned, boned, halved
¼ cup light soy sauce
¼ cup white wine
2 tablespoons sugar
½ teaspoon finely grated gingerroot or dash ground ginger
1 garlic clove, minced

Place chicken breast halves between pieces of plastic wrap; lightly pound with meat mallet or rolling pin to flatten. Place in shallow dish. In small bowl, combine remaining ingredients; mix well to dissolve sugar. Pour marinade over chicken. Cover; refrigerate 1 to 2 hours, turning several times. Drain chicken, reserving marinade.

Arrange chicken on lightly greased broiler pan. Broil 4 to 5 inches from heat for 5 minutes. Turn chicken; brush with marinade. Broil an additional 5 to 6 minutes or until chicken is tender. If desired, serve with hot cooked rice. **6 servings.**

NUTRIENTS PER ⅙ OF RECIPE

Calories 140	Dietary Fiber...........................0 g
Protein.....................................25 g	Sodium..............................230 mg
Carbohydrate............................1 g	Potassium.........................210 mg
Fat ....3 g	Calcium..............<2% U.S. RDA
Cholesterol..........................70 mg	Iron.......................4% U.S. RDA

Chicken Dinner in a Dish

2	whole chicken breasts, skinned, boned, halved
2	medium potatoes, quartered
2	carrots, cut into 2-inch pieces
1	large onion, cut into wedges
½	cup dry white wine or chicken broth
1	bay leaf
	Salt and pepper, if desired
8-oz.	pkg. frozen cut green beans, thawed, drained

Heat oven to 350°F. In ungreased 12x8-inch (2-quart) baking dish, arrange chicken, potatoes, carrots and onion. Pour wine over chicken; add bay leaf. Sprinkle with salt and pepper. Cover with foil. Bake at 350°F. for 1 hour. Add beans to chicken and vegetables. Cover; continue baking 10 to 15 minutes or until chicken is thoroughly cooked and vegetables are tender. **4 servings.**

NUTRIENTS PER ¼ OF RECIPE

Calories 180	Dietary Fiber...........................6 g
Protein.....................................21 g	Sodium..............................215 mg
Carbohydrate..........................22 g	Potassium.........................810 mg
Fat ....1 g	Calcium.................4% U.S. RDA
Cholesterol..........................70 mg	Iron.....................10% U.S. RDA

Chicken Breasts in Wine Sauce

2	tablespoons margarine or butter
3	whole chicken breasts, skinned, boned, halved
10¾-oz.	can condensed cream of chicken soup
¼	cup white wine or milk
	Dash pepper
1½	cups sliced carrots
4.5-oz.	jar sliced mushrooms, drained

In large skillet over medium heat, melt margarine. Brown chicken breasts about 5 minutes on each side. In small bowl, combine soup, wine and pepper; pour over chicken. Stir in carrots and mushrooms. Reduce heat. Cover; simmer 25 to 35 minutes or until chicken is tender. Serve with hot cooked rice, if desired. **6 servings.**

NUTRIENTS PER ⅙ OF RECIPE

Calories	240	Dietary Fiber	1 g
Protein	27 g	Sodium	550 mg
Carbohydrate	8 g	Potassium	510 mg
Fat	10 g	Calcium	2% U.S. RDA
Cholesterol	70 mg	Iron	8% U.S. RDA

Madras Skillet Curry

2	whole chicken breasts or 1 whole fresh turkey breast (about 2 lb.)
2	tablespoons flour
2 to 3	tablespoons curry powder
1	teaspoon salt
1	teaspoon paprika
½	teaspoon ginger
1½	cups (1 large) chopped onion
1	cooking apple, cored, cut into bite-size pieces
2	garlic cloves, minced
4 to 6	tablespoons oil
1	cup chicken broth

Hot cooked rice
Condiments: chutney, coconut, mandarin oranges, pineapple chunks

Remove skin from chicken breasts. Bone and cut in half. Place in freezer for 1 hour or until firm but not frozen; slice thinly across grain of meat. In large bowl or plastic bag, combine flour, curry powder, salt, paprika and ginger. Add chicken slices; stir to coat. In large heavy skillet or wok, saute onions, apple and garlic in 2 tablespoons hot oil until tender. Remove and set aside. Heat remaining oil. Add chicken slices with any remaining flour mixture; saute until chicken is lightly browned. Reduce heat to medium. Add chicken broth and onion-apple mixture. Cook until mixture boils and thickens, stirring constantly. Serve over hot cooked rice; top with condiments. **4 servings.**

NUTRIENTS PER ¼ OF RECIPE

Calories	510	Dietary Fiber	2 g
Protein	30 g	Sodium	790 mg
Carbohydrate	41 g	Potassium	520 mg
Fat	25 g	Calcium	6% U.S. RDA
Cholesterol	70 mg	Iron	20% U.S. RDA

Chicken Cordon Bleu

2   whole chicken breasts, skinned, boned, halved
2   oz. (½ cup) shredded Swiss cheese
¼   cup finely chopped, boiled ham
    Salt, if desired
2   teaspoons Dijon mustard
1   egg
2   tablespoons water
¼   cup all purpose flour
¼   teaspoon salt
⅓   cup dry bread crumbs
    Oil for frying

Place 1 chicken breast half, boned side up, between 2 pieces of plastic wrap. Working from the center, lightly pound breast with flat side of meat mallet or rolling pin until about ⅛ to ¼-inch thick; remove wrap. Repeat with remaining chicken breasts.

In small bowl, combine cheese and ham. Sprinkle chicken breasts lightly with salt; spread with mustard. Place scant ¼ cup of cheese mixture on center of each breast. Bring 1 end of breast over cheese mixture. Fold in sides; roll up jelly roll fashion, pressing ends to seal. Cover; refrigerate at least 1 hour. In medium bowl, combine egg and water. In shallow pan, combine flour and ¼ teaspoon salt. Coat chicken with flour mixture; dip in egg mixture. Roll in crumbs. Cover; refrigerate at least 1 hour.

Heat oven to 350°F. In small skillet, heat 1 inch oil over medium heat. Fry each chicken roll about 2 minutes or until golden brown. Place in ungreased 8-inch (2-quart) square baking dish. Bake at 350°F. for 25 to 30 minutes or until tender. **4 servings.**

VARIATION:

VEAL CORDON BLEU: Substitute 4 (4-oz.) boneless veal cutlets or 1 lb. veal round steak, cut into serving-size pieces, for the chicken.

NUTRIENTS PER ¼ OF RECIPE

Calories	310	Dietary Fiber	<1 g
Protein	34 g	Sodium	430 mg
Carbohydrate	13 g	Potassium	400 mg
Fat	12 g	Calcium	15% U.S. RDA
Cholesterol	150 mg	Iron	10% U.S. RDA

Citrus Chicken and Vegetables

½ lb. (1½ cups) fresh green or yellow beans, cut in
half
1 cup julienne-cut carrots
1½ cups sliced zucchini
¼ cup all purpose flour
2 tablespoons sesame seed
½ teaspoon salt
⅛ teaspoon pepper
2 whole chicken breasts, skinned, boned, cut into
bite-size pieces
3 tablespoons margarine or butter
¼ cup orange juice
1 tablespoon lemon juice
1 teaspoon rosemary, crushed
2 tablespoons chopped fresh parsley, if desired

Cook beans and carrots together in small amount of boiling
water until almost tender, about 10 to 15 minutes. Add zucchini; cook an additional 5 minutes. Drain; set aside.

Meanwhile, combine flour, sesame seed, salt and pepper in
plastic bag. Add chicken, ¼ at a time; shake gently to coat.
Melt margarine in large skillet. Saute chicken over medium
heat until completely cooked and golden brown, about 4 to
5 minutes. Remove from pan; set aside. Remove drippings
and excess crumbs from pan. Stir in orange juice, lemon
juice and rosemary; bring to a boil. Add cooked vegetables,
stirring until thoroughly heated. Add cooked chicken; toss
gently. Serve immediately. Sprinkle each serving with parsley. **4 servings.**

NUTRIENTS PER ¼ OF RECIPE

Calories	290	Dietary Fiber	4 g
Protein	25 g	Sodium	420 mg
Carbohydrate	17 g	Potassium	570 mg
Fat	14 g	Calcium	6% U.S. RDA
Cholesterol	60 mg	Iron	15% U.S. RDA

Chicken-Filled Crepes

Crepes (see Index)

FILLING

10¾-oz. can condensed cream of chicken soup
4 oz. (1 cup) shredded Cheddar cheese
⅔ cup milk
3 cups cubed, cooked chicken
2.5-oz. jar sliced mushrooms, drained
1 tablespoon chopped pimiento
¼ cup sliced almonds

Prepare 12 crepes. Heat oven to 350°F. In medium saucepan, combine soup, cheese and ⅔ cup milk. Cook until smooth and bubbly, stirring constantly. In medium bowl, combine chicken, mushrooms, pimiento and half soup mixture. Spoon about ⅓ cup chicken mixture down center of each crepe; roll up. Place seam side down in ungreased 13x9-inch (3-quart) baking dish. Pour remaining soup mixture over filled crepes. Bake at 350°F. for 15 to 20 minutes or until hot and bubbly. Garnish with sliced almonds. **6 servings.**

NUTRIENTS PER ⅙ OF RECIPE

Calories	390	Dietary Fiber	1 g
Protein	32 g	Sodium	245 mg
Carbohydrate	18 g	Potassium	400 mg
Fat	20 g	Calcium	25% U.S. RDA
Cholesterol	190 mg	Iron	10% U.S. RDA

Light Lemon Chicken

2 lemons
2 teaspoons cornstarch
1 teaspoon sugar
½ cup chicken broth
2 tablespoons dry sherry

      2 tablespoons soy sauce
    ¼ cup oil
      2 whole chicken breasts, skinned, boned, cut into
        ¼-inch strips
    ½ teaspoon salt
    ⅛ teaspoon pepper
4.5-oz. jar sliced mushrooms, drained
 6 to 8 green onions, cut diagonally into ½-inch pieces
      1 red bell pepper, cut into ¼-inch strips

Cut ⅛-inch thin strips of lemon peel from ½ of 1 lemon. Set aside. Slice other half and reserve for garnish. Squeeze juice from second lemon. In small bowl, combine cornstarch and sugar. Add 2 tablespoons lemon juice, chicken broth, sherry and soy sauce; blend well. Set aside.

Heat large skillet or wok over medium-high heat until hot. Add oil; heat until it ripples. Sprinkle chicken with salt and pepper. Stir-fry 3 minutes or until chicken is cooked. Remove chicken to serving platter; keep warm. Add mushrooms, onions and red pepper to skillet. Stir-fry 1 minute. Add lemon juice mixture to vegetables; stir fry 1 minute or until thickened. Return chicken to skillet; add lemon strips and stir-fry 1 minute. Serve with hot cooked rice, if desired. Garnish with lemon slices. **4 servings.**

NUTRIENTS PER ¼ OF RECIPE

Calories	310	Dietary Fiber	1 g
Protein	28 g	Sodium	1020 mg
Carbohydrate	10 g	Potassium	430 mg
Fat	17 g	Calcium	2% U.S. RDA
Cholesterol	70 mg	Iron	10% U.S. RDA

Colorful Chicken Fried Rice

 1 to 2 tablespoons minced, peeled gingerroot or 1 to 2
        teaspoons ground ginger
      2 tablespoons catsup

   1 tablespoon soy sauce
   ½ teaspoon salt
   ¼ teaspoon pepper
   1 whole chicken breast, skinned, boned, cut into thin
     bite-sized pieces*
   2 garlic cloves, minced
   3 tablespoons oil or margarine
   1½ cups frozen mixed vegetables, thawed, drained
8-oz. can pineapple chunks, drained
   2 cups cooked rice
   ¼ cup finely chopped onion

In small bowl, combine gingerroot, catsup, soy sauce, salt
and pepper; mix well. Add chicken to marinade; stir to coat.
Set aside.

In large skillet over medium heat, saute garlic in oil until
light golden brown, about 30 seconds. Add chicken and
marinade; stir-fry for 1 to 2 minutes or until chicken is no
longer pink. Add vegetables and pineapple. Increase heat to
high; stir-fry for 2 to 3 minutes. Reduce heat to medium.
Add rice and onion; stir-fry for 1 to 2 minutes or until rice
is thoroughly heated. **4 servings.**

NUTRIENTS PER ¼ OF RECIPE

Calories	350	Dietary Fiber	7 g
Protein	17 g	Sodium	670 mg
Carbohydrate	42 g	Potassium	420 mg
Fat	12 g	Calcium	4% U.S. RDA
Cholesterol	35 mg	Iron	10% U.S. RDA

Chicken Chow Mein

   1½ cups sliced celery
   2 tablespoons cornstarch
   3 tablespoons soy sauce
1½ to 2 cups cubed, cooked chicken
16-oz. can (2 cups) chow mein vegetables or bean
     sprouts, drained

4-oz. can (½ cup) mushroom pieces and stems, drained, or 8-oz. can (⅔ cup) water chestnuts, drained, sliced
1 cup water
1½ teaspoons instant minced onion or 1 tablespoon chopped onion
1 teaspoon chicken-flavor instant bouillon
Hot cooked rice or chow mein noodles

Place celery in 2-quart microwave-safe casserole. Microwave on HIGH for 2 to 3 minutes or until crisp-tender. In small bowl, combine cornstarch and soy sauce; stir into celery. Add chicken, chow mein vegetables, mushrooms, water, onion and bouillon. Microwave on HIGH for 11 to 13 minutes or until sauce is thickened, stirring once halfway through cooking. Serve over rice or noodles. **4 servings.**

NUTRIENTS PER ¼ OF RECIPE

Calories	290	Dietary Fiber	3 g
Protein	25 g	Sodium	1250 mg
Carbohydrate	37 g	Potassium	520 mg
Fat	3 g	Calcium	4% U.S. RDA
Cholesterol	50 mg	Iron	15% U.S. RDA

Chicken Rice Bake

1¼ cups uncooked regular rice
2 tablespoons chopped onion
½ teaspoon salt
1 stalk celery, chopped
2 cups water
10¾-oz. can condensed cream of chicken soup
4-oz. can (½ cup) mushroom stems and pieces, drained
2½ to 3-lb. frying chicken, cut up
2 tablespoons margarine or butter, melted
½ teaspoon salt
½ teaspoon paprika
¼ to ½ teaspoon poultry seasoning

Heat oven to 375°F. In ungreased 13x9-inch pan, combine rice, onion, ½ teaspoon salt, celery, water, soup and mushrooms; mix well. Arrange chicken skin side up on rice mixture; drizzle with margarine. Sprinkle with ½ teaspoon salt, paprika and poultry seasoning. Bake at 375°F. for 1 hour or until chicken is tender. **5 to 6 servings.**

VARIATION:

PORK CHOPS RICE BAKE: In large skillet, brown 6 pork chops. Arrange pork chops on rice mixture; omit margarine.

NUTRIENTS PER ⅙ OF RECIPE

Calories	470	Dietary Fiber	1 g
Protein	36 g	Sodium	890 mg
Carbohydrate	33 g	Potassium	420 mg
Fat	20 g	Calcium	2% U.S. RDA
Cholesterol	100 mg	Iron	15% U.S. RDA

Chicken Tetrazzini

        7   oz. uncooked spaghetti
        8   oz. fresh mushrooms, sliced (1½ cups)
       ¼   cup margarine or butter
        3   tablespoons flour
        2   cups chicken broth
       ¾   cup half-and-half
        3   tablespoons dry sherry, if desired
        1   tablespoon chopped fresh parsley
       ½   teaspoon salt
       ⅛   teaspoon nutmeg
            Dash pepper
        3   cups cubed, cooked chicken
       ¾   cup grated Parmesan cheese
            Fresh parsley, if desired

Cook spaghetti to desired doneness as directed on package. Drain; rinse with hot water. Keep warm.

Heat oven to 350°F. In Dutch oven or large saucepan over medium heat, saute mushrooms in margarine until tender. Reduce heat. Stir in flour. Cook 1 minute until smooth and bubbly, stirring constantly. Gradually stir in chicken broth. Cook over medium heat until mixture boils and slightly thickens, stirring constantly. Remove from heat. Stir in half-and-half, sherry, parsley, salt, nutmeg and pepper. Add chicken and cooked spaghetti; toss with sauce. Place in ungreased 13x9-inch (3-quart) baking dish; sprinkle with Parmesan cheese. Bake at 350°F. for 30 to 35 minutes or until thoroughly heated. Garnish with parsley before serving. **8 servings.**

NUTRIENTS PER ⅛ OF RECIPE

Calories	350	Dietary Fiber	1 g
Protein	28 g	Sodium	810 mg
Carbohydrate	25 g	Potassium	550 mg
Fat	14 g	Calcium	20% U.S. RDA
Cholesterol	50 mg	Iron	10% U.S. RDA

Easy-on-the-Cook Chicken Divan

16-oz.	pkg. frozen cut broccoli
2	cups cubed, cooked chicken
10¾-oz.	can condensed cream of chicken soup
½	cup mayonnaise
1	teaspoon lemon juice
2	oz. (½ cup) shredded Cheddar cheese
½	cup soft bread crumbs
2	tablespoons margarine or butter, melted

Heat oven to 350°F. Grease 12x8-inch (2 quart) baking dish. Cook broccoli as directed on package; drain. Arrange broccoli in prepared baking dish. Layer chicken over broccoli. In small bowl, combine soup, mayonnaise and lemon juice; mix well. Spread over chicken. Sprinkle with cheese. In small bowl, combine crumbs and margarine; sprinkle over top. Bake at 350°F. for 30 to 35 minutes or until thoroughly heated. **6 servings.**

MICROWAVE DIRECTIONS: Cook broccoli as directed on package; drain. In small microwave-safe bowl, microwave margarine on HIGH for 30 to 45 seconds. Add bread crumbs, mixing well; set aside. Arrange broccoli in 12x8-inch (2-quart) microwave-safe baking dish. Layer chicken over broccoli. In small bowl, combine soup, mayonnaise and lemon juice; mix well. Spread over chicken. Microwave on HIGH for 6 to 8 minutes or until thoroughly heated, rotating ½ turn and adding cheese and bread crumbs halfway through cooking.

NUTRIENTS PER ¼ OF RECIPE

Calories	360	Dietary Fiber	3 g
Protein	21 g	Sodium	695 mg
Carbohydrate	10 g	Potassium	430 mg
Fat	26 g	Calcium	15% U.S. RDA
Cholesterol	60 mg	Iron	8% U.S. RDA

Chicken Vegetable Country Casserole

FILLING

2	cups cubed, cooked chicken
17-oz.	can cream style corn
8.5-oz.	can early peas or sweet peas, drained
2.5-oz.	jar sliced mushrooms, undrained
1	cup milk
¼	cup chopped onion
4-oz.	mozzarella cheese, cut into 1-inch pieces
1	tablespoon chopped fresh parsley
1	tablespoon Worcestershire sauce
1	teaspoon fresh chopped chives or ¼ teaspoon dried chives
½ to 1	teaspoon pepper

TOPPING

　　1½　cups all purpose flour
　　½　cup cornmeal
　　⅓　cup grated Parmesan cheese
　　3　teaspoons baking powder
　　3　teaspoons fresh chopped chives or 1 teaspoon
　　　　dried chives
　　1　teaspoon salt
　　½　teaspoon garlic powder
　　1　cup milk
　　½　cup oil
　　1　egg, beaten

Heat oven to 400°F. Grease 13x9-inch (3-quart) baking dish. In large bowl, combine all filling ingredients. Pour into prepared baking dish. Bake at 400°F. for 20 minutes or until bubbling around edges.

Meanwhile in large bowl, combine flour, cornmeal, Parmesan cheese, baking powder, 3 teaspoons chives, salt and garlic powder; blend well. Add 1 cup milk, oil and egg; stir just until soft dough forms. Drop by tablespoonfuls on top of hot chicken mixture. Return to oven. Bake an additional 25 to 35 minutes or until topping is light golden brown. **8 servings.**

HIGH ALTITUDE: Decrease milk in filling to ½ cup.

NUTRIENTS PER ⅛ OF RECIPE

Calories	460	Dietary Fiber	5 g
Protein	23 g	Sodium	910 mg
Carbohydrate	42 g	Potassium	350 mg
Fat	22 g	Calcium	35% U.S. RDA
Cholesterol	80 mg	Iron	10% U.S. RDA

Chicken 'n Stuffing Casserole

2	cups seasoned stuffing mix
½	cup chicken broth
¼	cup margarine or butter, melted
1¼	cups cubed, cooked chicken or turkey
¼	cup finely chopped onion
¼	cup chopped celery
¼	cup mayonnaise or salad dressing
1	egg, slightly beaten
¾	cup milk
10¾-oz.	can condensed cream of mushroom soup, reserving half can for sauce
2	oz. (½ cup) shredded Cheddar cheese

SAUCE

2	tablespoons sliced pimiento-stuffed olives, if desired
¼	cup dairy sour cream
1	tablespoon milk
	Reserved cream of mushroom soup

In medium bowl, combine stuffing, broth and margarine; place *half* in ungreased 8-inch (2-quart) square baking dish. In small bowl, combine chicken, onion, celery and mayonnaise; spoon over stuffing layer. Top with remaining stuffing. In same bowl, combine egg and milk; pour over stuffing. Cover; refrigerate at least 2 hours or up to 12 hours.

Let stand at room temperature 20 minutes before baking. Heat oven to 325°F. Spread casserole with half can mushroom soup. Bake at 325°F. for 30 minutes. Sprinkle with cheese; return to oven and bake an additional 10 minutes or until cheese is melted. Cool slightly; cut into squares.

In small saucepan, combine sauce ingredients. Heat, stirring constantly, until heated. Serve with stuffing squares. **6 servings.**

MICROWAVE DIRECTIONS: Using 8-inch (2-quart) microwave-safe dish, prepare and refrigerate casserole as directed above. Let stand at room temperature 20 minutes; spread casserole with half can mushroom soup. Microwave on HIGH for 7 minutes, rotating dish ½ turn halfway through cooking. Sprinkle with cheese; microwave on HIGH for 1½ to 2½ minutes or until cheese is melted. Cool slightly; cut into squares. In small microwave-safe bowl, combine sauce ingredients; mix well. Microwave on HIGH for 45 to 60 seconds or until heated.

NUTRIENTS PER ¼ OF RECIPE

Calories	420	Dietary Fiber	1 g
Protein	19 g	Sodium	1110 mg
Carbohydrate	24 g	Potassium	330 mg
Fat	28 g	Calcium	20% U.S. RDA
Cholesterol	90 mg	Iron	10% U.S. RDA

Chicken a la King

¼ cup margarine or butter
¼ cup all purpose flour
1 teaspoon chicken-flavor instant bouillon
⅛ teaspoon pepper
  Dash thyme leaves
2 cups milk
2 cups cubed, cooked chicken or turkey*
9-oz. pkg. frozen peas, thawed, drained
2-oz. jar sliced pimiento, drained
6 Popovers (see Index)

In medium saucepan, melt margarine. Stir in flour, bouillon, pepper and thyme. Gradually add milk, stirring constantly. Cook over medium-high heat until mixture boils and thickens, stirring constantly. Stir in chicken, peas and pimiento. Simmer 5 minutes or until thoroughly heated. To serve, spoon chicken mixture into hot, split popover. **6 servings.**

MICROWAVE DIRECTIONS: In 2-quart microwave-safe casserole, microwave margarine on HIGH for 40 to 60 seconds or until melted. Stir in flour, bouillon, pepper and thyme. Microwave on HIGH for 30 seconds. Blend in milk; beat well with wire whisk. Microwave on HIGH for 6 to 7½ minutes or until mixture thickens and boils, stirring twice during cooking. Stir in remaining ingredients except popovers. Microwave on HIGH for 4 to 6 minutes or until thoroughly heated. Serve as directed above.

TIP: *Two 5-oz. cans boned chunk chicken can be substituted for the cubed, cooked chicken.

NUTRIENTS PER ¼ OF RECIPE

Calories	330	Dietary Fiber	1 g
Protein	23 g	Sodium	350 mg
Carbohydrate	28 g	Potassium	410 mg
Fat	14 g	Calcium	15% U.S. RDA
Cholesterol	130 mg	Iron	15% U.S. RDA

Frijoles-Zucchini Tortilla Pies

      6 (6-inch) flour or corn tortillas
  8-oz. pkg. Monterey jack or Cheddar cheese slices

FILLING

      1 cup (1 medium) coarsely chopped zucchini
     ½ cup thinly sliced green onions
     ¼ cup chopped green pepper
      1 tablespoon margarine or butter
      2 cups cubed, cooked chicken or turkey
     ¼ teaspoon garlic powder
     ½ cup prepared taco sauce
  15-oz. can kidney or pinto beans, drained, rinsed
     ½ cup dairy sour cream
  1 to 2 tablespoons thinly sliced green onions
         Taco sauce

Heat oven to 350°F. Gently press 1 tortilla in each of six un-greased 10-oz. custard cups or individual au gratin casseroles. (Heat tortillas to soften as directed on package, if necessary.) If needed, cut part of cheese slices to make six 4x4-inch squares; gently press 1 cheese square in each tor-tilla-lined custard cup. Cut remaining cheese slices into nar-row strips, 1 inch in length; set aside.

In large skillet, saute zucchini, ½ cup onions and green pep-per in margarine until crisp-tender. Stir in chicken, garlic powder, taco sauce and beans; simmer 3 to 5 minutes or until thoroughly heated, stirring occasionally. Spoon evenly into tortilla-lined custard cups; sprinkle with reserved cheese. Bake at 350°F. for 15 to 25 minutes or until cheese is melted and bubbly. Let stand a few minutes before serv-ing. Combine sour cream and 1 to 2 tablespoons onions. Serve with sour cream mixture and additional taco sauce to spoon over individual servings. **6 servings.**

MICROWAVE DIRECTIONS: Place tortillas in mi-crowave-safe baking dish; cover with microwave-safe plas-tic wrap. Microwave on HIGH for 1 to 1½ minutes or until softened. Gently press 1 tortilla in each of six 10-oz. mi-crowave-safe custard cups or individual au gratin casseroles. If needed, cut part of cheese slices to make six 4x4-inch squares; gently press 1 cheese square in each tor-tilla-lined custard cup. Cut remaining cheese slices into nar-row strips, 1 inch in length; set aside.

In large microwave-safe bowl, place zucchini, ½ cup onions, green pepper and margarine. Microwave on HIGH for 2½ to 3½ minutes or until crisp-tender, stirring once. Stir in chicken, garlic powder, taco sauce and beans; cover with waxed paper. Microwave on HIGH for 3 to 5 minutes or until thoroughly heated, stirring once. Spoon evenly into tortilla-lined custard cups; sprinkle with reserved cheese. Arrange custard cups in microwave in circle with one in the middle. Microwave uncovered on HIGH for 3 to 5 minutes or until cheese melts, rearranging once. Let stand before serving.

NUTRIENTS PER ⅙ OF RECIPE

Calories	410	Dietary Fiber	6 g
Protein	29 g	Sodium	630 mg
Carbohydrate	31 g	Potassium	530 mg
Fat	19 g	Calcium	10% U.S. RDA
Cholesterol	80 mg	Iron	15% U.S. RDA

Parmesan Chicken Fingers

    2 whole chicken breasts, skinned, boned, halved
   ¼ cup plain yogurt
   ⅓ cup dry bread crumbs
    3 tablespoons grated Parmesan cheese
   ½ teaspoon parsley flakes
   ⅛ teaspoon pepper
    4 French rolls (5 to 6 inches long)
    1 recipe Cucumber-Garlic Sauce
    1 large tomato, cut into 8 slices

Heat oven to 375°F. Lightly grease large cookie sheet. Place 1 chicken breast half between 2 pieces of plastic wrap. Working from center, lightly pound breast with flat side of meat mallet or rolling pin until about ¼-inch thick; remove wrap. Repeat with remaining chicken breasts. Cut each breast half into 3 strips.

In medium bowl, combine chicken and yogurt, stirring to coat chicken well. In small bowl, combine bread crumbs, cheese, parsley flakes and pepper. Roll yogurt-coated chicken strips in crumb mixture, coating evenly. Arrange in single layer on prepared cookie sheet. Bake at 375°F. for 15 to 18 minutes or until chicken is tender and golden brown.

Slice French rolls in half lengthwise. Place 3 chicken strips on bottom half of each roll; top each with ¼ cup Cucumber-

Garlic Sauce and 2 tomato slices. Cover each with top half of roll. **4 sandwiches.**

NUTRIENTS PER 1 SANDWICH

Calories	560	Dietary Fiber	2 g
Protein	34 g	Sodium	690 mg
Carbohydrate	40 g	Potassium	440 mg
Fat	29 g	Calcium	15% U.S. RDA
Cholesterol	90 mg	Iron	15% U.S. RDA

Cucumber-Garlic Sauce

In small bowl, combine 1 cup finely chopped cucumber, ½ cup mayonnaise or salad dressing, 1 teaspoon parsley flakes and ¼ teaspoon garlic powder. Cover and refrigerate at least 1 hour to blend flavors. **1 cup.**

California Chicken Pockets

   1 cup chopped, cooked chicken
   1 cup frozen cut broccoli, cooked, drained
   1 avocado, peeled, chopped
   ½ cup chopped tomato
   ½ cup cooked rice, if desired
   2 oz. (½ cup) shredded mozzarella cheese
   1 egg, hard-cooked, chopped
   ½ cup mayonnaise
   1 tablespoon Dijon mustard
   ¼ teaspoon celery seed
   4 pocket breads (6-inch diameter), halved

In medium bowl, combine chicken, broccoli, avocado, tomato, rice, cheese and egg. In small bowl, stir together mayonnaise, mustard and celery seed. Pour over chicken mixture; toss to coat. To serve, spoon approximately ½ cup mixture into each pocket bread half. **4 servings.**

TIP: Filling can be made several hours ahead; refrigerate until serving time.

NUTRIENTS PER ¼ OF RECIPE

Calories	670	Dietary Fiber	3 g
Protein	28 g	Sodium	320 mg
Carbohydrate	57 g	Potassium	610 mg
Fat	37 g	Calcium	20% U.S. RDA
Cholesterol	120 mg	Iron	25% U.S. RDA

Tostado Chicken Filling

2	tablespoons margarine or butter
¼	cup chopped onion
2	whole chicken breasts, cooked, skinned, boned
16-oz.	can (2 cups) tomato sauce
1	teaspoon sugar
½	teaspoon salt
½ to 1	teaspoon chili powder
¼	teaspoon cumin

In large skillet, melt margarine. Saute onion until tender. Shred chicken with 2 forks; add to onion mixture. Stir in remaining ingredients. Simmer 20 to 30 minutes until thoroughly heated and flavors are well blended, stirring occasionally. Serve filling with warm flour or corn tortillas. **3 cups.**

NUTRIENTS PER ¼ CUP

Calories	90	Dietary Fiber	<1 g
Protein	10 g	Sodium	310 mg
Carbohydrate	4 g	Potassium	185 mg
Fat	4 g	Calcium	<2% U.S. RDA
Cholesterol	20 mg	Iron	4% U.S. RDA

Roasting Poultry

• Use the following directions for roasting chickens, capons, turkeys, game hens, ducks or geese.

• Remove giblets from body cavity. Rinse bird inside and out with cold water. Drain; pat dry with paper towels. If bird will not be stuffed, cavity may be sprinkled with salt.

• To stuff, place bird breast side down and lightly fill neck cavity with stuffing. Pull neck skin over cavity; fasten skin to back with skewer. Turn bird over; loosely fill interior cavity with stuffing. Tuck drumsticks under band of skin across tail or tie to tail with string. Bend wing tips under back of bird.

• Place bird breast side up on rack in shallow roasting pan. Rub bird with oil or softened butter or margarine. Insert meat thermometer into the inside thigh muscle of the bird so that the tip does not touch the bone. Do not cover pan or add water.

NOTE: Since domestic ducks and geese have a higher proportion of fat, prick skin in several places before roasting to allow excess fat to escape. Do not rub skin with oil, butter or margarine. During roasting, skim off excess fat.

• Roast at 325°F. using Timetable for Roasting Poultry. Cooking times are only approximate because of differences in size, shape and variety. An unstuffed bird will take less time than a stuffed bird.

• During last half of roasting time, the bird may be basted with pan drippings or sauce. When it is two-thirds done, cut skin or string holding drumsticks. If bird begins to brown too quickly, cover loosely with foil to prevent overbrowning.

• With whole bird, begin checking for doneness during the last hour of cooking. It is essential that poultry be completely cooked. A thermometer is the most accurate guide for roasting poultry. Poultry is done when the internal temperature reaches 180 to 185°F. If the bird has been stuffed, the temperature of the center of the stuffing should be 165°F. If no thermometer is available, the bird is done when the legs move up and down easily and the flesh gives when pressed.

• For easier carving, allow bird to stand at least 15 minutes before carving to set juices. Cover loosely with foil to keep warm.

Timetable for Roasting Poultry

(Oven Temperature 325°F./
Thermometer Reading 180 to 185°F.)

Poultry	Weight Pounds	Total Roasting Time Hours
Chicken (stuffed)	2½ to 4½	2 to 3½
Capon (stuffed)	4 to 8	2½ to 4½
Turkey (stuffed)	4 to 6	2 to 3
	6 to 8	3 to 3½
	8 to 12	3½ to 4½
	12 to 16	4½ to 5½
	16 to 20	5½ to 6½
	20 to 24	6½ to 7
	24 to 28	7 to 8½
Cornish Game Hen* (stuffed or unstuffed)	1 to 1½	1 to 2
Duck (stuffed)**	3 to 5	2 to 3
Goose (stuffed)**	4 to 8	2¾ to 3½
	8 to 14	3½ to 5

*Roast at 350°F.
**Roast at 400°F. for 15 minutes, then at 325°F.

Hints for Handling Poultry

• Rinse whole bird or pieces and pat dry before beginning preparation steps.

• Cutting board, poultry shears and knives, dishes and hands coming in contact with fresh poultry must be clean. Wash with hot, sudsy water before and after preparation.

• To prevent bacteria growth, do not interrupt cooking process until poultry is completely cooked. Poultry must be transferred from microwave to oven or microwave to grill in a continuous cooking process.

• If poultry is to be transported after cooking, keep hot pieces hot and cold pieces chilled.

Carving Roasted Bird

Use a sharp knife or electric knife, always cutting across the grain. Cut through joint between thigh and body of bird to remove leg. Separate drumstick from thigh.

Make a deep horizontal cut to the bone into the breast meat just above the wing. Beginning near the front of the breast, cut thin slices down to horizontal cut. Repeat with other side of bird.

Bread Stuffing

1   medium onion, chopped
2   stalks celery, chopped
½   cup margarine or butter
8   cups dry bread cubes*
2   tablespoons finely chopped fresh parsley, if desired
2   tablespoons poultry seasoning, sage or savory
1   teaspoon salt
¼   teaspoon pepper
    About ½ cup chicken broth or water

In large skillet, saute onion and celery in margarine until tender. In large bowl, combine bread cubes, parsley, poultry seasoning, salt and pepper; mix well. Add broth and margarine-onion mixture, stirring until of desired moistness (stuffing will become a little more moist during cooking because it absorbs juices from bird). **9 cups.**

TIPS: *Day-old soft bread cubes can be substituted for dry bread cubes. Decrease broth to about ¼ cup.

Allow about ½ cup stuffing per pound of poultry. If necessary recipe may be halved, or bake any remaining stuffing in greased covered casserole at 350°F. for 30 to 45 minutes or until thoroughly heated.

VARIATIONS:

APPLE-RAISIN STUFFING: Add 2 medium peeled and chopped apples and ⅔ cup raisins. Decrease liquid by 2 tablespoons. (Apples will make stuffing more moist.)

CHESTNUT STUFFING: Roast chestnuts by cutting X-shaped slit on one side of shell. Place on ungreased cookie sheet. Bake at 400°F. for 15 to 20 minutes, stirring occasionally. Cool enough to handle; remove shell. Chop finely. Add desired amount to stuffing (1 cup added to this amount of stuffing will give a mild flavor).

CORN BREAD STUFFING: Use crumbled baked corn bread for part or all of bread cubes. Decrease poultry seasoning to 1 teaspoon. Corn Bread Stuffing is also good in the sausage variation.

MUSHROOM STUFFING: Saute 1 cup sliced or chopped fresh or drained canned mushrooms with onion and celery.

NUT STUFFING: Add ¼ cup chopped nuts—almonds, filberts, pecans, walnuts or peanuts. For a toasted flavor, saute nuts with onion mixture.

OYSTER STUFFING: Simmer ½ to 1 pint (1 to 2 cups) oysters with liquor for about 5 minutes or until oysters are set; drain. Chop oysters; add to stuffing.

SAUSAGE STUFFING: In small skillet, brown ½ lb. pork sausage; drain. Reserve drippings. Add sausage to bread cube mixture. Decrease poultry seasoning to 1 teaspoon and salt to ¼ teaspoon (sausage is highly seasoned). Drippings can be substituted for part of margarine used to saute onion and celery.

WATER CHESTNUT STUFFING: Add ½ to 1 cup chopped water chestnuts to stuffing.

NUTRIENTS PER ⅟₁₈ OF RECIPE

Calories	120	Dietary Fiber	<1 g
Protein	3 g	Sodium	330 mg
Carbohydrate	14 g	Potassium	55 mg
Fat	6 g	Calcium	2% U.S. RDA
Cholesterol	0 mg	Iron	4% U.S. RDA

Rice Stuffing

    2   tablespoons chopped onion
    ¼   cup margarine or butter
    2   cups cooked rice (white, brown, wild or
        combination)
    ½   teaspoon salt
    ½   teaspoon poultry seasoning

In medium skillet, saute onion in margarine until tender. Add cooked rice, salt and poultry seasoning; mix well. **2 cups.**

TIPS: Seasoned rice mixes can be substituted for rice; omit salt and poultry seasoning.

For variety, add any of the following to Rice Stuffing: ¼ cup chopped or slivered almonds or chopped pecans, ½ cup drained canned mushrooms, ¼ cup raisins or currants, 1 tablespoon grated orange peel, ½ to ¾ cup drained crushed pineapple or 1 stalk celery, chopped (cook with onion).

NUTRIENTS PER ¼ OF RECIPE

Calories	220	Dietary Fiber	<1 g
Protein	2 g	Sodium	400 mg
Carbohydrate	25 g	Potassium	45 mg
Fat	12 g	Calcium	<2% U.S. RDA
Cholesterol	0 mg	Iron	6% U.S. RDA

Wild Rice-Sausage Stuffing

       5 cups water
       2 teaspoons chicken-flavor instant bouillon or 2
          chicken-flavor bouillon cubes
    1½ teaspoons salt
       ¾ cup uncooked wild rice, rinsed
    1½ cups uncooked regular rice
       1 lb. pork sausage
    1½ cups chopped celery
       ¾ cup chopped onions

In large saucepan, combine water, bouillon and salt; bring to a boil. Add wild rice. Cover; simmer 20 minutes. Add regular rice. Cover; simmer an additional 25 minutes or until rice is tender and liquid is absorbed. Meanwhile, in large skillet brown sausage, celery and onions; drain. Combine sausage mixture and rice mixture. Use to stuff turkey or Cornish game hens.* **12 cups.**

TIP: *Bake any remaining stuffing in greased covered casserole at 350°F. for 30 to 45 minutes or until thoroughly heated.

NUTRIENTS PER ⅟₁₆ OF RECIPE

Calories	160	Dietary Fiber	1 g
Protein	4 g	Sodium	405 mg
Carbohydrate	22 g	Potassium	120 mg
Fat	6 g	Calcium	<2% U.S. RDA
Cholesterol	10 mg	Iron	6% U.S. RDA

Chicken or Turkey Gravy

   2   cups hot milk
   ¼   cup poultry drippings
   ¼   cup all purpose flour
   ¼   cup cold milk
       Salt and pepper

In skillet or roasting pan, add hot milk to drippings. Combine flour and cold milk; mix until smooth. Add flour mixture to hot liquid. Cook until mixture boils and thickens, stirring constantly. Season with salt and pepper. **2½ cups.**

TIP: If gravy is too thick, thin with additional milk. If too thin, thicken with additional flour dissolved in cold water. Heat to boiling, stirring constantly.

NUTRIENTS: Variables in this recipe make it impossible to calculate nutrition information.

Giblet Gravy

       Chicken giblets
       Water
   2   stalks celery, sliced
   1   medium onion, sliced
   1   teaspoon salt

¼ teaspoon pepper
3 tablespoons flour
3 tablespoons poultry drippings
  Milk or water
  Salt and pepper

In medium saucepan, cover giblets with water. Add celery, onion, salt and pepper. Simmer 1 to 2 hours or until tender.

In skillet or roasting pan, add flour to drippings. Cook over low heat until smooth and browned, stirring constantly. Add 2 cups giblet broth to drippings. (If necessary, add additional milk or water to giblet broth to make 2 cups.) Cook until mixture boils and thickens, stirring constantly. Chop giblets; add to gravy, if desired. Season with salt and pepper. **2 cups.**

TIP: Flour and drippings can be decreased to 2 tablespoons each for thin gravy; increased to 4 tablespoons for thick gravy.

NUTRIENTS: Variables in this recipe make it impossible to calculate nutrition information.

Orange Glazed Turkey Breast

4 to 5 lb. fresh or frozen whole turkey breast, thawed
   2 tablespoons oil
   1 teaspoon thyme leaves
     Salt
     Pepper
   1 medium onion, peeled, quartered
   1 garlic clove, peeled

ORANGE GLAZE

1 tablespoon margarine or butter
½ cup orange marmalade
⅓ cup frozen orange juice concentrate, thawed
½ teaspoon ginger

Heat oven to 350°F. Brush turkey breast on all sides with oil. Rub thyme inside and outside of cavity; sprinkle with salt and pepper. Place breast skin side up on rack in roasting pan. Place onion and garlic inside breast cavity. Bake at 350°F. for 30 minutes. Cover; bake for 2 to 2½ hours or until internal temperature reaches 170°F. and turkey is tender throughout.

In small saucepan, melt margarine. Add marmalade, orange juice concentrate and ginger. Cook over medium heat until smooth and bubbly, stirring constantly. Brush turkey with glaze. **8 to 10 servings.**

NUTRIENTS PER ⅒ OF RECIPE

Calories 280	Dietary Fiber...........................0 g
Protein...................................43 g	Sodium.............................140 mg
Carbohydrate.......................16 g	Potassium.........................490 mg
Fat ....5 g	Calcium.................2% U.S. RDA
Cholesterol......................120 mg	Iron......................15% U.S. RDA

Barbecued Turkey Breast

4 to 5 lb. fresh or frozen whole turkey breast, thawed

BARBECUE SAUCE
  ½ cup catsup
  1 tablespoon brown sugar
  1 tablespoon water
1½ teaspoons Worcestershire sauce
  1 teaspoon prepared mustard

MICROWAVE-TO-GRILL DIRECTIONS: Prepare charcoal fire for grilling. Rinse turkey breast; pat dry. Place skin side down in microwave-safe pan; cover with microwave-safe plastic wrap. Microwave on HIGH for 10 minutes. Turn turkey breast; cover again with microwave-safe plastic wrap. Microwave on MEDIUM for 15 to 20 minutes or until outer edges of turkey begin to cook. Meanwhile, in small bowl combine all sauce ingredients.

Immediately place turkey breast on grill 4 to 6 inches from medium coals; cover.* Cook 30 to 45 minutes or until internal temperature is 165 to 170°F. and juices are no longer pink when pierced with fork, turning turkey once halfway through cooking. Brush with sauce last 5 minutes of cooking. **10 servings.**

TIP: *If cooking on a grill without cover, a tent of aluminum foil can be used.

NUTRIENTS PER ⅒ OF RECIPE

Calories 220	Dietary Fiber.........................<1 g
Protein.....................................47 g	Sodium..............................240 mg
Carbohydrate...........................5 g	Potassium.........................510 mg
Fat ....1 g	Calcium.................2% U.S. RDA
Cholesterol.......................130 mg	Iron.....................15% U.S. RDA

Turkey Slice Saute

¾ lb. (about 2 cups) whole fresh green beans
1½ to 2 cups sliced carrots or baby carrots
1 cup sliced celery
1 to 1¼ lb. fresh turkey breast slices
2 tablespoons margarine or butter
1 cup sliced fresh mushrooms
¼ cup sliced green onions or 2 tablespoons finely chopped shallots
¼ cup dry white wine
2 tablespoons lemon juice
½ teaspoon salt
¼ teaspoon pepper

Place green beans, carrots and celery in steamer basket over boiling water. Reduce heat. Cover; simmer 10 minutes or until just tender. Keep warm.

Meanwhile, in large skillet over medium heat, saute turkey slices in margarine for 2 to 3 minutes, turning once. Stir in mushrooms, onions, wine and lemon juice. Reduce heat. Cover; simmer 3 to 4 minutes or until turkey is no longer pink. Sprinkle with salt and pepper.

Arrange steamed vegetables and turkey on warm serving platter. Spoon mushroom mixture and sauce over turkey. Serve immediately. **4 to 5 servings.**

MICROWAVE DIRECTIONS: Place green beans, carrots and celery in microwave-safe bowl with *½ cup water;* cover with microwave-safe plastic wrap. Microwave on HIGH for 8 minutes, stirring once halfway through cooking. Let stand covered while preparing turkey. In 13x9-inch (3-quart) microwave-safe dish, microwave margarine on HIGH for 30 to 45 seconds or until melted. Dip both sides of turkey slices in melted margarine; arrange in single layer around outer edge of dish. Add mushrooms and onions. Cover with microwave-safe plastic wrap. Microwave on HIGH for 3 minutes. Rearrange turkey slices with cooked portions at center of dish; add wine and lemon juice. Cover; microwave on HIGH for 2 to 4 minutes or until turkey is no longer pink. Sprinkle with salt and pepper. Serve as directed.

NUTRIENTS PER ⅕ OF RECIPE

Calories	290	Dietary Fiber	3 g
Protein	35 g	Sodium	410 mg
Carbohydrate	11 g	Potassium	770 mg
Fat	11 g	Calcium	8% U.S. RDA
Cholesterol	70 mg	Iron	15% U.S. RDA

Grilled Turkey Tenderloins

¼ cup oil
¼ cup soy sauce
¼ teaspoon basil leaves
¼ teaspoon marjoram leaves
¼ teaspoon thyme leaves
1 lb. fresh or frozen turkey tenderloins, thawed

In small bowl, combine all ingredients except turkey; mix well. Place turkey in 8-inch square (2-quart) baking dish; pour marinade over turkey. Cover; refrigerate 2 to 4 hours, turning occasionally.

When ready to barbecue, place turkey on grill 4 to 6 inches from medium-high coals. Cook 13 to 18 minutes or until no longer pink, turning once. **4 servings.**

BROILER METHOD: Prepare turkey as directed above. Broil 4 to 6 inches from heat for 18 to 20 minutes or until no longer pink, turning once.

NUTRIENTS PER ¼ OF RECIPE

Calories	180	Dietary Fiber	0 g
Protein	25 g	Sodium	320 mg
Carbohydrate	0 g	Potassium	270 mg
Fat	8 g	Calcium	2% U.S. RDA
Cholesterol	60 mg	Iron	8% U.S. RDA

Turkey Club Melt

    4 slices whole wheat bread, toasted
    4 tablespoons mayonnaise
    6 oz. sliced, cooked turkey
    4 slices tomato
    8 slices bacon, crisply cooked, crumbled
    1 avocado, sliced
    4 oz. (1 cup) shredded Cheddar cheese

Spread 1 tablespoon mayonnaise on one side of each bread slice. Top each bread slice with ¼ of the turkey, 1 tomato slice, ¼ of the crumbled bacon, ¼ of the avocado slices and ¼ of the cheese. Toast in toaster oven 3 to 5 minutes or until hot and cheese is melted. **4 sandwiches.**

TIP: To broil, prepare sandwiches as directed above. Broil 4 to 6 inches from heat for 2 to 3 minutes or until hot and cheese is melted.

NUTRIENTS PER 1 SANDWICH

Calories	530	Dietary Fiber	3 g
Protein	28 g	Sodium	660 mg
Carbohydrate	17 g	Potassium	670 mg
Fat	39 g	Calcium	25% U.S. RDA
Cholesterol	80 mg	Iron	15% U.S. RDA

Turkey Enchilada Bake

2	tablespoons margarine or butter
½	cup (1 medium) chopped onion
1	garlic clove, minced
½	cup sliced ripe olives
¼	cup chopped green chiles
½	cup dairy sour cream
10¾-oz.	can condensed cream of chicken soup
1½	cups cubed, cooked turkey or chicken
4	oz. (1 cup) shredded Cheddar cheese
¼	cup oil
8	corn or flour tortillas
¼	cup milk

Heat oven to 350°F. In medium saucepan, melt margarine. Add onion and garlic; saute until tender. Stir in ¼ cup of the ripe olives, chiles, sour cream and soup; mix well. Reserve ¾ cup sauce; set aside. To remaining sauce, add turkey and ½ cup of the cheese; mix well.

In medium skillet, heat oil; lightly fry tortillas to soften. Fill tortillas with turkey mixture; roll up. Place seam side down in ungreased 12x8-inch (2-quart) baking dish. In small bowl, combine reserved ¾ cup sauce and milk; spoon over filled tortillas. Bake at 350°F. for 30 to 35 minutes or until bubbly. To serve, sprinkle with remaining cheese and olives. **6 to 8 servings.**

MICROWAVE DIRECTIONS: In medium microwave-safe bowl, combine margarine, onion and garlic. Microwave on HIGH for 2 to 3 minutes or until onions are tender, stirring after 1 minute. Stir in ¼ cup of the olives, chiles, sour cream and soup; mix well. Reserve ¾ cup sauce; set aside. To remaining sauce, add turkey and ½ cup of the cheese; mix well. Wrap tortillas in microwave-safe plastic wrap. Microwave on HIGH for 30 to 45 seconds or until softened. Fill tortillas with turkey mixture; roll up. Place seam side down in ungreased 12x8-inch (2-quart) microwave-safe baking dish. Combine reserved ¾ cup sauce with milk; spoon over filled tortillas. Microwave on HIGH for 6 to 8 minutes or until thoroughly heated. Sprinkle with remaining cheese and olives. Microwave on HIGH for ½ to 1 minute or until cheese melts.

NUTRIENTS PER ⅛ OF RECIPE

Calories	340	Dietary Fiber	1 g
Protein	15 g	Sodium	520 mg
Carbohydrate	19 g	Potassium	180 mg
Fat	23 g	Calcium	20% U.S. RDA
Cholesterol	50 mg	Iron	10% U.S. RDA

Quickest-Ever Turkey Pot Pie

15-oz.	pkg. refrigerated pie crusts
1	teaspoon flour
6	tablespoons margarine or butter
⅓	cup flour
¼	teaspoon marjoram
⅛	teaspoon pepper
1	cup milk
10½-oz.	can condensed chicken broth
3	cups cubed, cooked turkey or chicken
16-oz.	pkg. frozen mixed vegetables, thawed*

Heat oven to 450°F. Allow 1 crust pouch to stand at room temperature for 15 to 20 minutes.** (Refrigerate remaining crust for later use.) Unfold pie crust; peel off top plastic sheet. Press out fold lines; sprinkle 1 teaspoon flour over crust. Turn crust, flour side down, on ungreased cookie sheet; peel off remaining plastic sheet. Invert 2-quart casserole over crust. With sharp knife, trace and cut around casserole rim; remove casserole. Trim an additional ¼ inch from edge of casserole-shaped crust. With cookie cutter or sharp knife, cut shapes out of crust. Cut additional shapes out of dough scraps, if desired; arrange over crust to decorate. Bake at 450°F. for 9 to 11 minutes or until light golden brown.

Meanwhile, in large saucepan, melt margarine. Stir in ⅓ cup flour, marjoram and pepper; cook until mixture is smooth and bubbly. Gradually add milk and chicken broth. Cook until mixture boils and thickens, stirring constantly. Stir in turkey and vegetables. Cook, stirring occasionally, until vegetables are tender, about 10 to 15 minutes. Spoon mixture into casserole; place baked crust on top. **6 servings.**

TIPS: *For quick thawing, place unopened vegetable package in warm water for 20 minutes.

**Crust pouch can be brought to room temperature in microwave. Microwave one pouch on DEFROST for 20 to 40 seconds.

NUTRIENTS PER ⅙ OF RECIPE

Calories 490	Dietary Fiber ....5 g
Protein ....28 g	Sodium ....760 mg
Carbohydrate ....35 g	Potassium ....540 mg
Fat ....26 g	Calcium ....8% U.S. RDA
Cholesterol ....70 mg	Iron ....15% U.S. RDA

Stir-Fried Turkey and Veggies

2	tablespoons sugar
2	tablespoons cornstarch
¼ to ½	teaspoon ginger
3	tablespoons soy sauce
1½	cups julienne-cut, cooked turkey or chicken
3	tablespoons oil

1 cup thinly sliced carrots
2 cups diagonally sliced broccoli
1 cup chicken broth
1 medium onion, thinly sliced
4-oz. can mushroom pieces and stems, drained
Chow mein noodles or hot cooked rice

In medium bowl, combine sugar, cornstarch, ginger and soy sauce; mix well. Add turkey and stir to coat. Let stand 15 minutes at room temperature to marinate. In large skillet or wok, heat oil over high heat. Add carrots and broccoli, stirring lightly to coat with oil; add broth. Cover; cook 2 minutes. Add turkey and soy sauce mixture; stir gently over medium heat. Add onion; stir-fry about 1 minute. Add mushrooms; stir-fry until mixture is hot. Serve over noodles or rice. **4 servings.**

NUTRIENTS PER ¼ OF RECIPE

Calories	300	Dietary Fiber	4 g
Protein	22 g	Sodium	1350 mg
Carbohydrate	20 g	Potassium	575 mg
Fat	15 g	Calcium	8% U.S. RDA
Cholesterol	50 mg	Iron	15% U.S. RDA

Sweet-Sour Turkey

8-oz. pkg. frozen cut green beans
⅓ cup firmly packed brown sugar
2 tablespoons cornstarch
⅓ cup vinegar
2 (8-oz.) cans chunk pineapple in its own juice, drained, reserving ⅓ cup liquid
2 tablespoons margarine
1½ cups cubed, cooked turkey or chicken
1 cup cherry tomato halves
2 cups hot cooked brown or regular rice
2 to 3 teaspoons toasted sesame seed, if desired

Cook green beans as directed on package; drain. In medium saucepan, combine brown sugar and cornstarch. Stir in vinegar, reserved pineapple liquid and margarine. Cook until sauce boils and thickens, stirring constantly. Stir in pineapple chunks, turkey, tomato halves and green beans. Continue to cook over medium heat until thoroughly heated, stirring occasionally. Serve over hot cooked rice. Garnish with sesame seed. **4 servings.**

NUTRIENTS PER ¼ OF RECIPE

Calories	440	Dietary Fiber	5 g
Protein	21 g	Sodium	545 mg
Carbohydrate	64 g	Potassium	630 mg
Fat	11 g	Calcium	6% U.S. RDA
Cholesterol	50 mg	Iron	15% U.S. RDA

Drumsticks Fricassee

4	turkey drumsticks or thighs (about 5 lb. total)
½	cup all purpose flour
2 to 3	tablespoons oil or shortening
1	teaspoon salt
¼	teaspoon pepper
1	chicken-flavor bouillon cube or 1 teaspoon chicken-flavor instant bouillon
	Water
10-oz.	pkg. (1½ cups) frozen peas and carrots
½	cup cold water
2	tablespoons flour

Rinse turkey; pat dry. Coat drumsticks with ½ cup flour. In large skillet or Dutch oven, brown drumsticks in hot oil; drain excess oil. Add salt, pepper, bouillon and just enough water to cover bottom of skillet. Cover; simmer 1½ hours or until turkey is tender, adding water as necessary. Add peas and carrots; cook about 10 minutes longer. Remove drumsticks to platter. In jar with lid, combine ½ cup cold water and 2 tablespoons flour; stir into broth and vegetables. Cook until mixture boils and thickens, stirring constantly. Serve sauce over drumsticks. **4 servings.**

NUTRIENTS PER ¼ OF RECIPE

Calories	760	Dietary Fiber	4 g
Protein	95 g	Sodium	1170 mg
Carbohydrate	23 g	Potassium	1440 mg
Fat	30 g	Calcium	10% U.S. RDA
Cholesterol	310 mg	Iron	50% U.S. RDA

Tortilla-Wrapped Mexican Sandwiches

6-oz.	container frozen avocado dip, thawed
3-oz.	pkg. cream cheese, softened
6	(8-inch) flour tortillas, softened
8	oz. thinly sliced, cooked roast beef or turkey
	Leaf lettuce
4	oz. (1 cup) shredded Monterey jack cheese
	Alfalfa sprouts
	Salsa (see Index) or taco sauce

In small bowl, combine avocado dip and cream cheese; blend well. Spread each tortilla evenly with avocado mixture to within ½ inch of edge. Arrange slices of meat, lettuce, cheese and sprouts over avocado mixture. Spoon on desired amount of salsa. (If sandwiches are made ahead, omit salsa and spoon onto portions just before serving.) Roll up each tortilla; secure with toothpicks. Serve immediately or wrap securely in plastic wrap and refrigerate until serving time. **6 sandwiches.**

NUTRIENTS PER 1 SANDWICH

Calories	300	Dietary Fiber	1 g
Protein	20 g	Sodium	480 mg
Carbohydrate	19 g	Potassium	220 mg
Fat	16 g	Calcium	25% U.S. RDA
Cholesterol	70 mg	Iron	10% U.S. RDA

Roast Duck with Plum Sauce

4 to 5-lb. duckling
Salt and pepper
1 orange, unpeeled, quartered
1 medium onion, quartered

PLUM SAUCE
½ cup firmly packed brown sugar
1 tablespoon cornstarch
1 teaspoon dry mustard
⅛ teaspoon ground cloves
17-oz. can (2 cups) purple plums, drained, pitted, reserving ½ cup plum liquid
⅓ cup orange juice

Heat oven to 400°F. Remove giblets from body cavity; refrigerate for later use. Rinse duckling inside and out; pat dry. Sprinkle cavity with salt and pepper. Place quartered orange and onion in cavity. Close body openings by bringing loose skin over openings and securing with metal skewers. Tie wings to body. Place breast side up on rack in shallow roasting pan. Bake at 400°F. for 15 minutes. Reduce oven temperature to 325°F. Bake 2½ to 3 hours or until meat is tender (about 180°F.), basting occasionally with drippings. To prevent spattering, remove excess drippings as they accumulate.

In small saucepan, combine brown sugar, cornstarch, mustard and cloves. Stir in plum liquid and orange juice until smooth. Cook until mixture boils and thickens, stirring constantly. Add plums. Cook until thoroughly heated. Discard stuffing from duckling. Serve sauce over duckling. **4 servings.**

NUTRIENTS PER ¼ OF RECIPE

Calories	880	Dietary Fiber	3 g
Protein	40 g	Sodium	130 mg
Carbohydrate	49 g	Potassium	740 mg
Fat	58 g	Calcium	6% U.S. RDA
Cholesterol	170 mg	Iron	40% U.S. RDA

Duckling a l'Orange

4½ to 5-lb. duckling
    1 teaspoon salt
    2 oranges, unpeeled, quartered
    3 peppercorns or ⅛ teaspoon pepper
    1 garlic clove, minced
3 to 4 tablespoons orange marmalade

ORANGE SAUCE
    2 tablespoons sugar
    1 tablespoon cornstarch
    1 tablespoon grated orange peel
    ⅔ cup orange juice
    3 tablespoons pan drippings
    2 tablespoons orange-flavored liqueur

    Hot cooked rice

Heat oven to 400°F. Remove giblets from body cavity; refrigerate for later use. Rinse duckling inside and out; pat dry. Sprinkle cavity with salt. Place oranges, peppercorns and garlic in cavity. Close body openings by bringing loose skin over openings and securing with metal skewers. Tie wings to body. Place breast side up on rack in shallow roasting pan. Bake at 400°F. for 15 minutes. Reduce oven temperature to 325°F. Bake 2½ to 3 hours or until meat is tender (about 180°F.), basting occasionally with drippings. During last 15 minutes of baking, spread with orange marmalade.

In small saucepan, combine sugar, cornstarch and orange peel. Stir in orange juice and 3 tablespoons drippings from roasting pan. Heat to boiling, stirring occasionally. Keep hot or reheat to serve. Stir in liqueur before serving. Discard stuffing. Serve duckling over rice with orange sauce. **4 servings.**

NUTRIENTS PER ¼ OF RECIPE

Calories 1010	Dietary Fiber...........................2 g
Protein.....................................41 g	Sodium..............................125 mg
Carbohydrate.........................57 g	Potassium.........................530 mg
Fat ....68 g	Calcium................4% U.S. RDA
Cholesterol.......................170 mg	Iron......................35% U.S. RDA

Sweet Sour Cornish Hens

         3 (1 to 1½-lb.) Cornish game hens
         2 tablespoons cornstarch
         1 teaspoon dry mustard
        ½ cup water
         2 tablespoons red wine vinegar
  1 to 3 teaspoons honey
         1 teaspoon soy sauce
   8-oz. can chunk pineapple in its own juice, undrained
         1 medium red bell pepper, cut into 1-inch pieces, if
            desired
         1 medium green pepper, cut into 1-inch pieces

Remove giblets. Rinse hens inside and out; pat dry. Halve
each hen. Place skin side up on rack in broiler pan or shallow roasting pan. Broil 4 to 6 inches from heat for 8 to 10
minutes or until skin is crisp; drain.

Heat oven to 325°F. Place halves skin side up in ungreased
13x9-inch (3-quart) baking dish. In medium bowl, combine
remaining ingredients; spoon over hens. Bake at 325°F. for 45
to 50 minutes or until tender, basting occasionally. **6 servings.**

MICROWAVE DIRECTIONS: Remove giblets. Rinse
hens; pat dry. Halve each hen. Place skin side down in 13x9-
inch (3-quart) microwave-safe dish; cover with microwave-
safe plastic wrap. Microwave on HIGH for 15 minutes;
drain well. Turn skin side up. In medium bowl, combine remaining ingredients; spoon over hens. Cover with microwave-safe plastic wrap; microwave on HIGH for an
additional 10 minutes or until meat is tender, spooning sauce
over once during cooking.

NUTRIENTS PER ¼ OF RECIPE

Calories	460	Dietary Fiber	1 g
Protein	47 g	Sodium	200 mg
Carbohydrate	13 g	Potassium	510 mg
Fat	23 g	Calcium	2% U.S. RDA
Cholesterol	150 mg	Iron	15% U.S. RDA

Microwave Cornish Hens

    4 (1 to 1½-lb.) Cornish game hens
    1 teaspoon salt
       Nut Stuffing using almonds (see Index)
  ¼ cup margarine or butter, melted
    1 teaspoon paprika

MICROWAVE DIRECTIONS: Remove giblets. Rinse hens inside and out; pat dry. Sprinkle cavities with salt. Lightly stuff body and neck cavity of each hen with stuffing. Secure body openings with toothpicks or wooden skewers. Cover ends of legs with small pieces of foil. Place inverted saucers or small casserole lids in 12x8-inch (2-quart) microwave-safe dish to hold hens out of juices. Place hens breast side down on saucers. Brush with mixture of margarine and paprika. Cover with microwave-safe plastic wrap. Microwave on HIGH for 12 minutes. Turn breast side up; rotate outside edges of hens to inside. Brush with remainder of margarine mixture. Cover with microwave-safe plastic wrap. Microwave on HIGH for 12 minutes or until meat thermometer registers 185°F. (will increase to 190°F. during standing).* Let stand covered 5 to 10 minutes. Remove toothpicks before serving. **4 or 8 servings.**

TIP: *Do not use conventional metal meat thermometer in microwave during cooking.

VARIATION:

WATER CHESTNUT STUFFED HENS: Use water chestnuts for almonds in stuffing. Brush hens with a glaze of 2 tablespoons melted margarine, 2 tablespoons soy sauce and 2 tablespoons dark corn syrup.

NUTRIENTS PER ⅛ OF RECIPE

Calories	690	Dietary Fiber	1 g
Protein	51 g	Sodium	1160 mg
Carbohydrate	25 g	Potassium	500 mg
Fat	42 g	Calcium	8% U.S. RDA
Cholesterol	150 mg	Iron	20% U.S. RDA

Apricot Glazed Cornish Hens

  6 (1 to 1½-lb.) Cornish game hens
     Salt
     Wild Rice-Sausage Stuffing (see Index)
12-oz. jar apricot preserves
  ½ cup water

Heat oven to 350°F. Remove giblets. Rinse hens inside and out; pat dry. Sprinkle cavities with salt. Lightly stuff body and neck cavity of each hen with about 1 cup of the dressing. Secure body openings with toothpicks or metal skewers. Tie legs together with string. Place in ungreased 15x10-inch jelly roll pan. In small saucepan, combine preserves and water. Bring to a boil, stirring constantly; set aside. Bake hens at 350°F. for 1½ to 2 hours or until tender. During last ½ hour of baking, baste hens frequently with preserves mixture. Remove strings and toothpicks before serving. If desired, split hens in half. **6 or 12 servings.**

NUTRIENTS PER ½ OF RECIPE

Calories 680	Dietary Fiber.........................1 g
Protein..................................53 g	Sodium..............................810 mg
Carbohydrate......................48 g	Potassium..........................570 mg
Fat...29 g	Calcium.................4% U.S. RDA
Cholesterol.....................160 mg	Iron.....................20% U.S. RDA

Glazes for Poultry

Each recipe makes enough glaze for 1 turkey or 4 Cornish game hens. Halve recipe for 1 chicken. Brush poultry frequently with glaze during baking.

TIP: If poultry becomes too brown, place piece of foil lightly over breast.

CURRY-PEACH GLAZE: Melt ¼ cup margarine or butter. Stir in ½ cup peach preserves and 1 teaspoon curry powder.

HONEY-LEMON GLAZE: Melt ¼ cup margarine or butter. Stir in ¼ cup honey and 1 tablespoon lemon juice.

ORANGE GLAZE: Melt 2 tablespoons margarine or butter. Stir in ⅓ cup thawed frozen orange juice concentrate or orange marmalade and ½ teaspoon ginger.

SOY-BUTTER GLAZE: Melt 2 tablespoons margarine or butter. Stir in ⅓ cup soy sauce, ¼ cup light or dark corn syrup and ⅛ teaspoon garlic powder.

Salads & Dressings

Salads & Dressings

What's in a salad? These days, just about anything you wish. Crisp greens, garden-fresh vegetables, colorful fruits, enriched pastas, protein-packed cheeses, eggs, meats, fish, poultry, legumes and other inviting ingredients. Mixed, molded, tossed or artfully arranged on chilled plates, salads reign supreme as appealing, nutritious staples on menus today.

Dressings, like the frosting on a cake, are selected to enhance and embellish salad ingredients. Using the freshest ingredients for both ensures that flavors and textures are at their absolute peak of perfection.

Nutritional contributions of salads to daily diets are impressively varied. From greens come vitamins A and C, calcium and iron. Fruits are especially rich in vitamins A and C and potassium. The hard-cooked eggs, meats, poultry, fish, and legumes added to salads contribute high-quality protein and amino acids along with B vitamins and iron. From cheeses come calcium, riboflavin and protein. Pasta additions help fulfill daily nutritional requirements by offering important complex carbohydrates, B vitamins, iron and protein. Fruits and vegetables contribute dietary fiber.

Green Salads

Selection

• When selecting greens, look for obvious indications of freshness and proper handling—bright color, blemish- and bruise-free leaves. For delicate flavor and tender texture, choose young shoots and leaves. Select heads of iceberg lettuce and cabbage that are firm.

• Choose a variety of greens to spark interest with complementary contrasts in flavor, texture and color. Although not all varieties are readily available year round, there are always several from which to choose. Use the salad greens identification descriptions to help in your selections.

Storing

• Store greens from garden or market washed or unwashed, according to preference, in refrigerator crisper section.

• Before washing, discard any discolored or blemished areas. Remove core from iceberg lettuce.

• To wash greens, rinse thoroughly and gently under cold running water or swish leaves through a water-filled sink without allowing them to soak longer than necessary.

• Drain and dry well to remove excess moisture that causes greens to deteriorate.

• Wrap greens in absorbent paper or clean cloth towel; place in plastic bag or container and refrigerate for several hours to crisp.

• Most greens are best when used within a few days. Iceberg and romaine lettuce will hold up to a week. Watercress, parsley and fresh herbs store about a week when refrigerated in tightly sealed jars.

Preparation

• Prepare greens for serving by trimming away tough ribs and stems and tearing leaves gently to avoid bruising and browning. Cut greens only when recipe calls for wedges or shredding. Large outer leaves can be used for "cups" to hold a variety of fillings.

• Gently combine greens and other ingredients just before serving. Ingredients that may break up in tossing, such as tomato wedges, can be placed atop greens after tossing.

Salad Greens Identification

• **Arugula:** Slender, notched leaves with an intense, bitter-sweet flavor. Use alone or mixed with other, milder greens.

• **Belgian or French Endive:** Smooth, elongated, compact heads of slender, crisp leaves; flavor is slightly bitter. Serve alone or mixed with other salad greens.

• **Bibb Lettuce:** Small heads of tender, buttery-feeling leaves with a slightly sweet mild taste. Serve alone or mixed with other greens.

• **Boston Lettuce:** Loose heads of tender, buttery-feeling leaves with flavor similar to Bibb lettuce. Serve alone or mixed with other greens.

• **Chinese Cabbage:** Long, slender, tightly closed heads of wide-ribbed, tender leaves, mild in flavor. Serve alone or mixed with other greens.

• **Curly Endive:** Fringed, curly leaves with a sharp bitter taste. Darker leaves will have a stronger flavor than the lighter inner leaves. Serve mixed with other, milder greens.

• **Escarole:** Wide, crisp, flat leaves with slightly curled edges. Flavor is slightly bitter. Serve mixed with other, milder greens.

• **Iceberg Lettuce:** Makes an especially crisp salad, very mild in flavor compared to other greens. Serve alone or mixed with other greens, especially those with a more pronounced flavor.

• **Leaf Lettuce/Red and Green:** Broad, tender, loose leaves with a mild, delicate flavor. May be curly, green or red-tipped. Serve alone or mixed with other greens.

• **Radicchio:** Tender, firm-textured, light red to rose-colored leaves, slightly bitter in flavor. Serve alone or mixed with other greens.

• **Romaine Lettuce:** Firm, crisp leaves with a mild, nutty flavor. Serve alone or mixed with other greens.

• **Savoy Cabbage:** A crinkly-leaved green cabbage with a milder flavor than red or green cabbage.

• **Sorrell:** Long, crisp, arrow-shaped leaves with a pungent, sour flavor.

• **Spinach:** Crinkled or flat, crisp leaves with a mild flavor. Trim away any tough stems or ribs. Serve alone or mixed with other greens.

• **Watercress:** Crisp, small, dark-leaved sprigs with a pungent, peppery flavor. Trim away tough stems. Serve alone or mixed with other greens.

Fruit and Nut Tossed Salad

```
    1   cup fresh spinach, torn into bite-size pieces
    6   cups romaine lettuce, torn into bite-size pieces
    1   cup seedless red or green grapes, halved
   ½   cup toasted slivered almonds*
11-oz.  can mandarin orange segments, chilled, drained
   ½   cup oil
   ¼   cup vinegar
   ¼   cup sugar
   ½   teaspoon salt
    1   small avocado, peeled, sliced, if desired
```

In large bowl, combine spinach, lettuce, grapes, almonds and orange segments. In jar with tight-fitting lid, combine oil, vinegar, sugar and salt; shake well. Just before serving, toss some of dressing with salad and garnish with avocado. Serve remaining dressing with salad. **6 to 8 servings.**

TIP: *To toast almonds, spread almonds on cookie sheet; bake at 350°F. for 6 to 8 minutes or until golden brown, stirring occasionally.

NUTRIENTS PER ⅛ OF RECIPE

Calories	230	Dietary Fiber	2 g
Protein	3 g	Sodium	145 mg
Carbohydrate	17 g	Potassium	295 mg
Fat	18 g	Calcium	6% U.S. RDA
Cholesterol	0 mg	Iron	8% U.S. RDA

Tossed Salad

4 cups assorted salad greens, torn into bite-size pieces
3 medium tomatoes, cut into wedges
1 medium cucumber, sliced
½ teaspoon salt
   Dash pepper
½ cup prepared French or other favorite dressing

In salad bowl, combine all ingredients; toss lightly. Serve immediately. **5 to 6 servings.**

TOSSED SALAD VARIATIONS: Any type of salad greens can be used such as:

Boston lettuce	Romaine
Bibb lettuce	Escarole
Iceberg lettuce	Spinach
Bronze lettuce	Watercress
Curly endive	

Vegetable additions:

Fresh Vegetables	**Cooked Vegetables**
Sliced zucchini	French fried onion rings
Cauliflower florets	Bamboo shoots
Shredded, thinly sliced or julienne cut carrots	Sliced water chestnuts
	Julienne-cut beets
	Artichoke hearts
Bean sprouts	Garden beans
Mushrooms	Garbanzo beans

Sliced green peppers
Sliced radishes
Thinly sliced onions
Sliced celery

Pimiento
Sliced olives

Fruit additions:

Thinly sliced avocado
Mandarin orange segments
Grapefruit segments
Seedless green or red grapes
Pomegranate seeds
Sliced unpeeled apples

Meat and cheese additions:

Cubed or shredded cheese
Anchovy fillets
Slices or wedges of hard-cooked eggs
Seafood
Cubed or sliced salami
Cubed or sliced summer sausage

NUTRIENTS PER ¼ OF RECIPE

Calories	110	Dietary Fiber	2 g
Protein	1 g	Sodium	180 mg
Carbohydrate	8 g	Potassium	270 mg
Fat	9 g	Calcium	2% U.S. RDA
Cholesterol	0 mg	Iron	6% U.S. RDA

Avocado and Orange Salad

SALAD

    Bibb or Boston lettuce, torn into bite-size pieces
3 large oranges, peeled and sectioned or sliced
1 medium cucumber, thinly sliced
1 large avocado, peeled, cut into ½-inch slices
    Pomegranate seeds, if desired

DRESSING

　½ cup oil
　¼ cup orange juice
　2 tablespoons sugar
　2 tablespoons lemon juice
　2 tablespoons sliced green onions
　½ teaspoon grated orange peel
　¼ teaspoon salt

On lettuce-lined platter or individual serving plates, arrange oranges, cucumber and avocado. In pint jar with tight-fitting lid, combine all dressing ingredients. Shake well to blend. Spoon dressing over salads. Sprinkle with pomegranate seeds. **6 servings.**

NUTRIENTS PER ⅙ OF RECIPE

Calories	310	Dietary Fiber	3 g
Protein	2 g	Sodium	90 mg
Carbohydrate	21 g	Potassium	590 mg
Fat	25 g	Calcium	6% U.S. RDA
Cholesterol	0 mg	Iron	6% U.S. RDA

Wilted Leaf Lettuce Salad

　6 cups leaf lettuce, torn into bite-size pieces
　2 tablespoons chopped green onions
　2 eggs, hard-cooked, chopped
　3 slices bacon, cut into ½-inch pieces
　¼ cup cider vinegar
　2 teaspoons sugar
　¼ teaspoon salt
　¼ teaspoon dry mustard
　⅛ teaspoon pepper

In large bowl, combine lettuce, onions and eggs; set aside. In small skillet, cook bacon until crisp. Add remaining dressing ingredients; heat until sugar is dissolved. Pour hot

bacon mixture over lettuce. Toss lightly. Serve immediately.
5 to 6 servings.

VARIATION:

WILTED SPINACH SALAD: Substitute 6 cups torn fresh
spinach for leaf lettuce.

NUTRIENTS PER ⅙ OF RECIPE

Calories	70	Dietary Fiber	<1 g
Protein	4 g	Sodium	155 mg
Carbohydrate	5 g	Potassium	200 mg
Fat	4 g	Calcium	2% U.S. RDA
Cholesterol	90 mg	Iron	6% U.S. RDA

Sweet 'n Sour Spinach Salad

DRESSING

   1   cup oil
   ¾   cup sugar
   ⅓   cup catsup
   ¼   cup vinegar
   2   teaspoons Worcestershire sauce
   ¼   teaspoon salt

SALAD

   8   cups fresh spinach or salad greens, torn into bite-
       sized pieces
   1   cup sliced fresh mushrooms
   ½   cup shredded carrots
   4   thin slices red onion, separated into rings
   2   hard-cooked eggs, chopped

In jar with tight-fitting lid, combine all dressing ingredients;
shake well. Refrigerate to blend flavors. In large bowl, combine all salad ingredients except eggs. Just before serving,
add enough dressing to coat greens; toss gently. Top with
chopped eggs. Serve immediately. Refrigerate remaining
dressing. **8 servings.**

NUTRIENTS PER ⅛ OF SALAD WITH 2 TABLESPOONS DRESSING

Calories 200	Dietary Fiber ....2 g
Protein ....3 g	Sodium ....125 mg
Carbohydrate ....14 g	Potassium ....220 mg
Fat ....15 g	Calcium ....2% U.S. RDA
Cholesterol ....70 mg	Iron ....4% U.S. RDA

Best Ever Vegetable Salad

> 1 cup chopped green pepper
> 1 cup sliced celery
> ½ cup sliced green onions
> 2 tablespoons diced pimiento
> 16-oz. can cut green beans, drained
> 12-oz. can whole kernel corn, drained
> ½ cup sugar
> ½ teaspoon salt
> ½ teaspoon white or black pepper
> ½ cup cider vinegar
> ¼ cup oil

In large bowl, combine green pepper, celery, onions, pimiento, green beans and corn. In small bowl, blend remaining ingredients and pour over vegetables; mix lightly. Cover; refrigerate several hours or overnight to blend flavors. **10 servings.**

NUTRIENTS PER ⅒ OF RECIPE

Calories 140	Dietary Fiber ....2 g
Protein ....2 g	Sodium ....355 mg
Carbohydrate ....20 g	Potassium ....195 mg
Fat ....6 g	Calcium ....<2% U.S. RDA
Cholesterol ....0 mg	Iron ....4% U.S. RDA

Marinated Multi-Vegetable Salad

    1½ cups cauliflower florets, cooked crisp-tender
    1½ cups thinly sliced carrots
     1 cup thinly sliced celery
17-oz. can peas, drained
16-oz. can cut green beans, drained
 2-oz. jar chopped pimiento, drained, if desired
    ¼ cup prepared French dressing
    ¾ cup mayonnaise
     1 tablespoon lemon juice
1 to 2 teaspoons dill seed

In large bowl, combine cauliflower, carrots, celery, peas, beans, pimiento and French dressing; mix lightly. Marinate at room temperature for 1 hour, stirring occasionally. Add remaining ingredients; mix well. Refrigerate until served. **12 servings.**

NUTRIENTS PER ½₂ OF RECIPE

Calories	160	Dietary Fiber	3 g
Protein	2 g	Sodium	285 mg
Carbohydrate	9 g	Potassium	170 mg
Fat	13 g	Calcium	2% U.S. RDA
Cholesterol	8 mg	Iron	6% U.S. RDA

Layered Lettuce Salad

     8 cups iceberg lettuce, torn into bite-size pieces
     3 cups coarsely chopped cauliflower
     1 cup thinly sliced carrots
     1 cup sliced fresh mushrooms
    ½ cup chopped sweet red onion
    1½ cups mayonnaise
2 to 3 tablespoons prepared mustard
     4 oz. (1 cup) shredded Cheddar cheese
    12 slices bacon, crisply cooked, crumbled

In 13x9-inch (3-quart) baking dish, layer lettuce, cauliflower, carrots, mushrooms and onion. Combine mayonnaise and mustard; spoon and spread evenly over onion
layer. Layer cheese and bacon over mayonnaise mixture.
Cover; refrigerate overnight. **12 servings.**

NUTRIENTS PER ¹⁄₁₂ OF RECIPE

Calories	310	Dietary Fiber	2 g
Protein	7 g	Sodium	390 mg
Carbohydrate	6 g	Potassium	280 mg
Fat	29 g	Calcium	10% U.S. RDA
Cholesterol	35 mg	Iron	6% U.S. RDA

Cauliflower and Broccoli Make-Ahead

- 4 cups (1 medium head) cauliflower florets
- 2 cups broccoli florets
- 1 cup peas
- ½ cup thinly sliced celery
- 2 tablespoons sliced green onions
- 1 cup mayonnaise or salad dressing
- ½ cup dairy sour cream
- 1 teaspoon sugar
- ½ teaspoon salt
- ½ teaspoon garlic salt
- 3 drops hot pepper sauce

In large bowl, combine cauliflower, broccoli, peas, celery
and onions. In small bowl, blend remaining ingredients.
Pour over vegetables; mix well. Cover; refrigerate until
serving time. **10 servings.**

NUTRIENTS PER ¹⁄₁₀ OF RECIPE

Calories	220	Dietary Fiber	2 g
Protein	3 g	Sodium	355 mg
Carbohydrate	7 g	Potassium	270 mg
Fat	20 g	Calcium	4% U.S. RDA
Cholesterol	20 mg	Iron	6% U.S. RDA

Simply Super Tomatoes

    6 medium tomatoes, peeled, cut into ½-inch slices
    ⅔ cup oil
    ¼ cup wine vinegar
    ¼ cup finely chopped fresh parsley
    ¼ cup finely chopped green onions
    1 garlic clove, minced
    1 teaspoon salt
    1 teaspoon dill weed
    1 teaspoon basil leaves
    ¼ teaspoon pepper

Arrange tomatoes in serving dish. In small bowl or jar with tight-fitting lid, combine remaining ingredients; mix well. Pour dressing over tomatoes. Cover; refrigerate 1 to 2 hours, spooning dressing over tomatoes occasionally. **6 servings.**

NUTRIENTS PER ⅙ OF RECIPE

Calories	240	Dietary Fiber	2 g
Protein	1 g	Sodium	360 mg
Carbohydrate	6 g	Potassium	265 mg
Fat	24 g	Calcium	2% U.S. RDA
Cholesterol	0 mg	Iron	4% U.S. RDA

Sweet 'n Sauerkraut Salad

  1½ cups sugar
    ¼ cup oil
    ½ cup cider vinegar
    1 quart (4 cups) sauerkraut, rinsed, drained
    1 cup chopped onion
    ½ cup chopped celery
    ½ cup chopped green pepper
2-oz. jar chopped pimiento, drained
    1 teaspoon mustard seed
    1 teaspoon celery seed

In large bowl, combine sugar, oil and vinegar. Add remaining ingredients; mix well. Cover; refrigerate 24 hours to blend flavors. **10 servings.**

TIP: Salad can be stored refrigerated, in a tightly-covered container, for up to 10 days.

NUTRIENTS PER ⅒ OF RECIPE

Calories	200	Dietary Fiber	3 g
Protein	1 g	Sodium	430 mg
Carbohydrate	35 g	Potassium	160 mg
Fat	6 g	Calcium	2% U.S. RDA
Cholesterol	0 mg	Iron	4% U.S. RDA

Tangy Carrot Raisin Salad

> 3 cups shredded carrots
> 1 cup raisins
> 3 tablespoons oil
> 2 tablespoons honey
> 2 tablespoons lemon juice
> ¼ teaspoon salt
> ⅛ teaspoon nutmeg

In medium bowl, combine carrots and raisins. In small bowl, combine oil, honey, lemon juice, salt and nutmeg; mix well. Pour over carrot mixture; toss until well blended. Refrigerate until serving time. **7 servings.**

NUTRIENTS PER ⅐ OF RECIPE

Calories	160	Dietary Fiber	3 g
Protein	1 g	Sodium	95 mg
Carbohydrate	26 g	Potassium	320 mg
Fat	6 g	Calcium	2% U.S. RDA
Cholesterol	0 mg	Iron	4% U.S. RDA

Marinated Garden Salad

⅓ cup tarragon vinegar
¼ cup oil
2 teaspoons dill weed
½ teaspoon salt
½ teaspoon dry mustard
⅛ teaspoon pepper
1 garlic clove, minced
1 head cauliflower, broken into bite-size pieces and cooked crisp-tender
2 cups cherry tomatoes, halved
2 cups (2 to 3 medium) sliced zucchini
6-oz. can (1⅓ cups) pitted ripe olives, drained

In small bowl, combine vinegar, oil, dill weed, salt, mustard, pepper and garlic. In large bowl, combine cauliflower, tomatoes, zucchini and olives. Pour dressing over salad mixture; toss well to combine ingredients. Refrigerate at least 1 hour to blend flavors. **12 servings.**

NUTRIENTS PER ¹⁄₁₂ OF RECIPE

Calories	90	Dietary Fiber	2 g
Protein	2 g	Sodium	210 mg
Carbohydrate	5 g	Potassium	235 mg
Fat	7 g	Calcium	4% U.S. RDA
Cholesterol	0 mg	Iron	4% U.S. RDA

Creamy Coleslaw

1 small head cabbage, shredded or thinly sliced
2 tablespoons sugar
2 tablespoons chopped onion
½ teaspoon salt
½ cup mayonnaise or dairy sour cream
1 teaspoon lemon juice

In large bowl, combine all ingredients; toss lightly. **10 servings.**

VARIATIONS:

APPLE SLAW: Add 1 large cubed apple, 1 teaspoon grated orange peel, ⅛ teaspoon cinnamon and ⅛ teaspoon cloves to cabbage mixture; omit onion.

COCONUTTY SLAW: Add ¼ cup chopped cucumber and ¼ cup flaked coconut to cabbage mixture; omit onion.

EXTRA CRISPY COLESLAW: Refrigerate shredded cabbage in ice water for 1 hour. Drain and combine with remaining ingredients.

FRUIT SLAW: Add 2 cups miniature marshmallows, 1 small stalk celery, chopped and 2 cups drained crushed pineapple to cabbage mixture; omit onion. Drained maraschino cherries can be used as a garnish.

SEAFOOD SLAW: Add ½ cup cooked crab meat, shrimp or lobster.

NUTRIENTS PER ⅒ OF RECIPE

Calories 110	Dietary Fiber ......1 g
Protein ......1 g	Sodium ......180 mg
Carbohydrate ......7 g	Potassium ......170 mg
Fat ......9 g	Calcium ......2% U.S. RDA
Cholesterol ......6 mg	Iron ......<2% U.S. RDA

Three Bean Salad

16-oz. can cut green beans, drained
16-oz. can cut yellow beans, drained
16-oz. can kidney beans, drained
   1 medium red onion, sliced, separated into rings
   1 green pepper, cut in 1-inch strips
   ¾ cup vinegar
   ½ cup oil
   ½ cup sugar

1 tablespoon chopped fresh parsley
1 teaspoon celery seed
¼ teaspoon pepper

In large bowl, combine beans, onion and green pepper. In small bowl, combine remaining ingredients. Pour dressing over bean mixture; mix lightly. Cover; refrigerate several hours or overnight to blend flavors. **12 servings.**

NUTRIENTS PER ¹⁄₁₂ OF RECIPE

Calories 150	Dietary Fiber ....4 g
Protein ....2 g	Sodium ....105 mg
Carbohydrate ....16 g	Potassium ....140 mg
Fat ....9 g	Calcium ....2% U.S. RDA
Cholesterol ....0 mg	Iron ....6% U.S. RDA

Cucumbers in Sour Cream

4 medium cucumbers, thinly sliced (4 cups)
1½ teaspoons salt
¾ cup vinegar
¾ cup water
1 cup dairy sour cream
1 teaspoon chopped fresh dill or ¼ teaspoon dill weed
1 teaspoon sugar
Dash pepper

Place cucumbers in medium bowl. Sprinkle with salt; add vinegar and water to cover cucumbers. Let stand 30 minutes; drain well. In small bowl, combine sour cream, dill, sugar and pepper; stir into cucumbers. Serve immediately or refrigerate. **8 servings.**

TIP: Thinly sliced onion rings can be added with dressing.

NUTRIENTS PER ⅛ OF RECIPE

Calories	80	Dietary Fiber	1 g
Protein	1 g	Sodium	420 mg
Carbohydrate	5 g	Potassium	150 mg
Fat	6 g	Calcium	4% U.S. RDA
Cholesterol	10 mg	Iron	4% U.S. RDA

Potato Salad

3 to 4	medium potatoes, cooked, peeled and cubed
3	eggs, hard-cooked, chopped
1	small onion, chopped or 6 green onions, chopped
2	stalks celery, chopped
¼	cup chopped pickle or pickle relish
1	teaspoon salt
⅛	teaspoon pepper
¾	cup mayonnaise or salad dressing
1	tablespoon prepared mustard

In large bowl, combine all ingredients; mix well. Cover; refrigerate until serving time. **4 to 6 servings.**

TIP: Other additions to potato salad include:

	cubed, cooked beef
1 to 2	tablespoons chopped green pepper or chives
4 to 5	sliced radishes
1	tomato, cut into wedges
	chopped cucumber or zucchini
½	cup cottage cheese
¼	cup sliced olives
¼	teaspoon curry powder or dill weed

VARIATION:

MARINATED POTATO SALAD: Toss warm potato slices, onion, pickle, salt and pepper with ¼ cup prepared French dressing. Cover; refrigerate several hours. Before serving, stir in eggs, celery and ½ cup mayonnaise; omit mustard.

NUTRIENTS PER ¼ OF RECIPE

Calories	310	Dietary Fiber	2 g
Protein	5 g	Sodium	640 mg
Carbohydrate	18 g	Potassium	350 mg
Fat	25 g	Calcium	2% U.S. RDA
Cholesterol	150 mg	Iron	6% U.S. RDA

German Potato Salad

4   slices bacon
½   cup chopped onion
¼   cup sugar
2   tablespoons flour
½   teaspoon salt
    Dash pepper
1   cup water
⅓   cup vinegar
4   cups cooked, peeled and sliced new potatoes
    Fresh parsley, if desired

In large skillet, fry bacon until crisp. Remove bacon; drain on paper towels. Saute onion in bacon drippings until crisp-tender. Add sugar, flour, salt and pepper; blend well. Cook until mixture is smooth and bubbly, stirring constantly. Gradually add water and vinegar. Cook until mixture boils and thickens, stirring constantly. Stir in potatoes; heat thoroughly. Spoon into serving dish. Crumble bacon; sprinkle over top. Garnish with parsley. **8 servings.**

MICROWAVE DIRECTIONS: Cut bacon into 1-inch pieces. Place bacon in large microwave-safe bowl; cover with waxed paper. Microwave on HIGH for 6 to 8 minutes or until bacon is almost crisp, stirring every 2 minutes. Remove bacon; place on paper towels. Add onion to bacon drippings; cover with waxed paper. Microwave on HIGH for 1½ to 2 minutes or until almost tender. Add sugar, flour, salt and pepper; blend well. Add water and vinegar; blend well. Microwave on HIGH for 3 to 5½ minutes or until mixture boils and thickens, stirring once halfway through cooking. Stir in potatoes; microwave on HIGH for 5 to 7 minutes or until thoroughly heated. Continue as directed.

NUTRIENTS PER ⅛ OF RECIPE

Calories	120	Dietary Fiber	2 g
Protein	3 g	Sodium	190 mg
Carbohydrate	22 g	Potassium	350 mg
Fat	2 g	Calcium	<2% U.S. RDA
Cholesterol	2 mg	Iron	4% U.S. RDA

Broccoli Tortellini Salad

7-oz.	pkg. cheese tortellini
1	cup fresh broccoli florets
½	cup finely chopped fresh parsley
1	tablespoon chopped pimiento
6-oz.	jar marinated artichoke hearts, undrained
2	green onions, chopped
2½	teaspoons chopped fresh basil or ¼ teaspoon dried basil leaves
½	teaspoon garlic powder
½	cup prepared Italian salad dressing
5 to 6	cherry tomatoes, halved
	Sliced ripe olives, if desired
	Grated Parmesan cheese, if desired

Cook tortellini to desired doneness as directed on package. Drain; rinse with cold water.

In large bowl, combine all ingredients except cherry tomatoes, olives, and Parmesan cheese. Cover; refrigerate 4 to 6 hours to blend flavors. Just before serving, add tomatoes; mix lightly. Serve sprinkled with Parmesan cheese. **6 servings.**

TIP: Salad can be made a day in advance and refrigerated. To avoid discoloration, just before serving add broccoli with tomatoes.

NUTRIENTS PER ¼ OF RECIPE

Calories 280	Dietary Fiber ....NA
Protein.......................................9 g	Sodium.............................560 mg
Carbohydrate.........................17 g	Potassium ....220 mg
Fat ....20 g	Calcium ....15% U.S. RDA
Cholesterol...........................45 mg	Iron.......................10% U.S. RDA

Garden Italian Salad

    1   cup orzo or rosa marina (rice-shaped pasta)
    1   cup thinly sliced zucchini
    ½   cup shredded carrot
    ½   cup sliced ripe olives
    ¼   cup sliced green onions
2-oz.   jar chopped pimiento, drained
    ½   cup prepared Italian salad dressing
    4   oz. mozzarella cheese, cut into ½-inch cubes
    1   tablespoon chopped fresh parsley

Cook orzo to desired doneness as directed on package; drain. Rinse with cold water.

In large bowl, combine orzo, zucchini, carrot, olives, onions and pimiento. Pour dressing over salad; toss well. Refrigerate at least 2 hours to blend flavors. Add mozzarella cheese just before serving; garnish with parsley. **5 servings.**

TIP: Two and one-half cups cooked macaroni rings or stars can be substituted for orzo.

NUTRIENTS PER ⅕ OF RECIPE

Calories 300	Dietary Fiber...........................1 g
Protein.....................................10 g	Sodium.............................410 mg
Carbohydrate.........................25 g	Potassium ....180 mg
Fat ....18 g	Calcium ....20% U.S. RDA
Cholesterol...........................10 mg	Iron.........................8% U.S. RDA

Macaroni Salad

4½ oz. (1 cup) uncooked elbow macaroni
1 stalk celery, chopped
¼ cup pickle relish or chopped sweet pickle
¼ teaspoon salt
1 tablespoon chopped onion
¾ cup mayonnaise or salad dressing

Cook macaroni to desired doneness as directed on package. Drain; rinse with cold water. In large bowl, combine macaroni with remaining ingredients; toss lightly. Cover; refrigerate until serving time. **5 to 6 servings.**

MACARONI SALAD VARIATIONS: Any of the following can be added:
2 to 3 hard-cooked eggs, chopped
1 to 2 cups cubed cheese
½ cup chopped nuts

Meat and seafood additions:
6½-oz. can tuna or crab meat, drained, flaked
½ to 1 cup canned salmon or shrimp, drained
1 to 2 cups cubed, cooked meat or sausage
Crumbled, crisply cooked bacon

Vegetable additions:
1 cup cooked peas or carrots
¼ cup stuffed olives or chopped cucumber
1 tablespoon chopped green pepper or pimiento
1 carrot, shredded

VARIATIONS:

MACARONI-FRUIT SALAD: Omit pickle relish and onion; substitute whipped cream or topping for mayonnaise. Fold in 1 to 2 cups cut-up fresh or drained canned fruit.

RICE SALAD: Substitute 2 cups cooked rice for the macaroni.

NUTRIENTS PER ⅙ OF RECIPE

Calories	290	Dietary Fiber	<1 g
Protein	3 g	Sodium	290 mg
Carbohydrate	20 g	Potassium	75 mg
Fat	22 g	Calcium	<2% U.S. RDA
Cholesterol	15 mg	Iron	4% U.S. RDA

Spinach-Rice Tomato Tulips

DRESSING

2	tablespoons tarragon vinegar
2	tablespoons oil
½ to 1	teaspoon dill weed
¾	teaspoon salt
¼	teaspoon garlic powder
¼	teaspoon dry mustard
	Dash pepper

SALAD

1½	cups cooked rice
10-oz.	pkg. frozen chopped spinach, thawed, squeezed to drain
1	cup chopped tomato
½	cup sliced green onions
½	cup sliced celery
6	large tomatoes, cut into tulip shape*
2	tablespoons sunflower nuts

In small bowl, combine all dressing ingredients; mix well. In medium bowl, combine cooked rice, spinach, tomato, onions and celery; mix well. Pour dressing over salad mixture; toss well. Refrigerate 1 hour to blend flavors. Spoon about ⅔ cup salad mixture into each tomato tulip. Sprinkle with sunflower nuts. **6 servings.**

TIP: *To prepare tomato tulips, hollow out stem portion at center of each tomato. Make 6 cuts from center of each tomato to outside, making sure not to cut through bottom skin.

NUTRIENTS PER ⅙ OF RECIPE

Calories	150	Dietary Fiber	3 g
Protein	5 g	Sodium	440 mg
Carbohydrate	20 g	Potassium	615 mg
Fat	6 g	Calcium	8% U.S. RDA
Cholesterol	0 mg	Iron	10% U.S. RDA

Tabbouleh

- 2 cups boiling water
- 2 cups cracked wheat or fine bulgur
- 3 medium tomatoes, chopped
- 1 medium cucumber, diced (1 cup)
- 1 cup finely chopped fresh parsley
- ½ cup finely chopped green onions
- 1 tablespoon dried mint leaves
- ½ cup lemon juice
- ½ cup olive oil
- 1 teaspoon salt

In large bowl, pour boiling water over cracked wheat; let stand 1 hour or until fluffy. Drain well; return to bowl. Add tomatoes, cucumber, parsley, onions and mint; mix well. Combine lemon juice, oil and salt; mix well. Stir into wheat mixture. Cover; refrigerate to blend flavors. **8 servings.**

TIP: One to 2 cups cubed, cooked beef can be added for a main dish salad.

NUTRIENTS PER ⅛ OF RECIPE

Calories	250	Dietary Fiber	5 g
Protein	5 g	Sodium	270 mg
Carbohydrate	29 g	Potassium	190 mg
Fat	14 g	Calcium	2% U.S. RDA
Cholesterol	0 mg	Iron	4% U.S. RDA

Fruit Salads

Selection

• When selecting fruits, choose produce of good color and shape with unbruised, unblemished skin that is firm enough to avoid a mushy interior.

• Specific guidelines vary according to variety. Fresh fruits like apples, cherries, citrus fruits, berries and grapes are ready to use as purchased. Others such as avocados, melons, bananas, kiwifruit, pineapple, papayas and pears may require additional ripening to bring out maximum flavor. Nectarines, peaches and plums should be purchased as near tree-ripened as possible for maximum flavor and sweetness as they do not ripen any further, just soften up a bit.

• For best fruit buys, purchase fresh fruits during their peak seasons when supply is most plentiful (see below for Fruit Availability Chart).

Storage

• Store fruits according to type and stage of ripeness. Some varieties like grapes, berries and citrus should be refrigerated immediately after purchase. Other fruits that need time to ripen or soften should be placed in a cool, dry place away from sunlight until they are ready to use, then refrigerate. Apples should be stored in a cool, dry place. Once fruits are fully ripe, they should be used promptly.

Preparation

• Prepare fruits for salads as close to serving time as possible (unless recipe indicates otherwise) to retain peak flavor, color and texture. Fruits such as apples, pears, bananas, peaches and avocados brown when cut. Dip these fruits in lemon juice or ascorbic acid solution to prevent discoloration.

• Add variety to fruit cups and combination salads by selecting colors, textures and flavors that complement one another and by cutting fruits in numerous ways.

• Frozen fruit salads can double as a light, refreshing dessert.

Fruit Availability Chart

With modern transportation and storage, many fruits that were once seasonal are now available year round. For best flavor, texture and price, however, fruits should be bought in their most plentiful months. Use this chart as a guideline.

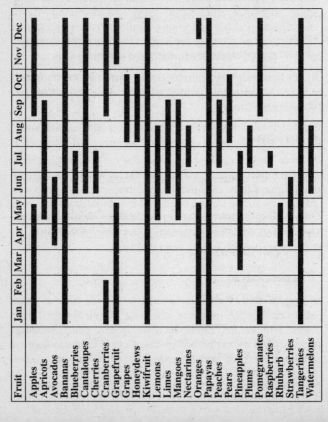

Watermelon Fruit Basket

To prepare watermelon basket, cut a thin slice from bottom of melon so it will sit flat, being careful not to cut through melon. With pencil and a 1½-inch wide cardboard guide, draw scallop design about one third of the way down from the top of the melon. On top half, mark handle. With sharp paring knife, carefully cut out scallops and handle; remove top sections. Scoop melon into balls or wedges; leave shell 1-inch thick. Wrap melon in plastic wrap; refrigerate until ready to serve. Fill with about 16 to 24 cups prepared fresh fruit just before serving. **48 servings.**

TIPS: Vary the fruit shapes and colors for an attractive salad. Include balls, spears, cubes and triangles.

To get the most out of melons, cut chunks or cubes rather than melon balls. Use grapes, cherries and strawberries for round shapes.

Blueberries and raspberries are best used as a garnish since they are fragile and easily bruised when tossed with other fruits.

Orange juice concentrate can be drizzled over or mixed lightly with fruit.

Fruit such as bananas, apples and peaches should be sprinkled with orange or lemon juice to prevent discoloration.

Fresh Fruit Quantities:

18½ lb. watermelon	=	16 cups
4 lb. pineapple	=	5 cups
3 lb. honeydew or cantaloupe	=	4 cups
1 pint strawberries, blueberries or raspberries	=	2 cups
1 lb. green grapes	=	2 cups
1 lb. red grapes	=	3 cups

NUTRIENTS: Variables in this recipe make it impossible to calculate nutrition information.

Waldorf Salad

¼ cup chopped nuts
¼ cup chopped dates or raisins
2 tablespoons sugar
4 medium apples, cored, cubed
1 stalk celery, chopped
⅔ cup mayonnaise or salad dressing*
1 teaspoon lemon juice

In large bowl, combine all ingredients; mix well. Cover and refrigerate. **6 servings.**

TIP: *Dairy sour cream or yogurt can be substituted for part of the mayonnaise.

NUTRIENTS PER ⅙ OF RECIPE

Calories	320	Dietary Fiber	3 g
Protein	1 g	Sodium	150 mg
Carbohydrate	24 g	Potassium	200 mg
Fat	24 g	Calcium	<2% U.S. RDA
Cholesterol	15 mg	Iron	2% U.S. RDA

Fruit 'n Yogurt Salad

20-oz. can pineapple chunks, drained, reserving liquid
11-oz. can mandarin orange segments, drained, reserving liquid
2 tablespoons cornstarch
8-oz. carton plain yogurt
1 tablespoon sugar
1 teaspoon vanilla or almond extract
1 cup seedless green grapes, halved
1 banana, sliced
1 apple, cored, sliced

In small saucepan, combine pineapple liquid and mandarin orange liquid with cornstarch; mix well. Cook over medium heat, stirring constantly, until thickened. Cool slightly. In large bowl, combine yogurt, sugar and vanilla; mix well. Stir in cooled mixture. Stir in pineapple, mandarin orange segments, grapes, banana and apple slices. Spoon into serving bowl. Cover; refrigerate about 4 hours or until completely chilled. **12 servings.**

NUTRIENTS PER ½ OF RECIPE

Calories	90	Dietary Fiber	1 g
Protein	2 g	Sodium	15 mg
Carbohydrate	20 g	Potassium	220 mg
Fat	1 g	Calcium	4% U.S. RDA
Cholesterol	0 mg	Iron	<2% U.S. RDA

Nectarine Salad Bowl

    4   medium nectarines, sliced (2 cups)
    ¼   cup sugar
    ½   teaspoon ginger
    1   teaspoon lemon juice
3-oz.   pkg. cream cheese, softened
    1   small head lettuce
    2   cups fresh raspberries or halved strawberries
    ½   cup seedless green grapes or blueberries

In medium bowl, combine nectarines, sugar, ginger and lemon juice; toss gently. Cover; refrigerate 1 hour. Drain nectarines, reserving liquid.

In small bowl, blend cream cheese and reserved liquid. To serve, line serving bowl with outer lettuce leaves; shred remaining lettuce and place in bowl. Arrange nectarines, raspberries and grapes on shredded lettuce. Serve with cream cheese dressing. **8 servings.**

NUTRIENTS PER ⅛ OF RECIPE

Calories 100	Dietary Fiber...........................4 g
Protein.....................................2 g	Sodium..............................35 mg
Carbohydrate........................16 g	Potassium.......................200 mg
Fat ....4 g	Calcium................4% U.S. RDA
Cholesterol.........................10 mg	Iron.......................4% U.S. RDA

Marinated Melon Melange

½ cup honey
¼ cup water
¼ cup lime juice
¼ cup light rum
1 cup watermelon balls or cubes
1 cup cantaloupe balls or cubes
1 cup honeydew balls or cubes
2 nectarines or peaches, sliced

In small saucepan, combine honey and water. Bring to a boil; reduce heat and simmer 5 minutes. Stir in lime juice and rum; cool.

In large bowl, combine watermelon, cantaloupe and honeydew. Pour cooled marinade over fruit. Cover; refrigerate 1 to 2 hours. Just before serving, add nectarines. **8 servings.**

NUTRIENTS PER ⅛ OF RECIPE

Calories 130	Dietary Fiber...........................1 g
Protein.....................................1 g	Sodium..............................10 mg
Carbohydrate........................30 g	Potassium.......................265 mg
Fat ....0 g	Calcium...............<2% U.S. RDA
Cholesterol...........................0 mg	Iron.......................2% U.S. RDA

Whipped Cream Fruit Salad

17-oz. can fruit cocktail, drained
1½ cups miniature marshmallows
¼ cup maraschino cherries, halved

2 medium bananas, sliced
1 medium apple, coarsely chopped
1½ cups whipped topping or sweetened whipped
    cream
    Lettuce leaves

In large bowl, combine all ingredients except whipped topping and lettuce, mixing lightly. Gently fold in whipped topping. Cover; refrigerate until served. Spoon salad onto lettuce-lined plates; garnish with additional maraschino cherries, if desired. **10 servings.**

NUTRIENTS PER ¹⁄₁₀ OF RECIPE

Calories	130	Dietary Fiber	1 g
Protein	1 g	Sodium	10 mg
Carbohydrate	19 g	Potassium	195 mg
Fat	7 g	Calcium	2% U.S. RDA
Cholesterol	0 mg	Iron	2% U.S. RDA

Lemony Fruit Salad

3¼-oz. pkg. lemon pudding and pie filling mix (not instant)
  ½ cup sugar
  ¼ cup water
  2 egg yolks
  2 cups water
  1 cup whipping cream, whipped
29-oz. can sliced peaches, drained
20-oz. can pineapple chunks, drained
11-oz. can mandarin orange segments, drained
16-oz. can sliced pears, drained

In medium saucepan, combine pudding mix, sugar and ¼ cup water. Stir in egg yolks. Add 2 cups water; mix well. Cook over medium heat, until mixture comes to a full boil, stirring constantly. Pour into large bowl; cool completely.

Fold in whipped cream. Gently fold in drained fruits. Cover; refrigerate several hours or overnight. **20 servings.**

NUTRIENTS PER ½₀ OF RECIPE

Calories 120	Dietary Fiber............................1 g
Protein......................................1 g	Sodium...................................25 mg
Carbohydrate.........................19 g	Potassium.........................145 mg
Fat ....5 g	Calcium.................2% U.S. RDA
Cholesterol.........................45 mg	Iron........................2% U.S. RDA

Molded Salads

Prized for their make-ahead convenience and spectacular appearance, molded salads range from vegetable-sparked aspics to shimmering fruit-flavored gelatins.

Molds

• Molds for salads can be as simple as an ordinary loaf pan or more decorative in individual or larger sizes. Whatever the shape, the mold should be the correct size for the recipe amount to retain an attractive shape. The size of any mold can be determined by filling it with water and measuring this amount.

• Molds of thin metal are easiest to unmold and brushing the interior lightly with oil before adding gelatin mixture facilitates unmolding.

• Unmolding must be done with care to keep gelatin firm. When ready to unmold, loosen the gelatin by running the tip of a pointed knife around edge of mold. If desired, moisten the surface of the serving plate to help position the gelatin in center of plate. Invert mold onto serving plate. Then apply a hot, moist towel for 1 minute to outside of the mold to loosen gelatin without overmelting it. Gently shake to release gelatin. Repeat hot, moist towel application, if necessary, until gelatin slides out easily.

Gelatins

• Gelatin can be either unflavored which is colorless and sugar-free, or flavored which is colored and can be purchased with or without sugar. Both types of gelatin must be thoroughly dissolved and combined with other ingredients according to recipe instructions for best results. Refrigerate at least 4 hours for a gelatin salad to set.

• To achieve evenly distributed additions of fruit or vegetables, refrigerate the clear gelatin mixture until it is the consistency of thick unbeaten egg whites and somewhat lumpy. Fresh, canned or frozen fruits and vegetables can be added to gelatins. However, *do not use uncooked* pineapple, figs, mangoes or papayas, as enzymes in these fruits prevent gelatin from becoming firm.

• To layer gelatin flavors for spectacular color effect, it is important to refrigerate the first layer only until set, but not firm, so layers will not slip apart when unmolded. The gelatin mixture for the second layer should be refrigerated until slightly thickened to prevent melting the first layer when added.

Jeweled Cranberry Shimmer

3½ cups cranberry juice cocktail
6-oz. pkg. lemon flavor gelatin
1 cup sliced, peeled peaches or nectarines
½ cup blueberries
½ cup seedless green grapes or pitted sweet cherries, cut in half
¼ cup slivered almonds

In small saucepan, bring 1½ cups of the cranberry juice cocktail to a boil. In large bowl, dissolve gelatin in hot cranberry juice; stir in remaining 2 cups cranberry juice. Refrigerate until thickened but not set, about 1 hour.

Lightly oil 6-cup mold. Stir fruits and almonds into thickened gelatin. Pour into prepared mold. Refrigerate about 4 hours or until firm. To serve, unmold onto serving plate. **8 to 10 servings.**

TIP: Frozen or canned fruit can be substituted for fresh fruit. No need to thaw frozen fruit; gelatin will set up in less time than stated above. Drain canned fruit well.

NUTRIENTS PER ⅒ OF RECIPE

Calories	160	Dietary Fiber	1 g
Protein	2 g	Sodium	60 mg
Carbohydrate	33 g	Potassium	135 mg
Fat	2 g	Calcium	<2% U.S. RDA
Cholesterol	0 mg	Iron	2% U.S. RDA

Ribbon Raspberry Salad

   2 (3-oz.) pkg. raspberry flavor gelatin
1½ cups boiling water
10-oz. pkg. frozen raspberries
   2 (8-oz.) cans crushed pineapple, undrained
   1 banana, sliced
   1 cup dairy sour cream

In large bowl, dissolve gelatin in boiling water. Add frozen raspberries; stir until thawed. Stir in pineapple and banana. Pour about ½ of gelatin mixture (2½ cups) into 8-inch square pan; refrigerate 30 minutes or until set. Carefully spread sour cream over gelatin; spoon remaining gelatin mixture over sour cream. Refrigerate at least 2 hours or until firm. **9 servings.**

NUTRIENTS PER ⅑ OF RECIPE

Calories	200	Dietary Fiber	2 g
Protein	3 g	Sodium	75 mg
Carbohydrate	37 g	Potassium	230 mg
Fat	6 g	Calcium	4% U.S. RDA
Cholesterol	10 mg	Iron	2% U.S. RDA

Gazpacho Guacamole Salad

SALAD

    2 envelopes unflavored gelatin
  ½ cup cold water
  ¼ teaspoon salt
   2 cups tomato juice
   3 tablespoons lemon juice
     Dash hot pepper sauce
   1 cup chopped seeded cucumber
   1 cup chopped tomato
  ½ cup chopped green pepper
  ¼ cup thinly sliced green onions

DRESSING

    1 cup mashed, peeled avocado
1 to 2 teaspoons thinly sliced green onions
   ¼ teaspoon salt
    2 tablespoons lemon juice
 3-oz. pkg. cream cheese, softened

In medium saucepan, soften gelatin in cold water; stir over low heat until dissolved. Remove from heat. Stir in salt, tomato juice, lemon juice and hot pepper sauce. Refrigerate until thickened but not set, about 20 to 30 minutes.

Lightly oil 5-cup mold or individual molds. Stir cucumber, tomato, green pepper and ¼ cup onions into thickened gelatin. Pour into prepared mold. Refrigerate about 4 hours or until firm. Meanwhile, in small bowl combine all dressing ingredients. Mix well. Cover; refrigerate at least 30 minutes to blend flavors. To serve, unmold salad onto serving plate; serve with dressing. **8 servings and 1 cup dressing.**

TIP: To prepare dressing in food processor or blender, cut avocado in large pieces and process until smooth. Add remaining ingredients; process just until blended.

NUTRIENTS PER ⅛ OF RECIPE

Calories 120	Dietary Fiber............................2 g
Protein.......................................4 g	Sodium..................................290 mg
Carbohydrate.............................8 g	Potassium...........................420 mg
Fat ....8 g	Calcium................2% U.S. RDA
Cholesterol..........................10 mg	Iron........................6% U.S. RDA

Cherry Burgundy Salad

In large bowl, dissolve 6-oz. pkg. cherry flavor gelatin in 1¼ cups boiling water; stir in ¾ cup red Burgundy wine or water. Refrigerate until slightly thickened but not set, about 50 minutes. Stir in 21-oz. can cherry fruit pie filling. Pour into 5-cup mold or individual molds. Refrigerate at least 3 hours or until firm. Unmold onto lettuce-lined serving plate. **9 to 12 servings.**

NUTRIENTS PER 1/12 OF RECIPE

Calories 150	Dietary Fiber.........................<1 g
Protein.......................................2 g	Sodium....................................45 mg
Carbohydrate...........................35 g	Potassium.............................50 mg
Fat ....0 g	Calcium...............<2% U.S. RDA
Cholesterol............................0 mg	Iron ....<2% U.S. RDA

Creamy Coconut Mold

1½	cups cold water
2	envelopes unflavored gelatin
24-oz.	carton (3 cups) cottage cheese
14-oz.	can sweetened condensed milk (not evaporated)
3-oz.	pkg. cream cheese, softened, cut into small pieces
1	cup coconut
1	cup chopped nuts
½	teaspoon almond extract
3	cups fresh fruit, cut into bite-size pieces

Lightly oil 1½-quart mold. In small saucepan, sprinkle gelatin over water to soften; stir over low heat until gelatin dissolves. Set aside. In large bowl, combine cottage cheese, sweetened condensed milk, cream cheese, coconut, nuts and extract; mix well. Stir in gelatin. Refrigerate until slightly thickened, about 10 minutes. Stir; pour mixture into mold. Refrigerate 3 hours or until firm. To release from mold, run knife around edges; turn onto serving plate. Serve with fruit. Garnish as desired. **12 servings.**

NUTRIENTS PER ½₂ OF RECIPE WITHOUT FRUIT

Calories	330	Dietary Fiber	1 g
Protein	14 g	Sodium	310 mg
Carbohydrate	31 g	Potassium	290 mg
Fat	17 g	Calcium	15% U.S. RDA
Cholesterol	30 mg	Iron	4% U.S. RDA

Frosty Fruit Salad

2	cups sugar
⅛	teaspoon salt
1	quart (4 cups) buttermilk
1	teaspoon vanilla
20-oz.	can crushed pineapple, drained
17-oz.	can fruit cocktail, drained

In large bowl, combine sugar, salt, buttermilk and vanilla until well mixed. Gently stir in drained fruits. Pour into 9-inch square pan. Freeze until firm. **9 to 12 servings.**

NUTRIENTS PER ½₂ OF RECIPE

Calories	200	Dietary Fiber	<1 g
Protein	3 g	Sodium	110 mg
Carbohydrate	46 g	Potassium	180 mg
Fat	1 g	Calcium	10% U.S. RDA
Cholesterol	2 mg	Iron	<2% U.S. RDA

Creamy Cucumber Mousse

8-oz.	can crushed pineapple in its own juice, drained, reserving 3 tablespoons liquid
2	envelopes unflavored gelatin
¾	cup water
¾	teaspoon salt
⅔	cup salad dressing or mayonnaise
1½	cups shredded cucumber
1	tablespoon finely chopped onion
2 to 3	drops hot pepper sauce
1	cup whipping cream, whipped

In small saucepan, soften gelatin in 3 tablespoons reserved pineapple liquid and water; stir over low heat until dissolved. Cool. In medium bowl, stir cooled gelatin and salt into salad dressing; refrigerate until slightly thickened but not set. Fold in cucumber, onion, hot pepper sauce and whipped cream. Pour into 6-cup decorative mold. Refrigerate until firm. To serve, unmold onto serving plate. **10 servings.**

NUTRIENTS PER ⅒ OF RECIPE

Calories	180	Dietary Fiber	<1 g
Protein	2 g	Sodium	205 mg
Carbohydrate	8 g	Potassium	70 mg
Fat	16 g	Calcium	2% U.S. RDA
Cholesterol	35 mg	Iron	<2% U.S. RDA

Orange Almond Salad

6-oz.	can frozen orange juice concentrate, thawed
⅔	cup water
3-oz.	pkg. orange flavor gelatin
⅔	cup lemon-lime flavored carbonated beverage, chilled
11-oz.	can mandarin orange segments, drained
½	cup slivered almonds
	Lettuce leaves

In large saucepan, heat orange juice concentrate and water to boiling; stir in gelatin until dissolved. Slowly add carbonated beverage; refrigerate until thickened but not set. Fold in mandarin orange segments and almonds. Pour into 4-cup mold. Refrigerate until firm. Unmold onto lettuce-lined serving plate. **8 servings.**

NUTRIENTS PER ⅛ OF RECIPE

Calories 150	Dietary Fiber ....1 g
Protein......................................3 g	Sodium..............................35 mg
Carbohydrate.........................26 g	Potassium.........................300 mg
Fat ....4 g	Calcium.................2% U.S. RDA
Cholesterol ....0 mg	Iron.......................2% U.S. RDA

Main Dish Salads

Particularly when weather is warm or anytime a light meal is desired, main dish salads offer a substantial, satisfying solution. And what an attractive way to utilize small amounts of leftover meats, poultry, seafood, cheese and hard-cooked egg. For make-ahead preparation, slice, dice or cube ingredients, wrap them separately and securely to retain moisture and flavor, and refrigerate. At serving time, arrange with greens and other ingredients for a chef's salad or combine with cooked, cooled rice or pasta and dressing. A colorful complementary garnish gives the salad its final festive touch.

Cobb Salad

1 cooked whole chicken breast, skinned, boned, cubed (about 1½ cups)
2 eggs, hard-cooked, coarsely chopped
6 slices bacon, crisply cooked, crumbled
4 cups salad greens, torn into bite-size pieces
1 large tomato, peeled, chopped
3 to 4 green onions, sliced (about ¼ cup)

  1 avocado, peeled, cubed, tossed in lemon juice
  4 oz. (1 cup) crumbled blue cheese
½ to 1 cup prepared Thousand Island dressing

To serve, arrange all ingredients except dressing in rows on large serving platter or in a 13x9-inch plastic cake pan with cover. Or, arrange each serving on an individual lettuce-lined serving plate. Spoon dressing over salad or pass dressing to be spooned over individual servings. **4 to 6 servings.**

NUTRIENTS PER ¼ OF RECIPE

Calories	420	Dietary Fiber	2 g
Protein	21 g	Sodium	680 mg
Carbohydrate	13 g	Potassium	670 mg
Fat	32 g	Calcium	15% U.S. RDA
Cholesterol	150 mg	Iron	15% U.S. RDA

Hot Chicken Fillet Salad

SWEET 'N SOUR DRESSING

  ½ cup oil
  ¼ cup cider vinegar
  ⅓ cup sugar
  ½ teaspoon dry mustard
  ¼ teaspoon salt

SALAD

  2 whole chicken breasts, skinned, boned, halved
  3 tablespoons flour
  ½ teaspoon salt
  ⅛ teaspoon pepper
  ¼ cup margarine or butter
  2 cups torn lettuce
  2 cups torn red leaf lettuce
 16 cherry tomatoes, halved
  1 ripe avocado, cubed

In jar with tight-fitting lid, combine all dressing ingredients; shake well. Refrigerate at least 1 hour to blend flavors.

Place 1 chicken breast half, boned side up, between 2 pieces of plastic wrap. Pound breast with meat mallet until about ¼-inch thick; remove wrap. Repeat with remaining breasts. In shallow pan, combine flour, salt and pepper. Coat chicken with flour mixture. In large skillet, melt margarine. Saute chicken 10 to 12 minutes or until no longer pink, turning once. Cut crosswise into ½-inch slices; keep warm. Arrange lettuce on 4 individual salad plates; top with chicken slices, cherry tomato halves and avocado. Serve with dressing. **4 servings.**

TIP: A 10-oz. pkg. of frozen breaded chicken fillets can be substituted for chicken breasts. Prepare according to package directions.

NUTRIENTS PER ¼ OF RECIPE

Calories	690	Dietary Fiber	3 g
Protein	27 g	Sodium	610 mg
Carbohydrate	30 g	Potassium	790 mg
Fat	51 g	Calcium	6% U.S. RDA
Cholesterol	70 mg	Iron	10% U.S. RDA

Chicken Salad

3 cups cubed, cooked chicken
2 stalks celery, chopped
¼ teaspoon salt
½ cup mayonnaise or salad dressing
2 tablespoons lemon juice

In medium bowl, combine all ingredients; mix well. Cover; refrigerate. Serve plain or use to fill green pepper, avocado or pineapple halves, hollowed out tomatoes or lettuce cups. **4 servings.**

TIP: For variety, add 3 slices bacon, crisply cooked and crumbled, ½ cup cubed jellied cranberry sauce, ½ cup toasted, sliced almonds, 1 cup seedless red or green grapes or 11 oz. can mandarin oranges, drained. Add additional mayonnaise, if necessary.

NUTRIENTS PER ¼ OF RECIPE

Calories	380	Dietary Fiber	0 g
Protein	27 g	Sodium	370 mg
Carbohydrate	2 g	Potassium	290 mg
Fat	29 g	Calcium	2% U.S. RDA
Cholesterol	100 mg	Iron	8% U.S. RDA

Turkey and Swiss Marinated Salad

11	oz. (2½ cups) uncooked elbow macaroni
1½ to 2	cups cubed, cooked turkey
8	oz. (2 cups) julienne-cut Swiss cheese
1	cup thinly sliced carrots
½	cup sliced celery
½	cup diced green pepper
¼	cup sliced green onions
2-oz.	jar chopped pimiento, drained
1	cup prepared Italian dressing
	Salt and pepper, if desired
	Lettuce leaves

Cook macaroni to desired doneness as directed on package. Drain; rinse with cold water. In large bowl, combine cooked macaroni and remaining ingredients; toss gently. Cover; refrigerate to blend flavors. To serve, spoon into lettuce-lined serving bowl. **12 servings.**

NUTRIENTS PER 1/12 OF RECIPE

Calories	340	Dietary Fiber	1 g
Protein	15 g	Sodium	555 mg
Carbohydrate	23 g	Potassium	145 mg
Fat	21 g	Calcium	20% U.S. RDA
Cholesterol	40 mg	Iron	6% U.S. RDA

Smoked Turkey Jarlsberg Salad Supreme

SALAD

12 oz. (2½ cups) smoked turkey breast, cut into
    1x¼-inch strips
 4 oz. (1 cup) Jarlsberg or Swiss cheese, cut into
    1x¼-inch strips
 1 cup seedless red grapes, halved
¾ cup slivered almonds, toasted*

DRESSING

⅓ cup mayonnaise
⅓ cup sour cream
1 to 2 tablespoons milk
    Salt and pepper, if desired

In medium bowl, combine all salad ingredients. In small bowl, combine all dressing ingredients; blend well. Pour dressing over turkey mixture; gently combine. Refrigerate until serving time. **4 to 6 servings.**

TIP: *To toast almonds, spread on cookie sheet; bake at 375°F. for 5 to 10 minutes or until light golden brown, stirring occasionally. Or, spread in thin layer in microwave-safe pie pan; microwave on HIGH for 3 to 4 minutes or until light golden brown, stirring frequently.

NUTRIENTS PER ⅙ OF RECIPE

Calories	360	Dietary Fiber	2 g
Protein	22 g	Sodium	800 mg
Carbohydrate	9 g	Potassium	350 mg
Fat	26 g	Calcium	25% U.S. RDA
Cholesterol	50 mg	Iron	4% U.S. RDA

Fruit and Ham Chef Salad

DRESSING

    1   peach or nectarine, peeled, sliced
    3   tablespoons orange juice
    ½   cup whipping cream, whipped

SALAD

    3   cups salad greens, torn into bite-size pieces
    2   cups cubed, cooked ham
    2   medium peaches or nectarines, peeled, sliced
    1½   cups blueberries
    ½ to 1 cup chopped celery

Place 1 sliced peach and orange juice in blender container. Cover; blend until smooth. Fold in whipped cream; refrigerate. On serving platter or 4 individual plates, arrange salad greens. Arrange ham, peaches, blueberries and celery over greens. Serve with dressing. **4 servings.**

NUTRIENTS PER ¼ OF RECIPE

Calories	370	Dietary Fiber	4 g
Protein	14 g	Sodium	660 mg
Carbohydrate	19 g	Potassium	580 mg
Fat	27 g	Calcium	4% U.S. RDA
Cholesterol	80 mg	Iron	15% U.S. RDA

Chef's Salad

    1   garlic clove, if desired
    1   head lettuce, torn into bite-size pieces (3 cups)
    ½   cup sliced cucumbers
    ½   cup chopped celery
    1   carrot, shredded
    3 to 4 radishes, sliced
    ¼   cup sliced green onions
    1   cup julienne-cut, cooked chicken or turkey
    1   cup julienne-cut, cooked ham

4 oz. (1 cup) julienne-cut Swiss or Cheddar cheese
3 eggs, hard-cooked, sliced
2 tomatoes, cut into wedges
½ cup croutons

Rub large salad bowl with cut garlic clove; discard garlic. Add lettuce, cucumbers, celery, carrot, radishes and onions; toss lightly. Arrange chicken, ham and cheese over lettuce. Top with eggs, tomatoes and croutons. Serve with an assortment of dressings. **6 servings.**

NUTRIENTS PER ¼ OF RECIPE

Calories 220	Dietary Fiber ....2 g
Protein ....22 g	Sodium ....450 mg
Carbohydrate ....8 g	Potassium ....480 mg
Fat ....11 g	Calcium ....25% U.S. RDA
Cholesterol ....180 mg	Iron ....10% U.S. RDA

Cheese and Pepper Salad

SALAD

8 oz. Monterey jack cheese, cut into thin strips
1 cup cubed, cooked ham
14-oz. can artichoke hearts, drained, cut in half
½ cup chopped red bell pepper
½ cup chopped green pepper
Lettuce leaves

DRESSING

½ cup oil
2 tablespoons red wine vinegar
1 tablespoon lemon juice
1 teaspoon chopped fresh parsley
½ teaspoon basil leaves
⅛ to ¼ teaspoon crushed red pepper

In medium bowl, combine cheese strips, ham, artichoke hearts and peppers; toss well.

In small bowl, combine all dressing ingredients. Pour dressing over salad mixture; toss until well coated. Refrigerate several hours to blend flavors. Spoon salad onto lettuce-lined individual salad plates. **4 servings.**

NUTRIENTS PER ¼ OF RECIPE

Calories	550	Dietary Fiber	1 g
Protein	23 g	Sodium	830 mg
Carbohydrate	11 g	Potassium	220 mg
Fat	46 g	Calcium	<2% U.S. RDA
Cholesterol	70 mg	Iron	8% U.S. RDA

Taco Salad

    1   lb. ground beef
    1   medium onion, chopped
1¼-oz. pkg. taco seasoning mix*
    ½   cup hot water
    ½   head lettuce, torn into bite-size pieces
 6-oz. pkg. corn chips
    3   oz. (¾ cup) shredded Cheddar or American cheese
    2   medium tomatoes, cut into wedges
    ⅓   cup chili sauce
    ¼   teaspoon hot pepper sauce

In large skillet, brown ground beef and onion; drain. Stir in dry taco seasoning mix and hot water; simmer 10 minutes over low heat, stirring occasionally. Line separate salad bowls or plates with lettuce; sprinkle with corn chips. Spoon about ½ cup beef mixture in center; sprinkle with cheese. Garnish with tomatoes. Serve immediately with combination of chili sauce and hot pepper sauce or with prepared French or Russian dressing. **4 to 6 servings.**

TIP: *To substitute for taco seasoning mix, add ½ cup chili sauce, 1 teaspoon salt, 1 teaspoon chili powder and ¼ teaspoon hot pepper sauce when adding hot water to beef-onion mixture.

NUTRIENTS PER ⅙ OF RECIPE

Calories 400	Dietary Fiber...........................3 g
Protein.....................................20 g	Sodium..............................620 mg
Carbohydrate.........................24 g	Potassium..........................420 mg
Fat ....25 g	Calcium...............25% U.S. RDA
Cholesterol........................70 mg	Iron......................20% U.S. RDA

Pepper Steak Salad

DRESSING

   ¼ cup oil
   ¼ cup red wine vinegar
   2 tablespoons Dijon mustard
   1 teaspoon soy sauce
   ½ teaspoon ginger
   ¼ teaspoon pepper
   1 garlic clove, minced, or ¼ teaspoon instant minced garlic

SALAD

   8 oz. cooked roast beef, cut into strips or chunks (about 1½ cups)
   1 cup cherry tomatoes, halved
   1 cup sliced fresh mushrooms
   ½ large green pepper, cut into julienne strips
   ½ cup sliced celery
   2 cups shredded Chinese or regular cabbage
   1 cup fresh bean sprouts, rinsed and drained

In small bowl or jar with tight-fitting lid, combine all dressing ingredients; blend well. In large bowl, combine all salad ingredients except cabbage and bean sprouts. Pour dressing over mixture; toss gently to coat. Cover; refrigerate 2 to 3 hours or until serving time. Just before serving, add cabbage and bean sprouts; toss. Serve immediately. **4 servings.**

NUTRIENTS PER ¼ OF RECIPE

Calories	280	Dietary Fiber	3 g
Protein	19 g	Sodium	260 mg
Carbohydrate	9 g	Potassium	580 mg
Fat	19 g	Calcium	4% U.S. RDA
Cholesterol	45 mg	Iron	20% U.S. RDA

Seafood Salad

1½ to 2 cups cooked or canned seafood*
¼ teaspoon salt
1 stalk celery, finely chopped
½ cup mayonnaise or salad dressing
1 tablespoon lemon juice

In medium bowl, combine all ingredients; mix well. Cover; refrigerate. Serve plain or use to fill green pepper, avocado or pineapple halves, hollowed out tomatoes or lettuce cups. **3 to 4 servings.**

TIPS: *Two cans (6½ oz. each) tuna, drained, flaked; 2 cans (7½ oz. each) crab or lobster meat, drained, flaked; 12-oz. package frozen shrimp, cooked, drained; 2 cans (4½ oz. each) shrimp, drained, chopped into pieces; or 16-oz. can salmon, drained and flaked can be used.

If desired, add 1 cup cooked rice or macaroni, shoestring potatoes or chow mein noodles for a heartier salad. Add additional mayonnaise, if necessary.

VARIATIONS:

Vegetable additions:
½ to 1 cup cooked vegetables such as mushrooms, peas, asparagus or beans
1 small cubed, peeled cucumber
2 tablespoons chopped green pepper
¼ cup sliced olives or pimiento
1 tablespoon chopped fresh parsley
1 tablespoon chopped chives

Protein additions:

    2 hard-cooked eggs, chopped
$\frac{1}{3}$ to $\frac{1}{2}$ cup cubed or shredded cheese
   $\frac{1}{2}$ cup chopped nuts

Fruit additions:

$\frac{1}{2}$ to 1 cup chopped fresh or drained canned fruit, such as pineapple, mandarin orange segments or avocado

Seasoning additions:

$\frac{1}{4}$ to $\frac{1}{2}$ teaspoon curry powder
   $\frac{1}{4}$ cup pickle relish
   2 tablespoons chopped chutney

NUTRIENTS PER ¼ OF RECIPE MADE WITH TUNA

Calories	320	Dietary Fiber	0 g
Protein	26 g	Sodium	330 mg
Carbohydrate	1 g	Potassium	290 mg
Fat	23 g	Calcium	2% U.S. RDA
Cholesterol	70 mg	Iron	8% U.S. RDA

Crab Louis

   2 (6-oz.) pkg. frozen crab meat, thawed*
   1 stalk celery, thinly sliced ($\frac{1}{2}$ cup)
   2 tablespoons sliced green onions
  $\frac{1}{2}$ cup mayonnaise or salad dressing
   2 tablespoons chili sauce
  $\frac{1}{4}$ teaspoon salt
     Dash white pepper
  $\frac{1}{2}$ cup whipping cream, whipped
   2 avocados, halved
     Lettuce leaves

Drain crab meat thoroughly on paper towels. In large bowl, combine celery, onions, mayonnaise, chili sauce, salt and pepper; blend well. Stir in crab meat; fold in whipping cream. Spoon carefully into avocado halves; arrange on lettuce-lined plates. Garnish as desired. **4 servings.**

TIPS: *Two 6-oz. cans crab meat, drained and flaked, can be substituted for frozen crab.

To prepare ahead, follow directions above, omitting whipped cream; refrigerate. When ready to serve, fold in whipped cream and spoon into avocado halves as directed above.

NUTRIENTS PER ¼ OF RECIPE

Calories	570	Dietary Fiber	1 g
Protein	18 g	Sodium	600 mg
Carbohydrate	12 g	Potassium	850 mg
Fat	50 g	Calcium	8% U.S. RDA
Cholesterol	140 mg	Iron	10% U.S. RDA

Crunchy Tuna Broccoli Salad

    2 (6½-oz.) cans water-packed tuna, drained, flaked
    2 cups chopped fresh broccoli
    ¼ cup chopped onion
    ½ cup chopped celery
    8 oz. can sliced water chestnuts, drained
    8 oz. can bamboo shoots, drained
    1 cup mayonnaise
    1 tablespoon lemon juice
    1 teaspoon dill weed
    ⅛ teaspoon pepper

In large bowl, combine all ingredients; mix well. Refrigerate several hours to blend flavors. **6 servings.**

NUTRIENTS PER ⅙ OF RECIPE

Calories	390	Dietary Fiber	2 g
Protein	20 g	Sodium	260 mg
Carbohydrate	10 g	Potassium	460 mg
Fat	30 g	Calcium	4% U.S. RDA
Cholesterol	60 mg	Iron	10% U.S. RDA

Nicoise Salad

- 2 tablespoons chopped green onions
- 2 tablespoons chopped fresh parsley
- ½ teaspoon dill weed
- ¼ teaspoon garlic salt
- 1 pkg. Italian salad dressing mix
- ¾ cup oil
- ¼ cup red wine vinegar
- 4 medium potatoes, cooked, peeled, sliced
- 1 lb. (3 cups) cut green beans, cooked, drained
   Lettuce leaves
- 16-oz. can salmon, drained, flaked
- 2 tomatoes, peeled, cut into 8 wedges
- 3 eggs, hard-cooked, quartered
- ½ cup pitted ripe olives, quartered

In jar with tight-fitting lid, combine onions, parsley, dill weed, garlic salt, dressing mix, oil and vinegar. Cover; shake well. In medium bowl, pour ¼ cup dressing over potatoes; toss to coat. Cover; refrigerate at least 2 hours. In another bowl, pour ¼ cup dressing over green beans; toss to coat. Cover; refrigerate until chilled.

To serve, line large serving platter with lettuce leaves. Spoon potatoes onto center of plate. Arrange salmon over potatoes. Spoon green beans around potatoes. Alternately place tomato wedges and egg quarters over beans. Garnish with olives. Pour remaining dressing over salad. **10 servings.**

NUTRIENTS PER ⅒ OF RECIPE

Calories	290	Dietary Fiber	3 g
Protein	12 g	Sodium	600 mg
Carbohydrate	13 g	Potassium	445 mg
Fat	22 g	Calcium	10% U.S. RDA
Cholesterol	100 mg	Iron	8% U.S. RDA

Garden-Style Tuna Salad

11 oz. (2½ cups) uncooked spiral or elbow macaroni
½ cup prepared Italian dressing
2 cups thinly sliced cucumbers
1½ cups diced tomatoes
½ cup sliced green onions
⅓ cup chopped green pepper
⅓ cup diagonally sliced celery
¾ teaspoon salt
¼ teaspoon pepper
1 cup mayonnaise
1 tablespoon prepared mustard
1½ teaspoons dill weed
2 (6½-oz.) cans tuna, drained, flaked
Fresh dill, if desired

Cook macaroni to desired doneness as directed on package. Drain; rinse with hot water. In large bowl, combine hot macaroni and dressing; toss gently. In large salad bowl, combine cucumbers, tomatoes, onions, green pepper and celery; sprinkle with salt and pepper.

In medium bowl, combine mayonnaise, mustard and dill weed; mix well. Add to macaroni mixture. Gently stir tuna and macaroni mixture into vegetables. Cover; refrigerate at least 4 hours before serving. **12 servings.**

NUTRIENTS PER ¹⁄₁₂ OF RECIPE

Calories 360	Dietary Fiber ....1 g
Protein ....13 g	Sodium ....470 mg
Carbohydrate ....24 g	Potassium ....160 mg
Fat ....24 g	Calcium ....2% U.S. RDA
Cholesterol ....30 mg	Iron ....8% U.S. RDA

Salad Dressings

Some dressings are designed as a topping—some as a light, mix-in coating for greens, and others as a binder. All should be prepared with the freshest ingredients and applied at the proper time with a light touch so they enhance rather than mask salad ingredients. Today, polyunsaturated oils, an abundance of fresh herbs, delicately flavored vinegars and low-fat ingredients for mayonnaise and for creamy dressings offer more wholesome, flavorful alternatives than ever before. The choice is yours.

Preparation

• Often homemade dressings can be prepared ahead and refrigerated to blend. For serving, dressings can be combined with other ingredients or served on the side. To maintain crisp textures, dressings should not be added to greens until just before serving. Many marinated salads with vegetables, pasta or rice can be made in advance to allow time for flavors to develop and blend. Vegetables, pasta or rice will absorb more flavor if warm when combined with a dressing.

Oils

Oils should be purchased in small quantities to ensure freshness and should be stored away from heat and light. If refrigerated, oil may need to be brought to room temperature before combining with other ingredients.

• **Olive Oil** is often favored for salads for its distinctive flavor, fruity aroma and richness. The highest-quality, most expensive olive oils are labeled "extra virgin" or "virgin" and come from the first cold-pressing of olives. Italian and French olive oils are fruity or nutty in taste with a light, easily digested consistency. Oils from Greece and Spain are heavier, stronger in taste and less easily digested. Fine-quality oils should have no aftertaste.

• **Peanut Oil,** also called groundnut oil, is a popular alternative to olive oil because of its pale color and delicate flavor. Its blandness, however, may require additional amounts of seasonings and vinegar or lemon juice.

• **Corn Oil,** an all-purpose oil, is chosen by many because of its subtle flavor but rejected by others who prefer lighter, less bland oils.

• **Safflower Oil,** a light, deep-golden oil, is high in polyunsaturates and so ideal for persons on low-cholesterol diets.

• **Sunflower Oil,** also high in polyunsaturates, is thin in texture, light-colored and mild.

• **Walnut Oil,** golden in color, is expensive but prized for a full-bodied nutty flavor. Buy in small quantities because of its short shelf life. Store in a cool place.

• **Sesame Oil** is available as two types. One, made from toasted sesame seed, is heavy in texture and has a strong taste. Use it sparingly to flavor dressings. The other, made from the untoasted seed, is lighter in texture and color and is comparatively quite bland in flavor.

Vinegars

Vinegars in their prime have a bright, unclouded appearance and fresh taste and aroma. We have included recipes for making flavored vinegars, which can also be used in sauces, marinades, soups and stews.

• **White Wine Vinegar** has a delicate flavor and aroma and pale coloring. A popular choice for salad dressings.

• **Red Wine Vinegar,** pale to deeper red coloring, has full-bodied flavor and is another excellent choice for salad dressings.

• **Herb-Flavored Vinegars** can be purchased or made at home. Generally, these vinegars have a red or white vinegar base with such flavor variations as tarragon, basil, thyme, rosemary, garlic, allspice or cloves.

• **Fruit-Flavored Vinegars** have a marvelous flavor and aroma. The infusion process for these vinegars requires a good deal of fruit, making them more costly than most other types.

• **Sherry Vinegar,** made from sweet sherry, takes on a nut-like flavor when combined with lemon juice for salad dressings.

• **White Vinegar,** also called distilled vinegar, is a colorless variety often used for pickling and seasoning, particularly when a colored vinegar would alter the appearance. Considered to be rather sharp and strong, it is not preferred for most salad dressings.

• **Cider Vinegar,** from a base of hard apple cider, is sharp-flavored and golden-colored. Like white vinegar, it is best used in pickling. Although often used in dressings, its over-powering taste is considered by many to be undesirable.

• **Rice Vinegar,** sweet with a delicate flavor, is often used in Asian cooking.

Vinegar and Oil Dressing

In jar with tight-fitting lid or blender container, combine ¼ to ½ cup oil, ½ cup vinegar, ½ teaspoon salt, dash pepper and ½ teaspoon Worcestershire sauce. Shake well or blend until well mixed. Cover; refrigerate. Mix well before serving. **¾ to 1 cup.**

NUTRIENTS PER 1 TABLESPOON

Calories 60	Dietary Fiber............................0 g
Protein....................................0 g	Sodium................................70 mg
Carbohydrate............................0 g	Potassium.............................0 mg
Fat ....7 g	Calcium...............<2% U.S. RDA
Cholesterol............................0 mg	Iron ....<2% U.S. RDA

Yogurt Dressing

8-oz. carton (1 cup) plain yogurt or dairy sour cream
1 tablespoon sugar or honey
¼ teaspoon onion salt
1½ teaspoons prepared mustard
1 teaspoon lemon juice

In small bowl, combine all ingredients; blend well. Cover; refrigerate. **1 cup.**

VARIATIONS:

CHIVE YOGURT DRESSING: Add 2 tablespoons chopped chives. If desired, add 2 slices crumbled, crisply cooked bacon, or 1 tablespoon bacon-flavored bits.

CHUTNEY YOGURT DRESSING: Add ¼ cup chopped chutney and 1 teaspoon curry powder.

CURRY YOGURT DRESSING: Add 1 teaspoon curry powder.

HORSERADISH YOGURT DRESSING: Decrease sugar to 1 teaspoon and add 1 teaspoon prepared horseradish and ½ teaspoon Worcestershire sauce.

NUTRIENTS PER 1 TABLESPOON

Calories	12	
Protein	1 g	
Carbohydrate	2 g	
Fat	0 g	
Cholesterol	0 mg	
Dietary Fiber	0 g	
Sodium	40 mg	
Potassium	35 mg	
Calcium	2% U.S. RDA	
Iron	<2% U.S. RDA	

Tangy French Dressing

½ cup firmly packed brown sugar
½ teaspoon salt
1 garlic clove, minced
½ cup vinegar

        ½ cup catsup
        ½ cup chili sauce
 ¼ to ½ cup oil
        ¼ teaspoon Worcestershire sauce
        Dash hot pepper sauce

In blender container or jar with tight-fitting lid, combine all ingredients. Blend at medium speed or shake well until smooth. Cover; refrigerate. Mix well before serving. **2 to 2½ cups.**

NUTRIENTS PER 1 TABLESPOON

Calories	50	Dietary Fiber	0 g
Protein	0 g	Sodium	135 mg
Carbohydrate	6 g	Potassium	45 mg
Fat	3 g	Calcium	<2% U.S. RDA
Cholesterol	0 mg	Iron	<2% U.S. RDA

Basic French Dressing

        ¾ cup oil
        ¼ cup vinegar or lemon juice
        1 teaspoon paprika
        ½ teaspoon salt
        ½ teaspoon dry mustard
        Dash pepper

In jar with tight-fitting lid or blender container, combine all ingredients. Shake well or blend at medium speed until smooth. Cover; refrigerate. Mix well before serving. **1 cup.**

TIP: For use with fruit, add ¼ cup sugar or 2 tablespoons honey.

VARIATIONS:

GARLIC FRENCH DRESSING: Add 1 garlic clove, crushed; let dressing stand several hours.

MINT FRENCH DRESSING: Add 1 to 2 tablespoons crushed mint leaves and 2 tablespoons sugar. Serve over fruit.

NUTRIENTS PER 1 TABLESPOON

Calories	90	Dietary Fiber	0 g
Protein	0 g	Sodium	65 mg
Carbohydrate	0 g	Potassium	0 mg
Fat	10 g	Calcium	<2% U.S. RDA
Cholesterol	0 mg	Iron	<2% U.S. RDA

Mayonnaise

    1 egg yolk
    ½ teaspoon salt
    ½ teaspoon sugar
    ¼ teaspoon prepared or dry mustard
       Dash pepper or cayenne pepper
    2 tablespoons lemon juice or vinegar
    1 cup oil

In small bowl, combine egg yolk, salt, sugar, mustard, pepper and 1 tablespoon of the lemon juice; blend well. Add oil by teaspoonfuls, beating at medium speed until half the oil has been added. Add the remaining 1 tablespoon lemon juice; blend well. Add the remaining oil by tablespoonfuls, beating until all the oil has been added and the mayonnaise is thick and smooth. Cover; refrigerate. **1 cup.**

TIP: If mayonnaise separates, in small bowl, slowly add curdled mixture to 1 egg yolk, beating constantly until it thickens again.

VARIATION:

BLENDER OR FOOD PROCESSOR MAYONNAISE: Use *1 whole egg or 2 egg yolks.* In blender container or food processor bowl with metal blade, combine egg, salt, sugar, mustard, pepper, lemon juice and 2 tablespoons of the oil.

Cover; blend until smooth or process with 5 or 6 on/off turns. With machine running, gradually add remaining oil in a slow, steady stream until thick and smooth. Cover; refrigerate.

NUTRIENTS PER 1 TABLESPOON

Calories	130	Dietary Fiber	0 g
Protein	0 g	Sodium	65 mg
Carbohydrate	0 g	Potassium	0 mg
Fat	14 g	Calcium	<2% U.S. RDA
Cholesterol	15 mg	Iron	<2% U.S. RDA

Cooked Salad Dressing

 2 tablespoons flour
 2 tablespoons sugar
 1 teaspoon salt
 1 teaspoon dry or prepared mustard
 ¾ cup milk
 1 egg, slightly beaten
 3 tablespoons vinegar
 1 tablespoon margarine or butter

In small saucepan, combine flour, sugar, salt and mustard; mix well. Stir in milk and egg; mix until smooth. Cook over medium heat until mixture boils and thickens, stirring constantly. Blend in vinegar and margarine. Cool. **1 cup.**

VARIATIONS:

COOKED FRUIT DRESSING: Cool cooked dressing. Before adding to fruit, fold in 1 cup thawed whipped topping or ½ cup whipping cream, whipped and sweetened.

SOUR CREAM COOKED DRESSING: Cool cooked dressing. Fold in ½ cup dairy sour cream. Serve on meat, seafood, potato and other vegetable salads.

NUTRIENTS PER 1 TABLESPOON

Calories 25	Dietary Fiber ....0 g
Protein ....1 g	Sodium ....150 mg
Carbohydrate............................3 g	Potassium ....25 mg
Fat ....1 g	Calcium...............<2% U.S. RDA
Cholesterol ....20 mg	Iron ....<2% U.S. RDA

Creamy Cucumber Dressing

In small bowl, combine ½ cup mayonnaise, ½ cup dairy sour cream, ½ cup chopped cucumber, 2 green onions, sliced, and ¼ teaspoon onion salt; mix well. Cover; refrigerate. **1½ cups.**

NUTRIENTS PER 1 TABLESPOON

Calories 50	Dietary Fiber ....0 g
Protein ....0 g	Sodium ....45 mg
Carbohydrate............................1 g	Potassium ....15 mg
Fat ....5 g	Calcium...............<2% U.S. RDA
Cholesterol ....4 mg	Iron ....<2% U.S. RDA

Thousand Island Dressing

1 cup mayonnaise
1 egg, hard-cooked, chopped
¼ teaspoon paprika
2 tablespoons sweet pickle relish
1 teaspoon finely chopped onion
2 tablespoons chili sauce
½ teaspoon Worcestershire sauce
Dash hot pepper sauce

In blender container or small bowl, combine all ingredients. Blend until smooth. Cover; refrigerate overnight to blend flavors. **1⅓ cups.**

NUTRIENTS PER 1 TABLESPOON

Calories	80	Dietary Fiber	0 g
Protein	0 g	Sodium	95 mg
Carbohydrate	1 g	Potassium	15 mg
Fat	9 g	Calcium	<2% U.S. RDA
Cholesterol	20 mg	Iron	<2% U.S. RDA

Delicious Bacon Dressing

½ cup mayonnaise
2 tablespoons lemon juice
1 tablespoon honey
Dash salt
2 tablespoons finely chopped onion
4 slices bacon, crisply cooked, crumbled

In small bowl, combine mayonnaise, lemon juice, honey and salt; blend well. Stir in onion and bacon. Serve at room temperature with green salads. **¾ cup.**

NUTRIENTS PER 1 TABLESPOON

Calories	90	Dietary Fiber	0 g
Protein	1 g	Sodium	105 mg
Carbohydrate	2 g	Potassium	15 mg
Fat	9 g	Calcium	<2% U.S. RDA
Cholesterol	8 mg	Iron	<2% U.S. RDA

Sour Cream Dressing for Fruit

½ cup dairy sour cream
¼ cup honey
2 teaspoons lime juice
⅛ teaspoon ground cardamom or nutmeg

In small bowl, combine all ingredients; blend well. Cover; refrigerate to blend flavors. Serve with fruit salads. **¾ cup.**

NUTRIENTS PER 1 TABLESPOON

Calories 45	Dietary Fiber...........................0 g
Protein.....................................0 g	Sodium................................5 mg
Carbohydrate..........................6 g	Potassium..............................20 mg
Fat ....2 g	Calcium..............<2% U.S. RDA
Cholesterol..........................4 mg	Iron ....<2% U.S. RDA

Creamy Blue Cheese Dressing

  4 oz. (1 cup) crumbled blue cheese
  ¾ cup oil
  1 cup dairy sour cream
  1 teaspoon salt
  ½ teaspoon sugar
  ⅛ teaspoon pepper
  1 garlic clove, minced
  ¼ cup tarragon vinegar
  ½ teaspoon Worcestershire sauce

In small bowl, beat blue cheese at low speed. Gradually add ¼ cup of the oil; beat until smooth. Gradually add remaining oil, beating continuously. Add remaining ingredients; beat until well blended. Cover; refrigerate. **2⅓ cups.**

NUTRIENTS PER 1 TABLESPOON

Calories 70	Dietary Fiber...........................0 g
Protein.....................................1 g	Sodium..............................105 mg
Carbohydrate..........................1 g	Potassium..............................20 mg
Fat ....7 g	Calcium..............<2% U.S. RDA
Cholesterol..........................4 mg	Iron ....<2% U.S. RDA

Sour Cream-Buttermilk Dressing

  1 cup dairy sour cream
  1 cup buttermilk
  ¼ cup mayonnaise or salad dressing
  ¼ cup vinegar
  2 tablespoons sugar

1   teaspoon salt
½   teaspoon celery salt
¼   teaspoon pepper

In small bowl, combine all ingredients; beat well. Cover; refrigerate. **2½ cups.**

NUTRIENTS PER 1 TABLESPOON

Calories	30	Dietary Fiber	0 g
Protein	0 g	Sodium	90 mg
Carbohydrate	1 g	Potassium	20 mg
Fat	2 g	Calcium	<2% U.S. RDA
Cholesterol	2 mg	Iron	<2% U.S. RDA

Tarragon Vinegar

2   cups white vinegar
3   sprigs fresh tarragon, 4 to 5 inches long

In small stainless steel saucepan, heat vinegar to boiling. Meanwhile, place tarragon sprigs in clean pint jar. Carefully pour hot vinegar into jar. Cover; let stand several days at room temperature to blend flavors. Remove tarragon. Store in cool, dark place. **1 pint.**

MICROWAVE DIRECTIONS: Place tarragon in clean pint jar; add vinegar. Microwave on HIGH 2½ to 3 minutes or until vinegar reaches 140°F. to 150°F. (jar will be warm to the touch). Continue as directed above.

NUTRIENTS PER 1 TABLESPOON

Calories	2	Dietary Fiber	0 g
Protein	0 g	Sodium	0 mg
Carbohydrate	1 g	Potassium	0 mg
Fat	0 g	Calcium	<2% U.S. RDA
Cholesterol	0 mg	Iron	<2% U.S. RDA

Summer Harvest Relish

2 cups diced zucchini
2 cups julienne-cut carrots
1½ cups cauliflower florets
1½ cups diagonally sliced celery
1 cup diced green pepper
½ cup sliced onion, separated into rings
2 teaspoons fresh minced ginger
2 teaspoons salt
1 teaspoon dry mustard
1 cup vinegar
12-oz. jar apple jelly

In 4-quart saucepan or Dutch oven, combine all ingredients. Bring to a boil, stirring occasionally. Reduce heat; cover and cook until vegetables are crisp-tender, about 10 minutes. Pack in airtight containers; store in refrigerator several days to blend flavors. **6 cups.**

NUTRIENTS PER ¼ CUP

Calories	50	Dietary Fiber	<1 g
Protein	1 g	Sodium	200 mg
Carbohydrate	13 g	Potassium	135 mg
Fat	0 g	Calcium	<2% U.S. RDA
Cholesterol	0 mg	Iron	2% U.S. RDA

Cranberry-Orange Relish

Cut 1 small unpeeled orange into eighths. Place orange, 12-oz. pkg. (3 cups) fresh or frozen cranberries and 1¼ cups sugar in food processor bowl with metal blade; process until finely ground. Refrigerate several hours to blend flavors. Store in refrigerator. **3 cups.**

TIP: To prepare relish in blender, grind half of ingredients at a time.

NUTRIENTS PER 1 TABLESPOON

Calories 25	Dietary Fiber............................0 g
Protein......................................0 g	Sodium....................................0 mg
Carbohydrate............................6 g	Potassium.................................5 mg
Fat ....0 g	Calcium..............<2% U.S. RDA
Cholesterol.............................0 mg	Iron ....<2% U.S. RDA

Whole Cranberry Sauce

In large saucepan, combine 1½ cups sugar, 1½ cups water and 12-oz. pkg. (3 cups) fresh or frozen cranberries. Bring to a boil, stirring occasionally until sugar dissolves. Continue simmering until most of berries pop, about 5 minutes. Cover; refrigerate. **2 cups.**

NUTRIENTS PER ¼ CUP

Calories 170	Dietary Fiber............................2 g
Protein......................................0 g	Sodium....................................0 mg
Carbohydrate............................42 g	Potassium.................................25 mg
Fat ....0 g	Calcium..............<2% U.S. RDA
Cholesterol.............................0 mg	Iron ....<2% U.S. RDA

Spiced Beets

2 (16-oz.) cans sliced beets, drained, reserving liquid
1 cup sliced onions
⅔ cup sugar
⅔ cup vinegar
1 cinnamon stick
5 whole cloves

If necessary, add water to reserved beet liquid to measure ⅔ cup. In large saucepan, combine all ingredients. Bring to a boil. Reduce heat; simmer 10 minutes, stirring occasionally. Refrigerate. Before serving, drain; remove cinnamon stick and cloves. **8 servings.**

NUTRIENTS: Variables in this recipe make it impossible to calculate nutrition information.

Quick Pickles

    3 cups thinly sliced, unpeeled cucumbers
    1 medium onion, sliced
    1 small green pepper, cut into strips
    1 small red bell pepper, cut into strips
    1 teaspoon salt
    1 garlic clove, crushed
       Ice cubes
  ¾ cup sugar
    1 teaspoon mustard seed
  ¼ teaspoon celery seed
  ⅛ teaspoon turmeric
  ½ cup white vinegar

In large bowl, combine cucumbers, onion, peppers, salt and garlic. Cover with ice cubes and mix thoroughly. Let stand 3 hours. Using colander, drain well. In large saucepan, combine remaining ingredients; add drained vegetables, mixing well. Heat just to boiling, stirring occasionally. Pack into refrigerator containers. Cover; refrigerate 24 hours before serving. **4 cups.**

NUTRIENTS PER ¼ CUP

Calories 45	Dietary Fiber.........................<1 g
Protein.......................................0 g	Sodium.............................135 mg
Carbohydrate........................11 g	Potassium............................60 mg
Fat ....0 g	Calcium...............<2% U.S. RDA
Cholesterol...........................0 mg	Iron........................2% U.S. RDA

Soups & Stews

Soups & Stews

Soups

Soups range from clear broths and consommes to robust chowders and gumbos and may well be the most versatile of foods. They may be served piping hot or icy cold and are fitting as an appetizer, elegant first course, main course and even dessert in some areas where frosty fruit soups are a fashionable menu finale. Great soups don't have to come from hours of preparation either. Convenience products such as canned soups and broth and frozen vegetables can offer sensational shortcuts.

Low in calories, simple broths are a dieter's delight. Soups laden with milk or cream, vegetables, meats, poultry or fish provide stick-to-the-ribs satisfaction as well as a multitude of vitamins and minerals. Soups can be economically prepared with fresh ingredients that need not be costly. Some of the most flavorful and nutritious combinations feature meat and poultry trimmings, bones and less tender cuts, seasonal vegetables, pasta, rice, dumplings and common seasonings.

Types of Soup

• **Broth,** or stock, is the thin liquid remaining after simmering and straining ingredients such as vegetables, meat or poultry. Broths can be time-consuming because long, slow simmering is required to achieve flavorful results, but they need little attention. Often used as a base for sauces, soups and gravies, homemade broth can be refrigerated several days or frozen.

• **Consommes** are broths made from beef, veal or poultry that have been clarified to make them clear.

• **Cream soups** are made with milk and/or cream and often thickened with flour.

• **Bisques** are rich creamed or pureed soups usually featuring additions of fish, vegetables and/or game.

• **Bouillabaisse** features several types of fish and shellfish seasoned with saffron.

• **Chowders** originally seafood-based, are now made as well with corn, potatoes, other vegetables and meats. Most often made with milk or cream, they are thick and hearty.

• **Cioppino** or fisherman's stew, contains various kinds of seafood.

• **Gumbos** are traditionally prepared with a variety of meats, seafoods and vegetables, particularly okra, a vegetable with a distinct flavor and thickening quality.

Equipment

For soup making, a large, high-quality stockpot is useful. The tall, narrow dimensions allow the liquid to bubble up through the ingredients for optimum flavor. A 5-quart Dutch oven can also be used. For stews, a Dutch oven or large casserole equipped with a tight-fitting lid is a practical investment.

A food processor is a valuable time-saver for tasks like slicing, chopping, pureeing and blending. Cheesecloth is helpful for straining broth, and smaller utensils like whisks of varying sizes, a slotted spoon, ladle, skimmer and sharp, high-quality cutlery add to speed and convenience.

Soup Making Hints

• For optimum flavor, select ingredients at their peak of freshness.

• For vegetable soups and stews, cut vegetables into similar-sized pieces for even cooking and attractive presentation.

• Add ingredients in order specified in recipe to avoid overcooking or curdling.

• Follow stirring and cooking instructions. Slow simmering extracts maximum flavor from ingredients and should not be rushed. Low heat and frequent stirring is essential for milk, cream, cheese, egg, seafood and other delicate ingredients; they should not be brought to a boil.

• For thickening, blend flour mixtures thoroughly to prevent lumping.

• You may prefer adding salt to taste after cooking.

• Many soups and stews are excellent make-aheads, which allows flavors a chance to blend.

• Serve soups and stews at the proper serving temperature. Cold soups should be thoroughly chilled, and on warm days are best served in chilled containers. Hot soups and stews are not at their best when served lukewarm.

Storing Soups and Stews

• Refrigerate immediately for quick and thorough cooling to avoid spoilage.

• For short-term storage of 3 days or less, refrigerate in plastic or glass containers with airtight lids.

• For long-term storage, freeze in single-serving or family-sized freezer containers allowing $1\frac{1}{2}$ inches of space at the top of each container. Label containers, freeze promptly and plan to use within 4 months. Soups and stews made with beans, vegetables or meats retain flavor and texture well when frozen and reheated. It is best to add thickening during reheating for soups and stews thickened with flour or egg. Recipes featuring eggs, cheese, and seafood are not recommended for freezing.

• To thaw frozen soups and stews, place container in refrigerator overnight or use microwave on defrost setting.

• When reheating, slowly heat only the amount to be served. The microwave is useful for reheating.

Keys to Successful Broth

• No need to peel or trim vegetables; wash thoroughly and cut into medium-sized pieces.

• Place ingredients in cold water to obtain optimum flavor from meats and vegetables as they cook.

• Simmer rather than boil mixture; bubbles should form slowly and burst before reaching the surface.

• Partially cover stockpot or Dutch oven with lid during cooking to help maintain proper simmering temperature, retain vitamins and prevent a cloudy appearance.

• Periodically remove yellowish scum which rises to the surface during the first 15 to 30 minutes of cooking. When it becomes white in color, no further skimming is required.

• Avoid overseasoning broths, especially with salt, as many flavors sharpen with storage.

• To strain broth when cooking is completed, ladle hot liquid into strainer or cloth-lined colander. Use cheesecloth or clean dishcloth; do not use terry-cloth fabric.

• Strained broth will still contain small particles which will make it appear cloudy. For crystal-clear broth, strained broth can be clarified. To clarify, combine ¼ cup water with 1 egg white and 1 eggshell, crushed. Stir into hot strained broth. Bring to a boil. Remove from heat and let stand 5 minutes. Strain broth through cheesecloth again. Discard egg.

• Ladle strained, hot broth into storage containers and refrigerate uncovered for fastest-possible cooling.

• Solidified fat can be lifted from top of broth after thorough cooling. However, since fat acts to seal in flavor, you may choose to do this step just prior to use.

• To store cooled broth, cover storage containers tightly. Refrigerate up to two days or freeze in convenient-sized quantities up to six months. For small quantities, freeze in ice-cube trays; when frozen, place cubes in freezer bags. (Ten cubes equal about 1 cup.)

Beef Broth

2	lb. meaty beef bones, such as shank, cut into 3-inch pieces, or short ribs
2	lb. beef bones, such as knuckle, cracked
1	cup cut-up carrots
2	celery stalks with leaves, cut into 2-inch pieces
2	small onions, quartered
10	cups water
8-oz.	can (1 cup) tomatoes, undrained, cut up
1½	teaspoons salt
½	teaspoon thyme leaves
5	peppercorns
2	fresh parsley sprigs
1	garlic clove, pressed
1	bay leaf
¾	teaspoon salt

Heat oven to 450°F. Place all bones in large roasting pan. Bake uncovered for 30 minutes. Add carrots, celery and onions. Bake, turning bones and vegetables occasionally, an additional 45 to 60 minutes or until bones are very deep brown (not charred).

Transfer ingredients from roasting pan to 8-quart saucepot or two 5-quart Dutch ovens. Discard fat in roasting pan. Add 2 cups of the water to roasting pan; heat and scrape to loosen any browned meat drippings. Pour hot liquid and remaining water over bones and vegetables in saucepot. Bring to a boil. Reduce heat; simmer partially covered 30 minutes. Skim off any scum that rises to surface. Add remaining ingredients except ¾ teaspoon salt; simmer partially covered an additional 5 hours. Remove bones; strain broth.* Stir in ¾ teaspoon salt. Cool uncovered in refrigerator. Cover and store in refrigerator or freezer. Skim fat from broth before using in recipe. **7 cups.**

TIP: *Remove meat from bones; refrigerate or freeze for later use.

NUTRIENTS: Variables in this recipe make it impossible to calculate nutrition information.

Hamburger Vegetable Soup

- 1½ lb. ground beef
- 6 cups water
- 3 beef-flavor bouillon cubes or 3 teaspoons beef-flavor instant bouillon
- 2 cups sliced carrots
- 1½ cups coarsely chopped onions
- 1½ cups coarsely chopped celery
- ½ cup coarsely chopped green pepper
- ⅓ cup barley
- 1 teaspoon salt
- ⅛ teaspoon pepper
- 2 bay leaves
- ¼ cup catsup
- 28-oz. can (3 cups) tomatoes, undrained, cut up
- 8-oz. can tomato sauce

In 5-quart Dutch oven, brown ground beef; drain. Stir in remaining ingredients. Bring to a boil. Reduce heat; cover and simmer 1 hour or until vegetables and barley are tender. Remove bay leaves. **10 servings.**

NUTRIENTS PER ¹⁄₁₀ OF RECIPE

Calories	220	
Protein	14 g	
Carbohydrate	18 g	
Fat	10 g	
Cholesterol	40 mg	
Dietary Fiber	4 g	
Sodium	900 mg	
Potassium	620 mg	
Calcium	4% U.S. RDA	
Iron	15% U.S. RDA	

Nacho Cheese 'n Beef Soup

      1   lb. ground beef
      2   cups beef broth
  8-oz.   jar picante sauce
    1/8   teaspoon cumin
    1/8   teaspoon pepper
 11-oz.   can condensed nacho cheese soup
          Tortilla chips
          Dairy sour cream

In medium saucepan, brown ground beef; drain. Add beef broth, picante sauce, cumin and pepper. Bring to a boil. Reduce heat; cover and simmer 15 minutes, stirring frequently. Stir in soup. Heat gently, stirring frequently. DO NOT BOIL. Pour into serving bowls; garnish with tortilla chips and sour cream. **4 servings.**

NUTRIENTS PER 1/4 OF RECIPE

Calories	410	Dietary Fiber	1 g
Protein	25 g	Sodium	1380 mg
Carbohydrate	17 g	Potassium	440 mg
Fat	27 g	Calcium	10% U.S. RDA
Cholesterol	80 mg	Iron	15% U.S. RDA

Italian Tortellini Soup

      1   lb. Italian sausage
      1   cup coarsely chopped onions
      2   garlic cloves, sliced
      5   cups beef broth
    1/2   cup water
    1/2   cup dry red wine or water
      2   cups (4 medium) chopped, seeded, peeled tomatoes

   1 cup thinly sliced carrots
  ½ teaspoon basil leaves
  ½ teaspoon oregano leaves
8-oz. can tomato sauce
 1½ cups sliced zucchini
 8 oz. (2 cups) frozen meat or cheese-filled tortellini or
        very small ravioli*
   3 tablespoons chopped fresh parsley
   1 medium green pepper, cut into ½-inch pieces
      Grated Parmesan cheese

If sausage comes in casing, remove casing. In 5-quart Dutch oven, brown sausage. Remove sausage from Dutch oven; reserve 1 tablespoon drippings in Dutch oven. Saute onions and garlic in reserved drippings until onions are tender. Add beef broth, water, wine, tomatoes, carrots, basil, oregano, tomato sauce and sausage. Bring to a boil. Reduce heat; simmer uncovered 30 minutes. Skim fat from soup. Stir in zucchini, tortellini, parsley and green pepper. Simmer covered an additional 35 to 40 minutes or until tortellini are tender. Top with Parmesan cheese. **8 servings.**

TIPS: *Eight oz. fresh meat or cheese-filled tortellini or very small ravioli can be substituted for frozen tortellini or ravioli. Simmer covered for 20 to 25 minutes or until tortellini are tender.

If tortellini or very small ravioli are not available, 2 cups bow-tie egg noodles or spiral macaroni can be substituted. Simmer covered for 20 to 25 minutes or until tender.

NUTRIENTS PER ⅛ OF RECIPE

Calories 240	Dietary Fiber ....3 g
Protein ....15 g	Sodium ....1130 mg
Carbohydrate ....17 g	Potassium ....560 mg
Fat ....12 g	Calcium ....15% U.S. RDA
Cholesterol ....60 mg	Iron ....10% U.S. RDA

Vegetable Beef Soup

2 to 3   lb. meaty beef bones, such as shank, cut into 3-inch pieces
6 to 8   cups water*
   2   beef-flavor bouillon cubes or 2 teaspoons beef-flavor instant bouillon
 1½   teaspoons salt
  ¼   teaspoon thyme leaves or marjoram leaves
  6   peppercorns or ¼ teaspoon pepper
  2   whole allspice
  1   bay leaf
  2   cups cubed, peeled potatoes
  1   cup sliced celery
  1   cup sliced carrots
  ½   cup chopped onion
16-oz.   can (2 cups) tomatoes, undrained, cut up
12-oz.   can whole kernel corn, undrained

In 5-quart Dutch oven, combine beef bones and water. Bring to a boil. Reduce heat; cover and simmer 30 minutes. Skim off any scum that rises to the surface. Add bouillon cubes, salt, thyme, peppercorns, allspice and bay leaf. Cover; simmer an additional 2½ to 3 hours or until meat is tender. Remove meat, peppercorns, allspice and bay leaf from broth. Remove meat from bones; cut into bite-size pieces. Skim fat from broth. Return meat to broth. Stir in remaining ingredients. Bring to a boil. Reduce heat; cover and simmer for 30 minutes or until vegetables are tender. **8 servings.**

TIP: *Three cups tomato or cocktail vegetable juice can be substituted for 3 cups of the water.

NUTRIENTS PER ⅛ OF RECIPE

Calories 250	Dietary Fiber ....4 g
Protein ....23 g	Sodium ....910 mg
Carbohydrate ....19 g	Potassium ....700 mg
Fat ....9 g	Calcium ....4% U.S. RDA
Cholesterol ....60 mg	Iron ....15% U.S. RDA

Chicken Broth

        2 lb. chicken backs, necks and/or wings*
        8 cups water
        2 small onions, quartered
        1 cup coarsely chopped celery with leaves
    ½ cup sliced carrots
        2 teaspoons chopped fresh parsley
        1 teaspoon salt
    ¼ teaspoon pepper
        1 bay leaf
    ½ teaspoon salt

In 5-quart Dutch oven, combine chicken and water. Bring to a boil. Reduce heat; simmer partially covered 30 minutes. Skim off any scum that rises to surface. Add remaining ingredients except ½ teaspoon salt; simmer partially covered an additional 4 hours. Remove bones; strain broth.**

Stir in ½ teaspoon salt. Cool uncovered in refrigerator. Cover; store in refrigerator or freezer. Skim fat from broth before using in recipe. **8 cups.**

TIPS: *Turkey pieces can be substituted for chicken.

**Remove meat from bones; refrigerate or freeze for later use.

NUTRIENTS: Variables in this recipe make it impossible to calculate nutrition information.

Lemon Chicken Rice Soup

        6 cups chicken broth
        1 chicken-flavor bouillon cube or 1 teaspoon
            chicken-flavor instant bouillon
    ⅓ cup uncooked regular rice
    ⅓ cup diced carrots

⅓ cup chopped celery
¼ cup finely chopped onion
1 cup cubed, cooked chicken
2 tablespoons margarine or butter
2 tablespoons flour
3 eggs
3 tablespoons lemon juice
 Salt and pepper
 Lemon slices, if desired
 Sliced green onions or chopped fresh parsley, if
 desired

In large saucepan, combine chicken broth, bouillon cube, rice, carrots, celery and onion. Bring to a boil. Reduce heat. Cover; simmer 20 minutes or until rice and vegetables are tender. Stir in chicken. Remove from heat.

In small saucepan, melt margarine. Stir in flour. Cook 1 minute until smooth and bubbly, stirring constantly. Gradually stir in 2 cups broth mixture; cook until slightly thickened, stirring constantly.

In small bowl, beat eggs until foamy. Gradually beat in lemon juice and 2 cups thickened broth mixture. Slowly add egg mixture to broth mixture in large saucepan, stirring constantly. Heat gently until soup thickens enough to coat a spoon, stirring frequently. Do not boil. Salt and pepper to taste. Garnish with lemon slices, green onions or parsley. **7 servings.**

NUTRIENTS PER ⅓ OF RECIPE

Calories 150	Dietary Fiber..........................1 g
Protein ....13 g	Sodium..............................690 mg
Carbohydrate........................11 g	Potassium.........................360 mg
Fat ....7 g	Calcium.................2% U.S. RDA
Cholesterol.......................130 mg	Iron........................6% U.S. RDA

Chicken Soup with Rice

2½ to 3-lb. frying chicken, cut up
          10 cups water
           ½ cup chopped onion
         2½ teaspoons salt
           ½ teaspoon thyme leaves, crushed
            6 peppercorns or ¼ teaspoon pepper
            1 cup thinly sliced celery
            1 cup thinly sliced carrots
           ½ cup uncooked white or brown regular rice

In 5-quart Dutch oven, combine chicken and water. Bring to a boil. Skim off any scum that rises to the surface. Reduce heat; cover and simmer 15 minutes. Add onion, salt, thyme and peppercorns. Simmer covered an additional 35 to 45 minutes or until chicken is tender. Remove chicken and peppercorns from broth; cool. Remove chicken from bones; cut into bite-size pieces. Skim fat from broth. Bring broth to a boil. Stir in chicken pieces, celery, carrots and rice. Reduce heat; cover and simmer 20 to 30 minutes or until vegetables and rice are tender. **10 servings.**

VARIATION:

Chicken Noodle Soup: Omit rice and add 1 cup uncooked egg noodles last 10 minutes of cooking time.

NUTRIENTS PER ¹⁄₁₀ OF RECIPE

Calories	160	Dietary Fiber	1 g
Protein	20 g	Sodium	590 mg
Carbohydrate	10 g	Potassium	220 mg
Fat	5 g	Calcium	2% U.S. RDA
Cholesterol	60 mg	Iron	6% U.S. RDA

Easy A-B-C Soup

    2   cups cubed, cooked chicken or turkey
    2   cups frozen mixed vegetables
  ½   cup chopped celery
  ¼   cup chopped onion
  ¼   teaspoon thyme leaves
    1   bay leaf
    6   cups chicken broth
    1   cup alphabet macaroni
        Salt and pepper

In 4-quart saucepan or Dutch oven, combine chicken, vegetables, celery, onion, thyme, bay leaf and broth. Bring to a boil. Reduce heat; stir in macaroni. Simmer 12 to 15 minutes or until vegetables and macaroni are tender, stirring occasionally. Remove bay leaf. Salt and pepper to taste. **10 servings.**

NUTRIENTS PER ⅒ OF RECIPE

Calories 130	Dietary Fiber ....1 g
Protein ....12 g	Sodium ....560 mg
Carbohydrate ....15 g	Potassium ....340 mg
Fat ....2 g	Calcium ....2% U.S. RDA
Cholesterol ....20 mg	Iron ....8% U.S. RDA

Easy Alphabet Vegetable Soup

    3   cups chicken broth
    3   cups tomato juice
  ¾   cup water
  ½   cup chopped celery
  ¼   cup chopped onion
  ¼   teaspoon basil leaves, crushed
    1   teaspoon Worcestershire sauce
1½   cups frozen mixed vegetables
  ⅔   cup alphabet macaroni

In large saucepan, combine chicken broth, tomato juice, water, celery, onion, basil and Worcestershire sauce. Bring to a boil. Reduce heat; cover and simmer 10 to 15 minutes or until celery and onion are crisp-tender. Stir in vegetables and macaroni. Cook covered over medium heat 20 to 25 minutes or until vegetables and macaroni are tender, stirring occasionally. **7 servings.**

TIP: For a heartier soup, add 1 lb. ground beef, cooked, drained or 2 cups cubed, cooked chicken with vegetables and macaroni.

NUTRIENTS PER ⅐ OF RECIPE

Calories	120	Dietary Fiber	2 g
Protein	6 g	Sodium	485 mg
Carbohydrate	23 g	Potassium	780 mg
Fat	1 g	Calcium	2% U.S. RDA
Cholesterol	0 mg	Iron	10% U.S. RDA

"Leftover Turkey" Soup

　　Bones and trimmings from 1 turkey or 3½-lb. frying chicken, cut up*
　8　cups water
　3　chicken-flavor bouillon cubes or 3 teaspoons chicken-flavor instant bouillon
　1　teaspoon salt
　¼　teaspoon poultry seasoning or sage
　1　bay leaf
　½　cup barley**
1½　cups sliced carrots***
　1　cup chopped onions
　1　cup sliced celery
　2　tablespoons chopped fresh parsley

In 5-quart Dutch oven, combine turkey bones and trimmings, water, bouillon cubes, salt, poultry seasoning and bay leaf. Bring to a boil. Reduce heat. Cover; simmer 1½ hours. Remove bones from broth. Remove turkey from bones. Strain broth; skim off fat. Return turkey to broth; stir in barley. Bring to a boil. Reduce heat. Cover; simmer 30 minutes, stirring occasionally. Stir in carrots, onions and celery. Simmer covered an additional 20 to 25 minutes or until vegetables and barley are tender. Stir in parsley. **8 servings.**

TIPS: *If using frying chicken, in 5-quart Dutch oven, combine chicken and water. Bring to a boil. Reduce heat. Cover; simmer 15 minutes. Skim off any scum that rises to the surface. Add bouillon cubes, salt, poultry seasoning and bay leaf. Simmer covered an additional 35 to 45 minutes or until chicken is tender. Remove chicken from broth. Remove chicken from bones; cut into bite-size pieces. Skim fat from broth; stir in barley. Continue as directed above.

**Three-fourths cup cracked bulgur, ½ cup uncooked regular rice or 1½ cups uncooked wide egg noodles can be substituted for barley. Omit 30 minute simmering time; add bulgur, rice or noodles with vegetables to broth. Continue as directed above.

***One cup corn, peas, diced potatoes, sliced zucchini or sliced mushrooms can be added with the carrots, onions and celery.

NUTRIENTS PER ⅛ OF RECIPE

Calories	160	Dietary Fiber	3 g
Protein	19 g	Sodium	725 mg
Carbohydrate	15 g	Potassium	385 mg
Fat	3 g	Calcium	2% U.S. RDA
Cholesterol	90 mg	Iron	8% U.S. RDA

Cream Soup

¼ cup finely chopped onion
¼ cup finely chopped celery
¼ cup margarine or butter
3 tablespoons flour

¼ teaspoon salt
⅛ teaspoon pepper
1½ cups chicken broth
1½ cups milk

In medium saucepan, saute onion and celery in margarine until tender. Stir in flour, salt and pepper. Cook 1 minute, stirring constantly, until smooth and bubbly. Gradually stir in chicken broth and milk; cook until slightly thickened, stirring constantly. Do not boil. Continue as directed in one of the following cream soup recipes or cover and store in refrigerator or freezer for later use. **4 servings.**

VARIATIONS:

CARROT CREAM SOUP: Stir in 2 cups sliced carrots, cooked and drained, ½ teaspoon grated orange peel and ⅛ teaspoon nutmeg. Heat thoroughly.

POTATO CREAM SOUP: Stir in 2 cups diced, cooked, peeled potatoes, 2 teaspoons Worcestershire sauce and ¼ teaspoon dry mustard. Heat thoroughly.

CAULIFLOWER CREAM SOUP: Stir in 2 cups cooked cut-up cauliflower and ½ teaspoon dill weed. Heat thoroughly.

BROCCOLI CREAM SOUP: Stir in 2 cups cooked cut-up broccoli, 2 teaspoons lemon juice and ¼ teaspoon garlic powder. Heat thoroughly.

NUTRIENTS PER ¼ OF RECIPE

Calories	190	Dietary Fiber	2 g
Protein	6 g	Sodium	610 mg
Carbohydrate	11 g	Potassium	270 mg
Fat	14 g	Calcium	10% U.S. RDA
Cholesterol	6 mg	Iron	2% U.S. RDA

Turkey Wild Rice Soup

3 (10¾-oz.) cans condensed chicken broth
2 cups water
½ cup uncooked wild rice, rinsed*
½ cup finely chopped green onions
½ cup margarine or butter
¾ cup all purpose flour
½ teaspoon salt
¼ teaspoon poultry seasoning
⅛ teaspoon pepper
2 cups half-and-half
1½ cups cubed, cooked turkey or chicken
8 slices bacon, crisply cooked, crumbled
1 tablespoon chopped pimiento
2 to 3 tablespoons dry sherry, if desired

In large saucepan, combine chicken broth and water. Add wild rice and onions. Bring to a boil. Reduce heat; cover and simmer 35 to 40 minutes or until rice is tender.

In medium saucepan, melt margarine; stir in flour, salt, poultry seasoning and pepper. Cook 1 minute, stirring constantly, until smooth and bubbly. Gradually stir in half-and-half; cook until slightly thickened, stirring constantly. Slowly add half-and-half mixture into rice mixture, stirring constantly. Add remaining ingredients. Heat gently, stirring frequently. Do not boil. Garnish as desired. **8 servings.**

TIP: *Uncooked regular long grain rice can be substituted for part or all of the wild rice; reduce simmering time to 20 to 30 minutes or until rice is tender.

NUTRIENTS PER ⅛ OF RECIPE

Calories	410	Dietary Fiber	1 g
Protein	20 g	Sodium	1130 mg
Carbohydrate	23 g	Potassium	445 mg
Fat	26 g	Calcium	8% U.S. RDA
Cholesterol	60 mg	Iron	10% U.S. RDA

Mushroom Cream Soup

  3 cups sliced fresh mushrooms
  ¼ cup finely chopped onion
  ¼ cup finely chopped celery
  ¼ cup margarine or butter
  3 tablespoons flour
  ½ teaspoon basil leaves, finely crushed
  ¼ teaspoon salt
  ⅛ teaspoon pepper
1½ cups chicken broth
1½ cups milk

In large saucepan, saute mushrooms, onion and celery in margarine until tender. Stir in flour, basil, salt and pepper. Cook 1 minute or until smooth and bubbly, stirring constantly. Gradually add chicken broth and milk. Cook until slightly thickened, stirring constantly. Do not boil. **3 servings.**

NUTRIENTS PER ⅓ OF RECIPE

Calories	260	Dietary Fiber	2 g
Protein	9 g	Sodium	710 mg
Carbohydrate	17 g	Potassium	655 mg
Fat	18 g	Calcium	15% U.S. RDA
Cholesterol	8 mg	Iron	6% U.S. RDA

Pumpkin Pot Pourri

16-oz. can (2 cups) pumpkin
   3 cups water
   3 chicken bouillon cubes
   ½ teaspoon salt
   ½ teaspoon cinnamon
   ¼ teaspoon nutmeg
     Dash pepper
   1 cup raisins

10-oz. pkg. frozen long grain white and wild rice in a pouch
2 tablespoons margarine or butter
½ cup chopped celery
½ cup chopped onion
2½-oz. jar sliced mushrooms, drained
2 cups half-and-half

In large saucepan, combine pumpkin and water; mix well. Stir in bouillon cubes, salt, cinnamon, nutmeg and pepper. Heat until bouillon cubes dissolve. Add raisins and rice; simmer. In skillet, melt margarine. Saute celery, onion and mushrooms in margarine until onion and celery are crisp-tender. Stir vegetables into pumpkin mixture; simmer until hot and flavors have blended, about 15 minutes. Add cream before serving; heat until hot. This soup thickens as it stands. **10 servings.**

NUTRIENTS PER ⅒ OF RECIPE

Calories	280	Dietary Fiber	3 g
Protein	3 g	Sodium	580 mg
Carbohydrate	23 g	Potassium	305 mg
Fat	20 g	Calcium	6% U.S. RDA
Cholesterol	20 mg	Iron	6% U.S. RDA

Cream of Tomato Soup

3 cups chopped tomatoes
⅓ cup chopped onion
2 teaspoons sugar
1½ teaspoons salt
1 teaspoon basil leaves
½ teaspoon thyme leaves
⅛ teaspoon pepper
6-oz. can tomato paste
¼ teaspoon baking soda
1 tablespoon margarine or butter
1 tablespoon flour
2 cups milk

In medium saucepan, combine tomatoes, onion, sugar, salt, basil, thyme, pepper and tomato paste. Cover; simmer 10 minutes. Press mixture through strainer or food mill to make puree; discard pulp. Stir in baking soda; set aside.

In large saucepan, melt margarine; stir in flour until well blended. Add milk all at once. Cook about 1 minute until thickened, stirring constantly. Stir in tomato puree. Cook until thoroughly heated; do not boil. **4 servings.**

MICROWAVE DIRECTIONS: In medium-size microwave-safe bowl, combine tomatoes, onion, sugar, salt, basil, thyme, pepper and tomato paste. Cover with microwave-safe plastic wrap; microwave on HIGH for 4 minutes. Stir; repeat. Press mixture through strainer or food mill to make puree; discard pulp. Stir in baking soda; set aside.

In 2-quart microwave-safe casserole, microwave margarine on HIGH for 45 seconds. Stir in flour until well blended. Add milk all at once. Microwave on HIGH for 4 to 5½ minutes or until thickened, stirring occasionally. Stir tomato puree into milk mixture. Serve immediately.

NUTRIENTS PER ¼ OF RECIPE

Calories	160	Dietary Fiber	4 g
Protein	7 g	Sodium	960 mg
Carbohydrate	23 g	Potassium	825 mg
Fat	5 g	Calcium	20% U.S. RDA
Cholesterol	8 mg	Iron	15% U.S. RDA

Lentil Soup

16-oz. pkg. (about 2½ cups) dry lentils
8 cups water
¾ cup sliced celery
⅓ cup sliced carrots
¼ cup chopped fresh parsley
2 teaspoons salt
¾ teaspoon oregano leaves

½ to ¾ teaspoon pepper
    1 medium onion, sliced
    1 garlic clove, minced
16-oz. can (2 cups) tomatoes, undrained, cut up
    3 tablespoons red wine vinegar

Wash and sort lentils. In 5-quart Dutch oven, combine lentils, water, celery, carrots, parsley, salt, oregano, pepper, onion and garlic. Bring to a boil. Reduce heat. Cover; simmer 1½ hours. Stir in tomatoes and vinegar. Cover; simmer an additional 30 minutes or until soup reaches desired thickness. **6 servings.**

NUTRIENTS PER ¼ OF RECIPE

Calories 290	Dietary Fiber ....16 g
Protein ....20 g	Sodium ....855 mg
Carbohydrate.........................52 g	Potassium ....885 mg
Fat ....1 g	Calcium ....8% U.S. RDA
Cholesterol ....0 mg	Iron.....................35% U.S. RDA

Easy Bean Soup

16-oz. pkg. (about 2⅓ cups) dry navy beans
    6 cups water
    8 cups water
1½-lb. ham shank
    1 cup chopped onions
    ¼ cup chopped fresh parsley
    1 teaspoon salt
    1 teaspoon basil leaves
    ½ teaspoon pepper
    ½ teaspoon nutmeg
    ½ teaspoon oregano leaves
    2 garlic cloves, minced
    1 bay leaf
    2 cups thinly sliced carrots
    1 cup chopped celery
    ½ cup mashed potato flakes

Wash and sort beans. In 5-quart Dutch oven, combine beans and 6 cups water. Bring to a boil. Reduce heat; simmer uncovered for 2 minutes. Remove from heat. Cover and let stand 1 hour; drain. Add 8 cups water, ham shank, onions, parsley, salt, basil, pepper, nutmeg, oregano, garlic and bay leaf. Bring to a boil. Reduce heat. Cover; simmer 1½ hours or until beans are tender. Remove from heat. Remove meat from bone; cut into bite-size pieces. Return meat to soup. Stir in carrots, celery and potato flakes until blended. Return to heat. Cover; simmer an additional 20 to 30 minutes or until carrots and celery are crisp-tender. Remove bay leaf. **9 servings.**

NUTRIENTS PER ⅑ OF RECIPE

Calories	250	Dietary Fiber	6 g
Protein	18 g	Sodium	845 mg
Carbohydrate	38 g	Potassium	900 mg
Fat	3 g	Calcium	10% U.S. RDA
Cholesterol	25 mg	Iron	30% U.S. RDA

Split Pea Soup

16-oz.	pkg. (2 cups) dry split peas
12	cups water
2	chicken-flavor bouillon cubes or 2 teaspoons chicken-flavor instant bouillon
1	cup finely chopped onions
½	teaspoon garlic powder
½	teaspoon oregano leaves
¼ to ½	teaspoon pepper
1-lb.	ham shank
1	bay leaf
1½	cups thinly sliced carrots
1	cup chopped celery

Wash and sort peas. In 5-quart Dutch oven, combine peas, water, bouillon cubes, onions, garlic, oregano, pepper, ham shank and bay leaf. Bring to a boil. Reduce heat; simmer 1½ hours. Remove meat from bone; cut into bite-size pieces. Return meat to soup. Stir in carrots and celery. Simmer an additional 1½ to 2 hours or until soup reaches desired thickness. Remove bay leaf. **6 servings.**

NUTRIENTS PER ⅙ OF RECIPE

Calories	350	Dietary Fiber	21 g
Protein	27 g	Sodium	665 mg
Carbohydrate	54 g	Potassium	995 mg
Fat	3 g	Calcium	6% U.S. RDA
Cholesterol	25 mg	Iron	30% U.S. RDA

Bean and Sausage Soup

2	slices bacon
½	cup chopped onion
1	cup sliced carrots
1	cup cubed, peeled potato
¼	cup chopped fresh parsley
½	teaspoon marjoram leaves, if desired
¼	teaspoon pepper
2	cups water
8-oz.	(1½ cups) thinly sliced smoked bratwurst, Polish sausage (kielbasa) or wieners
16-oz.	can cut green beans, undrained
16-oz.	can Great Northern beans or white beans, undrained

In large saucepan, cook bacon until crisp; drain, reserving 1 tablespoon drippings. Crumble bacon; set aside. Saute onion in reserved drippings until tender. Add carrots, potato, parsley, marjoram, pepper and water; bring to a boil. Reduce heat; cover and simmer about 20 minutes or until vegetables are tender. Add bratwurst, beans and reserved bacon. Cook until thoroughly heated. **6 servings.**

NUTRIENTS PER ⅙ OF RECIPE

Calories	260	Dietary Fiber	6 g
Protein	14 g	Sodium	440 mg
Carbohydrate	26 g	Potassium	670 mg
Fat	11 g	Calcium	8% U.S. RDA
Cholesterol	25 mg	Iron	15% U.S. RDA

Lemony Basil Soup

1¼	cups chopped onions
1	lb. fresh mushrooms, sliced
1	cup sliced celery
1	cup sliced carrots
4	garlic cloves, minced
¼	cup margarine or butter
6	cups water*
3	(10¾-oz.) cans condensed chicken broth*
10¾-oz.	can condensed cream of chicken soup
½	cup chopped fresh basil leaves**
1	teaspoon pepper
1	teaspoon lemon juice
½	cup uncooked wild rice, rinsed
¼	cup uncooked regular rice
	Lemon slices
	Grated Parmesan cheese

In 5-quart Dutch oven, saute onions, mushrooms, celery, carrots and garlic in margarine until tender. Stir in water, chicken broth, cream of chicken soup, basil, pepper, lemon juice, wild and regular rice. Bring to a boil. Reduce heat; cover and simmer 35 to 40 minutes or until wild rice is tender. Garnish each serving with lemon slice and Parmesan cheese. **16 servings.**

TIPS: *Ten cups Chicken Broth (see Index) can be substituted for the water and condensed chicken broth.

**One tablespoon dry basil leaves and a 10-oz. pkg. frozen chopped spinach, thawed and drained can be substituted for fresh basil leaves.

NUTRIENTS PER ¹⁄₁₆ OF RECIPE

Calories	120	Dietary Fiber	2 g
Protein	6 g	Sodium	590 mg
Carbohydrate	13 g	Potassium	395 mg
Fat	5 g	Calcium	6% U.S. RDA
Cholesterol	4 mg	Iron	8% U.S. RDA

French Onion Soup

    4   cups thinly sliced onions
    3   tablespoons margarine or butter
    5   cups beef broth
    1   beef-flavor bouillon cube or 1 teaspoon instant
        beef bouillon
    1   teaspoon Worcestershire sauce
        Dash pepper
 4 oz. (1 cup) shredded Swiss cheese
    ¼   cup grated Parmesan cheese
    6   slices French bread, toasted

In 5-quart Dutch oven, saute onions in margarine over low
heat 15 minutes or until onions are golden brown and tender.
Stir in beef broth, bouillon cube, Worcestershire sauce and
pepper. Bring to a boil. Reduce heat; cover and simmer 20
to 25 minutes. In medium bowl, combine cheeses.

Ladle soup into 6 ovenproof bowls. Top each with slice of
toasted French bread; sprinkle with about 2 tablespoons
cheese mixture. For ease in broiling, place bowls on cookie
sheet; broil about 3 to 5 inches from heat for 1 to 3 minutes
or until cheese is bubbly. Pass additional shredded cheese to
be added to individual servings as desired. **6 servings.**

NUTRIENTS PER ¹⁄₆ OF RECIPE

Calories	230	Dietary Fiber	3 g
Protein	14 g	Sodium	880 mg
Carbohydrate	19 g	Potassium	455 mg
Fat	13 g	Calcium	25% U.S. RDA
Cholesterol	20 mg	Iron	6% U.S. RDA

Minute Minestrone

¼ cup chopped onion
1 medium zucchini, sliced
2 tablespoons margarine or butter
9-oz. pkg. frozen baby lima beans
2 (10½-oz.) cans beef broth
16-oz. can whole tomatoes, undrained, cut up
1 cup water
½ cup broken vermicelli, uncooked
1 tablespoon grated Parmesan cheese
¼ teaspoon basil leaves
¼ teaspoon pepper
⅛ teaspoon garlic salt
Dash cayenne pepper

In large saucepan over medium heat, saute onion and zucchini in margarine until vegetables are crisp-tender. Remove frozen lima beans from pouch; add to sauteed vegetables. Stir in remaining ingredients. Simmer, stirring occasionally, about 15 minutes or until vermicelli is tender but still firm. **4 to 5 servings.**

MICROWAVE DIRECTIONS: In 2½-quart casserole, melt margarine. Stir in onion and zucchini; microwave on HIGH for 3 to 4 minutes or until vegetables are crisp-tender. Stir in remaining ingredients as directed above. Microwave on HIGH for 15 to 20 minutes or until vermicelli is tender but still firm.

NUTRIENTS PER ⅕ OF RECIPE

Calories	200	Dietary Fiber	4 g
Protein	11 g	Sodium	1160 mg
Carbohydrate	23 g	Potassium	640 mg
Fat	7 g	Calcium	8% U.S. RDA
Cholesterol	1 mg	Iron	10% U.S. RDA

Chunky Tomato Soup

10¾-oz. can condensed tomato soup
  1¼ cups water
   1 tomato, coarsely chopped
   1 green pepper, coarsely chopped
   1 zucchini, coarsely chopped
  ½ teaspoon beef-flavor instant bouillon
  ½ teaspoon basil leaves, crushed
  ¼ teaspoon Worcestershire sauce

In medium saucepan, combine all ingredients. Bring to a boil. Reduce heat; cover and simmer 3 to 5 minutes, stirring occasionally. Serve immediately. **4 servings.**

MICROWAVE DIRECTIONS: In 2-quart microwave-safe bowl, combine all ingredients. Cover with microwave-safe plastic wrap. Microwave on HIGH for 8 to 11 minutes or until fully heated, stirring once halfway through cooking.

NUTRIENTS PER ¼ OF RECIPE

Calories	70	Dietary Fiber	3 g
Protein	2 g	Sodium	580 mg
Carbohydrate	14 g	Potassium	350 mg
Fat	1 g	Calcium	2% U.S. RDA
Cholesterol	0 mg	Iron	10% U.S. RDA

Manhattan Clam Chowder

  5 slices bacon
  1 cup chopped onions
  1 cup chopped celery
  ¼ cup finely chopped green pepper
  3 cups water
  2 cups diced, peeled potatoes
  1 cup diced carrots
  1 tablespoon chopped fresh parsley
  1 teaspoon salt

¼ teaspoon thyme leaves, crushed
⅛ teaspoon pepper
3 (6½-oz.) cans minced clams, drained, reserving liquid
16-oz. can (2 cups) tomatoes, undrained, cut up
1 bay leaf

In large saucepan, cook bacon until crisp. Remove bacon from saucepan; drain, reserving 2 tablespoons drippings in saucepan. Crumble bacon; set aside. Saute onions, celery and green pepper in reserved drippings until tender. Add water, potatoes, carrots, parsley, salt, thyme, pepper, reserved liquid from clams, tomatoes and bay leaf. Bring to a boil. Reduce heat; cover and simmer 25 to 35 minutes or until vegetables are tender. Remove bay leaf. Stir in clams. Heat gently, stirring frequently; do not boil. Garnish each serving with crumbled bacon. **6 servings.**

NUTRIENTS PER ⅙ OF RECIPE

Calories 160	Dietary Fiber............................3 g
Protein....................................12 g	Sodium..............................560 mg
Carbohydrate........................20 g	Potassium.........................710 mg
Fat ....4 g	Calcium.................8% U.S. RDA
Cholesterol.........................35 mg	Iron.....................30% U.S. RDA

New England Clam Chowder

3 slices bacon
1 cup diced, peeled potatoes
½ cup chopped celery
¼ cup chopped onion
¾ teaspoon salt
⅛ teaspoon thyme leaves, crushed
⅛ teaspoon pepper
2 (6½-oz.) cans minced clams, drained, reserving liquid
¼ cup flour
3 cups milk

In large saucepan, cook bacon until crisp. Remove bacon from saucepan; drain, reserving 2 tablespoons drippings in saucepan.* Crumble bacon; set aside. Add potatoes, celery, onion, salt, thyme, pepper and reserved liquid from clams to reserved drippings. Bring to a boil. Reduce heat; cover and simmer 10 minutes or until vegetables are tender.

In 1-quart jar with tight-fitting lid, add flour to milk; shake well. Gradually stir into vegetable mixture. Cook over medium heat, stirring frequently, for 15 minutes or until thickened. Stir in clams. Heat gently, stirring frequently; do not boil. Garnish each serving with crumbled bacon. **4 servings.**

TIP: *If desired, omit bacon drippings and substitute 2 tablespoons margarine or butter.

NUTRIENTS PER ¼ OF RECIPE

Calories	230	Dietary Fiber	2 g
Protein	17 g	Sodium	1110 mg
Carbohydrate	25 g	Potassium	630 mg
Fat	7 g	Calcium	30% U.S. RDA
Cholesterol	50 mg	Iron	25% U.S. RDA

Light Fish Chowder

   1 cup chopped onions
   1 tablespoon margarine
   2 cups water
   1 large potato, cubed
   1 cup sliced carrots
  ½ cup sliced celery
   1 bay leaf
  ¼ teaspoon thyme leaves
     Dash pepper
   1 lb. fish fillets, cubed
   2 cups milk
   3 tablespoons flour

½ teaspoon salt, if desired
    Chopped fresh parsley, if desired
    Lemon wedges, if desired

In Dutch oven or large saucepan, saute onions in margarine until tender. Add water, potato, carrots, celery, bay leaf, thyme and pepper; bring to a boil. Cover; simmer about 20 minutes or until vegetables are tender. Stir in fish and 1¾ cups of the milk. Stir flour into remaining ¼ cup milk; stir into chowder. Cook until fish is opaque and chowder is thoroughly heated. Add salt. Serve sprinkled with parsley and a squeeze of lemon. **4 servings.**

NUTRIENTS PER ¼ OF RECIPE

Calories	330	Dietary Fiber	4 g
Protein	28 g	Sodium	465 mg
Carbohydrate	26 g	Potassium	935 mg
Fat	13 g	Calcium	20% U.S. RDA
Cholesterol	60 mg	Iron	8% U.S. RDA

Potato Corn Chowder

½ cup chopped celery
2 green onions, sliced
2 tablespoons margarine or butter
2 cups water
2 chicken-flavor bouillon cubes or 2 teaspoons instant chicken bouillon
⅛ teaspoon pepper
1 cup mashed potato flakes
17-oz. can whole kernel corn, drained
1 cup half-and-half

In large saucepan, saute celery and onions in margarine until tender. Add water, bouillon cubes and pepper. Cook over medium heat until bouillon is dissolved, stirring frequently. Remove from heat; stir in potato flakes and corn until blended. Add half-and-half. Return to heat. Heat gently, stirring frequently; do not boil. Garnish each serving with additional green onion slices, if desired. **4 servings.**

NUTRIENTS PER ¼ OF RECIPE

Calories	280	Dietary Fiber	6 g
Protein	6 g	Sodium	855 mg
Carbohydrate	35 g	Potassium	515 mg
Fat	13 g	Calcium	8% U.S. RDA
Cholesterol	25 mg	Iron	4% U.S. RDA

Hearty Catfish Gumbo

4	slices bacon
1	cup (2 medium) chopped onions
1	cup coarsely chopped green pepper
1	garlic clove, minced
16-oz.	can tomatoes, undrained, cut up
2	tablespoons chopped fresh parsley
½	teaspoon thyme leaves
¼	teaspoon pepper
1	cup water
¼	teaspoon hot pepper sauce
10½-oz.	can condensed tomato soup
10-oz.	pkg. frozen cut okra
1	lb. fresh or frozen catfish fillets, thawed, skinned and cut into 1-inch pieces

In large saucepan or Dutch oven, cook bacon until crisp; remove bacon from pan and crumble, reserving drippings. In bacon drippings, saute onions, green pepper and garlic until tender. Stir in remaining ingredients except catfish. Cover; simmer 30 minutes or until vegetables are tender. Add catfish; cover and simmer an additional 10 minutes or until fish flakes easily with fork. If too thick, add additional water. **8 servings.**

NUTRIENTS PER ⅛ OF RECIPE

Calories 130	Dietary Fiber...........................3 g
Protein....................................12 g	Sodium.............................440 mg
Carbohydrate........................13 g	Potassium.........................540 mg
Fat ....4 g	Calcium.................6% U.S. RDA
Cholesterol........................30 mg	Iron.....................10% U.S. RDA

Oyster Stew

2 cups milk
2 cups half-and-half
⅓ cup margarine or butter
3 cups fresh oysters, undrained*
¼ cup finely chopped onion
1 tablespoon chopped fresh parsley
1 tablespoon chopped pimiento
1 teaspoon salt
½ teaspoon pepper
⅛ teaspoon Worcestershire sauce
Oyster crackers, if desired

In large saucepan, combine milk and cream; heat slowly until bubbles appear around edges.

In medium saucepan, melt margarine. Add oysters and onion. Cook over low heat 8 to 10 minutes or until edges of oysters begin to curl. Stir oyster mixture, parsley, pimiento, salt, pepper and Worcestershire sauce into hot milk mixture. Heat gently, stirring frequently; do not boil. Garnish each serving with oyster crackers. **5 servings.**

TIP: *Three 8-oz. cans oysters, undrained, can be substituted for fresh oysters. Reduce salt to ¼ teaspoon. Cook over low heat 4 to 6 minutes or until edges of oysters begin to curl. Continue as directed above.

NUTRIENTS PER ⅕ OF RECIPE

Calories.....................................410	Dietary Fiber..........................0 g
Protein....................................19 g	Sodium............................845 mg
Carbohydrate........................19 g	Potassium.......................480 mg
Fat ....29 g	Calcium..............35% U.S. RDA
Cholesterol ....110 mg	Iron.....................45% U.S. RDA

Cajun Shrimp Soup

    ½ cup chopped green pepper
    ¼ cup sliced green onions
    1 garlic clove, minced
    1 tablespoon margarine or butter
    2 (12-oz.) cans (3 cups) vegetable juice cocktail
 8-oz. bottle clam juice
    ½ cup water
    ½ teaspoon salt
    ¼ teaspoon thyme leaves, crushed
    ¼ teaspoon basil leaves, crushed
 ⅛ to ¼ teaspoon red pepper flakes, crushed
    1 bay leaf
    ⅓ cup uncooked regular long grain rice
 12-oz. pkg. frozen cooked shrimp
    Hot pepper sauce, if desired

In large saucepan, saute green pepper, onions and garlic in
margarine until tender. Stir in vegetable juice, clam juice,
water, salt, thyme, basil, pepper flakes and bay leaf. Bring to
a boil. Reduce heat; add rice. Cover and simmer 15 to 20
minutes or until rice is tender. Stir in shrimp; simmer uncovered an additional 3 to 5 minutes or until shrimp are thoroughly heated. Remove bay leaf. Add hot pepper sauce to
individual servings as desired. **4 servings.**

NUTRIENTS PER ¼ OF RECIPE

Calories.....................................220	Dietary Fiber..........................2 g
Protein....................................22 g	Sodium..........................1300 mg
Carbohydrate........................25 g	Potassium.......................610 mg
Fat ....4 g	Calcium..............10% U.S. RDA
Cholesterol ....130 mg	Iron.....................15% U.S. RDA

Cioppino

28-oz. can (3 cups) tomatoes, undrained, cut up
16-oz. can (2 cups) stewed tomatoes, undrained, cut up
 8-oz. can (1 cup) tomato sauce
     1 cup sauterne wine or dry white wine
     2 teaspoons basil leaves
     1 teaspoon salt
    ¼ teaspoon pepper
    12 small clams in shells, washed
    ⅓ cup oil
  1½ cups chopped onions
     1 cup chopped fresh parsley
     1 lb. fresh medium shrimp, shelled, deveined*
     6 garlic cloves, minced
     1 lb. frozen snow or dungeness crab legs in shell,
           thawed, cracked
     1 lb. fresh halibut or cod, cut into 1½-inch pieces
           French bread

In 5-quart Dutch oven, combine tomatoes, stewed tomatoes,
tomato sauce, wine, basil, salt and pepper. Bring to a boil.
Reduce heat; simmer uncovered 10 minutes, stirring occasionally. Bring back to a boil; add clams. Cover tightly and
cook over medium heat 4 to 6 minutes or until clam shells
open.

In medium saucepan, heat oil. Stir in onions, parsley, shrimp
and garlic. Simmer covered 3 to 5 minutes or until shrimp
are light pink, stirring occasionally. Stir shrimp mixture into
tomato-clam mixture. Add crab. Simmer uncovered 5 minutes. Add fish pieces. Simmer uncovered an additional 2 to
3 minutes or until fish flakes easily. Serve with thick slices
of French bread to dip in rich broth. **6 servings.**

TIP: *One 12-oz. bag frozen medium shrimp, cooked and
drained, can be substituted for fresh shrimp.

NUTRIENTS PER ⅙ OF RECIPE

Calories 470	Dietary Fiber...........................3 g
Protein.....................................37 g	Sodium ....1180 mg
Carbohydrate.........................40 g	Potassium.......................1325 mg
Fat ....16 g	Calcium...............15% U.S. RDA
Cholesterol.......................160 mg	Iron.....................35% U.S. RDA

Bouillabaisse

      1 medium onion, chopped
      2 garlic cloves, minced
      2 tablespoons olive or cooking oil
     ¼ cup chopped fresh parsley
   2½ teaspoons salt
     ¼ teaspoon saffron or curry powder
     ¼ teaspoon pepper
      1 bay leaf
      4 cups water
      1 teaspoon lemon juice
      1 lb. fish fillets, cut into 2-inch pieces
 12-oz. pkg. (3 cups) frozen shrimp
  6-oz. pkg. (¾ cup) frozen crab or lobster meat
      1 pint fresh oysters or clams, undrained
  8-oz. can (1 cup) tomato sauce

In Dutch oven or large saucepan, saute onion and garlic in oil until tender. Add remaining ingredients; mix well. Heat just to boiling. Simmer covered over low heat, 20 to 30 minutes or until seafood is done, stirring occasionally. Remove bay leaf. Serve in large soup bowls. **10 to 12 servings.**

TIP: Any combination of fish or seafood can be used depending on availability and taste. Fish and seafood can be added either fresh or frozen, although fresh fish and seafood give the most flavor. Fish and seafood in the frozen state use the maximum cooking time. Fresh and thawed fish and seafood require the minimum cooking time.

NUTRIENTS PER ½ OF RECIPE

Calories 120	Dietary Fiber........................<1 g
Protein......................,...........16 g	Sodium............................800 mg
Carbohydrate.........................5 g	Potassium........................320 mg
Fat ....3 g	Calcium.................6% U.S. RDA
Cholesterol.........................80 mg	Iron.....................15% U.S. RDA

Cheddar Beer Cheese Soup

- ⅓ cup margarine or butter
- ½ cup all purpose flour
- 1 garlic clove, pressed
- 1 tablespoon grated onion
- 1 teaspoon Worcestershire sauce
- ½ teaspoon salt
- ½ teaspoon dry mustard
- ⅛ teaspoon white pepper
- 3 cups chicken broth
- 1½ cups half-and-half
- 1 cup beer
- 16 oz. (4 cups) shredded sharp white Cheddar cheese
  Buttered croutons, unsalted popcorn or chopped fresh parsley, if desired

In large saucepan, melt margarine; stir in flour. Cook 1 minute, stirring constantly, until smooth and bubbly. Add garlic, onion, Worcestershire sauce, salt, mustard and pepper; blend well. Gradually stir in chicken broth, half-and-half and beer; cook until thickened, stirring constantly. Add cheese; heat gently, stirring until melted. Do not boil. Garnish each serving with croutons, popcorn or parsley. **7 servings.**

NUTRIENTS PER ⅐ OF RECIPE

Calories 450	Dietary Fiber........................<1 g
Protein....................................20 g	Sodium............................980 mg
Carbohydrate........................12 g	Potassium........................235 mg
Fat ....36 g	Calcium...............50% U.S. RDA
Cholesterol........................100 mg	Iron.......................4% U.S. RDA

Vegetable 'n Cheese Soup

    3 tablespoons margarine or butter
    1 cup chopped celery
    1 cup shredded carrot
  ½ cup chopped onion
    3 cups water
    2 chicken-flavor bouillon cubes
    6 drops hot pepper sauce
    1 cup mashed potato flakes
    2 cups milk
  12 oz. (3 cups) shredded American or Cheddar cheese

In large saucepan, melt margarine; stir in celery, carrot and onion. Cook over medium heat for 5 minutes, stirring occasionally. *Do not brown.* Add water, bouillon cubes and hot pepper sauce, stirring until bouillon cubes are dissolved. Bring to a boil; cover and simmer 10 minutes or until vegetables are tender. Stir in mashed potato flakes. Add milk and cheese, stirring constantly until cheese is melted. Do not boil. **7 servings.**

NUTRIENTS PER ⅐ OF RECIPE

Calories	300	
Protein	....................................14 g	
Carbohydrate	........................13 g	
Fat	....22 g	
Cholesterol	........................50 mg	
Dietary Fiber	............................2 g
Sodium	............................1100 mg
Potassium	........................430 mg
Calcium	...............40% U.S. RDA
Iron	........................2% U.S. RDA

Cucumber Soup

TOMATO ICE

12-oz. can (1½ cups) spicy vegetable juice cocktail
  6-oz. can tomato paste
      1 tablespoon lemon juice

SOUP

4   large cucumbers, peeled, seeded, cut into chunks
     (about 4 lb.)
2   garlic cloves
1 to 2 tablespoons fresh parsley or coriander leaves
1   teaspoon salt
2   cups (1 pint) buttermilk, chilled
8-oz. carton plain yogurt
     Thin slices unpeeled cucumber

In small bowl, combine all tomato ice ingredients. Freeze in
ice cube trays with dividers until firm but not frozen hard,
about 2 hours. In blender container or food processor bowl
with metal blade, blend cubes, in batches if needed, until
smooth. Spoon into freezer container; cover. Return to
freezer until firm, about 2 hours, or until serving time.

In blender container or food processor bowl with metal
blade, puree half of soup ingredients at a time until nearly
smooth. Cover; refrigerate until chilled. To serve, ladle
about ¾ cup soup into each chilled bowl; scoop about ¼ cup
tomato ice into center of each serving. Garnish with cucumber slices. **8 servings.**

TIP: To prepare soup ahead, cover and refrigerate up to 3
days before serving.

NUTRIENTS PER ⅛ OF RECIPE

Calories	90	Dietary Fiber	3 g
Protein	6 g	Sodium	610 mg
Carbohydrate	15 g	Potassium	680 mg
Fat	1 g	Calcium	15% U.S. RDA
Cholesterol	4 mg	Iron	8% U.S. RDA

Cold Gazpacho

2   medium tomatoes, chopped
1   cucumber, thinly sliced
1   small onion, chopped

½ green pepper, chopped
1 garlic clove, minced
1 tablespoon oil or olive oil
1 tablespoon wine vinegar or lemon juice
   Dash hot pepper sauce
24-oz. can (3 cups) vegetable juice cocktail or tomato juice

In large bowl, combine all ingredients; cover and refrigerate
at least 6 hours. Serve chilled. **5 servings.**

NUTRIENTS PER ⅕ OF RECIPE

Calories 80	Dietary Fiber...........................3 g
Protein ....2 g	Sodium...............................540 mg
Carbohydrate.......................11 g	Potassium.........................470 mg
Fat ....3 g	Calcium................2% U.S. RDA
Cholesterol ....0 mg	Iron.......................6% U.S. RDA

Vichyssoise

3 medium leeks, sliced
2 tablespoons butter or margarine
3 medium potatoes, peeled, sliced
4 cups chicken broth
2 cups half-and-half
½ teaspoon salt, if desired
   Chopped chives

In large saucepan, saute leeks in butter until tender. Add
potatoes and chicken broth. Cover; simmer 15 to 20 minutes
or until potatoes are tender. Process in blender container or
food processor bowl with metal blade until smooth and
creamy. Stir in half-and-half and salt. Refrigerate until cold.
Serve garnished with chopped chives. **11 servings.**

NUTRIENTS PER 1/11 OF RECIPE

Calories 120	Dietary Fiber...........................1 g
Protein ....4 g	Sodium...............................420 mg
Carbohydrate...........................8 g	Potassium.........................250 mg
Fat ....8 g	Calcium................4% U.S. RDA
Cholesterol ....20 mg	Iron.......................2% U.S. RDA

Chilled Raspberry Soup

    2 cups fresh raspberries or 2 (10-oz.) pkg. frozen
       raspberries, thawed
 1½ cups water
    1 cup cranberry juice cocktail
  ¾ cup sugar
    1 cinnamon stick
    3 whole cloves
    1 tablespoon lemon juice
 8-oz. carton raspberry yogurt
  ⅓ cup dairy sour cream
       Cinnamon

Place raspberries and ¼ cup of the water in blender container; blend until smooth. In large saucepan, combine
pureed fruit, remaining 1¼ cups water, cranberry juice
cocktail, sugar, cinnamon stick and cloves. Cook over
medium heat until mixture begins to boil; remove from heat.
Cool. Strain soup into large bowl. Add lemon juice and yogurt; whisk until well blended.* Cover; refrigerate until
cold. Pour into individual serving dishes. Top each with sour
cream; sprinkle with cinnamon. **9 servings.**

TIP: *If desired, pour mixture into blender container and
blend at low speed until smooth.

NUTRIENTS PER ⅑ OF RECIPE

Calories	140	Dietary Fiber	2 g
Protein	2 g	Sodium	20 mg
Carbohydrate	29 g	Potassium	115 mg
Fat	2 g	Calcium	6% U.S. RDA
Cholesterol	4 mg	Iron	<2% U.S. RDA

Scandinavian Fruit Soup

  ½ cup sugar
    4 cups water
  ¼ cup quick cooking tapioca

½ cup raisins
8-oz. pkg. (2 cups) mixed dried fruit
½ lemon, finely chopped (including peel)
1 stick cinnamon

In large saucepan, combine sugar and water. Bring to a boil. Gradually add tapioca, stirring constantly. Add remaining ingredients; cover and simmer 1½ hours, stirring occasionally. Discard cinnamon stick. Serve hot. **10 servings.**

NUTRIENTS PER ⅒ OF RECIPE

Calories	130	Dietary Fiber	3 g
Protein	1 g	Sodium	5 mg
Carbohydrate	32 g	Potassium	250 mg
Fat	0 g	Calcium	<2% U.S. RDA
Cholesterol	0 mg	Iron	2% U.S. RDA

Cold Peach Soup

16-oz. pkg. frozen peach slices, thawed, reserving ½ cup peach slices
¾ cup pineapple juice
½ cup orange juice
3 tablespoons sugar
½ cup dairy sour cream
½ cup half-and-half
¼ cup dry white wine
1 tablespoon lemon juice
¼ teaspoon cinnamon

Place peaches, pineapple juice, orange juice and sugar in blender container or food processor; process until smooth. Add sour cream, half-and-half, wine, lemon juice and cinnamon; blend until smooth and creamy. Pour into large bowl. Cut reserved ½ cup peach slices into chunks; stir into blended mixture. Cover; refrigerate until serving time. **8 servings.**

NUTRIENTS PER ⅛ OF RECIPE

Calories 140	Dietary Fiber.............................1 g
Protein.....................................1 g	Sodium...................................15 mg
Carbohydrate.........................24 g	Potassium..........................180 mg
Fat ....5 g	Calcium.................4% U.S. RDA
Cholesterol..........................10 mg	Iron........................2% U.S. RDA

Stews

Stews are heartier, thicker versions of soup and often require long, slow simmering of ingredients in a covered container to achieve tenderness and rich flavor. With stew on the menu, you don't need to serve much more than good bread, and perhaps a salad.

Types of Stew

• **Ragout** is well-seasoned meat and vegetables in a thick sauce.

• **Brunswick** typically features two meats such as chicken and game plus vegetables.

• **Burgoo** is generally made from several kinds of meat and a variety of vegetables and is highly spiced.

• **Chili con carne** is a well-seasoned combination of meat, tomatoes and beans.

Hearty Beef Stew

1½ to 2 lb. boneless beef stew meat, cut into 1½-inch cubes
    ¼ cup all purpose flour
     2 teaspoons salt
    ¼ teaspoon pepper
     3 tablespoons oil
     2 cups water
8-oz. can (1 cup) tomato sauce

    2 beef-flavor bouillon cubes or 2 teaspoons beef-
       flavor instant bouillon
    2 stalks celery, cut into 1-inch pieces
    2 medium onions, quartered
    1 bay leaf
    6 carrots, cut into 1-inch pieces
    4 medium potatoes, cut into pieces
    2 tablespoons flour
  ¼ cup water
    1 cup frozen peas or cut green beans
       Chopped fresh parsley, if desired

Coat beef cubes with mixture of ¼ cup flour, salt and pepper. In 5-quart Dutch oven, brown meat in oil. Stir in 2 cups
water, tomato sauce, bouillon cubes, celery, onions and bay
leaf. Bring to a boil. Reduce heat; cover and simmer 1½
hours or until meat is tender.

Remove bay leaf. Add carrots and potatoes. Cover; simmer
an additional 30 to 40 minutes or until vegetables are tender.
In small jar with lid, add 2 tablespoons flour to ¼ cup water;
shake well. Stir into stew mixture. Stir in peas. Cook over
medium heat until mixture boils and thickens, stirring frequently. Garnish each serving with parsley. **6 servings.**

NUTRIENTS PER ⅙ OF RECIPE

Calories	480	Dietary Fiber	7 g
Protein	40 g	Sodium	1390 mg
Carbohydrate	40 g	Potassium	1330 mg
Fat	18 g	Calcium	6% U.S. RDA
Cholesterol	100 mg	Iron	35% U.S. RDA

Chili Con Carne

    1 lb. ground beef
  ½ cup chopped onion
  ¾ cup water
  ½ cup chopped green pepper
    3 teaspoons chili powder

½   teaspoon salt
¼   teaspoon pepper
¼   teaspoon hot pepper sauce
1 to 2   garlic cloves, minced
28-oz.   can (3 cups) tomatoes, undrained, cut up
10¾-oz.   can condensed tomato soup
6-oz.   can tomato paste
4-oz.   can chopped green chiles, undrained
15½-oz.   can kidney beans, undrained*

In medium skillet, brown ground beef with onion; drain. In large saucepan, combine ground beef mixture and remaining ingredients except kidney beans. Bring to a boil. Reduce heat; cover and simmer 1½ to 2 hours, stirring occasionally.** Stir in kidney beans; simmer until thoroughly heated. Garnish. **6 servings.**

TIPS: *One 15½-oz. can chili beans, undrained can be substituted for kidney beans.

**For use in slow cooker, proceed as directed above and cook on low setting for 5 to 6 hours. Add kidney beans; heat thoroughly.

NUTRIENTS PER 1¼ CUPS

Calories	320	Dietary Fiber	9 g
Protein	20 g	Sodium	1280 mg
Carbohydrate	33 g	Potassium	1080 mg
Fat	12 g	Calcium	8% U.S. RDA
Cholesterol	45 mg	Iron	30% U.S. RDA

Hearty Meatball Stew

1   lb. bulk pork sausage
2   tablespoons oil
¼   cup flour
⅛   teaspoon pepper
1   cup water
10¾-oz.   can condensed chicken broth

  3 carrots, sliced
  2 stalks celery, sliced
  1 large (1 cup) onion, sliced
12-oz. can vacuum packed whole kernel corn,
       undrained
  2 cups water
  1 medium head cabbage, cut into 8 wedges

Shape pork sausage into 25 to 30 1-inch balls. In large skillet or Dutch oven, brown meatballs in oil, carefully turning to brown evenly. Remove meatballs from skillet. Reserve 2 tablespoons meat drippings in skillet; stir in flour and pepper. Gradually add 1 cup water and chicken broth. Cook until mixture boils and thickens, stirring constantly. Add carrots, celery, onion and meatballs. Simmer uncovered for 20 to 30 minutes or until vegetables are tender and stew is thickened, stirring occasionally. Add corn; heat thoroughly.

In large skillet or saucepan, heat 2 cups water to boiling; add cabbage. Cover and cook 8 minutes or until crisp-tender; drain. Arrange cabbage wedges in a ring, cut side down, around edge of serving platter; spoon stew into center of cabbage ring. **6 servings.**

NUTRIENTS PER ⅙ OF RECIPE

Calories	330	Dietary Fiber	6 g
Protein	14 g	Sodium	960 mg
Carbohydrate	30 g	Potassium	870 mg
Fat	17 g	Calcium	10% U.S. RDA
Cholesterol	30 mg	Iron	10% U.S. RDA

Oven Baked Stew

  2 lb. beef stew meat
  1 tablespoon sugar
  1 teaspoon salt
  ⅛ teaspoon pepper
  ⅛ teaspoon thyme leaves
  ⅛ teaspoon marjoram leaves

⅛ teaspoon rosemary leaves
6 whole carrots, cut into chunks
3 stalks celery, thickly sliced
1 large onion, chopped
¼ to ½ cup red wine
16-oz. can (2 cups) tomatoes, undrained

Heat oven to 250°F. In ungreased 3-quart casserole, combine all ingredients; mix well. Cover; bake at 250°F. for 5 to 6 hours or until meat and vegetables are tender, stirring occasionally. **6 to 8 servings.**

NUTRIENTS PER ⅛ OF RECIPE

Calories	240	Dietary Fiber	3 g
Protein	27 g	Sodium	440 mg
Carbohydrate	12 g	Potassium	600 mg
Fat	8 g	Calcium	4% U.S. RDA
Cholesterol	80 mg	Iron	20% U.S. RDA

Best-Ever Lamb Stew

2 lb. boneless lamb for stew, cut into 1-inch cubes
½ teaspoon sugar
1 tablespoon oil
⅓ cup all purpose flour
2 tablespoons chopped fresh parsley
1 to 2 teaspoons salt
¼ teaspoon thyme leaves
¼ teaspoon pepper
1 garlic clove, minced
2 cups water
1 cup dry red wine or water
1 teaspoon Worcestershire sauce
1 bay leaf
6 to 8 carrots, cut into 1-inch pieces
4 stalks celery, cut into 1-inch pieces
4 small onions, quartered
2 to 3 medium potatoes, cut into pieces

Sprinkle lamb cubes with sugar. In 5-quart Dutch oven, brown lamb in oil. Stir in flour, parsley, salt, thyme, pepper and garlic. Cook 1 minute, stirring constantly. Gradually stir in water, wine and Worcestershire sauce. Add bay leaf. Bring to a boil. Reduce heat; cover and simmer 1½ hours or until meat is tender, stirring occasionally. Stir in vegetables. Cover; simmer an additional 30 to 45 minutes or until vegetables are tender. Remove bay leaf. **5 servings.**

NUTRIENTS PER ⅕ OF RECIPE

Calories	460	Dietary Fiber	5 g
Protein	26 g	Sodium	1015 mg
Carbohydrate	39 g	Potassium	955 mg
Fat	19 g	Calcium	8% U.S. RDA
Cholesterol	110 mg	Iron	20% U.S. RDA

Chicken Dumpling Stew

2½ to 3-lb. frying chicken, cut up
   2 tablespoons margarine or butter
   3 cups water
   2 chicken-flavor bouillon cubes or 2 teaspoons chicken-flavor instant bouillon
   1 teaspoon salt
   ¼ teaspoon pepper
   2 stalks celery, cut into 1-inch pieces
   1 medium onion, sliced
   1 bay leaf
   ⅓ cup all purpose flour
   ½ cup water
  1½ cups frozen mixed vegetables
   1 recipe Fluffy Dumplings (see Index)

In 5-quart Dutch oven, brown chicken in margarine. Add water, bouillon cubes, salt, pepper, celery, onion and bay leaf. Bring to a boil. Reduce heat. Cover; simmer 50 to 60 minutes or until chicken is tender. Remove chicken and bay leaf from broth. Remove chicken from bones; cut into pieces. Skim fat from broth.

In small jar with lid, add flour to water; shake well. Stir into broth. Cook over medium heat until mixture boils and slightly thickens, stirring frequently. Stir in chicken and vegetables. Bring to a boil. Drop dumpling dough by rounded tablespoons onto boiling stew mixture. Reduce heat. Cover tightly; cook 13 to 16 minutes or until dumplings are fluffy and no longer doughy on bottom. **6 servings.**

NUTRIENTS PER ¼ OF RECIPE

Calories	390	Dietary Fiber	5 g
Protein	30 g	Sodium	1180 mg
Carbohydrate	38 g	Potassium	525 mg
Fat	13 g	Calcium	8% U.S. RDA
Cholesterol	150 mg	Iron	15% U.S. RDA

Chicken Stew Oriental

- 2 whole chicken breasts (about 1 lb.), skinned, boned, cut into 1-inch cubes
- 2 tablespoons oil
- 1 garlic clove, minced
- 2 cups water
- 8¼-oz. can pineapple chunks in heavy syrup, drained, reserving syrup
- ⅓ cup uncooked regular long grain rice
- ¼ cup cider vinegar
- 3 tablespoons brown sugar
- 2 tablespoons soy sauce
- ½ teaspoon salt
- ½ teaspoon finely chopped gingerroot
- ⅛ teaspoon pepper
- ½ green pepper, cut into 1-inch pieces
- ½ red bell pepper, cut into 1-inch pieces
- 3 tablespoons cold water
- 2 tablespoons cornstarch

In large skillet, saute chicken and garlic in oil until chicken is partially cooked. Stir in 2 cups water, reserved pineapple syrup, rice, vinegar, brown sugar, soy sauce, salt, ginger-root and pepper. Bring to a boil. Reduce heat; cover and simmer 12 minutes or until rice is almost tender. Add green and red pepper and pineapple chunks. Combine 3 table-spoons cold water and cornstarch; quickly stir into stew mixture. Bring to a boil. Reduce heat; cover and simmer an additional 10 to 15 minutes or until rice and green pepper are tender. **4 servings.**

MICROWAVE DIRECTIONS: In 2-quart microwave-safe casserole, combine chicken and garlic. *Omit oil.* Cover with microwave-safe plastic wrap or cover. Microwave on HIGH for 3 to 4 minutes or until chicken is partially cooked, stirring once during cooking. Stir in *1 cup water,* reserved pineapple syrup, rice, vinegar, brown sugar, soy sauce, salt, gingerroot and pepper; cover. Microwave on HIGH for 12 to 15 minutes or until rice is tender, stirring once halfway through cooking. Stir in peppers and pineapple; cover. Microwave on HIGH for 1 minute. In small bowl, combine 3 tablespoons cold water and cornstarch; stir into chicken mixture. Microwave on HIGH for 1½ to 2 minutes or until slightly thickened, stirring once halfway through cooking.

NUTRIENTS PER ¼ OF RECIPE

Calories 360	Dietary Fiber............................1 g
Protein.....................................27 g	Sodium..............................840 mg
Carbohydrate..........................41 g	Potassium.........................420 mg
Fat ....10 g	Calcium.................4% U.S. RDA
Cholesterol.........................70 mg	Iron......................15% U.S. RDA

Vegetables

Vegetables

Leafy greens, potatoes, squash, corn, peppers, tomatoes, mushrooms, asparagus, onions, beans, broccoli, kohlrabi and others—vegetables have never been more enticing or exciting. Today, advanced cultivation and harvesting techniques, processing and shipping innovations have made it difficult to distinguish purchased vegetables from freshly picked and have also made possible the availability of a wide variety of fresh vegetables in our markets year round. In recent years, many vegetables new to our markets have been introduced, especially from Asia and Mexico, providing additional diversity to our meals. Vegetables bring distinctive flavors, bright colors, firm textures to menu planning and are rich sources of vitamins, minerals and fiber. No wonder vegetables are increasingly popular for main dishes as well as entreé accompaniments.

Purchasing

Vegetables are available in most markets in several forms—fresh, frozen, canned and dried.

• Fresh vegetables are usually least expensive and of best quality during their peak growing season. Unlike fruits, most vegetables are shipped at maturity and will not ripen further after harvesting (tomatoes are the exception). Look for freshness, crispness, good color, firm texture, unblemished skin and proper shape and size. Avoid vegetables with any signs of insects, wilting, bruising, spoilage or dryness. Vegetables such as potatoes, onions, squash and carrots retain their peak flavor and texture longer than others. For highest quality, we recommend purchasing most vegetables in amounts that can be used within several days.

The waxy coating found on vegetables like cucumbers, squash and turnips is used to guard produce against spoilage, to retain moisture content and improve appearance. This coating, approved by the Food and Drug Administration, is edible or may be gently scrubbed off with a vegetable brush.

• Frozen vegetables are generally of high quality because crops are harvested at the proper stage of ripeness when flavors and nutrients are at their peak. The processing, done as soon after picking as possible, consists of blanching so that vegetables closely resemble freshly picked in every way. Additives like sugar and salt are minimal unless the package contains a sauce. Select frozen packets that are firm with no evidence of thawing or freezer burn. In recipes, an equal amount of frozen vegetables can be substituted for fresh-cooked.

• Canned vegetables are now available with the options of less or no salt or sugar. Check label for selection guidelines. Avoid any cans with signs of leakage or bulging.

• Dried vegetables such as beans, peas and lentils provide an excellent, low-cost source of protein. Although there are individual color and flavor differences, these legumes can often be interchanged in recipes. Dried beans and peas increase in volume when cooked; on average, 1 cup dried beans yields 2½ cups cooked. Dried peppers and onions provide convenience for cooking and are available in the spice section of supermarkets. Store in a cool, dry place.

Storing

All vegetables—fresh, frozen and canned, lose nutrients during prolonged storage. Most fresh vegetables should be stored in the vegetable crisper compartment in the refrigerator, which is especially designed to provide optimum storage conditions. They can also be stored unwashed in plastic bags in the refrigerator. Keep unripe tomatoes at room temperature until they ripen, then refrigerate. Onions, garlic, potatoes, sweet potatoes, rutabaga and winter squash are best stored in a cool, dry, well-ventilated place out of direct sunlight. Onions and potatoes should be stored apart from each other to retard spoilage.

Vegetables purchased frozen should not be allowed to thaw before storing in freezer at 0°F. or lower. Canned and dried vegetables store best in a cool, dry place. Rotate cans as necessary so older purchases are consumed first.

To freeze most fresh vegetables, blanch first to retain flavor, true color, tender texture and nutrients and to prolong freezer life. Vegetables frozen as soon as possible after picking retain the most flavor, texture and quality.

Preparation

• Fresh vegetables require washing before cooking, but should not be allowed to soak. Just rinse or scrub quickly, drain and dry. Vegetables can be boiled, steamed, microwaved, baked, stir-fried, grilled or broiled. Whatever preparation method you prefer, use as little water as possible and avoid overcooking. To retain peak flavor, color and texture, as well as vitamins and minerals, cook vegetables until crisp-tender and still bright in color. Crisp-tender means that they are tender enough to pierce with a fork but still crisp to bite. Potatoes and beets should be tender throughout. Leafy greens should be wilted but bright in color.

• Commercially frozen vegetables should be prepared according to package directions. Canned vegetables need only be heated through in the liquid they are packed in.

Although many cooks prefer serving vegetables plain or just lightly seasoned, vegetables are congenial partners with a wide variety of toppings, sauces, glazes, stuffings, seasonings, flavored butters, and other additions. Seasonings can be combined with liquid as vegetables are cooking or with melted margarine or butter and tossed lightly with vegetables before serving. When microwaving vegetables, to avoid a speckled appearance do not season until after cooking.

Vegetable combinations are most attractive when there is a contrast in colors and textures with an emphasis on compatible flavors.

Fresh Vegetable Availability Chart

For best flavor, texture and price, purchase vegetables in their most plentiful months.

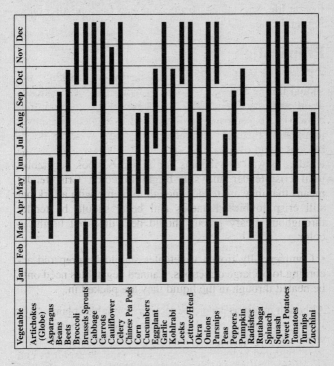

Tangy Artichokes

9-oz. pkg. (1 cup) frozen artichoke hearts
¼ cup dairy sour cream
1 tablespoon milk
2 teaspoons prepared horseradish
2 slices bacon, crisply cooked, crumbled

In medium saucepan, cook artichokes as directed on package; drain well. In small bowl, combine sour cream, milk and horseradish; mix well. Add sour cream mixture and bacon to artichokes, tossing to coat. **3 to 4 servings.**

NUTRIENTS PER ¼ OF RECIPE

Calories	80	Dietary Fiber	3 g
Protein	3 g	Sodium	100 mg
Carbohydrate	5 g	Potassium	55 mg
Fat	5 g	Calcium	2% U.S. RDA
Cholesterol	10 mg	Iron	<2% U.S. RDA

Asparagus Mornay Casserole

1 lb. asparagus*
1 tablespoon margarine or butter
1 tablespoon flour
½ teaspoon instant chicken bouillon
Dash nutmeg
1 cup half-and-half or milk
2 oz. (½ cup) shredded Swiss cheese
2 tablespoons crushed round buttery crackers

Remove tough ends from asparagus spears. Cook spears in small amount of boiling water until crisp-tender, about 10 to 15 minutes; drain. Arrange cooked asparagus in 12x8-inch (2-quart) baking dish. In small saucepan, melt margarine. Stir in flour, bouillon and nutmeg; cook 1 minute, stirring constantly, until smooth and bubbly. Gradually stir in half-and-half; cook until thickened, stirring constantly. Remove from heat; stir in cheese until melted. Pour evenly over asparagus; sprinkle with cracker crumbs. Broil about 6 inches from heat for 3 to 5 minutes or until lightly browned. Serve immediately. **4 servings.**

MICROWAVE DIRECTIONS: To cook asparagus in microwave, arrange spears in 12x8-inch (2-quart) microwave-safe dish; cover with plastic wrap. Microwave on HIGH for 4 to 6 minutes or until asparagus is crisp-tender, rearranging spears once during cooking; drain. In 4-cup glass measuring cup, microwave margarine on HIGH for 30 seconds or until melted. Stir in flour, bouillon and nutmeg. Microwave on HIGH for 30 seconds. Stir in half-and-half, blending well. Microwave on HIGH for 4 to 5 minutes or until thickened, stirring every 2 minutes; stir in cheese until melted. Pour evenly over asparagus; sprinkle with cracker crumbs. Microwave on HIGH for 1 to 2 minutes or until thoroughly heated.

TIP: *One 10-oz. pkg. frozen asparagus can be substituted for fresh asparagus.

NUTRIENTS PER ¼ OF RECIPE

Calories	200	Dietary Fiber	2 g
Protein	10 g	Sodium	170 mg
Carbohydrate	10 g	Potassium	440 mg
Fat	14 g	Calcium	25% U.S. RDA
Cholesterol	35 mg	Iron	6% U.S. RDA

Asparagus-Tomato Stir-Fry

1	tablespoon butter
1	lb. asparagus, cut diagonally into 1½-inch pieces
4	green onions, cut into 1-inch diagonal slices
4.5-oz.	jar sliced mushrooms, drained
2	small tomatoes, cut into thin wedges
1	tablespoon toasted sesame seed*
½	teaspoon grated lemon peel
1	tablespoon soy sauce

  2 teaspoons lemon juice
  ½ teaspoon sesame oil

Heat large skillet over medium-high heat. Add butter, asparagus and onions; stir-fry 3 to 4 minutes. Add mushrooms and stir-fry 1 minute. Stir in tomatoes, sesame seed, lemon peel, soy sauce, lemon juice and oil. Heat thoroughly. **8 servings.**

TIP: *To toast sesame seeds, spread on cookie sheet; bake at 375°F. for 3 to 5 minutes or until golden brown, stirring occasionally. Or, spread in thin layer in medium skillet. Heat over medium-high heat for 2 to 4 minutes or until light golden brown, stirring frequently.

NUTRIENTS PER ⅛ OF RECIPE

Calories 45	Dietary Fiber...........................2 g
Protein.......................................3 g	Sodium.............................190 mg
Carbohydrate...........................4 g	Potassium........................240 mg
Fat ....2 g	Calcium...............<2% U.S. RDA
Cholesterol...........................4 mg	Iron.......................4% U.S. RDA

Green Beans Polynesian

     4 cups cut green beans or 16-oz. pkg. frozen cut
         green beans
     1 large ripe pineapple, at room temperature
    ¼ cup chopped onion
     2 tablespoons margarine or butter
    ¼ cup sugar
     1 teaspoon dry mustard
     2 tablespoons vinegar
     2 teaspoons soy sauce
     1 tablespoon cornstarch
8-oz. can water chestnuts, drained, sliced

Cook green beans over medium heat until crisp-tender, about 8 to 12 minutes; drain.

Cut pineapple in half, keeping leaves intact. Hollow out pineapple, being careful not to puncture shell. Core and cube pineapple to make 1½ cups; reserve ⅓ cup pineapple juice. (Refrigerate any remaining pineapple cubes and juice for later use.)

In large saucepan or skillet, saute onion in margarine until tender. Stir in sugar, dry mustard, vinegar and soy sauce. Combine cornstarch and reserved pineapple juice; stir into onion mixture. Bring to a boil, stirring constantly. Add cooked green beans, water chestnuts and pineapple cubes; cook until thoroughly heated. To serve, spoon into pineapple shells. **10 servings.**

MICROWAVE DIRECTIONS: Place frozen beans in 1½-quart microwave-safe casserole; cover with microwave-safe plastic wrap or cover. Microwave on HIGH for 6 to 7 minutes or until crisp-tender, stirring once during cooking; drain. Prepare pineapple as directed above. In 2-quart microwave-safe casserole, microwave margarine on HIGH for 30 seconds or until melted. Add onion; microwave on HIGH for 1 to 2 minutes or until onion is tender. Stir in sugar, dry mustard, vinegar and soy sauce. Combine cornstarch and reserved pineapple juice; stir into onion mixture. Microwave on HIGH for 1½ to 2½ minutes until thickened and boiling. Add cooked green beans, water chestnuts and pineapple cubes. Microwave on HIGH for 2 to 4 minutes until thoroughly heated.

NUTRIENTS PER ⅒ OF RECIPE

Calories	100	Dietary Fiber	2 g
Protein	2 g	Sodium	105 mg
Carbohydrate	17 g	Potassium	240 mg
Fat	3 g	Calcium	4% U.S. RDA
Cholesterol	0 mg	Iron	4% U.S. RDA

Green Bean Casserole

Heat oven to 350°F. In ungreased 1½-quart casserole, combine 16-oz. can French-style green beans, drained, with 10¾-oz. can condensed cream of mushroom soup. Bake at 350°F. for 20 to 25 minutes or until bubbly. Top with 2.8-oz. can french-fried onions during last 5 minutes of baking. **4 to 5 servings.**

MICROWAVE DIRECTIONS: In 1-quart microwave-safe casserole, combine green beans and mushroom soup. Microwave on HIGH for 5 to 6 minutes or until thoroughly heated, stirring once halfway through cooking. Sprinkle french-fried onions over top. Microwave on HIGH for 2 minutes or until bubbly.

TIP: If desired, top with shoestring potatoes, potato chips or crumbled cheese crackers.

VARIATION:

ORIENTAL GREEN BEAN CASSEROLE: Add 8-oz. can sliced water chestnuts, drained, and ¼ teaspoon soy sauce to green bean mixture. Substitute chow mein noodles for onions.

NUTRIENTS PER ⅕ OF RECIPE

Calories	190	Dietary Fiber	1 g
Protein	3 g	Sodium	680 mg
Carbohydrate	14 g	Potassium	145 mg
Fat	14 g	Calcium	4% U.S. RDA
Cholesterol	0 mg	Iron	4% U.S. RDA

Boston Baked Beans

16-oz. pkg. (about 2⅓ cups) dry Great Northern or navy beans
  2   quarts water
  1   lb. smoked pork shank

½ cup chopped onion
½ cup molasses
2 tablespoons brown sugar
½ teaspoon dry mustard
¼ teaspoon ginger
¼ teaspoon allspice

In Dutch oven or large saucepan, cover beans with water. Soak overnight or at least 12 hours; *do not drain.* Add pork shank and onion to beans; bring to boil. Simmer 1 hour; drain, reserving 2 cups liquid. Heat oven to 300°F. Place drained beans and pork in ungreased 3-quart casserole or bean pot. In small bowl, combine remaining ingredients; stir in reserved liquid. Pour over beans. Cover; bake at 300°F. for 3 to 3½ hours or until beans are tender. Remove pork shank; trim meat off bone and return meat to casserole. Bake, uncovered, an additional 30 to 60 minutes or until liquid is absorbed and beans are tender. **8 servings.**

NUTRIENTS PER ⅛ OF RECIPE

Calories	260	Dietary Fiber	12 g
Protein	15 g	Sodium	305 mg
Carbohydrate	43 g	Potassium	850 mg
Fat	3 g	Calcium	10% U.S. RDA
Cholesterol	30 mg	Iron	30% U.S. RDA

Refried Beans

3 tablespoons margarine or butter
⅓ cup chopped onion
1 to 2 garlic cloves, minced
2 (16-oz.) cans kidney beans or pinto beans, drained
8-oz. can (1 cup) tomato sauce
2 tablespoons chopped green chiles
⅛ teaspoon salt

In large skillet, melt margarine; saute onion and garlic until tender. Add beans; mash with fork. Stir in tomato sauce, chiles and salt. Simmer 10 to 15 minutes to blend flavors, stirring occasionally. **6 servings.**

NUTRIENTS PER ⅙ OF RECIPE

Calories 100	Dietary Fiber...........................8 g
Protein......................................5 g	Sodium.............................350 mg
Carbohydrate...........................8 g	Potassium......................350 mg
Fat ....6 g	Calcium.................2% U.S. RDA
Cholesterol ....0 mg	Iron........................6% U.S. RDA

Dried Legumes

The legume family includes lentils, lima beans, black-eyed peas, soybeans, navy beans, split peas, kidney beans and pinto beans. Although there are individual differences in color and flavor, peas and beans of a similar type can be used interchangeably. Dried beans and peas need soaking to rehydrate before cooking. Lentils and split peas are the exception. They are small and do not have a skin, so they can be rehydrated by the cooking process. For dried beans or peas, allow 1 cup dried (½ lb.) for 4 servings. One cup dried will yield 2½ cups cooked.

Before rehydrating or cooking, wash and sort beans or peas. *To rehydrate,* let beans or peas stand in cold water overnight or about 12 hours. Or combine beans or peas and water; heat to boiling and boil 2 minutes. Remove from heat, cover and let stand 1 hour. With either method, retain the soaking water for cooking. *To cook,* heat beans and soaking water to boiling over high heat. Reduce heat; simmer covered over low heat until tender. To keep water from foaming, add 1 tablespoon oil during cooking. Salt, wine, tomatoes or other acidic foods tend to toughen the skins of beans and peas; do not add acidic foods until the final part of cooking.

Cooking Chart

Type	Amount Of Dried	Water	Soak	Cooking
Lentils	1 cup (½ lb.)	2 cups	No	30 to 35 minutes
Split Peas	1 cup (½ lb.)	2 cups	No	30 to 45 minutes
Whole Peas	1 cup (½ lb.)	2½ cups to 3 cups	Yes	1 to 1⅓ hours
Beans or Black-Eyed Peas	1 cup (½ lb.)	2½ cups to 3 cups	Yes	1½ to 2 hours
Soybeans	1 cup (½ lb.)	4 cups	Yes	2 to 2½ hours

Favorite Succotash

    1½ cups frozen baby lima beans
     1 cup sliced carrots
     2 cups frozen corn
    ¼ teaspoon garlic salt
       Dash pepper
     2 tablespoons margarine or butter

In medium saucepan, bring 1½ cups salted water to a boil. Add frozen lima beans and carrots. Bring to a boil. Reduce heat; simmer 6 minutes. Stir in frozen corn. Simmer an additional 6 minutes; drain. Stir in remaining ingredients. Cook until heated. **7 servings.**

MICROWAVE DIRECTIONS: In 1½-quart microwave-safe casserole, combine carrots and margarine; *omit water.* Cover with microwave-safe plastic wrap or cover. Microwave on HIGH for 2 to 3 minutes or until crisp-tender. Add remaining ingredients; recover. Microwave on HIGH for 6 to 8 minutes or until thoroughly heated, stirring once halfway through cooking.

NUTRIENTS PER ⅓ OF RECIPE

Calories	120	Dietary Fiber	5 g
Protein	4 g	Sodium	130 mg
Carbohydrate	18 g	Potassium	320 mg
Fat	4 g	Calcium	<2% U.S. RDA
Cholesterol	0 mg	Iron	4% U.S. RDA

Big Bean Pot

¾ lb. (18 slices) bacon, cut into pieces
3 medium onions, chopped
¾ cup firmly packed brown sugar
1 teaspoon garlic powder
½ teaspoon dry mustard
½ cup cider vinegar
¼ cup catsup
15½-oz. can kidney beans, drained
15½-oz. can butter or lima beans, drained
2 (21-oz.) cans pork and beans

Heat oven to 350°F. In Dutch oven, saute bacon and onions; drain. Add remaining ingredients; mix well. Bake at 350°F. for 60 to 70 minutes or until hot and bubbly. **16 servings.**

NUTRIENTS PER ¹⁄₁₆ OF RECIPE

Calories	220	Dietary Fiber	9 g
Protein	9 g	Sodium	510 mg
Carbohydrate	34 g	Potassium	340 mg
Fat	6 g	Calcium	6% U.S. RDA
Cholesterol	10 mg	Iron	15% U.S. RDA

Beets in Sour Cream Sauce

4 medium (2 cups) beets, cooked, peeled, cubed
1 tablespoon finely chopped onion
1 tablespoon margarine or butter

  1 tablespoon lemon juice
½ teaspoon salt
⅛ to ¼ teaspoon pepper
  3 tablespoons dairy sour cream
  1 egg, hard-cooked, finely chopped, if desired

In medium saucepan, combine beets, onion and margarine. Cook over low heat until thoroughly heated, stirring occasionally. Stir in lemon juice, salt and pepper. Add sour cream; mix well. Spoon into serving dish; sprinkle with chopped egg. **4 servings.**

NUTRIENTS PER ¼ OF RECIPE

Calories	110	Dietary Fiber	1 g
Protein	3 g	Sodium	365 mg
Carbohydrate	8 g	Potassium	235 mg
Fat	7 g	Calcium	4% U.S. RDA
Cholesterol	70 mg	Iron	4% U.S. RDA

Harvard Beets

  ¼ cup sugar
  1 tablespoon cornstarch
  1 teaspoon salt
     Dash pepper
16-oz. can sliced or diced beets, drained, reserving liquid
     Water
  3 tablespoons vinegar

In medium saucepan, combine sugar, cornstarch, salt and pepper. Measure reserved liquid; add water to make ¾ cup liquid. Gradually stir liquid and vinegar into sugar mixture; blend until smooth. Cook until mixture boils and thickens, stirring constantly. Add beets; cook until thoroughly heated. **4 servings.**

MICROWAVE DIRECTIONS: In 1-quart microwave-safe casserole, prepare mixture as directed above. Microwave on HIGH for 2 to 3 minutes or until mixture boils and thickens. Stir in beets. Microwave on HIGH for 2 to 4 minutes or until thoroughly heated.

NUTRIENTS PER ¼ OF RECIPE

Calories	90	Dietary Fiber	1 g
Protein	1 g	Sodium	830 mg
Carbohydrate	22 g	Potassium	160 mg
Fat	0 g	Calcium	<2% U.S. RDA
Cholesterol	0 mg	Iron	4% U.S. RDA

Sunny Sprouts

    2   (10-oz.) pkg. frozen Brussels sprouts
    1   cup thinly sliced carrots
    ½   cup thinly sliced celery
    1   cup water
    1   teaspoon salt
    1   teaspoon sugar
    2   tablespoons butter or margarine, melted
    1   teaspoon prepared mustard
    ¼   teaspoon salt
        Dash pepper

In medium saucepan, combine Brussels sprouts, carrots, celery, water, 1 teaspoon salt and sugar. Bring to a boil. Cook until crisp-tender, 10 to 12 minutes; drain. In small bowl, combine butter, mustard, ¼ teaspoon salt and pepper; add to vegetables and toss lightly. **10 to 12 servings.**

MICROWAVE DIRECTIONS: In 1½-quart microwave-safe bowl or casserole, place frozen Brussels sprouts, carrots, celery, salt, sugar and *2 tablespoons* water. Cover with plastic wrap. Microwave on HIGH for 7 to 9½ minutes or until carrots and celery are tender, stirring once halfway through cooking. Drain thoroughly. Add butter, mustard, salt and pepper. Microwave on HIGH for 2 to 3 minutes or until thoroughly heated. Stir mixture until butter is completely melted.

NUTRIENTS PER ½ OF RECIPE

Calories 50	Dietary Fiber ....2 g
Protein ....2 g	Sodium ....310 mg
Carbohydrate..........................6 g	Potassium ....230 mg
Fat ....2 g	Calcium................2% U.S. RDA
Cholesterol ....4 mg	Iron......................4% U.S. RDA

Broccoli with Orange Sauce

    1½ lb. broccoli, cut into serving-size spears
     2 (3-oz.) pkg. cream cheese
    ¼ cup milk
    ½ teaspoon salt
    ½ teaspoon grated orange peel
    ¼ teaspoon thyme leaves
    ¼ cup orange juice
 2 to 3 tablespoons chopped walnuts, if desired

In large saucepan, cook broccoli in boiling salted water until crisp-tender, about 7 to 12 minutes; drain well.

In small saucepan, combine cream cheese, milk, salt, orange peel and thyme. Cook over medium heat until smooth, stirring occasionally. Add orange juice; mix well. Place hot broccoli in serving dish. Pour orange sauce over broccoli; sprinkle with nuts. Garnish with orange slices, if desired. **6 to 8 servings.**

MICROWAVE DIRECTIONS: In 2-quart microwave-safe casserole or bowl, place broccoli and ¼ cup water; cover. Microwave on HIGH for 9 to 10 minutes or until crisp-tender; drain well. Place broccoli in serving dish; keep warm. In small microwave-safe bowl, combine cream cheese, milk, salt, orange peel and thyme. Microwave on HIGH for 2 to 3 minutes or until cream cheese is soft, stirring once. Stir until smooth. Add orange juice; blend well. Microwave on HIGH for 30 to 60 seconds or until hot. Continue as directed above.

NUTRIENTS PER ⅛ OF RECIPE

Calories	120	Dietary Fiber	2 g
Protein	4 g	Sodium	200 mg
Carbohydrate	5 g	Potassium	255 mg
Fat	10 g	Calcium	8% U.S. RDA
Cholesterol	25 mg	Iron	4% U.S. RDA

Broccoli-Mushroom Saute

  ¼ cup butter or margarine
  1 medium onion, thinly sliced
  4 cups bite-size broccoli florets
8 oz. fresh mushrooms, quartered
  ½ teaspoon garlic salt
  ⅛ teaspoon pepper

In large skillet, melt butter; saute onion until tender. Stir in broccoli, mushrooms, garlic salt and pepper; saute 1 to 2 minutes. Cover; cook over medium heat 5 to 7 minutes or until broccoli is crisp-tender, stirring frequently. **8 servings.**

MICROWAVE DIRECTIONS: In 3-quart microwave-safe casserole, microwave margarine on HIGH for 45 to 60 seconds or until melted. Stir in onion. Microwave on HIGH for 1 to 2 minutes or until crisp-tender. Stir in remaining ingredients; cover with microwave-safe plastic wrap or cover. Microwave on HIGH for 6 to 8 minutes or until broccoli is tender.

NUTRIENTS PER ⅛ OF RECIPE

Calories	120	Dietary Fiber	2 g
Protein	4 g	Sodium	260 mg
Carbohydrate	8 g	Potassium	460 mg
Fat	8 g	Calcium	4% U.S. RDA
Cholesterol	20 mg	Iron	6% U.S. RDA

Broccoli Ginger Stir-Fry

- 2 tablespoons oil
- 4 cups bite-size broccoli florets
- 2 garlic cloves, minced
- 1 tablespoon soy sauce
- 1 teaspoon minced gingerroot

Heat large skillet or wok over medium-high heat until hot. Add oil; heat until it ripples. Add broccoli, garlic, soy sauce and gingerroot; stir-fry 2 to 4 minutes or until broccoli is crisp-tender. **8 servings.**

NUTRIENTS PER ⅛ OF RECIPE

Calories 50	Dietary Fiber............................1 g
Protein......................................1 g	Sodium.............................140 mg
Carbohydrate...........................3 g	Potassium..........................150 mg
Fat ....4 g	Calcium.................2% U.S. RDA
Cholesterol...........................0 mg	Iron.......................2% U.S. RDA

Sauteed Cabbage

In medium skillet, melt 3 tablespoons margarine or butter. Stir in 4 cups (½ medium head) shredded cabbage, ½ teaspoon salt, ½ teaspoon dill weed and dash pepper. Cover; cook about 10 minutes or until cabbage is tender, stirring occasionally. **4 servings.**

TIP: Chinese cabbage can be substituted for cabbage.

NUTRIENTS PER ¼ OF RECIPE

Calories 100	Dietary Fiber............................2 g
Protein......................................1 g	Sodium.............................380 mg
Carbohydrate...........................4 g	Potassium..........................180 mg
Fat ....9 g	Calcium.................4% U.S. RDA
Cholesterol...........................0 mg	Iron.......................2% U.S. RDA

Cabbage Wedges with Veggie Cheese Sauce

½ medium head cabbage
1½ teaspoons margarine or butter
1 cup shredded carrots
1 cup thinly sliced celery
1 tablespoon flour
1 cup milk
2 oz. (½ cup) shredded Swiss cheese
½ teaspoon celery salt
¼ teaspoon nutmeg
⅛ teaspoon pepper

Cut cabbage into 4 wedges. Cook cabbage in lightly salted boiling water until crisp-tender, about 8 to 12 minutes; drain well. Meanwhile, in small saucepan melt margarine. Add carrots and celery; cook until tender. Remove from heat. Stir in flour. Gradually add milk. Cook until mixture boils and thickens slightly, stirring constantly. Add remaining ingredients; stir until cheese is melted. Place hot cabbage wedges on serving platter or in serving bowl. Pour sauce over cabbage. **4 servings.**

NUTRIENTS PER ¼ OF RECIPE

Calories	150	Dietary Fiber	3 g
Protein	8 g	Sodium	380 mg
Carbohydrate	15 g	Potassium	570 mg
Fat	7 g	Calcium	30% U.S. RDA
Cholesterol	20 mg	Iron	4% U.S. RDA

Sweet-Sour Red Cabbage

2 tablespoons margarine or butter
2 tablespoons chopped onion
6 cups (1 medium head) shredded red cabbage
1 small tart apple, thinly sliced
¼ cup firmly packed brown sugar

½ teaspoon salt
½ cup water
¼ cup vinegar

In large saucepan, melt margarine. Add onion; saute until tender. Add remaining ingredients; mix well. Cover; simmer 45 minutes or until cabbage is tender, stirring occasionally. **6 servings.**

NUTRIENTS PER ⅙ OF RECIPE

Calories 100	Dietary Fiber...........................2 g
Protein.......................................1 g	Sodium.............................240 mg
Carbohydrate........................16 g	Potassium........................220 mg
Fat ....4 g	Calcium.................4% U.S. RDA
Cholesterol..........................0 mg	Iron......................2% U.S. RDA

Honey-Glazed Carrots

½ cup water
1½ lb. small whole carrots, or carrots cut into
      2½x¼-inch strips
3 tablespoons butter or margarine
2 tablespoons honey

In medium saucepan, bring water to a boil. Add carrots. Cover; cook over medium heat for 8 to 12 minutes or until carrots are tender; drain. In large skillet, melt butter. Stir in honey. Add carrots. Cook over low heat, stirring constantly until carrots are well glazed. **12 servings.**

MICROWAVE DIRECTIONS: Place carrots in 1-quart microwave-safe casserole or bowl. Add *2 tablespoons* water. Cover with microwave-safe plastic wrap or cover. Microwave on HIGH for 10 to 13½ minutes or until carrots are tender, rotating once halfway through cooking.

In small microwave-safe bowl, combine butter and honey. Microwave on HIGH for 1 to 1½ minutes or until mixture boils; stir. Pour over carrots; toss until well coated.

Microwave on HIGH for 1 to 2 minutes or until thoroughly heated.

NUTRIENTS PER ½2 OF RECIPE

Calories	60	Dietary Fiber	2 g
Protein	1 g	Sodium	45 mg
Carbohydrate	8 g	Potassium	170 mg
Fat	3 g	Calcium	<2% U.S. RDA
Cholesterol	8 mg	Iron	<2% U.S. RDA

Carrots Supreme

- 2 tablespoons margarine or butter
- 2 cups thinly sliced carrots
- 1 cup thinly sliced celery
- 3 tablespoons water
- ¼ teaspoon salt
- ⅛ teaspoon pepper
  Dash dillweed or fresh dill
- 3 tablespoons half-and-half or whipping cream
- 1 teaspoon prepared horseradish

In medium skillet, melt margarine. Stir in carrots, celery and water. Cover; cook over medium-high heat for 3 to 5 minutes or until carrots are crisp-tender, stirring occasionally. Add remaining ingredients; mix well. Cook uncovered until liquid is almost evaporated. **5 servings.**

NUTRIENTS PER ⅕ OF RECIPE

Calories	80	Dietary Fiber	2 g
Protein	1 g	Sodium	210 mg
Carbohydrate	6 g	Potassium	270 mg
Fat	6 g	Calcium	4% U.S. RDA
Cholesterol	2 mg	Iron	2% U.S. RDA

Tangy Mustard Cauliflower

   1   medium head cauliflower
  ½   cup mayonnaise or salad dressing
1 to 1½ teaspoons prepared or dry mustard
   1   green onion, sliced
   2   oz. (½ cup) shredded Cheddar or American cheese
       Salted sunflower nuts, if desired

In large saucepan, cook cauliflower head in boiling salted water until crisp-tender, about 15 to 20 minutes; drain well. Place hot cauliflower in serving dish. In small bowl, combine mayonnaise, mustard and onion; spread over cauliflower. Sprinkle with cheese. Cover; let stand a few minutes until cheese is melted. Sprinkle with sunflower nuts. **8 servings.**

NUTRIENTS PER ⅛ OF RECIPE

Calories	160	Dietary Fiber	2 g
Protein	5 g	Sodium	140 mg
Carbohydrate	5 g	Potassium	240 mg
Fat	14 g	Calcium	8% U.S. RDA
Cholesterol	15 mg	Iron	4% U.S. RDA

Stir-Fried Oriental Celery

   2   tablespoons oil
   4   cups diagonally sliced celery
   8   oz. fresh mushrooms, sliced
   8   oz. pea pods or 6-oz. pkg. frozen pea pods, thawed, drained
   3   green onions, sliced
   1   tablespoon cornstarch
  ¼   teaspoon ginger
  ¼   cup corn syrup
   2   tablespoons orange juice
   1   teaspoon soy sauce
  ¼   cup slivered almonds
½ to 1 teaspoon grated orange peel

In wok or large skillet, heat oil. Saute celery in oil 3 minutes or until crisp-tender. Stir in mushrooms, pea pods and onions; saute 3 minutes. In small bowl, combine cornstarch, ginger, corn syrup, orange juice and soy sauce; pour over vegetables. Cook 1 minute, stirring constantly. Sprinkle with almonds and orange peel. **8 servings.**

NUTRIENTS PER ⅛ OF RECIPE

Calories 120	Dietary Fiber..........................2 g
Protein.....................................3 g	Sodium.............................145 mg
Carbohydrate........................16 g	Potassium.........................410 mg
Fat ....5 g	Calcium...............4% U.S. RDA
Cholesterol...........................0 mg	Iron.......................8% U.S. RDA

Corn Zucchini Saute

    1 medium red pepper, cut into strips
    1 medium green pepper, cut into strips
    3 cups (2 medium) sliced zucchini
   ¼ cup oil
    4 large ears (2 cups) sweet corn kernels, cut from
       cobs
    1 teaspoon garlic salt
   ½ teaspoon Italian seasoning

In large skillet, saute peppers and zucchini in oil until crisp-tender, about 5 minutes. Add corn, garlic salt and Italian seasonings; cook until thoroughly heated. **6 to 8 servings.**

NUTRIENTS PER ⅛ OF RECIPE

Calories 110	Dietary Fiber..........................3 g
Protein.....................................2 g	Sodium.............................240 mg
Carbohydrate........................11 g	Potassium.........................290 mg
Fat ....7 g	Calcium...............<2% U.S. RDA
Cholesterol...........................0 mg	Iron.......................4% U.S. RDA

Scalloped Corn

- ½ cup chopped onion
- 1 green pepper, chopped
- ¼ cup margarine or butter
- 16-oz. can cream style corn
- ½ cup seasoned bread crumbs
- 2 eggs, beaten

Heat oven to 375°F. Grease 1-quart casserole. In medium saucepan, saute onion and green pepper in margarine until tender; remove from heat. Stir in remaining ingredients; pour into prepared casserole. Bake at 375°F. for 35 to 40 minutes or until set. **6 servings.**

MICROWAVE DIRECTIONS: In 1-quart microwave-safe casserole, microwave margarine on HIGH for 45 to 60 seconds or until melted. Stir in onion and green pepper. Microwave on HIGH for 2 to 3 minutes or until tender. Stir in remaining ingredients, blending well. Microwave on HIGH for 8 to 10 minutes or until knife inserted in center comes out clean, stirring once halfway through cooking.

NUTRIENTS PER ⅙ OF RECIPE

Calories 190	Dietary Fiber............................2 g
Protein.......................................5 g	Sodium............................390 mg
Carbohydrate..........................22 g	Potassium.........................200 mg
Fat ....10 g	Calcium.................2% U.S. RDA
Cholesterol...........................90 mg	Iron.......................6% U.S. RDA

Fried Eggplant

- 2 eggs, slightly beaten
- 1 teaspoon salt
- 2 tablespoons milk
- 1½ lb. eggplant
- 1¼ to 2 cups dry bread crumbs
- ½ cup oil or olive oil

In small bowl, combine eggs, salt and milk. Peel eggplant; slice ¼-inch thick or cut into strips about ½-inch wide. Dip slices into egg mixture, then into bread crumbs. In large skillet, fry eggplant slices in hot oil until tender and golden brown. (Eggplant will absorb oil rapidly; add oil gradually as eggplant is fried.) Drain on paper towels. Place eggplant slices in warm oven until serving time. **4 to 6 servings.**

NUTRIENTS PER ⅙ OF RECIPE

Calories	350	Dietary Fiber	2 g
Protein	7 g	Sodium	630 mg
Carbohydrate	31 g	Potassium	280 mg
Fat	22 g	Calcium	8% U.S. RDA
Cholesterol	90 mg	Iron	10% U.S. RDA

Kohlrabi Parmesan

       2 tablespoons margarine or butter
       4 medium kohlrabi, peeled and sliced
      ¼ teaspoon marjoram leaves
      ¼ cup grated Parmesan cheese
          Salt and pepper

In medium skillet, melt margarine. Add kohlrabi and marjoram. Cook loosely covered over low heat for about 20 minutes or until tender, stirring occasionally. Add Parmesan cheese, mixing lightly to combine. Sprinkle with salt and pepper. **3 to 4 servings.**

NUTRIENTS PER ¼ OF RECIPE

Calories	100	Dietary Fiber	2 g
Protein	4 g	Sodium	320 mg
Carbohydrate	5 g	Potassium	260 mg
Fat	8 g	Calcium	10% U.S. RDA
Cholesterol	4 mg	Iron	2% U.S. RDA

Zesty Ratatouille

- ⅓ cup oil
- 2 lb. eggplant, cubed (6 cups)
- 2 medium zucchini, sliced (3 cups)
- 1 medium green pepper, cut into bite-size pieces (¾ cup)
- 2 stalks celery, cut into bite-size pieces (1 cup)
- ¾ cup sliced onions
- 1 to 2 garlic cloves, minced
- 3 medium tomatoes, peeled, cut into wedges (3 cups)
- 1 teaspoon basil leaves
- 1 teaspoon oregano leaves
- ½ teaspoon thyme leaves
- ¼ teaspoon pepper
- ½ teaspoon salt, if desired

In 4-quart saucepan, Dutch oven or wok, heat oil over medium heat. Add eggplant, zucchini, green pepper, celery, onions and garlic. Cook 7 to 10 minutes or until crisp-tender, stirring occasionally. Add tomatoes, basil, oregano, thyme, pepper and salt. Cover; simmer until thoroughly heated. **8 to 10 servings.**

TIP: One-half cup grated Parmesan cheese can be added with other seasonings, if desired.

NUTRIENTS PER ¹⁄₁₀ OF RECIPE

Calories	130	Dietary Fiber	2 g
Protein	3 g	Sodium	130 mg
Carbohydrate	12 g	Potassium	510 mg
Fat	8 g	Calcium	4% U.S. RDA
Cholesterol	0 mg	Iron	8% U.S. RDA

Creamy Basil Mushrooms

¼ cup margarine or butter, melted
1 lb. fresh mushrooms, sliced
2 tablespoons chopped green pepper
2 tablespoons chopped red bell pepper
½ cup whipping cream
2 tablespoons dry white wine
½ teaspoon salt
¼ teaspoon basil leaves

In large skillet, melt margarine. Add mushrooms and peppers. Saute over medium heat 5 to 7 minutes or until vegetables are soft, stirring occasionally. Remove mushrooms and peppers; keep warm. Add cream, wine, salt and basil to skillet. Simmer over low heat 5 to 7 minutes or until mixture thickens slightly, stirring frequently. Add mushrooms and peppers; cook until thoroughly heated. **6 servings.**

NUTRIENTS PER ⅙ OF RECIPE

Calories	160	Dietary Fiber	1 g
Protein	3 g	Sodium	290 mg
Carbohydrate	4 g	Potassium	340 mg
Fat	15 g	Calcium	2% U.S. RDA
Cholesterol	25 mg	Iron	2% U.S. RDA

English Mushroom and Cream Bake

8 oz. fresh mushrooms, sliced
2 tablespoons butter or margarine
1 teaspoon lemon juice
1 teaspoon Worcestershire sauce
6 oz. (1½ cups) shredded Gruyere cheese
1 cup whipping cream
4 eggs

Heat oven to 350°F. Generously grease 4 individual ramekins or four 10-oz. custard cups. In small skillet, saute mushrooms in butter, lemon juice and Worcestershire sauce; drain. To assemble each ramekin, sprinkle about 3 tablespoons of the cheese evenly over bottom. Pour ¼ cup whipping cream over cheese. Break 1 egg gently over cream; spoon ¼ of mushroom mixture evenly over egg. Top with ¼ of remaining cheese. In 13x9-inch pan, place ¾ inch hot water; carefully set ramekins in hot water. Cover pan with foil. Bake at 350°F. for 15 minutes. Uncover; bake an additional 10 to 15 minutes or until mixture is set and eggs are cooked. **4 servings.**

NUTRIENTS PER ¼ OF RECIPE

Calories	530	Dietary Fiber	1 g
Protein	21 g	Sodium	310 mg
Carbohydrate	5 g	Potassium	360 mg
Fat	47 g	Calcium	50% U.S. RDA
Cholesterol	420 mg	Iron	10% U.S. RDA

Southern Style Okra

3	slices bacon
⅓	cup chopped green pepper
1	medium stalk celery, chopped
1	small onion, sliced
1	teaspoon salt
	Dash pepper
1	cup coarsely chopped tomatoes
10-oz.	pkg. frozen cut okra
7-oz.	can whole kernel corn, drained

In medium skillet, fry bacon until crisp. Drain on paper towel; reserve drippings. Crumble bacon; set aside. To reserved bacon drippings, add green pepper, celery and onion. Saute until tender. Add remaining ingredients; mix well. Cover; simmer 10 to 15 minutes or until okra is tender, stirring occasionally. Sprinkle with crumbled bacon. **4 to 6 servings.**

TIP: One 16-oz. can cut okra, drained, and one 8-oz. can stewed tomatoes can be substituted for frozen okra and tomatoes.

NUTRIENTS PER ⅙ OF RECIPE

Calories	70	Dietary Fiber	2 g
Protein	3 g	Sodium	510 mg
Carbohydrate	10 g	Potassium	240 mg
Fat	2 g	Calcium	4% U.S. RDA
Cholesterol	2 mg	Iron	4% U.S. RDA

French Fried Onion Rings

Oil for deep frying
2 large yellow onions
2 eggs
1 cup milk
1⅓ cups all purpose flour
Salt and pepper

In heavy saucepan or deep fat fryer, heat 2 to 3 inches oil to 400°F. Slice onions into ¼-inch slices; separate into rings. In small shallow bowl, beat eggs. Add milk, flour, salt and pepper; mix well. Dip onion rings into batter; drain slightly. Fry onion rings in hot oil about 1 minute on each side or until golden brown. Drain on paper towels. **8 servings.**

NUTRIENTS PER ⅛ OF RECIPE

Calories	240	Dietary Fiber	1 g
Protein	5 g	Sodium	95 mg
Carbohydrate	19 g	Potassium	125 mg
Fat	16 g	Calcium	4% U.S. RDA
Cholesterol	70 mg	Iron	6% U.S. RDA

Peas with Dill

16-oz. pkg. frozen sweet peas
¼ cup chopped onion
2 tablespoons butter or margarine

2   tablespoons chopped pimiento
¾   teaspoon dillweed
⅛   teaspoon salt

Cook peas as directed on package; drain. In medium saucepan, saute onion in butter until tender. Stir in peas, pimiento, dillweed and salt; cook until thoroughly heated. **5 servings.**

MICROWAVE DIRECTIONS: Cook peas in microwave as directed on package. In 1-quart microwave-safe casserole, microwave margarine on HIGH for 30 seconds or until melted. Add onion. Microwave on HIGH for 1 to 2 minutes or until tender. Stir in peas, pimiento, dill weed and salt. Microwave on HIGH for 3 to 4 minutes or until thoroughly heated, stirring once halfway through cooking.

NUTRIENTS PER ⅕ OF RECIPE

Calories 120	Dietary Fiber ....2 g
Protein ....5 g	Sodium ....200 mg
Carbohydrate.........................13 g	Potassium ....170 mg
Fat ....5 g	Calcium ....2% U.S. RDA
Cholesterol ....10 mg	Iron ....8% U.S. RDA

Garden Fresh Stir-Fry

2   tablespoons oil
3 to 4   medium carrots, cut diagonally into ¼-inch slices (1½ cups)
1   cup broccoli florets, cut into 1-inch pieces
1   cup cauliflower florets, cut into 1-inch pieces
1   large garlic clove, minced
3   tablespoons water
1½   cups pea pods or 2 (6-oz.) pkg. frozen pea pods, thawed, drained
1   medium red bell pepper, cut into ¼-inch strips
¼   cup chopped onion
½   teaspoon salt

¼ teaspoon basil leaves
⅛ teaspoon pepper
⅓ cup whole cashews, if desired

Heat large skillet or wok over medium-high heat until hot. Add oil; heat until it ripples. Add carrots, broccoli, cauliflower and garlic; stir-fry 2 minutes. Add water. Cover; cook 3 to 4 minutes or until vegetables are crisp-tender. Add pea pods, red pepper, onion, salt, basil and pepper. Stir-fry about 2 minutes or until most of cooking liquid has evaporated and vegetables are crisp-tender. Sprinkle with cashews. **6 servings.**

NUTRIENTS PER ⅙ OF RECIPE

Calories	150	Dietary Fiber	3 g
Protein	4 g	Sodium	210 mg
Carbohydrate	15 g	Potassium	400 mg
Fat	8 g	Calcium	6% U.S. RDA
Cholesterol	0 mg	Iron	8% U.S. RDA

Louisiana Peppers

2 slices bacon, cut into 1-inch pieces
1 large green pepper, cut into ¼-inch strips
1 large red pepper, cut into ¼-inch strips
1 large yellow pepper, cut into ¼-inch strips
¼ teaspoon oregano leaves
2 tablespoons chopped fresh parsley

In large skillet, saute bacon until crisp; drain on paper towel. Reserve bacon drippings. Add pepper strips and oregano to skillet. Saute until peppers are tender. Stir in bacon. Spoon into serving dish; sprinkle with parsley. **6 servings.**

NUTRIENTS PER ⅙ OF RECIPE

Calories	35	Dietary Fiber	1 g
Protein	1 g	Sodium	45 mg
Carbohydrate	4 g	Potassium	180 mg
Fat	2 g	Calcium	<2% U.S. RDA
Cholesterol	2 mg	Iron	6% U.S. RDA

Baked Potatoes

Heat oven to 350°F. to 400°F. Select medium or large size (uniform for same baking time) raw white baking potatoes. Scrub potatoes. If desired, rub with small amount of shortening to soften skins. Prick with fork to allow steam to escape. Bake at 350°F. for 1 to 1½ hours or at 400°F. for 45 minutes to 1¼ hours or until tender. To microwave 1 potato, place in center of microwave. Microwave on HIGH for 3 to 4 minutes or until fork-tender. For each additional potato, add 2 to 3 minutes cooking time. Cover; let stand 2 to 3 minutes before serving. Using paper towels to protect hands from heat, roll potatoes between hands to make inside potato mixture light and mealy. Cut criss-cross slit in tops; gently squeeze lower part of potato to force potato up through slit. Top with margarine or butter, salt and pepper and/or one of these toppings:

Sour cream and chives
Crumbled cooked bacon
Sliced green onions
Crumbled blue cheese or shredded Cheddar cheese
Whipped cream cheese
Garlic or onion salt
One-half cup margarine or butter, whipped with 2 teaspoons
    lemon juice and 2 teaspoons chopped fresh parsley
One chopped onion sauteed in ½ cup margarine or butter
Cheese Sauce (see Index)

VARIATION:

QUICK BAKED POTATOES: Halve potatoes lengthwise; cut surfaces in criss-cross pattern (do not cut skins). Sprinkle lightly with onion and garlic salts. Dot with margarine. Place in ungreased shallow baking pan. Bake at 425°F. for about 30 minutes or until tender. Sprinkle with paprika. To microwave, prepare as directed above. Place 4 potato halves in 8-inch (2-quart) microwave-safe dish.

Cover with microwave-safe plastic wrap; microwave on HIGH for 10 to 12 minutes or until potatoes begin to feel tender, rotating potatoes once during baking. Remove from oven. Let stand covered 2 minutes. Sprinkle with paprika.

NUTRIENTS PER 1 POTATO

Calories	140	Dietary Fiber	3 g
Protein	3 g	Sodium	10 mg
Carbohydrate	32 g	Potassium	590 mg
Fat	0 g	Calcium	<2% U.S. RDA
Cholesterol	0 mg	Iron	2% U.S. RDA

Summer Salsa Potatoes

¾	cup finely chopped tomato
¾	cup finely chopped zucchini
¾	cup finely chopped cucumber
¼	cup chopped onion
2	oz. (½ cup) shredded Cheddar cheese
8-oz.	bottle mild taco sauce
6	medium raw baking potatoes, scrubbed
2	tablespoons margarine or butter, melted
¼	teaspoon garlic powder
12-oz.	carton creamed cottage cheese

In large bowl, combine chopped vegetables and cheese. Pour taco sauce over vegetables; toss until well coated. Allow vegetables to marinate at least 2 hours before serving.

Heat oven to 350°F. Pierce scrubbed potatoes with fork. Bake at 350°F. for 1 hour or until tender. Make a large slit lengthwise down center of each potato and push together at ends to create a well. Place potatoes in ungreased 13x9-inch (3-quart) baking dish. Combine melted margarine and garlic powder; spoon evenly over inside of each potato. Fill each potato with about ¼ cup cottage cheese. Spoon about ⅓ cup vegetable mixture over each potato. Return to oven and bake an additional 15 to 20 minutes or until thoroughly heated. Serve immediately. **6 servings.**

NUTRIENTS PER ⅙ OF RECIPE

Calories 290	Dietary Fiber..........................5 g
Protein ....15 g	Sodium..............................850 mg
Carbohydrate.........................40 g	Potassium........................920 mg
Fat ....8 g	Calcium..............15% U.S. RDA
Cholesterol ....20 mg	Iron......................8% U.S. RDA

Mashed Potatoes

Peel and cook 4 medium potatoes; drain. In large bowl, mash hot potatoes. Add 2 tablespoons margarine or butter and ½ teaspoon salt. Gradually add 2 to 3 tablespoons milk or sour cream, beating until light and fluffy. If desired, top with additional margarine and sprinkle with pepper or paprika. **4 servings.**

VARIATION:

CREAMED CHEESE MASHED POTATOES: Add 3-oz. pkg. cream cheese, softened with milk.

NUTRIENTS PER ¼ OF RECIPE

Calories 200	Dietary Fiber..........................2 g
Protein ....3 g	Sodium..............................370 mg
Carbohydrate.........................28 g	Potassium........................460 mg
Fat ....9 g	Calcium................2% U.S. RDA
Cholesterol ....0 mg	Iron.:......................2% U.S. RDA

American Fried Potatoes

Slice 6 peeled, raw potatoes. In large skillet, heat ⅓ cup oil. Add potatoes, 1 tablespoon finely chopped onion, if desired, and salt and pepper to taste. Fry over low heat, stirring occasionally, until light golden brown and potatoes are tender. **6 servings.**

NUTRIENTS PER ¼ OF RECIPE

Calories	200	Dietary Fiber	2 g
Protein	4 g	Sodium	100 mg
Carbohydrate	19 g	Potassium	620 mg
Fat	12 g	Calcium	4% U.S. RDA
Cholesterol	0 mg	Iron	25% U.S. RDA

French Fried Potatoes

In deep saucepan or deep fryer, heat oil or shortening (fill pan half full) to 375°F. Wash and scrub 4 medium raw potatoes. Peel or leave skins on. Cut into thin strips ¼ to ⅜-inch wide. Dry potatoes well with paper towels. Fry a few potatoes at a time 5 to 8 minutes, turning occasionally, until golden brown. Remove with slotted spoon; drain on paper towels. Salt to taste. **4 servings.**

NUTRIENTS PER ¼ OF RECIPE

Calories	470	Dietary Fiber	3 g
Protein	3 g	Sodium	280 mg
Carbohydrate	27 g	Potassium	810 mg
Fat	39 g	Calcium	<2% U.S. RDA
Cholesterol	0 mg	Iron	6% U.S. RDA

Crisp Browned Potatoes

  1 lb. (3 to 4 medium) raw potatoes, peeled, sliced
  ½ cup margarine or butter, melted
    Salt, if desired

Heat oven to 350°F. Place potatoes in ungreased shallow 1½-quart casserole. Drizzle margarine over potatoes. Sprinkle with salt. Bake at 350°F. for 45 to 55 minutes or until tender and golden brown. Baste occasionally with margarine from casserole. **4 servings.**

NUTRIENTS PER ¼ OF RECIPE

Calories	280	Dietary Fiber	2 g
Protein	2 g	Sodium	285 mg
Carbohydrate	18 g	Potassium	425 mg
Fat	23 g	Calcium	<2% U.S. RDA
Cholesterol	0 mg	Iron	2% U.S. RDA

Hash Browns

Shred 6 peeled, raw potatoes or cube 6 peeled, cooked potatoes (see Fresh Vegetable Cooking Chart). In large bowl, lightly toss potatoes with 1 tablespoon finely chopped onion; salt and pepper to taste. In large skillet, melt 6 tablespoons margarine. Add potatoes. Fry, partially covered, over low heat until bottom has a crisp golden crust and potatoes are tender. Turn; brown potatoes on other side. **6 servings.**

NUTRIENTS PER ⅙ OF RECIPE

Calories	230	Dietary Fiber	3 g
Protein	3 g	Sodium	230 mg
Carbohydrate	27 g	Potassium	820 mg
Fat	12 g	Calcium	<2% U.S. RDA
Cholesterol	0 mg	Iron	6% U.S. RDA

Lemon Buttered New Potatoes

    8 to 12 small raw new potatoes
       ⅓ cup margarine or butter
        2 tablespoons chopped fresh parsley
        1 teaspoon grated lemon peel
       ½ teaspoon salt
       ¼ teaspoon pepper
       ⅛ teaspoon nutmeg
        3 tablespoons lemon juice

Pare a strip around center of each potato, if desired. Cook potatoes in small amount of boiling water until fork tender;

drain well. In small saucepan, melt margarine. Add remaining ingredients; mix well. Cook until thoroughly heated. Place hot potatoes in serving dish; pour margarine mixture over potatoes. **4 servings.**

MICROWAVE DIRECTIONS: In 1½-quart microwave-safe casserole, microwave margarine on HIGH for 45 to 60 seconds or until melted. Add potatoes; stir to coat. Cover with microwave-safe plastic wrap or cover. Microwave on HIGH for 9 to 11 minutes or until tender, stirring once halfway through cooking. Stir in remaining ingredients. Microwave on HIGH for 1 to 2 minutes or until thoroughly heated.

NUTRIENTS PER ¼ OF RECIPE

Calories	320	Dietary Fiber	3 g
Protein	5 g	Sodium	450 mg
Carbohydrate	40 g	Potassium	950 mg
Fat	16 g	Calcium	2% U.S. RDA
Cholesterol	0 mg	Iron	8% U.S. RDA

Au Gratin Potatoes

  ¼ cup margarine or butter
  ¼ cup all purpose flour
  ½ teaspoon salt
  2 cups milk
  4 oz. (1 cup) shredded American or Cheddar cheese
  ½ cup grated Parmesan cheese
  5 cups (5 medium) peeled, sliced, raw potatoes
  ¼ cup dry bread crumbs
  1 tablespoon margarine or butter, melted

Heat oven to 350°F. In medium saucepan, melt ¼ cup margarine; stir in flour and salt. Add milk. Cook until mixture boils and thickens, stirring constantly. Stir in cheeses and potatoes. Pour into greased 2-quart casserole or individual casserole dishes. Combine crumbs with margarine; sprinkle over potatoes. Cover; bake at 350°F. for 1 to 1½ hours or until bubbly. If desired, garnish with chopped chives. **6 servings.**

TIP: Potatoes can be cooked before combining with other ingredients. Reduce baking time to 30 to 35 minutes.

NUTRIENTS PER ¼ OF RECIPE

Calories	370	Dietary Fiber	2 g
Protein	14 g	Sodium	790 mg
Carbohydrate	34 g	Potassium	860 mg
Fat	20 g	Calcium	35% U.S. RDA
Cholesterol	30 mg	Iron	8% U.S. RDA

Scalloped Potatoes

4	medium raw potatoes, peeled, thinly sliced
1	small onion, sliced, if desired
2	tablespoons margarine or butter
2	tablespoons flour
1	teaspoon salt
⅛	teaspoon pepper
1½	cups milk

Heat oven to 350°F. Place potatoes and onion in greased 1½ to 2-quart casserole. In medium saucepan, melt margarine. Blend in flour, salt and pepper; cook until smooth and bubbly, stirring constantly. Gradually add milk. Cook until mixture boils and thickens, stirring constantly. Pour sauce over potatoes. Bake at 350°F. for 1½ to 2 hours or until potatoes are tender. If desired, garnish with crumbled bacon. **4 servings.**

VARIATIONS:

SCALLOPED POTATOES WITH ONIONS: Place ⅓ of potatoes and ⅓ of onion slices in greased casserole. Sprinkle with 1 tablespoon flour, ½ teaspoon salt and dash pepper; dot with 1 tablespoon margarine. Repeat layering, ending with potatoes on top. Pour milk over potatoes. Bake as directed above.

CREAMY SCALLOPED POTATOES: Substitute one 10¾-oz. can condensed cream of mushroom or celery soup combined with ½ cup milk for the white sauce.

SCALLOPED POTATOES AND HAM: Add 1 cup cubed, cooked ham.

NUTRIENTS PER ¼ OF RECIPE

Calories	200	Dietary Fiber	3 g
Protein	7 g	Sodium	660 mg
Carbohydrate	27 g	Potassium	780 mg
Fat	8 g	Calcium	15% U.S. RDA
Cholesterol	6 mg	Iron	30% U.S. RDA

Glazed Sweet Potatoes

> 4 medium sweet potatoes*
> ¼ cup firmly packed brown sugar**
> ¼ teaspoon salt
> ¼ cup margarine or butter, melted

Cook sweet potatoes (see Fresh Vegetable Cooking Chart). Heat oven to 350°F. Peel cooked potatoes; cut into quarters or slice. Arrange in ungreased shallow baking dish. Combine remaining ingredients; drizzle over potatoes. Bake at 350°F. for 20 to 30 minutes or until glazed and thoroughly heated. Garnish with coconut, peanuts, macadamia nuts or miniature marshmallows. **4 servings.**

TIPS: *One 16-oz. can sweet potatoes, drained, can be substituted for fresh sweet potatoes.

**If desired, omit brown sugar and add ⅓ cup maple-flavored syrup.

To make ahead, combine all ingredients. Cover; refrigerate up to 2 days. Increase baking time to 30 to 45 minutes.

VARIATIONS:

FLAVORED SWEET POTATOES: Add one of the following:

- ½ teaspoon grated orange peel
- ⅛ teaspoon cinnamon or nutmeg
- ½ cup well-drained crushed pineapple
- ¼ cup orange or fruit juice
- 2 tablespoons rum or brandy

NUTRIENTS PER ¼ OF RECIPE

Calories	280	Dietary Fiber	3 g
Protein	2 g	Sodium	280 mg
Carbohydrate	41 g	Potassium	260 mg
Fat	12 g	Calcium	4% U.S. RDA
Cholesterol	0 mg	Iron	6% U.S. RDA

Mashed Rutabagas

- 2 to 3 medium rutabagas
- ½ teaspoon salt
- ⅛ teaspoon pepper
  Dash nutmeg, if desired
- ¼ cup hot milk
- ¼ cup margarine or butter

Peel, slice and cook rutabagas (see Fresh Vegetable Cooking Chart). In large bowl, mash hot rutabagas. Add remaining ingredients. Beat until light and fluffy. **6 servings.**

VARIATIONS:

MASHED TURNIPS: Substitute 2 lb. turnips for rutabagas.

MASHED PARSNIPS: Substitute 2 lb. parsnips for rutabagas.

NUTRIENTS PER ¼ OF RECIPE

Calories	100	Dietary Fiber	1 g
Protein	1 g	Sodium	290 mg
Carbohydrate	6 g	Potassium	240 mg
Fat	8 g	Calcium	4% U.S. RDA
Cholesterol	0 mg	Iron	2% U.S. RDA

Spinach Souffle

9-oz. pkg. frozen chopped spinach
   ¼ cup margarine or butter
   ¼ cup all purpose flour
   ½ teaspoon salt
   ⅛ teaspoon pepper
   1 cup milk
   3 eggs, separated

In medium saucepan, cook spinach as directed on package; drain well. Heat oven to 350°F. In small saucepan, melt margarine. Blend in flour, salt and pepper; cook until mixture is smooth and bubbly, stirring constantly. Stir in milk. Cook until mixture boils and thickens, stirring constantly. Remove from heat.

Blend small amount of hot white sauce into egg yolks, then add egg yolk mixture to remaining white sauce. Stir in spinach. In large bowl, beat egg whites until stiff peaks form. Stir ¼ of beaten egg whites into sauce mixture. Gently fold sauce mixture into remaining egg whites. Pour into buttered 1½-quart casserole. Set casserole in pan of water (1-inch deep). Bake at 350°F. for 40 to 50 minutes or until a knife inserted in the center comes out clean. Serve immediately. **4 servings.**

VARIATION:

ASPARAGUS SOUFFLE: Substitute 16-oz. can (2 cups) cut asparagus, drained, for spinach; decrease salt to ¼ teaspoon. Liquid drained from asparagus can be used for part of milk.

NUTRIENTS PER ¼ OF RECIPE

Calories 240	Dietary Fiber.........................2 g
Protein.....................................9 g	Sodium...........................530 mg
Carbohydrate........................12 g	Potassium........................360 mg
Fat ....17 g	Calcium...............15% U.S. RDA
Cholesterol.....................210 mg	Iron.....................15% U.S. RDA

Parmesan Squash Ring

  ½ cup chopped green onions
   2 tablespoons margarine or butter
   2 (12-oz.) pkgs. frozen mashed squash, thawed, or 3 cups mashed, cooked fresh squash
   1 cup grated Parmesan cheese
   4 eggs, beaten
1 to 2 tablespoons honey
  ½ teaspoon dry mustard
  ¼ teaspoon pepper

SAUCE
  ½ cup mayonnaise
  ½ cup dairy sour cream
   1 tablespoon chopped fresh dill or 1 teaspoon dillweed
   1 tablespoon lemon juice

Heat oven to 350°F. Oil 5-cup ring mold. In small skillet, cook onions in margarine until tender; set aside. In large bowl, combine squash, Parmesan cheese, eggs, honey, dry mustard and pepper; mix well. Add onions; stir gently. Spoon into prepared mold. Bake at 350°F. for 30 to 40 minutes or until set. Cool 10 minutes.

Meanwhile, in small bowl combine sauce ingredients; stir until well blended. To release from mold, gently run knife around edges; turn onto serving plate. Serve with dill sauce. Garnish as desired. **6 to 8 servings.**

NUTRIENTS PER ⅛ OF RECIPE

Calories	300	Dietary Fiber	2 g
Protein	9 g	Sodium	250 mg
Carbohydrate	15 g	Potassium	275 mg
Fat	23 g	Calcium	20% U.S. RDA
Cholesterol	160 mg	Iron	8% U.S. RDA

Dilly-Dilly Summer Squash

- 2 tablespoons sliced green onions
- 2 tablespoons margarine or butter
- 2 medium crookneck or zucchini squash, thinly sliced (3 cups)
- ½ teaspoon salt
- ½ teaspoon dillweed or 1½ teaspoons chopped fresh dill
- ¼ teaspoon pepper
- ¾ cup dairy sour cream

In large skillet, saute green onions in margarine 1 minute or until crisp-tender. Add squash, salt, dillweed and pepper. Cover; cook over medium-low heat until crisp-tender, stirring occasionally. Stir in sour cream. Garnish with additional fresh dill, if desired. **4 servings.**

NUTRIENTS PER ¼ OF RECIPE

Calories	170	Dietary Fiber	2 g
Protein	3 g	Sodium	360 mg
Carbohydrate	7 g	Potassium	280 mg
Fat	15 g	Calcium	8% U.S. RDA
Cholesterol	20 mg	Iron	2% U.S. RDA

Glazed Acorn Squash

- 3 acorn squash
- ¼ cup margarine or butter
- ¼ cup firmly packed brown sugar
- 2 tablespoons maple-flavored syrup
- ½ cup coarsely chopped walnuts

Heat oven to 350°F. Cut squash in half lengthwise; remove seeds. Cut squash halves crosswise into 1-inch thick pieces. Arrange in 13x9-inch (3-quart) baking dish; cover. Bake at 350°F. for 35 to 40 minutes or until nearly tender.

In small saucepan, melt margarine. Stir in brown sugar, syrup and walnuts; cook over medium heat just until sugar dissolves, stirring constantly. Spoon walnut mixture over squash. Continue baking an additional 10 to 15 minutes or until squash is tender, basting occasionally. **12 servings.**

MICROWAVE DIRECTIONS: Cut squash in half lengthwise; remove seeds. Cut squash halves crosswise into 1-inch thick pieces. Place fleshy portion up in 13x9-inch (3-quart) microwave-safe baking dish. Cover with microwave-safe plastic wrap. Microwave on HIGH for 12 to 16 minutes or until nearly tender, rotating dish ½ turn halfway through cooking. Allow to stand 5 minutes; drain thoroughly.

Sprinkle squash with walnuts. In small microwave-safe bowl, combine margarine, brown sugar and syrup. Microwave on HIGH for 1½ to 2 minutes; stir to combine. Pour sauce evenly over squash. Microwave on HIGH for 3 to 4½ minutes or until thoroughly heated. Spoon sauce over squash just before serving.

NUTRIENTS PER ½ OF RECIPE

Calories	140	Dietary Fiber	2 g
Protein	2 g	Sodium	50 mg
Carbohydrate	18 g	Potassium	420 mg
Fat	7 g	Calcium	4% U.S. RDA
Cholesterol	0 mg	Iron	6% U.S. RDA

Summer Squash Casserole

2	cups water
6 to 8	medium zucchini, sliced (6 cups)
1	cup shredded carrots
½	cup diagonally-sliced celery
½	cup chopped onion

    1   cup dairy sour cream
    ½   teaspoon dillweed
10¾-oz.   can condensed cream of chicken soup
  6-oz.   pkg. (4 cups) herb seasoned stuffing mix
    ½   cup margarine or butter, melted

Heat oven to 350°F. Grease 3-quart casserole. In 3-quart saucepan, bring water to a boil. Add zucchini, carrots, celery and onion. Cover; cook over medium heat about 5 minutes or until celery is crisp-tender. Drain. In small bowl, combine sour cream, dillweed and soup. Add to cooked vegetables; mix well.

In large bowl, combine stuffing mix and margarine. Spoon half of stuffing in bottom of prepared casserole. Spoon vegetable mixture over stuffing mixture; sprinkle with remaining stuffing mixture. Bake at 350°F. for 30 to 40 minutes or until golden brown and thoroughly heated. **18 servings.**

NUTRIENTS PER ¹⁄₁₈ OF RECIPE

Calories	140	Dietary Fiber	1 g
Protein	3 g	Sodium	330 mg
Carbohydrate	11 g	Potassium	180 mg
Fat	9 g	Calcium	4% U.S. RDA
Cholesterol	8 mg	Iron	2% U.S. RDA

Tomato-Zucchini Medley

  2   tablespoons butter or margarine
  3   medium zucchini, sliced
  ⅓   cup chopped onion
  2   medium tomatoes, peeled, cut into wedges
  ½   teaspoon basil leaves
  ½   teaspoon salt
  ⅛   teaspoon pepper

In large skillet, melt butter. Add zucchini and onion; saute until crisp-tender. Add tomatoes and basil; cook until tomatoes are hot. Season with salt and pepper. **8 servings.**

NUTRIENTS PER ⅛ OF RECIPE

Calories 40	Dietary Fiber..........................1 g
Protein.......................................1 g	Sodium............................160 mg
Carbohydrate..........................4 g	Potassium........................170 mg
Fat ....3 g	Calcium................2% U.S. RDA
Cholesterol ....8 mg	Iron.......................2% U.S. RDA

Vegetable Casserole

1½	cups cooked, drained cauliflower florets
1½	cups cooked, drained peas
1½	cups cooked, drained lima beans
1	cup cooked, drained sliced carrots
½	cup chopped onion
1	cup chopped celery
½	cup sliced water chestnuts
10¾-oz.	can condensed cream of celery soup
1	cup shredded American or Cheddar cheese
1	cup dairy sour cream
	Salt and pepper
½	cup bread crumbs
2	tablespoons margarine or butter, melted

Heat oven to 350°F. In ungreased 2-quart casserole, layer vegetables in order given. In small bowl, combine soup, cheese and sour cream; blend well. Season with salt and pepper. Pour over vegetables. Combine bread crumbs and margarine; sprinkle over top of casserole. Cover; bake at 350°F. for 20 minutes. Uncover; bake an additional 15 to 20 minutes or until thoroughly heated. **16 servings.**

NUTRIENTS PER 1/16 OF RECIPE

Calories 150	Dietary Fiber..........................2 g
Protein.......................................5 g	Sodium............................340 mg
Carbohydrate........................14 g	Potassium........................320 mg
Fat ....8 g	Calcium................8% U.S. RDA
Cholesterol ....15 mg	Iron.......................6% U.S. RDA

Creamed Vegetables

1 tablespoon margarine or butter
1 tablespoon flour
½ teaspoon salt
¼ teaspoon pepper
1 cup milk
2 cups cooked vegetables*

In medium saucepan, melt margarine. Blend in flour, salt and pepper; cook until mixture is smooth and bubbly, stirring constantly. Gradually add milk. Cook until mixture boils and thickens, stirring constantly. Stir in vegetables; cook until thoroughly heated. **4 to 6 servings.**

MICROWAVE DIRECTIONS: In 4-cup microwave-safe measuring cup, microwave margarine on HIGH for 30 seconds or until melted. Stir in flour, salt, pepper and milk until smooth. Microwave on HIGH for 2 to 3 minutes or until slightly thickened and boiling, stirring once halfway through cooking. Stir in cooked vegetables. Microwave on HIGH for 1 to 2 minutes or until thoroughly heated.

TIP: *Any one or more of the following vegetables can be used: cauliflower florets, peas, cubed or sliced potatoes or kohlrabi, onion or carrot slices, spinach, asparagus or cabbage.

NUTRIENTS PER ⅙ OF RECIPE

Calories 70	Dietary Fiber ....1 g
Protein ....3 g	Sodium ....220 mg
Carbohydrate ....8 g	Potassium ....210 mg
Fat ....3 g	Calcium ....6% U.S. RDA
Cholesterol ....2 mg	Iron ....2% U.S. RDA

Grilled Vegetables

CORN-ON-THE-COB: Husk corn; wrap in heavy duty foil. Place directly on the hot coals. Cook about 20 minutes, turning frequently until tender. Check doneness by pressing a kernel with your thumbnail. It should be tender but juicy.

CORN-IN-THE-HUSK: Pull husks back on ears of corn and remove silks. Replace husks. Soak in cold water about 30 minutes. Remove from water. Cook on grill about 4 inches from hot coals for about 20 minutes or until tender. Turn frequently to roast evenly.

MUSHROOMS: Large mushroom caps can be placed on skewers either alone or combined with meat. To prevent splitting, cook mushrooms in a small amount of boiling water for about 5 minutes before placing on skewers. Brush with melted or softened seasoned butter, meat marinades or basting sauces before grilling. Cook over coals about 10 minutes, brushing occasionally with melted or softened butter. Allow about 5 mushrooms per serving.

POTATOES: Scrub potatoes. Oil skin lightly and pierce with fork. Wrap each potato securely in squares of heavy duty foil. Place potatoes on grill 4 to 6 inches from hot coals. Roast about 1 hour or until tender, turning several times. Unwrap potatoes; slit top of each lengthwise. Serve with margarine, butter or sour cream.

SUMMER SQUASH: Small whole yellow zucchini or patty pan squash can be placed on skewers before grilling or put directly on the grill. One to 2-inch slices or quartered patty pan squash can be placed on skewers. Before grilling, brush with melted or softened seasoned butter or prepared French or Italian dressing. Cook over coals 20 to 30 minutes or until tender, brushing occasionally with melted or softened butter. Allow about 1 small squash per serving.

TOMATOES: Tomatoes cook more quickly than firmer vegetables. Both cherry and larger tomatoes can be used. No need to baste. Place small tomatoes on skewers or halves on the grill or on a sheet of foil to prevent skin from breaking. Small tomatoes cook in about 5 minutes; larger ones take about 10 minutes. Allow about 5 cherry tomatoes or 1 large tomato per serving.

Vegetable Tempura

In deep fryer or heavy saucepan, heat 2 to 3 inches of oil to 400°F. In small bowl, beat 1 egg slightly; add ½ cup cold water, ½ cup all purpose flour, 1 teaspoon sugar and ½ teaspoon salt. Blend until dry ingredients are moistened. Dip vegetables in batter; fry in hot oil about 3 to 4 minutes or until golden brown.* Drain on paper towels. Serve hot.

TIPS: *Crisp vegetable slices or pieces such as potato, green beans, green pepper, celery, cauliflower, onions, mushrooms, zucchini, eggplant or summer squash can be used for tempura.

Vegetables should be well dried with paper towels before dipping in batter.

Shrimp can also be used for tempura.

NUTRIENTS: Variables in this recipe make it impossible to calculate nutrition information.

Basic White Sauce

¼ cup margarine or butter
¼ cup flour
½ teaspoon salt
¼ teaspoon pepper
 2 cups milk

In medium saucepan, melt margarine. Blend in flour, salt and pepper. Cook until mixture is smooth and bubbly; gradually stir in milk. Stirring constantly, heat until mixture boils and thickens. **2 cups.**

VARIATIONS:

THIN WHITE SAUCE: Decrease margarine and flour to 2 tablespoons each.

THICK WHITE SAUCE: Increase margarine and flour to ½ cup each.

CHEDDAR CHEESE SAUCE: Decrease margarine and flour to 3 tablespoons each. Prepare white sauce; stir in 2 cups (8 oz.) shredded Cheddar cheese, 2 teaspoons Worcestershire sauce, dash Tabasco sauce and dash cayenne pepper. Heat over low heat and stir until smooth and cheese is melted. **3 cups.**

NUTRIENTS PER 1 TABLESPOON

Calories	25	Dietary Fiber	<1 g
Protein	2 g	Sodium	60 mg
Carbohydrate	1 g	Potassium	25 mg
Fat	2 g	Calcium	<2% U.S. RDA
Cholesterol	0 mg	Iron	<2% U.S. RDA

Buttery Amandine Sauce

In small skillet, over medium heat, heat ¼ cup butter until bubbly. Add 4.5-oz. jar whole or sliced mushrooms, well drained. Saute until golden brown, about 5 minutes. Stir in ½ cup slivered or sliced almonds; saute until fully heated. Pour over hot cooked green beans, asparagus or other vegetables. **About 1 cup.**

NUTRIENTS PER 1 TABLESPOON

Calories	50	Dietary Fiber	1 g
Protein	1 g	Sodium	50 mg
Carbohydrate	1 g	Potassium	35 mg
Fat	5 g	Calcium	<2% U.S. RDA
Cholesterol	8 mg	Iron	<2% U.S. RDA

Garlic Butter

In small bowl, combine ½ cup butter, margarine or unsalted butter, softened, and ⅛ to ¼ teaspoon garlic powder or 1 to 2 garlic cloves, minced. Beat 2 to 3 minutes at medium speed until light and creamy. Refrigerate 8 hours or overnight to blend flavors. Serve as a spread on French bread, as an accompaniment to steak, or as a topper for vegetables such as green beans or potatoes. **¾ cup.**

NUTRIENTS PER 1 TABLESPOON

Calories	70	Dietary Fiber	0 g
Protein	0 g	Sodium	80 mg
Carbohydrate	0 g	Potassium	0 mg
Fat	8 g	Calcium	<2% U.S. RDA
Cholesterol	20 mg	Iron	<2% U.S. RDA

Seasoned Butter

In small bowl, beat 1 cup butter or margarine, softened, until light and fluffy. Gradually beat in 3 tablespoons finely chopped fresh parsley, 1 teaspoon garlic or onion salt, ½ teaspoon pepper and 2 tablespoons lemon juice. Place in covered container. Store in refrigerator up to 1 month or in freezer several months. Use as a topper for any green vegetables. **1¼ cups.**

NUTRIENTS PER 1 TABLESPOON

Calories	80	Dietary Fiber	0 g
Protein	0 g	Sodium	190 mg
Carbohydrate	0 g	Potassium	10 mg
Fat	9 g	Calcium	<2% U.S. RDA
Cholesterol	25 mg	Iron	<2% U.S. RDA

Fresh Vegetables

Use the following chart and general cooking instructions as a guide for preparing and cooking fresh vegetables. Cooking times are based on 4 servings. Vary cooking times slightly to suit individual preference.

TO BOIL: Use shallow saucepan and about 1 cup water per pound of vegetable. Add ½ teaspoon salt per cup of water. Bring salted water to a boil over high heat; add vegetables. Return to a boil; begin timing. To preserve the natural color of green vegetables, boil uncovered for first 5 minutes. Cover pan and reduce heat; boil gently throughout the cooking time. Do not overcook.

TO MICROWAVE: Arrange vegetables in microwave-safe dish with thicker portions such as the stems of asparagus or broccoli toward the outside of the dish. Add 2 to 3 tablespoons of water; cover with lid or microwave-safe plastic wrap. Microwave on HIGH, stirring, rearranging or turning halfway through cooking. Remove at minimum time and let stand for time stated in chart, then check for doneness. If too crisp, continue cooking, checking frequently for doneness. Use care in releasing hot steam when removing lid or plastic wrap after cooking.

TO STEAM: Place vegetables on steaming basket over ½ to 1 inch of boiling water (water should not touch bottom of basket). Place whole vegetables in a single layer and layer cut-up vegetables no more than 2 inches deep. Cover tightly; reduce heat so water continues to boil and begin timing. Add more water during cooking if necessary.

Cooking Chart

Vegetable (4 servings)	Preparation	Cooking Time	Seasoning and Serving Suggestions
Artichoke (French/Globe) 4 medium	Wash. Trim off stem even with base and 1 inch off the top of the artichoke. Clip ½ inch off tips of leaves to remove thorns. Brush cut edges with lemon juice. Remove coarse outer leaves.	For boiling, use enough water to cover. Add 2 tablespoons lemon juice. **Boil:** 30 to 45 minutes. **Steam:** 25 to 35 minutes. **Microwave:** 9 to 14 minutes, let stand 3 to 5 minutes.	Serve hot with Hollandaise sauce or Garlic Butter. Serve cold with French or Italian salad dressing.
Artichoke (Jerusalem/Sunchoke) ¼ lb.	Wash. Peel; leave whole or slice. To keep from darkening before cooking, place in 1 quart of water with 3 tablespoons lemon juice added.	**Boil:** Whole, 10 to 20 minutes; Slices, 5 to 10 minutes. **Steam:** Whole, 15 to 20 minutes; Slices, 12 to 15 minutes. **Microwave:** 6 to 7 minutes, let stand 1 minute.	Serve raw in salads. Serve hot with butter, margarine or white sauce.
Asparagus 1 lb.	Wash thoroughly to remove dirt and sand. Snap off base of stalks (they will snap just	Tips will cook faster than the stalk. A bundle of spears can be placed upright so tips are	Serve hot with butter, margarine, Hollandaise sauce, fresh lemon, toasted

Asparagus Continued	between the tender and tough portions). Leave whole or cut into 1-inch pieces. Whole stalks may be tied together in a bundle before cooking.	above water. For cuts, tips may be added to boiling water a few minutes after stalk pieces. **Boil:** Whole, 10 to 15 minutes; Cuts, 5 to 8 minutes. **Steam:** Whole, 12 to 20 minutes; Cuts, 7 to 12 minutes. **Microwave:** 7 to 12 minutes, let stand 3 minutes.	almonds, grated Parmesan cheese or Italian salad dressing. Or, marinate cooked asparagus in French or vinegar and oil dressing; chill. Serve on lettuce.
Beans (Green and Wax) 1 lb.	Wash; trim off ends. Leave whole, slice diagonally into 1-inch pieces or slice lengthwise (French style).	**Boil:** Whole or 1-inch pieces, 8 to 15 minutes; French style, 10 to 12 minutes. **Steam:** 15 to 20 minutes. **Microwave:** 11 to 16 minutes, let stand 1 minute.	Season with Italian seasoning, basil leaves or add chopped onions during cooking. Serve with cheese sauce, sour cream and dillweed or sauteed mushrooms. Or marinate cooked beans in Italian dressing; chill and serve on lettuce.

Cooking Chart

Vegetable (4 servings)	Preparation	Cooking Time	Seasoning and Serving Suggestions
Beans (Lima) 3 lb. unshelled (1 lb. shelled)	Shell; wash.	**Boil:** 12 to 20 minutes. **Steam:** 20 to 25 minutes. **Microwave:** 16 to 18 minutes; stir twice. Let stand 1 minute.	Season with oregano, savory, tarragon or thyme. Serve with butter or white sauce.
Beets 1 lb. (4 medium)	Scrub with vegetable brush. Leave root ends and 2 inches of beet tops attached. Do not peel before cooking. Skins will easily slip off after cooking. Trim root and stem. Slice, dice, shred or leave whole.	For boiling, use enough water to cover. Add 1 tablespoon vinegar to preserve color. **Boil:** 35 to 40 minutes. **Steam:** 40 to 50 minutes. **Microwave:** 15 to 20 minutes; stir every 5 minutes. Let stand 3 to 5 minutes.	Season with cloves or thyme. Serve with butter, margarine, sour cream or orange sauce.

Vegetable	Preparation	Cooking	Serving
Broccoli 1 lb. (4 to 5 cups pieces)	Wash carefully; remove large outer leaves and tough portion of stalk. For uniform cooking, have stalks of similar size; split larger ones if necessary. Stems take longer to cook than florets.	**Boil:** 7 to 12 minutes. **Steam:** Spears, 12 to 14 minutes; pieces, 10 to 12 minutes. **Microwave:** 8 to 12 minutes, let stand 2 to 3 minutes.	Serve with butter, margarine, Hollandaise sauce, sour cream, cheese or mustard sauce, buttered bread crumbs, grated Parmesan cheese, crumbled cooked bacon or toasted almonds.
Brussels Sprouts 1 lb. (4 cups)	Remove wilted outer leaves; trim stems. Wash thoroughly.	**Boil:** 7 to 15 minutes. **Steam:** 15 to 20 minutes. **Microwave:** 6 to 9 minutes, let stand 3 minutes.	Season with curry powder, nutmeg or sage. Serve with butter, margarine, white sauce, cheese or mustard sauce, Hollandaise sauce, buttered bread crumbs, grated Parmesan cheese or chopped hard-cooked egg.
Cabbage (Savoy, Green, or Red) 1½ lb. (1 medium head)	Wash. Remove any wilted outer leaves. Cut into wedges or shred; discard core.	To preserve the color of red cabbage, add 1 tablespoon vinegar or lemon juice. **Boil:** Wedges, 8 to 12 minutes; shredded, 3 to 7 minutes.	Season with caraway, dill, nutmeg or oregano. Serve with sour cream, butter, margarine, crumbled cooked bacon, cheese or white sauce.

Cooking Chart

Vegetable (4 servings)	Preparation	Cooking Time	Seasoning and Serving Suggestions
Cabbage Continued		**Steam:** Wedges, 9 to 14 minutes; shredded, 5 to 8 minutes. **Microwave:** Wedges, 6 to 13 minutes; shredded, 7 to 13 minutes. Let stand 3 minutes.	
Carrots 1 lb. (about 2½ cups sliced or 3 cups shredded)	Peel with vegetable peeler to remove thin layer of skin. Remove ends; rinse. Leave baby carrots whole; cut larger carrots into slices or strips or shred.	**Boil:** Whole, 15 to 20 minutes; slices or strips, 8 to 13 minutes; shredded, 3 to 5 minutes. **Steam:** Whole, 20 to 30 minutes; slices or strips, 8 to 11 minutes. **Microwave:** Whole, 7 to 12 minutes, let stand 3 minutes.	Season with mint, cinnamon, ginger, nutmeg, chives or add raisins or chopped apple during cooking. Serve with butter, margarine, parsley, cheese sauce, honey, brown sugar, crumbled cooked bacon or sour cream.

Cauliflower 1¼ to 1½ lb. (1 medium head)	Remove outer leaves and excess portion of stem. Wash. Leave whole or cut into florets.	To cook whole head, place stem side down. **Boil:** Whole, 15 to 20 minutes; Florets, 8 to 15 minutes. **Steam:** Whole, 20 to 25 minutes; Florets, 10 to 18 minutes. **Microwave:** Whole, 8 to 15 minutes, let stand 3 minutes. Florets, 7 to 13 minutes, let stand 3 minutes.	Season with nutmeg, rosemary, basil leaves, caraway seed or tarragon. Serve with cheese, Hollandaise or mustard sauce, Parmesan cheese, buttered bread crumbs or sour cream.
Celery 1½ lb. (1 medium bunch or 4 cups sliced)	Separate stalks and wash thoroughly. Cut off bottoms, leaves or any blemishes. If outer stalks are especially stringy, remove larger strings with a vegetable peeler. Cut stalks into slices or 1-inch pieces.	**Boil:** 5 to 10 minutes. **Steam:** 18 to 20 minutes. **Microwave:** 3 to 6 minutes, let stand 3 minutes.	Season with bouillon, onion or dill. Serve with margarine, butter, cheese sauce, toasted almonds or grated Parmesan cheese.

Cooking Chart

Vegetable (4 servings)	Preparation	Cooking Time	Seasoning and Serving Suggestions
Chinese Cabbage or Celery Cabbage 1½ lb. (1 medium head)	Remove any wilted outer leaves. Wash. Cut off base. Slice crosswise.	**Boil:** 4 to 5 minutes. **Steam:** 4 to 6 minutes. **Microwave:** 5 to 8 minutes, let stand 3 minutes.	Season with ginger, garlic, onions or soy sauce. Serve with butter, margarine or sour cream.
Chinese Pea Pods (Snow Peas) 1 lb.	Wash; remove tips and strings along both sides of pod.	**Boil:** 2 to 3 minutes. **Steam:** 3 to 5 minutes. **Microwave:** 4 to 6 minutes, let stand 1 minute.	Season with garlic, ginger or bouillon. Serve with sauteed mushrooms, water chestnuts, soy sauce, toasted almonds or bean sprouts.
Corn 2-3 cups kernels (4 large ears)	Just before cooking, remove husks and silk; trim ends. Leave corn on cob or cut off kernels with sharp knife. If desired, corn on the cob can	Use unsalted water for cooking. **Boil:** Ears, 5 to 8 minutes; Kernels, 4 to 6 minutes. **Steam:** Ears, 5 to 9 minutes;	Season with sugar, curry powder, basil or green pepper. Serve with butter, margarine, seasoned butters, grated

Corn Continued	be microwaved with husks on. Strip back husks to remove silk, then pull the husks back over the corn. Or, remove husks and wrap each ear in plastic wrap or waxed paper for microwaving.	Kernels, 4 to 8 minutes. **Microwave:** 3 to 4 minutes per ear, let stand 2 minutes. Kernels, 5 to 9 minutes, let stand 1 minute.	Parmesan cheese, onion or chili sauce.
Cucumber 2 large	Wash. Peel, if desired. Slice, or cut into strips.	Generally served raw.	Season with basil, mint, dillweed or tarragon. Serve with sour cream or yogurt and chives.
Eggplant 1½ lb. (1 medium or 4 cups cubed)	Wash. Peel if skin is tough; cut off stem. Slice, cube or cut into strips. Dip in lemon juice to prevent darkening.	Slices are usually fried. **Boil:** 5 to 8 minutes. **Steam:** 5 to 9 minutes. **Microwave:** 5 to 7 minutes; stir every 2 minutes. Let stand 2 minutes.	Season with garlic, oregano, basil, thyme, rosemary, allspice, nutmeg or curry powder. Serve with grated Parmesan or shredded mozzarella cheese.
Kohlrabi 1½ lb. (4 small to medium)	Remove root ends and tops; wash, peel skin from bulb. Slice, cube or cut into strips.	**Boil:** 20 to 25 minutes. **Steam:** 25 to 30 minutes. **Microwave:** 10 to 12 minutes; stir twice. Let stand 5 minutes.	Season with nutmeg, garlic, basil, dill or chives. Serve with Parmesan cheese, cheese sauce, sour cream, butter or margarine.

Cooking Chart

Vegetable (4 servings)	Preparation	Cooking Time	Seasoning and Serving Suggestions
Kohlrabi Continued			Serve slices or strips raw in salads or with dip.
Leeks 1½ lb.	Remove root ends, tough outer leaves and tops, leaving 2 inches of dark leaves. Split lengthwise. Wash thoroughly.	**Boil:** 10 to 15 minutes. **Steam:** 10 to 15 minutes. **Microwave:** 4 to 7 minutes, let stand 3 minutes.	Season with dillweed, basil, thyme or rosemary. Serve with seasoned butter, crumbled cooked bacon or grated Parmesan cheese.
Mushrooms 1 lb.	Wash; pat dry. Cut off tips of stems. Do not peel. Leave whole or slice.	**Saute:** 4 to 5 minutes in 2 to 3 tablespoons butter. **Broil:** 8 to 10 minutes, 4 to 5 inches from heat, brushing with butter. **Microwave:** Omit water; add 3 tablespoons butter. Microwave 4 to 6 minutes covered with waxed paper. Let stand 2 minutes.	Season with white wine, garlic, green onions or chives. Serve with toasted almonds, dillweed or sour cream.

Vegetable	Preparation	Cooking	Seasoning and Serving
Okra 1 lb.	Wash pods thoroughly; cut off ends. Leave whole or slice.	For boiling, use enough water to cover. **Boil:** 5 to 10 minutes. **Steam:** 15 to 20 minutes. **Microwave:** 7 to 10 minutes, let stand 3 minutes.	Season with bacon, green peppers or celery. Serve with butter, margarine, buttered bread crumbs, tomato sauce, grated Parmesan cheese, French dressing, chili sauce or sour cream.
Onions (white, yellow or red) 1 lb. (2 large, 4 medium or 8 to 12 small)	, Trim stem and root ends; wash. Peel. Cut large onions into quarters or slices; leave small onions whole.	For boiling, use enough water to cover. **Boil:** Small whole, 15 to 20 minutes. Large whole, 20 to 30 minutes. **Steam:** Small whole, 20 to 25 minutes. Large whole, 35 to 40 minutes. **Microwave:** Small, 4 to 6 minutes, let stand 5 minutes. Large, cut into quarters, 5 to 6 minutes. Let stand 5 minutes.	Season with chicken bouillon, curry powder, caraway seed or parsley. Serve with white sauce, buttered bread crumbs or grated Parmesan cheese.
Parsnips 1¼ lb. (4 to 5 medium)	Wash. Peel. Cut off ends. Leave whole or cut in half, quarters, slices or thin strips.	**Boil:** Whole, 10 to 20 minutes. Slices, 8 to 15 minutes.	Season with nutmeg, onions or parsley. Serve with butter, margarine,

Cooking Chart

Vegetable (4 servings)	Preparation	Cooking Time	Seasoning and Serving Suggestions
Parsnips Continued		**Steam:** Whole, 15 to 25 minutes. Slices, 11 to 17 minutes. **Microwave:** Slices, 8 to 10 minutes, let stand 5 minutes.	brown sugar, honey, jelly, cheese or white sauce.
Peas 2 lb. unshelled (2 cups shelled)	Shell; wash.	**Boil:** 5 to 10 minutes. **Steam:** 8 to 12 minutes. **Microwave:** 5 to 7 minutes, let stand 1 minute.	Season with marjoram, savory, mint leaves, dill, basil or rosemary. Serve with butter, margarine, cheese or white sauce, crumbled cooked bacon, sauteed mushrooms, toasted almonds or sour cream.
Peas/Fresh Black-eyed 2 lb. unshelled (1 lb. shelled)	Shell; wash.	**Boil:** 20 to 25 minutes. **Steam:** 20 to 30 minutes. **Microwave:** 14 to 18 minutes covered with waxed paper, let stand 5 minutes.	Season with garlic, red pepper, cumin, chili powder or basil. Serve with butter, margarine, green pepper, cream or tomato sauce.

Peppers/ Bell (Green, red or yellow) 4 peppers or 2 peppers cut into halves	Wash. Remove stem and white membrane with seeds. Leave whole, cut in half, rings, or strips or chop.	**Boil:** Whole or halves in water to cover. 3 to 5 minutes to partially cook before stuffing. **Steam:** Whole or halves, 10 to 15 minutes. Rings or strips, 8 to 10 minutes. **Saute:** Strips or chopped in 2 to 3 tablespoons butter or margarine, 3 to 5 minutes. **Microwave:** Place 4 halves cut side down, covered with plastic wrap. Microwave 4 to 6 minutes; drain.	Season with basil, oregano, marjoram, onion or garlic. Serve with tomatoes, corn, shredded cheese. Serve raw in salads or with dip.
Peppers/ Hot (includes Jalapeño, Anaheim, Poblano, Serrano and over 200 other varieties)	When handling hot peppers, wear rubber or plastic gloves to protect hands from the chili oil or capsaicin. This oil is very irritating and can burn the skin. Avoid touching your face or eyes. Wash hands, utensils and cutting board thoroughly after cutting. Remove stems and seeds, then rinse with cold water.	Generally used as an ingredient in recipes.	Add to soups, stews and dips.

Cooking Chart

Vegetable (4 servings)	Preparation	Cooking Time	Seasoning and Serving Suggestions
Potatoes 1½ to 2 lb.	Wash and scrub. Peel if desired. Leave whole or cut in quarters, slices or chunks. To prevent peeled or cut edges from darkening before cooking, submerge in cold water.	**Boil:** Whole, 25 to 40 minutes; quarters, 20 to 25 minutes; slices or chunks, 15 to 20 minutes. **Steam:** Whole, 30 to 35 minutes; quarters, 20 to 25 minutes; slices or chunks, 8 to 12 minutes. **Microwave:** For whole potato with skin on, pierce in several places with a fork. Place at least 1 inch apart on paper towels in microwave oven. Microwave 12 to 16 minutes, let stand 5 minutes. Quarters, slices or chunks, 7 to 11 minutes, let stand 3 minutes. **Bake:** Pierce whole baking potatoes, with skin on, in several places with a fork. To	Season with onion, chives or rosemary. Serve with white or cheese sauce, butter or margarine, sour cream, chives, grated cheese or crumbled cooked bacon.

Potatoes Continued		soften the skin, if desired, rub with oil. Bake at 350°F. for 1 to 1½ hours or at 400°F. for 45 minutes to 1¼ hours.	
Potatoes/ New 1½ lb. (10 to 12)	Wash. Leave whole with skins on. If desired, peel a narrow strip around center of each potato.	**Boil:** 15 to 25 minutes. **Steam:** 18 to 22 minutes. **Microwave:** 8 to 12 minutes, let stand 3 minutes.	Serve with butter, margarine, grated lemon peel, chives, dillweed, sour cream, Italian dressing or grated Parmesan cheese.
Rutabagas (yellow turnips) 2 lb. (1 large or 2 medium)	Wash, peel. Slice, cube or cut into 2-inch pieces.	**Boil:** Cubes, 20 to 25 minutes; 2-inch pieces, 30 to 40 minutes. **Steam:** Cubes, 25 to 30 minutes; 2-inch pieces, 35 to 40 minutes. **Microwave:** Cubes, 14 to 18 minutes; stir every 3 minutes. Let stand 3 minutes.	Season with dillweed, cinnamon or nutmeg. Serve with brown sugar, maple syrup, butter or margarine.

Cooking Chart

Vegetable (4 servings)	Preparation	Cooking Time	Seasoning and Serving Suggestions
Spinach and Other Greens (beet tops, collards, turnip greens, mustard greens, kale, swiss chard) 1½ to 2 lb.	Wash and drain leaves several times. Remove tough stems and wilted leaves. Tear large leaves into bite-sized pieces.	Cook in water that clings to leaves from washing. **Boil:** Spinach, 3 to 5 minutes; other greens, 9 to 12 minutes. **Steam:** Spinach, 5 to 12 minutes; other greens, 10 to 15 minutes. **Microwave:** Spinach, 4 to 7 minutes; other greens, 7 to 9 minutes.	Season with garlic, onion, nutmeg, lemon or lime juice. Serve with crumbled cooked bacon, vinegar, soy sauce, white sauce, toasted sesame seed, sour cream or French dressing.
Summer Squash (pattypan, zucchini, straightneck yellow, crookneck yellow and cocozelle) 2 lb.	Wash but do not peel. Cut off stem and blossom end. If necessary remove seeds and fibers. Slice or cube.	**Boil:** 5 to 10 minutes. **Steam:** 5 to 10 minutes. **Microwave:** 7 to 11 minutes, let stand 3 minutes.	Season with oregano, basil, dillweed, nutmeg, ginger, allspice or rosemary. Serve with sour cream, butter, margarine, grated Parmesan cheese, parsley or crumbled cooked bacon.

Sweet Potatoes or Yams 1½ to 2 lb.	Wash but do not peel. After cooking, remove skins and slice or mash.	**Boil:** 20 to 30 minutes. **Steam:** 30 to 40 minutes. **Microwave:** 8 to 12 minutes, let stand 1 minute. **Bake:** Pierce whole sweet potatoes in several places with a fork. If desired, for softer skins rub with oil. Bake at 400°F. for 45 minutes to 1 hour.	Season with cinnamon, allspice or nutmeg. Serve with butter, margarine, brown sugar, maple syrup or honey.
Tomatoes 1½ lb. (5 medium)	Wash. Cut out stem. Peel if desired. (Dip tomato into boiling water 30 seconds, remove and dip into cold water; peel.) Leave whole, quarter or slice.	**Boil:** 7 to 15 minutes over low heat, cook covered without additional liquid, stirring occasionally. **Microwave:** Slices or wedges without additional liquid, 5 to 8 minutes, let stand 1 minute.	Season with basil, oregano, thyme, marjoram, sage or tarragon. Serve with sour cream, vinaigrette, grated Parmesan cheese or chives. Serve raw or as an ingredient in salads or with dip.
Turnips 1 lb.	Wash; peel. Leave whole or cut into slices or cubes.	**Boil:** Whole, 20 to 30 minutes; slices, 10 to 15 minutes. **Steam:** Whole, 25 to 35	Season with basil, dillweed, thyme or chives. Serve with butter, margarine, onion, crumbled cooked

Cooking Chart

Vegetable (4 servings)	Preparation	Cooking Time	Seasoning and Serving Suggestions
Turnips Continued		minutes; slices, 20 to 25 minutes. **Microwave:** 9 to 14 minutes, let stand 3 minutes.	bacon or brown sugar. Serve raw in salads or with dip.
Winter Squash (banana, butter-nut, hubbard, buttercup, acorn or spaghetti) 3 lb.	For boiling or steaming, peel and cut into cubes or slices. For baking or microwaving, cut in half or in serving-sized pieces. Remove seeds and fiber but not skin. For spaghetti squash, do not peel; cut in half lengthwise. Remove seeds and fibers.	**Boil:** Slices, 7 to 9 minutes; cubes, 6 to 8 minutes. For spaghetti squash, place cut side up; boil 25 to 35 minutes. **Steam:** Slices, 9 to 12 minutes; cubes, 7 to 10 minutes. **Microwave:** Do not use water. Spread cut surfaces with 1 to 2 tablespoons butter or margarine. Place in baking dish; cover with plastic wrap. Microwave 10 to 13 minutes, let stand 5 minutes.	Season with curry powder, nutmeg or sage. Serve with honey, brown sugar, maple syrup, cooked crumbled bacon, orange juice, butter or margarine.

| Winter Squash Continued | **Bake:** Place cut side up in shallow baking dish or pan. Add ¼ cup water. Dot squash with butter or margarine. Cover with foil. Bake acorn, hubbard, butternut, buttercup and spaghetti squash at 400°F. for 30 to 50 minutes, banana for 20 to 30 minutes. Serve as is or mashed. | |

Special Helps

Special Helps

Measuring

• **Liquid Measures:** To measure liquids, use standard liquid measuring cups that are available in 1-, 2- and 4-cup sizes with a pouring spout. Place cup on a level surface and fill to the required amount. Check at eye level.

• **Dry Measures:** To measure dry ingredients and solid fat, use standard dry measuring cups that come in sets of ¼, ⅓, ½ and 1 cup.

   • To measure shortening and brown sugar, firmly press into measuring cup, level off with spatula or knife. (Margarine or butter is often packaged in sticks and can be cut into desired amounts. Each ¼-lb. stick equals ½ cup or 8 tablespoons.)

   • To measure flour, granulated or powdered sugars and dry baking mixes, lightly spoon or pour ingredients into measuring cup and then level off with the straight edge of a spatula or knife. There is no need to sift flour before measuring.

• **Measuring Spoons:** Used for dry or liquid ingredients and available in standard sets of ¼, ½, and 1 teaspoon, and 1 tablespoon.

Equivalent Measures and Weight

dash = less than ⅛ teaspoon

3 teaspoons = 1 tablespoon

2 tablespoons = ⅛ cup or 1 fluid ounce

4 tablespoons = ¼ cup

5⅓ tablespoons = ⅓ cup

8 tablespoons = ½ cup

12 tablespoons = ¾ cup

16 tablespoons = 1 cup

1 cup = 8 fluid ounces

2 cups = 1 pint or 16 fluid ounces

4 cups = 1 quart

2 pints = 1 quart or 32 fluid ounces

4 quarts = 1 gallon

8 quarts = 1 peck

4 pecks = 1 bushel

16 ounces = 1 pound

1 ounce = 28.35 grams

1 liter = 1.06 quarts

Microwave Cooking

Whether used alone or in tandem with conventional cooking, the microwave oven can save both time and energy. From mini-meals to full-course old-fashioned dinners, the kitchen remains cool, cleanup is easier and foods retain color, texture, flavor, moistness and nutrients. Recipes in this cookbook have been tested in a *650-watt oven*. If the wattage of your oven is more or less than this, cooking times should be adjusted accordingly to avoid underdone or overcooked results.

Microwave Cookware

• Use only microwave-safe dishes and utensils. Glass, glass-ceramic, paper, dishwasher-safe plastics and pottery are generally acceptable because they allow microwaves to pass through and penetrate the food from all angles without harming the cookware or the oven itself.

• Avoid metal containers, dishes with metal trim, metal twist-ties and conventional meat and candy thermometers. Foil can be used only as oven manufacturer directs.

• Cookware shapes and sizes contribute to successful microwave cooking. Consider the size of the cooking dish when bubbling is likely and fill it only one-half to two-thirds full to avoid boilovers. Ring-shaped dishes are ideal for foods that cannot be stirred, and round shapes cook more evenly than square.

Microwave Cooking Techniques

• Arrange food to maximize the even penetration of microwaves. Foods of similar size (like potatoes for baking) microwave best when arranged in a ring. With foods of uneven thickness (like fish and chicken pieces), place smaller pieces and thinner areas to the center of the dish so dense portions can receive the most microwave energy.

• Appropriate coverings will add to cooking success. Glass lids and plastic wrap retain moisture and speed cooking. When using plastic wrap, fold back one corner to prevent excessive steam buildup. Microwave-safe paper toweling and napkins absorb moisture and grease and prevent spattering. Waxed paper prevents spattering and promotes even cooking.

• To promote even cooking, foods may be stirred from outside edges to inside to mix heated portions with unheated portions, rotated one-quarter turn when stirring is not possible, or rearranged or turned over according to recipe directions.

• Microwave cooking times for doneness, standing and holding are different from conventional cooking times. Test food for doneness at lowest time given whenever there is an option and return for additional time if necessary. Foods will continue to cook during standing time.

• Prick foods with thick skins (potatoes) or membrane coverings (egg yolks) to allow steam to escape to prevent bursting.

• Use a microwave thermometer for testing doneness of meats and other foods or remove meat from oven and test with conventional thermometer.

• When defrosting, place unwrapped food on microwave-safe rack or plate. Break up or separate pieces of food as soon as possible. If thin or small food areas begin to cook, allow food to stand for a short time or, if possible, remove defrosted portions and continue to defrost remainder. Large, dense foods may require standing times after microwaving to complete defrosting process.

Microwave Tips

• Add water sparingly for high-moisture foods like vegetables. Too much water drains color, flavor and nutrients and slows cooking.

• Foods with high-sugar areas, like sweet fillings and frostings, attract microwaves for quick heating. Monitor timing carefully to prevent overheating.

• Small quantities and piece sizes microwave more quickly than larger amounts, so vary times accordingly.

• Let the microwave speed up your cooking by handling such tasks as softening cream cheese, butter, margarine and ice cream; melting chocolate, butter or margarine and marshmallows; defrosting frozen foods; plumping raisins and other dried fruits; sauteing chopped vegetables for casseroles and stuffings and partially cooking foods to be finished in conventional oven or on the grill.

• Foods not recommended for microwave cooking are regular popcorn, liquor or liqueurs which are not combined with other ingredients, eggs in the shell, crusty breads, crispy fried foods, foam cakes, dried legumes and home canning.

Barbecuing

Safety First

• Read manufacturer's booklet accompanying grill to know proper operating and maintenance instructions.

• Before lighting, place grill in well-ventilated area away from anything that could catch fire and somewhat removed from center of activity. For charcoal grill, never use gasoline as a starter fuel.

• Never leave a lighted, hot grill unattended.

• Have a sprinkler bottle of water handy to control flare-ups.

• Invest in equipment for safe, convenient outdoor cooking, such as long-handled barbecue tools, heavily padded oven mitts and/or potholders, a large apron to cover clothing, skewers, heavy-duty foil, drip pan, hinged baskets, basting brush and a carrying basket for toting often-used utensils and seasonings.

• Be sure coals are under control or safely disposed of when finished.

Successful Cooking Suggestions

• For charcoal grills, purchase hardwood charcoal briquets. For special barbecue flavors, use wood chips from mesquite, fruit or nut trees. Avoid using resinous woods like pine, cedar, spruce and fir.

• For charcoal grills, the quantity and type of food to be cooked determine the amount and arrangement of the briquets. Generally there should be enough briquets to extend two inches beyond the food when it is placed in a single layer. If more briquets are needed after the fire is started, add them to the edges, gradually moving them into the center for even distribution. Rearrange briquets as little as possible after fire is established.

• Light charcoal or gas grill about 30 minutes before cooking food. Charcoal will be ready for cooking when partially covered with gray ash. When partially cooking foods in microwave oven or stove top before grilling, have grill ready when precooking is completed.

• Our recipes are tested with coals that are medium-high in temperature. To test temperature, hold your hand about 4 to 5 inches from coals. If you can hold that position for 3 seconds before the heat forces you to pull away, you are nearing this temperature.

• Trim meats before grilling to avoid uneven cooking, curling edges and flare-ups. Avoid grilling high-fat items like bacon.

• Baste with care, using small amounts of marinade to avoid flare-ups.

• Grill bone-in items bone side down first to help distribute heat throughout the food for slower, more even cooking.

• To prevent loss of juices, use tongs to turn meats and other foods.

• A band of foil secured around edge of grill can serve as a windbreak, and foil loosely tucked over food can serve as a grill cover.

• Use a meat thermometer whenever possible to determine doneness. And always pay close attention to food as it cooks to avoid overcooking or unsafe undercooking.

The Perfect Finishing Touch:

Garnishes

Entree & Salad Garnishes

• **Apple Feathers:** Select firm, unblemished apples. Using sharp knife, cut each into 4 wedges; remove core. From each wedge, cut a series of 3 to 5 gradually smaller V-shaped wedges; spread slices slightly so that contrasting cut surfaces are visible. Brush all cut surfaces with lemon juice. Use for salads and cheese plates.

• **Bacon Curls:** Fry or microwave bacon slices until browned but still limp; immediately roll up. Fasten with toothpick; drain. Use for salads and egg dishes.

• **Bell Pepper Flower Cup:** Select bell pepper of uniform shape, color and glossiness. Cut thin slice from bottom of pepper to form a flat base. With sharp knife, mark petal or zigzag design evenly around stem end of pepper; cut along markings with sharp-pointed knife to remove stem end of pepper. Remove membrane and seeds from inside of pepper. Use to hold salad dressings or dips, individual servings of salad or raw vegetable relishes.

• **Carrot Curls:** Using vegetable peeler, cut thin lengthwise strips of carrot. For curls, roll up; secure with toothpick. Place in cold water and refrigerate until crisp; drain. If desired, wrap carrot curls around olives, cucumber or celery sticks.

• **Citrus Cartwheels:** Thinly slice unblemished lemons, limes or oranges. Cut small V-shaped notches just into peel all around slice. Overlap or interlock 2 slices, if desired. Decorate with mint leaves.

• **Cucumber Twists:** For decorative effect, score cucumber with fork; cut into thin slices. Make a cut in each slice from edge to center. Twist slice and stand upright.

• **Fluted Mushrooms:** Wash, dry and trim mushrooms. Beginning at center of mushroom cap, using tip of knife, gently press V-shaped designs in circular pattern into cap. Refrigerate in plastic bag. If desired, mushrooms can be marinated or sauteed before using.

• **Green Onion Brushes and Curls:** Trim root end from onions. For brushes, remove most of the green top portion. With sharp knife, make 4 or more intersecting slashes at bulb end to make fringe. For curls, cut green top portion of onion lengthwise into several slivers without cutting into white portion. Place in cold water; refrigerate until curled.

• **Julienned Vegetable Bundles:** Select long, straight carrots and beans. Cut carrots lengthwise into very thin slices; cut each slice into thin strips or halve if desired. Cut beans into thin strips or leave whole. Cook or blanch vegetables until crisp-tender; season as desired. Divide into bundles. Tie using blanched green onion stems or chives as "ribbons" or drape thin slice of pimiento over the middle of each bundle. If desired, let vegetables cool, and marinate before serving.

• **Radish Pompons:** Remove thin slice from each end of radish. Starting at either end, cut each radish lengthwise into thin slices, cutting to but not through other end. At right angle to first cuts, make a similar series of parallel cuts to the same depth. Place in cold water; refrigerate until crisp.

• **Tomato Roses:** Select firm small yellow or red tomatoes. Using a very sharp knife and starting at bottom end of tomato, cut a thin slice for a base; do not sever. Beginning from base, cut a continuous narrow strip in spiral fashion, tapering to the opposite end to remove. (For wavy edges, use sawing motion when cutting.) Curl the strip onto its base in a rose shape. Use fresh herbs, celery leaves or green onion stems for leaves, if desired.

Dessert Garnishes

Dessert garnishes may be as simple or as elaborate as you wish. Choose them to complement and enhance the cake, pie or dessert.

• **Apricot Rose:** Sprinkle sugar on waxed paper. Place apricot halves over sugar. Sprinkle with additional sugar. Place second sheet of waxed paper over apricot halves. With rolling pin, roll out apricot halves until double in size. Roll one half tightly at a slight angle to form center of rose. Loosely wrap remaining halves around center, overlapping slightly and shaping edges like rose petals. Press together at base and trim if necessary.

• **Chocolate Curls:** Allow bar of chocolate to stand in warm place (80 to 85°F.) until slightly softened, about 10 minutes, or soften bar by wrapping in waxed paper and turning in hands to warm. Using vegetable peeler or cheese server, shave chocolate in long strands along smooth side of chocolate. For larger curls, draw blade over wide surface of chocolate; for small curls, pull blade along narrow side. Transfer curls with toothpick to dessert.

• **Chocolate-dipped Fruit or Nuts:** Melt semi-sweet chocolate. Partially dip fruits or nuts such as dried apricot halves, mandarin orange sections, strawberries, pecan halves or blanched almonds in chocolate; allow excess to drip off. Place on waxed paper. Refrigerate to set.

• **Chocolate Leaves:** To form chocolate into a leaf shape, melt unsweetened, semisweet, or sweet cooking chocolate or vanilla-flavored candy coating or almond bark. Brush melted chocolate evenly on underside of washed and dried nontoxic leaves (ivy, mint, lemon or rose leaves). Wipe off any chocolate that may have dripped to front side of leaf. Refrigerate leaves about 10 minutes or until chocolate is set. Apply second layer of chocolate over first layer. Refrigerate until chocolate is set. Carefully peel leaf away from chocolate. Store in refrigerator or freezer until ready to use.

• **Gumdrop Decorations:** Between sheets of waxed paper, roll out large gumdrops. Cut rolled candy into desired shapes using a sharp knife or small canape cutters.

• **Strawberry Fans:** Select firm strawberries with stems. Starting at a tip, cut thin slices almost to stem. Spread slices to form open fans.

• **Tinted Coconut:** In a bowl or covered jar, dilute a few drops of desired food coloring with 1 teaspoon water. Add 1 cup coconut and toss with fork or shake covered jar until coconut is evenly tinted.

Simple garnishes to make special designs or write out names:
  • Animal crackers or decorative cookies
  • Candied fruit
  • Candies such as mint wafers, jelly beans, gumdrops, peppermint candies, licorice strings or pieces
  • Chocolate or butterscotch chips
  • Chopped or whole nuts
  • Coconut—as is or tinted or toasted
  • Colored nonpariels or sugars
  • Fresh fruit or flowers
  • Miniature marshmallows
  • Raisins or candied fruit
  • Vary cake frosting by using a spatula or back of a spoon to smooth gently in swirls or spirals, create peaks or trace crisscross or zigzag.

Spices, Herbs & Blends

Spices, herbs and blends can add flavors, aromas and/or color to savory and sweet dishes. Use these seasonings judiciously, as flavors increase as food cooks and is stored. Many serve well as sodium and sugar substitutes.

- Spices consist of the seeds, buds, fruit or flower parts, bark or roots of plants.

- Herbs are the aromatic leaves.

- Blends are compatible mixtures which are combined commercially or by cooks according to taste preferences.

Purchasing:

Purchase in small amounts to use while flavor is at its peak. As a general rule, for 1 tablespoon of a snipped fresh herb, substitute 1 teaspoon dried or ¼ teaspoon of the powdered or ground form.

Storing:

Store fresh herbs in plastic wrap up to 2 weeks in the refrigerator. Store dried seasonings in a cool, dark, dry place away from damaging sunlight.

Food Storage

Proper storage—pantry, refrigerator and freezer—is absolutely essential for preserving the freshness and quality of food.

Dry Storing

- The best shelf and pantry storage areas are dark, dry and within a temperature range of 50 to 70°F. Avoid areas near heat sources and water pipes.

- Be alert to insects and help avoid the problem by keeping storage areas free of dust and food particles.

- Eliminate exposure to air, moisture and insects by storing foods in containers with tight-fitting lids. Rewrap packaged foods with torn or damaged wrappers and take time to reseal packages after use.

• Date foods not already marked by the manufacturer and use older items before more recently purchased products.

• Dispose of cans with bulges or leaks. Use contents of dented cans promptly.

• Store all food items away from household products to avoid any possibility of dangerous mix-ups.

Refrigerator Storage

• Maintain refrigerator temperature between 34 and 40°F. Check periodically by placing a thermometer inside.

• Refrigerate perishable items promptly after shopping.

• To allow proper air circulation for even cooling, don't overcrowd shelves.

• Store foods wrapped in plastic or in covered containers to prevent drying out and keep odors from spreading.

• Check expiration dates to use products before quality is jeopardized.

• Cover and refrigerate leftovers promptly. All high-moisture foods or those with meats, fish, poultry, eggs, custard and cream cheese fillings, cream sauces or cheeses are especially subject to bacteria growth at room temperatures.

• Use cooked meats and poultry within two days for optimum safety.

• Hot foods can be cooled in ice water to avoid raising refrigerator temperature above 45°F.

Freezer Storage

• Think of your freezer as a treasure chest, because that is exactly what it is if used to advantage. Freezing food is one of the best ways to prolong its life, to avoid waste and save time.

• Operate your freezer at the optimum temperature of 0°F. or below.

• Use quality containers and wraps designed especially for maintaining the freshness, texture and color of frozen foods. To protect foods from cold air deterioration use only moisture- and vapor-proof materials such as plastic containers with tight-fitting lids, freezer paper and heavy-duty plastic bags, wraps and foil.

• When filling containers leave room for expansion; when wrapping foods, press out air and wrap tightly.

• A wide variety of foods freeze beautifully, although there are some that alter unfavorably in texture, flavor and appearance. Among these are: salad greens, bananas, custard, mayonnaise and sour cream mixtures, luncheon and fried meats, hard-cooked egg whites and boiled frostings.

Safely Holding or Transporting Foods

• Safe temperatures for holding foods, according to the United States Department of Agriculture, are 140°F. or above for hot foods and 40°F. or below for cold foods.

• Use proper equipment for safe transport like thermal containers, ice chests and insulated coolers so that hot foods will stay hot and cold foods will remain chilled.

• Take extra precaution with any foods that are highly susceptible to bacterial growth, like dairy products, creamed and custard mixtures, meats, poultry, seafood and stuffings.

• Pack food and nonfood items separately and in the order you will need them. Pack thoroughly heated or chilled foods in separate containers.

• Pack liquids in tightly sealed containers and brace containers with other items to keep them upright.

• Do not leave any foods sitting in the hot sun. Even foods that might not spoil may deteriorate in quality.

• Take only as much food as you think will be eaten. Leftovers are best discarded.

• Hot foods will retain heat up to five hours if wrapped immediately upon removal from the oven in several layers of foil and then newspaper.

• Remember, FOOD SPOILAGE IN PROGRESS IS ALMOST IMPOSSIBLE TO DETECT. It takes only an hour for bacteria to grow in warm, moist conditions and this growth does not perceptibly alter taste, odor or appearance of most foods at the time they are being served and consumed.

Storing Foods in the Freezer

• When preparing foods to freeze, allow them to cool so their warmth does not raise the freezer temperature above zero. Then freeze them promptly. Season lightly because flavors can intensify during storage. After wrapping, label each package with contents, date to use before and number of servings or intended use. Periodic rotating of frozen foods is important to ensure use before quality diminishes.

• Food that has thawed should not be refrozen unless it is cooked first. Refreezing partially thawed goods still showing ice crystals often can be done safely; however, there may be a loss of quality. Thawed dishes containing a mixture of ingredients (stews, soups, pies, casseroles, etc.) cannot safely be refrozen.

• There are special packaging techniques particularly suited to small portions. For example, liquids such as stock, beverages, uncooked egg whites, and puree can be frozen in ice cube trays until firm, then removed and stored in plastic bags to use individual cubes as necessary. Ground meats can be divided into portions and frozen as is or formed into meat balls or patties to save time later and speed thawing. Some items, inconvenient when frozen in a large solid block (like berries and vegetables), can be spread on a tray, frozen until firm and then packaged in handier quantities. Make your own "TV dinners" by arranging slightly undercooked foods on divided foil trays. Fill air spaces with gravies and sauces, seal trays tightly with foil and freeze immediately.

Waxed paper between layers of flat foods like pancakes, chops, fish fillets, chicken pieces and steaks permit them to be easily separated for thawing. Freeze soups, stews and casserole mixtures in foil-lined dishes. When mixture is solid, remove dish for reuse and over-wrap food tightly with foil. To serve, unwrap and return food to casserole to heat.

Food Preservation:

Canning

Canning preserves the flavor of produce and allows you to store it for use at a much later date.

In the canning process, heat destroys food-spoiling agents such as yeasts, mold and bacteria. Some bacteria are killed by temperatures of 212°F. in the boiling water bath; other bacteria that cause botulism food poisoning are only destroyed by temperatures of 240°F. in the pressure cooker. Home canning is safe when canning procedures are carefully followed.

Keys to Successful Canning

• **Do Not Can Food in the Oven**
Conventional and microwave ovens are not satisfactory for canning because the jars may explode or the temperature of the food will not get high enough to kill botulism-producing bacteria.

• **Acid Foods**
Fruits and tomatoes need to reach boiling temperature (212°F.) to kill any organisms that could cause spoilage. The boiling water bath is one method used for canning these acid

foods. A container is needed that is large enough to hold the canning jars on a rack, allowing them to be covered with water that will boil. The pressure cooker may also be used for canning acid foods; 5 pounds of pressure is recommended and the time needed is shorter than in a boiling water bath. (During the hot summer this advantage may be important to you.) The open kettle method is no longer recommended for any fruits or tomatoes because it is impossible to prevent contamination at the time the jar is filled.

• **Low-Acid Foods**
Vegetables must reach a temperature higher than boiling water, so they are pressure-cooked to assure safe canning without danger of botulism. Follow manufacturer's directions carefully when using a pressure canner.

• **Jars**
Use standard canning jars that are specifically designed to withstand sudden changes in temperature or the high temperatures of pressure cooking.

Preparation of Jars

Select jars without nicks, cracks or rough spots on rim where lid will provide seal. Wash jars in hot soapy water, rinse well and let stand with hot water in them to warm the jars and prevent breakage when hot syrup is added. (Dishwasher may be used.)

Sealing of Jars

Vacuum-seal lids with metal screw bands are the easiest and most convenient to use. The seal can be checked at a glance by noting a depressed center of the lid when the jar is cooled. When using vacuum-seal lids, place in pan with water to cover; heat to boiling and keep hot during canning process.

Canning Fruits and Tomatoes Using Pressure Cooker Method

Follow directions for Canning Vegetables but use 5 pounds of pressure instead of 10 pounds.

Canning Vegetables Using Pressure Cooker Method

• Prepare vegetables and pack into jars according to Timetable for Canning Vegetables. Add boiling water, or the boiling water in which vegetables were heated, for packing as directed.

• To seal, wipe rim of jar with clean cloth to remove food particles that would prevent sealing.

• Place sealing compound rim of vacuum-seal lid on clean jar rim. Screw metal bands down tightly by hand.

• Place filled jars on rack in pressure canner containing 2 or 3 inches of hot water or the amount recommended by canner manufacturer.

• Place canner over high heat. Lock cover according to manufacturer's directions. Leave petcock or vent open for steam to escape.

• After steam has escaped for 10 minutes, close petcock or vent and let pressure rise to 10 pounds. Start counting processing time after it has reached 10 pounds. Watch heat to keep pressure at 10 pounds during processing time. (Fluctuating pressure causes the liquid to cook out of the jars.)

• When time is up, remove from heat and allow pressure to fall slowly to zero before opening. Slowly open petcock; if steam escapes, the pressure is not down yet. After petcock is open, remove cover.

• Remove jars from canner and cool upright 2 to 3 inches apart on wooden board, newspapers or several layers of cloth. Cool away from any draft that could cause hot jars to break.

• About 12 hours after processing, remove metal bands and make sure top of lid is depressed, which means the jar is sealed. (Lids are used only once; bands can be reused.) If jars are not sealed, store in refrigerator and use contents within a few days. Or, check jar top again for food particles; top with a new lid and process for original time.

• **Safety Note:** Before eating home-canned vegetables, bring the vegetables to a full boil, then cover and boil for 10 minutes. Boil corn 20 minutes. This is a safety precaution in case any phase of the canning process was not correct. The boiling destroys botulism toxins. If using home-canned vegetables for a salad, boil and cool before using.

Canning Fruits and Tomatoes Using Boiling Water Bath Method

• Prepare fruit and pack into jars. If fruits tend to darken, use ascorbic acid, according to manufacturer's directions. Add hot syrup or water as directed. Run knife between fruit and jar to remove any air bubbles. Add additional syrup if necessary.

Sugar Syrup for Fruits

| Allow 1 to 1½ cups syrup for each quart. | | | |
Type of Syrup	Sugar (Cups)	Water (Cups)	Yield (Cups)
Thin	1	3	3½
Medium	1	2	2½
Heavy	1	1	1½

• To seal, wipe rim of jar with clean cloth to remove food particles that would prevent sealing. Place sealing compound rim of vacuum-seal lid on clean jar rim. Screw metal bands down tightly by hand.

• Place filled jars on rack in a canner filled one third full of hot water. Add additional hot water as needed to cover jars 1 to 2 inches.

• Cover canner and heat water to boiling. Begin timing the processing when water boils. Reduce heat to hold water at a steady but gentle boil.

• Remove jars from canner and cool upright, 2 to 3 inches apart, on wooden board, newspapers or several layers of cloth. Cool away from any draft that could cause hot jars to break.

• About 12 hours after processing, remove metal bands and make sure lid is depressed, which means the jar is sealed. Do not retighten bands. (Lids are used only once; bands can be reused.) If jars are not sealed, store in refrigerator and use contents within a few days. Or, check jar rim again for food particles; top with a new lid and process again for 15 minutes.

• Store in a dark, cool area.

Food Preservation:

Jams & Jellies

Jams and jellies . . . not at all difficult or time-consuming to prepare with that same homemade goodness. Included are microwave-easy recipes particularly suited for today's smaller families and busy lifestyles.

Freezer Strawberry Jam

2 pints (1 quart) strawberries
4 cups sugar
1 cup water
1 pkg. (1¾ oz.) powdered fruit pectin

Crush strawberries or process in blender until in small pieces. Measure into a large bowl. Stir in sugar; let stand 10 minutes. In a small saucepan, combine water and pectin. Heat to boiling and boil 1 minute, stirring constantly. Stir into fruit mixture and continue stirring 3 minutes to dissolve most of sugar. Spoon into clean 8-oz. jar or moisture- vapor-proof freezer containers, leaving ½ inch of head space for freezer storage. Cool slightly; cover with tight-fitting lids. Let stand until set, about 24 hours. Store in freezer up to 1 year or in refrigerator 2 to 3 weeks. **5 cups.**

NUTRIENTS PER 1 TABLESPOON

Calories 45	Dietary Fiber ....NA
Protein ....0 g	Sodium.....................................0 mg
Carbohydrate...........................11 g	Potassium...........................15 mg
Fat ....0 g	Calcium...............<2% U.S. RDA
Cholesterol ....0 mg	Iron ....<2% U.S. RDA

Berry-Cherry Quick Jam

3	cups raspberries
16-oz.	can sweet cherries, drained (reserve liquid)
½	cup corn syrup
1	tablespoon lemon juice
5	cups sugar
	Reserved liquid plus water to make ¾ cup
1	¾-oz. pkg. powdered fruit pectin

Fully crush raspberries; measure 2 cups. Finely chop sweet cherries; measure 1 cup. In 4-quart bowl, combine raspberries, cherries, corn syrup, lemon juice and sugar; mix well. Let stand 10 minutes. In small saucepan, combine liquid and powdered pectin. Heat to full rolling boil, stirring constantly; **boil 1 minute.** Pour hot pectin mixture into fruit mixture; stir vigorously 3 minutes. Ladle jam into clean jelly glasses or moisture- vapor-proof freezer containers leaving ½ inch headspace. Cover with tight-fitting lids (no paraffin needed); label. Let stand for several hours at room temperature or until set. Store jam in refrigerator up to 3 weeks or in freezer up to 3 months. **8 cups.**

NUTRIENTS PER 1 TABLESPOON

Calories	40	Dietary Fiber	<1 g
Protein	0 g	Sodium	0 mg
Carbohydrate	10 g	Potassium	10 mg
Fat	0 g	Calcium	<2% U.S. RDA
Cholesterol	0 mg	Iron	<2% U.S. RDA

Berry Rosé Jelly

3½   cups sugar
1½   cups cranberry-raspberry drink
 ⅛   teaspoon cinnamon
 ⅛   teaspoon cloves
 ½   cup rosé wine
 1   pkg. (3 oz.) liquid fruit pectin

In large saucepan combine sugar, cranberry-raspberry drink, cinnamon and cloves. Bring to a boil, stirring to dissolve sugar. Boil 1 minute, stirring constantly. Remove from heat; stir in wine and pectin. Skim off foam with metal spoon. Spoon into clean 8-oz. jars or moisture- vapor-proof freezer containers, leaving ½ inch head space for freezer storage. Cool slightly; cover with tight-fitting lids. Let stand several hours at room temperature or until set. Store in refrigerator up to 3 weeks or in freezer up to 3 months. **3¾ cups.**

NUTRIENTS PER 1 TABLESPOON

Calories	50	Dietary Fiber	NA
Protein	0 g	Sodium	0 mg
Carbohydrate	14 g	Potassium	10 mg
Fat	0 g	Calcium	<2% U.S. RDA
Cholesterol	0 mg	Iron	<2% U.S. RDA

Fruit and Carrot Conserve

2 cups chopped peeled apples
1 cup chopped peeled pears
1 cup finely shredded carrots
3 cups sugar
¾ cup apple juice
2 tablespoons lemon juice
3-oz. pkg. peach gelatin

In large saucepan, combine apples, pears, carrots and sugar. Stir in apple juice and lemon juice. Over medium heat, bring mixture to a boil; boil 10 minutes, stirring occasionally. Remove from heat. Add gelatin; stir 1 minute. Ladle conserve into 4 clean 8-oz. jelly jars or moisture- vapor-proof freezer containers, leaving ½ inch headspace. Cover with tight-fitting lids. Refrigerate at least 24 hours. Store conserve in refrigerator up to 3 weeks or in freezer up to 3 months. **4 cups.**

NUTRIENTS PER 1 TABLESPOON

Calories	45	Dietary Fiber	<1 g
Protein	0 g	Sodium	5 mg
Carbohydrate	12 g	Potassium	20 mg
Fat	0 g	Calcium	<2% U.S. RDA
Cholesterol	0 mg	Iron	<2% U.S. RDA

Apricot-Pear Preserves

1 cup chopped dried apricots
1 cup water
1 tablespoon lemon juice
5 cups (6 medium) chopped, cored, peeled pears
4 cups sugar

In small saucepan, combine apricots, water and lemon juice; bring to a boil. Reduce heat; simmer uncovered 5 minutes. Set aside.

In large saucepan, combine pears and sugar. Over medium heat, bring mixture to a boil, stirring occasionally. Reduce heat; simmer uncovered for 25 minutes, stirring occasionally. Add cooked apricot mixture. Bring to a boil; boil 5 minutes. Spoon into clean 8-oz. jars or moisture- vapor-proof freezer containers, leaving ½ inch head space for freezer storage. Cool slightly; cover with tight-fitting lids. Refrigerate at least 24 hours. Store in refrigerator up to 3 weeks or in freezer up to 3 months. **4¾ cups.**

NUTRIENTS PER 1 TABLESPOON

Calories	50	Dietary Fiber	<1 g
Protein	0 g	Sodium	0 mg
Carbohydrate	13 g	Potassium	40 mg
Fat	0 g	Calcium	<2% U.S. RDA
Cholesterol	0 mg	Iron	<2% U.S. RDA

Citrus Marmalade

1	medium orange
1	medium tangerine
1	medium lemon
1½	cups water
⅛	teaspoon baking soda
3	cups sugar
3-oz.	pkg. liquid fruit pectin

MICROWAVE DIRECTIONS: Score outer peel of fruit into quarters. Remove thin layer of peel a quarter at a time. Discard white membrane from peel and fruit. Cut peel into very thin strips. In 2-quart microwave-safe bowl, combine peel, water and soda. Cover; microwave on HIGH for 5 to 8 minutes or until mixture comes to a full rolling boil; continue to boil for 10 minutes, stirring once halfway through cooking.

Meanwhile, in shallow bowl, finely chop fruit, being careful not to lose any juice. Add fruit with juice to peel mixture.

Cover; microwave on HIGH for 3 to 4 minutes or until mixture comes to full rolling boil; continue to boil for 10 minutes, stirring once halfway through cooking. Stir sugar and pectin into 2 cups of fruit mixture; discard excess mixture. Microwave on HIGH for 6½ to 9 minutes or until mixture comes to full rolling boil, stirring twice during cooking. Continue to boil for 1 minute.

Spoon into 3 clean, hot 8-oz. jars or moisture- vapor-proof freezer containers, leaving ½ inch head space for freezer storage; screw lids on firmly. Cool several hours. Store in refrigerator up to 3 weeks or in freezer up to 3 months. **3 cups.**

NUTRIENTS: Variables in this recipe make it impossible to calculate nutrition information.

Microwave Apple Butter

  8   cups (9 medium) cored, quartered, peeled apples
  2   cups apple cider or apple juice
1½ cups sugar
  ¾ teaspoon cinnamon
  ¼ teaspoon cloves
  ¼ teaspoon allspice

MICROWAVE DIRECTIONS: In 3-quart microwave-safe casserole, combine apples and cider. Microwave on HIGH for 12 to 15 minutes or until apples are tender, stirring twice during cooking. In blender or food processor bowl with metal blade, process apple mixture until smooth. Return to casserole. Add sugar, cinnamon, cloves and allspice; blend well. Microwave on HIGH for 25 to 35 minutes or until thickened and dark brown, stirring once halfway through cooking. (Mixture will thicken as it cools.) Spoon into 4 clean, hot 8-oz. jars or moisture- vapor-proof freezer containers leaving ½ inch head space for freezer storage; cover with tight-fitting lids. Store in refrigerator up to 3 weeks or in freezer up to 3 months. **4 cups.**

NUTRIENTS PER 1 TABLESPOON

Calories	30	Dietary Fiber	<1 g
Protein	0 g	Sodium	0 mg
Carbohydrate	8 g	Potassium	30 mg
Fat	0 g	Calcium	<2% U.S. RDA
Cholesterol	0 mg	Iron	<2% U.S. RDA

Food Preservation:

Pickles, Relishes & Sauces

Pickles, relishes and sauces are welcome additions as sandwich or meat accompaniments or as a salad. When preparing these condiments, choose produce at peak and wash under cold running water or through several changes of water.

Vinegar provides the acid solution to preserve pickles and relishes. Some of our recipes call for cider vinegar, which has a more mellow flavor than distilled white vinegar. When a sharper flavor or a light color of vegetable or fruit is desirable, distilled white vinegar is used.

Pickling salt is used instead of iodized salt, which causes pickles to darken or makes brine cloudy.

Because of variables in making pickles, we are unable to give specific nutritional information for each recipe. However, here is nutrition information for typical dill pickles:

NUTRIENTS PER 1 MEDIUM DILL PICKLE

Calories	7	Dietary Fiber	1 g
Protein	<1 g	Sodium	928 mg
Carbohydrate	1 g	Potassium	130 mg
Fat	<1 g	Calcium	<2% U.S. RDA
Cholesterol	0 mg	Iron	4% U.S. RDA

Dill Pickles

24 to 30 cucumbers, 3 inches long
12 to 16 sprigs fresh dill
    4 teaspoons mustard seed
    4 cups (1 quart) water
    2 cups cider vinegar
    2 tablespoons pickling salt

Wash cucumbers and pack in hot sterilized quart jars. To each jar, add 3 or 4 sprigs fresh dill and 1 teaspoon mustard seed. In large saucepan, combine water, vinegar and salt. Heat to boiling. Fill jars leaving ½ inch at top. Seal according to canning directions. Process in simmering water bath at 200°F. to 205°F. for 10 minutes. Store without removing screw bands. **4 quarts.**

TIP: A peeled garlic clove may be added to each jar along with dill.

NUTRIENTS: Variables in this recipe make it impossible to calculate nutrition information.

Microwave Quick Pickles

    3 cups thinly sliced unpeeled cucumbers
    1 medium onion, sliced
    1 small green bell pepper, cut into strips
    1 small red bell pepper, cut into strips
    1 small carrot, thinly sliced
    1 garlic clove, crushed
    1 teaspoon salt
    8 cups ice cubes
   ¾ cup sugar
    1 teaspoon mustard seed
   ¼ teaspoon celery seed
   ⅛ teaspoon turmeric
   ½ cup white vinegar

MICROWAVE DIRECTIONS: In large bowl, combine cucumbers, onions, peppers, carrots, garlic and salt. Add ice cubes and mix thoroughly. Let stand 3 hours. Using colander, drain well.

In 4-cup microwave-safe glass measuring cup, combine remaining ingredients. Microwave on HIGH for 2 to 5 minutes or until mixture boils; stir to dissolve sugar. Pack drained vegetables in 1-quart jar. Pour hot vinegar mixture over vegetables; cover. Let stand in refrigerator 24 hours before serving. Store in refrigerator. **4 cups.**

NUTRIENTS: Variables in this recipe make it impossible to calculate nutrition information.

Refrigerator Cucumber Pickles

    7 medium unpeeled cucumbers, thinly sliced
    1 tablespoon pickling salt
    2 medium (2 cups) onions, thinly sliced or chopped
    1 green pepper (1 cup), chopped
    2 cups sugar
    1 tablespoon celery seed
    1 tablespoon mustard seed
    1 cup vinegar

In large bowl, mix cucumbers and salt; let stand ½ hour. Drain well. Stir in onions and green peppers. In small bowl, combine remaining ingredients. Pour syrup over cucumber mixture; mix well. Store in covered container or pack in quart jars; refrigerate several hours or up to 3 months. **About 3 quarts.**

NUTRIENTS: Variables in this recipe make it impossible to calculate nutrition information.

Mixed Pickle Slices

5 quarts (20 cups) thinly sliced unpeeled cucumbers
  or zucchini
6 medium onions, thinly sliced
3 medium green peppers, thinly sliced
3 cloves garlic or ¼ teaspoon instant minced garlic
⅓ cup pickling salt
  Ice cubes
5 cups sugar
2 cups cider vinegar
2 tablespoons mustard seed
1½ teaspoons celery seed
1½ teaspoons turmeric

In large container, combine cucumbers, onions, green peppers and garlic. Sprinkle with salt and cover with layer of ice
cubes; mix lightly. Let stand 3 hours. Drain well; remove
garlic. In large saucepan, combine sugar, vinegar, seeds and
turmeric. Heat to boiling. Fill jars with pickle slices and
syrup, leaving ½ inch at top. Clean top of jar; seal with vacuum-seal lids. Process in simmering water bath at 200 to
205°F. for 5 minutes. **10 pints.**

NUTRIENTS: Variables in this recipe make it impossible to calculate
nutrition information.

Pickled Beets

16-oz. can (2 cups) sliced or whole beets, drained (reserve
  ⅓ cup liquid)
⅓ cup sugar
⅓ cup reserved beet liquid or water
⅓ cup vinegar
1 teaspoon pickling spice, if desired

In medium saucepan, combine drained beets, sugar, reserved beet liquid and vinegar. Tie pickling spice in cheesecloth and add to beets. Cook until mixture comes to boil, stirring occasionally. Cool and remove pickling spices before serving. Leftovers will keep several weeks in refrigerator. **2 cups.**

TIPS: If desired, use 3 whole cloves, 2 whole allspice and ½ stick cinnamon for pickling spice.

For longer storage, fill jars to within ½ inch of top with hot pickles and liquid; seal with vacuum-seal lids and process in boiling water bath at 212°F. for 30 minutes.

For pickles using fresh beets, cook beets as directed in Vegetables chapter. Continue as directed above.

NUTRIENTS: Variables in this recipe make it impossible to calculate nutrition information.

Marinated Cucumbers

    3 cups (2 medium) thinly sliced cucumbers
    1 medium red or green pepper, cut into thin strips
    ¼ cup chopped onions
    1 cup sugar
    1 teaspoon salt
    ½ teaspoon celery seed
    ½ teaspoon mustard seed
    ½ cup cider vinegar

In large bowl, combine cucumbers, peppers and onions. In small bowl, combine sugar, salt, celery seed, mustard seed and vinegar; blend well. Pour over cucumber mixture; toss to coat well. Cover; refrigerate at least 24 hours, stirring occasionally. If desired, drain before serving. **3 cups.**

NUTRIENTS: Variables in this recipe make it impossible to calculate nutrition information.

Pickled Peppers

1 tablespoon sugar
1 tablespoon salt
2 cups water
1 cup white vinegar
1 red bell pepper, cut into sixths
1 yellow bell pepper, cut into sixths
1 green bell pepper, cut into sixths
2 garlic cloves, halved
1 small onion, sliced and separated into rings
1 sprig fresh tarragon or ¼ teaspoon dried tarragon

MICROWAVE DIRECTIONS: In 2-quart microwave-safe bowl, combine sugar, salt, water and vinegar. Microwave on HIGH for 8 to 14 minutes or until mixture boils. In 1-quart jar, pack remaining ingredients. Pour hot vinegar mixture over vegetables; cover. Let stand in refrigerator 1 week before serving. Store in refrigerator. **1 quart.**

NUTRIENTS: Variables in this recipe make it impossible to calculate nutrition information.

Corn Relish

16-oz. can (2 cups) whole kernel corn, drained
⅓ cup pickle relish
⅓ cup chopped pimiento
⅓ cup chopped green peppers
¼ cup sugar
1 small onion, chopped
¼ cup vinegar
1 teaspoon cornstarch
½ teaspoon celery seed
1 tablespoon prepared mustard

In medium saucepan, combine all ingredients; mix well. Cook, stirring occasionally, until mixture comes to a boil and thickens slightly. Cool before serving. Store, covered, in refrigerator for 2 to 3 weeks. **2½ cups.**

TIP: Fresh corn may be substituted for canned. Cover, heat to boiling and simmer about 5 minutes.

NUTRIENTS PER ¼ CUP

Calories	70	Dietary Fiber	2 g
Protein	1 g	Sodium	190 mg
Carbohydrate	17 g	Potassium	100 mg
Fat	0 g	Calcium	<2% U.S. RDA
Cholesterol	0 mg	Iron	2% U.S. RDA

Fresh Vegetable Relish

    2 medium tomatoes, chopped
    2 medium cucumbers, chopped
    1 stalk celery, sliced or chopped
    1 small onion, chopped
    ¼ cup firmly packed brown sugar
    2 teaspoons salt
    ¼ cup vinegar
    ½ teaspoon mustard seed or dill weed

In 1-quart container, combine all ingredients; mix well. Cover and refrigerate several hours or up to 3 months. **3 cups.**

NUTRIENTS PER ¼ CUP

Calories	30	Dietary Fiber	<1 g
Protein	0 g	Sodium	360 mg
Carbohydrate	7 g	Potassium	125 mg
Fat	0 g	Calcium	30% U.S. RDA
Cholesterol	0 mg	Iron	2% U.S. RDA

Homemade Tomato Sauce

        2 cups (2 large) chopped onions
        2 garlic cloves, minced
      1/3 cup oil or olive oil
        8 cups (12 medium) coarsely chopped, peeled
           tomatoes
        1 tablespoon oregano leaves
        1 teaspoon sugar
        1 teaspoon basil leaves
        1 teaspoon rosemary leaves, crushed
      1/2 teaspoon salt
      1/4 teaspoon pepper
        2 cups water
   12-oz. can tomato paste

In 4-quart saucepan or Dutch oven, saute onions and garlic
in oil until tender. Add remaining ingredients; bring to a
boil, stirring occasionally. Store in refrigerator up to 1 week
or in freezer up to 3 months. **8 to 10 cups.**

NUTRIENTS PER 1 CUP

Calories	140	Dietary Fiber	<3 g
Protein	3 g	Sodium	380 mg
Carbohydrate	14 g	Potassium	550 mg
Fat	8 g	Calcium	4% U.S. RDA
Cholesterol	0 mg	Iron	10% U.S. RDA

Garlic Pesto Sauce

        4 cups lightly packed fresh basil leaves, rinsed and
           patted dry
        4 garlic cloves
        1 cup olive oil
      1/2 cup pine nuts or blanched almonds
        1 teaspoon salt
     1 1/2 cups freshly grated Parmesan cheese

In food processor bowl with metal blade, combine all ingredients except cheese. Process until smooth and well blended. Stir in cheese. Use immediately or store in jar with tight-fitting lid. Refrigerate up to 1 week or freeze for longer storage. Serve with gnocchi or cooked pasta. **2 cups.**

NUTRIENTS PER 2 TABLESPOONS

Calories 190	Dietary Fiber...........................1 g
Protein ....5 g	Sodium.............................310 mg
Carbohydrate...........................2 g	Potassium ....115 mg
Fat ....18 g	Calcium...............15% U.S. RDA
Cholesterol...........................6 mg	Iron........................8% U.S. RDA

Helpful Terms & Definitions

AL DENTE A food, usually pasta or vegetables, cooked until just firm to the bite. Italian, meaning "to the tooth."

ALMOND BARK (Vanilla-flavored candy coating) A compound made with vegetable fats instead of cocoa butter, with colorings and flavorings added. It is available in 1½-lb. packages or in blocks and round disks where candy-making supplies are sold.

ANTIPASTO Means "before the pasta" and includes an assortment of marinated vegetables, cheeses, sausages, anchovies, olives, seafood and other foods. Usually used as an hors d'oeuvre, but can be served as a first course, salad or light entree.

ASCORBIC ACID Vitamin C. Available commercially to keep cut fruit from darkening; often used in canning.

ASPIC A jelly, often clarified and made by chilling concentrated stock, used to cover or glaze chilled foods. Also refers to a jelly made by adding gelatin to fruit juice or meat and vegetable stocks.

AU GRATIN Dishes cooked with a sauce, usually containing cheese, and topped with buttered crumbs and/or cheese and browned.

AU JUS Served in juice or drippings; usually refers to meats.

BASTE To moisten food and add flavor by spooning or brushing pan drippings or other liquid over the food while cooking.

BEAT To combine ingredients, usually until smooth, using a spoon, whisk, hand beater or electric mixer.

BLANCH To immerse briefly in boiling water, usually followed by quick cooling in cold water, to precook briefly to set color and flavor or to loosen skin of foods such as tomatoes, peaches or almonds.

BLEND To thoroughly combine two or more ingredients by hand or using an appliance such as blender, mixer or food processor.

BOIL To heat a mixture until it bubbles continuously with bubbles breaking the surface. Bubbles form very rapidly with a rolling boil.

BONE To remove bones from meat, poultry or fish.

BRAISE To cook food slowly, often after browning, in a minimum amount of liquid using tightly covered cookware.

BREAD To cover a food with fine crumbs before cooking, usually after dipping in an egg or milk mixture.

BROWN To cook food in a small amount of hot fat on top of the range or by exposing it to dry heat in the oven to give appetizing color.

CARAMELIZE To stir sugar over low heat until it melts and develops a golden-brown color and distinctive flavor.

CHILL To refrigerate a food or cool completely in ice or iced water.

CHOP To cut into small pieces using a sharp knife or appliance.

CHUTNEY A relish combining fruits and/or vegetables and spices. Frequently served with curried dishes and meats.

CLARIFY To make a liquid clear. Often achieved by skimming or by adding eggshell to liquid, then straining. Particles adhere to egg white or shell.

COAT To cover food surface evenly with a mixture of seasoned flour, fine crumbs or batter.

COATS SPOON When a thin, even film covers a metal spoon after it has been dipped into a cooking mixture, removed and allowed to drain.

CONDIMENT An ingredient, usually pungent, added to or served with other foods to complement flavor.

CREAM To soften or combine one or more ingredients until the mixture is smooth and fluffy.

CUBE To cut a food into uniform squares, usually about ½ inch in diameter.

CUT IN To distribute shortening throughout dry ingredients using a pastry blender, two knives or fork.

DASH Less than ⅛ teaspoon.

DEEP-FAT FRY To cook in hot fat deep enough to immerse food being prepared.

DICE To cut into uniform-sized pieces smaller than ½ inch across.

DRIPPINGS Meat or poultry juices and fat remaining in pan after cooking. Often used to make gravies and sauces.

DUST To sprinkle lightly with flour or sugar.

DUTCH OVEN A deep, heavy pan with tight-fitting lid used for roasting meats or making stews and hearty soups.

ENTREE The main course or main dish of a meal.

FILLET A piece of fish or meat that has all bones removed.

FLAKE To separate layers of cooked fish lightly with tines of fork.

FLUTE To make a decorative pattern around edge of pastry or fruits and vegetables.

FOLD IN To combine a heavier mixture with a delicate substance such as beaten egg white or whipped cream without loss of air.

FONDANT A creamy sugar mixture used as a basis for confections.

FRY To saute or cook in a small amount of fat.

GIBLETS Heart, liver and gizzard of poultry.

GLAZE To coat with syrup, thin icing or jelly, either during cooking or after food is cooked.

GRATE To shred with a hand-held grater or with food processor.

GREASE To rub surface of dish or pan with solid shortening or margarine to prevent sticking during cooking or baking.

GRIND To produce food particles by forcing food through grinder.

HORS D'OEUVRE Small or bite-sized portions of various foods served as appetizers.

JULIENNE Food, usually vegetables, cut into thin, matchstick-like strips.

KNEAD To manipulate a dough or other mixture in a folding, pushing and turning motion to produce a smooth, elastic texture.

LIQUEUR An alcoholic beverage flavored with aromatic substances, often sweetened.

LOX Smoked salmon.

LUKEWARM A temperature of about 95°F. that feels neither hot or cold.

MARBLING Streaks of fat in meat.

MARINATE To let food stand in a seasoned liquid to tenderize and enhance flavor.

MERINGUE A mixture of stiffly beaten egg whites and sugar baked on top of a pie, or as a shell to be filled with whipped cream and fruit or ice cream.

MINCE To cut into very small pieces using a sharp knife or suitable appliance.

MONOSODIUM GLUTAMATE (MSG) A crystalline chemical food additive used to intensify natural flavors.

MOUSSE A light, delicate dish made with egg whites and cream usually combined with fish or seafood, or with chocolate or fruit for a dessert.

NEWBURG A rich sauce made from cream, butter, sherry wine and egg yolk; usually combined with lobster or other seafood.

NOUVELLE CUISINE A type of French cooking, less rich than traditional French food, that features small portions and lightly cooked vegetables and emphasizes interesting combinations of taste, color and texture.

PAELLA A Spanish dish consisting of rice, seafood and chicken seasoned with saffron.

PANBROIL To cook in an uncovered skillet, turning frequently and pouring off drippings as they accumulate.

PARBOIL To boil until partially cooked.

PARE To remove peel or other outer covering from a food.

PÂTÉ A highly seasoned meat spread served cold as an appetizer.

PITA OR POCKET BREAD Thin, flat rounds of bread

that bake attached around the edges only, and when split form a pocket for holding sandwich fillings.

POACH To cook in simmering liquid.

PREHEAT To heat a cooking appliance to the desired temperature before beginning cooking or baking. It is necessary to preheat an oven for foods that cook or bake in less than 1 hour. There is no need to preheat for foods requiring longer cooking or when broiling or roasting. An oven preheats in about 10 minutes.

PROSCIUTTO A salty Italian smoked ham, often served thinly sliced as an appetizer.

PUREE To convert food to a liquid or smooth, pastelike consistency.

QUICHE An oven-baked pastry shell with a filling of eggs, cheese, and ham or other ingredients; can be served as appetizer or main course.

RAMEKIN Individual baking dish.

ROAST To cook uncovered in an oven, using dry heat.

ROSETTE IRON A decorative iron with a long handle. It is heated in deep hot fat, dipped into batter and returned to hot fat to produce rosettes. Rosettes become cookies when sprinkled with powdered sugar or iced, or can be used as a base for main dishes.

ROULADE Usually refers to a thin slice of meat rolled around a filling.

ROUX A mixture of melted fat and flour cooked over low heat to a smooth paste and used for thickening soups, sauces and gravies. Can be light or dark in color depending on cooking time.

RUMTOPF Used to describe a fermented fruit mixture or the pot in which the natural fermentation process of the fruit and sugar mixture occurs.

SAUTE To cook in a skillet in a small amount of shortening, stirring until tender or browned.

SCALD To heat to just below the boiling point; to pour boiling water over a food to blanch; or to dip briefly in boiling water to loosen skin for peeling.

SCALLION A mild green onion.

SCORE To cut fat or other food surface with shallow grooves before cooking to increase tenderness, prevent fat from curling or for decorative purposes.

SEAR Using high heat to brown surface of meats quickly to seal in juices.

SEASON To add salt, pepper, herbs, spices or other seasonings.

SHRED To cut into thin slivers using a grater or knife.

SIMMER To cook in liquid just below boiling point so that tiny bubbles form on bottom or sides of pan.

SKEWER A metal or wooden pin on which food is placed; frequently used for kabobs.

SKIM To remove fat or scum from liquid.

SLIVER To cut into very thin, elongated pieces.

SMORGASBORD A buffet of Scandinavian origin featuring a variety of hot and cold dishes, often appetizers, smoked and pickled fish, hot and cold meats and cheeses.

SOFTENED Refers to margarine, butter or cream cheese in a soft state for easy blending.

STEAM To cook food in a rack or wire basket above boiling water.

STEEP To extract flavor and/or color from a food by allowing it to stand in a hot liquid.

STEW To simmer a food long and slowly in liquid in a covered pot.

STIR To combine ingredients with a spoon or whisk, using a circular motion.

STIR-FRY To cook sliced foods quickly in a little oil or liquid over high heat while continually stirring and tossing. An Oriental cooking method often done in a wok over high heat.

STOCK The liquid in which meat or poultry bones, fish or vegetables have been cooked. Used as a base for soups and sauces to enhance flavor.

TAPAS Snacks and hors d'oeuvres, Spanish in origin, usually consisting of marinated foods.

TART A small open-faced pie with fruit or a sweet or savory filling. Sometimes called a flan.

TENDER-CRISP Vegetables cooked only until tender but still crisp in texture.

TERRINE A well-seasoned pâté, usually of meat or game. Also refers to the baking dish itself.

TORTILLA A flat, unleavened pancake made from coarse cornmeal or flour and water and cooked on a griddle.

TOSS To mix food lightly and quickly using two utensils such as a salad fork and spoon.

TRUFFLE An aromatic and flavorful wild fungus used as a seasoning or garnish. Also a rich candy made of chocolate, butter and sugar shaped into balls and coated with cocoa.

TRUSS To close a cavity or otherwise secure poultry or meat using skewers or string.

VINAIGRETTE An oil and vinegar sauce with herbs and seasonings added. Used as a salad dressing or served over chilled vegetables, meats or fish.

WHIP To beat rapidly with a whisk or mixer to incorporate air into a mixture to lighten and increase volume.

WHISK A utensil with wire loops, balloon-shaped at the end, used for hand-beating foods to blend and/or add volume.

WOK An Oriental cooking pan with rounded bottom and wide, sloping sides, used for stir-frying foods.

ZEST The colored outer peel of citrus fruit, used to add flavor.

Flour Definitions

ALL-PURPOSE FLOUR All-purpose flour is the most widely used flour and is the one used throughout this cookbook unless otherwise specified. It is suitable for all kinds of baking, from yeast breads to delicate cakes. All-purpose flour comes bleached or unbleached. (Unbleached flour has not been whitened by a bleaching agent.) Bleached and unbleached flour can be used interchangeably.

BREAD FLOUR Bread flour is a wheat flour milled especially for yeast baking. It contains a higher amount of protein that enhances its bread-making qualities. Bread flour can be substituted for all-purpose flour in yeast bread recipes with the following recipe changes: Knead dough 10 minutes, allow a longer rise time and let dough rest 15 minutes before shaping.

CAKE FLOUR Cake flour is a very fine wheat flour milled especially for delicate cakes and pastries. A substitute for each cup of cake flour is 1 cup minus 2 tablespoons all-purpose flour.

OAT FLOUR Oat flour is made of finely ground oat kernels. It can easily be made by placing rolled oats in the blender and grinding until fine.

RYE FLOUR Rye flour is milled from rye grain and is available in light, medium and dark forms. Since rye lacks the proteins necessary for yeast bread structure, it is used in combination with bread or all-purpose flour.

SELF-RISING FLOUR Self-rising flour is an all-purpose flour to which 1½ teaspoons baking powder and ½ teaspoon salt per 1 cup flour have been added. It is ideal for making biscuits and muffins.

WHOLE WHEAT OR GRAHAM FLOUR Whole wheat or graham flour is milled from the entire wheat kernel. It may be ground to varying degrees of fineness. Baked products made with whole wheat flour are heavier and more compact.

Cake Definitions

ANGEL FOOD CAKES Angel food cakes contain no shortening, egg yolks or added leavening ingredients.

CHIFFON CAKES Chiffon cakes contain vegetable oil (do not substitute other types of shortening), egg yolks and leavening ingredients. Shallow cracks that appear on top of baked cake will be dry.

SPONGE CAKES Sponge cakes contain no shortening but use both yolks and whites of eggs. A leavening ingredient may be added.

TORTE A rich cake made with crumbs and eggs and containing fruit and nuts. Also refers to a multilayered cake.

Chocolate Definitions

CHOCOLATE-FLAVORED SYRUP A combination of cocoa, corn syrup and flavoring. It is available in various-sized jars or cans.

MILK CHOCOLATE Sweet chocolate made with milk and packaged in various-sized bars and shapes.

SEMI-SWEET CHOCOLATE Chocolate made with additional cocoa butter, flavorings and very little sugar. It is molded into 1-ounce blocks and packed eight to a carton or formed into chips and sold in 6- or 12-ounce packages.

SWEET COOKING CHOCOLATE (German's sweet chocolate) Similar to semi-sweet chocolate, but with a higher proportion of sugar. It is packaged in 4-ounce bars.

UNSWEETENED CHOCOLATE The basic chocolate from which all other products are made. It is molded into 1-ounce blocks and packed eight to a carton.

UNSWEETENED COCOA A powder made from roasted cacao beans with most of the cocoa butter removed. It is available in 8- or 16-ounce cans.

WHITE CHOCOLATE Not really chocolate in the true sense because it does not contain "chocolate liquor" from the cocoa bean. It is a blend of milk and sugar cooked until it condenses into a solid. Some types contain cocoa butter; others contain artificial flavoring. It is available in bars or chunks.

Index